Official Hayes Modem Communications Companion

AT Comm Reference

Note: This tear-out card li... commands. All modems do not use the same commands. See Appendix A for a more complete listing and details on using the commands.

AT Command Descriptions

Command	Description
ATA	Enter answer mode, go off hook, attempt to answer incoming call, and go online with another modem.
ATD	Enter originate mode, go off-hook, and attempt to go online with another modem. The dial modifiers tell the modem what, when, and how to dial.
ATDT	Dial by using tone method.
ATDP	Dial by using pulse method.
ATDT,	Dial by using tone method and wait two seconds.
ATH0	Hang up and place modem in command state.
ATL0, L1	Set low speaker volume.
ATL2	Set medium speaker volume.
ATL3	Set high speaker volume.
ATM0	Turn speaker off.
ATM1	Turn speaker on until carrier detected.
ATM2	Turn speaker on.
ATM3	Turn speaker on until carrier detected, except while dialing.
ATQ0	Return result codes.
ATQ1	Do not return result codes.
ATS*n*?	Read and respond with current value of register *n* (*n* is the register number; ? requests the value assigned to that register).
ATS*n=value*	Set the value of register *n* to value.
ATV0	Display result codes as numbers.
ATV1	Display result codes as words.
AT&F	Recall factory configuration as active configuration.
AT&Q5	Communicate in error-control mode.
AT&V	View active configuration, user profiles, and stored telephone numbers.
AT&W0	Write storable parameters of current configuration in memory as profile 0.
AT&W1	Write storable parameters of current configuration in memory as profile 1.
AT&Y0	Specify stored user profile 0 as power-up configuration.
AT&Y1	Specify stored user profile 1 as power-up configuration.

Result Code Descriptions

Number	Word	Description
0	OK	Command executed.
1	CONNECT	A connection has been established.
2	RING	Ring signal indicated
3	NO CARRIER	Carrier signal not detected, or lost, or inactivity for period of time set in the automatic timeout register (set with **S30**) caused the modem to hang up.
4	ERROR	Invalid command, checksum, error in command line, or command line exceeds 255 characters.
5	CONNECT 1200	Connection at 1200 bps (disabled by **X0**).
6	NO DIALTONE	No dial tone detected. Enabled by **X2** or **X4**, or **W** dial modifier.
7	BUSY	Engaged (busy) signal or number unobtainable signal detected. Enabled by **X3** or **X4**.
8	NO ANSWER	No silence detected when dialing a system not providing a dial tone. Enabled by @ dial modifier.
10	CONNECT 2400	Connection at 2400 bps (disabled by **X0**).
11	CONNECT 4800	Connection at 4800 bps (disabled by **X0**).
12	CONNECT 9600	Connection at 9600 bps (disabled by **X0**).

S-Register Descriptions

Register	Description	Range/Units	Default Setting
S0	Select ring to answer on.	0-255 rings	0
S1	Ring count (incremented with each ring).	0-255 rings	0
S2	Escape sequence character.	0-127 ASCII	43
S3	Carriage return character.	0-127 ASCII	13
S4	Line feed character.	0-127 ASCII	10
S5	Back space character.	0-32,127 ASCII	8
S6	Wait before blind dialing.	2-255 sec	2
S7	Wait time for carrier/silence.	1-255 sec	50
S8	Duration of delay for comma.	0-255 sec	2
S9	Carrier detect response time.	1-255 1/10 sec	5
S10	Delay carrier loss to hang up.	1-255 1/10 sec	14
S11	Duration/spacing of DTMF tones.	50-255 msec	95
S12	Escape sequence guard time.	0-255 1/50 sec	50

Official Hayes Modem Communications Companion

Official Hayes Modem Communications Companion

by Caroline M. Halliday

Foreword and Introduction by
Dennis Hayes
President and Founder
Hayes Microcomputer Products, Inc.

IDG BOOKS

IDG Books Worldwide, Inc.
An International Data Group Company

San Mateo, California ✦ Indianapolis, Indiana ✦ Boston, Massachusetts

Official Hayes Modem Communications Companion

Published by
IDG Books Worldwide, Inc.
An International Data Group Company
155 Bovet Road, Suite 310
San Mateo, CA 94402

Library of Congress Catalog Card No.: 9475047

ISBN: 1-56884-072-1

Printed in the United States of America

10 9 8 7 6 5 4 3 2 1

1C/QU/RZ/ZU

Distributed in the United States by IDG Books Worldwide, Inc.

Distributed in Canada by Macmillan of Canada, a Division of Canada Publishing Corporation; by Computer and Technical Books in Miami, Florida, for South America and the Caribbean; by Longman Singapore in Singapore, Malaysia, Thailand, and Korea; by Toppan Co. Ltd. in Japan; by Asia Computerworld in Hong Kong; by Woodslane Pty. Ltd. in Australia and New Zealand; and by Transword Publishers Ltd. in the U.K. and Europe.

For general information on IDG Books in the U.S., including information on discounts and premiums, contact IDG Books at 800-762-2974 or 415-312-0650.

For information on where to purchase IDG Books outside the U.S., contact Christina Turner at 415-312-0633.

For information on translations, contact Marc Jeffrey Mikulich, Foreign Rights Manager, at IDG Books Worldwide; FAX NUMBER 415-358-1260.

For sales inquiries and special prices for bulk quantities, write to the address above or call IDG Books Worldwide at 415-312-0650.

 is a registered trademark of IDG BooksWorldwide, Inc.

 The text in this book is printed on recycled paper.

About the Author

Caroline M. Halliday

Caroline M. Halliday shares her passion for PCs and telecommunications with her husband. They like to explore new BBSs and online services and keep abreast of current trends in the industry. Unfortunately, Caroline keeps stumbling across new computer games that divert her attention. Her husband can pick up the slack, however, and keep their phone companies profitable.

To pay for these exploits, Caroline uses her electrical engineering degree to write books and magazine articles for the PC industry. She focuses particularly on making the technology understandable to the home user and small-business owner. Caroline is on the *InfoWorld* review board, and her other best-selling book is *PC SECRETS*, also published by IDG Books Worldwide.

About IDG Books Worldwide

Welcome to the world of IDG Books Worldwide.

IDG Books Worldwide, Inc., is a subsidiary of International Data Group, the world's largest publisher of computer-related information and the leading global provider of information services on information technology. International Data Group publishes over 195 computer publications in 62 countries. Forty million people read one or more International Data Group publications each month

If you use personal computers, IDG Books is committed to publishing quality books that meet your needs. We rely on our extensive network of publications, including such leading periodicals as *Macworld*, *InfoWorld*, *PC World*, *Computerworld*, *Publish*, *Network World*, and *SunWorld*, to help us make informed and timely decisions in creating useful computer books that meet your needs.

Every IDG book strives to bring extra value and skill-building instructions to the reader. Our books are written by experts, with the backing of IDG periodicals, and with careful thought devoted to issues such as audience, interior design, use of icons, and illustrations. Our editorial staff is a careful mix of high-tech journalists and experienced book people. Our close contact with the makers of computer products helps ensure accuracy and thorough coverage. Our heavy use of personal computers at every step in production means we can deliver books in the most timely manner.

We are delivering books of high quality at competitive prices on topics customers want. At IDG, we believe in quality, and we have been delivering quality for over 25 years. You'll find no better book on a subject than an IDG book.

John Kilcullen
President and CEO
IDG Books Worldwide, Inc.

IDG Books Worldwide, Inc. is a subsidiary of International Data Group. The officers are Patrick J. McGovern, Founder and Board Chairman; Walter Boyd, President. International Data Group's publications include: **ARGENTINA'S** Computerworld Argentina, Infoworld Argentina; **ASIA'S** Computerworld Hong Kong, PC World Hong Kong, Computerworld Southeast Asia, PC World Singapore, Computerworld Malaysia, PC World Malaysia; **AUSTRALIA'S** Computerworld Australia, Australian PC World, Australian Macworld, Network World, Mobile Business Australia, Reseller, IDG Sources; **AUSTRIA'S** Computerwelt Oesterreich, PC Test; **BRAZIL'S** Computerworld, Gamepro, Game Power, Mundo IBM, Mundo Unix, PC World, Super Game; **BELGIUM'S** Data News (CW) **BULGARIA'S** Computerworld Bulgaria, Ediworld, PC & Mac World Bulgaria, Network World Bulgaria; **CANADA'S** CIO Canada, Computerworld Canada, Graduate Computerworld, InfoCanada, Network World Canada; **CHILE'S** Computerworld Chile, Informatica; **COLOMBIA'S** Computerworld Colombia; **CZECH REPUBLIC'S** Computerworld, Elektronika, PC World; **DENMARK'S** CAD/CAM WORLD, Communications World, Computerworld Danmark, LOTUS World, Macintosh Produktkatalog, Macworld Danmark, PC World Danmark, PC World Produktguide, Windows World; **ECUADOR'S** PC World Ecuador; **EGYPT'S** Computerworld (CW) Middle East, PC World Middle East; **FINLAND'S** MikroPC, Tietoviikko, Tietoverkko; **FRANCE'S** Distributique, GOLDEN MAC, InfoPC, Languages & Systems, Le Guide du Monde Informatique, Le Monde Informatique, Telecoms & Reseaux; **GERMANY'S** Computerwoche, Computerwoche Focus, Computerwoche Extra, Computerwoche Karriere, Information Management, Macwelt, Netzwelt, PC Welt, PC Woche, Publish, Unit; **GREECE'S** Infoworld, PC Games; **HUNGARY'S** Computerworld SZT, PC World; **INDIA'S** Computers & Communications; **IRELAND'S** Computerscope; **ISRAEL'S** Computerworld Israel, PC World Israel; **ITALY'S** Computerworld Italia, Lotus Magazine, Macworld Italia, Networking Italia, PC Shopping Italy, PC World Italia; **JAPAN'S** Computerworld Today, Information Systems World, Macworld Japan, Nikkei Personal Computing, SunWorld Japan, Windows World; **KENYA'S** East African Computer News; **KOREA'S** Computerworld Korea, Macworld Korea, PC World Korea; **MEXICO'S** Compu Edicion, Compu Manufactura, Computacion/ Punto de Venta, Computerworld Mexico, MacWorld, Mundo Unix, PC World, Windows; **THE NETHERLANDS'** Computer! Totaal, Computable (CW), LAN Magazine, MacWorld, Totaal "Windows"; **NEW ZEALAND'S** Computer Listings, Computerworld New Zealand, New Zealand PC World; **NIGERIA'S** PC World Africa; **NORWAY'S** Computerworld Norge, C/World, Lotusworld Norge, Macworld Norge, Networld, PC World Ekspress, PC World Norge, PC World's Produktguide, Publish& Multimedia World, Student Data, Unix World, Windowsworld; IDG Direct Response; **PANAMA'S** PC World Panama; **PERU'S** Computerworld Peru, PC World; **PEOPLE'S REPUBLIC OF CHINA'S** China Computerworld, China Infoworld, PC World China, Electronics International, Electronic Product World, China Network World; IDG HIGH TECH BEIJING'S New Product World; IDG SHENZHEN'S Computer News Digest; **PHILIPPINES'** Computerworld Philippines, PC Digest (PCW); **POLAND'S** Computerworld Poland, PC World/Komputer; **PORTUGAL'S** Cerebro/PC World, Correio Informatico/ Computerworld, MacIn; **ROMANIA'S** Computerworld, PC World; **RUSSIA'S** Computerworld-Moscow, Mir - PC, Sety; **SLOVENIA'S** Monitor Magazine; **SOUTH AFRICA'S** Computer Mail (CIO),Computing S.A.,Network World S.A.; **SPAIN'S** Amiga World, Computerworld Espana, Communicaciones World, Macworld Espana, NeXTWORLD, Super Juegos Magazine (GamePro), PC World Espana, Publish, Sunworld; **SWEDEN'S** Attack, ComputerSweden, Corporate Computing, Lokala Natverk/LAN, Lotus World, MAC&PC, Macworld, Mikrodatorn, PC World, Publishing & Design (CAP), DataIngenjoren, Maxi Data,Windows World; **SWITZERLAND'S** Computerworld Schweiz, Macworld Schweiz, PC Katalog, PC & Workstation; **TAIWAN'S** Computerworld Taiwan, Global Computer Express, PC World Taiwan; **THAILAND'S** Thai Computerworld; **TURKEY'S** Computerworld Monitor, Macworld Turkiye, PC World Turkiye; **UKRAINE'S** Computerworld; **UNITED KINGDOM'S** Computing /Computerworld, Connexion/Network World, Lotus Magazine, Macworld, Open Computing/Sunworld; **UNITED STATES'** AmigaWorld, Cable in the Classroom, CD Review, CIO, Computerworld, Desktop Video World, DOS Resource Guide, Electronic Entertainment Magazine, Federal Computer Week, Federal Integrator, GamePro, IDG Books, Infoworld, Infoworld Direct, Laser Event, Macworld, Multimedia World, Network World, NeXTWORLD, PC Letter, PC World, PlayRight, Power PC World, Publish, SunWorld, SWATPro, Video Event; **VENEZUELA'S** Computerworld Venezuela, MicroComputerworld Venezuela; **VIETNAM'S** PC World Vietnam

Dedication

For all who "push the envelope of technology," particularly in the fields of medicine and computers.

Acknowledgments

I want to acknowledge *all* the talented staff at Hayes Microcomputer Products, Inc., for their help, particularly the founder and president, Dennis Hayes.

Special thanks to Peggy Ballard, who focused much of her time and energy on this product.

Thanks to Dwayne Arnold and Ricky Lacy for enriching my list of frequently asked questions.

Thanks to Paul Curtis, partner at The Coastal Group, for sharing his information for the "First BBS Teleconference to the USSR" sidebar.

Thanks to Alan Fuerbringer at Mustang Software, Inc., for his useful solution.

Thanks to Bruce Ansley for reviewing the chapter on the Internet.

Thanks to Tim Stanley for modifying the AT Command Quick Reference Card.

Thanks to H. Leigh Davis and Sandy Reed for excellent editing and support.

Thanks to Dow Jones News Retrieval, Dialog, and America Online.

Thanks to Hayes for supplying various supporting materials.

Software Creations BBS screens are used with permission of Dan Litton.

Credits

VP & Publisher
David Solomon

Managing Editor
Mary Bednarek

Acquisitions Editor
Janna Custer

Production Director
Beth Jenkins

Senior Editors
Tracy L. Barr
Sandra Blackthorn
Diane Graves Steele

Production Coordinator
Cindy L. Phipps

Associate Acquisitions Editor
Megg Bonar

Editorial Assistant
Darlene Cunningham

Project Editor
H. Leigh Davis

Copy Editor
Sandy Reed

Technical Review
Hayes Microcomputer Products, Inc.

Production Staff
Tony Augsburger
Valery Bourke
Mary Breidenbach
Chris Collins
Sherry Gomoll
Drew R. Moore
Kathie Schnorr
Gina Scott

Proofreader
Henry Lazarek

Indexer
Steve Rath

Book Design/Jigsaw Puzzle Illustrations
Jo Payton

Contents at a Glance

Table of Contents

Part II: Communications Basics 54

Foreword and Introduction to the Book

At Hayes, we built the on-ramp to the information highway. Over the last decade, computers revolutionized the way we work and play. Computer communications made it possible for online information services to grow in popularity and to increase in number and type of services available. With the widespread use of modems over the global telephone network, it's now possible for computers at virtually any location to connect. As the speed of communications technology increases, new applications are opening that will allow the novice as well as the experienced computer user to conduct business or enjoy entertainment interactively at any time with information systems or people who may be located anywhere. All this — and at prices that almost everyone can afford.

For the last 15 years, we at Hayes Microcomputer Products, Inc. have worked very hard to take the mystery out of modems and computer communications. In fact, I felt so strongly about providing a resource to eliminate the discomfort you may feel about computer communications that we did something at Hayes that we've never done before. We provided Caroline Halliday and IDG Books with an inside look at Hayes that no one else has ever seen. She interviewed our research and development engineers, talked at length with our technical service and support team, toured our labs, and spent a lot of time getting to know Hayes from the inside. That insight, coupled with her vast knowledge of the computer industry and her successful track record as a writer, provides you with the most thorough and detailed computer communications guidebook ever written.

This authoritative reference taps into the Hayes knowledge base unlike any other book ever written. We have a unique perspective concerning what people want to know about using modems and computer communications. Our customer and technical support team members speak with more than one million modem users every year. I know firsthand that this type of interaction can build a huge information and knowledge base among Hayes employees. I say that because I answered the phones myself during our early years, and today I spend much of my time talking with customers and use what I learn from them to improve our products and our company. Now, you can benefit from our years of experience and enjoy the exciting world of computer communications like never before.

When my partner, Dale Heatherington, and I began our company some 15 years ago, our goal was to make our company a global leader in computer communications. We wanted to do that by making products that took computer communications out of a technical environment and let them migrate to the real world where almost anyone could use them productively. Our first goal was to take the mystery out of modems. It is now my desire that the *Official Hayes Modem Communications Companion* become an extension of that vision, which can take the mystery out of modem communications for you.

When the first Hayes Smartmodem shipped on June 16, 1981, a new era in computer communications began. We introduced the Hayes Standard AT Command Set to allow software to use a command language for controlling modem features, such as Auto Dial and Auto Answer. Up to that time, most early modems were not intelligent devices but simply translators that required complicated technical setup for a specific use. Now, thanks to the original Hayes Smartmodem, a modem is a system element that is easier to integrate into the computer environment. Its ease of use was coupled with a powerful capability that had been unavailable prior to 1981. That capability was a standard set of commands we designed to make it easy for software to tell the modem what to do — the Hayes Standard AT Command Set. It has been adopted worldwide for modem communications and continues to be copied "more or less" by most modem manufacturers and supported by communications software developers. Its use is so widespread that it gave birth to the term *Hayes-compatible* or *AT-compatible* products, a whole new category of modems known as PC modems.

In hindsight, I think you can look at that first Hayes Smartmodem as being the foundation for the on-ramp to the information highway and, when coupled with communications software and the telephone network, a whole new world of information at a user's desktop. In the 1980s, we weren't contemplating the superhighway that is receiving so much attention today. But in the beginning stages, the information highway needed explorers to open new territories for dial-up communications. I'm very proud that our company was there as a pioneer.

Speed has also played a great role in our ability to use the information highway and is increasingly more important to what we can reasonably do with the infrastructure. That first Hayes Smartmodem was a 300 baud modem. Since then, modem speeds have doubled about every 18 months. With today's files and programs being measured in megabytes and telephone charges being measured in dollars per minute, we need faster modems. With a 300-baud modem, transferring a megabyte of data would take more than 9 hours! Today, our OPTIMA 288 V.FC + FAX supports data-throughput speeds of up to 230,400 bps, hundreds of times faster than our first modem! That's a megabyte of data transferred in less than a minute, an increasingly valuable capability when you consider the vast number of huge data, graphics, and program files being transferred today. These increases in speed translate into shorter transfer times, lower operating costs and phone charges, and more convenience. That's good news for every user. Advances in speed have also led to exciting, powerful communications applications for remote control, remote LAN access, and multimedia applications that are ready to burst onto the scene with information services and bulletin boards supporting pictures, video, and desktop conferencing.

Our design philosophy today is a direct reflection of our vision from the early 1980s — design a product that is technologically complex and powerful on the inside, yet simple to use from the outside. Furthermore, we want to bring the product to the market at a price that makes the technology more available to growing and varied segments of the marketplace. So, whether it's Hayes LANstep, our network operating system, or Smartcom for Windows communications software, our design philosophy is the same as it was in the beginning. Time has shown that our philosophy is sound and that it has provided a solid foundation for future computer communications technology.

One of the most gratifying aspects of the success of our design philosophy is knowing that because modems no longer require a technical expert, we have freed users to go on a nearly limitless journey beyond their desktops. The telephone network has become the largest computer peripheral in the world, with the modem providing the electronic link to a wide array of communications applications and information available from such industries as the medical, legal, and entertainment fields, as well as the government. You may have already experienced the communications excitement of calling an online service, like CompuServe, America Online, or Prodigy, or explored the variety of topics and people who communicate regularly on one of the more than 200,000 bulletin board systems around the world that represent special interest groups as diverse as home improvement, botany, computer clubs, or business communications systems for customer service.

Whether you need to maintain a worldwide, intercompany e-mail system, use your modem as a fax machine, oversee a network for placing orders with suppliers, or play a game, modems provide the critical link. From the very practical to the ridiculous, computer communications has something for everyone.

I'm excited about the possibilities for you when you combine the capabilities of your modem and communications software with the wealth of information in this book. So, no matter what your communications application might be, go ahead and start your own computer communications revolution and jump on the information highway. The on-ramp is only an AT command away.

Dennis Hayes
President and Founder
Hayes Microcomputer Products, Inc.

I

PART

An Armchair Tour

Part I of the *Official Hayes Modem Communications Companion* introduces this book, the communications world, and the technology. You learn about the necessary elements to make efficient and productive use of the remaining parts of the book.

Chapter 1 introduces the important elements in the book. It gives an overview of telecommunications, how the material is presented in the book, and what to look for when using the book as reference material.

Chapter 2 introduces the communications world and defines communications, what you can communicate with, and what you need to communicate. It also includes information on interesting and unusual applications for telecommunicating. You don't need any technical knowledge to understand this chapter.

Chapter 3 introduces the technology. You learn about data modems, fax modems, and their associated software. This chapter focuses on a general understanding and serves as a springboard for the more technical details introduces in later parts.

1

CHAPTER

A Guide to Using This Book

Welcome to the *Official Hayes Modem Communications Companion*! This authoritative guide to PC communication will make you comfortable with the technology, improve your productivity, and widen your horizons. Above all, it is a benefits-oriented practical tool that addresses the most frequently asked questions about communication.

This chapter is the guide to the rest of the book and introduces the following topics:

❖ Electronic communication

❖ What is and is not in this book

❖ Keys to finding information

❖ Where to go from here

Changing World

Electronic communication is one of the most rapidly changing and exciting technologies of this century. It has radically altered our view of the world. No longer do we hear about revolutions or natural disasters in distant places months or years after they occur. Now, we see and hear events as they happen and can even communicate directly with people involved.

Not only has our perspective of the world changed, but our everyday lives are also different. It is inconceivable to run any business without a telephone, and even the smallest business typically has a fax machine, voice mail, or an answering machine.

Modems and all the associated technology are now available to anyone with a computer at an affordable price and in an understandable presentation. In the same way that millions who use PCs now would never have imagined using a computer 10 to 15 years ago, millions now use modems, faxes, and other telecommunication tools as easily as an ordinary telephone or television. Telecommunication has become a major application for computers, now ranking in importance with word processors, spreadsheets, and databases.

It was natural for personal computers to evolve to include communication facilities. After all, mainframes have used modem technology since the 1960s. Telephones had become commonplace, inexpensive, and a primary means of communication. In fact, modems have been available for personal use since before the IBM PC and date back to the first microcomputers, which came in kits, such as the Altair.

Modems used with mainframes required dedicated phone lines. To link with another modem, you specified the phone number so mechanical switches could be set internally. If you needed to access a different phone number, the modem's switches had to be adjusted — usually by a qualified technician.

Dennis Hayes, founder of Hayes Microcomputer Products, learned about telephone networks while at Georgia Tech as a co-op student with AT&T Long Lines. After leaving Georgia Tech, he joined National Data Corporation. NDC ran a service bureau that handled electric membership cooperatives, which provide power and telephone service to rural communities. Part of Hayes job was to help the local independent telephone companies install modems.

Realizing how cumbersome the modem installation and configuration process was, Dennis Hayes and Dale Heatherington pioneered the concept of a microprocessor-controlled modem rather than having to call a technician every time a parameter needed changing.

In 1977 — four years before the introduction of the IBM PC — Hayes and his partner, Dale Heatherington, built a microprocessor-controlled modem that could be directly controlled by computer software. The first models were aimed at the hobbyists who were building microcomputers from kits, particularly the S100, and soon after that Apple II computers.

Although the first models were for hobbyists, the potential for personal and small-business use was obvious. Additionally, Hayes realized that the early computer companies did not have experience in data communication and that the large established companies, such as AT&T and IBM, would not immediately recognize the potential of the small-user market.

What became Hayes Microcomputer Products was incorporated by Hayes and Heatherington, an engineer, as D.C. Hayes Associates in January 1978. The voracious appetite of typical early microcomputer users for things to do with their computers spurred modem sales. For example, Hayes sold more than 1,000 modems for the Apple II before Apple introduced a hard disk drive.

Early modems worked only with specific computer models. Customer requests for modems to connect to computer A or computer B quickly drove Hayes to look for device independence in the modems. This would enable the company to build a single model modem that would connect to any computer, whether it was a minicomputer or a microcomputer or mainframe.

Linking modems to each other was not a problem, because all modems had to meet a specific standard. The problem was getting the electronic signals from the modem to a computer. The computers all had their own method of connection and used different standards.

This device independence was a driving force in the Hayes modem design. Each had to be able to be connected to a terminal, a microcomputer, or a printer. Additional features could not compromise this criterion. As a result, intelligent modems (with microprocessors that can accept commands from external software) became the standard means for linking computers, terminals, and printers.

By 1982, only a year after the IBM PC's introduction, Hayes annual sales hit $12 million, and in 1983 the company added Smartcom II software for the IBM PC to its product line. Since then, modems have become a standard part of many PC setups and are increasingly important for both business and home use.

Nowadays, modems are used most frequently to link two computers, but they continue to be able to link other devices, such as a terminal or printer, to a computer as well. Throughout this book, I assume you will be using a PC and a modem as one end of the connection. You may, however, be linked to another computer or a printer. Using a modem with a dedicated terminal rather than a PC, although feasible with modems, is not covered in this book.

What Is in This Book

Although communication is no longer limited to a technical audience, the perception lingers that modems are complicated "black boxes." This book, for introductory and intermediate users, focuses on the essential tools needed to take advantage of your modem, PC fax, and the telecommunication world. It is a practical reference that introduces the necessary concepts and terms and shows how to apply them.

The decision of what material to include in this book and what to omit was based in part on using the concept of providing answers to commonly asked communication questions. I gathered these questions from a variety of sources including the Hayes customer support staff, electronic bulletin boards, user groups, magazines, and, of course, my own experience.

This book explains PC communication, modems, faxes, and how to link to and exchange data with other computers. You learn what modems and faxes are, how to choose them, when to use them, and how to use them most effectively.

The early chapters lay the groundwork for the intermediate and more-advanced chapters. Armed with the concepts, you can move on to selection, installation, and configuration. After "getting it to work," you can discover how to streamline your communication and optimize your configuration to minimize online costs.

The gigantic array of online information is another main focus. Just as a library is a much wider resource than is your personal book collection, online information can expand your personal program library into a huge collection and give you limitless information on any topic.

However, just as a specialized library may be better in some instances, information may exist in various forms in different places online. To avoid frustrations, online services should be considered carefully and used appropriately.

Online information is not just reference material. A worldwide community of people use PC communication to share and exchange messages and information. They are not elite or (typically) eccentric, but they do have a desire to communicate.

Telecommunicating makes this possible 24 hours a day, seven days a week. Not only is the world becoming a smaller place, but time-zone differences, national borders, and even continental boundaries are irrelevant. Access to all this information can be as close as a local phone call.

The different types of online services are introduced in this book, and a sample session of each type illustrates applicable techniques that you can use to tap into this incredibly rich resource.

What Is Not in This Book

This book is not an encyclopedic tome that incorporates every tiny detail relating to communication. Because it is a practical tool, unnecessary engineering detail is not included. I do not, for example, describe the intimate details of how a modem or fax is designed so that you can design one for yourself. However, I provide sufficient conceptual information so you are able to appreciate what a modem or fax does, why it does it, and how to optimize its performance.

This book does not cover the details of linking a terminal to a modem. However, it does explain how to use your PC as a terminal to link to other computers. The information relating to terminals linking to remote computers tends to be very vendor specific.

This is not a speculative book. If the technology is not widely available and actually being used in practical situations, it is not covered in detail. Wireless communication, for example, is not included.

Although an important focus for this book is the available online services, both commercial and free, my intent is to give you a solid understanding of the possibilities and typical flavor of these services — not to provide an exhaustive guide. Once you have chosen an online service that suits your needs, you can probably find other books that focus on that particular service.

How the Parts Fit Together

The *Official Hayes Modem Communications Companion* is divided into four main parts: "An Armchair Tour," "Communications Basics," "Survival and Efficiency Tools," and "The Online World Tour." The book introduces terms and techniques so beginners will understand the necessary concepts and can apply their knowledge. It also includes, as sidebars, in-depth explanations for readers interested in more details or background.

Part I, "An Armchair Tour," introduces the concept of the whole communication picture being composed of a variety of connected but separate elements. It serves as a guide to the rest of the book. It introduces the technology, explains what is included in the book and what is excluded. It shows what is possible with communication, what you need to achieve your goals, and how the parts of the book fit together.

Part II, "Communications Basics," introduces the fundamentals necessary to use modems and PC faxes effectively. It covers the important terms and elements needed to communicate. By the end of this section, you know when to use a fax and when to use a modem, as well as how to select, install, and make a connection with another computer. You understand the essentials of serial ports, telephones, modems, communication software, connecting, terminal emulation, file transfer, and disconnecting.

Part III, "Survival and Efficiency Tools," moves you from the elementary connection to making the most of the modem, fax, and communication software. By the end of this section, you understand modem features and know what to look for in communication software, such as dialing directories, scripts, and file-transfer protocols. You understand your fax software and OCR software. Additional chapters cover other automation techniques, such as off-line readers, methods for reducing costs, and remote control software.

Armed with the techniques from earlier sections, Part IV, "The Online World Tour," introduces the wide scope of available online services. The perspective is practical, emphasizing what each type of service should be used for, and includes a brief tour. This makes you aware of the potential for online communication rather than providing a reference guide to any particular service. With the fear of the unknown removed, you gain the confidence to use a particular service without mentally counting the costs. As general topics, the covered services include BBSs, the Internet, message-based services such as MCI Mail, information-exchange services such as CompuServe and Prodigy, and information-searching services such as Dialog and Dow Jones News Retrieval.

Part V includes four appendixes to serve as references: "AT Command Set," "Resource Guide to Popular Online Services," "Guide to Smartcom for Windows LE," and "100 Most Frequently Asked Questions."

Keys to Finding Information

Three design elements used throughout the book help guide you when using the book as a reference, provide more technical detail for the interested reader, and emphasize the authoritative practical tools included.

The sidebars

Each chapter in Parts II through IV also includes sidebars. These are usually one page in length and allow the inquisitive reader to gain an in-depth understanding of a specific topic. You often see sidebars in magazines. They are separate boxed areas of text, often with a shaded background, that stand separately from the main text but are related to the subject.

How to Identify a Sidebar

Boxed sidebars introduce additional details, historical or more advanced information on a particular topic. They are set apart from the main text by being boxed and have a shaded background.

For example, Chapter 4, "Selecting Your Equipment," includes a sidebar on understanding a UART

(Universal Asynchronous Receiver/Transmitter). Although this is an important topic that will be of interest to most readers, it is not essential reading for understanding the concepts introduced in the chapter.

The questions

Throughout the book, you will see commonly asked questions in large type. These questions are used as a graphical element throughout the book to stand apart from the main text. The questions start in the margin, appear in italics, and are surrounded by quotation marks to indicate that these are questions that many readers have.

"How do I find answers to my communications questions?"

The main text surrounding the question will directly answer the question. This element also helps you focus on a particular problem by posing questions likely to occur.

Appendix D lists these commonly asked questions and provides a page cross-reference to where you can find the answers in the book.

The jigsaw puzzle

At the beginning of each chapter, the jigsaw puzzle shows how the particular chapter relates to the whole book. This will serve as a quick guide for the reader interested in exploring only particular features. (See Figure 1-1.)

Each of the 12 jigsaw puzzle pieces represents a benefit or feature of communications. For example, the picture of winged running shoes represents speeding your communications, and the envelope being mailed represents sending mail electronically. The puzzle pieces in the chapter opener show the major topics covered in that particular chapter. For example, the chapters that have the winged running shoes as one of the chapter opener puzzle pieces include sections that help speed your communications.

The 12 puzzle pieces represent the following concept:

1	Time savers
2	Speeding communications
3	Automating communications
4	Transferring files
5	Chatting online
6	E-mail and messaging
7	Broadcasting your messages
8	Reading online
9	Researching online
10	Entertainment and games online
11	World exploration
12	Reaching an audience around the world

Figure 1-1: The 12 jigsaw puzzle pieces used in this book.

Where to Go from Here

Typical readers of the *Official Hayes Modem Communications Companion* include:

1. Non-computer people, probably professionals and business owners, who recognize the need to expand their understanding and use of communication to compete in the market.

2. Home users who dabble in communication and want their children to have access to online information and games.

3. Network administrators, again possibly non-computer professionals, who are expected to expand a company's information base or implement electronic mail services both internally and externally.

4. Modem owners who want to better understand the technology. They are likely to be user-group members and extensive magazine readers.

These readers need to know how to select, install, configure, and use the equipment and software they have or need to buy. They are looking for a fundamental understanding of what they are doing, where to go for data sources, and how to collect the data, but they do not want a lecture in electronics or speculative information on future technologies.

When the basics are understood, these readers want real solutions and practical methods to reduce expenses by getting the required data as fast and as inexpensively as possible. Even without understanding the technology, many readers are aware that ongoing costs are necessary for phone service but want to feel in control of their expenses.

If you are a newcomer to communications, although you may be a PC expert, Chapter 2, "Understanding the Communications World," and Chapter 3, "Understanding the Technology," are essential reading. These chapters show the full scope of communication and serve as a launching point for exploring the remainder of the book.

Even if you already own and use a modem, these chapters may let you discover new opportunities. Skim through them quickly to get an idea of all the concepts before moving on.

Part II, "Communications Basics," is the next stopping place for all readers. The essential concepts and practical methods introduced in this section are built on in later chapters. If you know what you want to do but do not know quite how to do it, this is the place to start. Along with Part III, "Survival and Efficiency Tools," it is also the section to read if you are considering purchasing equipment or software.

Intermediate users can go directly to Part III to learn how to make the most of the equipment they already have up and running. If terms that you do not understand are used, they will have been explained in Part II, so you may need to refer back for areas where you are less knowledgeable. Part III can also help in purchasing decisions.

As Part II introduces the essentials to make a connection, communicate with another computer, and transfer files between computers, Part III shows the myriad of tools that make this connection more efficient, streamlined, and cost-effective. If you are upgrading equipment, Part III shows what might be missing from your current configuration. Chapter 12, "Special Purpose Communications," focuses on less-common connections, such as remote control software, communicating on the road, and international communication. These are becoming increasingly important but need special consideration to be feasible.

Part IV, "The Online World Tour," is beneficial for all readers. It shows what you can connect to. This is the section for finding where to look for computer games, doing patent searches, getting a pen pal in Siberia, or finding technical support for your favorite word processor. It is also the place to find where to market and distribute the programs you have written, advertise your better mousetrap, or tout your solution to world poverty.

Summary

This chapter described the general scope of the book and explained the design elements that will help you find the specific techniques you are looking for.

If you're new to telecommunications, thoroughly read Chapters 2 and 3. If you already know some basics about your modem, skim Chapters 2 and 3, and move on to Part II.

2

CHAPTER

Understanding the Communications World

This chapter introduces the concept of human communications and telecommunications. You will learn about the following topics:

- ❖ Understanding human communications
- ❖ Understanding telecommunications
- ❖ Appreciating the many reasons for communicating
- ❖ Knowing what you need to communicate

Defining Communications

As humans, we no longer depend on our ability to hunt, kill, and keep away animal predators but instead have established an elaborate set of social skills and methods of interacting for survival. In many ways, we still use our hunting and survival skills, but we depend heavily on communications rather than actually killing our prey. We typically define successful people as those who have made better business decisions, can manage more people, and have accumulated more money. The respected "tribal" leader is no longer the man who has killed the most animals, but now is the person who has the most control of money, people, and data.

We also continue to be social animals and communicate in many different ways. The most obvious is speech, but mime, body language, and the written word are also important elements, as well as the more recent radio, television, and computer communication.

Data communications, or *telecommunications*, where information is transferred between two computers, is a logical extension of human communications skills. We are by nature inquisitive and have extended our skills, moving from semaphore to telegraph, telephone, and the current computer electronics era. There is little doubt that this evolution will continue, and the next generation will have even more data at its fingertips.

Communications on a computer can seem like a daunting field that you will never understand. Even a PC expert may find all the new terminology intimidating. However, once you have learned a couple of basic items, PC communications is easier to understand than many other PC concepts.

Before discussing computer communications, let's briefly consider human communication in general. These analogies illustrate successful and unsuccessful communication. As I introduce you to the various telecommunications techniques throughout the rest of the book, I will restate the "human" equivalent so that you have a quickly understandable comparison.

Let's first consider communication between two people. One person signals in a way that must be understood by the receiving person. Despite the apparent simplicity of this scenario, many different parameters need to be satisfied for successful communication. For example, the two people need to be within earshot, speak the same language, and be ready to listen and talk to each other.

In conversation, the sending and receiving often occurs at the same time in both directions. One person smiles as the other says something funny, or one person's blood pressure rises as another person shouts abuse. You have direct feedback as to whether your message is being received as you desire and, if necessary, can alter your response until the desired effect is found.

As humans, our speech involves a lot of body language, voice intonation, and other signals that impart more than the words themselves. Some forms of communication remove some of the human senses and reduce the ease of communication. For example, the telephone removes sight from the interchange. Unless the receiving person provides verbal feedback, you cannot tell whether your message is being understood or misinterpreted. Some people, including myself, continue to use hand signals while on the telephone even though they cannot be heard or seen by the receiver.

Other forms of communication can still involve two people but are less direct, such as letter writing. One person writes a letter and mails it; at a later time, the recipient reads the letter. Parameters similar to those for direct communication must be satisfied, such as language barriers and correct routing of information (equivalent to being within earshot). This indirect approach can also have problems if that information is lost along the way or misinterpreted or if the situation changed between its being sent and received.

Mail, like the telephone, removes senses from the communication, both sound and vision. However, its indirectness—the information is not read as soon as it is written— is a tremendous advantage. You can read what you have written before sending it and reconsider your phrasing. Ultimately, however, the indirectness means you are unable to see the recipient's immediate reaction.

Strictly speaking, books are also a form of communication that involves two people. The author has written material that is mass produced and read at a later time. As before, the communication requires correct routing of information and no language barrier, but you can also look at this form of communication in a different way.

The author has gathered and arranged related material that is intended to be seen as a single entity by the reader. A major application for telecommunications involves the electronic equivalent of a library. You browse through "book" titles and select topics of interest so that you can withdraw books or abstracts from books for later reading. In this communications example, the emotional response of the reader is less important than the usefulness of the material itself. The best communication is achieved by the "library" that has the most accurate and accessible indexing system.

Most types of communication are variations on the three basic forms: conversation, mail, and books. These have direct equivalents in telecommunications: chatting, messaging, and databases.

The Potential for Communications

Webster's Ninth New Collegiate Dictionary defines *telecommunication* as "communication at a distance (as by telephone or television)" and *teleconference* as "a conference among people remote from one another who are linked by telecommunication devices (as telephones, televisions, or computer terminals)."

Although accurate, this definition only hints at the reality and potential for telecommunications with your PC. Even if you know little about computers, you can appreciate the potential by considering what you can do with television and existing technology. The telecommunication problems you will run into have parallels with typical telephone, television, and VCR use.

You can use an antenna and pick up local television stations, or you can connect to a cable television company and pick up more stations. If you use a satellite dish, however, you have many more television stations from all around the world available at the click of a button (or two).

Not only can you get access to more television stations, but with newer televisions, you can also watch more than one channel at once, get better quality sound, bigger (and smaller) pictures, and automate your watching by having the television turn off after a predefined time or blocking out specific channels.

If you add a VCR, your resources multiply. You can watch prerecorded tapes, record your own tapes, watch the television while recording another channel, get higher resolution pictures on your television, and program the VCR to turn on and off automatically. Now add a video camera, and you can videotape your family and friends, record events that are remote from your VCR, and bring them into your home.

Each of these devices has more options and gizmos each model year, and whatever you buy now will be outdated in a couple of years. If you wait a while before purchasing, you will be able to do more things than present equipment will permit. However, while you wait, you are missing out on many possibilities.

Telecommunications on your PC is comparable. Armed with a modem, communications software, and a phone line, you have access to limitless resources bounded only by your imagination. The field is so wide that generalizations are essential.

As discussed previously, communications can be divided into three main topics: speech, mail, and books. Telecommunications has equivalents: chatting, messaging, and databases.

You can use your modem, communications software, and phone line to communicate with another modem that is attached to another computer. You can, for example, call a friend or business colleague. Depending on your communications software, you can "chat" with your friend by typing on your keyboard and waiting for him to type a response, send a message to the other computer so that your business colleague will read it when she returns to her computer, transfer files between the two computers, or look something up on your friend's computer.

However, except in special circumstances, you are unlikely to want to communicate only with a particular friend. All around the world, in rapidly increasing numbers, online services supply the same features as the simple scenario of communicating with a friend but on a much grander scale.

Online services, covered in detail in Part IV, are computers with modems and specialized communications software that act as repositories for the database information and messages that are exchanged between modem owners. Most have multiple phone lines, and several, if not thousands, of people can be calling the same computer at the same time. Some systems even include features that allow you to "chat" or play games with other people who are currently calling the same computer.

As with many new technologies, a large variety of terms are used for similar items. *Online services* is a general term that encompasses such well-known commercial services as CompuServe as well as the estimated 200,000-plus *bulletin board systems* (BBSs) available in the U.S. Although many of these BBSs are run as hobbies from basements, do not assume that they are amateurish. Each online service is unique and offers different features and contents.

Databases

The most popular application for online services is the collection of software. People want to extend their personal software libraries, and literally millions of computer files are available online. You simply call up the online service and transfer the file to your computer.

The types of files available online are even more varied than the people who run the services. Many programs, utilities, and data are free for the taking. For example, one file may be a template to create newsletters in Microsoft Publisher, another may contain a spreadsheet model template for calculating your mortgage payments in Lotus 1-2-3, and another may be clip art. Each file was created by someone and transferred to the online service for anyone to access and use.

The First BBS

Across the nation, thousands of people sign on to bulletin board systems everyday to perform a wide range of tasks, from downloading important business information to ordering groceries. The inventors of the first BBS didn't have such commercial uses in mind on a snowy Chicago day in 1978. Ward Christensen and Randy Suess were simply two snowbound computer hobbyists who needed an easier way to transfer data to one another than sending cassette tapes in the mail.

The preceding summer, Dennis Hayes shipped the first hobbyist modem, the 300-baud internal modem. Hayes built the first Smartmodems on his kitchen table in small production runs of five. The Smartmodem was the missing component needed to make the connection between computers and telephone lines easily. In the setup manual, Hayes wrote that modems could be used for a number of applications, including establishing a bulletin board.

Christensen and Hayes knew each other from industry meetings. So, when Christensen called Hayes on that snowy Saturday, Hayes agreed to donate a modem for use in their history-making project.

Christensen and Suess then developed software and hardware for the first BBS in a short two weeks. Two years earlier, Christensen had written software to allow him to "beep" the contents of a floppy disk to a cassette tape by using an acoustic coupler. Although Christensen didn't know it at the time, he had just invented the 128-byte Xmodem standard, which is still used today.

While Suess worked on the hardware side, Christensen wrote a bulletin board program patterned after corkboard bulletin boards used to post information for a computer club. With that program finished, all the components — computer, phone line, modem, and software — came together to produce the first, and to this day, the oldest BBS in the world.

The most important file type found in online services is called *shareware*. These commercial products, often of a very high quality, are distributed by using the shareware principle, which means you can obtain and copy these programs for no charge. You can use them for a limited period to see whether they fit your needs. If they do, you pay the registration fee to the original author. If you do not find the program useful, you simply delete it from your computer and owe nothing.

Shareware programs, like programs found in retail and mail-order outlets, vary in quality. However, you have to pay only if you actually like the product. Even if you do not like the product, you are more knowledgeable about what to look for in another company's product.

I find that about half of the programs I use on a regular basis are shareware and are much better than typical commercial equivalents because they fit my needs more closely. This is due in part to the fact that I can actually try them out before purchase.

In particular, I find that shareware products, such as communications programs, bookkeeping programs, electronic databases, and virus detectors, often incorporate valuable additions much more quickly than do their commercial counterparts. For example, if I am concerned that my antivirus program is out of date, I can get the latest update within minutes by using telecommunications.

Programs found online really do include the full gamut. Games are extremely popular, as are utility programs, but you can find almost anything you need. If you cannot find it, ask by leaving a message and you are very likely to be directed to several files fitting your needs.

Do not overlook telecommunications as an economical means of file distribution as well as file collection. For private use, you can rapidly distribute updated sales reports, new form layouts, and other data by using your modem instead of an overnight courier service or mail. The data arrives almost instantaneously for the cost of a phone call.

For more public consumption, you can rapidly get your program seen by more people than is possible through traditional selling channels. Do not assume that if you use the shareware approach you will not get registrations. If your product is any good, people will register. Recent reports estimate that the top shareware antivirus program manufacturer made $2 million in profits in a single quarter. Although multimillion-dollar enterprises are in the minority, many shareware authors make a reasonable living by supporting and updating their programs. Shareware is also distributed by other methods, but the primary sources are online services and disk vendors that charge a small disk-copying fee.

The other more specialized application for online databases is research. Some online services are organized as huge reference libraries. You pick a topic and gradually focus in on the data you are looking for. For example, you may need to know how and why the economy of China has changed over the last 100 years, or you may need to know current financial information for your stock portfolio.

By accessing the most appropriate online service, you can sift through enormous databases and rapidly focus on the information you need. When you find the data, you will be able to extract only the information you need and ignore the rest.

Some companies offer a service in which their staff will do the searching for you. You might use this, for example, as a newspaper clipping service, where you hire a company to read particular newspapers and magazines and provide copies of articles mentioning your company's or your competitors' name. Because the search is done electronically (most newspapers and magazines are now available in electronic form), searching can be much more accurate and inclusive than depending on a human to spot the names.

Messages

Apart from files, most online services include a messaging system. *Messages* are usually divided into *topics*, often known as *conferences*. You look at the conferences or topics, choose the ones of interest to you, and read the messages being sent. You can also type in your own message in response to someone, or you can start a new series of messages. Topics or conferences are very diverse and are not necessarily computer related. A few examples are politics, cooking, word processing, science fiction, and geology.

Messaging is typically designed for public discussion. Although messages can be marked as private, they are not private in the sense that they cannot be read by anyone. They can be read by the computer operators who run the computer system. You might use a private message to invite a fellow computer user to a movie, but you would not disclose confidential information that you didn't want anyone other than the recipient to read.

Messages are a mainstay on online services. They come in various guises but can provide more diverse and rapid information than other means. Many PC vendors, such as Hayes, Borland, Microsoft, and WordPerfect, have their own conferences on at least one popular online service. You can read information about upcoming products, get detailed qualified technical support, and find out what other people are complaining about or praising in a new product.

You can also contact many vendors by using their bulletin boards. When you purchase a computer product, the documentation often includes the phone number for a BBS. A vendor's BBS may include tips on configuration, updated documentation, or even full technical support resources. Companies with BBSs include Hayes, Microsoft, and Symantec. Online With Hayes, for example, enables users to read information about new products, obtain technical support, and download files (800-874-2937).

Some online services offer variations on the messaging system. You can do online shopping, make airline reservations, find the weather, or obtain stock market information, for example. This is an area where there is a blurring between using the online service as a database and using it as a messaging system.

Online services also provide interest at a variety of levels. You can find local, regional, national, and international information if you look in the right places. In many cases, all of these services are only a local phone call away.

Messages are intended to be an open forum type of mail. However, private mail, known as *electronic mail* or *e-mail*, is also available on some online services. These services, or this aspect of a service, are equivalent to the U.S. Postal Service or a courier service providing a mechanism for private delivery of your mail. In these cases, neither the online service operators nor other subscribers to the online service can read the information.

You can send your message to anyone who subscribes to the same service as you do or who subscribes to a service that can exchange data with your service. This interchange of data between services is an evolving feature that is gradually becoming less of an issue as more services can interconnect.

With e-mail, you write a message to be sent to a particular person or group of people, and the service distributes the information. Depending on the service, the message can be text only, or you may be able to attach a binary file, such as a program, to the message so that the file and message are sent together.

Some e-mail services offer more than mail service to their subscribers. MCI Mail, for example, will send a message to the addressed person. However, if the person is not an MCI Mail subscriber, the message will be printed and mailed via U.S. mail from the closest service location to the recipient. In many cases, this is faster than using U.S. mail directly and, for short messages, costs less than an overnight courier service. It is also more convenient.

Before using one of these services, be sure to understand whether anyone else, such as the system operator, is able to read your mail. Although you probably do not care if someone reads that you are holding a meeting in Chicago on Tuesday, you may care if others learn that you are about to make a hostile takeover of a competitor. This can be important when you are sending mail from one service to another because the receiving service may not offer the same privacy as the sending service.

Another major application for telecommunications and mail is PC faxes. You can use a PC fax modem, which is now often incorporated into the modem board in your computer, in the same way you would use a stand-alone fax machine. You choose what you want to send from your computer and send it via the fax software. In this case, the receiving computer is a fax machine and may or may not be a PC fax modem. Chapter 3, "Understanding the Technology," details the differences between a data modem and a fax modem. However, for this chapter, you need to understand that a PC fax modem provides a method of sending data to a potentially non-PC end user and that the fax received is a graphical representation of the text or material sent. You would not use a fax modem to communicate with an online service.

You need to understand that the data you send is not limited to being read the instant it is sent. The computer or remote fax is a storage medium, equivalent to a mail box. The information is read or retransmitted only when the receiver is ready.

Chatting

The database and messaging information found on online services share both a big advantage and a big disadvantage. You can access any of the information at any time of the day or night, but you are not directly interacting with the sending person.

However, direct interaction, known as *chatting*, is available in various forms on many online services. Some online services offer conferences where you can "chat" with other people online. Suppose, for example, that when you are online, you choose to look at a chat conference. You would type the command to join the conference and a message would appear on everyone's screen in this conference saying that you joined. You would then watch for a few moments while you read what everyone is discussing. Suppose the topic is local restaurants. A typical message may ask "Where do I go for good seafood?" When you want to add your input, you type your comment at the keyboard, and your comment is shown to everyone in the chat conference.

While discussing local restaurants may seem trivial, another section of the same conference might include a guest "speaker," such as a famous author, politician, or industry leader, giving you the opportunity to ask questions of people you would not normally be able to meet. This type of chatting is often advertised by the service. When you connect with the service, a list of upcoming "events" shows you who will be chatting when.

Interactive games are an increasingly popular application for online chatting. Unlike ordinary computer games in which you pit yourself against a computer opponent, with *interactive games,* you call an online service with your modem and participate in computer games where the other players are also "humans" calling in from their respective computers. This is like a computerized version of the very popular Dungeons and Dragons role-playing games. The games offered, however, are not all mystical characters. There are also plenty of opportunities to drive a tank and shoot your opponents, for example.

Another minor application for chatting online may occur when you call a BBS, especially if it is a small local BBS. The system operator, the person who runs the BBS, may see that you are having difficulty doing something or may want to respond to a message you are leaving immediately, and will chat with you by interrupting the bulletin board software and typing a message to you on the screen.

I regularly call a couple of local bulletin boards very early on Saturday mornings. The system operator of one of them (run from the local vet's office!) does system maintenance at about the same time as I call. He often breaks in to have a quick chat. We discuss, for example, what we have read in the trade journals or what new software or hardware we have seen or bought. This is unlikely, if not impossible, on many of the large online services.

Technology potential

Technology is changing so rapidly that even the most detailed description of online applications barely scratches the surface of the potential.

In the same way that PCs have completely changed the way we do business and how we need to present ourselves to look "professional," telecommunications has and will continue to change the way we use our computers.

Consider, for example, how word processors changed mass mailing. You now regularly receive mail with your name seamlessly included in the address and main text of a letter, as if it had been written specially for you. You can do similar things with telecommunications. With a single phone call, you can communicate with hundreds of thousands of people. It's up to you what you want to say to them or hear from them.

First BBS Teleconference to the USSR

"Greetings from the United States of America. This moment shall go down in history because it marks the beginning of the Global User Group, a momentous occasion." With these words, the first International BBS Teleconference involving uncensored access to the then-USSR was conducted on June 15, 1990.

It all started when Paul Curtis, systems operator for GLOBALNET, the worldwide electronic bulletin board system of the Association of PC User Groups (APCUG), wrote a White Paper in April 1989 describing the possibilities and opportunities for reducing tensions among nations of differing political and economic systems. With the help of GLOBALNET sponsor Borland International and equipment donations from other U.S. software and hardware manufacturers, Curtis' possibility became a reality.

The first BBS teleconference to Russia used Hayes modems and was held at the First International Computer Forum in Moscow. At the Moscow site, the entire teleconference was projected on a large screen so that the audience could observe the proceedings and ask questions. "There was such disbelief that such a thing could even take place or that the technology could make it possible," Curtis remembers.

Through this historic event, channels of communication were opened between the East and the West that had never been opened before. "The combination of communicating and computing is an empowering technology," emphasized Curtis.

Using Modems in One of the First Closed Loop Traffic Systems

If you've ever been stuck in traffic because of a malfunctioning traffic light, you can appreciate the role Hayes modems played in helping to revolutionize traffic control systems.

Until the early 1980s, traffic control was monitored by urban traffic-control systems that only connected traffic-control boxes at intersections to a mainframe computer. These systems were expensive and often inefficient. Complaints about traffic light malfunctions had to be checked through the mainframe or in person.

Cities needed a decentralized system that would allow traffic-control monitoring at the desktop. In the early 1980s, Transyt Corporation in Tallahassee, Florida, developed such a system. Using Hayes

Smartmodems, Transyt's Closed Loop System connected intersections on the airport loop road in Atlanta to PCs operated by the city's traffic-monitoring team. Hayes modems, installed in traffic-control boxes near the intersections, allowed the traffic team to monitor traffic lights, change traffic patterns, and watch intersections on the airport loop without leaving their desks or logging on to a mainframe.

The Transyt Closed Loop System was a huge success, and the Transyt Corporation currently has approximately 2,000 systems installed internationally. More than 11 years after the first installation, the primary communications link from the office to the field continues to be the Hayes modem.

What You Need to Communicate

To communicate, you ultimately need at least two people: one to send information and one to receive it. Telecommunications is similar in that you need to send information and have it received.

As a general rule, a telecommunications link has five elements: the sending computer, sending modem, telephone link, receiving modem, and receiving computer. The electronic devices that you use to connect your computer with another computer are called *modems* (short for *modulator/demodulator*). The transmitting modem accepts signals from the sending computer and translates (*modulates*) data into a form that can be sent on a telephone line. The receiving modem, attached to the other end of the phone line, translates (*demodulates*) the received data and passes the signals to the receiving computer. The receiving modem may be attached to a printer rather than to a computer.

A modem can be an external device, the proverbial "black box," or a device installed inside your computer. Chapter 3, "Understanding the Technology," introduces modems and their purpose in more detail. For this chapter, you need to understand that you link two modems together and control them from computers to make a telecommunications link.

As a modem owner, you will need communications software. This software does two things: it controls the connection and is responsible for sending or receiving the desired data. This connection control involves controlling the link between the modem and the computer as well as the link between the modems. Chapter 1 explains how Dennis Hayes realized the value of being able to control a modem by sending it commands from software, cofounded Hayes Microcomputer Products, and created the PC modem industry. This allows you, the computer operator, the ability to control the modem via software commands.

Most modems come with communications software. Some of these programs are very elementary and provide only the minimum required to make a connection, and others are flexible and versatile enough to fit all of your communications needs. If you prefer, you can purchase communications software from a third-party company or another modem manufacturer.

The typical stumbling block for most new modem users is establishing the first connection and transferring the first file. The ease of doing this is directly related to the communications software. Before you give up telecommunications as a very technical and overwhelming topic, try and judge whether your frustration is due to communications software that is unnecessarily difficult to use.

Communications software has two primary purposes. First, it controls the modem. Second, it sends and receives your data to and from another modem. The modem must be controlled to make it operate with appropriate parameters (equivalent to talking the same language in human communication) as well as to establish and maintain the link between the two modems (equivalent to dialing the correct phone number and keeping the phone off the hook).

The receiving computer must also use communications software to control its modem and open the way to allow the data to be received. The receiving computer does not have to be the same type of computer as the sending computer, nor does it have to be running the same communications software. But the two modems must be able to communicate with each other for the communications link to work. The receiving device can be a printer, and the printer can accept the control codes and data sent from the originating computer to print a document. In this case, the printer sends data back to the originating computer and signals its status.

With the two modems, and consequently the two computers, linked, you use the communications software to send data to and receive data from the other computer. Regardless of whether you are chatting, messaging, or using a database, the communications link involves sending and receiving data between two modems that are controlled by computers with communications software.

The automation possible with computers can remove the need for a second person to be active in a telecommunications link. However, it does not usually remove the need for a second computer. In many cases, such as when you call an online service, you are able to control the communications software attached to the remote modem (the modem at the other end of the phone line). You instruct the online service to accept your message or file without direct interaction with anyone at the service.

Using a PC fax modem instead of a data modem is a similar conceptual connection. The fax software on your computer controls the PC fax modem. It sends signals to the fax modem that make the fax modem adjust its parameters or establish a connection with another fax modem and send or receive data. Although you may have a PC fax modem and a data modem as a single expansion board or device, you actually have two separate devices: a data modem and a fax modem. A telecommunications link can either link two faxes together or can link two modems together. You use communications software to link two data modems together and fax software to link two faxes together.

Strictly speaking, the term modem means modulator/demodulator. Types of modems include data modems, fax modems, and voice modems. As is typical with PC terminology, the terminology has become abbreviated, and *data modems*, which are used to transmit data from one place to another, are known simply as modems. Now that fax modems are also available for the PC, the terminology is more confusing. A *fax modem* can send data that conforms with the fax standards from one place to another.

If you think about it, the term fax is meaningless. Does it refer to the hardware, the paper, the action of transmitting, or the printed document? A stand-alone fax machine is actually a fax terminal, because it is a terminal device capable of sending and receiving faxes. When installed in a PC, the equivalent device lacks the terminal capabilities but includes the modem features for sending and receiving documents to fax communication standards.

In this book, the term *modem* is used to mean *data modem*, and the term *fax modem* relates to the electronic device installed or attached to a PC that can receive and send facsimiles of documents.

Summary

This chapter introduced the concept of telecommunications. Telecommunications between computers is an extension of human communications. By considering the three main means of human communication—conversation, mail, and books—you can understand the three main types of telecommunications—chatting, messaging, and databases.

You use telecommunications to transfer data between two computers. The other computer can be the same as or completely different from yours. You make your computer communicate with your modem. Your modem communicates with another modem, which in turn communicates with its computer. For the connection to be successful, the two modems must be able to communicate with each other.

Chatting is equivalent to holding a conversation with another person. When connected to another computer, you type on your keyboard, and someone else types on his/her keyboard in response. *Messaging* is when you type a series of sentences, a "message," that is stored on another computer and can be read by the recipient. Messaging lacks the direct interaction available with chatting but is the most typical way of interacting when online.

Much data stored online is in databases and can be divided into two general types. One database type is a collection of files and programs that you can gather by using your modem. The other is more of a research resource that you search for pertinent information on a particular topic. This type is roughly equivalent to a sophisticated encyclopedia.

Online services include large-scale commercial services, such as GEnie, as well as bulletin board systems. A typical commercial service can handle thousands of users calling at once; a BBS typically handles only tens of concurrent users. However, each online service has an individual character and offers unique features. A data modem is typically referred to as a modem, and a fax modem is a modem that can transmit and receive facsimiles of documents.

Chapter 3 builds on the knowledge gained from this chapter to introduce the specifics of telecommunications as it applies to PCs.

Understanding the Technology

This chapter introduces telecommunications technology. You learn about the following topics:

❖ Understanding data modem and fax modem communication

❖ Understanding data modem and fax modem hardware

❖ Knowing your data modem and fax modem software

❖ Understanding remote control software

This information provides the basic knowledge to enable you to take advantage of the *Official Hayes Modem Communications Companion.* Subsequent chapters are more specialized and will focus on one or more of the topics covered in this chapter. The terminology introduced in this chapter will be assumed in later chapters.

Introducing Modem Communications

As explained in Chapter 2, a telecommunications link involves five main elements. A computer with communications software is linked to a modem. The modem is linked to a phone line and subsequently to another modem. This remote modem is in turn linked to another computer with communications software or to a printer.

The two computers, two communications software programs, and the two modems do not need to be the same. In fact, you do not actually have to use a phone line to link the two modems; a cable will serve but obviously has distance limitations.

The key to a communications link is making the two modems communicate with each other. This involves making the communications software at each end of the connection control the modems appropriately so the modems will interact.

Introducing a modem

To understand modem communication, you need to understand the basics. A *modem* (*mo*dulator/*dem*odulator) is a piece of electronic hardware that you attach to your computer. As shown in Figure 3-1, it can be an external box that is connected to your computer by a cable, or as shown in Figure 3-2 and Figure 3-3, it can be an internal device that is plugged into your computer directly.

Note: Many newer modem models include a PC fax modem as standard. If you purchase a data and fax modem, you have essentially bought two different devices in a single unit. You have the ability to connect by using the modem portion or the fax modem portion of the data and fax modem. This section of the chapter refers only to the data modem. Fax modems and their software, because they are used for different purposes than data modems, are detailed in subsequent sections.

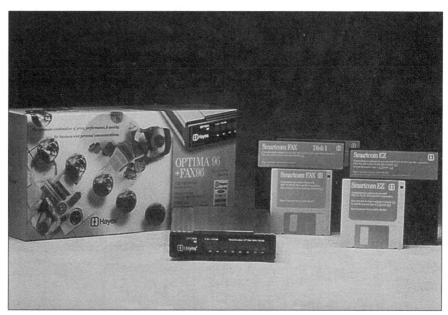

Figure 3-1: An external modem, the Hayes OPTIMA 96 + FAX96 is a data and fax modem combined in a single unit.

Figure 3-2: An internal modem, the Hayes OPTIMA 144B + FAX144 is a data and fax modem with a communications accelerator combined in a single expansion board.

Figure 3-3: A PCMCIA modem, the Hayes OPTIMA 144 + FAX144 is a data and fax modem combined on a PCMCIA expansion board used in some laptop and notebook computers.

As an external unit, a modem is typically a small rectangular box with a series of LEDs (light-emitting diodes) along the front and a series of connectors and an on/off switch on the back. Most modems also include a separate power supply, a small black cube with an incorporated electrical plug, that you plug into the electrical outlet and the rear of the modem.

An external modem typically has two or three other connectors. The larger connector, known as a *DB25 connector*, is the data connector that accepts the cable linking your computer and the modem. You will need a cable that can join this connector to a serial port on your computer.

Serial ports are covered in detail in Chapter 4, "Selecting Your Equipment." For this chapter, you need to understand that your modem is controlled by your computer via this cable.

The other one, or two, connectors are *RJ-11 phone jacks*. These are the same as the connectors typically found on telephones and telephone outlets. They are used to connect your modem to the phone line and possibly to another telephone extension.

Do not be embarrassed if you did not realize that you need to connect the modem to the phone line. It may be very obvious once you know, but an acquaintance of mine spent more than an hour trying to help someone call a BBS with a new modem and software without thinking to ask whether the modem was connected to a phone line.

A modem's electronic circuitry includes a microprocessor. You control the modem from your computer by using communications software, which sends two types of information to the modem: data and modem commands.

A special sequence of characters, known as the *escape sequence*, switches the modem into command mode so that it is ready to accept instructions. These instructions tell the modem to perform such tasks as the equivalent of picking up the phone receiver, dialing a phone number, and making a connection with another modem.

A modem can accept many more commands than those necessary to simply dial the telephone. Successful telecommunication involves many more parameters and coordination between the two modems. Commands can set the desired speed of data transfer between the modems, the number of times the phone should ring before the modem answers, and the form of modem status information that is sent back from the modem to the computer.

Chapter 5, "Understanding Your Modem," explains the essentials of these commands; but for this chapter, you need to understand that the modem is a microprocessor-controlled box that interfaces between your computer and your phone line. You control it from communications software on your computer. The modem can accept commands when in command mode and can send and receive data to the other computer when not in command mode.

Linking the computer to the modem

Your PC is a digital computer. A bit of data has one of two discrete levels, on or off, also known as high or low, or one or zero. The patterns generated by your PC, the sequences of ones and zeros, make up the data that you see as characters on the video screen, numbers in a spreadsheet, or keystrokes on the keyboard, for example.

In a telecommunications link, you are sending digital data from one computer to another. However, the telephone system is an analog system designed to accept the human voice. Although parts of it take advantage of digital electronics technology to move the speech more efficiently, the telephone system in its current form is intended for speech and not a series of ones and zeros. Analog signals do not have discrete levels like the zeros and ones in digital signals, but can have any value between the minimum and maximum.

An ordinary light switch provides an approximate analogy. The on/off switch is considered digital because the light bulb is either on or off. If you replace the light switch with a dimmer switch, the light bulb's glow is considered analog because its brightness can have a variety of levels between on and off.

You can think of your PC as a microprocessor with memory and a series of devices attached to it. The devices include the keyboard and display. However, the PC system architecture allows you to add other devices, such as a printer or mouse, via standard connections, known as serial and parallel ports. Most printers, for example, are connected to your computer via the parallel port.

A modem is a serial device and is attached to the PC's microprocessor via serial port. Unfortunately, despite the simplicity of the concept, attaching a modem to an available serial port in a way that everything continues to work in your PC is not necessarily simple. Chapter 4 shows logical approaches to making your modem installation easy.

If you have an internal modem, the modem is plugged into the computer and the modem acts as a serial port. If you have an external modem, the electronics that make up the serial port are located in your PC and you connect a cable from a serial port to the modem.

Your communications software sends the digital data to be transmitted to the other computer to the modem via the serial port, and the modem translates this data into an analog form that can be transmitted efficiently along the phone line to the receiving modem. The receiving modem translates the analog data back into digital data and passes this digital data on to the receiving computer via the serial port.

Your communications software also sends digital data to the modem to control the modem. The modem is able to determine when the data is to be used for control and when it is to be transmitted.

Introducing the link between two modems

So far, you have learned that the PC sends digital data to the modem via the serial port and the modem can translate this into an analog form that can be sent down the telephone line for the receiving modem to translate back again. The translation from digital data to the analog form is known as *modulation*, and the translation from the analog form to digital data is known as *demodulation*.

You no doubt have encountered the term modulation in radio and television transmission. Consider the AM and FM bands on your radio. AM is the abbreviation of *amplitude modulation,* and FM is the abbreviation of *frequency modulation.* Television is also transmitted by using modulation techniques. You listen to a particular radio station by setting your radio's tuning circuits to a particular frequency where the radio station transmits its signal, for example, 98.1 MHz FM.

You can think of the modulation process as the radio station transmitting a steady signal, known as the carrier signal (98.1 MHz in the example) and then superimposing the music and speech on top of this carrier. The way the music and speech are superimposed is the modulation technique. In the same way, the sending modem modifies (modulates) a tone or tones by the digital data. The receiving modem recovers the digital data from the modulated tone or tones.

Your radio picks up the signal transmitted by the radio station (the carrier and music or speech combined). The radio can strip away (demodulate) the carrier signal from this combined signal and leave the music and speech. The music and speech are then sent to the radio's speaker for your listening pleasure.

The modulation techniques used by modems are more complex than the radio example and, depending on the particular communications standard being used, may even involve no carrier signal being sent. However, you can think of the procedure as the sending modem modulating (encoding) the data in some known way and sending the digital data in a form suitable for analog phone lines. The receiving modem, because it knows how the data was modulated, can perform the reverse and demodulate the data to change it into digital form for transmission to the receiving computer.

For a successful communications link, the two modems must be able to communicate with each other. The receiving modem must know, for example, what modulation method or methods are being used, what the carrier signal frequency or frequencies are, how fast the data is being sent, and the form of the data.

In the same way that there are a variety of PCs manufactured by different manufacturers and with different microprocessors and performances, there are different modems that conform with different standards and operate at different speeds. To someone who has been involved only with PCs, telecommunications standards can seem unnecessarily complicated. The PC industry has become so large that it has been able to create its own unique standards, or variations on more universal standards, that are commonly accepted. It is easy to assume that there are no other computer standards. However, telecommunications is not isolationistic and, unlike computers, can be used to link.

PC owners, for example, have a tendency to dismiss mainframe computers and Amiga personal computers, for example, as remote and irrelevant. Standards that apply to mainframes or Amigas may not seem to have any significance to a PC owner. Owners of IBM PC-compatible systems and Apple Macintosh computers often have similar views about the importance of each other's standards.

However, it is vital to realize that telecommunicating has been around longer than PCs, is not a PC standard, and is independent of the computers attached to the modems. Early telecommunication standards, still in use today, were different in the U.S. from the rest of the world. However, the more-recent communications standards, now the most common primary standards, are truly international.

The communications standards dictate details such as the carrier signal frequencies, how the data is modulated, and how fast data is transmitted. Your modem will conform with at least one of these standards, and you can communicate with another modem that conforms with the same standard. Chapter 5, "Understanding Your Modem," explains the relevant specifics of some of the communications standards.

To create a communications link, both modems must be working to the same standard or they will not be "speaking the same language." The modem and communications software can automate the creation of a successful link. The bleeps, clicks, and hisses you hear when your modem makes a connection are part of the automated linking procedure. Chapter 5 explains the important aspects of this automation.

Introducing Communications Software

You need communications software to make your modem operate. This software may have been supplied with the modem, or you may have purchased it elsewhere. The software must serve two basic purposes but will probably include many additional features.

When you run the communications software, you issue commands that control your modem. These set such items as the speed you want the modem to try and connect at and whether to answer the telephone line when it rings. Other commands make the modem do the equivalent of picking up the phone, listening for a dial tone, and dialing a phone number.

When another modem answers the phone, the two modems establish a communications link. This connection is a negotiation procedure trying to find the highest common standard at which both modems can communicate. Once found, the two modems use this standard, and you can start to communicate with the other computer.

You also use communications software to send data from one computer to the other via the established communications link. You can type on your keyboard and have the characters control the other computer, or you can transfer a file between the computers. When you have finished communicating, you tell the communications software to instruct the modem to hang up the phone, and the modem terminates the phone connection.

Communications software comes in many forms, ranging from the most elementary to the most sophisticated. You can compare the range with the range of word processors available. A word processor at its most simple is a text editor.

At its simplest, when in a text editor, you type characters on the keyboard; they appear on-screen and can be stored in a file. Different fonts and special formatting, such as centering or automatic word wrapping at the end of a text line, may not be available. Even inserting, moving, or copying text may require knowledge of some esoteric command names and methods. These programs are usable but are not particularly user-friendly.

At its most sophisticated, a word processor can do advanced desktop publishing. You can use lots of fonts, reformat whole manuscripts with a single command, insert and manipulate graphics with ease, and produce masterpieces with every bell and whistle possible. These programs are undoubtedly the best if you need most of their features.

Hundreds of word processors fall between the extremes. The most suitable one is the one that includes at least all the features you need or will want in the near future but is easy to use with logical commands.

Communications software is comparable. You will be more successful rapidly with communications software that is beyond the most basic, because you will find it much easier to use. On the other hand, you do not need to rush out and buy the most sophisticated program unless you need a particular feature.

Chapter 8, "Beyond the Basics," and Chapter 9, "Making the Most of Your Modem and Software," introduce all the features a communications program needs to be reasonably easy to use and perform all the communications tasks. When you understand these features, Chapter 10, "Streamlining Your Communications," shows the extra features you can look for in a communications program that make telecommunicating easier, faster, and more streamlined.

Introducing Fax Machine Communication

The popularity of fax machines has expanded dramatically in the last few years. Faxing is an economical way to transfer printed material almost instantly from one location to another.

Like a modem, a fax machine is a microprocessor-controlled device that links with another fax machine via a telephone line. The telecommunications link is similar to that shown in Chapter 2. A computer is linked to the fax modem, which is in turn linked to the phone line, another fax modem, and another computer.

Unlike modems, which are available only as computer peripheral devices, many fax machines are stand-alone units and do not attach to a computer. Most of these incorporate a telephone and may include an answering machine as well. These fax units combine the computer and modem portions of the connection.

A modem is designed to link you with another computer and communicate directly with that computer. A *fax machine*, as its full name *facsimile machine* suggests, produces a replica of a document found on the sending fax machine on the receiving fax machine's paper. The methods used to generate the data for sending and printing at the receiving end are totally different than for modem communication.

When the fax machine sends a fax document, you can think of it as a scanner and modem. The scanner portion reads the page for transmittal as a series of dots, one line at a time. This data is sent from the scanner portion to the modem portion as a series of ones and zeros representing the presence or absence of a dot on the original document.

The modem portion modulates this data into a form suitable for transmission on the phone line. This modulated data conforms with a telecommunications standard. However, the standards used for fax transmittal are different from the standards used for data modem transmittal.

The receiving fax machine can be thought of as a modem and printer. The modem demodulates the transmitted data and passes the series of ones and zeros to the printer portion. The printer portion of the receiving fax machine takes the data and either prints or does not print a dot in the corresponding place on the page to replicate the original document.

PC fax modems are a further development from stand-alone fax machines. Rather than needing to print a document or graphic before it can be transmitted to another fax machine, PC fax modem boards send the document directly from the PC without the need for printing first and then passing it through a fax machine. Similarly, when receiving a fax document on your PC fax modem, rather than it being printed, the image of the page is stored in a file on your computer.

As shown in Figure 3-4, you can purchase PC fax modems as expansion boards that fit into your PC and provide fax machine services.

Figure 3-4: The Hayes JT FAX 144B Dual, a PC fax modem that provides similar services to a stand-alone fax machine but is controlled from the PC to support high-density enhanced fax servers as well as LAN fax servers on gateway applications.

However, many new modems also include fax modem features so you can purchase a combined unit on a single expansion board, or as an external unit.

To avoid confusion between when to use a modem and when to use a fax modem, consider the two features — the data modem and the fax modem — as two separate items, even though they are located on a single expansion board or external case and use the same cables. You cannot, for example, use communications software to send a fax document and you cannot use a fax machine to send a computer file.

Fax machines (whether stand-alone or PC fax modems) are preferable in some situations, and modems are preferable in others. Knowing when to use which device is important.

Think of a fax machine as a device that can replicate a document or graphic by scanning the document and sending the scanned image to the other fax machine for printing. The receiving fax modem may be located in another computer, or it may be a stand-alone fax machine. A modem can send electronic files and characters to another computer.

When you receive a fax document, even if you receive it via your PC fax modem and it is stored on your computer, you have a series of dots that make up a scanned image. You do not have text; you have a picture of text.

Chapter 7, "Understanding Your Fax Modem," introduces how to use your fax modem and Chapter 11, "Making the Most of Your Fax Modem," shows how to make the most of your fax modem and its software.

Introducing Fax Modem Software

If you have a stand-alone fax machine, the buttons and displays serve as the controls for it. A PC fax modem, even though it includes a microprocessor, is controlled by fax modem software installed on your computer.

The fax modem software has two main purposes: preparing your document for transmittal or display and controlling the fax modem board for transmittal or receipt.

First consider sending a document. The fax modem software is responsible for converting your document or graphic image into a series of scanned lines made up of dots and spaces. In a stand-alone fax, a scanning head actually views the page and detects dark and light areas on a scanned line. In a PC fax modem, the software performs an equivalent function.

Note: This is not the same as reading your text. The PC fax modem software takes your document regardless of its type and reads it as a series of a narrow lines, called *scan lines.*

The fax modem board's control for transmittal or receipt of documents is equivalent to that of a data modem, except that different communications standards are used.

The fax modem software tells the fax modem board to perform such functions as the equivalent of taking the phone off the hook, dialing the phone number, and establishing a mutually compatible communications standard with the receiving fax machine.

When connected, the document is transmitted between the two fax machines. If the receiving fax machine is a stand-alone unit, the document is reproduced one scan line at a time as the data is transmitted. If the receiving fax modem is a PC fax modem, the document is reconstructed electronically and is stored as a single graphic file on the computer.

Fax modem software, like communications software, is available in a variety of different flavors, but you are most likely to use the software supplied with your fax modem board. The commonality between modems doesn't exist between fax modem boards, so you need fax modem software that supports your particular fax modem board.

Some PC fax modems come with very basic fax modem software, and others are supplied with more-advanced software. Some PC fax modems also come with extra utilities that can help with file conversion so that your fax document can be loaded in other PC programs.

The basic fax modem software can send a graphic file to the specified phone number and receive faxes when the phone rings and a fax transmission is detected. More-advanced fax modem software may allow you to send the same document to multiple people by one selection or to group your commonly used lists of recipients. The utility software may include programs to convert from one graphic format to another or may include an OCR (optical character recognition) program that can convert your graphic file into text.

The typical home user can make do with less-advanced fax modem software and supplement the functionality by using other PC software such as graphic conversion programs or OCR programs available from other vendors. Unlike communications software, where there are literally hundreds of extra things beyond the basics that can be added to the software, far fewer bells and whistles can be added to fax modem software.

However, the business user can purchase more-specialized software for specific applications needs, such as using a fax modem as a fax-back server, which gives an automated fax response to a phone call. For example, some companies have automated telephone numbers you can call, and they automatically fax you sales literature.

The appeal of fax machines is their ubiquitous presence in so many locations, including rest stops on interstate highways, hotels, and businesses of all sizes. You do not need a computer to send a fax. In many situations, a fax document is considered written confirmation; consequently it is used for quotations, purchase orders, and many other business applications. It has become the equivalent of permanent voice mail. Rather than leaving a telephone message, people send confirming faxes.

Introducing Remote Control Software

Another interesting application for modems is remote control software. This is an extension of more-typical modem communication. You link the two computers as you would for a normal telecommunication connection and can operate the remote computer (the one at the far end of the telephone connection) as if it were in front of you.

For example, remote control software enables you to call your office computer from home and use all of the usual application programs, such as word processors and spreadsheets, that are located on the office computer. You see on your home monitor the same thing as on your office computer, and when you press a key on your home keyboard, your office computer behaves as if you had pressed a key on its keyboard.

Being able to use your main computer remotely allows you, for example, to take advantage of all the applications software on the remote computer. You do not have to have that software on the computer in front of you. You can use the large hard disk on the remote computer and do not have to have such resources on your connecting computer.

Remote control software also may enable you to perform maintenance and configuration changes remotely. Because you have control of the remote computer, your keyboard causes actions on the remote computer, and your monitor displays the correct screen, you can rearrange the hard disk contents and alter configurations at will.

It also can provide remote technical support and training in a way not possible unless you are physically in the same room as the remote computer. As discussed in Chapter 2, "Understanding the Communications World," the telephone removes the sense of sight from a communication. In a way, remote control brings sight back into the situation.

Suppose that you install a spreadsheet on a customer's computer. When that customer needs to know how to enter a formula into a cell, he or she may call you for technical support. With remote control software, you can see the same screen that your customer sees and press keys for him or watch him press keys. If you have ever done technical support via telephone, you will appreciate how remote control software can be a boon to productivity.

One problem with remote control software is that both computers must have the software installed and ready to use, so it typically is employed in situations where you know you are going to need it rather than being a coincidental part of most PC users' software set.

Other problems relate to compatibility and system resources. You need to run applications programs that will allow the remote control software to operate correctly, but not all application programs will support the software, and not all computers have adequate resources to allow both the application and the remote control software to run at once.

However, the advantages of remote control software for technical support and home/office use can be tremendous. Chapter 12, "Special Purpose Communications," explains remote control software in more detail. It also includes information on using your communication software's host mode, which makes your remote computer behave like a bulletin board, allowing you to exchange files or find files on a remote computer without needing to be at that location.

Where to Go from Here

To choose and install your modem and communications software, you need to read Chapter 4, "Selecting Your Equipment," next. Chapter 5, "Understanding Your Modem," which deals with actually making the connection, communicating, and disconnecting, assumes your modem and software are installed correctly.

To choose and install your PC fax modem and its software, you also need to read Chapter 4 next. Chapter 7, "Understanding Your Fax Modem," covers actually sending and receiving your fax document, but it assumes you have a PC fax modem already installed.

Other variations on telecommunications, such as remote control software, international communications, and using modems on the road, are also covered in Chapter 12. This chapter assumes you understand how and when to use your data modem and fax modem in more common situations. This information is found in Chapters 4 through 11.

Summary

Part I introduced the world of telecommunications. It showed what communication is, what you can communicate with, and what you need to communicate.

It introduced the major items involved in telecommunications: modems and their software, fax modems and their software, and online services.

Although it avoided detail, Part I also showed the basics of a modem connection and fax modem connection, knowledge that is assumed in subsequent chapters.

Part II, "Communications Basics," details how to choose the equipment, install it, and get it up and running. You can begin to focus more on a particular chapter to identify the specific items you need to make a successful communications link.

When you have your modem or fax modem up and running, you can examine Part III, "Survival and Efficiency Tools," to learn more about making the most of what you have, and Part IV, "The Online World Tour," to discover the limitless opportunities for online data resources.

II

PART

Communications Basics

Part II introduces the concepts and practical tools you need to make your data modem or fax modem work. By the end of this part, you will have your equipment up and running and will know enough to make a connection, communicate with another computer, and transfer files and fax documents between the computers. However, you will not necessarily know the most efficient or fastest way to make the transfer or know streamlining and automation techniques. These techniques are covered in Part III.

Chapter 4 introduces selecting your equipment and installing it. By the end of this chapter, you know whether you want to use a modem or fax modem and will be ready to make your first connection.

Chapter 5 explains how to make a telephone connection with your modem and how to communicate with another computer via modem. You learn such terms as terminal emulation as well as how and when to use AT commands.

Chapter 6 extends your modem use to include file transfer. You learn how to transfer a file to and from another computer and when to use which file-transfer protocol.

Chapter 7 explains how to make a connection with your fax modem. You learn the pros and cons of PC fax modems as well as fax machines and how to send and receive fax documents.

4
CHAPTER

Selecting Your Equipment

This chapter covers the essentials for selecting and installing your data modem or fax modem. Even if you already own a data modem or fax modem, this chapter shows the important features you should understand to make the first connection. Most new modems include a plethora of features, and you only need the essentials to start with. In particular you will learn about the following concepts:

- ❖ Understanding telephone essentials and serial ports
- ❖ When to choose a data modem and what to look for
- ❖ When to choose a fax modem and what to look for
- ❖ Installing your data modem or fax modem and making it work

Serial Ports, RS232, and Telephone Essentials

Installing and operating your data modem or fax modem is the most important part of telecommunications. When you have the data modem working, you can start choosing from all its options. You can think of this process like installing a VCR: Until you can make a tape play on your television, learning about setting the clock and automatic programming isn't worth too much.

Before you learn when to use a fax modem and when to use a data modem, you need to understand a little about the telephone connection and serial ports in your computer. You make a connection between two computers and two modems by connecting the first computer to a modem and the modem to a telephone line; the second computer is connected to its modem, which is in turn connected to the phone line.

Telephone line essentials

Using a phone line is a convenient way of linking the two modems. The whole country, and most of the world, has telephone lines linking businesses and residences. In concept, these telephone lines are cables that connect one place with another. In reality, there are a wide variety of methods for actually making the connection, but you can think of it as a long cable.

The telephone exchanges include switching equipment that route the telephone call in different directions, and the actual route may not include a physical cable. For example, most international and some long-distance calls are transmitted to a satellite in space and sent back down to earth in or near the receiving area. In most connections, different types of cables are used. The phone cable that is actually attached to your phone outlet is probably a four-wire cable; when that cable reaches a junction box, the connection is continued via cables with many more wires or wires that use more advanced technology, such as fiber optics and packet-switch networks, so that many phone calls can be routed along the same cable.

As a modem user, you should understand that the phone companies involved make the connection in many different ways. This variation, as well as other factors, including the weather, can affect the quality of your connection. For example, you may get a very clear connection one time you call your mother but a noisy line the next, even if you hang up the phone and redial immediately. When you use a modem, you do not actually hear the clarity of the connection, although its effect is noticeable when you try to communicate or transfer files.

If your connection and transfer run smoothly, you do not need to think about the telephone connection. However, when you experience intermittent problems, such as losing data or getting random or unexpected characters appearing on-screen, remember that your equipment and settings may be perfect, but the phone line connection may be noisy.

The telephone is designed to transmit the human voice from one location to another via cable. As explained in Chapter 3, the human voice is *analog*, rather than *digital*, and consists of a variety of signal levels. Digital data has only two states, on or off, which are often referred to as zeros and ones.

To transfer information between two computers, the digital data must be converted into a form suitable for transmission along telephone lines that are designed for analog data transmission. The modem *modulates* the data into a form for transmission and also *demodulates* the data for the receiving computer or device. The modem does not change the data — only the form of the data.

Modem technology is reaching the point where increasing the speed of data transmission (shoving more data down the line at once) will require better connection equipment. The fastest modems currently available, when used with all the special data-compression features, are stretching the limits of analog phone connections. To move beyond this speed, replacement connections will be necessary. Although the majority of users do not need to transmit faster, the new technology is available in some geographical areas, and some people have started to use it. However, not every phone connection will ever exceed the current analog telephone standards.

Three types of telephone lines are typically available: voice grade, conditional voice grade, and leased lines. The vast majority of phone lines are voice grade; they are designed to be of a sufficiently high quality for transmitting the human voice well. However, if you have special needs, such as transmitting a lot of data, you can get higher-grade lines. You will pay more for these lines and may need to pay for their installation at your location and at any receiving locations.

The conditional voice grade line provides a better-quality phone line by using more-modern technology, such as packet-switched networks. A leased line, as its name implies, is a phone line that you lease. It is "permanently" connected to a particular phone and is used most frequently for connecting terminals, which may be PCs, to a minicomputer or mainframe. This permanent attachment means that you do not have a dial tone and you do not have the ability to dial a phone number.

Why Not More Data, Faster?

You may wonder why the modem manufacturers do not make faster and faster modems. The problem is not with the modems but with the relatively antiquated analog phone system. Because the phone system is designed for the human voice and consequently analog data, the digital data from your computer is modulated into analog form for transmission down the phone line.

The current modems, such as V.FC and V.FAST, are transmitting data at just below the theoretical limit of the phone lines. They probably could send data just a little bit faster, but not reliably, with every phone connection in the world.

There are two ways of increasing data rate. You either send the data faster or send more data at once. However, it requires power to send the data along the telephone line, there is inherent noise on the telephone line, and there is a limited amount of bandwidth on the telephone line. You are limited by the physical limitations.

This limitation, known as Shannon's Law — after Claude Shannon who proved the limits for an ideal situation — shows it is related to the power of the signal, the power of the noise, and the bandwidth of the channel. In reality, this limit cannot be reached because of other problems found in a practical situation. (For example, Shannon's Law assumes only random noise.)

The amount of power available is limited by the design of the telephone system. The bandwidth of the telephone system, which can be thought of as the amount of room available to send multiple bits of data at once, is limited. You reach a point where you cannot distinguish the difference between two bits of data being sent at the same time, you cannot distinguish between two bits of data being sent one after the other, and the signal is so weak that you cannot distinguish the bits of data from the noise on the phone line.

"Do I need a special telephone line for my modem?"

All home users and most small- to medium-sized businesses will need only a voice-grade phone line. Specialized needs, such as typesetting or printing services that transmit data more or less continually to the printers, are possible exceptions. If you have applications that need these capabilities, you will probably be told by your software or hardware supplier as well as the phone company.

Most telephone companies offer a variety of extra services on the standard voice-grade line. Some of these are beneficial to modem users. Others are hazardous.

One option is pulse or tone dialing. A pulse dial phone sends a series of pulses that sound like clicks when you dial the phone. When you press 6, for example, you hear six clicks on the line. A tone dial phone sends a different tone for each digit on the keypad. (When I lived in Florida, I regularly called a local engineering company regularly whose number sounded like "Mary had a little lamb!")

Tone dialing is an extra cost item in most areas; in others, it is a standard part of the service. Tone dialing is much faster, and when using a modem, which sends tones or pulses down the phone line faster than you can dial manually, the extra cost is well justified. If you have tone dialing, you can use pulse dialing, but in some cases, if you only have pulse dialing, the telephone exchange equipment that routes your call will not be able to recognize the tones as digits in the dialed number.

Another option increasingly being offered by telephone companies is call waiting. Call waiting adds a signal to the phone line — in some areas, it sounds like a beep, in others a clicking noise — to indicate that someone else is trying to call your phone number.

Although you may not consider it rude or inconvenient to have someone interrupt your phone call, because you can keep talking without interruption, the modem cannot ignore the signal. You may lose some data, or you may lose the connection completely because the two modems lose track of each other.

"How do I disable call waiting?"

You have two alternatives for call waiting besides not subscribing to the service in the first place. You can disable call waiting before making a phone call. This typically involves dialing *70 from a tone phone or 1170 from a rotary phone. You can program your modem to send this dialing sequence before dialing the desired phone number. Chapter 9 explains how to do this with communications software, and Chapter 11 explains how to do this with fax software.

However, there are several problems. Your phone company service may use a different number sequence or may not allow you to disable call waiting. Additionally, if you are receiving the phone call rather than dialing out, call waiting is not disabled.

Another technique, which requires some experience to set up properly, involves setting a parameter in your modem so that the modem ignores interruptions that are only as long as the call-waiting beep. However, this technique requires a balancing act of making the modem ignore the call-waiting signal while recognizing interruptions that prevent corrupted data. If at all possible, disable call waiting before making a phone call.

If you have a single phone line into your home, you should be able to use this to connect a modem. All PC modems that connect directly to the phone line use a modular connector known as an *RJ-11* jack. You plug a phone cable into the modem in the same way that you plug a phone cable into an extension phone.

Most homes now use these modular connections rather than the previous four-terminal system. If not, you can inexpensively purchase adapter kits that convert to the modular jack system, or you can get a telephone installer, such as the phone company, to make the conversion for you.

To give your modem the best line possible, remove as many other phone extensions as possible. The more telephone extensions you have attached to the phone line, the more potential for problems. In particular, be wary of very cheap phones, especially old ones, because they can cause many problems related to noisy phone lines and poor data connection. Cordless telephones are another potential problem.

"Can I use my telephone at the same time as the modem?"

In the same way that call waiting adds beeps to the phone line that interfere with the data connection made between the modems, picking up a telephone receiver while a modem is using the phone line introduces extraneous noise (even if you only listen and do not talk). This noise may cause your computer to receive or send corrupt data or lose the telephone connection between the two modems.

If you use a modem in a house with many phone extensions, create a system so that people do not inadvertently use the phone when the modem is connected. For example, you may decide that a second phone line is justified specifically for the modem.

Although a typical phone wire to your house includes four wires, only two are used to make a connection to a typical phone. The phone cables you attach have a similar modular RJ-11 jack that can accommodate the four wires, but only two of the wires may be connected. These two wires are named *tip* and *ring* and harken back to the early days of telephones when a telephone operator at the local telephone exchange made the connection for you.

"How do I attach a modem to my second phone line?"

In many cases, your home may be already wired for two telephone lines. The second two wires in the four-wire cable, also named *tip* and *ring* but for a second phone number, allow you to have a second phone number. To use this second line with a telephone, you purchase a two-line phone or you buy an adapter.

A two-line phone uses an *RJ-12* jack instead of an RJ-11. These are physically the same size, but all four wires are connected and used with the RJ-12. The phone has a button of some sort that connects with the first or second phone line.

Depending on your modem, you may be able to use the second phone line in an RJ-12 jack (or even other less common phone jack types that are most typically found in businesses). However, this feature, which you may need to enable using software, is not available on all modems.

A more common alternative is purchasing an adapter that makes the second phone line appear like the first phone line to the modem. To connect a modem or single-line phone to the second phone line, you can purchase an adapter that is sold at most electronic stores or your local telephone store. This adapter is a small plug that plugs into your phone outlet and has three sockets in it. One socket is labeled *L1+L2*, another *L1*, and the third *L2*. To plug a modem or phone into line 1, you can use the L1+L2 or L1 socket. To plug a modem or phone into line 2, you use the L2 socket. The L2 socket makes the third and fourth wires in your phone outlet appear in the locations normally used for the first and second wires. (To plug a two-line phone into this adapter, use the L1+L2 connector.)

In a business situation, or in homes with more than one phone line, you may have different types of telephones. If your company uses a private branch exchange (PBX), you may or may not be able to attach a modem so that it goes through the exchange. You may need a separate phone line that bypasses the PBX to connect your modem to the phone line. In particular, if you have a digital PBX, you cannot connect a typical modem. However, you can purchase modems designed to work on digital PBXs.

In some business environments, you can't know whether someone is already using the phone line that is attached to a modem because each extension attached to the same line may be in a physically different location. Additionally, you may not want to supply all users with their own modems but may want them to share a modem or a few modems. In this situation, consider a more advanced connection arrangement, known as *modem pool*. If your users are connected via a *local area network* (LAN), you can probably add a modem so that multiple people can share a single-user modem. This is comparable to sharing a printer on a LAN. Only one person can use each modem at a time, but the arrangement can be economical if implemented sensibly.

Other more-specialized telephone situations include using a modem in situations where modular telephone jacks are not feasible, such as in a hotel room or at a public telephone. A device known as an *acoustic coupler* may help in these cases. This kludgy-looking device connects a typical phone handset and a modem's RJ-11 jack. Chapter 12 includes examples of unusual situations, especially when using a modem on the road, and explains acoustic couplers in more detail.

Serial port essentials

A modem is the interface between the computer and telephone line. After deciding that you can plug the modem into a telephone line, you need to determine how to plug the modem into the computer. Unfortunately, this is not always as easy as plugging into the phone line.

As explained in Chapter 3, you can consider your PC as a microprocessor with a series of devices attached to it. These devices are attached via a connection known as a *port*. Typical devices are the keyboard and monitor. The PC also includes support for two additional, industry-standard ports, known as a *serial port* and a *parallel port*.

You can attach serial devices to serial ports and parallel devices to parallel ports. Because the PC's ports conform to an industry standard, rather than a PC-specific standard, you can choose from a wide variety of serial and parallel devices rather than having to buy a PC-specific device.

Most PC users know the general definitions of bits and bytes and serial and parallel. However, these bear repeating. Digital data consists of ones and zeros, known as *bits* of data. In a PC, these bits are typically moved around in groups of eight. These groups are known as *bytes* of data.

A typical printer is a *parallel* device that can accept data one byte at a time. A typical mouse, digitizer, or external modem is a *serial* device and can accept data one bit at a time. A typical internal modem is a *serial port* and modem combined into a single expansion board that you plug into your PC.

The parallel port in a PC can take the data given to it and arrange it in a form so that one byte of data is sent out of the port at a time. The parallel port communicates with the device, such as a printer, to coordinate the sending of data at a rate that the device can accept.

The serial port is similar, but its job is more involved. A serial port takes the data presented to it as a byte of data and arranges it so that the data is sent from the port one bit at a time. Similarly, the serial port accepts data one bit at a time and rearranges the data into bytes so that the PC's microprocessor can manipulate the data. This conversion is done by an *integrated circuit* (a chip), known as a *universal asynchronous receiver/transmitter* (UART), and its supporting circuitry.

The following sidebar gives you more detail on this process. For the purposes of making your modem work, you probably do not need to understand more than the preceding paragraph. However, to take full advantage of the faster transmission speeds, you need more-detailed knowledge to understand terms like overrun and to know what type of UART is in your serial port and understand its speed limitations.

"What do RS-232 and RS-232C mean?"

The serial port on a PC is said to conform with the Electronic Industries Association's (EIA) standard number RS-232. (The RS stands for *recommended standard.*) The C is added after the name to refer to the revision level of the standard. Formally, the RS-232 standard specifies the interface between data terminal equipment (DTE) and data communication equipment (DCE) using serial binary data interchange. In other words, the standard gives details on sending serial data from one piece of equipment to another.

The RS-232 standard is a written document that actually specifies only a limited portion of what has come to be known in the PC world as the RS-232 standard. For example, revision C does not specify the shape of the connector. However, it does specify the connector's gender—whether it has pins or holes. IBM, and as a result almost all PC-compatibles, use the wrong gender connector for their serial ports according to the specification.

Revision D of the standard is now released and actually makes some PC-compatibles even less in compliance because it specifies a 25-pin D-type connector. Many PCs, most notably AT-compatibles, use 9-pin connectors for their serial ports.

Understanding a UART

In most situations, such as using a serial mouse, the speed at which data is sent from or received by the serial port is relatively slow, and no problems occur. However, problems can occur when using high-speed modems because the UART and the way in which it interacts with the PC may not be fast enough to avoid data loss.

For example, the UART may signal to the microprocessor that it has data to be transferred, but the microprocessor may be busy doing something else and take too long to respond. If the UART receives more data than it has room to store, data will be lost. This is known as *dropping characters* or *overrun*. In modem communications, this phenomenon manifests itself as lost data or data that appears to be corrupted. Your file transfer may abort because too many errors in the data were detected.

The early PCs used a UART chip from National Semiconductor called an 8250B. Faster PCs, such as AT- and 386-based computers, used a functionally comparable chip called the 16450. The 16450 is typically placed in a socket in your computer, rather than being soldered directly into the circuit board.

These UART chips include a serial port and baud rate generator. In simplistic terms, the *baud rate generator* is the mechanism that controls when, what, and how fast data is sent from the serial port.

The 16550AFN UART is used in IBM PS/2 computers and some newer PCs. This UART is a direct pin-for-pin replacement for the 16450. It includes a serial port and baud rate generator but has the advantage of also including a 16-character FIFO buffer on both the receiver and transmitter portions. A FIFO buffer is a *first-in first-out* storage area. The first character to be placed in this buffer is the first character read from the buffer.

This UART is less likely to experience overrun because a temporary storage area exists for the characters that are waiting for processing. As a minimal cost upgrade, many communications experts recommend replacing the 16450 with the 16550AFN.

If you are not using high-speed communications (say 9600 bps or higher), this upgrade is unnecessary. If you are using high-speed communications, it is an inexpensive alternative where physically possible, but it is not a panacea. Be sure to examine other potential causes of data loss, such as unshielded long wires or noisy phone connections.

Some manufacturers offer alternative solutions, such as replacement serial ports, sometimes known as communications accelerators. These are introduced in Chapter 9.

Now that I've stated that PCs do not conform with the RS-232 standard and have probably confused you, you should realize that the PC conforms with the RS-232 standard well enough so that if you can make your PC talk to the serial port and connect the modem to that port, you probably can make the modem talk to the computer and make the appropriate connections.

Port addresses, interrupts, and names

For most PC operations, you do not need to know the technical details of how the application program uses the operating system and how the operating system controls the microprocessor and hardware. However, this detail becomes important when installing or configuring software that needs to use extra hardware, such as mice and modems. It's a pity that you can't learn about the detailed stuff after you have the program working, but unfortunately, you need the knowledge to make it all work together.

Because you are adding a serial device to your computer when you add a data modem or fax modem—regardless of whether the modem is internal or external—you need to know what serial ports you have, what they are named, and part of how they are configured. The PC can only control one thing at a time, so your addition must appear to the software as a distinct and separate item. If, for example, you have a mouse and a modem both responding to the microprocessor's instructions at once, neither device will work correctly.

This basic understanding is the most confusing part of installing a modem. When it is installed and configured appropriately, you can forget most of the detail until you install new software or replace or rearrange your hardware.

First, the information you probably know. Your application programs, such as word processors or communications software, interface with the operating system, which in turn manipulates the computer hardware. The most prevalent operating system on the PC is DOS.

DOS Version 3.3 or later supports up to four serial ports. Earlier DOS versions support up to two serial ports. These ports are named by DOS as COM1, COM2, COM3, and COM4. In your communications software, you probably need to specify which serial port your modem is attached to.

The microprocessor communicates with the devices by using I/O (input/output) addresses commonly referred to as *port addresses*. The port addresses can be thought of as the "positions" of the devices. Each serial port is assigned a group of eight port addresses. (You specify the first address, and the subsequent seven addresses are assigned as the rest of the group.)

Additionally, each serial port is assigned an *interrupt* number. An interrupt number is often referred to as an interrupt level or interrupt request level. Interrupt level 3, for example, is abbreviated to IRQ3, and interrupt level 5 is abbreviated to IRQ5. An interrupt is a signal line that the serial port uses to indicate to the microprocessor that it needs attention. For example, the serial port may signal that it has some data ready for the microprocessor to collect.

"What are the typical address and interrupt assignments for serial ports, such as COM1?"

You can (theoretically) assign an address and interrupt to a particular serial port, such as COM1 or COM2. In fact, the flexibility of this assigning depends on the sophistication of your software. The typical assignments are shown in Table 4-1.

Table 4-1	Typical Serial Port Assignments	
Port name	**Address**	**Interrupt**
COM1	3F8	IRQ4
COM2	2F8	IRQ3
COM3	3E8	IRQ4
COM4	2E8	IRQ3
COM3 (PS/2)	3220	IRQ3
COM4 (PS/2)	3228	IRQ3

Notice that COM1 uses the same interrupt as COM3, and COM2 uses the same interrupt as COM4. This is because the PC was actually designed to support only two serial ports, and the addition of COM3 and COM4 are workarounds.

IBM PS/2 computers have a different I/O address map, and you can assign different addresses to your additional serial ports.

You need a unique name, interrupt, and address for each serial port in your computer. For example, if you have a mouse, you place it on one serial port and your modem on another.

The usual approach is to attach your first serial device to COM1 and the next to COM2. Wherever possible, avoid reconfiguring the devices you already have installed. If you change them, you will probably need to change the configuration of each of the software programs that use that particular device.

For example, if you have a mouse on COM1, avoid moving it to COM2 if at all possible. If you move it, you may need to change the configuration of each of your application programs that use a mouse.

To attach a serial device to your computer, you need a serial port. DOS can access them only if they are physically present on your computer. As explained earlier, a serial port comprises electronic circuitry that contains a UART or equivalent chip that performs the necessary data manipulation for serial data to be sent from the port.

Most PCs, made after about 1985, include two serial ports as standard. These may be built into the computer's main system board or may be in an expansion board. Earlier PCs typically had only one serial port. However, you can purchase inexpensive expansion boards that contain a serial port (or two), or you can purchase an internal modem that incorporates a serial port.

All serial ports that you can plug serial devices into are revealed by a connector in the computer's case. This connector will be either a 25-pin D-type connector (so called because it is D-shaped) or a 9-pin D-type connector. The typical PC standard is for this connector to be male (have pins rather than holes), but some early PCs had female connectors. (The serial port on an internal modem cannot be used to plug in a different serial device.)

If your display adapter is an EGA or earlier, it may also have a 9-pin D-type connector. This must be used to attach your monitor and is not a serial port.

To communicate by conforming with the RS-232 standard, you do not actually need to use all the wires in the 25-pin connector. In fact, all the required connections can be made with the 9-pin connector. IBM used the 9-pin connector in the IBM AT for space considerations (a 9-pin connector is much smaller than a 25-pin connector). Consequently, many PC compatibles also use the 9-pin connector.

Note: The serial ports with a 9-pin connector cannot be used for synchronous communication because this requires more than 9 wires for the signals. Unless you are using a leased line (covered earlier in this chapter), you will be using asynchronous communication and can use the 9-pin connectors without a problem.

You typically assign a serial port's name, address, and interrupt number by altering switches or changing jumpers on the circuit board. Some serial ports can be adjusted by using configuration software instead of physically changing switches.

If you are adding an internal modem, the serial port is incorporated into the expansion board, and you need to assign an available port name, address, and interrupt number.

As with the serial ports, this may be achieved by physically altering switches on the board or by running software. The manufacturer's documentation is essential reading.

An external modem can be plugged into an available serial port in your computer. Whether you add an internal or external modem, you need to write down the serial port name, address, and interrupt number. You need this information for your communications software. If any of your hardware or software does not work after installing a modem, the first question asked by technical support will be "Do you know your serial port name, address, and interrupt number?"

As more and more PCs include extra devices, such as sound boards and network adapters, the port address and interrupts become an important issue. There are a limited number of addresses and an even more limited number of interrupts. Because you only want one device to respond at a time, the assignments can become tricky.

For example, most network adapters are configured to use interrupt 3 when supplied. If you then try to add a second serial device, you may experience conflicts because the second serial device may be configured to also use interrupt 3. These conflicts may not occur when you are not actually using the second serial port but *do* occur when you try to add a modem. In this case, you may need to change the interrupt number assigned to your network adapter or to your second serial port.

Several programs — commercial, shareware, and free — are available that will interrogate your computer hardware and tell you what devices are assigned to which ports. Microsoft Diagnostics (MSD), shipped as part of DOS 6 and later, is particularly convenient, but your computer or modem may be supplied with a utility program. Many Gateway 2000 computers, for example, are supplied with QA Plus, and Qualitas' 386MAX memory management program is supplied with ASQ, a system analysis program.

You can use a serial device on COM1 and another on COM3, and similarly a serial device on COM2 and another on COM4, if you usually only use one serial device at a time.

For example, you may have a mouse on COM1 and a plotter or serial printer on COM3. Because you use the printer only when printing and the mouse to move the cursor around the screen, you can probably make both devices work successfully.

Problems arise when you try to use both devices at once. For example, if your program moves the mouse around while printing to a serial device, you can end up sending incorrect information to the mouse and the serial printer, and neither will work correctly. (This does not occur with parallel printers and mice, because the mouse and printer are configured as different devices with different port addresses.)

This conflict is particularly important for modems and mice. As a general rule, if you are using a mouse on COM1, avoid COM3 for your modem; and if you are using a mouse on COM2, avoid COM4 for your modem. Read the documentation that comes with your modem to help avoid problems.

Choosing a Modem

Like PCs, modems are advertised with lots of buzzwords, and different manufacturers emphasize different features to make a particular modem stand out from the crowd.

Also like PCs, your particular needs will be different from other people's requirements, and selection really is a matter of personal preference. You can buy very inexpensive modems that will probably operate under most conditions but may lack the extra features, technical support, warranty, or company reputation, and not be tolerant of slightly noisy phone lines or work with all other modems.

In contrast, you also can buy expensive top-of-the-line modems from well-known companies with every conceivable feature, excellent technical support, and good warranties. However, you may not need all these features and may be wasting your money.

One important difference between modems and PCs is that you need two modems to communicate, but many PCs never have their compatibility with other PCs tested. Any modem you buy, including fax modems, must be able to establish, maintain, and disconnect with another modem, which may or may not be of the same brand or standard.

Choosing a data modem, fax modem, or combined unit

Your first choice is relatively easy. Decide whether you need or will need a data modem, a fax modem, or a modem that combines data and fax capabilities. (Many new model modems automatically include a fax modem.)

If you know you want to transfer files between computers, call such online services as CompuServe or BBSs, or link your computer to another computer through telephone lines, you need a data modem.

If you want a substitute for a stand-alone fax machine and want to send documents (equivalents of pieces of paper), consider a fax modem. As the concept of the electronic desktop becomes more of a reality, where nothing is handed around on pieces of paper, the desirability of PC fax modems increases. As discussed in a later section, choosing a fax modem requires careful consideration.

Choosing the modem's form factor

After deciding whether you need a data modem or combined data modem and fax modem, you need to assess your current computer system, because this may limit your options. If you are going to use the modem with a desktop or tower computer, you have two main choices: internal or external.

An *internal modem* fits into an expansion slot inside your computer and incorporates a serial port. You need an available slot in which to place it, and you need to assign it an unused serial port name. If you already have four serial ports on your computer, you need to remove one to use an internal modem.

If you have a PS/2 computer and want to use an internal modem, you may need to select one that uses the Micro Channel Architecture (MCA) bus connection rather than the more common Industry Standard Architecture (ISA) or PC bus connector. (Not all PS/2 computers have the MCA bus; some low-end computers, such as the Model 25, use the ISA bus.)

If you want an external modem, you have two general choices. The typical box style is about 6 inches wide, 1½ inches high, and 10 or 11 inches deep, although some companies offer futuristic shapes rather than the boring box. Alternatively, you can choose a small modem, often known as a *pocket modem*, that can be used with a desktop or tower computer or (because of its small shape) taken on the road with a laptop.

If you want to use a modem with a laptop or notebook, you can use an external modem and attach it to a serial port. Some laptops come with built-in modems or modems that are available from the computer manufacturer as upgrade options. Alternatively, if your computer has a PCMCIA type 2 slot, you can purchase a PCMCIA modem that plugs into the expansion slot in your notebook. (These may be products offered by the computer manufacturer or a third-party company.) These modems are also small and lightweight for relatively easy travel.

If you are not limited in your choice, consider the following advantages of external modems:

- Most external modems have LEDs (light-emiting diodes) on the front that give an indication of the current modem status.

- You can use the serial port for other purposes, such as attaching a plotter.

- You can move the modem from one computer to another. This is good if you own multiple computers or decide to upgrade your computer.

- External modems have a separate power supply and do not use PC power. (This is only a factor with older PCs that don't have a power supply sufficient to power the modem along with everything else.)

Consider the following advantages of internal modems:

- Internal modems do not need a data cable connecting the serial port to the modem.

- Internal modems come with a built-in serial port.

- You don't need extra room for the modem on the desk.

- You don't need an extra electrical outlet for the modem's power supply.

Apart from the physical shape of your modem, you need to consider its features. Some modems can transfer data faster than others. The majority of buzzwords, in particular the ones that are not acronyms or abbreviations, used by communications people are related to the communications standards. These standards dictate the speed at which data can be transferred from one computer to another. In some standards, more data is sent at once. In others, the data is compressed before transmission and uncompressed by the receiving modem, which results in more data being sent in a certain amount of time.

Selecting compatibility

For PCs, the first consideration is to buy only a Hayes-compatible or AT-compatible modem. (As explained in Chapter 5, the AT is not the same as IBM's AT but refers to the two characters that are used as the start of modem commands.)

The analogy with PCs is worth reiterating here. The term PC-compatible has come to mean PCs that run and support all software and hardware designed for the IBM PC. In some cases, the PC-compatible standard has been expanded and enhanced by other manufacturers, and these extras may be desirable features. In other cases, increasingly less significant nowadays, PC compatibility may mean supporting almost all software and hardware designed for the IBM PC. This is where name brand — not necessarily IBM, but a major computer manufacturer — plays an important part in the support you will get from the computer manufacturer and software vendors when you find an incompatibility. They are more willing to support a computer that has brand recognition, because there are more likely to be many customers with the same computer.

The term AT-compatible is comparable. Buying a modem that claims to be AT-compatible is essential for you to use PC-communications software easily and consequently make a connection with another modem easily. However, it does not guarantee full compatibility and/or it may buy you extra features that are not available on all other AT-compatible modems.

For most PC users, there is only one type of telecommunication, and you use an AT-compatible modem to link with other modems. This type of communication is called more formally *asynchronous communication*. Asynchronous (as opposed to synchronous) communication is communication that occurs between two computers without regard to the precise clock timing sequences of the connected computers.

Synchronous communication is used between two computers when the events at each end of the phone line must occur in sync with (or in step with) the devices and computers attached to each other. People who need synchronous communication are usually aware of it, because they either have specialized computer knowledge or are supported by people who do. The most common implementation is linking a terminal to a mainframe computer. You can purchase specialized adapter boards for your PC that perform this type of communication.

However, if you need synchronous communications, you can purchase modems that will do both asynchronous and synchronous communication. You can do synchronous communication on dial-up phone lines and don't need a specialized synchronous communication adapter.

Note: The Hayes AutoSync protocol handles the situation this way. The synchronous application talks to the AutoSync driver, and the AutoSync driver sends special formatting signals to the modem so that the modem can convert the data. The modem has firmware in it that converts the asynchronous data into synchronous and puts it out on the phone line. Between the computer and the modem, the connection is asynchronous, but to the software, it appears to be a synchronous channel, and the data going over the phone line is properly formatted synchronous data. It's a clever way of tricking the hardware to do what the software needs to do.

Modem communications standards

Modems can operate at a variety of speeds and with different options that affect the effective data rate and insensitivity to data errors. A modem's data transfer rate is specified in bits per second (bps). However, this is not the only number you need to consider. When choosing a modem, you want to pick the most advanced standard you can afford.

Remember, however, that you must communicate with a second modem. The fastest and the highest standard that you will be able to communicate to second modem is the *highest common denominator*. For example, if you are only going to communicate with a 1200 bps modem, you do not need the fastest modem on the market.

The history of the modem provides insight into the apparently random numbering of communications standards and the apparent duplication of standards for certain data rates. You simply need to understand that from the time of the very first modem in the 1920s, people have wanted to send more data faster.

As a consequence, when a national or international standard for faster transmission had not been defined but public demand existed, manufacturers created proprietary standards to accommodate their customers. However, in most cases, the manufacturers also supported existing standards as fallback positions. If a modem was not connected to a modem that could support the faster standard, a fallback, and probably slower, standard was agreed on by the modems and used instead.

You don't have to worry about whether the modem you are calling has a particular standard. You set your modem to communicate with all its features, and it negotiates with the other modem automatically to find the best common denominator. However, when you buy a modem, you need to know which features you want, because its top feature will be the best at which you can communicate.

In the U.S., early microcomputer modems conformed with the Bell 103 standard. This transmits data at 300 bps. Although now rarely used, it is still supported by most high-speed modems as the final fallback standard. The next standard in the U.S. that is still used is Bell 212A. This transmits data at 1200 bps.

However, in Europe and the rest of the world, the two equivalent standards that were adopted were specified by the United Nations agency Consultative Committee on International Telephony and Telegraphy (CCITT) and were V.21 for 300 bps transmissions and V.22 for 1200 bps. CCITT is now renamed ITU-T (International Telecommunication Union).

Unless you purchase a very old modem, most modems support both Bell 212A, Bell 103, as well as V.21 and V.22. Bell 212A or V.22 are likely to be the lowest standards your modems will ever use.

For speeds above 1200 bps, U.S. manufacturers tend to adopt the international standards as they become available. However, there are some modems that also incorporate proprietary standards that you can use only when calling a modem of the same brand.

The 2400 bps standard is V.22bis (pronounced *bizz* or *biss* depending on who you talk to), and the 4800 bps and 9600 bps standard is V.32. The 14,400 bps standard is V.32bis.

So far, apart from slightly strange numbers, the bigger the standard number, the faster the modem, and the addition of *bis* to the standard number means a faster modem. As an additional help, most manufacturers use the data speed as part of the product's name to indicate its maximum speed.

Two more important standards are commonly available on newer modems: V.42 and V.42bis. Both of these standards may be available on any 1200 bps or faster modem.

A modem that supports V.42 can do error-checking on your data to help ensure that the data received is the same as the data sent. (Error-checking is explained in more detail in Chapter 6.)

A modem that supports V.42bis can compress and uncompress the data you are transmitting. As a consequence, you send more data between the modems in a given amount of time. Although manufacturers clearly tout the V.42 and V.42bis support, they do not usually make the potentially faster data-throughput speed with data compression part of the product name. The amount of data compression you actually get depends on the data that you are sending.

The ITU-T will agree on a further communications standard called V.FAST in 1994 and will probably name it V.34. This was intended to be the fastest possible standard possible on typical analog phone lines. In fact V.34bis is already being discussed. However, eventually further speed advancements beyond a standard will require specialized telephone lines and other techniques as yet not considered.

However, V.FAST has been very slow in being defined and agreed upon, and many people are clamoring for faster modems now. As a result, several U.S. manufacturers, headed by Multi-Tech Systems Inc., AT&T Paradyne, and AT&T Microelectronics, created a standard known as V.32terbo as an interim solution. This standard has a maximum speed of 19,200 bps. (As with memory capacities, 19,200 bps is usually represented as 19.2 kbps and is often spoken of as nineteen dot two.)

Understanding Modulation

Although you don't need to know the intimate details of the communications standards, a conceptual understanding of *modulation* is valuable. It will help you understand commonly confused terms, such as *speed* and *baud*, and understand why the current analog phone line cannot transmit data infinitely faster. These topics are covered in Chapter 5.

A covered in Chapter 3, the modem is a modulator/demodulator. When sending data, the modem modulates digital data into an analog form, and when receiving data, it recovers the data and changes it into a digital form again.

There are many different ways of modulating data, and each communications standard uses one or several different methods. To understand the basics, consider that steady alternating signal, known as a *carrier signal,* is transmitted at a particular frequency with a particular amplitude. The data signals are detected as changes in the carrier signal. The carrier signal is a *sine wave*, which you may remember from high school mathematics. All modulation schemes use amplitude, frequency, or phase modulation, or a combination of them.

Consider first *amplitude modulation*, which is similar to AM radio. The amplitude, or signal level, of the carrier is changed to indicate the data. A carrier signal with a normal signal level may represent a zero, and a carrier signal with a slightly lower signal level may represent a one. The carrier's signal level goes up and down to represent the data bits. Amplitude modulation on its own is not used in data modems.

In *frequency modulation*, which is like FM radio, the carrier signal's frequency is altered to indicate the data bits. Low-speed modems use frequency modulation.

The third type of modulation is called *phase modulation*. This requires two sine waves with the same frequency to be sent. A sine wave is an oscillating wave; at one point in time, its signal level is a minimum; at another, it is at a maximum. The number of times per second the signal is at a maximum (or at a minimum) is the signal's frequency. Phase modulation delays or advances the second sine wave relative to the first sine wave.

Depending on the communications standards, the modems use one or more of the modulation methods to transmit data. The details of what represents a one and what a zero are part of the communications standard. However, in many of the standards, you are sending more than one bit of data at a time.

Using amplitude modulation again as the example, because it is the easiest to visualize, a normal carrier signal amplitude may represent two zeros in a row. A slightly lower signal may represent a zero followed by a one. A slightly lower signal may represent a one followed by a zero, and a slightly lower signal still may represent two ones in a row. Consequently, each change in the carrier signal represents more than one bit of data. Sending two data bits at a time rather than one means that twice as much data can be sent in a given time.

In a separate effort, a different group of manufacturers, including Rockwell International Corp. and Hayes Microcomputer Products, has created another standard called V.Fast Class or V.FC. Rockwell has developed a modem chip that is available to all modem manufacturers as well as computer manufacturers. Computer manufacturers may include this chip on a system board so that the modem is an integral part of the computer. This standard has a maximum speed of 28,800 bps.

Many manufacturers have announced support for this V.FC standard, but it should be considered an interim standard. If you need to communicate at 28,800 bps now, rather than waiting for V.FAST standard to be finalized, V.FC is of interest. If not, it is worth waiting for the new standard modems.

Table 4-2 summarizes the specification numbers in increasing speed order. Remember that any modem 1200 bps or faster may include V.42 and V.42bis features. Both of these standards are desirable features for your modem to support.

Table 4-2	Summary of Modem Specification Numbers
Speed	**Standard**
300	103 or V.21
1200	212A or V.22
2400	V.22bis
4800	V.32
9600	V.32
14,400	V.32bis
19,200	V.32terbo
28,800	V.FC or V.FAST (V.34)

Note: V.42 and V.42bis are available on modems 1200 bps or faster. V.42 adds error-detection and V.42bis adds data-compression.

Selecting extras

Besides communications standards and physical shape, you should consider the extras that come with your modem when considering price. The warranty, technical support, or any money-back guarantee offered may be important to you.

If you buy a modem that supports a new or less commonly used standard, examine the upgrade path being offered. The biggest complaints I hear on bulletin boards are from modem buyers who thought they would be able to upgrade their modems inexpensively, but when the time came, the upgrade cost a couple of hundred dollars.

The analogy with PCs applies here again. In most cases, PC upgrades are not as smooth or inexpensive as you may think. A modem is not the same as software, and upgrading costs the modem manufacturer more than the shipping costs.

If you are purchasing a data modem and fax modem combination, take special care to read the product's specifications. Fax modems follow different communications standards than data modems. As a result, you may think that you are purchasing a modem with a particular speed when you are actually reading the fax modem's specification. Consider your data modem needs and your fax modem needs separately, and then look at products that can fill both needs. The following section on choosing a fax modem gives details on what to look for in fax modems.

The other extras that come with modems are the cables and communications software. The cables, typically a data cable for external modems and a phone cable for all modems, are fairly inexpensive to buy for yourself, but you do need to remember to purchase them. Check with the supplier regarding the length of the phone cable in case you need a longer one to reach the phone outlet.

For external modems, check whether a data cable is supplied and the type of connector on the end. You may need to buy a different cable to fit your serial port. Remember that serial ports on the PC may have a 9-pin or 25-pin connector. You can purchase a 25-pin to 9-pin adapter cable or complete replacement cables if necessary. These cables are called a variety of names, including serial cables, RS-232 cables, and DTE to DCE cables.

"Do I need a null modem cable?"

You sometimes hear about a null modem cable, and people get confused about whether this is the cable they need to connect their modem. A *null modem cable* is a cable that allows you to link two pieces of equipment together without using modems. It is also known as a crossover cable, a modem eliminator cable, or a DCE-to-DCE cable, or DTE-to-DTE cable. You don't need one for connecting your modem to a PC.

You also do not want to purchase a specialized plotter cable to use with a modem because, like the DCE-to-DCE cable, the connectors on the ends may be right, but it may not have the correct wires going to the correct pins. This specialized plotter cable may be a DCE-to-DCE cable, which will not work correctly connecting a modem to a PC, or it may be a completely custom cable for a specific plotter configuration.

Understanding Flow Control or Handshaking

The concept of flow control is fairly simple. The flow control settings establish "who talks, when". A ham radio operator, for example, uses the term "over" to signal when it is time for the listener to speak. A committee discussion may use rules so that the person speaking stands up; when the speaker sits down, another person can stand up and speak. This controls the flow of information and prevents two people speaking at once.

The RS-232 specification, used by the serial ports in your computer, supports two forms of flow control, known as *hardware handshaking* and *software handshaking*. As the names vaguely suggest, controlling data flow with software handshaking involves sending a signal within the data stream (comparable with saying "over" in the ham radio example). Controlling data flow with hardware handshaking involves using extra signals separate from the data stream (comparable with the committee discussion example).

In a typical communications connection, you have two areas of flow control. The *local flow control* dictates the type of handshaking used between the serial port and the modem. The *end-to-end flow control* dictates the type of handshaking used between the two modems.

The end-to-end flow control is determined automatically by the error-control features in your modem or by the file-transfer protocol from the communications software you are using. (File transfer is covered in Chapter 6.)

You can alter the local flow control method and choose between hardware and software handshaking. Lower-speed modems may only support software handshaking, in which case you have no choice. However, most higher-speed modems, which include error-correction features, support both hardware and software handshaking. When transmitting data at higher speeds, hardware handshaking is preferable.

Hardware handshaking involves two signal lines called clear to send (CTS) and request to send (RTS). When a serial device (modem or computer, for example) is ready to receive data, it raises the CTS line. When the serial device is ready to send data, it raises the RTS line. When both the CTS and RTS lines are raised, the data is sent. When the CTS or RTS line is lowered, the data transmission between the two serial devices is stopped.

Software handshaking involves characters added to the data stream that signal the beginning and end of the transmission. The XON character (pronounced ex-on) starts the transmission, and the XOFF character stops the transmission. The XON character is the character sent when you press Ctrl+S and XOFF character is the character sent when you press Ctrl+Q.

Occasionally, the XON or XOFF character appears in the middle of a file transmission, due to the particular combination of bits, and the receiving computer gets confused. It sends a message, or your communications program issues a message, depending on which program detected the XON or XOFF in an unexpected location, that indicates an XON or XOFF character was found.

For example, if the data stream starts with an XON character, the receiving program is expecting to see an XOFF to indicate the end of the transmission. If a file contains an XON character, the receiving program may send a message. You can manually send an XON or XOFF character as required, by pressing the relevant keystrokes.

Because it is likely that XON or XOFF may appear occasionally in a file, hardware handshaking is preferable to software handshaking. However, apart from the local control, the handshaking type is determined by the communications protocols and not by the user.

Table 4-3 lists the pin assignments needed to connect a 9-pin serial port connector to a modem. (The names of the signals are also included for reference.) A 25-pin serial port connector needs a straight-through cable where pin 1 at one end of the cable is connected to pin 1 at the other end, and pin 2 is connected to pin 2. You actually need only nine wires connected, but some serial cables have all 25 wires connected at each end of the cable.

Table 4-3	Serial Port Pin Assignments
9-pin Serial Port	**25-pin modem connector**
1 (CD)	8
2 (RD)	3
3 (SD)	2
4 (DTR)	20
5 (SG)	7
6 (DSR)	6
7 (DTR)	4
8 (CTS)	5
9 (RI)	22

The RS-232 standard works well only with short cables. It is not intended for use with cables much longer than a yard. If you use a longer cable, you are more likely to pick up extraneous noise and consequently data errors. You are better off with a longer phone cable and short serial port cable, although longer phone cables are also susceptible to noise. The serial cable should also be shielded. Many users make an inexpensive cable by using *ribbon cable* (a flat strip of wires frequently used to connect different internal parts within PCs). These will work under ideal conditions, but if you experience data loss, your serial cable may be at fault. Consider investing in a shielded serial cable before blaming noisy phone lines. (You can buy shielded ribbon cable.)

Besides cables, you need communications software to operate your modem. Almost all modems come with some sort of communications software, but the available features in this software vary dramatically, depending on the modem. Choosing communications software is covered later in this chapter.

If you want a data modem and fax modem, you need communications software to operate the data and fax communications software to operate the fax modem. These are two separate communications programs, although a future trend will be to make a single program perform both tasks. As with the data and fax modem combination, you should still consider your needs for transferring data and faxing separately and then compare them with the software's features.

Choosing a Fax Modem

Fax modems are, on the one hand, obvious add-on products for PCs, but on the other hand, they are not totally suited for the job of faxing and receiving documents. The suitability of fax modems depends on what you want to send out, what you want to receive, and what you want to do with the received fax documents.

Note: Fax is short for *facsimile.*

Data modems are well suited to PCs because they transfer data that is stored on a computer to another computer or peripheral device. Fax documents can be documents or drawings that are stored on a computer, but they are just as likely to be handwritten material, including signed documents or drawings, sales brochures or other informational material.

A brief summary of the advantages of fax machines over fax modems and fax modems over fax machines is worth considering.

The advantages of fax machines over fax modems include the following:

- ✤ You can use any fax machine from more or less anywhere. You do not have to carry a computer and fax modem around with you.

- ✤ You can send information that is not stored on the computer, such as handwritten notes, sketches, and printed brochures.

- ✤ The recipient does not need to own a computer. You can arrange for fax documents to be received at local service centers, hotels, or your customer's site.

- ✤ In theory, a fax document is easier to send than a file.

- ✤ You can use the fax machine (but not a fax modem) as a low-volume copy machine.

The advantages of fax modems over fax machines include the following:

- You can transfer large files, such as text, programs, or graphic files, complete and without degradation. A fax document is always received as a relatively low-resolution *graphical* representation of the original.

- You can typically transfer the file faster than a document.

- You can do far more with a fax modem than a fax machine. For example, you can do online research. You can send electronic mail intended for many possibly unnamed people to read.

Choosing a fax modem first involves deciding whether you need a fax modem or a stand-alone fax machine. There is no slot for you to insert your paper on a PC fax modem. This may seem obvious to many people, but it is asked about more often than you would think.

Considering sending documents

First consider the material you want to send. If you send only information you have previously printed from your PC, you may make good use of a fax modem. However, if you send handwritten information or signed documents, the fax modem is less applicable because you must find some way of getting the written material into your computer.

The signed-document issue is worth emphasizing. It is actually relatively easy to add a graphic image of your signature onto a fax document in your PC. However, you need to be very comfortable with your PC security before you would want to use that type of mechanism due to the legal implications of anyone having access to your signature.

Sending handwritten or preprinted documents with a fax modem and performing the equivalent of stuffing the document in the fax machine's slot are time-consuming and require extra software and hardware. You need a scanner and scanning software. The scanner translates your paper document into an electronic form and stores it as a file on your computer. You can then use the fax modem and its software to send the document as if you had created it on your computer. The scanning process often takes as long as, if not longer than, sending the document.

Considering receiving documents

To receive a fax document on a fax modem, your computer must be turned on and the fax communications software loaded. (There are ways to install the software so that you can work on your computer while waiting for a fax.)

However, you cannot use the fax modem and the data modem at the same time. Nor can you use a telephone attached to the same phone line. They can share the telephone line, but only one device can use the line at a time.

The fax modem behaves like a fax machine. It can answer the phone, establish a communications link with the sending fax machine, and collect the sent document.

Received fax documents are always graphical representations of the original material. Graphic files are large compared to typical text files.

A single-page document that is 4 KB when stored as ASCII text, might be 1 MB — about 250 times larger — when stored as a graphic file. If you expect to receive 10 to 20 pages of fax documents a week and have a need to keep them all, you can rapidly fill your hard disk.

You can print the graphic file and then delete it from your hard disk if you do not actually need to store the received fax on your PC. Many stand-alone fax machines, particularly the less expensive ones, use photosensitive paper that curls and fades with time. Most PC printers use ordinary paper, so the output from the printer may be better than from the stand-alone fax machine.

However, you need a printer that can print graphic files, and you need to consider the time needed to print. A laser printer, for example, can take several minutes to print a page with a graphic image.

If you need to use the received fax on your computer to make modifications, for example, you probably need to convert the received graphics file into text. This can be done by using an optical character recognition (OCR) program. A few fax communication programs include OCR programs, and many other OCR programs are available. Chapter 11 details the advantages and disadvantages of these programs.

An OCR program looks at the graphic file and tries to interpret the shapes into text characters. Depending on the OCR program, this method is very successful for clear typewritten and printed documents and is useless for handwritten, dirty, or complex documents including a mixture of fonts. For example, it is quicker to retype a document with handwritten marked-up notes and pictures than to try to make the OCR program convert it accurately.

Another potential problem with handling documents received by a PC fax modem is your filing system and organization. The documents are saved with a DOS filename, and you need suitable software that can identify the document easily, or you may spend hours trying to find the fax again.

With printed documents, even if you don't have a filing system, you can skim and dismiss a document within a couple of seconds. On the computer, you will be loading and unloading large graphic files unless you have a good filing system that can identify the document without reading it.

Text documents that you are going to alter rather than just read and throw away are much more appropriate for sending with a data modem than a fax modem. However, fax modems are relatively inexpensive ways of providing yourself with faxing capabilities, especially if you purchase a data modem and fax modem combination. The ability to give people a fax number is becoming an essential part of business today.

If you are buying a data modem anyway, consider getting a combined data modem and fax modem to supplement a stand-alone fax machine. You can use the PC fax modem for outgoing faxes that are documents you created on your PC and the stand-alone fax machine to send pre-printed or handwritten material.

Choosing a fax modem's form factor

As with data modems, you need to consider the physical attributes of the PC fax modem as well as the communications standards. The previous section on choosing a data modem's form factor applies equally to your fax modem.

A PC fax modem will probably be an internal device. However, the data modem and fax modem combinations are commonly available as external units. You need to select an internal fax modem that conforms with the expansion bus of your computer. For example, if you have a PS/2 computer, you may need a fax modem with a Micro Channel Architecture connector, or you may want a PCMCIA fax modem for your laptop.

The fax modem is similar to the data modem in that it uses the serial port to connect to your PC. If you already have four serial ports in your computer, you will have to remove one to make a serial port available for an internal fax modem. An external fax modem needs one of the serial port connectors.

Choosing fax modem compatibility and communications standards

Fax machines (stand-alone and PC fax modems) send documents between each other by using established communication standards. These standards predate PCs and are different from all the standards covered earlier in this chapter for data modems.

However, these standards were established by the same United Nations group, ITU-T (previously CCITT), as for data modems. Fax machine communication standards are known as Groups, and there are standards for Group 1, Group 2, Group 3, and Group 4. Almost all fax machines produced today are Group 3 compliant.

Group 1 and Group 2 fax machines are analog devices and do not include modems. Group 3 faxes are digital devices and scan the document, convert the digital data, and then modulate it for transmission. Upon receipt, they demodulate the data back into digital data for printing. Group 4 fax machines can transmit the fax data over digital telephone lines, such as leased lines or ISDN lines. They are not covered in this book.

"What are fax modem communications standards?"

The group number may be abbreviated in the manufacturer's specification. For example, Group 3 may be referred to as G3. Choose a fax machine or fax modem that is Group 3 compliant. Group 3 modems use ITU-T communications standards that specify how the data is modulated for transmission. Like data modems, the different modulation schemes result in different speeds of data transmission.

The V.21 Channel 2 standard is used for 300 bps fax transmission. V.27ter is used for 4800 bps transmission with 2400 bps transmission as a fallback speed. V.29 is used for 9600 bps transmission with 7200 bps fallback speed. V.17 is used for 14,400 bps fax transmission with 12,000 fallback speed. Table 4-4 lists the standards.

Table 4-4	Fax Modem Standards
Maximum Speed	**Standard**
300	V.21 Channel 2
4800	V.27ter
9600	V.29
14,400	V.17

As with PC data modems, you should buy the fastest fax modem you can afford. When buying a data modem and fax modem combination, be sure to read carefully and determine which is the data modem's speed and which is the fax modem's. You can, for example, buy a 9600 bps data modem that has a fax modem capable of 14.4 kbps transmission. This will not give you a 14.4 kbps data modem.

PC fax modems, rather than fax machines, also conform with other standards. These standards are the equivalent of AT-compatibility and dictate how the PC will communicate with the fax modem. The standards do not affect how the fax data is transmitted so are not relevant to stand-alone fax machines.

The command set used by the PC to communicate with the fax modem is determined by the fax modem's Class. The Telecommunications Industry Association (TIA, also referred to as EIA/TIA) has established the Class standard for fax modems. However, some PC fax boards, including the most popular, use a proprietary standard.

Class 1 fax modems conform with EIA/TIA-578 and are the most commonly found PC fax modems. Class 2 is a fairly recent new standard that is likely to be more popular than Class 1 because of performance improvements.

The selection of a Class 1, Class 2, or a proprietary fax modem depends on the software you are using. The Class standard for the fax modem affects how the PC talks to the fax modem, not how the data is sent over the phone line. The issue for fax modems is a matter of fax communications software support. A Class 1 or Class 2 fax modem will be supported by almost all fax communications software. If you pick a popular proprietary fax modem, such as Hayes JT Fax or Intel SatisFaxtion, any supplied fax communications software will support it. Do not consider proprietary fax modems that are not specifically supported by the fax communications software you are considering.

A fax modem using proprietary techniques for communicating between the data and fax modem may outperform or be more flexible than Class 1 or Class 2 fax modems. For example, you may be able to send a fax document in the background more efficiently while working on another program. Now that Class 2 fax modems have become available, this is a preferable choice to Class 1 fax modems. (The Class 3 standard is also being discussed.)

Fax modem extras

As with the data modem, you need to consider the extras that may or may not be supplied with your fax modem. This includes such physical items as the phone cable as well as the warranty, technical support, and money-back guarantee. The previous section on modem extras applies to fax modems as well, except that you are less likely to have an external fax modem and consequently will not be concerned about data cables.

The fax communications software is typically a weak point with PC fax modems. The programs work satisfactorily, but you may need other programs to provide file management or conversion utilities. The following section on choosing communications software and Chapters 7 and 11 provide more detail.

Choosing Communications Software

Most modems come with communications software, and most fax modems come with fax communications software. You should consider only modems with associated software. This helps with installation and fault-finding, because the supplier will be unable to argue that they have not tried that particular communications program.

The software supplied with data modems and fax modems varies in quality and features. However, most will probably get you up and running even if they do not include all the extra features you may want when you can do the basics.

You have a wide choice of communications programs to choose from. The most appropriate choice depends on what you want to do. For example, if you want to call BBSs, you will want a different program than if you want to call Prodigy, an online service that requires its own communication software. You probably want a general-purpose communications program and should be prepared to get add-on programs or specially written programs as you communicate with different online services.

For example, a general-purpose communications program will allow you to connect with a friend or business colleague as well as get access to most online services. However, you will dramatically reduce your online charges, which in some cases include a charge for the time you are connected to the service in addition to the telephone connection charges, by using a product that streamlines your actions while connected. If you need a special program to connect with a particular online service, you purchase this program as part of the start-up kit when you first subscribe to the service.

The best communications program to use is the one that includes the features you need and you can get the most help with. It's rather like word processors — you get the best help with your word processor if you talk to other people with the same program.

As a starting point, use the communications software supplied with your modem. If you are unable to make it work and cannot get adequate help from the modem manufacturer, choose a well-known third-party program that supports your modem. For example, QModemPro from Mustang Software and Procomm Plus from Datastorm Technologies are two of the most popular programs used on BBSs. If you are using Microsoft Windows, choose a communications program designed to work with Windows, such as Hayes Smartcom for Windows or DCA's Crosstalk for Windows.

As mentioned in Chapter 3, do not give up on telecommunicating because you cannot understand the communications software supplied with your modem. Chapter 5 introduces the basics of making a connection, and Chapter 6 covers how to transfer files between computers. Your communications software should be able to perform both of these tasks.

Part III explains specific features supplied in communications programs and shows how to consider whether you need a better program than that supplied with your modem. In most cases, if you do more than the very occasional connection, you will want to take advantage of software with more features. If you catch the telecommunications bug, you will have very specific requirements.

Fax communications software is slightly different in scope. Most fax modems are supplied with software. Do not consider a fax modem unless it comes with software. Unlike data modems, where you have a lot of control over the communications parameters, you cannot do many different things with a fax modem. You simply send a document or receive a document.

The fax modem communications software must be able to the basics, such as sending and receiving documents, but needing extra features, such as viewing the received document or converting the file into another form, depends on your application. Rather than expecting your fax communications software to do much more than communicate, you may consider third-party utility programs.

For example, fax software can save your graphic file. To work with the received file, you want a graphic viewing or editing program. You may need to convert the graphic file into another file format before you can edit it in your editing program. You may choose a third-party (or is it sixth-party?) program that can do the file conversion. If you want to convert the file to text, you need an OCR program. OCR programs are sophisticated and will probably not be included in your fax modem.

Chapter 7 shows how to send and receive a fax. The supplied fax communications software should be able to perform this task. Part III explains the extra desirable features, such as file management, that you may want for use with your fax modem. When considering the cost of modems and in particular fax modems, assess the associated software carefully.

Installing Your Equipment and Software

As an external unit, a modem is typically a small rectangular box with a series of LEDs (*light-emitting diodes*) along the front and a series of connectors and an on/off switch on the back. Most modems also include a separate power supply, a small black cube with an incorporated electrical plug, that you plug into the electrical outlet and the rear of the modem. (See Figure 4-1.)

There are typically two or three other connectors on an external modem. The larger connector, known as a DB 25 connector, is the data connector and accepts the cable linking your computer and the modem. You need a cable that can join this connector to a serial port on your computer. Serial ports are covered in detail earlier in this chapter.

The other one, or two, connectors are RJ-11 phone jack connectors. These are the same as the connectors typically found on telephones and telephone outlets. They connect your modem to the phone line and possibly to another telephone extension.

You link one connector, probably labeled *Line* or *Telco*, to your phone line via a normal phone cable. This links your modem to the phone line in the same way that a phone is linked to the phone line. When you issue the appropriate instructions in the communications software, the modem can perform the equivalent of taking the phone off the hook and dialing a phone number.

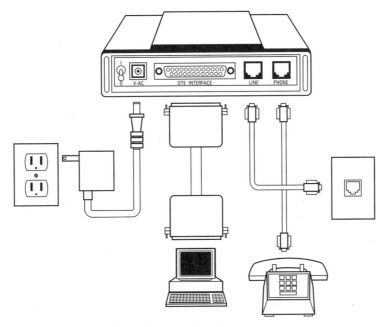

Figure 4-1: The setup of a typical external modem.

The other RJ-11 phone jack, when present, will probably be labeled *Phone* or *Ext.* You can connect a phone via a phone cable to this connector. If there is only one connector on the rear of your modem and it is labeled *Phone*, you should use a phone cable and this connector, the telephone line, and not an extension phone.

Don't be embarrassed if you didn't realize that you need to connect the modem to the phone line. It is very obvious once you know, but an acquaintance of mine spent more than an hour trying to help someone call a BBS with a new modem and software and did not think to ask whether the modem was connected to a phone line.

On some modems, the RJ-11 connectors are not labeled. In this case, they often are linked internally; it doesn't matter which one you use to connect to the phone line and which to an extension phone. However, check your modem documentation to be sure. If the documentation tells you to use a specific one for the phone line and the other for the extension phone, take the time to label the connectors so you avoid confusion later.

If the space around your computer is limited, you should label the cables themselves as you install them. It is surprising how often you have to unplug your external modem to move telephones or computers around.

An internal modem, as its name suggests, is plugged into your PC, laptop, or notebook. It draws its power from the computer and does not include a separate power supply. You can put the modem into any available slot that it will fit into. (See Figure 4-2.)

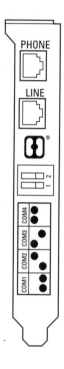

Figure 4-2: A typical internal modem.

Modems have moderate power supply needs, and if you are using a laptop or notebook, you will quickly run down your battery. Wherever possible, plug your laptop or notebook into the main power when using your modem. Because you must be near a telephone anyway to transmit, the addition of external power to the computer is not normally a big problem.

An internal modem has fewer visible connectors than an external modem. The data connector is not required because the computer is linked to the modem via the expansion board or PCMCIA connector.

Like the external modem, the internal modem has one or two, RJ-11 telephone connectors on the rear panel. (The PCMCIA modem also has an RJ-11 connector.) If there is only one connector, you plug a phone cable into the rear panel of the modem and into the telephone outlet in the wall.

If there are two connectors, one probably will be labeled *Line* and the other *Phone* or *Ext*. Use a phone cable to join the connector labeled *Line* to the telephone outlet in the wall, and use a phone cable to join the other connector to a telephone if you prefer.

Tip: Even if you do not want to leave a telephone attached permanently, it is worth adding a telephone while you install your modem and make it work. You can then check that you are actually getting a dial tone and can dial numbers manually from the modem's location.

If there are two connectors and they are not labeled, check the modem documentation for details. As with the external modem, if you must use one for the phone line and one for the extension phone, take the time to make a sticky label and label the connectors so that you avoid confusing the connections.

Take the time when installing your modem to label your phone cables as well as the connectors. This is especially important with internal modems. You will probably need to unplug your modem from the phone line every time you move your computer. Reconnection is much quicker with labeled connectors.

With the hardware installed, you need to install the communications software supplied with your modem. This usually involves running an installation program that copies and uncompresses the files onto your computer. Refer to your modem or communication software documentation for specific details.

After copying the files to your hard disk, you need to configure the software to fit your computer hardware configuration and the modem. This can involve such items as specifying the serial port, its address, and interrupt level, as well as choosing niceties such as screen color.

The actual process depends on the specific modem as well as the specific software. Some communications programs can examine your hardware and determine the modem's location automatically. Others will supply lists for you to choose from, and still others will require to do all the specifying explicitly.

Note: Hayes modems support a feature called AutoStart that enables software to automatically determine the modem capabilities and feature set and configure the software to support them. This feature is supported through the I4 command. With Smartcom for Windows, for example, the software automatically interrogates the modem to find the speed and feature set and can set up the software to support those feautures.

Make sure that your modem is turned on before starting your communications program. (An internal modem gets its power from the PC and is "turned on" whenever your PC is turned on.) In this way, any initializing or interrogation done by the communications program will occur automatically.

"Why doesn't my communication software start when I type AT and press Enter?"

Although this chapter introduces the concept of modems being Hayes-compatible or AT-compatible and mentioned the term AT commands, this is not the name of your communications software program. AT commands are used within your communications software program to communicate with your modem. In most cases, the software program sends the commands and you do not type them separately.

To start your communications program, you need to type its DOS filename at the DOS command prompt and press Enter. (Although this may seem obvious to experienced DOS users, it can be confusing because an operating mode found within communications programs, known as *terminal mode,* can look deceptively like a DOS command mode.)

The communications program's name will probably be the product name or an abbreviation of the name. For example, you run QModemPro by typing **qmpro** and Smartcom Exec by typing **exec** and pressing Enter.

Your fax software is comparable with the data communications software. Installing involves copying and uncompressing files onto your hard disk or creating working copies. This process is usually automated and may or may not include configuring your fax modem. Be sure to turn your fax modem on before doing the configuration. (As with data modems, if the fax modem is internal, the fax modem is powered on whenever your computer is turned on.)

Your data modem or fax modem requires a communications program to be running as well as the modem being powered on to communicate.

Chapter 5 shows how to communicate with your modem, make your modem communicate with another modem, and create a communications link. Chapter 6 explains file transfer, which you can do after you understand how to make the two modems talk to each other. Chapter 7 shows how to establish a connection and send or receive fax documents at your fax modem.

Summary

This chapter introduced the telephone and RS-232 port essentials. You learned the type of phone line you need and techniques for getting the best service from that line. You also learned the basics on serial ports, their DOS names, port addresses, and interrupt levels.

You determined whether you need a data modem, fax modem, or a combination data and fax modem. The selection depends on many factors, including the specific types of information you want to exchange, the computer's form factor, and other criteria such as warranty or technical support.

You were introduced to the ITU communications standards used in data modems. Some of these specify the speed at which your modem can communicate, and others add data-compression or error-detection into the process.

You also were introduced to the ITU communications standards for fax modems. These are not the same as the standards used for data modems.

This chapter covered installing your modem and communications software in preparation for the subsequent chapters. Chapter 5 introduces data modem communication, and Chapter 7 introduces fax modem communication.

5

CHAPTER

Understanding
Your Data Modem

This chapter explains how to communicate by using your data modem. You learn the following important steps:

❧ Preparing to communicate

❧ Issuing commands to a modem

❧ Establishing a connection

❧ Communicating with another computer

❧ Breaking the connection

This chapter does not explain how to send a fax but focuses on data modems. Chapter 7 is the equivalent chapter for fax modems. Your modem and communications software should be installed before using the techniques in this chapter. Chapter 4 explains modem selection and installation.

Preparing to Communicate

Unless you have used your modem recently and made successful connections, it is well worth checking that you have the following connected:

- ♣ A phone line plugged into the rear of the modem and the telephone outlet in the wall

- ♣ The data cable for an external modem plugged into the rear of the modem and into the serial port on your computer

- ♣ The power supply for an external modem plugged into the rear of the modem and into an electrical outlet

If you find a missing cable or loose connection, be sure to turn off the computer and modem before correcting the problem. When you plug in a connector, you actually make and break the connection multiple times. This can damage the electrical equipment it is attached to. For example, plugging in the power supply to the modem when it is already plugged into the electrical outlet can break your modem. It rarely happens, but there is a chance.

After checking the cables, turn on your modem and start your communications program. An external modem may have an LED to indicate that the power is on and will probably light at least one of the LEDs on its front panel.

An internal modem lacks these LEDs, but you may use a terminate-and-stay-resident (TSR) program on your computer to display the equivalent of the LEDs on your computer screen. A TSR is a program you load into your computer, typically from AUTOEXEC.BAT. It remains in memory and you can run your normal programs with the TSR still resident.

Your internal modem may be supplied with a program of this type or you can obtain one from a computer user group or BBS. These programs remove the disadvantage of not having visible LEDs on an internal modem but may not allow all your other application programs to run successfully. This program is worth considering when you are experiencing problems rather than being a requirement for all situations.

Table 5-1 lists the most common LEDs found on external modem front panels and gives a brief description of their purpose. You will not need to look at these LEDs other than to check that power is on, but they are a valuable tool in troubleshooting. For example, if you do not hear a dial tone when you ask the communications software to dial a number, you can look at the OH LED and see whether the modem performed the equivalent of lifting the phone receiver.

Table 5-1		Modem LEDs
LED	**Name**	**Description when lit**
HS	High Speed	Modem is operating at what it considers to be a "high speed."
AA	Auto Answer	Modem answers when phone rings.
CD	Carrier Detect	Modem detects a carrier signal from other modem.
OH	Off Hook	Modem has done equivalent of lifting phone receiver.
RD or RX	Receive Data	Data is being sent from modem to computer.
SD or SX	Send Data	Data is being sent from computer to modem.
TR	Terminal Ready	Computer and modem are linked via serial port.
MR	Modem Ready	Modem is turned on.
DC	Data Compression	Modem is able to compress data.
EC	Error Control	Modem is able to detect errors.

You need to know five items in order to connect with another modem:

1. The phone number
2. Whether you are calling the other modem or the other modem is calling you
3. The *character format*
4. If you are doing the calling, the fastest desired transmission speed
5. The *terminal emulation* both computers will use

Each of these items is detailed in the following sections. Most communications programs include all of these settings within their menus. However, you also can control your modem by sending commands directly. Issuing commands to your modem is covered later in this chapter.

Knowing where you are calling and how

To make a communications link, two modems are connected via a telephone line.

If you are calling another modem, you need to know its phone number. You also want to choose whether you use tone or pulse dialing. As covered in Chapter 4, tone dialing is faster, but you need a phone line that can accept it.

When dialing another modem, you are originating the call. You may need to select this option, called *modem originate*, in your communications program. In most programs, this is the default setting, and if you select a phone number to dial from your program's *dialing directory* (list of phone numbers), this setting is assumed.

If another modem is calling your modem, you need to know the phone number that your modem is attached to. Remember that you cannot use the phone for a voice call at the same time as the modem.

When a modem calls your modem, your modem answers the phone. You need to select the *auto-answer* option or the *modem answer* option in your communications software. This instructs the modem to listen for the phone ringing and then pick up the phone call.

Choosing character format

As explained in Chapter 4, your computer sends serial data to the modem, which is modulated and sent to the other modem for translation back into digital data, where it is accepted by the receiving computer's serial port.

Although the data is sent from the serial port one bit at a time, it is arranged in groups known as *characters*. The character format is comprised of three parts: start bits, data bits, and stop bits. Both computers need to be set to send and receive characters with the same character format.

You define the character format for your connection by choosing the number of *data bits* (7 or 8), the number of *stop bits* (1 or 2), and the *parity* (None, Even, Odd, Mark, or Space).

"What do 7E1 and 8N1 mean?"

The sidebar, "Understanding Character Format," explains parity and gives more detail on how the character is actually formatted when you change these parameters.

In general, if you are calling another PC, such as a BBS or your office personal computer, you will want to choose eight data bits, no parity, and one stop bit. If you are calling a mainframe computer — many commercial online services are run on mainframes — you will probably need to choose seven data bits, even parity, and one stop bit. These are commonly abbreviated to 8N1 and 7E1 respectively.

These values can be changed in most communications programs in a variety of places. The menus are typically named *port settings, device settings,* or format settings. In many programs, you can choose a setting that will be the default if you do not specify a different one, and you can specify a different setting for a particular telephone number. (Choosing default settings and customizing settings for particular places you call are covered in Chapter 8.)

For example, you may set 8N1 as the default because you will usually be calling bulletin boards. However, your settings for when you call the online service Genie may be 7E1.

Understanding transmission speed

In addition to specifying the format of the character, the serial port must be set to transmit data to the modem at a particular speed. Surprisingly, the maximum possible speed is not always the most desirable.

With a few exceptions, which are noted in the following sidebar, choose a transmission speed that matches your modem's maximum speed or choose the *automatic* or *maximum* speed option. For example, if you have a 2400 bps modem, choose 2400. If you have a 9600 bps modem, choose 9600.

Many users, experts included, use the term *baud,* or *baud rate,* instead of or as well as *speed* or *bits per second* (bps). You can provoke many arguments trying to understand the correct definition. The technical sidebar "Understanding Baud and Data Rates" addresses these debates.

Understanding Character Format

Your computer sends data to the serial port one byte at a time. The UART and other circuitry rearrange this data into serial data form for transmission from the serial port. The receiving serial port accepts the data one bit at time.

So that the receiving port understands where one byte begins and ends, the bits of data are arranged into characters. The data bits have extra bits known as *framing bits* added on either end of the byte of data. You can control the format of the character by altering the number of data bits, the number of stop bits, and the parity.

The sending and receiving serial ports must be set to use the same character formats to translate the data correctly. Some computers, typically mainframes, can use only seven data bits in a byte, and consequently, the PC, which can use eight data bits in a byte, must alter its serial port settings to conform with the more limiting standard.

Similarly, some serial ports expect one bit to indicate the end of a character being sent on the serial port, and others expect to see two bits to indicate the end of a character.

Using human communication as a comparison, think of needing the same character format at both ends as the difference between local accents. I was in a car accident once in Texas, and the other driver came from New York. I could not understand the slow-talking Texas policeman who left gaps in the middle of words as well as between them. I spoke very precisely with my British accent, pronouncing every syllable, and the policeman had problems understanding me. The New Yorker, who talked extremely fast with no gaps between sentences, let alone words, ended up repeating what the policeman and I said so we could all communicate with each other. You would not have believed that we were all talking English.

The parity bit is an error-checking mechanism that can be added to the data. The parity bit is added so that the receiving serial port has a check that the character sent is the same as the character received. The receiving serial port compares the *parity bit* in the character with the *parity* of the received character. If the two are the same, there is a reasonable assurance that the character actually received is the same as what was sent.

To understand a character's parity, consider a character containing eight data bits, which is a row of eight ones and zeros. The character is considered to have even parity if there is an even number of ones in the row and is considered to have odd parity if there is an odd number of ones in the row.

If you set even parity on your serial port, the serial port will make the parity bit a one or a zero to make the character along with its parity bit have an even number of ones in the row of data. For example, if the eight data bits were 10011001, the parity bit would be a zero to maintain an even number of ones.

You may have odd, even, mark, space, or none parity. Odd parity is similar to even parity, except that the parity bit is made a one to make an odd number of ones in the character. No parity, usually designated as a setting of none, does not add a parity bit.

Mark and space are also no parity, in that they do not represent the parity of the character, but they do add a bit in the parity bit location. Mark adds a one in the parity bit location, and space adds a zero in the parity bit location. They are used most frequently in serial device applications, such as plotting, other than modems.

If you want to avoid the detail, understand that baud (pronounced *bod*) and baud rate are most frequently used incorrectly. As a modem user, talk about your modem's speed in bits per second or bps and you will be correct. I think the confusion has arisen because baud is easier to pronounce than bps.

Your communications software, and other documentation, such as guides to online services, may use the term baud or baud rate to mean transmission speed or data rate. This is where you set the transmission speed. (The modem's actual baud is defined by the communications standard being used and is not directly controlled by the user.)

The speed of the modem you are connecting to is usually not important to the data speed setting. Your modem will try to connect at the fastest speed you specify, and if this is not possible will automatically negotiate a slower speed with the other modem.

The following three sections address the times when you will not want to set the communication software's transmission speed to the maximum value.

Slow modem, fast software

Your communications software may be able to send data at rates that your modem cannot handle. For example, if you have a 2400 bps modem, you don't want to set the port speed to 115200 bps. If you do not pick an appropriate speed, you may experience overrun or dropped characters. (Chapter 4 explains overrun.)

Connect charges

Many online services charge you a connect time charge. You pay an hourly rate for the length of time you are connected to the service. Because you can get more data in a given amount of time if you connect at a faster speed, these services often charge more per hour if you use a faster speed.

For example, you may pay $1 per hour if you connect at 2400 bps or $5 per hour if you connect at 9600 bps. As a beginner, do the basic mathematics to choose the best connection speed. In this example, 2400 bps seems a better choice. You will need to set your communications program to the slower speed, or your modem will try to connect at the faster speed, and you will connect at the higher hourly rate.

As you become more familiar with communications, this is an area well worth revisiting, because understanding the true cost of a connection can save you a lot of money. Even in the preceding example, you may want to use the faster speed for certain operations and the slower speed for others. For your first few connections, the difference of a few cents an hour is probably less important than actually making the connection and doing the communicating. However, when you are spending ten hours a week online, the few cents add up. Part IV explains how to find out your true online costs and what choices are available.

By the way, if spending ten hours a week online seems a lot to you, consider this. A popular online service changed its rate schedule from a fixed monthly charge to an hourly rate. Many people (home computer users) complained that this would be cost prohibitive for them because they spent in excess of 200 hours a month online to this particular service!

Understanding Baud and Data Rates

When a modem manufacturer called me in 1986 to tout a brand new product that was a 9600 bps proprietary modem with 7.5 baud, I realized I needed to brush up on my engineering degree. I didn't know how to repsond. I knew the terms but bandied them around haphazardly. Baud and data rates are the most abused and confusing terms in modem technology.

First the definitions. *Data rate* is the amount of data that is transmitted in a given amount of time. For example, a data rate of 2400 bits per second means that 2,400 bits of data are sent every second. *Baud* is the signaling rate. For example, 2400 baud means that data is sent 2,400 times per second. (Notice that this definition does not say how much data is sent, only how often data is sent.) Strictly speaking, there is no such thing as *baud rate*. It is like saying "frequency rate" rather than frequency.

Any modem that conforms with the commonly accepted standards, such as V.22bis or V.32, and operates faster than 1200 bps has a baud rate lower than the data rate. To conform with the standards and make best use of the telephone system, more than one bit of data is transferred between the modems at a time.

For example, a 2400 bps modem operates at 1200 baud. Two bits of data are being sent every 1/1200 of a second. The faster modems, such as the 9600

bps modems, have even lower baud rates because even more data is being sent at one time. In my earlier example of 9600 bps at 7.5 baud, 1,280 bits of data were being sent at a time, and they were sent 7.5 times per second.

Many communications programs include a baud setting rather than a bps setting, and many people, including modem manufacturers, refer to their modems as being, for example, 9600 baud modems. In fact, the communications programs are correct and the modem manufacturers are wrong!

Your communications program communicates with your modem through the serial port. The baud setting you choose in the communications program dictates the data speed between the serial port and the modem. Because the data is only sent out of the serial port one bit at a time, the signaling rate is the same as the data rate.

However, the data being sent between the two modems may or may not be sent one bit at a time. The baud is decided by the modems and not the user. In some cases it is chosen based only on the communications standards being used, in others it depends on the standard as well as on the amount of noise on the phone line. When you refer to a modem, you should talk about the data rate and ignore its baud.

Data-compression included

You want to pick a sufficiently fast speed for your communication, which may not be the specified speed of your modem. As explained in Chapter 4, the V.42bis communication standard adds data compression features to your modem. V.42bis is a feature that may be available on all 2400 bps or faster modems.

Other modems may use different data compression methods. These may be proprietary to the particular brand and model of modem or may conform with another fairly common standard called MNP Level 5.

When your modem uses a compression standard, such as V.42bis or MNP Level 5, it compresses the data supplied from the computer and transmits it to the other modem. The receiving modem uncompresses the data and passes it on to the receiving computer. This compression results in more data being passed between the modems in a particular length of time than if the data is sent uncompressed.

In this case, if you set the serial port to the maximum speed of the modem, such as 9600 bps, the modem will not be sending data the whole time because it will compress the data and wait for more data. In effect, the compression will not increase the overall throughput.

However, if you set the serial port speed on both the receiving and the transmitting computer to faster than the modem's speed, the overall throughput can exceed the modem's maximum transmission speed. The sending modem collects a chunk of data and compresses it, then it sends the smaller-sized data to the other end for uncompression or extraction. The data transmission speed (the number of bits per second) remains the same, but the amount of data contained in those bits is more due to the compression.

The amount of compression, which may be none, depends on the type of data being sent. If you have used file compression programs, such as PKZIP, you may be familiar with the concept that certain file types compress more than others. A typical text file, for example, can be compressed by a substantial amount, but a typical program file can be compressed only a small amount.

This compression is possible because of the actual patterns in the data bits and the type of compression techniques used. Text files, for example, include a lot of repetitive characters; words such as "the" or "and" or lots of space characters in a row may occur frequently. A compression technique may take advantage of this to reduce the amount of data sent. Consider the difference in voice communication between ordering "Same again" in a restaurant as opposed to "I'll have a gin and tonic with lots of ice and a lime twist, please."

As a beginner, you don't need to worry about the degree of data compression possible on the material you are sending or receiving. Because the maximum data-throughput with data compression can be eight times your modem speed, you should set your serial port speed higher than your modem speed. (If you do not know about the receiving computer, set the speed higher and be prepared to lower it at a future time if you experience data loss.)

Choosing between compressing data before transmission or using a modem's compression techniques is an intermediate topic that is addressed in Part III. Chapter 9 expands on the possible approaches. Like using the most economical speed if you are being charged based on the time you are on-line, you also want to reduce the time you are on line by using the best compression method.

Understanding terminal emulation

In addition to setting the speed and format of the transmitted information, you need both computers to operate with the same or compatible *terminal emulations*. The parameters discussed previously allow the data to be sent and received at their respective serial ports. The terminal emulation is what the two computers mean by the data that is being sent.

You must remember that you are actually linking two modems together with a communications link. Although each modem may be attached to a computer, the computer types do not have to be the same. Additionally, a second computer does not have to be involved. One modem may be attached to a printer or a device called a terminal.

Terminals consist of a video screen, keyboard, and some control electronics and are typically used to attach to minicomputers or mainframes. They do not contain the processing power of a PC, nor do they usually contain disk drives, but they use the communications link to connect the keyboard to the programs and data on the minicomputer or mainframe. The remote computer in turn controls the terminal. It may send particular data or controlling codes to alter the terminal's operation.

There are a variety of terminal types. Logically, each type is used to connect to each type of computer. Some are very simple, and others are more sophisticated with many more functions available. You can make your PC appear to the other computer as a terminal, hence the name *terminal emulation*. The two computers are able to "talk" to each other because they are using the same terminal emulation.

Using voice communication as a comparison, the terminal emulation is equivalent to establishing the language you are going use, such as French or Spanish. If the two people talking to each other do not use the same language, some information may be heard correctly, but other information may be misinterpreted.

The voice communication analogy can be extended beyond language to gestures and expressions. This is equivalent to the computer sending controlling data and expecting a certain result. In America, looking at the person you are speaking to shows a degree of interest and respect. But in another culture, say Japan, you show respect by keeping your eyes and head lowered. Hand gestures in particular have very different meanings around the world. Even within Europe, a relatively small geographical area, a polite gesture in one country may be lewd in another.

The terminal emulation you choose dictates the effect of your pressing a key on the keyboard and what the receiving computer thinks that key means. For example, when you press an A on your keyboard, the receiving computer considers it as an A. However, if you press F1 on your PC, this may have no meaning to the computer at the other end. Additionally, the remote computer will send data to your computer, and you need to choose the terminal emulation mode that will respond in the expected way to the data or control information sent.

The most basic terminal emulation is known as TTY. This is supported by most computers but has the disadvantage of providing only basic functionality. (TTY was used for teletype machines, an early form of fax machines still in use in many places around the world.) If you do not know what sort of computer you are connecting to, you are unlikely to fail with TTY. Even if the other computer is actually using another terminal emulation, you may still be able to understand most of the characters because TTY is a subset of many more-advanced terminals.

"How do I make BBS menus appear in color?"

If you are connecting with another PC — and most BBSs are run on PCs — you should choose ANSI as the terminal emulation being used by your communications program *and* the BBS. This allows you to see characters in color, bold, or flashing where applicable. Additionally, you will be able to see line characters. These are the characters that make your menus have lines around them instead of funny looking characters.

"When I log on to a BBS, I see funny characters around the menus. Why?"

If there is a mismatch between your terminal emulation selections, your screen will not appear as intended. The BBS probably offers a menu option, and you can adjust the setting in your communications program.

You may have seen similar funny characters by pressing Print Screen and printing a screen with menus on to a laser printer or dot matrix printer.

A recent addition to many BBSs is a graphical user interface called RIP (Remote Image Protocol). This allows you to see graphical menus and to use your mouse on-line. To take advantage of RIP, you need to use RIP Script or RIP emulation as your terminal emulation. As graphical user interfaces on BBSs become more popular, this will become a preferable alternative to ANSI.

The other terminal emulation types found in many communications programs are very important if you need to connect to other types of computers and are features worth looking out for in your communications software. As a PC user, you will probably be told whether you need to use one of these other emulations. Common terminal emulations include VT 52, VT 100, VT 102, VT 220, and VT 230. These are Digital Equipment Corporation (DEC) terminal emulations. Other popular ones are Wyse 50, IBM 3101, and Heath 19; Prestel and Teletel are widely used in Europe.

When you connect with a system for the first time, you will often be given a choice of terminal emulations. You will probably want to choose the most advanced one your computer can support. If you do not know which to choose, make a note of all of them and try them in turn. For example, choose RIP over ANSI, and choose ANSI over TTY.

The more-advanced terminal emulation may make the system less responsive. For example, the time it takes to redraw the screen with RIP may be much longer than with TTY. If you have a fast modem and fast computer, you may not see any significant difference between the speeds and can enjoy the "pretty screens". However, on slow computers with relatively slow modems, the redrawing can be annoying.

Issuing Commands to a Modem

Almost all communications software includes a menu system that allows you to choose the phone number, character format, transmission speed, terminal emulation, and if necessary an auto-answer feature. You pick the relevant menu and select from a list of options. You are then ready to make a connection.

However, the ease with which you can select these items varies dramatically with the software program. This may be the point where you decide that the communications program provided with your modem is unusable.

As explained in Chapter 3, AT-compatible modems can be controlled from software. (You, or more likely a telephone technician, made adjustments in early modems by opening it up and altering switches inside the cover.) When you make a selection from a menu, the communication software sends commands to the serial port and modem to make the appropriate adjustments.

You can also make these and many other adjustments directly rather than using the communications software. As you become more experienced with communications, you are more likely to need to make the adjustments directly, because your software may not include all the particular modem-controlling commands you need.

For example, you are likely to want to configure your modem in a particular way every time you start your communications software. One method of doing this is to make your software issue a series of commands to the modem, known as an *initialization string*, when you start the communications program. Initialization strings are covered in Chapter 10, because they are an intermediate-level topic. However, controlling the modem directly is an introductory topic.

When you turn on your modem, it powers up in *command mode* and is ready to accept commands that are sent from the computer's serial port. The modem commands (with two exceptions) all begin with the prefix **AT,** and sending commands directly to the modem is commonly referred to as issuing *AT commands*. For example, the command to dial the phone number 555-1111 is ATD555-1111.

"What does AT stand for?"

AT is not an abbreviation but is used by the modem to determine the character format and transmission speed being used by the serial port. The AT allows the modem to self-calibrate. It is expecting to see the two characters AT and can adjust its internal settings so that it will understand the subsequent characters sent as commands from the serial port.

This AT character sequence is not the same as IBM's PC AT computer designation. The AT in an IBM AT computer is an abbreviation for Advanced Technology, because it is a more advanced computer than the IBM PC.

To issue AT commands, you need a method of sending characters from the serial port. For modems, this is done from within your communications program. Your communications program will have a mode where, when you type characters on-screen, they are sent to the serial port. This is most frequently known as *terminal mode* or the *terminal screen* (because you are using the PC as a terminal).

This is the area on your screen where you see data from the computer you are connected to. In a DOS-based communications program, the terminal screen is typically a blank screen with a line of status information at the top or bottom of the screen. In a Windows-based communications program, it is usually a blank window.

*"When I type **AT** at the DOS command prompt, nothing happens. Why?"*

Because the terminal screen is mostly blank or has a series of commands with the cursor at the bottom, it can be confused with the DOS prompt screen that may be displayed when you turn on your computer. The two screens may appear similar, but they serve different functions.

The DOS prompt screen, which usually has a drive letter and path, such as C:\>, followed by the cursor, is used to issue commands to DOS. The terminal screen is within your communications software program.

To reach a terminal screen, you need to type the name of your communications software program, such as **qmodem** or **exec**, and load your communications software then access the terminal screen. The method for accessing this screen varies, but you may automatically be in this screen when you load the program or may need to press Esc to remove a dialing directory (list of places you can call). Alternatively, your communications program may use the term direct connection to give you access to the terminal screen. Some communications programs do not include a method for you to enter AT commands directly.

When at the terminal screen, the keys you press on your keyboard are sent to the modem. If your modem is in command mode, the keys you press are considered modem commands and the modem tries to respond to them. If your modem is not in command mode (it is in *online mode*) and is connected to another modem, the keys you press are sent to the modem, passed to the other modem, and in turn passed onto the other computer.

You will need to issue AT commands in two typical situations: configuring and trouble-shooting. You may want to change some modem settings, such as how long the modem is to wait after dialing before giving up on making a connection or how many times the phone must ring before your modem should answer it. You may also need to use AT commands to find problems, such as verifying that your modem actually can communicate with the computer or hang up the phone when the remote computer appears to be unresponsive.

There are literally hundreds of AT commands, and no single modem supports them all. Some of these commands are found on all modems, some are found on specific modems, and some are applicable only to fax modems. In most cases, a particular AT command is used in the same way on each modem that supports that command. However, there is no clear-cut definition that says "buy a modem that supports the following AT commands and you won't go wrong." In general, an AT-compatible modem will include support for sufficient AT commands to make communications successful.

Unfortunately, there is no definitive core AT command set. The TIA/EIA 602 standard for data modems, TIA/EIA 578 for Class 1 fax modems, and TIA/EIA 592 standard for Class 2 fax modems are minimum lists of AT commands that a modem or fax modem will include. However, these lists are not enough for most modem use.

This book presents the AT commands in various forms. This chapter includes seven AT commands that all users should memorize. Even if you know about AT commands, you should read the following section because it defines terms like result codes that are used throughout the book.

Appendix A includes a list of the AT commands. Your modem will include many of these commands, but it may include additional ones as well.

Verifying that your modem is there (AT)

The first command all users should know is AT. From the terminal screen, type **AT** and press Enter. As you press each character, it is sent to the modem. However, the modem will not respond until you press Enter to indicate that the command is completed.

Most modems are not case-sensitive, so you can type **AT** or **at**. However, some modems are case-sensitive and only respond **to AT**.

"Can I type *at* or must AT commands be capital letters?"

Your modem should respond, by displaying on your terminal screen, with OK or less commonly 0. If you do not see the OK or 0, you typed the command incorrectly or your modem is not responding. Check that your modem is turned on and verify that your cables are plugged in. (You may need to exit your communications program and restart it if your modem was not turned on.)

The OK and 0 are called *result codes* and are the modem's method of signalling its status as a result of the commands you have sent. Modems support two types of result codes: verbose and short form. As the name suggests, one is brief and the other is more descriptive. See the ATV and ATQ commands later in this section.

If you make an error when typing a command, you cannot use the backspace key to erase it because the modem has already received it. Press Enter and retype the command; remember to press Enter at the end.

You may not see the letters AT on-screen as you type them. You can make them appear by using another AT command (**ATE1**) to make the modem echo the commands back to the screen. However, some communications programs do not operate correctly when you do this, so if you do it for testing, use the **ATE0** command to turn the echo off before resuming normal communication. See the later section on "Communicating" for more information on the local echo command.

Making your modem go off hook (ATH1)

Use **ATH1** to make your modem do the equivalent of picking up the phone receiver. You can use this to make sure that the modem is plugged into a phone line. Type **ATH1** and press Enter. The modem performs the equivalent of taking the phone off the hook. It will return the result code OK or 0, and you should hear a dial tone through your speaker and the OH LED on your modem should light. Type **ATH** or **ATH0** to hang up the phone.

If you type the **AT** correctly, but the modem is unable to understand the rest of the command, your modem will respond with ERROR or 4. You can reissue the command.

If you do not hear a dial tone, your modem may have its speaker volume turned down or off. (Some modems do not include a speaker.) Early-model modems have a knob on the back that you turn to alter the speaker volume. Newer modems use two AT commands to alter the sound from the speaker. **ATM1** turns the speaker on, **ATM0** turns the speaker off. **ATL0** provides the lowest volume and **ATL2** a medium volume.

Making your modem dial (ATD)

The ATD command is used to make the modem dial a phone number. On its own (without the accompanying number), you can use it like ATH1 to make sure the modem is plugged into a phone line. Type **ATD** and press Enter.

To make the modem dial a phone number, you add the phone number to the ATD command. For example, to make it dial directory inquiries, you type **ATD555-1212** and press Enter.

There are many modifiers to this command so that you can make the modem dial in different ways and with different delays. For example, you can add a T to the command to make it dial in tones or add a P to the command to make the modem dial in pulses. You can add a W to make the modem wait until it hears a dial tone before dialing or add a comma (,) to make it pause while dialing.

For example, the command **ATDTW9,555-1212** dials the same number as before but will use tone dialing, will wait to hear a dial tone before dialing the 9, and will pause before dialing the rest of the number. As you may have guessed by now, there are additional AT commands to alter the length of time the modem will pause when you include a comma in the dialing command and additional modifiers that affect the dialing.

You may need any or all of the modifiers depending on how you are configured. For example, many company phone systems require you to dial a 9 to get an outside line, and you may have to pause for a couple of seconds before you get the line.

As a beginner, you do not need to learn all the modifiers, but you should understand that your communications program is issuing these instructions to your modem. It will probably require you to add such items as commas to indicate delays and add the number you would dial to get an outside line.

Getting result codes (ATQ and ATV)

It is much easier to fault find if your modem is supplying result codes. If you are having trouble connecting with a new online service, any one of many things may be going wrong. You may not be dialing the right number, the phone line may not be working, your modem may not be working, the phone number may be busy or ringing with no answer, et cetera, et cetera.

The ATQ command enables and disables the result codes. If you type **ATQ0** and press Enter, result codes are enabled; if you type **ATQ1** and press Enter, result codes are turned off.

The ATV command enables and disables the verbose result codes. If you type **ATV1** and press Enter, you will get verbose result codes that are much more meaningful than the short form. Typical examples include OK, RING, BUSY, CONNECT 2400, CONNECT 9600, and COMPRESSION: V.42BIS.

The short form codes, enabled by typing **ATV** or **ATV0**, return a one- or two-digit number. Most PC users will not use these codes, although obscure communications programs may require their use. These codes are used most frequently when the modem is attached to specialized equipment, such as control circuitry. Rather than the circuitry needing to translate long words, it can translate the number.

Making your modem hang up (ATH)

After the AT command, the most important command you can learn is how to hang up the phone. The AT command to make your modem hang up the phone is ATH or ATH0. Type **ATH** and press Enter or type **ATH0** and press Enter. Your modem should hang up the phone.

This is not as easy as it sounds and is explained in more detail in the section on disconnecting later in this chapter.

Resetting your modem (ATZ)

To reset the modem to a predefined state, use the ATZ command. Type **ATZ** and press Enter.

If no one has reconfigured your modem, this returns you to the factory default settings. However, you should be aware that you can store your own selection of settings in many modems. These settings are known as a *profile*. Profiles are an intermediate topic and are covered in Chapter 9. When you use the ATZ command, the *preferred* profile that you have previously chosen is restored.

Connecting

To make a connection with another modem, you need to set the phone number, character format, transmission speed, and terminal emulation for your connection. This can be done via menus in your communications software or, if necessary, by issuing AT commands directly to your modem.

When each item is chosen, you select the dial command in your communications software to start the connection process. The communications software sends the commands to the modem, which in turn alters its settings where necessary, takes the phone off the hook, and dials the specified number.

The terms *local* and *remote* are frequently used in communications. As with Einstein's theory of relativity, the terms you use depend on your frame of reference. The local computer and the remote computer may vary, depending at which end of the phone connection you are standing. For the following explanation, assume that the local computer is the one you are dialing from (the *originating* modem) and the remote modem and computer (the *answering* modem) are the ones at the other end of the phone line receiving the phone call.

At the other end, the remote, or answering, modem is set to auto-answer and performs the equivalent of picking up the telephone receiver when the phone rings.

(If the phone number is busy, your modem may signal to your communications software that it is busy or it may continue to wait for an answer.) You can make adjustments to many modems (by using AT commands) that alter how long the modem should wait for a connection.

The tones, bleeps, buzzes, and squeals you hear while your modem is making the connection indicate the negotiation process. When the remote modem answers the phone, it sends a tone or series of tones to the local modem that originated the phone call. The particular tone or series of tones specify the particular speed and particular modulation scheme that it is able to connect at.

The local modem either responds or fails to respond to the tones sent from the remote modem. The two modems negotiate the highest possible connection speed that both modems can achieve (or have been set to achieve). Depending on the particular speed and modulation protocol established, the two modems may exchange further information. This information is used, in part, to further tailor the connection by altering the modems' electronics. In this way, the best possible connection, with the least noise and potentially the most error-free transmission characteristics, for the particular phone line connection is made.

On modems that do not support data compression or error detection, when the highest mutually acceptable speed and modulation standard has been agreed to by the modems, the connection is complete, and the modem sends the result code indicating connection at a particular speed to the communications program (unless the result code feature has been disabled).

However, on modems that support data-compression or error-detection, such as V.42, V.42bis, or MNP 5, the connection is not yet complete. The modems do further negotiation to agree on the data compression or error-detection standards. When complete, the modem sends the result code to indicate the connection speed and the compression or error detection to the communications program.

When you are connecting with another modem, look out for this result code. You will not see codes that your modem is not capable of achieving, but you may see standards that are lower than you are expecting.

For example, if you have a 9600 bps modem and connect with a BBS, you may see a result code such as `CONNECT 2400`. This means you are connected at 2400 bps, not 9600 bps. Read the BBS's menus carefully because you may find that if you call an alternate number, you can connect to the BBS at a faster speed, such as 9600 bps. Typically, the commonly advertised phone number for online services is a 2400 bps number.

As another example, you may see a connect result code that says, `CONNECT 2400, COMPRESSION: V.42bis, PROTOCOL: V.42/LAPM` indicating that you have connected at 2400 bps, but the modems are able to use V.42bis compression and V.42 error detection.

After the negotiation, the two modems "keep in touch" with each other by establishing a signal between them, known as a carrier signal. This is the signal that is modulated to transmit the digital data between the modems. Chapter 4 introduces modulation and carrier signals. When a modem stops detecting a carrier signal, the connection is lost. You will have to reestablish the connection by redialing the phone number.

Communicating

After the modems finish negotiating and establish the carrier signal, the two computers, or the computer and the remote serial device, can communicate with each other by using the chosen terminal emulation.

When you press a key on your keyboard, it is received by the remote computer, and if the remote computer sends characters to your computer, you see them on-screen. The computer you call, such as an online service, usually displays a prompt, such as `Last`

`Name`, or will display a screen of information and a menu. If you call a friend, rather than an online service, you see the modem result codes, and when you press keys on your computer, they will display on your friend's computer screen. When your friend presses keys on the keyboard, you will see them on your screen.

Part IV explains in more detail the type of information you see when you access an online service. For this chapter, you need to understand that the remote computer is running a program that you control when you call it. This program will probably ask for your name and password before providing access to its resources. If you follow the prompts and type carefully, you will quickly reach the menus for the system. If this is the first time you access the system, you may need to register with the system or fill out a questionnaire, but the remote computer sends characters (or graphical images depending on the terminal emulation) that are displayed on your screen.

You respond to the prompts sent from the other computer, and the remote computer follows your instructions. For example, you may ask to read mail or send a message. Depending on what computer you are connected to and what program is running on that computer, you may have to alter a further communications setting. If you do need to alter this setting, make a note of it and set it before the next time you connect with this system.

As explained in the section on issuing AT commands to your modem, when you power up your modem, it is in command mode and your modem tries to interpret any keys you press on the keyboard as commands. When you make the modem dial a phone number, the modem switches from command mode to online mode, and any key you press on the keyboard is passed to the remote modem and onto the remote computer.

"Why do I see repeated characters when I connect to a particular computer?"

In most cases, the remote computer echoes (repeats) the character in the data it sends back to the local computer, so when you press a key, it appears on your screen. However, some computers, depending on how they are configured, do not do this echoing. The remote computer will still accept and process the key press correctly, but you will not see it on the screen. You can correct this by turning on *local echo* and making the local modem echo the characters you press back to your screen.

In the opposite case, where you have local echo turned on and the remote computer also sends back the characters you press, you will see double characters. For example, if you type **hello** you would see HHEELLOO. In this case, turn local echo off.

Local echo is turned on and off either directly from a command in your communications program or by issuing an AT command to your modem. In many communications programs, it is a single key combination to toggle the setting. For example, QModem uses Alt+E and calls it *Duplex toggle;* Smartcom Exec uses the term *Echo typed characters* and you choose yes or no. The AT command to turn echo on is ATE1 and to turn echo off is ATE0.

Unfortunately, this is another area like baud and data speed where terms are misunderstood. Local echo on is sometimes called full duplex, and local echo off is sometimes called half duplex.

Strictly speaking, the terms full duplex and half duplex refer to how the data is transmitted between two serial devices. In half duplex, data is sent in only one direction at a time; in full duplex, data is sent in both directions at once.

As covered in Chapter 6, some file transfer protocols are full duplex and others are half duplex. This is different from local echo being on and off. Local echo on makes the connection between your computer and modem a duplex connection and has nothing to do with the connection between the two modems.

In most cases when you are calling an online service, you want local echo set to off, and the remote system will echo the characters you press. You are most likely to need to turn local echo on when you call a friend's computer and not a BBS. In the calling-a-friend situation, the symptoms of not having local echo on will show as you seeing what your friend types but not what you are typing. Similarly, if your friend can see what you type but not what he is typing, he needs to turn local echo on his computer.

Apart from local echo, communication between the two computers involves you sending characters, which are created by pressing keys on your keyboard, and the remote computer sending characters back to you. Even the graphical interfaces are doing a similar thing — when you pick a menu item this is translated into a series of characters that are accepted by the remote computer. This *character transfer* will allow you to read the information and send information between the two computers.

However, on many occasions, you will send more information than you can type easily at your keyboard, and you will want to send or receive files of information that may or may not consist of characters. *File transfer* is an important part of modem communications and is introduced in detail in Chapter 6.

As a beginner, you should differentiate between *character* and *file transfer* so that you know when you are doing one and when the other. When you press a key, you are doing character transfer, and when you activate a command (run a program) comparable with the DOS copy command, you are doing a file transfer between the two computers.

ASCII, which is an abbreviation for American Standard Code for Information Interchange, is a national and international standard for representing characters that are used on most computers. The internationally approved ASCII character set includes representations for all the alphanumeric keys and punctuation keys and many symbols. There are 128 characters in the set, although not all of the characters are printable. For example, one character represents a carriage return. You can represent 128 characters with seven bits of binary data.

The IBM PC popularized a variation of the standard character set, called the extended character set. This included an additional 128 characters and requires eight bits of binary data for the full set.

"Why do I see gibberish when I connect?"

Sometimes when you are online, you see characters that look peculiar, including for example, smiley faces, squiggles, and other strange shapes. This is a mismatch between your communications program's terminal emulation and the terminal emulation being used on the remote computer.

Your terminal emulation is taking the number of the ASCII character and displaying the character from the extended character set instead of from the basic character set. For example, instead of displaying 2, which is ASCII character number 50, the screen will actually display the extended ASCII character number 178 (128 + 50), which is a shaded rectangle.

Most communications programs have a command that switches the representation so that you see the correct character. This is often called 8-bit toggle or 8-bit on and off, and in QModemPro is toggled by pressing Alt+8. Note that changing this option does not affect characters that are already displayed, but will affect any new characters sent from the remote computer to your screen.

Disconnecting

In theory, disconnecting from the remote modem and computer appears easy. Unfortunately, it is not always simple to make the modem perform the equivalent of hanging up the phone.

When you have made a connection, the modems are transparent to the connection, and you are linked to the remote computer. You expect any data that you send from your computer to the other computer or that you receive from the remote computer to be passed on by the modems and not be changed en route.

However, when you want to hang up the phone, you need to make your modem hang up the phone or the remote computer needs to make the remote modem hang up the phone. You need the modem to stop passing the data it receives onto the other modem and accept an AT command to hang up the phone. When one modem hangs up the phone, the carrier signal is lost and the other modem is aware the connection has been broken.

Unless configured differently by the use of AT commands, Hayes-compatible modems monitor the connection by two methods. They look in the stream of data being sent for a special sequence of characters, referred to as an escape sequence to instruct the modem to switch from on-line mode to command mode. Additionally, they look for the presence of a carrier signal.

When you want to make the modem pay attention to you, rather than pass data onto the other modem, you issue this escape sequence and the modem switches to command mode and awaits AT commands. When you have made any adjustments you need, you can issue a final instruction to make the modem return to online mode if applicable.

"How do I hang up?"

Because the modem uses three different ways to determine whether it can send data, you can use two different ways to break the connection yourself, or you can get the remote computer to break the connection.

If you are connected to an online service, you can use the remote computer program's commands to break the connection. A typical menu will include a command option such as goodbye or logoff. When you enter this command, you will be disconnected from the service. Wherever possible, particularly if you are paying a connect time charge for the service, use the facilities offered by the remote computer to disconnect. In this way, you can be certain that the remote computer considers you disconnected immediately and does not wait until nothing happens for a certain length of time before considering you disconnected.

If you need to hang up at a time when you do not have a menu option, use your modem to break the connection. For example, if the remote computer locks up or you are unable break out of a file transfer, you can try to make your modem hang up.

The easiest method, and the one you should always use first if you are breaking the connection, is the hang up command. The hang up command in your communications program issues the escape sequence followed by the hang up command. Your modem detects the escape sequence, switches to command modem, then accepts and acts on the hang up command.

Alternatively, you can issue the hang up command directly. You first need to switch the modem to command mode using the escape sequence and then issue the ATH command as described earlier.

The term *escape sequence* does not mean the Esc key on your keyboard. It is a series of keystrokes that you designate as "the keys I want the modem to pay attention to." By default, it is assigned to the plus key, but, surprise, surprise, you can use AT commands to alter the assignment.

To explain the escape sequence, assume the default setting of the plus key. For a true AT-compatible modem, the escape sequence is a period of no data of at least one second (where nothing is typed on the keyboard or is being sent to the modem) +++ followed by another period of no data of at least one second. These no-data periods are known as Guard Time. Hayes Microcomputer Products has a patent on this escape sequence, and other modem manufacturers have been issued a license by Hayes to use it in their modems. This escape sequence is formally called Hayes Improved Escape Sequence with Guard Time.

When the modem sees this escape sequence, it switches to command mode and accepts AT commands. (The escape sequence is one of the two commands that does not use the prefix AT.)

Some modems do not require the Guard Time and will respond to an escape sequence of +++AT followed by a carriage return in most cases without needing a no-data period before or after it. This escape sequence is formally called Time Independent Escape Sequence (TIES).

Understanding an Escape Sequence

Dale Heatherington, inventor of the Hayes Smartmodem along with Dennis Hayes, very carefully chose the escape sequence needed to switch the modem from online mode to command mode. The idea was to create a sequence of characters that would not appear in any data being sent from one modem to the other.

Suppose that the escape sequence had been "cat." The internal electronics in the modem would have been programmed so that when it saw the sequence of characters "c a t," it would switch from online mode to command mode. This would mean if any file transferred with the word "cat" in it — or whenever you typed the word cat when connected — the modem would stop passing data to the other modem and wait for AT commands. The likelihood of the word "cat" occurring in files is high, especially if you consider it as part of other words, such as catalog, advocate, or scathing, and the escape sequence would interrupt far too many transmissions.

On the other hand, you cannot pick an obscure sequence of bits because the user must be able to type it at the keyboard. Remember that the modems were designed to work with any computer, so unusual keys, such as the function keys on a PC or special keys found on terminals, were not suitable.

The addition of Guard Time before and after the escape sequence reduces the chance that a file will switch the modem to command mode. Using the "cat" example again, the need for you to leave a one second no-data period before and after typing the word "cat" probably makes it unlikely that the word catalog or advocate will make the modem switch to command mode. File transfer, which is a continual stream of data, is very unlikely to trigger the modem.

The default escape sequence chosen was a one second no-data period +++ followed by a one second period of no data. On most modems, you can reprogram this sequence to be another character, such as !!!, if you prefer.

The sidebar uses a specific example to explain the escape sequence. However, for a beginner, you need to understand that the modem is designed to respond and switch to command mode when it sees the escape sequence. If you transfer files or data that contain the escape sequence, the modem will assume that the sequence of data bits was intended for it and will interrupt the data transmission by switching to command mode.

The issue is how often the escape sequence actually occurs during data transmission. If you never send a file that has the particular sequence of bits that make up the escape sequence, you will detect no difference between the two types of modems (the one that uses Guard Time and the one that is time-independent).

However, you will not be able to send a file or sequence of characters that make up the escape sequence without the modem switching to command mode and disrupting the transmission. By employing Guard Time, where nothing is transmitted for a second before and after the escape sequence, it is far less likely, as in almost improbable, for the escape sequence to be detected in a normal data stream.

On the other hand, the Guard Time requirement can make it harder to attract the modem's attention. If, for example, you want to sever a connection while a file is being transmitted or streams of characters are scrolling across your screen, the one-second delay without transmission can seem impossible. In this case, you must resort to one of the other methods for breaking the connection.

However, Guard Time may be preferable to you because the transmission will not be broken unintentionally by the data that is being transmitted. Although it is harder to interrupt and get the modem's attention, it is not due to strange — and probably unrecognizable to the user — data content.

The other method for hanging up the phone is to remove power from the modem. Use this as a last resort. An external modem is relatively easy to turn off at its power switch. Exit your communications software, turn your modem back on, and restart your communications software before making another connection.

With an internal modem, you can only remove power by turning off the computer or by pressing the reset button. (This is not the same as pressing Ctrl+Alt+Del.) Wherever possible, exit your communications program before turning off. If you turn your computer off, rather than pressing the reset button, wait until the hard disk drive and cooling fans have stopped before turning it back on again.

Summary

This chapter introduced the basics of making a connection with your modem. You learned the five items needed before making a connection: phone number, call originator, character format, data speed, and terminal emulation. You also learned that you may need to adjust local echo to be able to see the characters you type.

In most cases, the communications program can issue the commands to the modem, but as you become more experienced, you will need to be able to issue AT commands to your modem directly. This chapter explained that modems can accept commands when in command mode and pass on the data you send from your computer to the other modem when in online mode. You can issue AT commands from the terminal screen, and you were introduced to seven of the most frequently used AT commands in this chapter.

Before reading the next chapter on file transfer, you should understand the three stages of a connection: dialing, connecting, and disconnecting. You should also understand the difference between character transfer, which uses terminal emulation and transfers one character at a time, and file transfer, which uses the equivalent of a DOS copy command to transfer groups of data.

6

CHAPTER

Understanding File Transfer

After users learn to make their modems call other modems and they have access to all these online services, file transfer becomes the primary application. You can copy files from your computer to another, or you can copy files from the other computer to your computer.

This chapter introduces file-transfer protocols. Specifically, you will learn the following techniques:

❖ Extending your communication to include file transfer

❖ Understanding the importance of the appropriate file-transfer protocol

❖ Defining the types of available file-transfer protocols

❖ Choosing a file-transfer protocol

Extending Your Communication to Include File Transfer

Chapter 5 introduces how to establish a connection with another modem. When you are linked to another computer via two modems, you can type characters on your keyboard and control a program running on the remote computer.

In many cases, in addition to typing messages, you need to transfer files between the two computers. File transfer is comparable to using the DOS copy command: You want to move a file from one computer to another.

However, because different computers are involved, and you probably won't have the same communication software running on both computers, and you may not even have the same operating system running on both computers, you need to use commands that will operate on both computers.

These commands are actually small programs that you run on both computers. You have a choice of programs that you can run. These programs support a particular standard, and the standards are known as *file-transfer protocols*.

In human communication, the analogy for file-transfer protocols is mailing a letter. In most countries, the general principle is to write the address on an envelope, put a stamp on it, and mail the letter in a mailbox. The postal service handles the routing and delivery.

In reality, the precise rules vary from country to country. In the U.S., for example, mail boxes are blue; in England, post boxes are red. In Germany, you typically place the town below the name and the street below that. In the U.S., the street address comes below the name and the town on the subsequent line. However, you can still send mail from one country to another without worrying about the details related to the receiving countries.

"What are uploading and downloading?"

In modem communication, the terms *uploading* and *downloading* refer to sending and receiving a file respectively. Like the remote and local computers, if you are standing at the other end of the connection, the uploading and downloading terminology is reversed.

The general procedure is to prepare the communication program at one end of the connection to send or receive the desired file and then start the program at the opposite end. For example, if you are calling an online service and want to download a file to your computer, you issue the command on the remote computer to start the download. Then you issue the command to your communication software to accept the downloaded file.

In most cases, when you control the program at both ends of the connection, you start the process at the remote end and then instruct your program to receive or send the file. If you are calling a friend, one of you should prepare to accept the file, and the other can instruct the communication program to send it. The typical procedure is to start the download command (the Page Down key in many communications software programs), and then start the upload command (the Page Up key in many communications software programs).

Remember that you are uploading the file from the sending computer. The receiving computer, which is accepting the file, needs to use the download command to receive the file. In the case of an online service, both ends use the terms downloading or uploading, because the program is only being controlled from one end. In the case of you and a friend, you are both controlling your own ends of the connection.

Although you probably will not use exactly the same file-transfer *program* at both ends of the connection, both computers must agree on the file-transfer *protocol*. There are a variety of protocols in use; some are variations on each other; others have specialized applications.

Although the technical detail may seem cumbersome to understand, you should realize that the faster the protocol you use, the faster the file is transferred. Different file-transfer protocols operate at different speeds and have different levels of error-checking.

On the other hand, it does not matter how fast the file is transferred if it is received inaccurately. Inaccuracies occur during file transfer because of noise on the telephone lines. You do not get 10, 20, or 30 minutes of completely noise-free phone lines. When you are talking, you can easily repeat a sentence or stop talking when the noise occurs; but in telecommunications, you need a mechanism to verify that what was sent is what is received.

Understanding Error-Correction

Apart from ASCII, the file-transfer protocols, such as XMODEM and ZMODEM, are *error-detecting* protocols, although they are often referred to as *error-correction* protocols. As a modem user, you should understand the difference between error-detection and error-correction, because you may need to be the judge of how long you are prepared to let a poor transfer last.

An error-detection protocol can identify when an error has occurred during transmission. It then signals the equivalent of "That can't be right" and resends a portion of the file.

An error-correction protocol, which is not employed by the file-transfer protocols, is actually able to *correct* an error rather than *detect* it. This is much more difficult than simply detecting the error.

Suppose that I send you an equation, and I tell you that it will be three numbers added together, such as 8 + 6 + 3 = 17. If you actually receive 8 - 6 + 3 = 17, you know there is an error and can correct the minus sign to a plus sign. On the other hand, if you actually receive 7 + 6 + 3 = 17, you know there is an error, but you cannot tell which number is incorrect.

The different error-detection methods, such as checksum, 16-bit CRC, and 32-bit CRC, offer different levels of error-detection. You can think of them as providing different levels of detail about the transmitted block. The additional detail gives the receiving computer more of a chance of detecting an error.

File Compression (Zipped Files)

File transfer takes time. Anything you can do to reduce this time saves you in telephone and connect-time charges. Most files stored by online services ready for you to download are stored in compressed form. This makes the file much smaller and consequently reduces the file transfer time.

The most commonly used file compression program is PKZIP, a shareware program from PKWare. This program can compress a file or many files into a single file. The compressed file is typically referred to as being *zipped* and has a file extension of .ZIP. Other file compression programs include ARC, from SEA, and LHA, a public domain program created by Haruyasu Yoshizaki (familiarly known as Yoshi).

However, you cannot run these files in their compressed form. After you download them, you need to uncompress them before use. Consequently, one of the first files you should obtain is the set of zipping and unzipping programs. This file, which has a name that includes its version number, such as PKZ204G.EXE, which means Version 2.04 of PKZIP, is available on most online services as well as from most user groups. It is a special type of zipped file, known as a *self-extracting* file, which can uncompress itself to give you the various utility programs and documentation.

If you find an online service using a different file compression program, you need to obtain the equivalent program. In general, you can find the appropriate file compression program for a particular online service in the files listing for that service.

"What do I do with this zipped file?"

PKZIP, which zips the files, and its partner, PKUNZIP, which unzips the files, are a vital part of your PC utility programs. If you intend to do any telecommunicating, you will use PKZIP on a regular basis and should register your shareware copy.

The PKZIP utility is used to group files together and enables you to download a single file to obtain all the elements you need. Suppose that you download a popular game with the filename MICEMN.ZIP. This single zipped file contains all the files you need to play, configure, and register the game, including the documentation.

You look for the game in a files list on the online service and download it to your computer. You then exit your communications program and issue the command **PKUNZIP MICEMN.ZIP**, at the DOS prompt. PKZIP uncompresses and separates all the files, and you have the game file, MICEMEN.EXE, the documentation, MICEMEN.DOC, and other supporting files.

Many online services accept files that you upload. However, many require you to zip the files before you upload them to save disk space and online time. Zipping files involves compressing them, which is the reverse of unzipping them. This process is easy when compressing only one file but requires a little care when compressing multiple files into a single zipped file. However, the documentation supplied with PKZIP provides good instructions.

Determining when to use PKZIP and when to take advantage of your modem's compression is an intermediate topic covered in Chapter 9.

File-Transfer Protocols

The following sections introduce the popular file-transfer protocols. Although you do not need to remember the technical details, you should understand the basics and make sensible selections. Additionally, this section can be used as a reference when you have trouble matching a file-transfer protocol available in your communications program with a file-transfer protocol available on an online service.

ASCII

The most basic file-transfer protocol is *ASCII*, which is used to transfer *text* files between computers. As Chapter 5 explains, ASCII is used on most computers throughout the world, and IBM PCs and compatibles have popularized the extended character set, which provides even more characters. The ASCII file-transfer protocol is *not* used to transfer programs. (Hayes communication software, including Smartcom for Windows LE, uses the term *autotype*.)

The ASCII file-transfer protocol sends each character in the file in turn as if you had typed it on the keyboard. It does not include error-checking features nor any compression features.

Understanding File Compression

File compression is extremely important when doing file transfer because it can dramatically reduce the size of your files and consequently reduce the file-transfer time. For example, I regularly capture screen shots for inclusion in magazine articles, and a file-compression program can compress the file to about 4 percent of its original size.

There are many ways to compress files, and a good file-compression program will use the best method for each particular file. Some compression algorithms are quite complex, but an understanding of simple algorithms can help you understand why some files cannot be compressed and others can be compressed substantially.

If a file contains truly random data, it cannot be compressed. However, most files, including program files, contain repetitive patterns. A file-compression program looks for these repetitions and, instead of sending the full pattern each time, sends an abbreviated version.

One approach is to eliminate the repetition in a series of bits. For example, a typical bit-mapped screen (without color) is a series of black dots and a series of white dots. Instead of sending the code for "white, white, white, white, black, black, black," the compression program may say "four whites, three blacks."

Another, much more involved approach is to use substitution and send the decoding instructions for the substitution. For example, if the text of this chapter was considered, the words *communications* and *file-transfer protocol* would occur very frequently. If I said "substitute Fred for communications and Jane for file-transfer protocol," I could save a lot of space.

This substitution approach is complicated because the substitutions are not the same for each file. For example, if the file was a bird-watching guidebook, the expression *file-transfer protocol* would not occur. However, *Fred* could be used as a substitute for *binoculars* or *winter habitat*.

XMODEM

XMODEM is the next most common file-transfer protocol found on PCs after ASCII. XMODEM was invented by Ward Christensen, the designer and programmer of the first BBS (see sidebar in Chapter 2). It is known as a half-duplex, error-correcting protocol. In fact, it is an error-detecting protocol and not an error-correcting protocol. *Half-duplex* means that data flows in only one direction at a time.

The file is divided into blocks that are 128 bytes in length, and a checksum is added to each block. The *checksum*, which is, as its name suggests, a number that verifies the data within a block, serves a similar purpose to a parity bit. See the sidebar "Understanding Error-Correction" for more detail.

The transmitting computer sends the first block of data along with its checksum. The receiving computer calculates the checksum for the block and compares its compared value with the checksum value sent with the block.

If the two checksums are the same, the receiving computer sends a character, called an *ACK* (for acknowledge), to the originating computer. The originating computer then sends the next block of data and its checksum.

If the checksums do not correspond, the receiving computer sends a *NACK* character (for no acknowledge) to the originating computer. The originating computer resends the block of data and its checksum.

"Why is the file bigger after I download it?"

The process of sending a block, verifying the checksums, and sending the next block continues. The last block of data in the file contains a special code called an *EOT* (end of text) code that logically indicates the end of the file. When the receiving computer gets the EOT code, it combines all the blocks received into a single file and completes the file transfer.

XMODEM blocks are all 128 bytes in length. If your file is not an even multiple of 128 bytes, XMODEM adds bits to the last block to make it a complete block. These are not removed by the receiving computer. Consequently, you may see a slightly larger number of bytes in the file on the receiving computer than on the sending computer. This does not affect the file because the end-of-file indicator within the last block is unchanged, but the padding on the end is stored on the disk.

XMODEM variations

Several variations on the basic XMODEM protocol are used in the PC environment. *XMODEM/CRC* uses a *cyclic redundancy check* (CRC) instead of a simple checksum. The CRC is a two-byte code that provides better error control than the one-byte checksum. Its value is derived from a more complex algorithm, and as a result, any transmission errors are more likely to be detected.

In many cases, XMODEM/CRC has replaced the original XMODEM. Consequently, you may run into poor nomenclature and find an online service referring to XMODEM/CRC as XMODEM. If you choose XMODEM in your communications program and XMODEM on the online service, but have trouble with a file transfer and none of the blocks are accepted, the nomenclature may be the problem. Try setting XMODEM/CRC in your communications program, keep XMODEM on the online service, and try again.

Although XMODEM, with its 128-byte blocks, is reliable, it is not particularly fast. Additionally, the transfer protocol does not provide a method of keeping the time and date stamp for the file. For example, if you download a new version of your favorite game by using XMODEM, the date and time that appears with the filename is the date and time of your downloading and not the file-creation date.

XMODEM-1K is another variation of XMODEM. It is similar, except that the block size is 1,024 bytes (1 KB) instead of 128 bytes. The larger block size gives a faster transfer rate because the receiving computer sends fewer ACK or NACK signals. Terminology is mixed with XMODEM-1K, too. Some online services use XMODEM-1K but call it *YMODEM.* YMODEM is explained in the following section. You may need to choose XMODEM-1K in your communications software to use the YMODEM protocol on the online service.

YMODEM

YMODEM is an extension of XMODEM-1K but includes two important but optional extra features: time and date stamp transfer and batch file transfer. YMODEM uses a 1 KB block size but also transfers such file information as the file date and time stamp.

You can also specify more than one file at a time to be transferred. This is known as a *batch-file-transfer protocol*. YMODEM is used on many online services but is often not implemented with the batch-file-transfer protocol feature and is sometimes not implemented with the time and date stamp transfer.

ZMODEM

ZMODEM has become the most popular file-transfer protocol in recent years. It is faster than the XMODEM variations and is usually implemented with the batch-file-transfer protocol and is more tolerant of errors.

In a ZMODEM transfer, the blocks are sent continuously to the receiving computer. Each block includes a 16-bit or a 32-bit CRC. The 32-bit CRC picks up more errors than the 16-bit CRC, in the same way that the 16-bit CRC detects more errors than a checksum. Consequently, you can be more confident that your data-transmission errors (due typically to noise on the telephone line) will be detected.

The sending computer does not expect to receive an ACK signal until the file is completely sent. If the receiving computer detects an error, however, it sends a NACK signal immediately and specifies which block contained an error. On receipt of the NACK signal, the sending computer aborts and restarts the file transmission, beginning with the incorrectly received block. ZMODEM also supports batch-file transfer; you specify a series of files and start uploading or downloading. ZMODEM automatically handles each file in turn.

ZMODEM is faster than the other file-transfer protocols because even less response is necessary from the receiving computer. If there are no detected errors, the receiving computer acknowledges at the end of a file transfer. However, its recovery from errors is particularly desirable. If you are downloading (or uploading) a file and start to see a lot of errors, you can assume that the telephone line has become noisy. You can hang up the phone, redial, and restart the file transmission. ZMODEM will not retransmit the whole file but will start from where it left off.

Suppose that you are downloading a 1 MB file and have received half of it when lots of errors start appearing. With the other file-transfer protocols, such as XMODEM, it's a toss-up whether it's quicker to let the file transfer continue with the error detection and retransmission or hang up and start all over again. With ZMODEM, when you try to download the file again, only the unreceived part is sent.

Other protocols

Several other file-transfer protocols are used in PC communications, and new ones are developed as new technology is available or programmers become more creative. Some are used for specialized purposes, and others are enhancements that can squeeze that extra ounce of performance for you.

When selecting communications software, look for a program that supports all the file-transfer protocols you need and that has the capability to add additional file protocols through add-on programs. In this way, you can expand your communication program's features without buying a whole new program.

For example, HSLINK is a relatively new file-transfer protocol that is not yet supported in every communications program but may be very popular in the online services you choose to frequent. You can buy an add-on program that allows you to use HSLINK with a communications program that supports external file transfer protocols. DSZ and GSZ, enhanced implementations of ZMODEM, are other examples of external protocols you may need.

The communications programs that support external file-transfer protocols allow you to select them from the upload or download menu as if they were part of the main program. In fact, the communications program passes control to the external file-transfer program and waits until the file-transfer program passes control back again to continue.

The following sections introduce two specialized but important file-transfer protocols: CompuServe B and Kermit. You may never run into these, but if you need them, nothing else will suffice.

CompuServe B

As its name suggests CompuServe B, along with its close relatives CompuServe B+ and Quick B, are proprietary file-transfer protocols used by the popular online service CompuServe. They are optimized for use with the particular software used by CompuServe. If you do not subscribe to CompuServe, you won't need it. On the other hand, if you do subscribe to CompuServe, it's the file-transfer protocol of choice.

Kermit

Kermit is another specialized file-transfer protocol. It is actually very flexible but has not become popular in the PC-to-PC communications world. It's the only commonly available file-transfer protocol for transferring 7-bit files.

As described in earlier chapters, you are not necessarily connected to another PC when you use your modem. The remote computer may be a minicomputer or mainframe. Most mainframes use 7-bit characters and not the more familiar (to PC users) 8-bit characters. You need to use Kermit to transfer files to a system that uses 7-bit files.

Kermit transfers can include blocks with varying sizes. This feature is useful if the receiving computer can accept only particular block sizes, but it is also particularly useful on noisy line conditions. When a line is clear, the blocks can be larger and received accurately, but when the line is noisy, smaller blocks are sent, which reduces the number of retransmissions of data necessary to receive the file accurately.

Kermit also allows you to specify wild-card transfers, (similar to the DOS wild-card feature) and employs some file-compression techniques. However, all this flexibility can make successful Kermit transfers difficult because of the number of options that must match, and consequently, it has not gained extensive popularity in the PC communications world, although it is used extensively in academic circles.

HSLINK

HSLINK is a bidirectional file-transfer protocol that is used with full-duplex modems, and both computers can send data at the same time. For example, you can use HSLINK with 9600 bps modems that support V.32, V.32bis, and V.FC communications standards. (As other communications standards bocome able to connect at full-duplex, they will also be able to use HSLINK.) HSLINK takes advantage of this feature and allows you to upload and download files at the same time.

This bidirectional protocol has tremendous performance advantages because you can transfer your files more rapidly. However, because it only works on high-speed modems that are operating in full-duplex, it is not very popular yet.

GSZ and DSZ

The ZMODEM file-transfer protocol was developed and put into the public domain by Chuck Fosberg. He also created two popular ZMODEM implementations called DSZ and GSZ. These shareware products are examples of add-on products that can supplement your communication software. Other add-ons for different purposes are covered in Chapter 10.

GSZ (an implementation of ZMODEM that uses graphical characters) and DSZ (an earlier implementation) include ZMODEM compression and MobyTurbo (TM) accelerator features. You may see 2-5 percent improvements in the time required to download a file when you use this program. Although this may seem small, every minute you save online is saved connect time and, where applicable, phone call expenses; these minutes leave you with more time for other online activities when you call a time-limited system that may, for example, allow only 90 minutes connect time each day.

Selecting a File-Transfer Protocol

With the exception of ASCII transfer, which is used for a particular purpose, you can choose any file-transfer protocol that your communications software and the remote computer's software support. However, there is a significant difference in performance between the protocols, and faster is probably better.

When to use ASCII

You are most likely to use the ASCII file protocol for uploading messages you have previously typed. For example, if you are looking for information on a new type of motor car oil you heard about, you may want to leave the same message on several online services. Typing the message before going online will save typing the same thing several times. Alternatively, you may want to ask detailed questions about a problem you are having with configuring your word processor, and writing the message before going online will ensure accurate typing.

Which protocol to choose

If you are transferring a file of data, rather than a text file, you cannot use ASCII and must choose another protocol. As a general rule, choose ZMODEM. Remember that the chosen protocol must be supported by the receiving *and* sending computers. If ZMODEM is not supported by your computer or the receiving computer, choose XMODEM. Although it's not a particularly faster protocol, it is widely supported.

The following are exceptions to this rule:

- When transferring 7-bit files, choose Kermit.

- When transferring from CompuServe, choose CompuServe B or one of its variants.

- If you have a modem that supports V.32 and are connected to a modem that supports V.32 and HSLINK is supported, HSLINK is preferable.

- If you have a modem operating in full-duplex mode at 9600 bps or higher and HSLINK is supported, HSLINK is preferable.

Summary

This chapter introduced file transfer, the other application for communication by modem besides sending and receiving messages. In particular, you learned that most files are stored in compressed form. You need a file compression and uncompression utility, such as PKZIP, to use the compressed files that you obtain.

You also learned that you upload a file from your computer to another computer and download a file from a remote computer to your computer. You must choose the same file-transfer protocol at both ends for the transfer to occur. In general, you should choose ZMODEM or XMODEM, except in specialized situations. You choose ASCII to upload or download text.

Chapter 7 introduces fax modem use. Part III extends your modem knowledge so that you can streamline your modem use and make the best use of your communications software.

7

CHAPTER

Understanding
Your Fax Modem

This chapter shows how to use your fax modem to send and receive documents. There are distinct differences between sending and receiving fax documents on your PC fax modem. Consequently, this chapter separates these two major functions. The following specific items are covered in this chapter:

- ❖ Preparing your fax document
- ❖ Sending your fax document
- ❖ Receiving fax documents
- ❖ Handling a received fax document

Preparing to Communicate

On the one hand, your fax modem is similar to a stand-alone fax machine; on the other hand, it is similar to a data modem. A stand-alone fax machine is like a long-distance copy machine. Your job is to prepare the document and dial the phone number. You feed a document into the fax machine, and it produces a copy at a remote location. When receiving, you simply verify that the fax machine is on and pick up the pages as they are received.

A fax modem needs preparatory work similar to a data modem as well as document preparation. (The preparatory work for a data modem is presented in Chapter 5.) However, after you dial the phone number, the fax modem behaves like a stand-alone fax machine, and you don't need to be actively involved in the process; the document sending is automated. In fact it's easier, because you don't have paper jams and misfeeds, unless the receiving modem runs out of disk space, which is equivalent to running out of paper.

With a data modem, you typically perform tasks, such as reading messages or performing file transfer, while online. The connection, when you are actually linked to another modem via the telephone line, is an interactive one. Although you can automate various parts of the process, your actions generally are a necessary part of the connection.

Receiving a fax document with a fax modem can be as easy as receiving with a stand-alone fax machine, if your computer is configured to accept a fax document. However, unlike a fax machine, which only serves one purpose, you can use your computer for other purposes, and you might change the computer's configuration and leave your fax modem inoperative and not prepared to receive documents at any time.

Chapter 4 explores the differences between using a stand-alone fax machine and using a fax modem. A PC fax modem can only *send* documents that it has in electronic form. *There is no paper slot in a fax modem.* You must prepare the document on your computer or use a scanner to convert a paper document to electronic format for transmittal.

Similarly, a PC fax modem *receives* documents in electronic form as graphic images. You can print the document as a graphic image, or you can use another program, usually not supplied with the fax modem, to convert the file into a text form so that you can edit it in your word processor. Keep in mind that graphic images are large, and storing many fax documents in graphic form on your computer can rapidly fill hard disk space.

Before considering the necessary preparation of your fax document, you need to install your fax modem and its software. This process is explained in Chapter 4. Like a data modem, unless you have used your fax modem recently and successfully sent or received a fax document, you should check the following connections:

❖ A phone line plugged into the rear of the fax modem and the telephone outlet in the wall

❖ The data cable for an external fax modem plugged into the rear of the modem and into the serial port on your computer

❖ The power supply for an external fax modem plugged into the rear of the modem and into an electrical outlet

If you find a missing cable or a loose connection, be sure to turn off the computer and fax modem before correcting the problem. After checking the cables, turn on your fax modem and start your communications program. An external modem may have an LED indicating that power is on, and at least one of the LEDs will light on its front panel. An internal modem is powered on whenever your computer is turned on.

Fax Limitations

Consider the following topics before using a fax modem extensively:

If you are dealing with computers, transferring files by a data modem is preferable in most cases to using a fax modem or stand-alone fax machines. If you have only a computer at one end of the connection, fax modems are a good alternative.

A fax machine sends a graphic representation of a document between two modems. If you need to send text, it is converted to a graphic image (a series of dots) before transmission.

The received image is in black and white — not color. If the sent image was stored electronically in color, the color is lost during conversion.

File conversion from one format to another is rarely perfect. The reason that different formats exist is that different application programs offer different features. Every time a file is converted into another format, you will probably lose detail. Wherever possible, minimize the number of file-format conversions to get the best possible translation.

Fax resolution is relatively low. The typical resolution is 300 dots per inch in a horizontal direction and 150 dots per inch in a vertical direction. This is lower than most laser printers and newspapers. You will see little detail on a fax document.

Sending a Fax Document

Sending a fax document by using a fax modem requires the document preparation, cover sheet preparation, and fax modem preparation. You can then actually send the document to another fax machine. The following sections detail these steps.

Preparing your fax modem to send a fax document

When the fax software is installed and loaded into memory (by typing the program's name at the DOS prompt or choosing the program from Windows), your fax modem is comparable to a stand-alone fax machine. The software incorporates the features you get on most fax machines — such as adding a line to each page of the document with your fax phone number and company name, or programming frequently dialed numbers to dial automatically.

You need to consider two sets of parameters: those that will apply to every fax you send and those that apply only to the particular document you are sending. The general parameters that apply to every document can be configured once and remain unchanged, but other parameters are part of the document preparation. Document preparation is covered in a later section.

The available general parameters vary, depending on the particular fax software you are running. However, they usually include communication configuration information, such as the fax modem's serial port assignment, dial type (tone or pulse), and the number of times you want a busy phone number to be redialed. Additional information that you can set is the filename for your fax cover page, word processor types, and a DOS directory name as a location for your dialing directory of commonly called numbers.

As a beginner, you should choose only the parameters you need, such as the port assignment. Chapter 4 gives the information you need about your serial ports and installation. Chapter 11 explains methods for streamlining your fax transmission and receipt, which include setting up directories to store your received fax documents and dialing directories.

Unlike a data modem, you don't have to be concerned about data-connection speeds and standards with a fax modem. These settings are important when you purchase the modem but are used automatically when you send or receive a fax document.

If the software is installed and loaded, you need to decide on three items before sending a fax: the document you want to send, the phone number of the fax machine you are sending it to, and whether you want to add a cover sheet.

Knowing whom to call

The fax software can perform the equivalent of dialing the phone number of the receiving fax machine for you. As explained in Chapter 5, the modem accepts commands from the software and can do the equivalent of taking the phone off the hook, dialing the number, and making the connection.

You need the phone number of the receiving fax machine and need to enter it into the fax software. Depending on the software, you may simply need to add the phone number to the cover page, or you may need to type it when you make the actual call.

Dialing directories, where frequently called numbers are stored for easy retrieval, and other automating techniques are covered in Chapter 11. This chapter covers the essentials of sending a fax that are applicable to all fax modems and software. Chapter 11 includes desirable rather than essential features that you can use with your fax software and hardware.

Knowing what to send

The concept of sending a fax document seems obvious: You find the document and press the equivalent of a start button. However, in practice, a fax modem requires different considerations than a stand-alone fax machine.

The document you want to send must be stored in electronic form; it can be a text file or a graphic image. Although you don't need a hard copy of the document, you must have a file that you can print or an image you can display on-screen. For example, you can print a word processing document or a spreadsheet. Although you may not have a color printer, a color graphic image is printable and can consequently be sent by fax.

You cannot send handwritten notes or drawings, marked up documents, or preprinted forms or brochures unless you can convert them to electronic form. (You can make this conversion by using a scanner and scanning software.)

"How do I load my document into the fax software?"

Your document files are stored on your computer in a variety of formats. Files are usually in the format appropriate for the particular application program software that you use to generate them. For example, a document created in WordPerfect is in a different electronic format than a spreadsheet created in Excel.

Depending on the sophistication of your fax software, you may be able to use some document files directly, and you will need to convert others into a form that can be used as input for the fax software. This is explained in more detail in the following section.

Another alternative, suitable for such short fax documents as a brief memo, is to use the text editor supplied with your fax software program to type your fax directly into the fax software.

Preparing the fax document

A typical fax document includes a cover sheet that specifies the number of pages in the accompanying document, who the fax document is for, and who sent the document. Most fax communication software includes a sample that you can use. (Some feature many samples—serious and frivolous.)

Your fax document is a file stored on your computer. The cover sheet is a separate file, rather than part of your document, that is sent before your fax document file. Some software programs give you the option to send a document without this cover sheet if you prefer.

Consider the form of your electronic document. Your application program, such as the word processor or spreadsheet, probably allows you to add such items as different fonts, centering, and other formatting features that make your document look professionally produced. You want your fax software to preserve these elements wherever possible.

Read your fax software documentation carefully, and consider these features prior to purchasing it. The manual should include a list of application programs and file format types that can be entered into the fax software without conversion by you. (The fax software converts the file into a graphic image for transmission.)

For example, typical fax software may support: ASCII text, WordPerfect, Microsoft Word, and WordStar word processors as well as PCX, TIFF Class F, or TIFF uncompressed graphic files. Any file that you can create in one of these listed formats probably won't need modification before sending. However, before sending a critical document to an important customer, experiment with samples and, when available, use the preview image to verify that what you are sending is what you expect. Remember that when you upgrade an application program, such as a word processor, the fax software may not be able to accept this new version directly.

If you use a word processor or other application program that does not create a supported file format, you need to convert your file into a format that *is* supported. For example, you can save your document as an ASCII text file from most word processors. If you change a document's file format—save it as a text file, for example—you may lose formatting and other items that make the document look professionally prepared.

Similarly, although many graphics programs use proprietary file formats, you can usually save the image as a PCX or TIFF format file. If you use this approach, you should check the fax image you are sending so that there are no surprises. TIFF files, for example, can be one of five or six different formats, and your fax software may only support one variation.

You can take another approach if the fax software accepts print files. This approach is useful because it can be applied in unusual situations. Most applications support a wide variety of printer types. In your application program, choose a printer type that is acceptable as an input file type for your fax software. For example, you may be able to choose a Hewlett-Packard LaserJet or an IBM Proprinter.

You create a document in your application program and issue the Print to File command. This creates a file that contains all the necessary codes to print the document on the specified printer type. You then use this print file as the input to your fax software. Keep in mind that the output quality of your document is only as good as the printer type you select.

Your fax software may include other utilities that can help automate more unusual situations, including print-capture and screen-capture utilities. Again, your results may vary, depending on the specific software (the application program and the fax software).

A print-capture program is a *terminate-and-stay-resident* (TSR) program that you load before starting your application program. You create the document in your application program as normal. To create a file suitable for your fax software, you activate the print-capture TSR and print your document. The TSR takes the output intended for the printer and saves it in a form suitable as input for the fax software.

A screen-capture program is similar. It also is a TSR that you load into memory before starting your application program. You create the document page or display the image on-screen. You then activate the TSR to capture the displayed image. The TSR saves the image in a format suitable as input for the fax software.

As explained in the "Preparing to receive a fax document" section, TSRs are a mixed blessing. They may be too large so that you do not have sufficient room in memory to run your application program. TSRs may or may not operate correctly with a particular application program, and they may or may not capture the correct image. Even if your fax software does not include conversion utilities or features, you can purchase third-party conversion utilities that produce excellent results and may enable you to send documents not possible otherwise.

I frequently capture program screens for inclusion in magazine articles and books. I also frequently need to convert files between different formats. Sometimes, my editors do not have the same word processor; sometimes, they use different graphic formats. I have a large collection of screen-capture programs and a couple of file-conversion programs. Although I have my favorites, I cannot use a single product for every occasion, and in some situations, I am unable to capture or convert an image.

In addition to using the fax preview mode of your fax software, it is worth noting that fax documents are in black and white, not color, although standards for color fax documents are being discussed. If you send a color picture, it appears in shades of gray. In some cases, this is difficult to view or read. If you use the fax preview mode, you will be able to see which shades of gray were used when the fax software changed your color image into black and white. It gives you the opportunity to alter the colors in the original and make a better selection for transmission in shades of gray.

Tip: If you find yourself somewhere without a printer but with a fax machine, you can always fax your document to the fax machine and get a hard-copy printout. This is especially useful when staying in hotels. Send yourself a fax to the hotel's fax machine. (Some hotels charge for incoming faxes.)

Connecting to send

After you prepare the document for sending and arrange the cover sheet, the hard work is over. You instruct your fax software to send the fax document to the desired number. The fax software issues the appropriate instructions to the fax modem. (These instructions are AT commands, comparable to those being used by data modems.) The modem dials the telephone and waits for the receiving fax machine to answer.

"Why do I hear a beep after dialing with my fax modem?"

When the receiving fax machine answers the phone, the two modems must establish a mutually acceptable communication standard. Like data modems, they negotiate this standard by exchanging signals that you hear as bleeps and whistles.

Unlike data modems, you don't have to worry about the standard that is actually chosen. The selected speed will be the fastest possible. Although you may have some documents transfer more slowly because they are connected to a slower fax machine, you cannot improve the situation by altering settings or precompressing files as you can with data modems.

After connection, your modem sends the document to the remote fax machine. It takes the document one page at a time and converts it into a series of horizontal lines that are sent between the modems. The receiving fax machine either prints the document one line at a time or, if it is a fax modem, saves the image in a file for later viewing or printing.

Receiving a Fax Document

When a fax machine calls your fax machine's phone number, your fax machine answers, negotiates a communication standard with the sending fax machine, and then the sending fax machine sends the document to your machine. On a stand-alone fax machine, the fax document is printed onto paper; on a fax modem, the document is stored as a file on your computer's hard disk. To read your fax, you must use the fax communications software supplied with your fax modem to display it on-screen, print it, or convert it into another file format to view in another application program.

Preparing to receive a fax document

Using a stand-alone fax machine to receive documents is easy. When it is plugged in and turned on, you only need to check the paper supply periodically. A power break may disrupt your settings, but you can check it when you reset the clocks or the answering machine.

A fax modem requires similar preparation but different knowledge. The power to an internal fax modem is available whenever the computer is turned on, and the MR LED on an external fax modem is lit when power is applied. However, this isn't enough to receive fax documents.

You need a program loaded into your computer's memory that can detect the telephone line ringing and activate the fax modem. Your fax software will probably include a utility for this purpose, usually a terminate-and-stay-resident (TSR) program you load whenever you expect a fax. You can load it from your AUTOEXEC.BAT file so that it is loaded into memory automatically when you turn on your computer.

A TSR will, as its name suggests, sit in memory until the ringing telephone line activates it. The fax software then leaps into action and performs the necessary tasks, such as answering the phone, sending the appropriate connection signals, and receiving the fax document.

TSRs are good and bad. They are good because you can run other software while they are waiting for the correct moment to activate. They are bad because you cannot always run other software while they are loaded into memory. A TSR may occupy too much memory so that you don't have sufficient memory remaining to load your other program, such as a word processor or spreadsheet. (This is true even if you have several megabytes of total memory in your computer.)

Alternatively, a TSR may not be completely compatible with your other software. This may be due to poor TSR program, but you can't do two things with the same serial port. For example, if you want to use an external fax modem to receive fax documents, you cannot use that serial port for any other purpose, such as attaching a mouse or plotter.

If you can make your application programs operate with the fax software's TSR program, you can load it each time you start your computer and be ready to receive a fax whenever the phone rings. If you load and unload the fax software TSR into memory, you must be aware of when you can receive a fax. Think of it as having a telephone answering machine that you must remember to turn on. If you want to receive a fax, the computer must be turned on. This means you will probably want the computer turned on all the time — at night and on weekends.

I do not use a fax modem for receiving fax documents unless I am expecting to receive a document within the next few minutes. I use my stand-alone fax machine and have it turned on permanently so that I do not miss a fax document. I change my computer configuration too often to be certain that the fax software will always be loaded.

Depending on your fax software program, the installation and removal of the TSR may be automated. Read the supplied documentation carefully to understand how you verify that you are prepared to receive fax documents.

Besides needing the software loaded in memory, you need the equivalent of having enough paper available. As explained in Chapter 4, fax documents are received as graphic images, and graphic images can be very large. You must always have plenty of room on your hard disk to accept the documents. Avoid using floppy disks for receiving many or long documents because their capacity is so limited.

This disk space requirement is another reason that I don't use a fax modem to receive documents. The usual document that I need to edit is written electronically, and I can use the data modem to transfer it as a text file, probably in my word processor's format, including all the style and page formatting. The usual fax document I receive is intended for reading and then discarding. It may be page proofs of an article, sales literature, or a confirmation of a fact.

Note: You cannot use the serial port or the phone line that is waiting for a fax document for another purpose at the same time. For example, you cannot use your data modem and receive a fax at the same time. Although this is obvious when sending a fax, it is not so obvious when you are using the computer for other purposes and expect the fax modem to automatically answer the phone.

Connecting to receive

If you have the fax software's TSR program for receiving a fax loaded into memory, you can use your computer as normal while waiting for a fax. When the phone rings, your fax modem will answer it. It then exchanges signals with the sending fax machine to establish a mutually compatible communications standard.

Unlike a data modem, where you can select a different transmission speed than the maximum, you want the fax modem to connect at the highest possible speed so that you receive the document as fast as possible. The fax machines will agree on a mutually compatible communications standard, and the document transfer will begin.

The sending fax transmits the document one line at a time. The receiving fax takes the data and stores it on the disk as a graphic image. When all the pages of the document have been received, or the transmission is stopped for some reason, the fax modem saves the document in a file on your hard disk. It is then available for viewing.

Knowing what you have received

It is vital that you understand that your fax modem saves a graphic image of a document. You have not received a document that can be directly edited in a word processor. The graphic image is stored as a series of bits of data, representing black dots on a white page of paper. The fax software probably includes a viewing utility so that you can see this image on-screen. If you have a printer that can print graphic images, you can print your document to your printer. This is equivalent to printing the document on a plain-paper stand-alone fax machine.

"How do I read my fax document?"

The viewing features in your fax software, if available, provide a way of reading your document. For single-page fax documents, such as a memo or short note, these features are adequate because you can read the information and then delete the file.

Pictures, sketches, and handwritten notes also can be read efficiently with your fax software's viewing features. Some viewers are quite sophisticated and include extra features. For example, some allow you to rotate the image, if the sender put a sheet of the document in upside down. Others allow you to adjust the contrast so that the document becomes more legible.

Multi-page documents can also be read in this way. However, as with all long documents on a computer, reading them from a video screen is not very efficient. You cannot see much at once, and you cannot refer to several places in the same document at once.

Avoid sending fax documents, particularly text, by inserting a page into a fax machine sideways, because the human eye can read text more easily with the lines of text running horizontally across the page. The problem is compounded with smaller text. The *vertical resolution* (the number of dots per inch) on a received fax document and its *precision* (its alignment with the previous row of dots) are much lower than the horizontal resolution and precision. On a fax modem, the precision is unaffected by the rotation, because the document is not physically moved through the fax machine, but the resolutions are still different. (If you don't believe me, try it and see.)

You have two alternatives to using your fax software's viewing features. You can print your document so that you have a hard copy to work from, or you can convert your fax file into another format so that it can be edited with your other application program. In some cases, conversion utilities are supplied with the fax software, and in most cases, so is a printing utility.

Printing your fax document

The print utility in your fax software will print your document on a printer that can print graphic images. These include Hewlett-Packard LaserJet, Epson graphic printers, and many other printers. The image stored as a series of dots is copied to your printer.

Printing fax documents can be extremely slow because the information is usually sent to the printer one line at a time. A single page may take several minutes to print. Again, the important thing to remember is that the fax document file is a graphic image and not text.

The fax modem has a tremendous advantage over many stand-alone fax machines because most printers use ordinary paper but most stand-alone fax machines use light-sensitive paper. The light-sensitive paper, as its name suggests, is affected by light. Fax documents, even when stored in file folders, tend to fade with time and should not be considered permanent. You must photocopy fax documents from most stand-alone fax machines to preserve the image. You only need to print fax documents from a fax modem to get a permanent image. (You can purchase stand-alone fax machines that use ordinary paper, but they tend to be more expensive.)

Converting your fax document

If you want to edit the fax document, you need to convert the received fax document into another form so that you can use it in other application programs. This file conversion falls into two main categories: graphic-image conversion and graphic-image-to-text conversion.

Some fax software includes graphic-file conversion utilities. You may have used the utility to change the graphic image form so that you could send a document. However, the reciprocal utility that can convert the received fax document format into another graphic-image format may not be available.

For example, the fax software may be able to convert from PCX and several different TIFF formats but only able to convert back to PCX format. Read the supported file format documentation very carefully. A third-party file-conversion program, such as HiJaak from Inset Systems, may be a valuable addition to your software library if you intend to handle graphic images in many forms.

Note: Even if the fax document sent was in color, the fax document is received in black and white. A conversion program is not going to restore the color for you.

"How do I get a text file from my fax document?"

Conversion of graphic images into text files, known as *optical character recognition* (OCR), is the only alternative for converting your fax documents into a form that can be read by a text editor or word processor. OCR software is not usually supplied with the fax software that is bundled with your modem.

Some scanners are supplied with OCR software, and many OCR programs are available from third parties. Some of these programs are excellent, fast, and accurate, and others are more or less useless. Because of its importance, OCR is covered in more detail in Chapter 11.

Beginners need to understand that OCR software takes the image of the page with text on it and examines what it considers to be a single letter. This small image is compared with the OCR software's library of letters, and a letter is chosen. The software then takes the next area and runs a similar comparison to determine the next letter.

In some cases, using OCR software is the only method of getting a document into electronic form. However, if you find you are making this conversion frequently with fax documents, evaluate whether you are making more work than is necessary. If the original document was in electronic form, you can probably use a data modem to transfer the file in electronic form. Even if you need to add formatting, such as fonts and centering, this approach probably will be more accurate and faster than using OCR software.

Summary

This chapter introduced sending and receiving fax documents with your fax modem. Although fax modems are an inexpensive form of fax machine, they require different preparation and document handling than stand-alone fax machines.

When sending fax documents, the document must be prepared in electronic form, converted into a form that the fax software can accept, and then sent, with or without a cover sheet. If you convert the file before sending, verify that the converted document looks as you expect.

When receiving fax documents, a TSR program must be loaded so that the fax modem is prepared to answer the phone. The received document can be viewed, printed, or converted into another file format. If you find that you are converting received documents frequently, consider using a data modem instead.

Part III takes you beyond the basics so that you can choose the best communications and fax software, streamline your communications, and perform special purpose communications.

Survival and
Efficiency Tools

Part III extends your communications knowledge beyond the basics of getting up and running. By the end of this part, you will know how to make the best use of your data modem, fax modem, communications software, and fax software.

Chapter 8 provides the launching point for this part. It introduces the types of opportunities for possible improvement. It explains whether the additional feature is software or hardware related or elementary or more advanced, so that you can read the details in the subsequent chapters.

Chapter 9 explains how to make the most of your data modem and its software. The chapter presents optimization guidelines that help you choose the most appropriate modem and software options.

Chapter 10 shows how you can streamline your communications. You learn when and how to use your communications software programming features and how to remove the drudgery and repetition. By employing these techniques, you can minimize your online expenses.

Chapter 11 explains how to make the most your fax modem and its software. It covers automation techniques and methods of reducing your expenses. It also provides guidelines on how to improve fax document quality and translation from graphics to text.

Chapter 12 covers special purpose communications. This includes using modems on the road, international communication, and communicating with a Macintosh. It also covers methods of controlling a remote computer, such as using remote control software or host mode in your communications software.

8
CHAPTER

Beyond the Basics

This chapter suggests many ways to make your modem communication easy, faster, and more efficient. Subsequent chapters provide more detail on the methods, but this chapter divides the possibilities into categories so that you can rapidly explore the opportunities. This chapter covers the following topics:

- ✜ Making the most of your equipment
- ✜ Potential software and modem improvements
- ✜ Potential fax software and fax modem improvements
- ✜ Alternative uses for modems or fax modems.

Making the Most of Your Equipment

Although electronic communication can be intimidating until you make a few connections and transfer a few files, the procedure soon becomes more routine. The general method of deciding who and what you are calling, dialing the phone number and making the connection, controlling the remote software and exchanging files, and then terminating the connection is the same for all the connections you are likely to make. These procedures apply regardless of whether you are using a data modem or a fax modem.

However, there are many ways you can improve your modem use beyond the basics. These techniques are similar to the difference between making yourself understood in a foreign language and holding an interesting conversation in that language.

As discussed in earlier chapters, telecommunicating involves making two modems communicate with each other over a telephone line. Each modem is attached to another device, such as a computer or printer, and you can control the remote device from your PC. Your task as a computer user is to choose options and settings that enable the modems and devices to establish and maintain a connection. The process is a logical series of events, and each stage has a variety of options.

Part II removes as many of the choices as possible so that you can make your first connection. As you may have noticed, however, there are many opportunities for improvements. These make establishing the connection more automated, make your actual communications faster, reduce your online time, or, in the case of fax documents, make the results higher quality.

Part III divides the improvements in each chapter. Chapter 8 sets the stage for the remaining chapters in this part. This chapter divides the potential improvements by separating the fax modem changes from the data modem and making two classes for data modems.

The first set of improvements (see Chapter 9) for the data modem connections is possible with most modems and communications software. The second set of improvements (see Chapter 10) applies mostly to communications software and gives you some indication of the power of the more advanced communications software. Fax modem techniques are discussed in Chapter 11. Chapter 12 discusses techniques possible in only the most advanced communications software.

Understanding Modem Features

Your modem is the serial device that takes the serial data supplied from your PC's serial port and modulates it into a form suitable for transmission along the telephone line. Similarly, the modem can take data sent from a remote modem and demodulate it into a form suitable for transmission from your modem to the serial port.

The modem is also programmable and can respond to commands sent from your PC. When you first power up, the modem is in *command mode* and ready to accept instructions. When switched to *data mode*, any data sent is passed to the remote modem. You can switch the modem from data mode to command mode by sending an escape sequence. You can then issue AT commands to instruct the modem.

"What other types of AT commands exist?"

The basic instructions, discussed in Chapter 5, include dialing a phone number or hanging up the phone. Most modems actually include many more commands; some support more than 100.

Although some commands are unique and you are unlikely to use them except in special circumstances, many are more general. For example, some modems (especially newer ones) have a speaker that can be controlled by AT commands. If your modem is buried in modular furniture, you may need to turn up the volume to hear it dial the phone. Conversely, if you use your modem late at night and do not want to wake other family members, you may want to turn down the speaker volume. (See Chapter 9, the section "Adjusting your speaker volume.") Obviously this is not an essential command, but it is valuable.

Your modem determines how it responds to commands and the other modem by examining internal storage areas. The modem's storage areas include integrated circuits or chips known as *read-only memory* (ROM) as well as memory areas known as *S-registers*. These areas are explained in more detail in Chapter 9, but the ROM contains unchangeable information placed by the modem manufacturer. Some S-registers contain information that remains stored in the modem even when the power is turned off; others give ongoing information about the modem's current status, but much of the information can be changed by using the appropriate AT commands. The S-registers contain information that determines such items as result codes (explained in Chapter 4) or how fast to dial a phone number.

"What's an S-register?"

Although you may need to alter a few S-registers, you won't need to change them all. Most people have only one or two preferred configurations. Your modem comes preprogrammed with the factory default settings. Some modems allow you to store other configurations as an alternative. This configuration, which allows you to store a collection of all your preferred S-register settings and other settings, is known as a *profile*.

"What is a profile?"

Additionally, you may wish to issue the same series of instructions to your modem every time you start your communications program. In this way, you can be certain that the modem is configured in the way you expect. You can configure your communications program so that it sends an *initialization string* of commands to your modem as soon as you start it.

"Why do I need an initialization string?"

Profiles and initialization strings are very important, especially if you will be calling different locations. If you only call your office PC, you will always use the same parameters. If you call, for example, several different BBSs or online services, the profiles and initialization strings become much more important.

Additionally, if you use more than one communications program, profiles and initialization strings are valuable. They enable you to use each program in the best possible way. Many modem owners may use multiple communications software programs without even realizing it. For example, you may use fax software and data communications software, or you may use a front-end program, such as that supplied when you register with Prodigy or another online service, and data communications software, such as QModem, Smartcom Exec, or Smartcom for Windows.

The optimum settings for your modem when you send a fax document may be completely different from the setting you use when you call a particular online service, which may in turn be completely different from the best settings for calling your office computer.

You can often adjust your modem settings from menu options within your communications programs. The more sophisticated the program, the more adjustments you can make without specifically issuing AT commands. For example, you may be able to choose the number of times the phone rings before the modem answers from a menu selection, such as Modem Configuration, or you may need to issue the AT command itself.

Altering the speaker volume or number of rings are commands that can be considered useful but not essential in particular user situations. Chapter 9 explores many available commands. However, no modem has all possible commands. Older modems in particular will have fewer available commands.

Other AT commands are more technical and control whether the modem uses error correction or compression when available or modem control when operating in synchronous mode. For most users, these settings should not be changed.

Besides the modem settings, your modem use will improve if you clearly understand how your modem is operating. As mentioned in Chapter 5, when your modem makes a connection, it sends result codes to your communications software that you may be able to see on-screen. For example, your screen may say `CONNECT 2400`.

To reduce online time, you should usually make the fastest connection possible and take advantage of error correction and compression. Although you may set these options, however, your modem can apply them only if the other modem can conform with these standards.

Chapter 9 discusses looking for information on how your modem has actually connected and how this knowledge affects your other selections, such as file-transfer protocol.

More on AT Commands

Chapter 5 introduces seven of the most important AT commands found in all AT-compatible modems. All modems include more commands than these seven, and some include more than 100 commands. Although there is an approved standard for AT commands, these represent only a small number of those actually found in modems.

Over the years, as communications standards have evolved, many manufacturers have produced modems that conform with the generally accepted previous AT commands and add new AT commands. Some of these additions may add proprietary communications standards, and others add user configuration convenience.

For example, when 9600 bps modems first became available, there were several different proprietary standards. If you had a 9600 bps modem, you could only communicate at 9600 bps with another modem of the same type. You could, however, communicate with other modems at 2400 bps by using the existing standards. These modems used (and still use) new AT commands to select the faster speed or otherwise change the modem configuration.

Other additions to the AT commands came from manufacturers trying to gain a market edge and have something different in their modems. Commands to store profiles, for example, are an enhancement to the standard AT command set.

The result is that there is no such thing as the complete AT command set, and even the most advanced modems do not include all the AT commands. In some cases, particular AT commands are implemented in different ways by different modems. These differences may be subtle or significant.

It doesn't matter that your modem does not include every single AT command. However, it is important that you know what AT commands your modem can support and use your communications software to take the best advantage of the commands that you do have. If you are purchasing a new modem or are using more than one modem type, you should compare the commands available in the two modems and see whether you need to reconfigure or even replace your communications software to get the best use out of your new modem.

For example, I own a very inexpensive but fast modem that does not perform as well as its more expensive competitors on noisy phone lines. A local BBS is a particular problem. As a result, I use a particular configuration with my inexpensive modem to help it connect with this BBS. It is not an ideal configuration, because the settings increase the chances of my getting communications errors. However, it makes the difference between being able to connect or not. When I use a different modem, I change its configuration to give me the best performance.

Understanding Communications Software Features

Your modem is controlled by software on your PC. Your communications software does not need to include many features. It must be able to send data to and receive data from the serial port and support a terminal emulation.

Even the most basic communications programs usually include the capability to send some AT commands to the modem by selecting options from the program's menus. However, these commands may be limited to resetting the modem, dialing a phone number, and hanging up the phone. You should be able to issue other AT commands directly from the terminal emulation screen.

To use this primitive type of communications program, you must be a sophisticated user or have very simple needs. As discussed in Chapter 4, if you find you have a primitive communications program and need more support, consider another program before giving up on telecommunicating.

"What extras are in my communications software?"

Most communications programs offer many more features than the absolute minimum. Your modem will work more or less with any of these programs, but you will get the best from your modem by using a good-quality communications program suitable for your task. This may involve using more than one communications program.

For example, the CompuServe Information Manager program supplied when you subscribe to CompuServe is not the most sophisticated communications program available, but it is one of the best for finding your way around CompuServe. It is written specifically to navigate CompuServe and help you read mail and find user forums, technical support areas, games areas, and other services without effort.

On the other hand, QModem is a more general-purpose communications program with some excellent advanced features. These include its "learn" feature where you can call a particular service or BBS and have the communications program record your keystrokes. With a little work, you can then use this learned sequence, known as a *script*, every time you call the service. The communications program will replay your keystrokes, saving you the repetition.

The most basic options in your communications program will include choosing the character format, speed, and terminal emulation. In almost all cases, your program will include a method of storing telephone numbers for online services that you call regularly.

Most communications programs, such as QModem and ProComm, have a dialing directory, which is equivalent to an electronic list of phone numbers. You can store some settings with each phone number. For example, apart from the phone number and name of the service, you can usually store such settings as the character format and speed. When you run your communications program, you select the service to connect with from this dialing directory.

Other communications programs, such as Smartcom Exec, organize around activities rather than using a dialing directory. Others, such as Smartcom for Windows, use both concepts. This metaphor is used on Apple Macintosh computers where all activities are stored as separate documents. Each online service or place you call with your modem is considered a separate activity. You select the activity by filename rather than from a list within your communications program.

The ease with which you can add more numbers to dial and the required specifications, such as speed and character format, also varies with the communications program. In most cases, you configure your communications program with a default set of information and then only customize the settings for specific connections.

Beyond the more basic options, a good communications program includes extra items that can streamline your modem use. The number and type of file-transfer protocols supported will affect your communications performance. You want a program that supports ASCII, XMODEM, and ZMODEM as a minimum. However, Kermit and YMODEM are desirable extras.

One particularly good alternative is to choose a communications program that allows you to add additional programs that can expand your communications features. Then, when a new file-transfer protocol becomes available, you can find an add-on program that supports the new standard and continue to use your current communications program. For example, the ZMODEM file-transfer protocol is available as an add-on program for many communications programs. You may be able to update your older communications program to include the relatively new standard.

"*What is a capture file?*"

You probably will want a communications program that supports session capture. The interaction that takes place from when you call the other modem until you hang up the phone is considered a *session.* The *capture file* stores a record of your online proceedings in a file on your disk so that you can read the events again. It's like tape-recording your online connection. You turn on or open the capture file, and everything you type and everything displayed on your computer screen is saved in this file. After you turn off or close the capture file (or exit the communications program), the file can be read by using a text editor, such as the EDIT program in MS DOS 5 or later versions.

You can use the capture file for a variety of purposes, including reading messages at leisure or listing the options available on the service you called. For example, if you call a new BBS, you can open a capture file, have a quick look around the service and list a few menus to see what's available, and then disconnect. By reading your capture file, you can determine whether the BBS includes messages or file areas or chat areas without reading and digesting all your options while online. Consider a capture file as a tape recorder that records everything that happens in session. It does not do anything more than record.

Scripts and *key macros* are another option in better communications programs. Scripts and key macros are similar to playing back portions of a recorded tape. A key macro feature allows you to assign a series of keystrokes to a single key press. For example, you may want to assign your password to a single key, such as F4. (Consider your security before you automate your passwords.) In this example, when an online service prompts you for your password, you can press F4 instead of typing all the characters of your password.

"Are scripts only for programmers?"

A script file is more complicated than a key macro, but all users can benefit from them. As its name suggests, script files play back information like a film script that contains instructions and dialog. For example, you can create a script that responds by typing the letters in your last name when it sees the prompt Last Name: from the online service. More-sophisticated script files can automate most, if not all, of your communications session.

You usually create a key macro for something you use in a variety of sessions. However, a script is tailored to a particular online service. For example, you may have one script file for calling your local BBS and another for calling the electronic mail service MCI Mail.

More-advanced communications software programs include a variety of tools for creating script files. Some have a programming language that you can use. For example, you may be able to include lines in the script that perform the equivalent of waiting for 10 seconds before responding, or pressing Y every time you see the prompt `More (Y/N)`.

Some communications programs make creating script files relatively easy by including a learning feature that records the information sent by the remote computer and your responses and makes the first draft at generating a script.

"Why do I need an offline reader?"

Another feature, particularly useful when calling BBSs for messages, is a communications program that supports an *offline reader*. The offline reader may be incorporated into the communications program or may be available as an add on product.

An offline reader is useful when you call a BBS or other online service that also supports offline readers. You choose a special menu item and the BBS automatically collects all the messages you have requested into a file and downloads that file to your computer. You then log off from the BBS and read the messages with your offline mail reader without being connected to the BBS.

Chapters 9 and 10 discuss making the most of your communications program and consequently making the most of your modem. To make all your options digestible, Chapter 9 focuses on your software configuration, including modem profiles and initialization strings. Chapter 10 partly assumes an understanding of Chapter 9 and covers the options possible with some communications programs to remove the repetitious portions of communicating and speed your communications so that you reduce online time.

Although you may not want to get involved with the details of configuring your modem, Chapter 10 can automate your connection at a simple level. For example, you can use a script (rather like replaying a series of recorded keystrokes) to automate connecting with online services.

More-sophisticated scripts and offline readers can completely automate your connection. For example, I call a national BBS and automatically download messages, find new files, and log off the system. I only select the phone number to dial; the rest is automated. I am only online for 10 to 15 minutes, but I collect messages that take me between 1 and 2 hours to read, which enables me to keep current at minimal expense. (See Chapter 10, the section, "Understanding offline mail readers.")

Tip: When you use a front-end communications program, supplied with your subscription to an online service, such as CompuServe, Prodigy, or America Online, many of the enhancements suggested in this section are not possible. The front-end program does a good job of streamlining your interface with the system, because the communications program is tailor-made for that service. However, you should look at the configuration settings in these programs to see whether you can make some alterations. For example, you may be able to send an initialization string before connecting, but you are unlikely to be able to alter all aspects of your connection.

Understanding Fax Features

As with stand-alone fax machines, you can purchase fax modems with varying degrees of sophistication. At its most basic, the fax modem must be able to take a file containing the image you want to send and deliver it to the remote fax machine as well as receive the image from a remote fax machine and save the image as a file. It must be able to dial the phone number, establish the connection, transfer the file, and break the connection.

Fax modems in PCs are a more recent development than data modems. Additionally, the task involved in transferring the file from one modem to the other involves fewer options and variables than are possible with data modems.

Like data modems, fax modems accept AT commands, and different fax modems support different AT commands. However, like data modems, all fax modems support the minimum necessary AT commands, and many support additional ones.

You can generally buy a data modem and use any communications software with it. The modem is independent of the communications software. Your modem may not support all the features of your communications software, but you can successfully use the software with any modem.

Apart from speed, you have far fewer features to choose from when selecting a fax modem. Most of the variability of features between fax modem features comes from the supplied software rather than the hardware, and fax modems are not as independent as data modems. When choosing a fax modem, choose carefully. Unlike data modems, which will work with your selection of communication programs, your fax modem may not work with alternative fax software.

Understanding Fax Software Features

Because of the typical fax modem's lack of independence, you probably will use the fax software supplied with your fax modem rather than purchasing separate fax modem software. However, you should consider third-party utility software to enhance your fax modem's software.

The fax software must be capable of taking an image stored on disk and getting it to the remote fax machine. Additionally, it must be capable of receiving a fax document.

"What extras do I need in my fax software?"

The desirable extras for fax software fall into two categories: control and flexibility preparing *for* and *during* the communications session and flexibility with document handling *before* transmission and *after* receipt. The control you want for preparing the document is comparable to the control and flexibility you want from a data modem. The document-handling features are unique to fax documents and do not have a data modem equivalent.

Your fax modem can accept AT commands like a data modem. However, it uses fewer AT commands because there are fewer necessary alternatives. For example, your fax modem must be able to dial the telephone and hang up the phone. Your fax communications software will probably hide most of the communications features within menu selections, which usually are named System Configuration.

After you choose the desired configuration, you probably won't change it again. Unlike a data modem, where you need different configurations depending on the service you are calling, almost all of your fax documents will be sent to similar systems, and reconfiguration is not necessary. However, you may be able to improve your configuration after the initial installation. After you have managed to send and receive a couple of fax documents, you should review your configuration to see whether any changes can be made.

The fax modem configuration is the area you need to consider if you find that your fax modem is no longer working. This will probably occur because you changed your computer configuration in some way. For example, if you change CONFIG.SYS or AUTOEXEC.BAT, your fax modem may no longer work. Chapter 11 provides a checklist of techniques for reviewing your fax software configuration.

As explained in Chapter 7, consider your fax modem like a stand-alone fax machine or an answering machine. You can receive faxes only if your computer is turned on and the terminate-and-stay-resident (TSR) program is loaded. Most problems with receiving fax documents relate to this TSR.

Your software may have different options for receiving fax documents. You may, for example, be able to print each document automatically upon receipt or place the documents into a separate area of your hard disk. Other desirable options for sending fax documents relate to ease of use and quality of the document. You can store fax machine phone numbers in a dialing directory, for example. Or, you can optionally enhance the fax document you send by adding a cover sheet to your document or by adding your company logo or signature to the document.

More-advanced fax software may allow you to prepare multiple fax documents and send them all at one time. Alternatively, you can send the same fax document to multiple people. Or, you can schedule the document sending time to take advantage of lower telephone rates. In this case, a feature for turning off the modem's speaker may be very important. You might want to keep a transaction log showing what you sent to whom and when. (See Chapter 11.)

When sending documents, you must import your document in a format that your fax modem software can understand. As explained in Chapter 7, there are several approaches to this, including using screen capture utilities or capturing the output from an application program by using a fax software utility program that can capture the data you would ordinarily send to a printer. Few, if any, fax software programs are exceptional in this area.

However, many third-party programs can perform good file translation when your fax modem software does not match your application software file formats. Remember that your application program, such as a word processor or spreadsheet, may be able to do the translation so that your fax software can accept the document.

When you receive documents, you want to read them and possibly convert them into another format, including text. Again, fax software programs usually are not exceptional in this area. Ideally, your fax software should include the capability to view your received documents and rotate them so they are readable without you standing on your head. Documents can easily be sent sideways or upside-down from a stand-alone fax machine.

Like sending documents, you can use third-party file-conversion programs to change the format of the received document into a format that one of your graphic programs can read. However, you may wish to convert a received fax into text so that it can be edited as text.

Be certain that you are using the correct tool for the job. If you want to edit a text document, consider the possibility of transferring the document as a file by using a data modem rather than a fax modem. This will preserve the accuracy of the file as well as keep all the formatting features of the document.

If the document was not in electronic form, or a data modem is not available, you need to use an optical character recognition (OCR) program to convert the received fax, which is a graphical image of the document, into text. Chapter 11 presents OCR software and techniques you can use to help improve your conversion accuracy. It also includes techniques for improving the document quality of sent and received faxes.

Understanding Remote Control Software

As covered in Chapter 5, you can make your modem communicate with another modem via your communications software. This remote modem is also controlled by communications software. In the case of online services, the remote computer runs special communications software, often BBS software. In the case of your calling a friend or your office, the remote computer is probably running a general-purpose communications program similar to your own.

When you call an online service, you can control your end of the communications link and the remote end. The remote computer displays lists of available commands, and you type your requests. When you call your friend, however, you have two people involved—one at each end of the connection. Each person controls his or her own end of the connection.

To transfer a file from one computer to another, the following is the general procedure:

1. The first person activates the upload command and specifies the filename and file-transfer protocol.

2. The second person activates the download command and specifies the filename and file-transfer protocol.

3. The second computer recognizes the signals to transmit being sent from the first computer, and the file transfer occurs.

Having two people involved in the connection is often not practical. The person calling the remote computer wants control of both computers. This is important in two situations, the previously described case where you want to transfer information from one computer to another and the case where you want to control the remote computer as if you were sitting at the remote computer.

The first case, where you only want to control both ends of the connection to save someone typing commands at the remote computer, is possible with more-advanced communications programs. You don't have to use special BBS software but can activate a feature in your communications software known variously as *host mode* or *remote access*.

"How do I control my office computer from home?"

Again, the performance and flexibility of these features depends on the communications program. However, the general idea is that you can set up your computer so that it is like a mini-BBS. The caller can control both ends of the connection and download or upload files or perhaps read messages as if he or she were calling a BBS. You may want to set up your office computer in this mode so that you can call and collect data when you are at home.

I find this setup particularly useful when someone needs to call me and collect files, but he or she has only one phone line. The host mode provides the caller with menu prompts and options. If I am controlling my end of the connection, I need to talk someone through the process on a second phone line, or I need to switch between chatting and file transfer. This can be especially disconcerting for callers who have not done much telecommunicating.

The other situation where you want control of the remote computer is when you want to use the remote computer as if you were seated at the remote computer's keyboard. For example, you may want to call your office from home and use the word processor and files stored on your office computer as if you were actually in the office. You want to press keys on your home computer and have the appropriate keystrokes activate the commands on the remote computer.

This type of software is called *remote control software*. You run a TSR on your office computer, and when you call from home by using the special communications software, you can control the remote computer. This is like your office computer having two keyboards and two displays — with one keyboard and one display in your home. Host mode and other remote control operations are covered in Chapter 12.

Understanding Special Situations

Most of this book has focused on the most general communications situations where you call another modem from your computer, but your computer is always located in the same place and is attached to the same telephone line.

In some cases, you need to use your modem or fax modem in more unusual situations. You may want to use your modem from a hotel room or send a fax from a public pay phone. Using your modem on the road is becoming easier every day as more hotels, airports, and even road rest areas become aware of communication needs. However, these special situations bring their own unique problems to the table, and Chapter 12 solves the most common.

Other special communication situations may or may not pose a problem. In some cases, the problems are perceived rather than real, such as taking your modem overseas and calling overseas with your modem. Calling overseas is at one level a perceived problem in that you only add more numbers to the dialing string. However, you may be dealing with different standards, and the two modems may not talk to each other because each follows its own standard. Taking your modem overseas and getting it through customs and plugged in and working are very real problems. In some cases, you will have your equipment confiscated at the border. Plugging in is often impossible if not illegal.

You also can use your modem to communicate with another type of computer. The perceived problem is linking with another computer type. Remember that your modem is communicating with another modem. The remote modem can be attached to any sort of computer, including Macintosh or mainframe. Chapter 12 covers the potential problems, typically perceived rather than real, of communicating with another computer type.

Summary

This chapter introduced some of the myriad ways you can enhance your communicating beyond the basics. These improvements include simple tasks, such as reconfiguring your communications software and your modems to use them to their full potential, as well as more-involved options, such as taking advantage of extra features in your communications programs.

Depending on your specific communications needs, you may want to make elementary changes that make the best use of the hardware and software that you own. These enhancements are covered in Chapter 9. Chapter 10 extends these enhancements to cover features possible only with more-sophisticated communications programs or by using add-on programs with your current communications program.

Your fax modem can be a particularly useful tool when used correctly—or a boat anchor when not used appropriately. Chapter 11 shows how to make the best use of your fax modem and its software for sending and receiving fax documents. The value of third-party software is also included in the discussion in that chapter.

9

CHAPTER

Making the Most of Your Modem and Software

This chapter presents techniques for making the most of your modem and communications software. In particular it covers the following topics:

- ❖ Configuring your modem
- ❖ Using AT commands to tailor the configuration
- ❖ Understanding profiles and initialization strings
- ❖ Understanding connection speed and compression
- ❖ Choosing serial port options

Reconfiguring Your Modem and Software

After making your first connections and transferring a few files, you should reconsider your modem's configuration and the communications software configuration. As you become more experienced with calling other modems, you move from needing guidance every step of the way to connecting faster, wringing an extra ounce of performance from your modem, and streamlining your communications.

This chapter focuses on choosing the best configuration for your modem in your particular situation and for your communication needs. These techniques take your configuration from a general-purpose modem to an optimized version. Most suggestions in this chapter relate to improving how your modem works, and Chapter 10 focuses on methods for streamlining the communications session itself.

You may find that you cannot achieve all the optimization suggested. You may not have a modem that contains all features, or you may not have a communications program with all the relevant options.

Modem type selection

When you first install your modem and communications software, you make selections relating to the serial port assignment and port addresses. You probably select the modem type from a list within your communications program. (Some communications programs can automatically choose a modem type, and others allow you to choose for yourself.)

Unless you can see the precise modem model on your communications software list of selections, you probably choose the option of Hayes-compatible, AT-compatible, or generic Hayes modem. You may choose based on your modem's speed, such as 2400 bps or V.32.

Consider re-examining your modem type selection to see whether a better match exists for your modem. Although your modem may claim to be "fully Hayes-compatible," there is actually no such thing. Not only do the modem manufacturers have their own interpretation of compatible, but the communications software manufacturers also have their own version.

"What modem type do I choose in my software?"

Additionally, some modems may have different models with the same features, and your communications program may supply the best configuration for one version but you own another.

Selecting the most appropriate modem type in your communications software is like understanding local dialects or even more subtle language differences, such as the difference between the American and English pronunciations of *mall*. Americans make "mall" rhyme with "doll," and the English make it rhyme with "shall." In both cases, the same word is being spoken, but they are not heard as the same word.

You should pay special attention to your modem type selection if you have an unusual modem or one that supports a proprietary standard. Some differences exist because the 9600 bps standard was slowly accepted over a period of years. Users were clamoring for faster speeds before there was a 9600 bps standard that was affordable for PC modems. Several modem manufacturers created a proprietary standard. These modems could communicate at 9600 bps with another modem from the same manufacturer but only at 2400 bps with another manufacturer's modem. Since that time, the V.32 standard has been accepted, and 9600 bps communications between different manufacturers' modems is possible.

However, if you have one of these older USRobotics 9600 bps modems, it may support the HST proprietary standard. This is not compatible with the older equivalent (speed-wise) Hayes V-Series 9600 bps modem when the modems try to operate at 9600 bps. If you choose the Hayes V-Series instead of the USRobotics in your communications software, you will not connect at 9600 bps — but only at 2400 bps.

In addition to the modem's communications standards, there are differences between the supported AT commands. For example, one modem may allow you to store two profiles while another allows three. If you choose the modem type that supports only two profiles in your communications software, you won't have access to the third profile. There also may be differences between the way two modems from different manufacturers implement the same AT command.

Even if your communications software lists your modem's product name specifically, you may want to alter or add to its configuration. Most communications software programs allow you to choose and add to the supplied settings. Wherever possible, retain the original configuration, and create a copy of it for experimentation. You can then return to the original if necessary.

Finding what your modem can do

Before exploring details of S-registers and other configuration settings, you need your modem operating manual to determine whether particular AT commands are available. The manual supplies lists and tables showing the available commands and summaries of their purposes.

Some modems, such as the Practical Peripherals 9600 SA modem, include an AT command that supplies information about the modem. From your communications program's terminal screen, type **AT$H** and press Enter. If the command is supported, you see the first of several screens of information about your modem, including the supported command list. Use Print Screen to print this information to your printer for reference. If your modem does not support this command, you will see the message ERROR when you press Return.

Understanding S-Registers

As explained in Chapter 8, your modem contains storage areas where data is stored. Some data is permanent, and some can be adjusted by the user. The permanent data is stored in *read-only memory* (ROM), and the more alterable data is stored in *nonvolatile memory*. Nonvolatile memory is memory for which the current contents are preserved when you remove power. However, you can change the contents by sending appropriate AT commands.

"*What is an S-register?*"

The memory areas can be compared with the memory areas in a PC. The ROM in a PC contains permanent data that is used, in part, to boot the computer when you first turn it on. The PC (except for early models) also contains nonvolatile memory. This memory contains, in part, the date and time. Although the date and time are preserved when you turn off power to the computer, you can issue a DOS command to alter the date or time.

The ROM in a modem contains a variety of information, including the factory default configuration. Part of the nonvolatile memory area is a series of storage locations called S-registers. The S-registers, which are numbered, contain the settings that your modem uses. For example, one register named S0 contains the setting for the number of rings the modem must receive before answering the phone. The register S1 contains the number of rings the modem has received. (Register S0 is a register you may wish to change, but register S1 is a register you won't want to change.)

For the most part, the S-registers are implemented in the same way regardless of the modem. However, different modems contain different S-registers. For example, a 2400 bps modem may contain 28 S-registers, and a 9600 bps modem may contain 96 S-registers.

Note: Arbitrarily changing the values of S-registers may make your modem stop working or work erratically. Change only the registers you need, and learn the reset command to remove any errors you have made.

Reading S-registers

Before changing any S-registers, you need to know what they currently contain. To view the contents of a particular S-register type **ATSn?** (where n is the particular S-register number) and press Enter. For example, to view the contents of S1, you type **ATS1?**. To view the contents of S0, you type **ATS0?**.

You can view the contents of several registers at once by stringing your requests together on a single command line. For example, to view the ASCII values for the Escape code character, the carriage return character, the line feed character, and the backspace character, stored in registers S2, S3, S4, and S5 respectively, you type **ATS2?S3?S4?S5?** and press Enter.

Your modem returns with something comparable to the following:

```
OK
ATS2?S3?S4?S5?
043
013
010
008
OK
```

(If you can't see what you're typing on-screen, remember to turn on local echo so that the modem will echo the characters back to the screen.)

Note: Local echo is typically a toggle in your communications program. For example, it is assigned to Alt+E in QModemPro, and is an option called Local character echo in the terminal settings in Smartcom for Windows. (Chapter 5 covers this in more detail.)

The example shows the values you probably will find in your modem. However, as covered in Chapter 5, you can change any of these values.

You probably will view an S-register's contents just before changing it. For example, if you think that your modem is dialing slowly, you will at the relevant S-register (S11) determine the meaning of its value and change to a new value that makes the modem dial more quickly.

If you want to know the values of all your alterable S-registers, you will probably view the profile for your modem — if your modem supports profiles — rather than explicitly calling each S-register's value. Profiles are covered in the later section, "Understanding Profiles."

Changing an S-register

You can change the value stored in an S-register by using the appropriate AT command. You type **ATS***n***=***value* and press Enter.

For example, to change the value of S0 to four and instruct the modem to answer the phone after four rings, you type **ATS0=4** and press Enter. Your modem responds with OK to indicate that it has accepted and executed a command. In this case, the number you type is an actual number and represents the number of rings the modem should receive before answering the telephone.

However, other S-registers, such as S2, contain a number, but the number represents something other than a number. For example, S2 contains the ASCII code for the Escape-code-sequence character. S12's contents determine the amount of guard time around the Escape-code sequence, expressed in 0.02 seconds (1/50 seconds). If you enter the value 50, the guard time is one second.

You should verify that you changed the register you intended by issuing a read command and checking that the new value is in the register.

You may never need to alter an S-register setting. But, by reading your modem manual carefully, you can get a performance improvement in many cases (by increasing the speed of dialing, for example) or can otherwise tailor the configuration to your particular situation (by instructing the modem to answer the phone only after ringing five times, for example).

However, you need to understand S-registers and know how to change them in two circumstances. If your modem starts behaving strangely, you may need only to change an S-register value. Alternatively, if you find something slightly unusual about your configuration, such as your modem dialing a telephone number before it gets a dial tone, you can change the S-register to make the modem work in your situation.

If you do need to alter an S-register's setting, look carefully to see whether you can make the change once and make the modem and communications software change the setting automatically each time by using profiles and/or initialization strings. These topics are covered later in this chapter in the sections "Understanding Initialization Strings," and "Understanding Profiles."

Valuable Commands

Chapter 5 introduces seven AT commands that all modem users should know. These include dialing a phone number and hanging up the phone. Even when explaining only the basic AT commands, other AT commands crept into the explanation to give you some idea of the flexibility of your modem's configuration.

So that your modem works when you first install it, your modem manufacturer creates a default configuration that works for many installations. However, most modems, especially the newer more advanced ones, have settings that involve personal preferences. As a result, you may prefer to make adjustments away from the factory default.

Before changing any modem settings, verify that your modem and communications software are installed and operating. The time to fine-tune your installation is after you have the basics working. Do not try to change everything at once.

The following sections introduce AT commands that have widespread usefulness. If you have a special situation, you may need other commands that are not included in this chapter. Refer to Appendix A, "AT Command Set," for ideas for further changes you might make.

Modifying your dial command

As presented in Chapter 4, the dial command is ATD followed by the desired phone number. To dial by using tones, you use ATDT, and to dial by using pulses, you use ATDP. So, to call 555-5555, you might issue the command **ATDT 555-5555**.

The sequence of characters the command comprises are known as a *string*. In this case, the characters ATDT 555-5555 are the dialing string. Most modems ignore spaces, hyphens, or parentheses in the dialing string, so you can add them for clarity. However, your modem dials fractionally faster if you leave them out.

If you use your communications software to issue this command, you probably will select tone or pulse dialing during the installation and enter the phone number in the dialing directory.

However, in many cases, you need to use a different arrangement. Keep in mind that the modem does exactly as you instruct and will probably do it faster than you could manually. If you need to pause during dialing, you will need to tell the modem to pause. If you need to dial a 1 in front of the number, you need to tell your modem.

The pause modifier

Including a comma (,) in your dialing string makes the modem pause. For example, if you use **ATDT 9,555-5555,** your modem dials the 9, pauses, and then dials the rest of the phone number.

The modem waits for the number of seconds specified in S-register S8. The factory default is usually two seconds.

The wait modifier

The wait modifier is different from the pause modifier. When you issue the dial command, the modem usually takes the phone off the hook and waits for a specified period of time before dialing. The modem does not attempt to detect a dial tone. The length of time that the modem waits is specified by the contents of S6, which usually is set as a default of 2 seconds, and on most modems, the minimum wait is 2 seconds regardless of the S6 contents.

Note: Whether to look for a dial tone when issuing a dialing command without the wait modifier is enabled and disabled as one of the result code options. If you choose a particular version of extended result code (by issuing the AT command ATX2), you can make the modem always look for a dial tone.

Including a W in your dialing string makes the modem wait for a dial tone before continuing. When the modem processes the W in the dialing string, it waits until it hears a dial tone, in which case it continues to process the rest of the dialing string, or if it does not hear a dial tone within the time specified in S7, it hangs up the phone. Depending on the selected result code format, you may see the `NO DIALTONE` result code if the dial tone is not detected within the specified time.

S7 is used for two purposes. If you use the W modifier in your dialing string, it controls the time the modem must wait before giving up on finding a dial tone. S7 also controls the amount of time the modem must wait before giving up on getting a carrier signal from a remote modem. The default value in S7 is often 30 seconds or greater. This allows time for the modem to dial the number, the remote telephone to ring, and the remote modem to pick up the phone and send a carrier signal.

You can use the W modifier in front of your phone number or in the middle of the number. In a situation where you get a dial tone when you pick up the phone receiver, you can allow the modem to "dial blind" and not actually listen for a dial tone. You probably need to use W in the middle of a dialing string when you have to dial a number to get an outside line and then have to wait for a telephone exchange to give you a dial tone. The necessary delay may vary, and in some cases, you may not get a dial tone if all the outside lines are busy. In this case, the W modifier can be a better alternative than the pause modifier.

Note: Your modem can detect only a normal dial tone. Other dial tones may not be recognized by the modem, such as separate tones for internal and external phone lines.

To instruct the modem to wait for a dial tone, place the W within the dial string. For example, if you use **ATDT 9W555-5555**, your modem takes the phone off the hook, pauses for the time specified in S6 or 2 seconds (whichever is longer), and then dials 9. It then waits until it hears a dial tone or for the time specified in S7. If it hears a dial tone, it continues dialing 555-5555. If it does not hear a dial tone, it hangs up the phone and sends the result code `NO DIALTONE` to the serial port.

Dealing with long dialing strings

When you issue a dialing command, the command is accepted by the modem and temporarily stored in a buffer. This buffer is limited in size, and as a consequence, there is a limit to the length of a dialing string. For example, the buffer may be limited to 36 characters.

The length of the dialing string does not include the spaces, hyphens, or parentheses if your modem ignores them, but it does include the ATDT in front. In some cases, especially if you are calling internationally or from a hotel room, this limitation can be a problem.

"How do I dial a long telephone number?"

When you issue a dialing command, the modem usually dials the number and then switches out of command mode in preparation for communicating with the remote modem. If you end your dialing string with the semicolon modifier (;), you can make the modem stay in command mode, ready to receive another AT command.

You can use this modifier to divide your dialing string into multiple parts and over-come the buffer size limitation. Suppose that you want to call a modem from your hotel room and want to use a long-distance telephone service credit card. You may need to dial a digit to get an outside line, an 800 number to access the long-distance service, enter your security code, and then dial the actual phone number. The two telephone numbers are 10 or 11 digits each, and the security code may be 14 digits, and that does not include any pauses or waits or the ATDT portion. You can quickly rack up long strings.

Additionally, you may want to keep the dialing string portion related to the long-distance carrier separate from the actual phone number your are dialing in your communications program. Most communications programs allow you to specify a prefix that must be added to all telephone numbers, and some allow you to store multiple prefixes. When you work from your office, you use the simple prefix; when on the road, you use the more extensive one.

The semicolon must appear as the last digit of your dialing string. Your modem responds with `OK` after each dialing string is sent. Remember not to put a semicolon at the end of the last portion of the dialing string so that the modem will switch out of command mode and prepare for a connection.

For example, you may issue the following command:

```
ATDT 9,1-800-555-1212;
```

The modem responds with `OK`, and then you can issue the remainder of a dialing string, such as:

```
ATDT ,555-5555
```

The modem treats the two strings as if they were a single one. Remember that you must issue the dialing command itself both times, and you do not place the semicolon after the final dialing string.

Monitor for busy

Another feature that can speed your dialing and redialing is making the modem detect a busy signal. When a busy signal is detected, the modem hangs up the phone and awaits your next command, which probably will be repeat the last command so that you can retry the number as soon as possible (see the section "Repeat the last command").

To monitor for busy, you must know the various result codes options. The AT command that adjusts the result codes is **ATXn,** where n is 0, 1, 2, 3, or 4.

The command **ATQ** or **ATQ0** enables result codes. To disable result codes, use **ATQ1**. In almost all circumstances, you need result codes enabled. The factory default typically enables result codes.

The command **ATV** or **ATV0** enables the short form of result codes. As explained in Chapter 5, short result codes return a number rather than a word such as CONNECT or BUSY. In most cases, you want to enable the long version of result codes unless you are using specialized computer equipment. Use the command **ATV1** to enable them. The modem's factory default typically enables long result codes.

After you enable result codes and choose the long version of result codes so that words rather than numbers are returned from the modem, you can choose between the various ATXn commands.

ATX0 offers 300 bps compatibility. The modem does not recognize dial tones or busy signals. However it does send the result code CONNECT when a connection is made.

ATX1 is slightly more advanced than ATX0. The modem returns such result codes as CONNECT, CONNECT 1200, or CONNECT 2400 depending on your connection speed (300, 1200, or 2400 bps respectively in this example). As with ATX0, the modem does not recognize dial tones or busy signals.

ATX2 is slightly more advanced than ATX1. The modem looks for a dial tone before dialing and reports NO DIALTONE if one is not found within 5 seconds. It sends the connect result codes found with ATX1.

ATX3 is similar to ATX2 except that it does not recognize a dial tone and does recognize a busy signal.

ATX4 is the most advanced and usually the preferred setting for result codes because it supplies the most information and detects the most things. You see the connect messages that tell you how fast your connection speed is, and the modem can detect a dial tone and busy signal. On most modems, ATX4 is the default setting; however, your communications program may change this value.

By making your modem detect a busy signal, you can learn sooner whether your telephone connection can be made and attempt a redial. These result codes are particularly important when you use a modem without a speaker or with the speaker volume turned down. Some modems may dial the number very loudly, but the busy signal or ringing may be much fainter.

You may need to select a redial-enabled option in your communications program. The communications program probably can look for a BUSY result code from your modem and act on it by automatically redialing the number. However, some communications programs make this an optional part of the configuration.

In QModemPro, for example, you specify the modem result codes that QModemPro should consider as a successful and unsuccessful connection. (The typical values are supplied.)

Repeat the last command

The A/ command allows you to repeat the last command. You use this command when you dial a number and find it is busy. Your communications software may use this command automatically if it has an automatic redialing feature.

Note: This is one of the two commands that do not start with AT. (The other is the escape sequence.)

To repeat the last command, you type **A/**. Unlike the other AT commands, you do not follow it by pressing Enter.

Adjusting speaker volume

Most early model modems that included a speaker had a knob on the back that you could adjust to alter the volume of the speaker. You can change the volume of newer modems that have a speaker by using AT commands.

You should choose a modem that contains a speaker so that troubleshooting is easier. However, you might choose a modem without a speaker in special situations. For example, a portable modem that you want to take on the road may be smaller if it does not include a speaker. The weight and size benefits may outweigh the benefits of having a speaker.

"How do I turn off the speaker?"

The speaker can be enabled or disabled by using the **ATM***n* command. ATM0 turns the speaker off all the time. ATM1, usually the default setting, leaves the speaker on until the data carrier signal is detected.

ATM2 leaves the speaker on all the time. In this case, you can hear the noise made as data is sent between the two modems. Although this is interesting, when you've heard it once, it's not usually a desirable option.

ATM3 turns the speaker on after dialing and leaves it on until the data carrier signal is detected. This allows you to hear the negotiation for the transmission speed and protocols between the two modems, but you do not have to listen to the phone being dialed.

Most people want the speaker to be set with the ATM1 command. Of more interest is the speaker volume command. The volume is controlled with the **ATL***n* command where n is 0, 1, 2, or 3. ATL0 and ATL1 make the volume low. ATL2, usually the default, gives a medium volume and ATL3 a loud volume.

Warning: Depending on your modem, the speaker can be extremely loud and even make the unit vibrate. I had a modem that had a volume control knob on the back, and the slightest adjustment changed the volume from a discrete set of bleeps to an alarm clock that could wake the dead. A different modem, controlled by software commands, literally shakes when set to a high speaker volume. (I assume that the speaker is not mounted firmly in the chassis. It is still under warranty, but it seems a petty thing to send it back for repair!)

Understanding Initialization Strings

As explained earlier in this chapter, your modem contains two main areas of memory: ROM and nonvolatile memory. The ROM contains information that cannot be changed; the nonvolatile memory contains information that can be changed. The S-registers are numbered storage areas in the nonvolatile memory. Some S-registers are intended to be changed by the user, while others are changed by the modem during operation.

Your modem contains a set of default settings that are applied each time you turn on your modem. The stored configuration is called the *factory configuration* or *factory profile.*

You may be able to specify an alternative group of settings that are automatically loaded when you turn on the modem. (See the section "Understanding Profiles.")

The default settings applied when you turn on your modem are copied into the from the factory profile into another set of memory. This copy is called the active configuration. This is the copy that you alter when you issue AT commands and alter S-registers.

Certain parameters, although they can be changed by your issuing AT commands, are not saved when you turn off the modem. When you turn the modem back on again, the factory settings are placed in the active configuration.

For example, the ASCII value for the carriage return character, stored in register S3, is restored to the factory default whenever the modem is repowered or reset.

"What is an initialization string?"

Most communications programs include an option in the modem configuration that allows you to change the modem's configuration from the default to your desired setting. This *initialization string* is a sequence of AT commands that is sent to the modem every time you start your communications program.

Note: The initialization string provides a method of sending a predefined set of commands to your modem using your communications program. A profile on the other hand is the modem's method of being able to restore a standard configuration to itself.

Some communications programs, such as Smartcom for Windows, include additional configuration commands that are comparable to an initialization string. For example, in Smartcom for Windows you can save two different modem setups (two initialization strings), a string that is sent prior to dialing, a string that is sent before answering, and a string to send after hanging up.

If you use your modem's profiles, you will be able to select a profile in the initialization string. If you are not using an alternative profile from the manufacturer's default, you can send a series of AT commands that change the desired parameters by saving it as an initialization string.

If you are using profiles, your best initialization string is probably ATZ0 or ATZ1 which reset the modem and restores the profile number 0 or 1 respectively.

The initialization string is particularly important if you use more than one communications program. You will have a preferred set of parameters for each program, and using an initialization string makes it possible to assume that the modem is the same configuration each time you run a program.

As you investigate the online world, you will find that initialization strings are a regular topic in messages. Although there is actually no perfect initialization string, the sequence of commands AT&F&C1&D2 is a good generic command string. However, because it restores the factory defaults, it does not include any personal preferences described in this chapter.

&F restores the factory defaults, &C1 makes the modem track the status of the remote modem's carrier signal, and &D2 makes the modem track the computer's data terminal ready (DTR) signal and hang up the phone and return to command mode when DTR is lowered.

My personal initialization string is only ATZ, but I use profiles to store a long sequence of AT commands that set many options, including the speaker volume, result code format, as well as making the modem track the remote modem's carrier signal and monitoring DTR.

Understanding Profiles

As discussed earlier, your modem may include the ability to store one or more configurations known as profiles. The modem will come with a factory default profile in ROM; however, you may be able to add alternatives.

By using an AT command, you can load a profile from nonvolatile memory into your modem's active configuration. This command overwrites the configuration currently stored in the active configuration with the information stored in the profile.

You can use other AT commands to write the information currently stored in the active configuration into a profile. Other AT commands allow you to select one of the profiles as the one that is loaded into the active configuration when you turn on your modem. You can also restore the factory default profile with another AT command.

Viewing the stored profile

The profile includes AT commands and some S-register settings. You can view the profiles stored in your modem by typing **AT&V** command and pressing Enter. Figure 9-1 shows an example of the response from a modem.

```
OK
at&v
ACTIVE PROFILE:
B1 E0 L2 M1 N1 Q0 T V1 W2 X4 Y0 &C1 &D2 &G0 &J0 &K3 &Q5 &R0 &S0 &T4 &X0 &Y0
S00:000 S01:000 S02:043 S03:013 S04:010 S05:008 S06:002 S07:060 S08:002 S09:006
S10:014 S11:050 S12:050 S18:000 S25:005 S26:001 S36:007 S37:000 S38:020 S44:003
S46:138 S48:007 S49:008 S50:255

STORED PROFILE 0:
B1 E0 L2 M1 N1 Q0 T V1 W2 X4 Y0 &C1 &D2 &G0 &J0 &K3 &Q5 &R0 &S0 &T4 &X0
S00:000 S02:043 S06:002 S07:060 S08:002 S09:006 S10:014 S11:050 S12:050 S18:000
S25:005 S26:001 S36:007 S37:000 S38:020 S44:003 S46:138 S48:007 S49:008 S50:255

STORED PROFILE 1:
B1 E1 L2 M1 N1 Q0 T V1 W2 X4 Y0 &C1 &D2 &G0 &J0 &K3 &Q5 &R0 &S0 &T4 &X0
S00:005 S02:043 S06:002 S07:060 S08:002 S09:006 S10:014 S11:050 S12:050 S18:000
S25:005 S26:001 S36:007 S37:000 S38:020 S44:003 S46:138 S48:007 S49:008 S50:255

TELEPHONE NUMBERS:
0=12125551212                              1=
2=                                         3=

OK

 ANSI    Offline 38400 8N1  [Alt+Z]-Menu   HDX 8 LF X ♪ ♪ CP LG ↑ PR  16:47:09
```

Figure 9-1: Viewing a modem's profiles. The modem has a currently active configuration as well as two user-created-and-saved configurations.

This modem has four stored profiles. One is the *factory default,* which is not displayed when you issue the AT&V command. Another contains the current settings, known as the *active profile.* The other two profiles are named *stored profile 0* and *stored profile 1.*

This modem also can store four telephone numbers. In Figure 9-1, only the first telephone number storage area has a number in it. The display from the profile viewing command shows the contents of each profile. The profiles consist of various AT command selections and a list of the contents for many S-registers.

Note: Not all S-registers are suitable for alteration by the user, and not all S-registers that can be altered by the user are stored within a profile.

The two profiles stored in this modem are very similar and differ only by one command and one S-register. Stored profile number 1 uses the E0 command rather than E1. The E0 and E1 are the second commands in the line below the stored profile's name.

The E0 setting makes the communications software responsible for echoing the characters you type at the keyboard while in command mode. The E1 setting makes the modem echo the characters you type at the keyboard while in command mode.

The other difference between the two profiles is in the contents of S-register S0. The S-register contents are listed on the line below the command settings. They are in the form Sxx:yyy, where xx is the S-register's number and yyy is the S-register's contents. In Figure 9-1, register S0 contains a zero in stored profile 0 and 5 in stored profile 1. The contents of S0 specify the number of rings the modem must hear before answering the phone.

To copy a profile to the active area, you use the **ATZ*n*** command, where n is the number of the stored profile. To restore profile number 0, for example, type **ATZ1** and press Enter.

Storing a new profile

If you want to store a profile, use a two-step process. First, make all the changes you want to the modem by using AT commands and adjusting S-register contents. When you have precisely the configuration you want, you can write it to a stored profile.

Note: You should use this command with care because it overwrites the existing profile. You should keep a record of the profiles before you start playing with them. (Press Print Screen with your printer turned on after issuing the AT&V command.)

Use the AT&V command to view the current profiles. Verify that the active profile contains what you expect. Then write the profile to a stored area by typing **AT&W0** to write it to profile 0 or **AT&W1** to write it to profile 1. After writing, use the view command again to make sure you performed the operation correctly.

Selecting the factory default profile

Your modem is supplied with a default profile that is the active profile unless you or your communications program make any changes. A copy of these settings is stored in ROM. This allows you or your modem manufacturer to have a complete configuration that is always the same.

Be prepared to use the factory default profile when troubleshooting. If you have made changes to the profiles, you probably will need to print a copy of their contents before restoring the factory defaults. Although the factory defaults are restored to the active configuration, you also may want to copy them into a profile to remove a problem setting.

This procedure is equivalent to having a floppy disk containing DOS that you can use to boot your computer. (DOS 6 includes features that perform the equivalent procedure without actually needing a disk.) Booting your computer from a floppy disk gives you a "clean" configuration. It allows you to troubleshoot when you have problems making all the parts of your computer work together.

To restore the factory defaults, type **AT&F** and press Enter. This copies all the factory settings from ROM into the active configuration. This is not the same as turning off the modem's power and turning it back on again. Nor is it the same as issuing the reset command.

When you purchase the modem, the profiles probably contain copies of the factory default settings. However, if you have changed profiles, it is the changed profile that is loaded into the active configuration when you turn the modem on — not the factory defaults.

Selecting a stored profile on power up

Your modem may allow you to save more than one profile, and one of these profiles is copied into the active configuration when you apply power to the modem. You can change which profile is loaded by issuing an AT command.

If you type **AT&Y0** and press Enter, profile number 0 is loaded when you apply power. If you type **AT&Y1** and press Enter, profile number 1 is loaded when you apply power.

Resetting your modem

If you want to restore a known configuration to your modem, you may need to issue the reset command. The reset command copies a profile into the active memory area. If the modem is online, the connection will be broken.

If you type **ATZ** or **ATZ0** and press Enter, the modem is reset and profile number 0 is loaded into the active configuration. If you type **ATZ1** and press Enter, the modem is reset and profile number 1 is loaded into the active configuration.

Note: Using the reset command does not have the same effect as turning the modem on and off. When you turn the modem on and off, the setting of AT&Y determines which profile is loaded. When you use the reset command, the form of the reset command determines which profile is loaded.

Connecting at an Optimum Speed

When you make your modem call another modem, you can specify whatever speed and other communications standard you prefer. However, this standard is applied only if the modem that is being called is capable of achieving that standard.

When the second modem answers the phone, the two modems negotiate first for a connection speed and then, if applicable, for other protocols, such as compression and error-correction. The modems select the highest mutually acceptable standard.

The result is that the communications speed and other protocols that you think you have selected may not be what you have actually achieved. However, there are a couple of different ways you can tell what communications standards are being used.

Dialing the correct number

If you set your communications speed and options within your communications program to the fastest your modem can achieve, your modem will connect at that speed wherever possible. For any given connection, your modem will choose the standards that achieve the highest possible data throughput. The compression standard, for example, is not "faster," but you push more data across because it is stored in a smaller space.

Faster Serial Ports

DOS is a *single-tasking* operating system. This means it can only do one thing at a time. Other operating systems, such as OS/2 and UNIX, are *multi-tasking* operating systems and can do multiple tasks at one time. In fact, they also do only one thing at a time, because there is only one microprocessor in the computer, but they are able to divide the available time between several different tasks so that it appears to you that multiple things are happening at the same time.

Microsoft Windows is an operating environment that runs on DOS. (It actually depends on your precise definition of operating system whether you consider Windows as an operating system in its own right.) Windows is a multi-tasking environment and can do multiple things at the same time by allocating small amounts of time to each task.

You can buy a communications program that runs under Windows and can run it at the same time as other application programs. However, you may experience problems when running at high speed due to limitations in the PC.

In a multi-tasking operating system, each task running is given a small amount of time to run before the next task is given some time. For example, the communications program may have time to pick up a few characters from the serial port, and then it is the next task's turn to have control of the microprocessor. The data being sent to the serial port by the other computer, however, continues to arrive, although the communications program cannot look at it.

The PC's serial port contains a *buffer*, a temporary storage area, where received characters are stored until the communications program is able to collect them. However, the storage area is not very big, and at high data speeds, there is a possibility that some characters will be received but lost because there was not enough room in the buffer.

This is not a problem for DOS communications programs, because the communications program

has complete control of the microprocessor and is able to process the data as fast as the modem can send it. However, in a multi-tasking operating system, such as Windows, you can reach situations where the serial port in the PC is inadequate.

As the new V.FAST modems become readily available, the capability of your serial port to handle the faster data speed starts to become an issue regardless of whether you are running DOS or Windows. The problem is more likely in Windows, because there is more chance the communications program will not have uninterrupted control of the serial port.

You can purchase special serial port boards, such as Hayes ESP Communications Accelerator, or internal modems with a faster serial port, that ease the problems. As covered in Chapter 4, the serial port in a PC contains a UART (universal asynchronous receiver/transmitter) chip with other support circuitry. The particular chip used is not the most advanced available, and the faster serial port boards use more-advanced circuitry. For example, the more-advanced circuitry may operate faster and include more buffers. Consequently, you are less likely to get data loss because of overrun.

Note: Because you are using different serial port circuitry, the communications program must recognize the different serial port. This requires your communications program to support it directly, or you must choose a faster serial port that includes the necessary device driver program. For example, if you are running under Windows, you need a special Windows device driver; if you are running under another operating system, such as OS/2 or DOS, you will need different device drivers.

The boards can be configured to behave like typical PC serial ports, but in this mode you will probably lose the advantage of the extra features. However, if you are using high-speed modems (over 9600 bps) with Microsoft Windows, you should consider a faster serial port to make the connection as error free as possible.

However, many online services, particularly BBSs, offer a variety of phone numbers that you can call. The modems attached to these phone numbers will probably vary in type, and you may be able to achieve faster speeds by calling a number other than the one most widely publicized.

For example, my local BBS advertises one phone number. However, if you call on this number, you can connect at only 2400 bps. On the opening screen, this BBS shows its other numbers and encourages 9600 bps modem owners to call an alternate number so that they can connect at 9600 bps.

The slower number is advertised because it is a single number that will allow anyone to connect. The sysop is trying to discourage people with only 2400 bps modems from calling the 9600 bps lines. If they do, the people with 9600 bps modems will have to call the 2400 bps number and only connect at 2400 bps.

To understand whether you have connected at 2400 bps or 9600 bps or are using any data compression features, you need to watch your communications program carefully while it makes the connection. The following section illustrates a suggested procedure.

Understanding modem speed and compression

As covered in Chapter 4, the maximum possible data-throughput speed for the top-of-the-line modems has increased over the years. The early modems were only capable of transferring 300 bps, but new modems can transfer many thousands of bits in a second.

Early modems transferred one bit of data at a time, but the new modems transfer many bits at once. Additionally, modems that support a data-compression standard compress the data before sending it and uncompress it at the remote end. This compression results in the same amount of information being stored in a smaller number of bits. Consequently, the total amount of data being sent in a particular time frame is more if compression is being used.

Your modem negotiates a connection with a remote modem in two stages. It first establishes a connection speed and then negotiates any further communications protocols.

Most communications programs display the result codes being sent by your modem during the connection process. When calling another modem, you should watch the result codes carefully to see the agreed modem speed.

However, the level of detail supplied by these result codes, assuming that you can see them, may not be sufficient to supply the full connection story. For example, it may tell you that error-correction protocol is being used but not indicate which one.

If you have your modem speaker turned on, you also hear the negotiation process as the two modems exchange tones with each other. After you have connected a few times while watching the result codes, you will quickly learn to identify the difference between the sounds of the connections.

For example, it is quite easy to recognize (although impossible to describe in words) the negotiation and carrier signal for a 2400 bps connection as compared with a 9600 bps connection. You can also gain clues from the length of time it takes to negotiate the connection. (Usually, the negotiation process takes longer the faster the resulting connection.)

When the modems have agreed on a connection speed, the connection is complete, but they continue negotiation to establish any possible compression or error-correction.

Knowing what your modem is doing

The result codes sent to your modem during connection can vary on the speeds and communications standards being applied as well as the settings in various S-registers. For example, your modem may return CONNECT as a result code. Depending on your S-register settings, this may mean you have connected at 300 bps or at 19,200 bps!

Alternatively, you may see the message CONNECT 19200/ARQ, which means you have connected at 19,200 bps and are using some type of error-control technique. However, it does not tell you the precise standard, such as MNP (Microcom Network Protocol) or V.42's LAPM (Link Access Procedure for Modems).

On the other hand, if you adjust all the required S-registers so that the modem supplies full details of the connection, you may not actually achieve the connection because your communications program may not be able to handle more than one line of result code.

Exploring how to get the best connection from your modem will be pointless in some circumstances and will make tremendous differences in others. The first criterion is whether you have an alternate phone number for the online service you are calling.

When to investigate your connection if you have no alternate phone number

If you have only one phone number to call, your modem is going to connect with only one type of modem, and your connection speed and compression options will always be the same — unless you alter the options in your communications program before making the connection. In the case of only having one phone number to call, there is only one variable that can affect your transmission speed (apart from a noisy phone line). If you are transferring a lot of data across this connection, it is worth investigating the connection type.

The issue of compression type arises when you transfer files between two modems that use the MNP Level 5 compression protocol. This compression standard compresses all files sent from one modem to the other regardless of whether they have been compressed already.

In most cases, you will use a compression program, such as PKZIP, to compress the files prior to transmission. When you use MNP Level 5, the modem tries to compress the file further and actually generates a file that is larger than the compressed file. This obviously takes longer to transmit.

If you use MNP Level 5, you should compare the file-transfer speed you obtain when you transfer a file that is compressed with the same file uncompressed. The results you get will depend on the file size and in many cases only make a difference of a second or two. However, if you are transferring many files, the second or two for each file may make a big difference.

The other modem compression standards, including V.42bis, can detect whether a file is incompressable and automatically disable their own compression during the time you transfer the compressed file.

Besides investigating whether you are using MNP Level 5, if you only have one phone number to call a service, there is nothing you can do to speed the connection, except make sure that your communications program is trying to apply the maximum communications standards that your modem can achieve.

When to investigate your connection if you have alternate phone numbers

As discussed in the preceding section, if you have only one phone number for the service you are trying to connect to, you have no chance of improving your connection speed and communications standards. However, many online services, in particular BBSs, offer several different phone numbers you can call.

Data-Compression Alternatives

As you transfer a file between computers, your communications program often reports on the number of characters per second being transferred. The faster your connection speed, the more characters per second that are transferred.

If you are viewing text messages while online, you don't have the same quantitative number showing your connection speed. You can see the difference between 2400 bps and 9600 bps in the speed that messages and menus appear, but you cannot see small incremental differences so easily. However, for most people, the file-transfer speed is of more interest than the speed screens appear.

Keep in mind that the smaller the file, the faster it is transferred. If you can compress your file, it will be transferred faster because the information is stored in a smaller number of bytes. However, you need to consider whether it is better to compress the file before sending it, by using PKZIP for example, or by allowing the modem to compress it for you, by using a compression standard, such as V.42bis or MNP Level 5.

If you are using V.42bis compression, it doesn't matter where you do the compression. V.42 modems can automatically detect whether the file is compressed and will suspend their compression while the compressed file is being transferred. However, MNP Level 5 cannot make this detection and tries to compress all the data being sent from your computer. The result is that compressed files become larger with MNP Level 5 transmission.

Many online services expect you to send only compressed files. They in turn only keep compressed files in their file libraries. Most adhere to one particular standard, most commonly PKZIP. This minimizes the storage space needed to keep the files. When you call these services, you should disable MNP Level 5 compression to get the best file transmission speed. (You don't have to disable V.42 compression.)

If you use an offline reader, however, the situation may be different. Offline readers, covered in Chapter 10, allow you to collect all the messages you want to read on an online service and download them as a file for later reading. This file, which contains your particular selection of messages, is generated when you call the service; it is not stored on the online service.

The sysop may choose not to compress the file, because it takes time to collect the information and it also takes more time to compress it prior to sending. When you are using a modem that has compression features, the data can be compressed during transmission, and the time the system would need to compress the file prior to sending is wasted. If you do not have compression active in your modem, the uncompressed file will take longer to transmit than if the system had compressed it prior to transmission.

I call three BBSs regularly and use their offline reader features. One does not compress the file prior to transmission, and I see a transfer speed of about 2,733 characters per second versus 1,622 when I call the other services and get a precompressed file.

At first glance, this may suggest that 2,733 characters per second is preferable to 1,622 characters per second; this is not true. Suppose that the file I wanted is 100 KB of text. It will take approximately 37 seconds to download at 2,733 characters per second. However, if the file is precompressed by using PKZIP, the 100 KB of text may be only 50 KB in size and will consequently take approximately 31 seconds to download at 1,622 characters per second. When using a modem that can compress if the file is compressable, you get the best performance possible even if the file is not compressed prior to transmission.

Advanced modem users can make the best use of their modem by considering the various options for data compression. You may want to select different configurations for when you call different online services so that you always get the data at the fastest possible speed. This does not necessarily mean you always pick every compression option available.

To find the different phone numbers, look carefully at the BBSs or online service opening screens. Make a note of the alternate numbers and also note the modem names, when available, alongside the numbers.

For example, a local BBS lists five numbers and the modem type attached to each number. The sysop uses a Smart One 2400 as the modem on node 1 (the number he advertises) and USRobotics Sportster 14400s on two of the other nodes. A Twincom 9600 and a USRobotics Dual Standard HST 16800 round out the five nodes.

The packet-switching networks, such as Tymnet and Sprintnet, often supply different local phone numbers. Some of these may be 1200 bps and some 2400 bps with MNP. It is probably worth paying slightly more for the local access call to a 2400 bps with MNP connection than to connect at 1200 bps or even 2400 bps without compression where you may have to spend twice as long on the phone.

My husband and I spent some time analyzing our local and long-distance phone rates. We determined that it was better to call long-distance to a particular online service so that we could connect at 9600 bps and get off the phone sooner than to pay the local phone company charges and connect at 2400 bps with MNP. The situation was complicated by surcharges during the day for one of the connections, different local phone call rates at different times, and different long-distance rates at different times. The results were different from when we last assessed it six months ago.

By the way, look carefully at your long-distance service. Many of them offer special promotions, such as cheap rates on weekends or reduced rates to a special person. You can probably nominate a BBS or online service for the discount. They may only apply for a few months, but you will often only want to call a BBS for a few months and then move on to new adventures. I hate to confess it, but we call a particular BBS more often than we call our family.

The following section explains a method of determining what speed and with what compression and error-detection standards you are connecting to a particular number. You should use this approach to find your best alternative and then use your normal dialing procedures for calling on future occasions.

Finding the full connection story

The general principle described in this section alters S-registers so that you see all the result codes sent from your modem. You apply this method to each of the available phone numbers for an online service and then choose the one that offers you the fastest connection.

Before calling your preferred selection, make certain that you restore your modem's profile to its normal configuration. The described method is intended only as a fact-finding approach — not the best configuration for communicating all the time.

The procedure involves three stages: altering your active configuration to get as many result codes as possible, dialing the required numbers and monitoring the result codes, and restoring your previous configuration.

Check your current configuration by using the view command and the S-register value view command described earlier. Make particular note of the settings for X, W, and S95. The values for X and W are displayed when you issue AT&V, and the value for S95 when you issue ATS95?. (They probably will be X4, W0 or W2, and S95 equal to 0 or 3.)

To alter your active configuration, perform the following steps:

1. Type **ATX4** and press Enter to enable the extended result codes. (This is usually the factory default setting.)

2. Type **ATW1** and press Enter to make the modem return the negotiation progress messages. (The factory default is typically ATW0 with these negotiation messages disabled.)

3. Type **ATS95=44** and press Enter to make the contents of S95 equal to 44. This enables the carrier, protocol, and compression messages.

To dial the number experimentally and record the result codes, perform the following steps:

1. Turn on your printer.

2. Dial the BBS's number manually by using the manual dial feature of your communications program or by issuing the command **ATD** followed by the phone number.

3. Listen to the two modems negotiate, and then as soon as the result codes are displayed, press Print Screen to print the screen's contents. (You may have to be quick to press the Print Screen key before the online service sends a new screen.)

   Alternatively, you can use the capture file feature in your communications program to capture this information. Chapter 10 explains capture files.

4. Issue the **ATH** command (or use the hang up command in your communications program) to hang up the phone and free the BBS for other callers.

5. Examine your printed results. The following example shows the results from calling one number for a local BBS:

```
CARRIER 2400
PROTOCOL: NONE
CONNECT 2400
```

Although my modem is a 9600 bps modem, it could connect only at 2400 bps. The two modems could not agree on a compression protocol, so the connection speed is the same as the carrier speed.

6. Repeat the dialing procedure for the BBS's other phone numbers if necessary.

For example, when I call the same local BBS on another number, I get the following result codes:

```
CARRIER 14400
PROTOCOL: LAP-M
COMPRESSION: V.42BIS
CONNECT 38400
```

This phone number takes advantage of all my modem's features. It uses LAP-M error-control protocol (used with V.42) and uses V.42bis. The carrier transmits data between the two modems at 14,400 bps, but because of the compression, I am actually transmitting data between the two computers at 38,400 bps. This is the phone number I want to use all the time.

7. Reset your modem's parameters. You can use the reset command to restore a saved profile. You also can exit your communications program, turn off your modem, turn it back on again, and restart your communications program. Another method is reissuing the ATX, ATW, and ATS95= commands so that the previous values are restored. Again, use the view commands to verify that your original configuration is restored.

8. Enter the most appropriate phone number for the online service in your dialing directory or activity so that you always call the best number.

Summary

This chapter showed how to make the most of your modem. This involves making adjustments to the modem's configuration to suit your needs as well as connecting to an online service at the best available connection speed.

The modem settings are adjusted by issuing AT commands. You can use *profiles* within your modem to save a series of settings. Additionally, you can issue a series of AT commands to your modem, typically known as an *initialization string*, when you start your communications program. These tools help ensure that your modem is always operating in a known configuration.

Chapter 10 introduces the extra features found in more-advanced communications programs. These help streamline your communications and remove much of the repetition and manual operation. Consequently, you will be able to reduce costs by spending less time online.

10

CHAPTER

Streamlining Your Communications

This chapter discusses features that are available in more-advanced communications software programs. In particular, you will learn many methods for automating your communications, including:

- ❖ Exploiting dialing features
- ❖ Capturing your online session
- ❖ Understanding key macros
- ❖ Using script files
- ❖ Creating script files easily
- ❖ Using offline mail readers

Taking Advantage of Convenient Extras

More-sophisticated communications programs include many features beyond the minimum tools necessary to make a connection with a modem. You should explore to see what tools you can use in your particular situation. A good way to start looking is by examining the chapter headings in the documentation for your communications software. You might find that your communications software includes special features for calling a particular service, or you may be able to create separate dialing directories for each user of your computer.

Each communications program has its own advantages and limitations, and you will probably have your own particular favorite. This chapter explores three main areas of potential communications software commands. The first section gives examples of three typical features that help keep you organized. All users will benefit from these and other comparable features.

Later sections cover three other important features: macros, scripts, and offline mail readers. (You can use offline mail readers even if your communications software does not support them directly. However, some communications programs incorporate them.) In their simplest form, these features benefit all users. However, at their most advanced, they can require extensive knowledge of what you are doing.

The three examples of extras that your communications program may have are *capture files*, *dialing directory options*, and *redialing features*. Your communications software may include exactly the same options as explained here or may have other variations.

Capturing features

Your communications program may have several ways for you keeping a record of what has occurred during a communications session. One feature may be called a *capture file*, *disk capture*, or *printer capture*. Another feature may be called a *scroll back buffer* or a *peruse buffer*.

Peruse buffer

The *peruse buffer*, or *scroll back buffer*, is a temporary storage area. As you communicate, the communications program keeps the information that has "scrolled off" the top of the screen. You can use the peruse buffer to look at something you missed.

"How do I look back at material scrolled off the screen?"

Suppose that you call an online service and use the help command. You see a list of commands or an explanation of a particular command. Assume that you want to know how to edit a message you just entered and used the help edit command to get details. You then use the information to edit your message, but you forget how to tell the remote computer you're finished. You can use the peruse buffer to scroll back your screen and reread the help information.

If your communications program supports a peruse buffer, it's probably active automatically. However, you may be able to alter its size as a configuration option within your program. This size will alter how far back through your communications session you can scroll. With a PC that is not severely limited in memory, you can probably keep at least the equivalent of 10 pages of text.

The actual command for activating the read buffer varies with the communications program. If you press Alt+up-arrow key in QModemPro, you activate the read buffer and you can scroll back. You can then use cursor-direction keys, such as the arrows and Page Up and Page Down, to move around the stored information. You press Esc to return to the terminal screen.

Smartcom for Windows also includes a peruse buffer. You use the up and down scroll arrows in the scroll bar to the right of the online window to access different areas of the temporarily saved information. This is similar to scrolling through information in other Windows applications.

Although using the capture-file options is the preferred way to save a record of your communications session, your communications program probably includes a command for saving the contents of your peruse buffer to a file on disk. This command can be a lifesaver when you make a simple error.

For example, I recently logged onto an online service to send an Internet message to my brother in England. I did not turn on a capture file because I wasn't planning anything that needed saving. However, when I sent the message, it was rejected by the online service.

I wasn't very familiar with the user interface and couldn't quickly find how to read the message I tried to send. I used the peruse buffer to scroll back and find where I had written the message and found the error in my brother's address.

Then, I couldn't find the command to correct the address and decided it was quicker to delete the message and rewrite it. However, I hate retyping. I used the save peruse buffer command and logged off the online system. I used a text editor to isolate the message portion of the saved buffer and saved it as a file.

I then logged onto the online service again and created a new message (while taking a lot of care over typing the address). I then used ASCII upload to rewrite the message text and send the copy of the message. This was not rejected, so I deleted the incorrectly addressed message and logged off the system.

If I'd been better prepared, I would have written the message offline in the first place. However, my original one sentence message expanded when I was actually online, and I had to resort to the peruse buffer to bail myself out of trouble.

Capture file

If your communications program does not include capture-file features, you should consider buying a new program. The capture file feature is invaluable for beginners and advanced users — regardless of whether you are calling a new online service or the same one every time.

Unless you are using offline mail readers (which are discussed later in this chapter), capture files are the easiest and fastest way to gather the large volumes of textual information you see online. They can help you reduce your online time substantially and consequently can reduce your online costs.

Although very useful, the capture file's function is very simple. It saves to disk every action taken and displayed during an online session. This gives you a record of what occurred in the session.

"How do I keep a record of what I've done online?"

The general procedure is to turn on and provide a name for your capture file before making the connection. You then make the connection and perform all the online activities as normal. After logging off the system, you turn the capture file off.

The capture file is an ASCII text representation of your session. You can read it in a text editor, such as DOS 6's EDIT program or Windows Notepad. It shows all the menus and what you typed as well as all the information you read, such as messages and file lists.

If you do not want to save the whole session, you can turn the capture file on and off during the session if you prefer. Other options for this feature vary with the communications program, but they typically include a print capture, where every action is printed on your printer.

If you use scripts to automate your communications session, turning a capture file on and off is one of the most common items you would add to the script. Scripts are covered later in this chapter.

I keep a different capture file for each service that I call. For example, DIALOG.CAP contains a record of my activity with Dialog Information Services and GATEWAY.CAP contains a record of my activity with Gateway 2000's BBS.

Depending on your particular option selections, you can typically make your communications program append new information to the end of an existing capture file or overwrite the existing file.

Note: When you run out of space on your hard disk, examine your capture files to see whether you can delete any of them. Although they are very useful immediately after your communications session, they don't usually have long-term value.

"How do I reduce my online time?"

Capture files can speed your online communication because you don't have to take the time to read everything while you are online. Because you have a faithful record of the events, you can let information scroll by and read it at leisure when your phone bill is not mounting.

Suppose that you call a BBS each week, read the new messages, look and see what new files have been uploaded, and log off. If you are not using a capture file, you must read each message carefully and perhaps take notes on the interesting new files. If you use a capture file, you can save online time in several ways: first when reading messages; and second when looking at file lists.

An online service presents information to you one screen at a time. If you ask to read all the new messages, you see one screenful and then are prompted to press a particular key to see the next screenful. Without a capture file, you have to read these messages one screen at a time. However, with a capture file, you can select the "non-stop" option and scroll all the messages past you at once. You can't read them as they fly by, but they are saved in the capture file. You can then read them offline.

Files lists are similar. Because the list is saved to disk, you can read it offline rather than needing to take notes while online. The capture file also can be useful when more than one person is interested in the information, because the record is permanent, and all the interested people do not need to be present when the information is recorded.

When calling a new online service, particularly one that only gives you limited access until you are registered or subscribe, the capture file is helpful. It allows you to do a lot more in a limited time because you don't have to read everything in detail. You can rapidly explore the service's menus and a few sample messages or file directories and study them at leisure.

Dialing directories

Most PC-based communications programs use the concept of dialing directories. At their most basic, they keep a list of who you want to call and the applicable phone numbers.

Some communications programs, such as Smartcom for Windows, support both analogies, dialing directories and activities and connections list. You can choose the interface that suits you best.

However, your dialing directory or activity and connection documents can keep far more information. After you become familiar with communications, look again at these elements and see how much more streamlining you can do.

A dialing directory entry usually contains additional information other than the number and name. You can usually specify such items as the modem you want to use or the communications parameters, including speed and character format.

When you add new entries, consider basing your entry on an existing entry and using a copy entry command in your dialing directory.

For example, I use two main sets of parameters: one for calling BBSs and one for minicomputers. BBSs are typically PC-based and use the character format of 8N1, and most commercial online services are on minicomputers and use 7E1 as their character format. Additionally, I usually use a packet-switched network, such as Tymnet or Sprintnet, to connect with the commercial online services, and my fastest connection is often only 2400 bps with compression.

When I add a new commercial service, I copy the entry with the 7E1 and slower speed settings. When I add a BBS, I copy a BBS entry. Then, I only need to change a few settings for my new entry.

"Is there an easy way to deal with those busy signals?"

Your dialing directory may allow you to enter multiple phone numbers for the same service. The communications program tries each number in turn. This can be useful when calling a popular BBS. If one number is busy, you can try another.

Note: Many BBSs have a special telephone connection system (supplied by the phone company) that automatically routes calls to another number. You call one number and may actually be connected via another number. Sometimes, calling the alternate number doesn't buy you anything because the BBS will route you there if possible.

Your communications program may allow you to specify a group of entries to call. It then tries each entry in the list in turn. I use this feature regularly. I call about five BBSs early on Saturday morning. I make a group of these BBSs and make the communications program try each one in turn until it gets through to one.

I then collect the mail and other items of interest and log off. Because I use scripts and offline mail readers, most of the actual communications session is automated. When I log off, the communications program continues calling the remaining BBSs in the group. I don't have to supervise closely until it connects with another service.

Other useful dialing directory features include different ways of sorting your entries. For example, you may be able to make your list alphabetical. Of more interest, however, are sorting features that allow you to sort based on the number of times you have called the entry or based on the last date that you called the entry.

I regularly sort my dialing directory based on the number of times that I have called the service. This puts my favorite BBSs and online services at the top of my list.

Dialing features

Your communications program probably includes many options for dialing and redialing. You may, for example, be able to set how long the program should wait before redialing a number or how fast to dial the number.

These options adjust modem settings, some of which are discussed in Chapter 9. For example, a setting in your communications program may change your modem's result codes so that it can detect a busy signal and you can redial the number faster.

"How do I get through to an online service faster?"

Settings, such as speed of dialing and time to wait before redialing, have default values that work for most people. However, with a little trial and error, you can tailor the settings to your situation.

You can make your modem dial a number painfully slowly, and it can take say 10 seconds to dial a number. Obviously, you can make it dial faster and save a few seconds on the connection. However, you also can set your modem to dial so fast that the telephone call does not go through because the telephone exchange (supplied by local phone company) misses some or all of the digits. You need to choose a setting that is fast enough to connect every time but not too slow to waste time.

You can probably alter the time your communications program pauses before dialing the next number. Again, you can make this a very long time and waste time. If you are trying to redial a busy number, someone else might manage to dial between your calls and you will never get through.

On the other hand, if you make the pause time too slow, your phone may not have time to break the connection. You may have experienced that when you hang up the phone and pick it up again immediately; you may have been fast enough that the previous caller is still on the line.

In my situation, I need to make the delay before redialing quite long. I live in a rural area, and my local phone service seems slow to disconnect. Additionally, I use an electronic device called a *fax switch* to monitor my incoming calls and switch automatically to the stand-alone fax machine if the incoming call is from a fax machine. This switch is slow to terminate a connection.

You need to explore your communication program's documentation in detail to find many of the less commonly used features that you may find a boon. (See Appendix C for details on using Smartcom for Windows LE.) I make a point of occasionally going through the online help indexes in all my application programs, including my word processor and spreadsheet, to find words that I am not familiar with. In this way, I can learn new topics and take advantage of some less-known features. I have found many tips on solving computer games this way too!

Your communications program may include other options for dialing. For example, your communications program probably includes a feature that allows you to specify a prefix to your phone numbers. You may be able to specify several of them. This can be used, for example, to dial 1 or 9, a pause, and then 1 in front of long-distance numbers you call from your office. You may be able to keep another prefix for use when you are on the road.

"How do I disable call waiting?"

You should use the prefix feature to disable call waiting. Call waiting and modem use are incompatible. You need to disable call waiting before making a call with a modem. If you don't and a call comes through, the modem assumes that the beep or tone is data and tries to pass it to your computer. Your computer assumes it is data and will make it part of the file you are downloading or try to display it. At best, you will see some random and weird characters on-screen. At worst, your modem and computer will hang and you will have to reboot.

If you add the digits required to disable call waiting (often *70 or 1170) as the prefix sent when you dial a phone number, you don't have to add it to every entry in your dialing directory.

Note: The code for disabling call waiting may vary, depending on where you live, and you may not be able to disable it before a call. *Note:* The dialing prefix does not disable call waiting when someone calls you by modem.

Automating the Communications Process

After you make a few connections, you will begin to realize how much of what you are doing is repetitious. For example, every time you call CompuServe, you always set the same communications parameters, dial the same number, and enter the same series of information, such as user name and password, to connect with the online service.

"How do I avoid all the repetitious typing?"

Your communications program includes many features that remove the repetition in the preparation and connecting process. You also can automate the actual connection in several ways.

If you intend to call a particular person or service only once, you don't need to automate the process. However, you may want to call the same service many times and do the same things each time.

For example, you may want to call your local BBS, read all the new mail in the general section and the word processing section, see any new files that have been uploaded, and check out any new message areas. For the most part, these tasks are repetitious. There may be a different number of messages or files to see, but you will be selecting the same commands each time.

Your communications program probably includes two important features that remove the drudgery of entering the same commands and information each time: *key macros* and *scripts*.

Understanding key macros

A key macro allows you to assign a series of keystrokes to a single key. When you press that key, the communications program sends that string of characters to the modem as if you had typed them at the keyboard.

For example, you can assign your password, last name, and first name to function keys. Then, when you log onto a system and it asks for your last name, you press one key. When it prompts for your first name, you press another key. When you are prompted for your password, you press another single key.

"How do I remember my account numbers?"

You also can assign your online service account number to a key. Because this is often a number, using a key macro removes the need for you to remember it.

Although this is convenient, you need to think carefully about security before programming your password into a key macro. Read your communications software documentation to determine whether anyone else can find your password if you assign it to a key.

This security does not just apply to whether someone will "steal" your online account. If you have children and want to restrict their access, don't use key macros. Most children are completely uninhibited with computers and will press keys to see what will happen.

If you do decide to assign your password to a key, you should use the same password with all your online services. This is relatively easy for BBSs, which allow you to choose your own password. However, most commercial online services assign you with a password, and you may not be able to change it to your favorite. However, to make the best use of most commercial services, you will be using a different communications program that is tailored to that service. In this case, because you will only be calling the one service from this program, a key macro feature will not be applicable anyway.

Using script files

The other automation feature available in more-sophisticated communications programs is scripting. As its name suggests, a script file is a list of events and activities that you want followed exactly. For example, a script file may contain the information necessary to type your last name when the computer you are calling sends the prompt `Last name:`.

You create this script for an entry in your dialing directory or an activity. The script is activated when you dial the particular number. Scripts range in complexity from very simple to very complex.

The ease of creation, maintenance, and flexibility of script files are a major consideration when choosing a communications program. The particular selection depends on your programming ability. The communications program includes what is known as a *scripting language* to help you create these script files.

"*I can't program. Can I use a script?*"

If you have no programming experience, you should choose a communications program that has a scripting language that looks like English. Try reading the examples in the manual to get an idea of whether you will understand the commands. Do not expect to understand everything without experience, but you should at least have some idea of the general tasks being scripted.

Some communications programs include a "learn" feature that can automatically create a script file for you. In fact, you still need to edit the resulting file, but the learning feature can often take you most of way towards creating the file.

The useful qualities of scripts cannot be emphasized enough. This chapter can only scratch the surface of script file potential, but two points are important. Anyone can create scripts and use them. More-sophisticated scripts require more knowledge, but this should not prevent you from experimenting.

The examples in the remainder of this chapter assume a basic understanding of online services, including BBSs and commercial online services. You need to know that you call an online service to read and send messages and find files. The messages may be divided into topic areas known as *conferences*. The files are stored in areas called *libraries*, and the libraries may also be divided by topics. You may also call an online service to *chat* with other people.

When you call an online service, you are prompted for your name and a password. You then move around an online service to the areas of interest by selecting commands from menus. The process involved can be the same every time you call, although the details of what you read, collect, or send may vary each time. Consequently, you can use script files to remove the repetitious portion of the connection.

Calling a BBS with a script

Hayes Smartcom uses simple English to develop scripts. The following script was generated with Smartcom for Windows. It automatically connects to the Online With Hayes BBS and issues your name and password. By examining this script, you can learn how to create and modify your own scripts.

```
START CONNECTION , "9, 1 800 874 2937" ;
IF NOT CONNECTED THEN STOP "Failed to connect." ;
WAIT FOR PROMPT "First Name?" ;
TYPE LINE "Caroline" ;
```

```
TYPE LINE "Halliday" ;
WAIT FOR PROMPT "Is this correct?" ;
TYPE TEXT "y" ;
WAIT FOR PROMPT "Enter Your Password:" ;
TYPE LINE @"330<J#~6SD$ ; {Scrambled}
WAIT FOR PROMPT "-Press Any Key;" ;
TYPE KEY RETURN_Key ;
WAIT FOR PROMPT "Command:" ;
```

This Smartcom script is written in simple English to make developing scripts as easy as possible. Don't be intimidated by the appearance of this script. Ignore how it looks and concentrate on what it says, and you'll find it relatively easy to understand.

This script begins by using a START CONNECTION command to dial the Online With Hayes BBS telephone number. Then, the script waits until the BBS asks you to enter your name and password, which it enters automatically. The password is scrambled in the script for your security.

Tip: If you don't know exactly what the remote system's prompt is, enter a WAIT FOR statement that continues after 5-10 seconds. This tip is useful if you know that the service will ask you for your name or other information, but you don't know the exact prompt.

Tip: A WAIT FOR TIME OF DAY statement or similar delay statement can be used to start a script when you are away from your desk, such as at night when the rates are lower.

Using a script editor

To edit the preceding script, you use a script editor within the communications software or use a text editor. Smartcom for Windows LE (included with this book) can run but not create and edit scripts. Smartcom for Windows can run, create, and edit scripts by using SCOPE, (Simple COmmunications Programming Environment).

Most script editors enable you to use all of the major commands, such as connecting, printing, saving, typing, sending, receiving, waiting, hanging up, and quitting. These commands can be combined to automate almost any activity that you can perform manually with your communications software.

The preceding script can be extended to download all of your new mail messages, check for new files in your favorite area, or print all of your mail messages and log off. You can also modify this script to call other online services.

The following section shows a simple script file that was automatically generated by using the communications program learn feature. The section following takes this script file and enhances it.

Using learn features

A good communications program will include a scripting language feature and will have a command that automatically generates scripts for you. The learn feature is similar to a tape recorder. The program watches all the activities and learns that when you see a particular prompt from the remote system, you want to type a particular response.

"How do I create a script file?"

Because each online service you call is different, you need to generate a script file for an entry in your dialing directory. In most communications programs, one of the fields in the directory is for the script file's name. After the script file is written and associated with a dialing directory entry, the script file is executed every time you call that dialing directory entry.

The script creation procedure in QModemPro, used as the example in this chapter, is comparable with other communications programs. You start the communications program and reach the dialing directory. You select the entry of interest and activate the learn command.

In QModemPro, this is done by pressing **Q** to activate the QuickLearn command. If you have not specified a name for your script file, you are prompted to enter a filename. Type a name that relates to the entry you have chosen. For example, if you call your local BBS regularly and it is called the Nearby BBS, you may want to create a script file called NEARBY.

QModemPro displays a Q next to the entry, showing that when you dial this entry, it will generate a script file automatically. You then call the online service and go through your usual connection process.

You will create the best script file if you type carefully and only add activities that you will perform every time you call. Remember that you are recording your activities so that they can be repeated. For example, if you want to automate reading the mail, you do this activity when QuickLearn is active. However, you probably will not want to reply to a message each time, so you would not do that during this session.

The following is a sample script file generated by using QuickLearn.

```
;
;   QuickLearn Script generated at 06:53:56   02-24-94
;   May require editing before use.
;
TurnON    8_BIT
TurnOFF   LINEFEED
TurnOFF   XON/XOFF
TurnON    NOISE
TurnON    MUSIC
TurnON    SCROLL
TurnOFF   PRINT
TurnOFF   SPLIT
TurnON    STATUSLN
TurnOFF   DOORWAY
TurnOFF   CAPTURE
Capture   C:\QMPRO\CAPTURE\NEARBY.CAP
TimeOut   30      ; Set Waitfor for 30 seconds
Waitfor   "What is your first name?"
Delay     100
Send      "caroline^M"
Waitfor   "What is your last name?"
Delay     100
Send      "halliday^M"
Waitfor   "Password? [                ]^[[15D"
Delay     100
Send      "secretone^M"
Waitfor   "ue, [N]onStop, [S]top? [C]^[[D^[[D"
Delay     100
Send      "^M"
Waitfor   "ue, [N]onStop, [S]top? [C]^[[D^[[D"
Delay     100
Send      "^M"
Waitfor   "ue, [N]onStop, [S]top? [C]^[[D^[[D"
Delay     100
Send      "^M"
Waitfor   "iew the bulletin menu? [Y]^[[D^[[D"
Delay     100
Send      "n^M"
Waitfor   "Command >> ?"
Delay     100
Send      "m"
Exit
```

This script automatically types my name and password, provides appropriate responses to reach the BBS's main menu, and then selects the Mail menu.

"What's in a script file?"

The problem many nonprogrammers have with understanding programs is that programs normally contain introductory information before they get to the meat of the program. The introductory information is important because it sets the rules that apply to the whole program, but it can be difficult to understand for a beginner.

Unfortunately, script files are similar, but fortunately, the introductory material is brief. Consider this script file as having a title and three parts. The title section is the lines beginning with semicolons. Part one contains the preparatory settings and consists of the lines beginning TurnON and TurnOFF. Part two is the line beginning TimeOut, and the remainder is part three of the script.

The first few lines that begin with semicolons are comments and make up the script's title. They explain that the script file was created by using the QuickLearn feature.

The next group of lines, the initial settings, beginning with TurnON and TurnOFF, are the QModemPro settings that were current when the script was created. For example, the TurnON NOISE line means that when a beep or bell is sent, you will hear it.

The TurnOFF CAPTURE line closes any open capture file. It means that if you have just called another service and have forgotten to stop recording the session, you will not record this new session with the other one.

The next line in the script turns on the capture file for your current session. In this example, it is a file named NEARBY.CAP and is saved in the subdirectory on drive C named \QMPRO\CAPTURE.

The next section in the script file contains the rules you want applied to everything in the remainder of the script. In this example, there is only one line, but this is the area where you probably will want to add lines to the script file. Before considering the TimeOut line, look at the remainder of the script.

The remainder of this script file is a series of groups of three lines. The first line in each group starts with a Waitfor instruction; the second line is a Delay; and the third line is a Send instruction.

Each set is similar; you want the script to wait until it sees a particular prompt. Then you want it to pause momentarily, and then send a particular response. However, there is a chance that the BBS or online service you call may change its menus, and your script file may never see the precise prompt. Consequently, it will then wait for a response forever.

The line beginning TimeOut specifies that if at anytime the script had waited longer than 30 seconds, you will be told so you can abort running the script.

The core of the script is the sets of three lines. Examine the first one in detail. This line instructs the script file to pause until the remote system sends the sequence of characters What is your first name?.

Note: The information in quotes must be received exactly for the script file to respond.

When you call an online system with this script, it processes the beginning of the script up to the first line beginning with WaitFor. It then stops until it sees the appropriate characters.

After these are received, you want the script to pause briefly. The Delay 100 line makes the script pause for 1/10 of a second. You need this delay because some online services get confused if you respond too quickly. They send the characters and must prepare for a response. If you respond too quickly, they may miss your response.

Another script language may not use precisely the same commands, such as WaitFor and Delay; however, it will have comparable ones with similar names. This is similar to word processors that have slightly different commands for doing the same thing.

After the delay, the Send command instructs the script to send the characters enclosed in quotes. In this example, it is the sequence caroline followed by Enter.

The actual line in the script has a caret (^) symbol followed by an M. The ^M is this script language's representation of the Enter key. Because the QuickLearn function recorded this, you would not have to know this to write the script, but you need to know to understand what the script instruction is.

The next three lines in the script are similar to the previous three. The script file sends my last name followed by Enter when it sees the prompt What is your last name?.

The next three lines are worth looking at closely to understand. The first line seems simple except for the ^[[15D on the end. This is similar to the ^M in that it is the script language's method of writing down an action that is not normally written.

To understand it (and the ^M), you need to remember that you are using a particular terminal emulation to communicate with the remote computer. In this example, the BBS is using ANSI emulation.

In your communications manual, there will be a table listing the program's representations of the special characters used in the current terminal emulation. For example, ANSI emulation has special characters for carriage return, clear screen, and delete.

The QModemPro emulation shows that the character represented by ^[[D is cursor left. The line that shows ^[[15D means that the cursor is moved 15 positions to the left. This is because when you are prompted for your password, the remote computer writes the prompt Password?, then a space, then an opening square bracket. It then leaves 14 spaces and places the closing square bracket. When it moves the cursor 15 spaces left, the cursor appears to you immediately after the opening square bracket waiting for you to type your password.

The script then delays and sends the password followed by Enter. By the way, as covered in Chapter 14, choose your password carefully. The example given is not suitable because it is easy to guess.

The remainder of the script gets you past the introductory material on the BBS and to the main menu. At the main menu, the prompt on this sample BBS is Command >> ?. For the example, the mail command is chosen, and the script ends with the Exit command.

At this point, you have gotten past all the repetitive material you have to do every time you log onto the system and have reached the part you are really interested in — the message area in this case.

Creating script files

You can generate scripts that are as simple as the previous example, or you can create more complex ones. For example, if you always check the new files and the new messages on a BBS, you can extend your script to look at these items automatically.

Depending on the sophistication of the script language supplied with your communications program, you can make the script do more-complex things, such as download and upload files, run other scripts from within a script, wait for a specific time, or signal you at specific points.

You can create script files from scratch. They are only ASCII text files. However, it is much easier and more efficient to base them on a QuickLearn version of the procedure. You are less likely to make mistakes.

As an example of the type of thing all users are likely to want to do to improve a script file, the following example extends the preceding example. The preceding example performs the log on process and moves you to the message menu. You might extend it to read new messages, perhaps in several conference areas, and get lists of the new files.

When you add more tasks to your script, you can quickly make very long scripts due to much repetition. Consider the preceding example.

The prompt `"ue, [N]onStop, [S]top? [C]^[[D^[[D"` appears three times. This is the last characters of the prompt `[C]ontinue, [N]onStop, [S]top?`. You are expected to press C to see the next screen of text, N to make the material scroll by nonstop, and S to stop reading. The actual syntax of this prompt varies with the online service, but all the services include a similar prompt.

If you use a capture file, you don't need to see the material one screen at a time and can let it scroll by continuously because you will be reading it at a later time. Additionally, if you are reading messages, the number of pages of text that displayed depends on how many messages there are. Using the nonstop answer in your script will work for more situations than using the continue answer.

You can write a line for your script file that looks for this prompt and supplies the same response every time it occurs. This command goes in the early section of the script file along with the time-out command. The `When` command can be used to make the script file look for alternate text strings when the `WaitFor` command is active.

To change this script, you would add the following line:

```
When "ue, [N]onStop, [S]top? [C]^[[D^[[D" "n^M"
```

This line goes immediately after the `Timeout` line and before the main portion of the script. Whenever the script is waiting for a particular prompt from the remote computer, it also looks for the prompt in the `When` line. When it sees this prompt, it will send `n` followed by `Enter` to make the computer display the information nonstop.

In QModemPro, you can have up to 20 `When` commands active at once. Other scripting languages will have slightly different commands and will have different limitations. You use the `When` command to amalgamate the repetitive sections in your script file only if you always want to respond in the same way.

Another modification to the script file is moving the turning on of the capture file after you enter your password. This prevents recording your last name and first name every time in the capture file. However, many online services display the time and date when you first log on and list important new information, such as new features and new phone numbers, so you shouldn't move the capture feature too far down or you will miss information.

Be sure to read your script file before using it. As the comment in the title says, you may need to edit it before using. This is particularly true if you are a poor typist. You need to correct your typing errors rather than make the same mistakes every time you call a particular online service.

Script files can be compared with DOS batch files. Everyone needs a couple of batch files, even if only AUTOEXEC.BAT. But with a little practice, you can create very sophisticated batch files that automate many tasks. Programmers have developed whole systems successfully with DOS batch files.

Similarly, script files can be elementary, such as the example here, or can be very advanced. I use a script file for almost all the online services I call. At the very least, they log me on and turn on a capture file. The more-sophisticated ones allow me to do all of my online activity without my physical intervention. I am on and off online services within 15 minutes and have literally hours worth of information to read.

Understanding offline mail readers

Offline mail readers are becoming increasingly popular, especially as we connect with more and more people online. These programs can be features in your communications program or, more typically, programs that you use in association with your communications program.

"How can I collect lots of messages fast?"

When you call an online service that supports offline readers, BBSs most commonly, you can download your mail as a file instead of reading it while you are online. This is comparable to reading your mail while standing at the mail box or being able to collect and deliver your mail but going home to read and respond to all your mail.

The general principle is that you call an online service and download a file known as a *mail packet* that contains all your messages. You then log off from the service. You then run your mail reading program and read the messages. As you read the messages, you may choose to save them, reply to them, or discard them. Any replies you create are saved in a file and are uploaded when you next collect messages.

Your communications program may include an offline mail reader, or you can obtain an offline mail reader as a separate program. Many readers are shareware and are available for downloading from online services. Although different mail reader formats are used, by far the most common is the QWK format (pronounced *quick*).

Because the online service you call must support the offline mail reader that you use, you can only use the offline mail reader format that is supported by the online service that you call.

Resource Guide to Offline Readers

Offline readers are incorporated as a part of some communications programs and are also available as stand-alone products. The following are some available products:

1stReader
Sparkware
P. O. Box 386
Hendersonville, TN 37077-0386

Blue Wave Offline Mail Reader
Cutting Edge Computing
P.O. Box 90476
Burton, MI 48509
(313) 743-9283

OFFLINE
Harvey Parisien
Box 323, Station A
Kingston, Ontario, Canada K7M 6R2

Off-Line Xpress (OLX)
Mustang Software Inc.
P.O. Box 2264
Bakersfield, CA 93303
(805) 873-2500

QModemPro
Mustang Software Inc.
P.O. Box 2264
Bakersfield, CA 93303
(805) 873-2500

Robomail
Parsons Consulting
5020 S. Lake Shore Drive, Suite 3301
Chicago, IL 60615-3249

Silver Xpress
Santronics Software
30034 S.W. 153 Court
Leisure City, FL 33033

WinQwk
Doug Crocker
PO Box 1454
Kent, WA 98035-1454

The online service can choose where to place the available commands. Consequently, you may find different commands in different places, depending on the service that you call. However, the majority of BBSs put the commands that access the mail reader with the other mail or message commands.

For example, Figure 10-1 shows the main menu from Software Creations BBS. The QMail Door option is listed at the bottom of the Mail Commands.

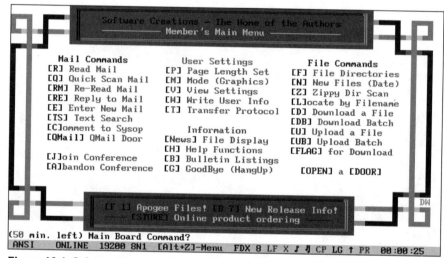

Figure 10-1: Software Creations Main Menu. The QMail Door command provides access to the mail reader features of this BBS.

Other BBSs may require you to choose mail or messages from a main menu and then list the commands for using a mail reader within the mail or message menu itself.

A *door* on a BBS is a method that allows the BBS to add extra programs and consequently extra functionality that the BBS software does not support directly. As a user, you select a door and gain access to other features. In the case of a mail reader, you access the program that creates the mail packet file that is downloaded to your computer.

When you first choose the Quick Mail Door on a BBS (or other similarly named feature), you have to perform a configuration procedure. The BBS has a series of conferences and message areas that are shown to you. You then specify the conferences of interest by choosing from the list.

When the configuration is complete, you can choose to download your selected mail. The BBS's mail reader program collects all the selected mail and makes it into a single file. You download this file to your computer and exit from the mail reading area of the BBS.

After you get offline, you start your mail reading program (from within your communications program—if it is included—or from the DOS prompt). The mail reader shows you a list of the mail packet files you have collected. You will have one for each of the services that you have accessed and used their mail reader functions.

After choosing the mail packet by name, the mail reader uncompresses the mail packet and displays a list of the conferences you have chosen to scan.

Note: As mentioned in Chapter 9, not all online services compress their mail packets.

Figure 10-2 shows a typical example collected from Mustang Software Inc., manufacturers of QModemPro communications software and WildCat BBS software.

A *mail packet* contains messages from the conferences you have expressed interest in. In Figure 10-2, you see a list of conferences. Eight of the conferences have a dot between the number and its name. This dot indicates that on this occasion (in this mail packet) you downloaded mail from those conferences. The conferences without a dot do not include mail this time (in this mail packet).

```
 File  Edit  Search  View  Message  Options  Window  Help      | Mem: 172k
[■]                            MUSTANG                              2=[↑]
 Hello  Session  News  Bulletins  Files  Goodbye  Attachments  Conference

        Outbox      (0/0)         17   WC!IMDigi
        Inbox       (0/0)         18   Alias
   0   Private                    21  •WC!UUCP        (36)
   1  •WILDCAT!      (246)        24  •RIPGraphic     (39)
   2  •QMODEMQMP     (68)         35   UUCP-EMAIL
   3  •DoorHelp      (42)         36   UUCP-QM
   4   ExtProtos                 37   UUCP-WC
   5   Net&Echo
   6   ModemHelp
   7   LANtastic
   8  •Novell        (16)
   9   DESQview
  10   TOMCAT!
  11   SysopChat
  12   OLX-SLMR
  13  •wcPRO!help    (6)
  14  •3rdParty      (14)
  15   QMODEM-TD
  16   WILDCAT-TD
                                                            4:47 pm
 F1-Help  Enter-Open  Ins-Index
```

Figure 10-2: Typical mail packet conference list. The conferences and the selected messages are shown in this summary.

Figure 10-2 shows that eight conferences contain mail that was downloaded in this packet. They have a dot between the conference number and its name. For example, the RIPGraphic conference (number 24) contains 39 messages for reading.

You then read the messages in turn and can discard, save, or reply to them as you choose. The precise methods depend on the particular mail reader.

When you next access the online service and select the BBS's mail reader features, any messages that you have replied to are uploaded as a file. The selected conferences are scanned for new messages, and the resulting file is downloaded to your computer.

Taglines

One area of lighter online entertainment is message taglines. As you read messages online, you will find that many have cute footnotes. These are known as *taglines*. Most offline readers include the capability to add a tagline to your replies. You also can find many utilities for creating, managing, and adding your own taglines to your messages.

Many taglines are extremely corny, but they certainly help liven some of the messages. It is considered acceptable to "steal" someone else's tagline and use it in another message. Although not included in the following examples, some taglines make good use of ASCII characters, such as happy faces and musical notes. Others use emoticons, such as :), to show emotions. You typically read an emoticon by tilting your head to the left. For example, :) is a smiling face with the colon as the eyes and the parenthesis as the mouth.

The following are examples of taglines:

```
"640K ought to be enough for anybody." - Bill Gates 1981
"Age and treachery beat youth and talent every time."
"Creativity is the result of a BOARD mind"
"Daddy, what does FORMATTING DRIVE C mean?"
"He's dead Jim! Get his tricorder, I'll get his wallet."
"I need a home run hitter" he said ruthlessly.
"Is that computer still on the phone?"
"Misspelled? Impossible. Error-correcting modem."
"Press to test." <click> "Release to detonate."
"Put knot yore trussed in spel chequers!"
"When in doubt, use a bigger hammer."
```

Combining the script feature with a BBS's mail reader program can make your connections completely automated. My typical script file is the same as in this chapter, except that the final command accesses the Quick Mail reader rather than the mail reading command.

When the mail reader is accessed, the script selects the commands for downloading a mail packet. You can add the commands to disconnect from the system and make the whole process automatic. However, my script finishes and sounds an alarm after downloading the mail packet. This allows me to download any files from the file library that I am interested in.

Summary

This chapter introduced a variety of methods for streamlining your communications sessions. These procedures include taking advantage of the many features in your communications program. These can be organizational and involve options in your dialing directory and other connection options.

Your communications program will probably include commands that help streamline your communications while online. Most important of these features are key macros and scripts. If you are interested in messages, offline readers are important, either as a feature of your communications program or as a separate program.

Chapter 11 explains ways that you can make the most of your fax modem.

11

CHAPTER

Making the Most of Your Fax Modem

This chapter covers tools and techniques for making the most of your fax modem. Specifically, this chapter discusses the following topics:

- Reconfiguring your fax modem
- Choosing file formats
- Adding company logos and signatures
- Streamlining fax document sending and receiving
- Using special fax software features, such as mail merge and transaction logs

Essentials for Fax Software

A typical fax modem has fewer adjustable features than a typical data modem. When you send or receive a fax document, the transmission portion is automated and does not require user intervention. The user must prepare the document for sending and read the received document but does not need to interact during the transmission process itself.

A data modem, in comparison, typically requires user interaction during the communications session, but less preparatory work is necessary.

As Chapter 4 explains, your fax modem requires a serial port and comes supplied with its own fax software. Although fax modems communicate with each other by using internationally accepted standards, there is less uniformity in the way the modems are controlled by the fax software.

Consequently, you are more limited with your fax modem software selection than you are with your data modem communication software. You probably will use the fax software supplied with your fax modem and not purchase an alternative. However, you may want to supplement the fax software by using other software utility programs. You will use the fax software for the actual document transmission but are more likely to do some, if not all, of the document preparation with alternative software.

As Chapter 7 explains, your fax software can accept documents in a variety of formats and may be capable of preparing such items as a cover sheet. It can dial a telephone number and send the document to a receiving fax. The fax software also includes programs that allow you to receive a fax document and save it as a file on your disk. It probably includes a file viewer so that you can see the received document.

Although fax software is not usually as sophisticated as data modem communication software, you can look for various options when choosing a fax modem. Additionally or alternatively, you can supplement the software with other utilities.

This chapter focuses on the extras that are found in some fax software programs. In most cases, these are equivalent to the extras found in communications programs. For example, a fax program may include many options in the dialing directory configuration that allow you to sort in various ways or have several directories.

Exploiting Your Fax Software Features

This chapter divides the extra features possible in your fax software into two general topics: the features that affect your productivity by streamlining fax transmission and receipt and the features that affect the quality of the fax document and the feasibility of sending it.

Productivity features include mail merging, batch sending, and transaction logs; and feasibility features include appropriate configuration, optimum file format, and adding signatures and company logos to your fax document.

Knowing what you have

Like data modems and communication software, if you already own and use a fax modem, you should look carefully at your documentation to see whether there are any features you are not using. Check the table of contents and the index for feature names you aren't familiar with.

For example, you may find that your fax software includes a screen-capture program. This may enable you to send an image stored in a format that the fax software cannot accept directly. You can load the screen capture program, display the image, and capture it in a format acceptable to the fax software.

To make the best use of your fax modem, you also should be familiar with the other application programs you use, such as word processors and spreadsheets. The other application programs fall into two categories: the programs you use to create a document for fax transmittal and utility programs that can help prepare the document after creation.

Reconfiguring your fax modem

When you first installed your fax modem, you probably selected the default settings or only changed the minimum number of settings to make your fax modem work. You should take the time to look again at your fax modem configuration and determine whether other changes are appropriate.

"How can I make the fax modem work faster?"

Although fewer options are available than with a data modem, first look at the configuration of your fax modem to see whether you selected the correct device. Most fax modem software is written to work with several different fax modems, and you should choose the exact model name and number wherever possible. If you choose a different model, you may still be able to use your fax modem, but you may not be using all the advanced features.

The fax modem configuration, particularly if you have a data modem and fax modem combination, probably includes other options that you may not have bothered to alter when you installed the modem. Many of these settings are parallel with those found on a data modem. For example, you may be able to choose between tone and pulse dialing, alter the speed of dialing, make the fax modem detect busy signals, and alter the delays before redialing.

Chapter 10 explains some of these types of options in more detail. You can typically shave seconds off every dialing procedure and minimize wasted time by choosing appropriate configuration settings. The manufacturer chooses default settings that are going to work in almost all situations. Because these settings are conservative, you can probably get better performance.

For example, I have a less-than-optimum phone system partly due to my electronic switch that routes my phone calls. It takes several seconds for the electronic switch to hang up the phone. Consequently, I cannot reduce the delay between when the fax modem detects a busy signal and hangs up the phone and when it redials. However, when I have a dial tone, my telephone system accepts tone signals very fast, so I can increase the dialing speed and save time.

You also should check your communication parameters to verify that you are selecting the fastest speed that your fax modem can use. If the fax machine you are communicating with is not as fast as yours, the two fax modems will negotiate a lower speed automatically. Consequently, you can always configure your fax software so that it tries to operate at the fastest speed.

On a data modem, there are times when you won't want your modem to try to connect at the fastest possible speed, such as when you pay an online service for connect time. The faster speed often has a premium cost, and the slower speed may be more economical although it takes longer to get the data. Chapters 5 and 13 cover the topics of reducing online costs for data modems.

File format options

Although file formats for your fax modem are introduced in Chapter 7, this chapter revisits the topic because understanding and selecting appropriate file formats for your fax documents is the key to making the most of your fax modem.

Fax software is usually relatively unsophisticated when compared with desktop publishing programs or word processors. If you only want to send a short text message, you can use the editor in your fax software and don't need to consider many of the advanced options. However, if you send longer documents, particularly if these documents were created in a variety of application programs, you need to consider your options carefully.

Think of it as the difference between typical documents that you distribute in printed form. If you use a Post-It note or other scrap of paper, you're only scribbling a quick note and attaching it to another prepared document. If you send an internal memo, it may have a standard layout, but you don't usually need to be too concerned about its appearance or the detailed contents. However, if you prepare a document that has a wider distribution, especially when it's being sent to customers, the presentation becomes important. Not only is the content important, but the precise layout may need to conform with a corporate image.

"How do I get a document into the fax software?"

The editor in your fax software probably can handle the simple text messages where the content is brief and the format is not particularly important. You can probably create a standard fax cover sheet or use one of the supplied examples to provide a consistent image. However, you won't want to depend on this editor for long document creation, particularly when the presentation is important.

Your fax software can accept documents from your other application programs. However, it can support only a limited number of file format types, and even those it may not support completely.

Every application program has its unique way of storing the data from your documents. For example, a word processing document includes text and the special codes that indicate the word processor formatting for the text. One code indicates that the line is centered, and another shows a font change. Although you may not actually see these codes when you use the word processor, they are important when you try to send the document as a fax document with your fax software.

Note: Your fax software may accept files from WordPerfect and Microsoft Word. However, it will not support the formats from future versions of the software. Suppose that your fax software supports WordPerfect Version 5.1 but not 6.0 or later. You must understand how this affects the document you send. If WordPerfect 6.0, for example, uses different codes for centering text or creating tables than WordPerfect 5.1, your fax software cannot translate a document created in WordPerfect 6.0 correctly.

You have various alternatives for getting your document in a form suitable for sending as a fax document. You may be able to save your document in a different format from within your application program. For example, almost all word processors can save documents as ASCII text, and almost all fax software can accept ASCII text. However, ASCII text does not include different fonts or many text formatting features. Your word processor may be able to save your document in a format comparable with a previous version, as WordPerfect 6.0 can save files in WordPerfect 5.1 format.

Many word processors, spreadsheets, databases, and other application programs also can save files in alternative formats. Not only does this make it easier to transfer document files between application programs, but it gives you a better chance of being able to send a fax document that looks as much like the original as possible. A less desirable option is to use a utility program that captures the file from within your application program.

"Why doesn't my fax document look right?"

Even if your fax software claims to support a particular word processor, you need to experiment to see how complete the support is. Using an alternative file-saving format from your application program might give better output. You should do this experimentation before you have an impending deadline.

You should experiment by sending some sample documents. Examine any document viewer available in your fax software before the document is sent. Then send the document to another fax machine. (If you have two phone lines, you may want to borrow a fax machine from a friend to try this in the privacy of your own home.) Compare the received document with the original and see where the differences occur.

You won't have many problems if you send text, but you can run into problems when you send other document types. Try to include in your sample document any features you may be using in real documents. For example, if you use tables in your word processor, add graphic images on your pages, or send spreadsheets, see whether these are accepted by the fax software. If not, devise an alternative method of document preparation. This may involve using screen-capture programs, using print-capture programs, or adjusting the fonts and features you use in your documents.

Similar rules apply to graphic files. Your fax software may accept files in different graphic formats, but the level of support varies greatly. Graphics often have additional problems that you may not be aware of. Your fax modem sends documents in black and white—not color. (Color fax machines are likely to become available in the next couple of years but not yet.)

Improving Your Fax Quality

Fax modems remove one of the problems found with paper documents. You won't send a dirty document. For example, your manuscript won't have a coffee mug circle on it, dirty fingerprints, or creased pages. However, you can run into problems that affect the quality of the document you are sending.

A stand-alone fax machine is like a copy machine. The received document will look like the original document. The clarity will not be as good, but the layout, content, and completeness will be the same.

When using a fax modem, you need to consider the document's layout, content, and completeness. Experiment with your fax software so that you understand what the cover sheet and a document created in the fax software's text editor will look like. If your document is imported from another application, such as a word processor or graphic program, use the fax software's viewer to preview the fax and check the format of the document that you actually send. Many formatting details may be lost in the translation from your application program to the fax software's format.

You need to carefully consider sending color documents. Your fax modem will send documents in black and white. When you send a color document, the results are often surprising and very difficult to read. Colors that contrast well on-screen don't have the same contrast when sent in black and white.

I regularly create screen shots for publication with my articles and books. Many are reproduced in black and white. Some magazines specify the color combinations I should use to create a well-contrasting screen. I have a special color scheme for Windows, for example. It looks hideous in color, but it looks very good in black and white. I often change the background color in other application programs so that they reproduce well in black and white. If you send color pictures by fax modem, you should apply similar modifications for clarity.

Most graphic programs are in color. When you send a color graphic image, your fax software converts it to black and white before sending. This can dramatically affect the clarity of the received document, because colors that contrast well do not necessarily get converted to shades of gray that contrast well.

Graphic file formats are more standardized in some ways and more subject to different interpretation than text files in other ways. Most fax software accepts graphic images in at least PCX and a TIFF format. However, there are a couple of variations of PCX format and several different standards for TIFF files. Because you cannot read the files, finding the correct format to save the file and the correct format to import the file into the fax software is a question of experimentation.

If you cannot find a suitable format to save your files and import them into your fax software, consider a separate file-conversion program.

You also need to consider the file format for the documents that you receive. Remember that you only receive a graphic image. If you want to do more than view the document and discard it, you need a graphic program that can accept a file format that can be generated by your fax software. Again, a file-conversion program may be necessary.

"Will an OCR program save me retyping fax documents?"

To convert a received document into text, you need an OCR (optical character recognition) program. This is unlikely to be supplied with your fax software, although some manufacturers are adding it as a premium option. OCR programs vary in their capability to translate the graphics into text. Some are practically useless, and others do a reasonable job. The best can often achieve accuracy exceeding 99 percent.

Note: 99.9 percent accuracy on a single page of text still results in about two errors per page. If the document is in an unusual font or is not a particularly clean image, it may be quicker and more accurate to have the document retyped.

If you find that you regularly convert fax documents into text, consider whether you are using the correct tool for the job. You may be better off using a data modem to transfer the document as a file rather than as a fax document. PCs and modems are inexpensive enough so that purchasing an additional PC and modem may be justified when you consider the time and costs involved in conversion of graphic files to text and correction or retyping.

How OCR Works

When you receive a fax document, it is stored as a graphic image. A particular page of information is represented as a series of rows of dots. The usual description is black dots on a white page. There are typically 300 dots per inch in the horizontal direction and 150 rows per inch in the vertical direction. Text documents are also represented in this way.

The human eye is easily deceived and, rather than seeing the page as lots of dots, sees the dots in groups. You see lines of text. They might appear a bit grainy, but you usually can interpret the dots correctly.

However, your word processor, spreadsheet, database, or other text application cannot interpret the dots as text, and to load the fax image into a text application for editing, you must convert the dots into text by using an optical character recognition (OCR) program.

An OCR program is designed to look at a page of dots and "see" the dots in groups; hopefully each group is a character of text. After dividing the page into these groups, it looks at each group in turn and tries to match the pattern of dots with a character in its font library. OCR is essentially a guessing program. The program guesses each of the characters on the page.

On a clean fax document where the background is not smudged, the lines of text are straight, and the font is not too ornate, the OCR program can make very good guesses, and you probably will only need to correct a few characters. You then save the interpreted page as a text file and can put it into your text application for editing. An OCR program can only interpret the material it is given and can only match it to the character shapes it understands. You won't get good results from poor-quality fax documents.

If the page is too light, the characters will have parts missing, and the OCR program may choose the wrong character. For example, if the descender on a *y* is light, the OCR program may think the correct letter is a *v* or a *u*. On the other hand, if the fax document is too dark, the letters will be blurry, and the OCR program will have too much information for a character. For example, it will have trouble discriminating between *m* and *rn*.

Handwritten documents are not written with the same accuracy as typed or printed documents. Even if you look at one person's handwriting, the characters are not written the same each time. One time, a letter may be smaller than another or written at more of an angle. OCR programs do not do a good job of interpreting handwriting.

The OCR program will also have trouble interpreting some fonts, even ones that appear simple. Most people understand why interpreting script fonts, which emulate ornate handwriting, is difficult. However, many OCR programs have trouble even with simple italic fonts. The characters in an italic font lean, and the OCR program usually tries to divide the graphic image into a row of rectangles. When it does this with an italic font, it is more likely to get part of the previous character and possibly the next character in a rectangle it considers a character.

Adding a company logo

Your fax software may include features that allow you to add clip art or other graphic images to your fax document. You can use this feature to add a company logo or a signature.

The flexibility of this feature depends on the individual fax software. However, the general principle is to place a graphic image in a small area of your document. In the case of a company logo, you may want to place this on the cover sheet for your fax so that your fax cover sheet maintains your company image and reflects your standard letterhead.

Some fax software enables you to add several graphic images on a page and have flexible placement options. Others are more restricted in number and location for these images.

"How do I sign a fax document?"

You can treat a signature in the same way as a logo or clip art image. You place it as a graphic image in the desired location. Again, the flexibility in placement depends on the fax software. Usually, however, you can add this image only to your cover sheet or a document you have created in the fax software's text editor.

To add this image, either as a logo or a signature, you need to get the desired graphic into electronic form. The most common method is to use a scanner and scan the image into your computer. Alternatively, you may be able to use a graphic program and re-create the image electronically.

You can purchase scanners that range from very inexpensive hand-held devices, to large, fast, page scanners that can scan engineering drawings. In general, you get what you pay for. However, many scanners include an OCR program as part of the supplied software.

Note: You should think carefully before putting your signature on your computer in electronic form. You must understand the security implications and your vulnerability. Anyone who has access to the files on your computer will have access to your signature. On the other hand, having your signature stored electronically compensates for one of the fax modem's shortcomings: its inability to send handwritten material.

Streamlining Your Fax Sending and Receiving

Because you don't interact with your fax modem while it sends or receives a fax document, the methods you employ to streamline your fax use relate more to the preparation and organization of your document and phone books than to techniques applicable during the actual transmission.

Document organization

Your fax software may include various options that can help you organize your fax documents. You usually can select directories where your received fax documents are placed. You may have other organizational options, such as a default directory for a copy of sent documents, or other storage aids.

"Where are my received fax documents?"

If you will send or receive many fax documents, you should decide on a procedure so that you know where you stand. You should employ a file-naming method that you can understand so that you can separate the read files from the unread files.

Think about your file-naming and organization system carefully. DOS has a serious limitation by allowing only eight characters in the main part of a filename. You need to choose a naming system that you will understand several months or years from now.

You also need to separate fax documents into different locations. At its simplest, you need an area for documents ready to send, another for sent documents, another for received documents, and another for received and read documents. Bear in mind that the received document is a graphic file, and graphic files tend to be extremely large. You can rapidly fill a hard disk if you get a lot of fax documents.

I use a system where my data files are divided by project. When I contact a potential customer, the information is stored in a directory named JOBS. When the job becomes a reality, it gets its own directory based on the customer's name. When the job is completed, I back up all the files and remove the directory.

I divide customer directories into project directories when applicable. It takes a couple of minutes to make sure that any generated document, such as a received fax, is immediately transferred to the correct directory, but it makes it very easy to find later. (It also has the added benefit of appearing efficient to my customers.)

My file-naming system is not very imaginative and varies with my mood. However, I always separate the files by projects and take care to name the files by type, such as .FAX for fax documents and .WP for word processing files. This means I am only looking through a few files when I search for information.

Transaction logs

Many stand-alone fax machines offer a feature known as *transaction logging*. The machine keeps lists of all the fax documents that have been sent or received. It also typically notes whether the document was sent or received successfully. Your fax software may offer a similar feature so that you can track your fax documents. Desirable extras for this feature include a record of the filename of the document.

"Can I keep a record of the fax documents I've sent?"

Although you won't suffer from document paper jams when you send a document by fax modem, your document may not be sent completely for other reasons. These include the receiving fax machine running out of paper or disk space or some sort of error with the document you are sending where the fax software is unable to convert the supplied file into a form suitable for transmission.

Mailing lists

Your fax software probably can store the names and fax phone numbers for the people you call. This capability is equivalent to the dialing directory for data communications software.

Some fax software includes extra features in the dialing directory area. If you need to send the same document to multiple locations, you may be able to establish mailing lists. These lists are equivalent to a circulation list on a memo.

"How do I send the same fax to many people?"

If you need the fax software to send a copy of the document to each person on the mailing list, this task can be implemented in a variety of ways. You may need to choose several people from your dialing directory and then issue the command to send a fax document. Alternatively, when you fill out the cover sheet, the fax software may be able to pick up the addressees automatically.

The flexibility of specifying what you want and then letting your computer software handle the distribution list is a feature that separates fax modems. Look carefully at this area when you choose a fax modem.

Mail merging

In some cases, you need to send the same message to a variety of people, but you don't want the other people to know. This process is equivalent to doing a mass mailing.

In the mass mailing situation, your needs are different than when you want to send a document to a circulation list. A good mass mailing uses personalized features that tailor each document to the receiving person.

Consider the customized junk mail you receive that says "Dear Mr. Smith. We are currently offering discounts on aluminum siding for people located in the Boston area." At first glance, the letter looks individually written but is in fact a mass mailing where the "Mr. Smith" and "Boston" are inserted automatically.

Like the group mailing feature, mass mailing features separate various fax modems. Some fax software does not support this type of feature; other fax software has particularly flexible mail merging options.

For example, some fax software allows you to use a special coding system when preparing your cover sheet or document. You write something like **%%FAXNAME%%** in your document where you normally write the name of the recipient and **%%FAXTEL%%** where you normally place the recipient's fax telephone number. You generate a separate text file that contains a list relating all the names you want to place in the `%%FAXNAME%%` and `%%FAXTEL%%` locations. The fax modem software takes the sample document file and the name file and generates a fax document for each person listed in the text file and then sends it to the specified number.

Choosing whether to use the fax software's mail merging capabilities can be a trade-off. Most good word processors include mail merging capabilities that far exceed any of the mail merging features found in a fax software program. However, if you use the word processor, you need a way to tell the fax software that you have a list of files to be sent as fax documents. You also need to tell the fax software which telephone number to dial for each document. The balance between how much to do in your word processor and how much to do in the fax software varies with the particular fax software.

Scheduling fax delivery

When you use a fax modem as a major source of document distribution, you can see the cost of telephone calls mount. Although sending a single page fax document can be less expensive than regular mail, when you start sending multipage documents, the costs mount rapidly and quickly exceed the costs of overnight courier services.

"How do I cut my phone costs?"

One way to reduce costs is to use the scheduling feature of your fax software. You can write and schedule your faxes for delivery but delay the actual sending until a later time. For example, you can delay the actual sending until the telephone rates go down in the evening or on the weekend.

Although I am only a small business and have very tight control of my expenses, I can reduce my phone bill by about a third by calling internationally during reduced times and delaying sending faxes within the U.S. until the evening.

Scheduling the fax transmittal until a later time has two additional advantages. If you wait until evening or night time to send the fax to a business, you are more likely to get straight through without a busy signal.

Additionally, delaying the fax sending also gives you a performance advantage. Most fax software can send your fax and allow you to continue using your computer while the fax document is being sent. Because the computer is dividing its resources so that it can do more than one thing simultaneously, it is less responsive to you while it sends the fax document. Delaying the actual sending until you are no longer using the computer allows you to continue working without a performance degradation.

Summary

This chapter showed how to make the best use of your fax modem. Most optimization features involve streamlining your document preparation and file handling. You need to determine the best combination of file formats to give you the best results.

Other keys to making the most of your fax modem involve using the extra features supplied with your fax software. The software may include flexible mail merging, logging, and scheduling features that can reduce your online costs.

Chapter 12 introduces special-purpose communications, such as using your modem on the road, using remote control software, and connecting internationally.

12
CHAPTER

Special-Purpose Communications

This chapters covers special-purpose communications, including the following topics:

- Understanding remote control software
- Using your modem on the road
- Using your modem internationally
- Creating a mini-BBS by using host mode
- Communicating with computer types other than PCs

Understanding and Using Host Mode

Bulletin board systems are introduced in Chapter 13 and are explained in detail in Chapter 14. They are probably the most common application for modems. You use your modem and communications software to call a remote computer. The remote computer runs special communications software, known as bulletin board software. This allows you to control both ends of the connection.

When you are connected, the BBS software displays a menu of selections, and you choose from that menu. You can read stored messages or select a file for transfer. The BBS software is designed to allow you access to the remote computer.

"Can I turn my computer into a BBS?"

Although BBSs use special communications software, there are many instances when you can benefit from having your own "mini-BBS." You can set up a computer as a BBS and call it from a remote location, for example. Suppose that you are on the road but need to pick up some files from your computer. If you leave your computer configured as a BBS, you can call in and collect the files without coordinating with someone else.

Alternatively, if you want to exchange files with a friend, it is much easier to set up one of the computers as a BBS and have the other person call this computer remotely. Then, when you connect, rather than typing messages to each other like **I am going to download the file now**, you can select from menus.

Apart from being an additional program you need to purchase, BBS software is very sophisticated and can do far more than the relatively simple task of downloading or uploading a couple of files. However, many communications software programs include a feature, known as *host mode*, that acts like a mini-BBS.

"Why would I use host mode?"

When you activate host mode, you make your communications program wait for an incoming phone call. It answers the phone, establishes the connection, and presents a menu of selections for your caller. You use host mode only on the remote computer;

the person calling the remote computer uses the typical communications program mode to dial a phone number and connect with the other computer.

Although limited in features, host mode usually has several essential security features that you can activate. First, most programs only allow the caller to access a particular subdirectory on your hard disk. If the file the user wants is not in that subdirectory, the user cannot access the file. This feature allows you to copy the files you want the caller to access to that subdirectory yet protect the other files on your disk.

Another common feature is password-protection. The caller must give a name and password that are acceptable to your system before seeing the host mode menus. The need for this feature depends on your circumstances. If you leave your computer in host mode for hours or days at a time, an unauthorized person could call the number with his/her modem and have access to your system. (Some people call numbers randomly with a modem in an attempt to find computer systems that they can access.)

I don't bother using the password feature. I set host mode on my computer only when I know a friend is going to call in the next few minutes. The extra configuration necessary to set up the password checking and tell the friend the password does not seem worth it for my potential exposure. However, I do take advantage of the other host mode features that allow access only to a particular directory. This way, the friends calling can easily remind themselves of the names of the files they want to download without wading through hundreds of other files on my computer.

Note: Although host mode allows you to control the activities you want to perform on a remote computer, it does not give you access to the programs on the remote computer. The typical activities involve downloading and uploading files and reading or leaving messages. You cannot, for example, run a spreadsheet on the remote computer. This requires remote control software.

Understanding Remote Control Software

Remote control software allows you to connect with another computer from a remote location by using modems and operate the remote computer as if you were sitting at the remote computer itself. For example, you can use remote control software to call your office computer from home and use the word processor or spreadsheet located on the office computer. It's like giving a computer an extremely long keyboard and display cables.

Consider a typical communication session when you use your normal communication software. You call another modem by using your modem, and the two modems connect. You run communication software on your computer, and the remote computer also runs communication software. The remote computer may run communication software similar to yours, or it may run specific software, such as bulletin board software. As explained earlier in the chapter, some communication software includes host mode, which is equivalent to running BBS software. When the remote computer uses communication software, you need someone to operate the remote computer. In the case of BBS software, you can control the remote computer by using the remote computer's communication software. However, you are only controlling the communications software on the remote computer—not any of the other programs on that computer.

When two people are involved in using communication software, your communication session involves transferring files from one computer to another or typing messages to each other. When you call a computer running BBS software, the processes are similar, but you control both ends of the connection. You transfer files from one computer to another or you send and read messages.

"How can I run my computer's programs remotely?"

Remote control software is different because it seems like you are sitting in front of the remote computer. For example, you can see a DOS prompt, use DOS commands, or type the command to start your word processor. You can run your word processor and save files to disk. The disk the files are saved on is the one on the remote computer.

This type of software is useful in two specific situations. First, you can use it to operate the computer from a remote location—to use the office computer when at home, for example. Second, it can be used as a technical support tool.

Suppose that you supply technical support to a remote location and are responsible for training users in their word processors. If someone has a problem, you can connect with his computer by modem and run remote control software. You can then watch him operate the word processor and see the mistakes he's making. Additionally, you can operate the application program by remote and show the user how to perform a task. The keys the user presses on his keyboard cause the application program to respond, and the keys you press on your keyboard also cause the application program to respond.

This can be an invaluable tool compared to a typical telephone technical support call. When you make a telephone call, communicating can be difficult because you don't have visual feedback from the other person. Remote control software helps you "see" what the other person is doing with the computer.

To run remote control software, you install the software on two computers, the one you will call from and the one you will operate remotely. Depending on the particular product chosen, this may require you to purchase a copy of the program for each end of the connection. When comparing prices, look carefully to determine how many copies of the software you need. Because you will run the communications software on two computers, you probably will need two copies of the software. This may be supplied in a single box, or it may require two complete copies.

Resource Guide to Remote Control Software

Close-Up
Norton Lambert Corp
P.O. Box 4085
Santa Barbara, CA 93140
(805) 964-6767

Central Point Commute
Central Point Software, Inc.
15220 NW Greenbrier Parkway, Suite 200
Beaverton, OR 97006
(800) 445-2110

Carbon Copy for DOS
Microcom Inc.
500 River Ridge Dr.
Norwood, MA 02062
(617) 551-1000

Crosstalk Remote2
DCA Inc.
1000 Alderman Dr.
Alpharetta, GA 30201
(404) 998-3998

Norton pcANYWHERE
Symantec Corp
10201 Torre Ave.
Cupertino, CA 95014-2132
(408) 253-9600

PC MacTERM
Symantec Corp
10201 Torre Ave.
Cupertino, CA 95014-2132
(408) 253-9600

To simplify the remaining explanations, consider the following remote control connection. Suppose that the computer containing the application software, such as a word processor, is the remote computer in your office, and the computer linking to the remote computer is in your home.

You run remote control software by loading a TSR (terminate and stay resident) program on your office computer. This makes the office computer answer the phone and give you control of this computer when you call it from your home.

You run the companion portion of your remote control software from your home. In most cases, this is the same product as installed on your office computer, but some remote control products allow you to call from ordinary communications programs by running a special script file. (Script files are covered in Chapter 10.)

After you have established the connection between your home computer and office computer, you can run your application programs. The communications software can display the same thing on your home computer's screen as on the remote computer's screen. The software can deal with such items as different video screen resolutions and keyboards to make your home computer appear as close as possible to your office computer.

"Why can't I use remote control software to receive faxes?"

For remote control software to work, the TSR must be loaded in the office computer. Consider a fax modem, where you can't receive fax documents unless you have the relevant TSR loaded into memory. You can't have multiple TSRs loaded into memory when they try to do the same job. A fax modem TSR uses the modem to answer the phone when it rings, as will a remote control TSR. You have to choose which one you load in memory. For similar reasons, you can't use remote control software to run communication software on your office computer. You are already using the modem to make the connection.

Remote control software has various other limitations. Most are due to the computer hardware rather than the remote control program limitations. The problems relate to available DOS memory and the differences between your screen at home and in the office.

In reference to the memory limitations, when you call your office computer, the TSR activates itself to make the connection. This program is always running while you are connected to the office computer. Consequently, it always uses some of the memory on your office computer. This leaves less memory available for your application program. You may not be able to load your application program because you don't have enough memory available after the remote control software's TSR is in memory.

This limitation can apply even if you have 16 MB of RAM in your office computer. The critical memory is the amount of base memory available to DOS. You can determine this by using the DOS MEM command. Most application programs, such as word processors and spreadsheets, specify that they need a certain amount of free memory to load, such as 480 KB. This amount must be available after you load the remote control software's TSR.

There are many techniques for maximizing the amount of free base memory in your computer, especially in 386-based computers (or better). These techniques can involve using memory-manager programs, altering your CONFIG.SYS and AUTOEXEC.BAT files, or using different command line switches when you start your application program.

In addition to memory limitations, you may encounter device limitations with the remote control software. These problems depend on the particular combination of software and hardware that you run. For example, you may not be able to access a CD-ROM drive using remote control software, or you may not be able to see the correct screens on your home computer. In most cases, there are workarounds that can solve your problems, but you may need to spend some time with the remote control software technical support technicians to make your particular configuration work.

You should consider the impact of your computer crashing while running remote control software. Regardless of the configuration, you probably will need to reboot the remote computer at some time. Look carefully at the remote control software to determine what happens if someone breaks the connection while in an application program. This may happen intentionally or accidentally. Remember that you are depending on a telephone connection to maintain the link between the two computers. You may get a noisy connection or may be unexpectedly disconnected.

It is very inconvenient to need to reboot the office computer by being physically present. After all, the whole point of remote control software is being able to use your computer when you are not sitting at it. Being able to reboot remotely is a good feature but can expose you if the wrong people can reboot the computer.

Consider the situation where you set up a remote computer with a database library on it. You can supply many people with the remote control software to access this computer remotely. Because only one person can be connected to the computer at one time, you aren't violating any copyright rules on the database software, yet many different people have access to this computer. In the case of some very expensive databases, such as medical or legal libraries, the remote control software costs are minimal compared with supplying multiple copies of the database.

However, if the users accessing the database hang up without exiting the database, the database will not be available to any user until you reboot the remote computer unless your remote control software can handle the rebooting automatically. If you are offering access to the database as a service, having the database unavailable due to the system needing rebooting is probably unacceptable.

Other issues you should examine relate to security. If you leave your office computer in a mode where you can connect to it remotely, you leave it in a mode where others also can connect to it. When using host mode in your communication program, you only expose one or two directories on your hard disk to the caller. In the case of remote control software, you expose your application programs to the caller.

Be sure to look at the security features in the remote control software. These include password security access. They also may include callback features where the remote computer calls the caller back at a previously specified number. This enables you to make the office computer pay for the phone call but limits where the caller can be located.

Remote control software provides features not usually found in other communication programs. You may be able to run the desktop publishing program in your office from your laptop or finish other projects from your home. You may be able to reduce the number of on-site technical support calls you need by using remote control software and linking to a consultant's or trainer's office.

In the past, remote control software was not particularly popular because of the programs' responsiveness. The modems had to pass a lot of information between the two computers, resulting in sluggish application program response. The new generation of high-speed modems are fast enough that you will be able to run most applications without unacceptable speed reductions because the two modems will be able to transmit and receive the necessary data fast.

However, remote control software is more difficult to set up and manage than typical communication software. If you only want to exchange a few messages or transfer files, stick with ordinary communications programs. As its name suggests, remote control software is suitable when you want to actually operate a computer remotely.

Communicating with a Macintosh

In a way, this section is unnecessary in this book, but a frequently asked question is "How do I connect with a Macintosh or other computer?" The earlier chapters emphasize that when you make a telecommunication connection, you control a modem with your computer. The modem connects with another modem, which in turn is connected to another computer or device.

The two computers at each end of the connection don't have to be the same. You can link PCs, Macintoshes, minicomputers, or mainframes, and any combination of computers. Each computer must be able to communicate with a modem, and the two modems do the actual linking. Because modems adhere to international communication standards (not computer standards), the computer types do not matter.

Now that I've said that you can link any two computers, there are limitations as to the value of linking the two computers. Most computers support the sending and receiving of ASCII text, so you can type information on your keyboard and have it appear on the remote computer, and the remote computer can send ASCII text to your computer and it will appear on your screen.

However, the ASCII character set on one computer may not be the same as the ASCII character set on another computer. The ASCII character set consists of 128 defined characters. However, on computers that can store information in 8-bit characters (chunks of data) rather than the 7-bit characters found on mainframe computers, the ASCII character set is extended another 128 characters. (There are 128 unique combinations of bits with 7 bits of binary data and 256 unique combinations with 8 bits of binary data.) Because these are not part of the internationally accepted standard, many different variations occur. If you only exchange data with PCs within the U.S., you'll probably always use the same character set. However, there are different standards for different countries as well as different standards for special purposes. The differences may allow you to use accented characters, different punctuation symbols, or different line drawing characters.

Apart from character transfer, most communications programs support file transfer, regardless of the computer they run on. If the two computers support the same file-transfer protocol, you can transfer files between the two computers. The important issue is what can be done with the files after they are transferred. Suppose that you transfer a spreadsheet file from a PC to a Macintosh. You can only use that PC file on the Macintosh if you have a Macintosh application program that can read the PC spreadsheet file. This applies to any file. The file may be transferred correctly, but it can only be used if the receiving computer's application program can read it.

Note: This disregard for *computer type* is why commercial online services can work. You transfer your file to the online service, even though the computer may be a mainframe computer. The online service never actually uses the file; it only stores it. Another user downloads the file from the online service to his PC and then uses it.

As more people connect different computer types together, more DOS-based and Apple-DOS application programs support a common file format so you can use a file on either computer, which makes transfer between computer types more valuable and more streamlined. This occurs frequently when you use application programs that are available on different platforms, such as WordPerfect and Microsoft Excel, which are available for the PC and the Macintosh. You are more likely to be able to use files created by the other computer type than if you try to import a file created by a less common application program.

Remote control software also allows you to link your PC to a Macintosh. For example, with the right software, you can call a PC from your Macintosh and run PC applications on your remote PC.

Using Your Modem on the Road

As covered in Chapters 7 and 11, your fax modem can accept and send fax documents as if it were a stand-alone fax machine. If your fax modem is installed in or attached to your laptop, you can send and receive fax documents wherever you are located—if you know the receiving fax machine's telephone number.

Data modems also can be installed in most laptop computers or can be attached to a laptop's serial port. Although you can use a full-sized external modem with a laptop, you can also purchase small-sized modems (and some that are combination fax and data modems) for use with your laptop. Chapter 4 explains modem selection and the relevant considerations and trade-offs when selecting a modem and communications software for your laptop.

If you have access to the RJ-11 jack for a telephone, you can attach your modem to the telephone system and send data via modems. However, using your modem while traveling can be more difficult than when in a home or office. The problems are not usually due to the modem but relate to how you connect to the telephone system.

"How do I use my modem in a hotel room?"

Hotels and conference centers are becoming more aware of the traveler with a laptop computer, and they make RJ-11 sockets increasingly available for their visitors. They often advertise their modem support in their hotel guides. In some cases, there is an extra socket on the telephone, and you just plug your modem into it. In other cases, the hotels have only a few phones with the modem socket on it, and you have to ask for the correct phone to be installed in your room. In other instances, you may have to use the hotel or conference center's business office. Although frustrating, this latter alternative is preferable to not being able to connect at all.

Tip: If you are in a hotel and do not have a printer, sending a fax to the hotel's fax number is an alternative for printing a document.

I make a point to ask a hotel about connecting my modem to the phone when I confirm my reservation. (I also ask about any fees for receiving fax documents.) I am unlikely to stay at a hotel without convenient modem hookups more than once.

If you have doubts about whether the plug in the back of a hotel phone really is an RJ-11 and is not a similar-looking connector, ask the hotel staff. If you make the wrong judgment, you can damage your modem permanently. Some, if not most, hotels use a special telephone system, similar to a company using its own telephone exchange system (PBX). Depending on the type of PBX and the equipment installed, you may not have suitable access to the telephone service by simply plugging in your modem.

"How do I use my modem from a public pay phone?"

If you do not have a phone jack connector suitable for your modem, you still have several other options. You can purchase a device called an *acoustic coupler* to make the connection. You may have seen pictures of these in movies that now seem antiquated. The telephone receiver is placed in a box that has two cradles for the earpiece and mouthpiece. Other acoustic couplers are two round cups that you strap onto the telephone receiver, usually with Velcro straps. The cups or box are attached to a cable with an RJ-11 connector on the end, and you can plug your modem into this connector.

Note: Acoustic couplers, as the name implies, use the microphone and speaker in the telephone receiver. They "listen" to the data being sent and "talk" into the telephone mouthpiece. This connection is less ideal than sending and receiving the data directly from the phone cable. However, this provides a method of connecting a modem to a public pay phone as well as an obscure hotel telephone.

Even with the modem physically connected, making a connection is typically more complicated when staying in a hotel or sending data from an airport than when dialing from your home or office. It is often a balancing act of dialing the correct sequence of numbers with the appropriate delays. In some cases, you can create a dialing string in your communications program. In others, you will have to dial the number by hand and then transfer control from the telephone handset to your communication program.

When you first learn to make a telecommunication connection, you must consider the steps involved in the process. These involve connecting the modem to the telephone line, configuring the modem correctly, dialing the required numbers, letting the modems negotiate a connection, and then performing the character and file transfer desired. When considering telecommunication on the road, you need to reconsider these steps. The first hurdle is the physical connection, and the second is dialing the correct number.

Earlier chapters, including Chapter 9, show techniques for using dialing string prefixes and dealing with extra-long dialing strings. You may need to employ these techniques when using an unusual telephone.

For example, you may need to use a long-distance calling card. You will probably need to dial an access number as well as account number information before dialing the telephone number of the computer you are calling. If you are calling from a hotel room, there may be additional numbers required to actually get a normal telephone company dial tone.

One of the problems with using the modem to do all the dialing is that you have to add delays into your dialing string. This gives the hotel's telephone system time to give you an outside line. Then, after you connect with your long-distance telephone service, it gives time for the long-distance service's computer to accept your account information.

Additionally, the typical default S-register setting (S7) for the length of time between when you start to dial and when the modem expects to negotiate a connection is only 30 seconds. It can take longer than that to dial all the relevant digits. You may need to alter S7's contents to allow for the longer time required. Chapter 10 covers altering the S-register contents. As you move from location to location, the necessary dialing sequence may vary. For example, one hotel may need a 9 and another an 8 to get an outside phone line.

It may be easier to manually dial the necessary phone numbers and only use the modem after the phone number is dialed. To do this, you need the phone and the modem connected at the same time. You can purchase adapter cables, known as RJ-11 splitters, that consist of a single RJ-11 connector at one end of the cable and two RJ-11 connectors at the other. You connect one end into the phone jack in the wall and the other ends into the phone and modem. Alternatively, you can use the acoustic coupler system and strap the handset onto the acoustic coupler after you dial the number.

This procedure involves telling the modem when you want it to start controlling the connection. You can configure some communication programs, such as Smartcom for Windows, so you can switch from voice to data with a keystroke. In other cases, you need to issue the **ATO** command from the terminal screen. You make adjustments by choosing the Settings menu on the main menu bar and then choosing Modem. From the Select Modem & Settings box, you choose Settings. You then uncheck the Monitor call for dial tone and Monitor call for busy signal checkboxes. Then, when you select the phone icon, you do not enter a phone number but press OK and connect.

Because you want to switch from voice to data quickly, you must set up your communication program and modem so that you can switch with a single keystroke. Turn on your modem, load your communications program, and get to the terminal screen.

As explained in earlier chapters, when you type at the terminal screen, the keystrokes are passed to the modem. However, the modem does not accept a command until you press Enter at the end of the command string. When you turn on your modem, it comes up in command mode, ready to receive instructions.

Type **ATO** at the terminal screen in preparation for completing the command. (The ATO command makes the modem take the phone off the hook.) Then, manually dial the required number with the handset.

When you hear the remote modem signal that it has answered the phone, transfer control to the modem. (If you use an acoustic coupler, quickly strap it onto the phone.) Press Enter to send the ATO command to the modem, and the modem negotiates the connection. You can hang up the handset.

You may need to perform a comparable procedure when sending a fax document with your fax modem. You prepare the fax communication software so that a single keystroke will take the phone off hook, and then you dial the phone manually. When the other fax machine answers, you transfer control to the fax modem. This also can be achieved by strapping on an acoustic coupler and pressing the correct key to complete the command or pressing the correct key to complete the command if the fax modem and the phone are attached to the phone line.

International Communication

The telephone system in the U.S. is taken for granted by most of the population. Stories of waiting six months to be assigned a phone number and phone charges that are a substantial portion of a paycheck seem incredible to Americans. However, these facts not only apply to Third World countries but also apply in many other countries throughout the world.

In many countries, the telephone company is government controlled, and in many cases, funds are not assigned for delivering phone lines to all residences. The concept of a phone being a necessity rather than a luxury is really only prevalent in the U.S.

International telephone communication may also be limited in other countries. Remember that when you make a telephone call, you actually are making a link between the location you are calling from and the location you are calling to. Although the signal may be transmitted between two points, the route must be available for the connection to be made. Although there are many international phone lines connecting the U.S. with other countries, another country may only have a few international connections. In some countries, you even need to schedule international phone calls.

"Can I call internationally with my modem?"

The easiest way to connect reliably with other countries is to use a commercial online service, such as CompuServe. You then make a local phone call and post your message or file. The recipient makes a phone call, local or long distance, to connect with the same service and pick up the sent information.

Part IV covers the various online services available. Many are available overseas. Alternatively, many offer connection to the Internet, an international network system. You send a message to the Internet through a commercial online service, and your recipient connects to a different online service available in his country to pick up the message. (Chapter 17 discusses the Internet exclusively.)

Some Internet connections offered by commercial online services only include messaging services and not file transfer. However, the Chapter 17 sidebar, "Transferring Binary Files with 7-Bit Systems," shows another method that allows you to transfer files over an Internet connection, even if file-transfer facilities are not available.

"Can I use my modem in Europe?"

Using your modem overseas is more complicated and may be illegal. Just as the modem you use in this country must be approved for use on the phone system in this country, most other countries also insist that telephones, modems, and other devices must be approved for use in that particular country. In many cases, this means you must use a modem supplied by the telephone company in that country.

Each country has its own standards, and these are probably not the same as the ones used by the U.S. Although many modem manufacturers sell their modems in different countries, the exact settings or modem models may be different to conform with local regulations. (Hayes modems are available in more than 65 countries worldwide.) This variation applies in Europe from country to country as well as in Asia, Africa, and the Middle East.

Note: Different countries also have different AC power circuits. The U.S. standard of 115V 60Hz AC is not typical. Different countries use different power cables as well as different voltages and frequencies. Your computer and modem must be able to connect to these services unless you are only running from a battery or are able to use appropriate adapters and transformers.

If you want to travel to other countries and use a modem, the best advice is to set it up beforehand and make arrangements to buy or borrow equipment in the relevant country. If you want to call another country from the U.S., the procedure is the same as if you are calling within the U.S., except that the telephone number is typically longer. You may need to adjust the S7 S-register to allow time for a connection to be made. However, if you use a modem that supports a V.21 or better standard, and the other modem also supports that standard, you will be able to make a connection.

Some early U.S. modems only support the Bell 103 or Bell 212A standards. These are U.S. standards and were not adopted internationally.

Note: The quality of phone line connections in the U.S. is substantially better than in many other countries and is improving. You may not be able to connect internationally at high speed without getting some data errors. Be sure to use error-detection wherever possible.

Summary

This chapter introduced some of the more unusual connections you may make with your modem. These include using the host mode in your communication software to set up a mini-BBS or using remote control software to run application programs from a remote location.

Other topics covered include communicating with other types of computers, such as a Macintosh, and communicating internationally.

Part IV, "The Online World Tour," introduces the wide variety of online services available to you. Chapter 13 provides an overview of the various services, and later chapters focus on more-specific applications.

IV

PART

The Online World Tour

Part IV introduces the limitless world of online data. Thanks to the remarkable proliferation of computers and telephone systems throughout the world, we can access more information from more sources, faster and more economically than previously possible.

Chapter 13 introduces all the online database services in a general way and differentiates between the most popular services based on their most common uses. Chapter 13 also introduces packet-switched networks, which allow you to access the online services potentially at a more economical telephone service rate, and the variety of ways that online services interconnect to provide you with more opportunities for reaching a wider user base. The subsequent chapters, Chapters 14 through 18, focus on each of these major purposes for online services in turn.

Beginners should read Chapter 13 carefully to determine what type of service is useful and then focus on the following corresponding chapter for more detail. Experienced modem users should skim the introduction to online databases in Chapter 13 to understand the divisions made before exploring the more detailed chapters. You may find a different service fits more of your particular needs than the one you were considering.

13

CHAPTER

Choosing
the Data Source

This chapter covers the following main topics:

❖ Understanding online databases

❖ Introducing bulletin board systems

❖ Introducing messaging services

❖ Introducing information-exchange services

❖ Introducing information-searching services

❖ Appreciating packet-switched networks

❖ Getting online with the whole world

Introduction to Online Databases

Armed with a computer, modem, and telephone line, the world is literally at your fingertips. If you can think of the question, it can be answered by telecommunicating. You can perform obvious tasks like calling your office, collecting or sending files, or sending messages to your colleagues. However, there literally are thousands of specialized online services that you can call. Chapter 2 introduces the three main purposes for telecommunicating and online services: chatting, messaging, and exchanging files.

Chatting is connecting to another computer via modems and interacting with the other computer operators. You type on your keyboard, and the words appear on the other computer screens. The other computer operators in turn type responses on their keyboards. This interaction is often called *conferencing* because it is very like holding a conference call. (***Note:*** The term conference is also used with messaging as a method of dividing the messages into related topics known as *conferences.*)

"Why would I want to chat online?"

If you've never chatted online, it may seem strange that people want to interact this way — especially if you aren't a rapid typist. However, consider the anonymity factor. You can't be seen or known by the other participants. Everyone is truly equal. Consequently, you can express views that you ordinarily wouldn't and not be judged by your sex, age, race, profession, or religion, unless you choose to disclose such information. Even poor spelling may be disguised as bad typing.

Although online services usually require you to register your correct name, for chatting, you can usually choose a name that is shown to the other users on the system. This pseudonym is often referred to as a *handle.* Handles can preserve your anonymity or reveal a lot. Consider the images portrayed by: Fred the Brain, Conan the Great, and Jill the Joker — compared with Jo or Al.

Online services are more frequently used for *messaging.* You send a message to someone specific or to all the users on a system. You can read messages sent to other people if they are marked for public viewing, and if you desire, you can join in with the exchange by replying to the messages. The primary advantage of messaging over chatting is that you are not present when the message is posted, and you can read the exchanges when you choose to get online. Another advantage is that you have the chance to get replies from more than the people currently online.

"Can anyone read a message I send?"

Depending on the service, messaging can be public or private. In a public message, the idea is to exchange information with other users — perhaps giving you a forum for your opinions or a searching tool to find help with specific questions or problems. In a private message, the idea is an alternative to the mail system. You can send messages and perhaps files that are intended for specific individuals. These individuals can call the online service from anywhere and collect their messages.

Although chatting and messaging aspects are important in specific instances or for particular personalities, the file exchange aspects of telecommunicating are cited as the most important reason individuals purchase modems and get online. People want more software for their computers.

Online services can provide you with far more software, both programs and data, than you can possibly ever use. In most cases, you can obtain a particular file from a variety of different sources. If file collection is your primary motivation for telecommunicating, regularly reconsider the most economical method to find and download the file.

"Which is the best online service?"

Some online services offer chatting, messaging, and file exchange, and others only offer one or two of these main functions. As you investigate online services, keep in mind the type of information you want to find and the typical user of that service.

For example, if you want to play interactive computer games, do not expect to find many kids playing on an expensive business-oriented system. If you want to talk to a Russian rocket scientist, you are unlikely to find a suitable candidate on a small local BBS that is not connected to other BBSs.

Generally, you can divide the available services into two categories: BBSs and commercial online services. That doesn't mean that all BBSs are free and none are run as commercial ventures; it is more a statement about how you learn where the systems are. In fact, any generalization you make about the available online services is inaccurate or incomplete. Because they are all essentially a community of computer users, trying to categorize is like trying to pigeonhole people. Bear this in mind as this chapter tries to divide the online world into meaningful categories.

Understanding Viruses

It is a fallacy that you are bound to get a computer virus by using a modem. However, the more files you exchange with other computers, the more likely you are to expose your computer to a computer virus. As you use a modem, you are more likely to increase the number of files you exchange and consequently increase your risk.

You can minimize the risks by understanding the following concepts:

♣ Viruses are small programs that can self-replicate and can damage system areas and files on your computer. They are hidden in files or on computer disks.

♣ You can get a virus only by transferring an infected file onto your computer or by accessing an infected disk.

♣ Although there are thousands of different viruses, very few have caused any widespread damage. The majority of reported incidences are either isolated cases, instigated by personal revenge motives, or are operator or system errors.

As a modem user, use the following procedures to minimize your exposure:

♣ Check that all your computers are currently virus-free. Several virus-checking programs, shareware and retail, are available.

♣ Establish a virus-checking procedure and follow it religiously. This is even more important than following a backup procedure for your hard disks.

♣ Immediately after hanging up the phone, verify that each file you transfer onto your computer does not contain a virus. (You need to uncompress the file and run the virus-checker.) Do not try the programs first.

♣ If you think you have a virus, stop. Don't do anything with your computer. Note any displayed messages and call the virus-checker manufacturer's technical support for assistance.

Although viruses are widely publicized, they are extremely rare. However, they can cause such devastation that precautions are worthwhile. Remember that your exposure is not limited to the files you obtain from online services; the disk you receive from a friend and even retail software is a potential risk.

A *BBS* (bulletin board system) is typically run from a PC or a series of networked PCs. Many are run by hobbyists from their basements and have only one telephone line. However, some have more than one hundred phone lines and are frequently used by thousands of users.

Commercial online services are typically run from minicomputers or mainframes and are linked via local telephone access number throughout the country. As some BBSs increase in popularity and offer local telephone access, the distinction can become blurred.

Some important commercial online services are focused for a business audience. They offer private messaging services or information searching in specialized categories, such as medicine, investment, or law. Others focus on information exchange via messages, chatting, and file exchange.

The following sections introduce the four categories for online services: BBSs, messaging systems, information exchange, and information searching. Appendix B is a resource guide to online services and gives phone numbers for reaching them.

Understanding BBSs

BBSs are almost always run from PCs, advertised by other BBS operators or users, and with more than 200,000 BBSs estimated in the U.S., they make up the bulk of online services.

BBSs are relatively easy to set up. You need a phone line, modem, special communication software, and your PC. In fact, some communication software includes commands that let you set up a mini-bulletin board. (Chapter 12 covers host mode.) As a result, many hobbyists set up BBSs as an extension of their PC hobby.

Besides the BBSs run from a hobbyist's basement, you probably have many other BBSs in your geographical area. Your local library probably has a card catalog system online where you can find books, reserve them, and even find out if there is a copy on the shelf. The Internal Revenue Service has a BBS you can call to get tax information, and the Social Security Administration has a BBS you can call to get information on your Social Security benefits. NASA also has a BBS that provides information on the space program.

In the last couple of years, with the dramatic cost reductions in the PC market, many PC software and hardware companies are looking to BBSs to reduce their technical support costs by supplying a BBS that their users can call. Other companies, professional associations, and volunteer groups are also finding BBSs a convenient and inexpensive way to disseminate and collect information.

Many local computer clubs have BBSs that tell you about upcoming meetings, exchange information, and want ads. Many associations use BBSs as means of communication, including membership lists, want ads, and general information exchange.

"What's the cheapest online service?"

BBSs are the best online services to try as a beginner to communications. This is particularly true if you are comfortable with your computer but not with the telephone charges. They are typically run by volunteers for fun, so you can often get help and make friends at the same time.

However, if new software intimidates you, consider a graphical online service, such as Prodigy or America Online, as a starting point. These are considered information exchange services and are detailed later in this chapter and in Chapter 16.

BBSs also are the best resource if you are very price conscious. Many BBSs are free or charge a nominal annual fee, and you only pay for the phone call.

I find BBSs the best online service for regional information. If I want to know what people think of a new restaurant, where to buy new carpeting, or find information on the latest local tax hike, I go to a local BBS. When I lived in Chicago, there were more than 300 BBSs within my local calling area. Even in the rural area where I now live, there are several within a few miles.

There are less than a dozen popular BBS software companies that sell the computer programs necessary to make a BBS. Consequently, you will find many common elements between different BBSs. For example, a main menu on one board will have similar choices to another board.

"Are all BBSs alike?"

When you try a couple of BBSs, you will be able to call almost any BBS and transfer your knowledge to the new BBS. The BBS software can be, and often is, customized, depending on the system operator's (known as a *sysop*) choices, but you are unlikely to have difficulty with operating a different BBS. BBSs do have character, however, and these are typically a reflection of the system operator's characters and the regular users. If you do not like a BBS, try a different one.

Chapter 14 covers BBSs in more detail and gives you a sample guided tour. Appendix B gives a sampling of a variety of boards arranged by area code so you can find ones in your region.

Understanding message-based services

Electronic mail, frequently abbreviated to *e-mail,* has been an integral part of some companies' communication system for many years. One person types a message on a computer or computer terminal and sends it to another person. The recipient reads the mail from the computer or computer terminal.

In some cases, all the users are operators of terminals attached to a central computer; in others, they are linked by a local area network (LAN). Some companies extend this connection further in a variety of ways and allow users to call via modem and collect their messages.

Some commercial online services offer a comparable service independent of your company. You purchase an account and can call the service, send a message to another subscriber to the service, and have the message delivered automatically and instantaneously. Some services allow you to attach a file to a message.

These services are equivalent to a mailing service. You direct your message to another user, and only the recipient can receive and read the message or the accompanying file.

"How do I send private messages instantly?"

The three major advantages of a message-based service are the inexpensive cost, more or less instantaneous delivery, and the service's accessibility from any location. The user is identified by name and password. You don't send the message to the recipient's physical location.

The typical home user isn't interested in this type of service, but this is the only electronic online service described that sends messages privately. In all other services, someone else, even if it is only an employee of the online service, has accessibility to the messages and in some cases the power to censor them. The cost per message is equivalent to typical mailing charges, but it is less expensive than courier services. Message-based services are alternatives to fax machines and fax modems, particularly if you need to keep the message private.

Apart from the basic concept of sending a message to someone else subscribing to the same service, the messaging services offer more-sophisticated and alternative options. In many cases, they provide links to other online services, so if you subscribe to one service, you can often send messages to or receive messages from subscribers to another service. Chapter 15 explains the potential problems with this approach in reference to security.

Additionally, the messaging services may include other mailing services. For example, you may be able to send a message to a recipient who is not a subscriber and who is on the other coast. The message is transmitted to the closest physical office to the recipient, printed, and then mailed automatically. You then save the time necessary to transport the mail coast to coast and reduce your costs by not using an overnight courier service. (Chapter 15 explains additional options for messaging services. However, most are of particular interest to sales personnel for links to the central office and pursuing sales leads.)

Understanding information-exchange services

Apart from BBSs, information-exchange services are the most widely known online services available. These commercial services can be thought of as very large BBSs. They are run from minicomputers or mainframes — in most cases, multiple minicomputers or multiple mainframe computers. They offer messaging and file exchange and, to a lesser extent, chatting.

These services should appeal to all users because they have so many different services and features. They do, however, cost money to access. Depending on the service, it may be a flat monthly fee, but in most cases, there is an additional charge, called a *connect charge*, where you pay for the time that you are actually connected to the service.

"What types of commercial online services are available?"

From a user interface standpoint, there are two types of services: *graphical interface* and the more traditional *text interface*. The graphical online services are particularly appealing to those intimidated by learning new software or who do not want to learn any commands. However, in comparison to the information-exchange services with a text interface, graphical services are incredibly slow.

In many cases, people initially subscribe to a graphical online service, and after gaining experience, consider the alternative services. This migration depends on your goals. The other online services tend to attract more computer literate users who are interested in computer topics, and the graphical services offer more readily accessible general material to a less technical audience.

For the home user, any of these services is desirable, and the most applicable depends on your particular interest. Chapter 16 gives examples of topics on some services and a guided tour to a graphical and textual information exchange service.

You will find advocates of each service. I find the graphical services frustrating because I am not interested in reading the news or seeing a weather forecast from my computer. However, these are precisely the reasons cited by a very technical friend of mine. She does not have time to read a newspaper, and the graphical service gives the information to her quickly in a format she likes.

The textual online services include vast amounts of information, and if you know where to look, you can find almost anything. However, because you are being charged a connect time charge, you need to be as efficient as possible. The major services offer software, in most cases for free, that help you navigate the areas of interest very rapidly. Chapter 10 details the advantages of this type of product. (There are equivalent products for BBSs.)

The messaging facilities available on these commercial information-exchange services are equivalent to BBSs in that you can read messages related to a particular topic and respond if you desire. However, because of the larger number of subscribers to the services, you will see opinions from a larger pool of people. As with the messaging services, you can send messages to other subscribers to the service and, in many cases, can send messages to subscribers to other services.

Understanding information-searching services

Another type of specialized online service is the *information-searching service*. These services are huge databases of information that are regularly updated. You call the database and search for information of interest.

These services are expensive when compared with the other online services and are not intended for the casual home computer user. It is not unusual to spend hundreds if not thousands of dollars a month to use them. However, for the right purpose, they are invaluable and cannot be underestimated. Additionally, many service companies, sometimes owned by the online services themselves, will inexpensively and automatically do the searching for you. In some cases, you can establish search criteria and have the online service automatically supply any data as it becomes available.

"How can online research help me?"

Chapter 18 covers these information-searching services in detail and gives a guided tour of one of them. Because they are designed for very specific purposes, a general description is too superficial to be illuminating, but consider the following applications.

You may need a newspaper clipping service. The online service may carry the full text of hundreds if not thousands of different newspapers from around the world. You can search for any references to your company, your industry, or your competitors. You can typically read an abstract of a reference and obtain full text of desired articles. Electronic document searching is much more accurate than any visual system.

The online service may catalog patent applications, current government legislation, and stock information. You can do a patent search and see what patents your competitor has filed or bought. You can keep current on new regulations that may affect your business or investment information. The information is not always so directly related to business. One particular service specializes in chemical compound information; another specializes in current law. Other equivalent services specialize in other areas.

If you are not currently doing business involving database searching, this type of service may seem fanciful and impractical. Although it has been made a cliché by the media, the world *is* getting smaller, and you must think globally to stay competitive. If you don't know what the competition is doing, understand market trends, or have the latest in technology, you may not survive.

Different Connections

The following sections cover alternative ways you can connect with your favorite online service and introduce some of the ways the online services connect with each other to your benefit.

Understanding packet-switching network access

As covered extensively in early chapters in this book, you make a connection between two modems by dialing a telephone number. The two modems negotiate a connection, and your computer is linked to the serial device that is connected to the other modem. In the case of online services, the other modem is attached to a computer. This other computer may be a PC, minicomputer, or a mainframe. It runs computer software that you control from your PC.

> *"Should I call the local phone number or the long-distance one?"*

In most cases, if you call a BBS, you dial the BBS directly. When you dial the number, the modem attached to the BBS detects the phone ringing and answers the phone. The actual routing of the telephone call from the outlet in your wall to the receiving computer's outlet is under the control of your local or long-distance telephone company. The receiving computer does not care whether you are calling from around the corner or around the world.

Commercial online services and a few very large BBSs offer an alternative method of connecting. Rather than dialing the computer directly, you call a local telephone number. This is the number for a telephone service called a *packet-switched network*. Two popular examples are Sprintnet and Tymnet.

A packet-switched network is a computer-controlled telephone system with digital telephone lines that can route your telephone call more efficiently and with higher fidelity than the regular analog telephone system. It is so-named because it divides the data being transmitted into small chunks called packets. (In some cases, your ordinary long-distance telephone call may be routed through a packet-switched network for part of its route.)

When you call the packet-switched network, you connect with the packet-switching network's computer. You identify the online service you wish to connect to by following the instructions supplied when you register with your chosen online service, and the packet-switching network links you to your online service's computer.

The online service has established an account with the packet-switched network company and pays the packet-switched network for the time that you are connected. The online service typically passes these charges on to you. For example, the online service may quote one price per hour of connect time if you call a particular number and a different price if you call a different number.

As covered in the sidebar "Calculating Connect Charges" it may be more economical to call a service directly, or you may save money by using a packet-switched network connection. Be sure to review your selection regularly, because this is one of the charges that varies over time as the online services offer different deals.

Linking with the world

Although interconnection between online services has been around for many years, it is probably the fastest growing area of interest in PC telecommunications. As more people accept modems as a commodity rather than a specialized device that you only own if you have a particular task to do, the communicating itself is becoming more commonplace. A few years ago in most circles, it was an adventure to link with a few hundred other users and find their opinions and exchange files with them. Now it is possible to link with literally millions of users worldwide.

In the BBS world, several fairly informal systems were established for allowing BBSs to exchange messages. This procedure usually is called *echoing mail.* The most common are Fidonet and RIME. You call your local BBS and read the messages relating to a particular topic, and you can respond to some of the messages. The sysop (system operator) of the BBS calls another BBS and, through the specialized software, passes on the messages you responded to and receives the new messages. When you next call the BBS, the new messages are available. Each BBS passes the information to the next link in the chain. Each sysop pays only a small portion of the cost because he or she is usually calling a nearby BBS.

Calculating Connect Charges

The relative costs of different online services can be dramatic. One may be free — another may cost tens of dollars an hour. The charges may vary depending on your modem speed and which phone number you use to access the service.

The costs fall into two categories: the access charges for the service and the telephone costs. Many services offer discount schemes, and you need to compare the costs to choose the best for you. Unfortunately, it is like a school mathematics exercise.

For example, a service may have a fixed monthly charge of $15 with five hours connect time free and $6 an hour after that. Compare this with $4 an hour all the time. You need to judge whether you will use the service less than three hours a month or more than eight hours.

Remember to regularly reassess the amount you use an online service because your needs change with time. For example, one year I spent hundreds of dollars with a particular service submitting my magazine articles. The following year, a different magazine was my major customer, and I stopped using the service but didn't cancel my subscription. However, it was only when I got the annual renewal bill for the service that I realized I was wasting my money. The service was just as good, but my needs had changed.

When comparing the services, don't overlook the other costs: telephone charges. The online services do not factor in these charges because they vary, depending on your location. Consider all the different ways in which you can access the service when considering relative costs. You may be able to call a local phone number, an intrastate state number, a long-distance number, or an 800 number.

Commercial online services often offer a regional phone number for access and not just a single national number. If you call the national number, you are paying the long-distance telephone charges. If you call the local access number, you pay the local telephone call charge, and the online service pays for the long-distance charge. This charge is often passed on to you by a higher cost in accessing the service through this local number.

Depending on where you live, the local access method may prove more expensive than using a direct long-distance number, and the cost difference may surprise you. Take the time to calculate the relative costs by making an estimate of your online time. For example, calculate the per hour costs for being online.

Do not overlook the special discounts offered by long-distance telephone companies. Many relate to calling the same number or set of numbers regularly. Because I live in a rural area, for example, the local access numbers for online services are intrastate calls. (Even the local pizza store is long-distance, although they do deliver.) I have joined every special program offered by my long-distance phone company and added the online service phone numbers to my "calling list." In most cases, it is cheaper for me to call the national number and pay the long-distance carrier than to pay the local telephone company.

As the cliché goes, "your mileage may vary," but I estimate that I have saved hundreds of dollars by regularly reconsidering how I access online services and how much I am actually using them. (Although calling online services is a passion for me, my combined online service charges are less than my electricity bill.)

You may wonder why a sysop would be interested and willing to bear the cost. Depending on the geographical location, a local BBS has a limited population of callers. To attract these people, the messages need to be of interest and current. To help make running the BBS interesting, the sysop also wants to reach other people who are not local. Picking up the messages from one of these mail-echoing exchanges gives the appearance of a BBS having more users and helps provide interesting interchanges.

"What is the Internet?"

Another much older network has only relatively recently become accessible to PC users. All the descriptions are rather vague because it is such a mixture of computers, located in a mixture of establishments, in many different countries. Chapter 17 covers the Internet in more detail.

The Internet is a network of networks that can all communicate with each other. They use a protocol (equivalent of language) called TCP/IP (Transmission Control Protocol/Internet Protocol) as the basis for that communication, and each attached computer is allocated a name. The connected computers are in universities, research establishments, government sites, and commercial companies.

In a way comparable to Fidonet and RIME, where each participating BBS bears a small portion of the cost, the sites connected to the Internet freely exchange electronic mail and files with each other. If you can find a way to connect with a computer on the Internet, you can literally exchange messages with the world for free.

Although The Internet Society allocates ID numbers to various Internet sites, the Internet itself is not a fixed entity and has seen explosive growth recently as many PC users have found ways to access the system. As a PC owner, you can access the Internet in one of several ways. Keep in mind that you can do two things with the Internet: send and receive messages and send and receive files. A supplier may only offer messaging services and not file-exchange services.

Note: People make a big deal about whether you are *on* the Internet. In general, almost all PC owners are not on the Internet. However, you can send and receive messages or files to a computer that is on the Internet.

At the most sophisticated end, beyond the scope of this book, you can set up an Internet node, get an ID from The Internet Society, and you are connected. In this case, you are considered *on* the Internet. However, this connection is not particularly straightforward because The Internet Society has procedures and rules that must be followed.

At a simpler level, more appropriate for almost all PC owners, you can access the Internet via most online services including from BBSs. Commercial online services are rapidly responding to customer pressure and are supplying Internet electronic mail services. A few have added file-exchange services as well.

As the popularity increases, the current limitations imposed by commercial services will probably disappear. For example, an online service may limit the amount of electronic mail or files that you can receive or send via the Internet in a month. Commercial online services typically charge you to send messages via Internet. In some cases, this is per message; in others, it is a nominal monthly charge with volume limitations.

This topic is probably the most speculative of all the topics covered in this book because it is changing daily. However, even with the online service charges, connecting is inexpensive. For example, I currently pay $3 a month and can send up to 50 messages. (I send some to my brother in England who works for a research establishment on the Internet. Now if I could just persuade him to reply. . . .)

Access to the Internet has also become popular with BBSs. The new versions of BBS software have, or will soon have, the necessary facilities so that BBSs can be on The Internet. One concept is that the BBS software manufacturer becomes an Internet node, and each BBS that uses that manufacturer's software becomes a user on the BBS software manufacturer's Internet node. You, the caller to the BBS, are considered a user of the BBS and can in turn access the Internet.

Summary

This chapter introduced online services. You can use your modem for three main functions while online: chatting, messaging, and file exchange. Each online service supplies one or more of these features. However, most online services emphasize a particular aspect.

BBSs are the most common online service. They vary in size from being operated from a single telephone line to hundreds of telephone lines. They are typically smaller in scope than the commercial online services. They are often regional or specialized on a particular topic. Increasingly, BBSs are being used by PC companies to provide technical support, and many national groups have one. Most BBSs offer file exchange and contain libraries of software you can download. Most BBSs also offer messaging where all the callers can read the messages and contribute responses. Less commonly, BBSs offer chatting, where you can interact with other users on the system.

Some online services emphasize messaging. They are like electronic mail services that extend beyond the bounds of your company. The message you send is not read by the online service and is only accessible to the recipient. In some cases, you can attach a file to a message. Messaging services do not have public forums, file libraries, or offer chatting. They are like a form of postal service.

Other online services emphasize information exchange. They also usually support messaging, but the messages are not completely private. They are intended as forums for exchanging information with an unknown group of individuals. Like BBSs, the information exchange services typically have large file libraries of software that you can download. Depending on the service, they may also offer chatting.

Another online service category is information-searching services. These are typically more expensive and are aimed at business or professional users. They have enormous, continually updated databases that you can search. They are the equivalent of electronic libraries. They do not offer messaging, chatting, or file exchange, except that you can usually obtain the full text of a reference you have found. A typical application is using the service as a newspaper clipping service.

This chapter also introduced packet-switched networks, which are used by many online services as means for connecting to their computers.

The global nature of communication is becoming a reality for PC users as an increasing number of methods emerge for exchanging messages and files economically with people around the world. The long-established Internet is now becoming available to PC users and is likely to become a favorite.

Chapter 14 explores BBSs in more detail. Chapter 15 focuses on messaging services, and Chapter 16 covers information-exchange services. Chapter 17 introduces the Internet. Chapter 18 explores information-searching services.

14

CHAPTER

BBSs for Everyone

This chapter introduces the immense world of BBSs. In particular, the following topics are covered:

- ❖ Types of BBSs
- ❖ A sample tour of two BBSs
- ❖ What to look for on a BBS
- ❖ How to find BBSs

Understanding BBSs

BBSs are the most common type of online service available. As covered in Chapter 13, BBSs offer messaging, chatting, and file exchange. Some offer each function and are general purpose, and others specialize by focusing on a particular topic, geographical region, or function.

Regardless of your taste, there are many BBSs around that are suitable for you. Everyone who calls BBSs is exercising the human desire to communicate. Some people only call to collect software — others only to espouse their favorite political agenda. However, they are all communicating.

Any BBS you call, and for that matter any online service you call, is made up of two components: the computer with its software and the other BBS users. The other BBS users make up a community, and the BBS software supplies the neighborhood.

A BBS really is a living, breathing community of people. Just as in real life, you'll meet people you love, hate, or share some similar opinions with. Some BBS users, often known as *lurkers*, are invisible to the community because they look around but do not contribute. Other BBS users are loudmouths who have an opinion on everything and can't let a single topic go by without extensive comment. Another element, often known as *flamers*, extends their opinions to personal affronts and can make discussions escalate into nuclear war very rapidly.

Unless you call for the file-exchange services only, you will run into the other members of the community, and you will be considered part of that community. The success or failure of a BBS depends on that community. If you do not like the atmosphere on a BBS, either work to correct it or go somewhere else. In telecommunicating, you don't have to move your home to meet new neighbors.

"Where do I get help on a BBS?"

Because all BBS users are trying to communicate, you will find that almost without exception they are very willing to help. Don't be afraid to ask where to find information. When approached appropriately, almost all users like to help because it gives great satisfaction to be needed or considered authoritative.

On-Line Etiquette

When you communicate with an online service, you connect to someone else's computer, and they are entitled to set the rules you must conform to. For example, a BBS typically limits how long you can be online each day so that many users get the opportunity to call. Other rules may apply to how many files you can download without uploading files.

Most of the operational rules are easy to live with. However, when you start reading messages or chatting, you can quickly meet people who intentionally or unintentionally abuse the system.

As a neophyte leaving messages, the first rule is to keep it simple and do not type your whole message in uppercase letters. Typing with Caps Lock on is considered shouting, and someone will reprimand you. If you read a series of messages and come across one that is written in uppercase letters, it seems to leap off the screen. If you cannot touch type well, do not use any uppercase letters at all.

Poor spelling and bad grammar are fine online, but bad taste is not. It is always exaggerated online and often quickly escalates into war. An offhand comment that your friends may think is funny, because they know your character, religion, and national origin, can be especially offensive. For example, ethnic jokes are not funny even if you are from an ethnic minority. You are not in that minority when online.

Before writing or sending a message, take a second to be certain that you did not miss a critical "not." Before responding to an apparently inflammatory message, reread it to be sure you did not misread. A sysop described his golden rule of etiquette to me as "Take aim at the topic and not the author".

You can get a lot of help online with solving your PC problems. Remember that not all the advice supplied will be accurate, but you should, more importantly, supply feedback when a solution is found. It is not only a matter of courtesy to thank someone for free consulting services, but it supplies the confirmation many other readers of the messages may be looking for.

In some cases, particularly on the larger and more complex boards, you may be guided to another area of the BBS to pose your question. In other cases, you can find the name and number of another BBS that can fill your need.

For example, if you want to find a BBS that has users interested in genealogy (a surprisingly popular topic), ask. Many BBS users frequent multiple boards, and unless you ask, they are unlikely to mention it. Many sysops encourage you to explore other boards. It either shows how much better their own is, or it allows them to focus on the topics of interest to them instead of needing to be all things to all callers.

The following sections introduce a few of the myriad types of BBSs. The purpose is to show you what is available — the list is not exhaustive. As mentioned in Chapter 13, each online service is unique, and you can find what you are looking for in a variety of different places. The key to the best use of online services is finding the most appropriate mix of services for the most economical use of your time and money.

Understanding local BBSs

One of the first BBSs you are likely to try calling is your local BBS. At its most expensive, it will cost you the price of a few local phone calls while you get the hang of it. Many local BBSs are run by PC enthusiasts as extensions of their hobby. They often have only one telephone line and are located in someone's basement. For the most part, especially when they are first established, they are general purpose and offer messaging and file exchange.

They do not usually offer chatting services. It is obvious why chatting is not supported. Chat boards require a minimum of two phone lines so that you can chat to the other person online, and until there is a core of users on the board, you will be the only one calling at one time even if there are two phone lines. If a board is being run by volunteers, the cost of one or two phone lines may be an acceptable burden to a sysop, but having many more phone lines installed makes it much more of a serious business proposition.

Many local BBSs are free and have no annual maintenance charges. Some do not charge but have certain usage rules. For example, you may have to upload one new file for every five that you download, or you have only a very limited time online unless you contribute financially or materially with new files for the file library. Other BBSs charge a nominal annual fee, which is intended to defray expenses. For example, several of my local BBSs charge $25 per year. This is probably enough for the sysop to pay the phone bill and buy a couple of CD ROM disks for the file library each year.

Local BBSs vary in quality and diversity. If you live near a major metropolitan area, you can easily have tens if not hundreds to choose from. Appendix B lists a selection of BBSs arranged by area code. Some magazines publish lists from time to time, and most BBSs contain a file that lists hundreds of BBSs. The section on invaluable files later in this chapter explains more about this list.

Obviously, the larger BBSs must be located locally to some people, so you may be fortunate to have one that is only a local phone call for you. The character of a BBS is reflected in its callers. Many local BBSs have less than 100 regular callers, and you can really get to know the individuals more easily than with services who get hundreds of callers a day.

Many local BBSs are extensions of the local computer club and are particularly beneficial for meeting people who know about PCs (or think they do). You must remember that the advice you see on a BBS is only as good as its source. I have seen many beginners who did not know what question to ask or where to start sorting out a problem get guidance from BBS users.

"What will I find on a local BBS?"

You will typically find file exchange and messaging on your local BBS. Depending on the number of users, you may find only one communal message area, or you may find a main area and a couple of specialized topic areas called *conferences*, on such topics as politics, parenting, or word processing. Messages are often referred to as *mail*.

There is an increasing interest in parents letting children use BBSs to exchange information. The local BBS is a great place to let your child communicate with friends and make new friends. It is a safe environment and can provide excellent education. You should to take an active interest in your child's online activities. Apart from the potential increase in telephone bills, insidious elements in our society are just as present here as everywhere else.

BBSs are great places to frequent when there are national or local crises occurring. If you listen to the radio, watch TV, or read a newspaper, you are presented with a diluted compilation of information. If you get on a BBS and read the messages, you get much more of a raw opinion and typically get another perspective on the topic. For local news, local BBSs provide a different gauge of interest.

Do not assume however, that a local BBS will not have up-to-date files available. You may be able to get the new printer driver for Windows from your local BBS within a couple of days of release and not have to subscribe to a national service to get it.

For example, I subscribe to a national BBS because some of my interests are not served by my local BBSs. I am very interested in the latest in PC communications information and several very specific PC topics but have not found other fanatics near me.

I am also addicted to computer games, particularly those that are not "shoot-em up" ones. I get the games from the national board and immediately upload them to my local BBS. You can get the new public domain or shareware games from my local BBS within a couple of days of their release. I call my local BBS for local information because the BBS picks up some messages on PC communication from a national source.

Listening for New Technology

Browsing around BBSs is an excellent way to keep in touch with new technology and new issues. For example, when the former U.S.S.R. collapsed, thousands of computer users around the world followed the action by communicating via BBSs with Russians. The Russians were sending messages to the West, and these messages were echoed throughout the world.

On a less world-shaking level, you can often pick up information on new technology or different interests from BBSs. You can certainly hear about the obvious, such as a new computer from IBM or new prices for online services. But more interestingly, you can hear how people like these new things and what they use them for. For example, the popularity of the Internet for PC users mushroomed in the space of only a few months because of BBSs. The Internet was not news; it had been in place for over two decades; but PC operators had only recently discovered it.

The timetable for acceptance of V.34 modems will depend on the reaction of BBS operators. Many people will not purchase new technology until they read about success stories on the BBSs. Offline readers are gaining in popularity rapidly because of the "good press" they are receiving online. RIP (Remote Image Protocol), a graphical interface for BBSs, is gaining in popularity because of the interest by users of BBSs.

You can also learn about other interests. Because these may never have a big following but are of particular interest to a small group of people, the international nature of BBSs gives these interests a forum. For example, a class of programs known as *demos* are popular in Europe and are gaining an interested following in the U.S. via BBSs. A demo is a program written typically as a collaborative effort by programmers. There is a competition each year for the best. A demo is intended to show the skills of the programmers.

Demos are typically self-running and show lots of objects moving around on your screen. You have probably seen pictures of bouncing balls on chessboards on the television. These demos are similar but are written for the PC. A casual PC user probably would look at a couple of demos and say, "Pretty pictures — so what?" However, to someone with programming knowledge, even very elementary knowledge, the programming skills required are apparent.

I consider it mutual cooperation. I get the PC communication information from my local BBS because the sysop collects and posts it, and he gets the latest games because I collect them and pass them on. By the way, supporting your local BBS is one of the best ways to get involved in BBSs, especially if you are considering running your own BBS. Many sysops welcome volunteers, and many waive subscription fees if you prove an asset to the BBS.

For example, you may volunteer to moderate some of the chat or message areas or help with the routine maintenance. Running a BBS is rather like running a restaurant, however. The image portrayed to the public ignores the mundane essential tasks, such as dishwashing and trash collection. Additionally, the sysop and his helpers supply a service — not the loudest voice.

Understanding national BBSs

Some BBSs have become so popular that they have become known nationally and have avid followers. They are no different than the local BBS except that they manage to pull users from all over the country. If a board is popular, it has lots of callers, and its user community gets larger and more diverse. However, if you call the board and only get busy signals, you will try another board. Some local BBSs are so popular, they do not have the phone line capacity.

The incremental cost for sysops to add more than a second phone line begins to mount because they need special computer hardware to allow multiple users on the BBS and have sufficient serial ports to attach to the phone lines. This is in addition to the costs involved with having many phone lines installed.

Consequently, there is a division between a local BBS and a BBS with many phone lines. The BBSs with more phone lines tend to be run more as commercial enterprises. Although only a few are big money-makers and allow the sysop to be a full-time BBS operator, many make small supplemental incomes for the sysops.

"What do I find on a national BBS?"

These boards tend to have more of everything. The national BBSs tend to have faster computer equipment, so they are more responsive, and have faster modems, so you can connect with a fast modem. Additionally, they often have more storage space, so they can hold more files. The larger user base encourages more messages, so they tend to have more general messages and many more topical conferences.

Additionally, the national BBSs tend to be more involved with interconnection. They often pick up echo mail, from such networks as Fidonet or RIME, or have links into the Internet. If you want to know what it is like to live in Israel, Estonia, or Australia, you only have to send a message to find out.

Chat boards

BBSs that offer chatting are far fewer in number than those that only offer messaging and file exchange. However, as a BBS becomes sufficiently popular to justify more than one telephone line, chatting is often listed as a feature even if it is not used all the time.

Next time you are on your favorite BBS, look carefully at the menus because you may see an option that says something like "who's on." This tells you the name of any other caller who is currently online. Depending on how the sysop has set up the system, you may be able to invite someone to chat with you. If he or she agrees, you type your message, and he or she types an answer.

A few BBSs have expanded their chat features so that they are a major or the only focus of the BBS. These typically charge a few cents an hour for you to chat with other callers. As with most BBSs, you can typically look around for a limited time for free. You may, for example, be able to chat for ten minutes a day for a month before subscribing.

"*What will I find on a chat board?*"

As covered in Chapter 13, chatting permits individuals to exploit their alter egos. Because of the relative anonymity, you can express opinions that you would not ordinarily do. If you are someone who carefully weighs everything you say before speaking, stay off the chat boards and stick with messaging systems or elementary chatting to find out who else is on the same BBS as you. If you are easily offended, by perhaps a comment on the President's new health plan, or whether women should stay at home and have babies, keep away. If you enjoy a good argument, try a chat board.

Some of these BBSs are adult only — others are not. However, even the adult boards have various sections. For example, an area may support very heated political or religious discussions, and another support more sexually oriented topics.

Another form of chatting is interactive game playing. You call a BBS and play a game with other users who are online. For example, you may choose to play a game where you are driving a tank and you fight other tanks that are controlled by other users.

A more common interactive game involves role playing and is similar in concept to the popular Dungeons and Dragons game. It is actually a form of chatting that follows rules while you express an alter ego. Interactive games are usually found as part of national BBSs. Some commercial online services also offer this and chat forums as does the Internet.

Messaging boards

Messaging boards are commonly found on local and national BBSs. Again, the character of the board is dictated by the users who call it. The more diverse the user base, the more diverse the topics under discussion.

As shown in the guided tour later in this chapter, boards that focus on messaging segregate the messages into topics. These topic areas are often called *conferences*. They permit you to call the board and read only the messages that may be of interest to you. Many boards get hundreds of messages a day, and you are unlikely to be interested in every topic. When you call the board, you look only at the message conferences that interest you. For example, you may look at the general conference, the education conference, and the movie review conference.

Many of the national messaging boards emphasize a particular topic and often name their boards appropriately to attract interested people. For example, there is at least one BBS focused on gay rights, another on education, and another on bird watching. The messaging boards typically include file libraries in addition to messaging. Many also pick up echo mail, such as Fidonet, RIME, or the Internet, to expand their message base.

Messaging boards can be a lot of fun, but the volume of messages can be overwhelming. Offline mail readers quickly become valuable, and you need to call a BBS regularly if you want to follow the messages on an ongoing basis. Calling occasionally often makes the messages seem very disjointed.

File library boards

Many message boards that are not focused on a particular topic also carry many file libraries. Many other BBSs tend to have minimal messaging areas but have gigabytes of files for downloading. Collection of new software is the most frequent reason given by users for using BBSs and online services.

Like message boards, the large file libraries are typically divided into topic areas to help you find things. For example, you may choose between word processing, games, utilities, and general. You can typically search for files in a variety of ways, including by filename, key topics, or date. You also can search for new files — perhaps files that have been added since you were last on the BBS.

Your best approach with a new board is to get an idea of the topics for the files and download the file or files that contain the lists of all the BBS files. Most BBS software can be set up automatically to create this file, so it will probably be updated regularly by the sysop. A later section explains what typical file names to look for.

"What files can I get from a BBS?"

You should understand clearly the type of files that are available online and the type of files that are suitable for uploading to BBSs. Software falls into one of three general categories: commercial, shareware, and public domain. WordPerfect is an example of commercial software; PKZIP is an example of shareware; and LZH (another file compression program) is an example of public domain software.

Public domain software, as the name implies, is available to everyone, and you can use it freely and copy it for your friends. Shareware programs are commercial programs distributed in a unique way. You may freely copy shareware programs. You may use shareware programs for a limited period, typically 30 days, free of charge. However, if you continue to use a shareware product, you must register it with the vendor. The registration form is included with the product files. If you do not use the shareware product, you are obliged to delete it from your computer. Shareware works as an honor system; if you use it, you are required to register it.

Some of the very best software available is shareware, and it is hard to use BBSs without encountering shareware. PKZIP, an essential program for BBS users, is a shareware product, and if you download files, you should be using a registered version of PKZIP. Some communication software does not support the ZMODEM file-transfer protocol, and you may decide to use the shareware add-on program. Again, this product should be registered. The most popular antivirus programs, SCAN and CLEAN, also are shareware programs.

Commercial software should not be found on BBSs, and you should not upload it. For example, it is illegal to upload WordPerfect, Windows, or DOS onto a BBS. Although most sysops go to great lengths to check that none of the files on their BBS are commercial, some programs slip by them. If you find that you have downloaded one, delete it, and leave a message for the sysop next time you call the BBS.

By the way, some people alter commercial software and upload it with the copyright screen removed or some other such modification. I am highly suspicious of programs obtained from a BBS that appear to be commercial even if I do not see any real evidence of tampering. I feel that someone who is corrupt enough to modify a commercial program and pass it off as public domain software may have the mentality necessary to place a virus within the modification.

There are several variations on the general definitions of shareware and public domain software. Some people distribute limited versions of their products for free and provide the full working version when you register the software. (These are not considered true shareware as approved by the Association of Shareware Professionals.)

Note: Software can be copyrighted even if it is public domain. This usually means you are not allowed to modify the software and pass it off as your own.

You may find files that are supplied by a commercial vendor on BBSs. For example, you may find a new mouse driver, video driver, or a bug fix for a program. Although these are parts of commercial products, they are typically legal on the BBS. On their own, these little files are useless, but if you own the relevant product, these files can upgrade your setup. These files are found most often on technical support BBSs.

For example, Qualitas had an interim update for their product 386MAX on their BBS. Users downloaded the file and ran the program. The program looked for 386MAX on your hard disk, and if it found it, updated it. If you did not have 386MAX installed on your hard disk, the downloaded file was of no use to you.

Another type of file that is fairly popular on BBSs is graphic files showing high-resolution pictures. Unfortunately, this area is very controversial because it is difficult to control for two reasons. As mentioned before, many BBSs expect you to maintain a particular upload-to-download ratio. For example, you may need to upload one file for every five that you download. Where do you get the files from? Some people use a scanner and scan pictures from magazines and books and upload them to a BBS. This is illegal. The photographer or publisher of the magazine or book owns the copyright on the printed photograph, and you may not copy it. You can scan only your own photographs and upload them.

The other problem associated with these graphic files is adult material and pornography. There are well-defined laws defining pornography and who can have access to it, but these are not yet well defined in the electronic media and specifically on BBSs. Ignoring the legal implications, there is no doubt that you can obtain plenty of pornographic pictures from some BBSs. As with the chat boards, if you find this material offensive, avoid the adult file areas, and if you let your children have free rein on BBSs, be aware that they may find access to this type of material.

Technical support boards

As the price of computer software and hardware continues to tumble, many companies are reassessing how to provide quality technical support at a more economical price. One solution is running a technical support bulletin board.

BBSs have the advantage that the user can call any time and the messages can be processed at a different time. Technical support technicians are regularly asked the same questions, and a BBS enables a company to post the most frequently asked questions so that they can be read without requiring a technician's intervention.

Technical support boards also offer the opportunity to provide software bug fixes or new printer or display drivers inexpensively. The user calls the BBS and downloads the driver of interest. The user also can leave messages for a technician to answer. In general, the messages on these BBSs are not read by all the users but are earmarked for the receiving technicians. (Companies offering technical support boards include Hayes, WordPerfect, and Gateway 2000.)

The problem with technical support BBSs is that some are very good and some are very bad. In many cases, the user calling needs to be fairly sophisticated to know what information to supply with a question and how to handle a modem and communications software. The lack of direct interface between the technician and the user can be frustrating because the user may omit information when asking the question, or the technician may omit information when answering the question. Consequently, getting the answer to a relatively simple question may take a couple of iterations.

I find the technical support BBSs very useful, but I am also very willing to call technical support directly when I have problems. I use the BBS to find out whether there is a new driver or any known incompatibilities. I call technical support by telephone when I have a question that cannot be asked in a couple of sentences.

Some technical support BBSs boast an interactive database where you can search for keywords and find any questions and answers that have been asked on a similar topic. I have been unsuccessful with these because I do not use quite the right search word. For example, I may ask for *printer, page jamming* when I should have asked for *printer problems, output.*

Some BBSs also offer a fax-back service. (Some telephone systems also offer this.) You call the BBS, request information, and it is faxed to the number you request within a few minutes. This is particularly useful for application notes that are so detailed it is hard to communicate them verbally. For example, an *application note* (a written piece of paper that shows how to do something specific) may show the switch settings for a sound board or the pin connections for an audio cable.

Association and government agency boards

In the current electronic world, you can find a BBS relevant to whatever topic you can conceive. Many associations, societies, and clubs use BBSs as a communication medium. In some cases, the organization may have an area on a commercial online service and require membership to subscribe to the service.

Additionally, many government agencies run BBSs that can be accessed by the general public. These include the IRS, Social Security Administration, Department of Defense, Department of Energy, Environmental Protection Agency, and Small Business Administration. Some of these even have 800 numbers.

Files containing lists of these BBSs are found on most BBSs. The one for the government agencies is commonly called GOVT.ZIP. A later section in this chapter lists the typical file names to look for and how to go about extending your search.

Overview of Your First Encounter with a BBS

The first time you call a BBS is different from the rest. In almost all cases, you are expected to register with the BBS. This allows the sysop to have a record of who you are and how to contact you. Although you may consider this information prying and unnecessary, bear in mind that you are actually using someone else's modem and computer. The sysop is entitled to know some basic information.

The typical information that you will be asked for is your name, address, phone number, and the password you want to use to access the system. In some cases, you are also given the opportunity to choose how your name will appear in messages. This is known as your *handle*. You may be named Frederick, for example, but want to be known on the board as Fred or even Skip. Another common option allows you to pick a default file-download protocol. If your communications program supports ZMODEM, and it is offered as an option, you will want to choose ZMODEM.

If you consider asking for this information prying, you probably will not find any online service satisfactory, because they all want it. In some cases, the BBS uses a callback system, where the BBS automatically calls you back at the given phone number to verify that you are a legitimate user. Beware of this if you call a BBS from work but give your home phone number, for example.

You need the name and password each time you call a BBS. Be very careful about what you use as a password. Most people choose a child's, pet's, or spouse's name, or their telephone number. Avoid this, especially if you are paying for the service, because it is very easy to guess a password and someone else can access the system by using your name. Consider basing it on a phone number that you remember, perhaps the local dry cleaner's or your doctor's.

Some BBSs ask for additional information, such as the type of computer you are using, the modem type, and other computer information. From the sysop's viewpoint, it is interesting to know something about the demographics of the callers. Filling out this information is typically a condition of becoming registered with the BBS. I think of it as a rite of passage. You are unlikely to be asked for the information again. It may prove useful to you. If you have a fast modem, for example, you may encourage the sysop to add a fast modem to the BBS by filling out this form.

"Why do I have to register with a BBS?"

However, some BBSs also ask for information that you may not be willing to give, such as age and gender. Before refusing to give your age, consider the board you are calling. If it contains adult material, the sysop must provide some method of filtering minors. Although it is less offensive to some people to be asked whether you are over 21, some people get upset however the question is phrased. Some BBSs require proof of age in writing before you are accepted to the BBS. This is often a copy of your driver's license.

You also may be asked for a credit card number. Again, consider the BBS carefully before giving this number. You should have an opportunity to explore the board in a limited way without subscribing, and you should be able to send a check instead of using a credit card if you prefer. However, the sysop is entitled to make sure the check clears before altering your access status to the board.

In addition to filling out some type of questionnaire, you will be shown the rules of the BBS. This will include the subscription charges, time limitations, and other details. For example, a BBS may have a rule of no profanity or that messages must be less than 25 lines. Remember that you are a guest on someone else's computer. If you do not like the rules, find another BBS.

After completing the questionnaire, you will have the opportunity to explore the BBS a little or will be instructed to call back the next day. The sysop takes the supplied information and upgrades your status on the BBS so that you have access as a registered user.

Note: Every time you call the BBS, you will be asked for your name and your password. These are the keys to your access. You must use exactly the same name each time you call. For example, Jon Smith is a different person than J Smith, or Jonathon Smith.

If you do forget your password, reregister by using a slightly different name; use your initial instead of your full name. Then leave a message for the sysop explaining why you are reregistering and specifying what you actually want your name and password to be. The sysop will compare the other information you gave, such as your address and phone number, and will clear up your error for you.

Five-Minute Tour of a BBS

Assuming that you are registered with a BBS, you will be able to access it by supplying your name and password when the BBS answers your phone call. The process of accessing the BBS is known as *logging on*. Similarly, the process of leaving the BBS is known as *logging off*.

BBSs are typically running one of about a dozen popular BBS software programs. However, each board has an individual character. Some are rather clinical and austere; others are so user-friendly that you have to plow through lots of menus to get anywhere.

To get around a BBS, remember the following hints:

- Read the menus and prompts carefully.
- If all else fails, log off and recall the system.
- Use the capture feature of your communication software and look at it offline.

For a brief introduction to a BBS, I called Software Creations, the largest BBS in the U.S. Figure 14-1 shows the opening screen.

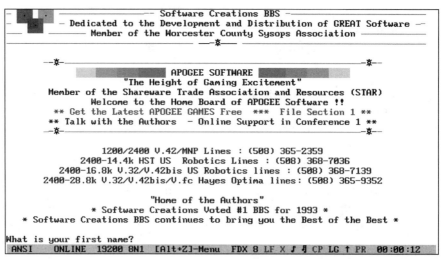

Figure 14-1: Software Creations opening screen. A BBS's opening screen should show the phone numbers for access as well as give a brief overview of where you have called.

The first prompt on most BBSs is for your first or last name. This is the first step in the logon process. The Software Creations opening screen is fairly typical although more colorful than many BBSs.

Notice the useful list of phone numbers in the center. If you have a faster modem, you can call a different number and log on at a faster speed. Software Creations is a national BBS that offers subscribers alternative phone numbers that are less likely to be busy. As it is an extremely popular BBS, the subscription is well worth the money.

After typing your first name, you are prompted for your last name. The BBS then repeats your name and your location and requests your password. You type your password, and when the BBS verifies it, you are logged onto the BBS. You continue to follow any prompts, such as Do you want to read your mail before proceeding? and then you reach the main menu.

The Main Menu shown in Figure 14-2 is an example of a particularly well-equipped BBS. However, it is very similar to many BBSs. The available items are arranged in groups, such as mail commands, user settings, and file commands. Within each group is a list of available commands, such as read mail or enter new mail. The letter or letters enclosed in square brackets before the command name are the letters you must press at the prompt to access the command. The overall menu is surrounded by a border that helps give the BBS character.

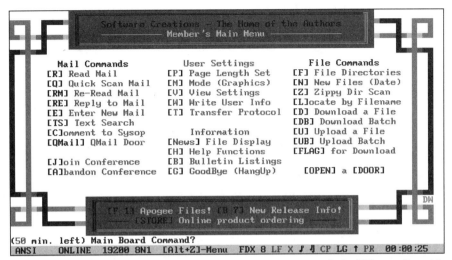

Figure 14-2: Main Menu. The actual items on this menu can vary with the BBS as well as with your status on that BBS.

Notice in particular the information displayed at the command prompt. On the sample screen, the very bottom line is displayed by the communications software and gives status information, such as the terminal emulation, the character format, and the amount of time since the connection was made. The line above is the terminal screen and shows the BBS's command prompt. In this case, the prompt is (50 min. left) Main Board Command?.

The prompt will show you where you are in the BBS. For example, it will say the Main Board, File Menu, or Mail Read menu. It usually also shows how much longer you have for today. Many boards restrict the length of time for which you can access the board in a single day so that other users get a chance to use it too.

You type the command of interest at the command prompt. In this example, I press R to read mail and get to the read mail command prompt. At this prompt, I could press H to get help on the available read commands or type a read command immediately. Pressing R S, for example, is the quick way to read all messages since you last read messages.

For this example, I press J to join a mail conference. This opens the mail conference menu, as shown in Figure 14-3.

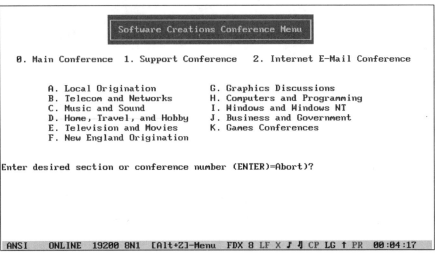

Figure 14-3: Software Creations mail conferences. The mail is divided into topics known as conferences.

This BBS has many different conferences available. Figure 14-3 shows the summary screen. The conferences are divided into categories based on subject, such as Music and Sound or Business and Government. There are further conferences for e-mail of a general nature, such as Internet e-mail or for users of this particular BBS. You press the number or letter for the conference of interest. For example, if you want to read the messages on the main board, you press 0, or if you want to read about games, you press K. Figure 14-4 shows the first screenful of gaming conference selections. The selections are color-coded to show their origin. This particular screen, the first of two, shows conferences from the Internet as well as from echo mail and a local conference. Again, you select the number of the conference of interest. For example, you type 52 to read about Nintendo gaming or 89 to read about Sega gaming.

When you are in a conference, you will be reading mail relating to that particular conference topic. You can read as many or as few messages as you like and can choose different conferences. However, if you are going to do much exploring of the messages, you will probably want to read the messages offline. As explained in Chapter 10, an offline reader can automatically create a file containing the messages from your chosen conferences and download it to your computer. You then log off from the BBS and read the messages at your leisure without incurring the telephone charges while you read.

When you finish reading the messages of interest, you can return to the main menu for other commands (or to log off). To illustrate a file library system, Figure 14-5 shows the screen displayed if you press F at the main menu.

```
Enter desired section or conference number (ENTER)=Abort)? k

Yellow = local     Cyan = Internet     Green = Echo

Gaming Conferences

1    Software Support                Talk to the authors here
9    INFINITY Machine                Support and codes from REM Software
14   comp.sys.ibm.pc.games          General Games Discussions
33   rec.games.design               Game Design
52   rec.games.video.nintendo       Nintendo Gaming
86   rec.puzzles                    Puzzles and Crosswords
89   rec.games.video.sega           Sega Gaming
90   alt.netgames.bolo              Bolo Network Gaming
111  rec.games.hack                 Nethack, Rogue, et al
130  rec.games.board                Board Games
131  rec.games.pinball              Pinball Games
132  rec.games.trivia               Trivia Style Games
134  rec.games.video                Video Games - Atari, 3DO, etc.
142  comp.sys.ibm.pc.games.action   Action Games Discussion
143  comp.sys.ibm.pc.games.adventure Adventure Games Discussion
144  comp.sys.ibm.pc.games.announce Announcements of Game Releases
145  comp.sys.ibm.pc.games.flight-sim Flight Simulators
(55 min left), (H)elp, More?
 ANSI    ONLINE   19200 8N1  [Alt+Z]-Menu   FDX 8 LF X ♪ ♫ CP LG ↑ PR   00:06:10
```

Figure 14-4: Software Creations Gaming Conferences. The mail that you can select from is obtained from a variety of sources.

```
 ☀─────────── Software Creations * Home of the Authors ───────────☀
   ┌───── Apogee Software ─────┐      ┌───── Software Creations ─────┐
   │ Apogee Releases ........... 1    │ SWC Releases ............... 3
   │ Apogee Dist. Network ....... 2   │ SWC Vendors/Sysops ........ 38
   ──── You Can Also Order These File Areas By Mail - Open Door #5 ────
   │ Arcanum Computing... 4   Id Software ...... 47   Boxer Software..... 6
   │ Alive Software .... 63   Boardwatch Contest. 62  ImagiSOFT ......... 61
   │ Gamer's Edge ...... 5    Favorite Authors....65  GameByte Magazine.. 66

Educational ........ 7    Utils, Files ....... 16   Windows, Games ..... 67
Games A-L .......... 8    Utils, Printers .... 17   Windows, General ... 20
Games M-Z .......... 9    Utils, Video ....... 18   Windows, Fonts ..... 69
Game Accesories .... 10   Utils, Menus ...... 102   Windows, Wallpaper . 70
MS-DOS ............. 15   Utils, Memory ..... 103   Windows, Drivers ... 71
OS/2 ............... 98   Utils, Keyboard ... 104   Windows, Printers .. 72
Unix ............... 99   Utils, Disk/Tape ... 14   Windows, Video ..... 73
Multi-tasking .... 100    Music/Sound Programs 11   Windows, Icons ..... 74
Device drivers ... 101    Music/Sound Files .. 12   Windows, Programing  75
4DOS Related ...... 79    Windows: Utils ..... 68   Windows, Sound ..... 76

(52 min left), (H)elp, More?
 ANSI    ONLINE   19200 8N1  [Alt+Z]-Menu   FDX 8 LF X ♪ ♫ CP LG ↑ PR   00:08:34
```

Figure 14-5: The Software Creations File menu. This BBS divides its huge file collection into directories by topic.

Again, Software Creations has an extensive list of available topics. You choose your topic by its number and can see a list of available files. If you choose topic number 39, Astronomy, for example, you see a screen similar to Figure 14-6.

```
(H)elp, (1-200), File List Command? 39
Filename      Size    Date     Description of File Contents
===============================================================================

ACE1.ZIP     163028  12-13-93  General Purpose Astronomy Software Package
                               Files: 12  Oldest: 9/26/86  Newest: 1/24/87
                               Uploaded by: Steve Meade
ALW32S.ZIP  1322267  07-14-93  ASTRONOMY LAB version 1.2
                               for Windows 3.1 and Windows NT
                               includes win32s for W31
                               brought to you by HZZ
                               Files: 3  Oldest: 5/28/93  Newest: 7/14/93
AMKP0111.ZIP  13202  09-02-92  AMSAT-formatted satellite elements as of
                               01/01/92.
AMST0111.ZIP  14320  09-02-92  AMSAT-formatted orbital elements as of
                               01/11/92.
ASTINFO.ZIP  101984  08-12-93  Astrological Information Viewer
                               Shows BioRythm etc..
                               Files: 4  Oldest: 1/17/93  Newest: 1/17/93
ASTLAB.ZIP   661111  11-22-93  Astronomy Lab for Windows
                               Files: 20  Oldest: 6/10/92  Newest: 10/2/93
                               Uploaded by: Bob Oxberger
(52 min left), (H)elp, (V)iew, (F)lag, More?
ANSI    ONLINE  19200 8N1  [Alt+Z]-Menu  FDX 8 LF X ♪ ♪ CP LG ↑ PR  00:09:19
```

Figure 14-6: File library list. The directory listing shows the available files.

On this BBS, you can continue to get a list of filenames with short descriptions of the files, or you can flag a particular file for downloading. If you choose flag, you are prompted for the filename, and it is marked as being a file you want to download. You then continue looking at lists of files and can download all your chosen files at once.

On many BBSs, there are literally hundreds of files on a particular topic, and you shouldn't search through them all. As shown later in the chapter, most BBSs have a file or series of files that you can download. These files contain a list of all the available files on the BBS. If you download one of these, you can then just look at any new files when you log onto the board.

In the same way that the mail menu has read commands that allow you to read only the messages you have not read since a particular date, the file menu has equivalent commands so that you can see which files have been added since you were last on the board or since a particular date.

If you need help at any time, you can press H or type **help** at the command prompt for a list of the currently available commands. As a newcomer to a BBS, you should choose one command at a time. However, as you gain experience, you can learn how to get through the menus more rapidly or activate a series of commands with a single command line.

To leave a BBS, you must log off from the system. In most cases, the command is G, **goodbye**, or **bye**. Remember that you can use this to exit the BBS when you get lost in the menu structure. Whenever you re-call the BBS, you start at the main menu again.

Logging off from a system rather than just issuing the hang up command to your communication software is a useful habit to cultivate. If you are paying for your online time, the BBS will not know immediately that you have hung up and will assume you are about to type on your keyboard. It will hang up eventually, but the few seconds to few minutes before it considers you to have hung up because there is no activity will cost you. Even if you are not paying for the time but have a restricted amount of time online, the BBS will continue to count your time down until it resets itself.

One-Minute Look at a Graphical BBS

A new generation of BBSs is gaining popularity. These use a graphical user interface called RIP (Remote Image Protocol) as the terminal emulation. If your software can support RIP — and increasingly communications software is supporting this standard — you can use your mouse online and have screen buttons to press instead of commands to type.

Note: All BBSs that support RIP also support another terminal emulation standard such as ANSI. To take advantage of RIP, you need to choose RIP emulation before dialing the BBS.

As an example of how RIP can completely change a BBS's user interface, see Figures 14-7 and 14-8. Figure 14-7 is the main menu from a BBS I called by using ANSI terminal emulation, and Figure 14-8 is the same BBS I called by using RIP terminal emulation.

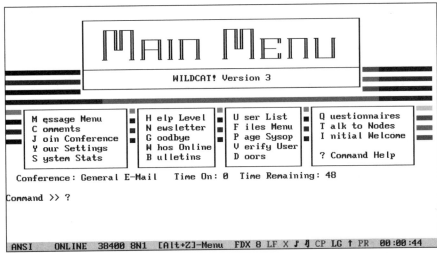

Figure 14-7: BBS main menu with ANSI terminal emulation. ANSI terminal emulation gives colors but is totally textual in appearance.

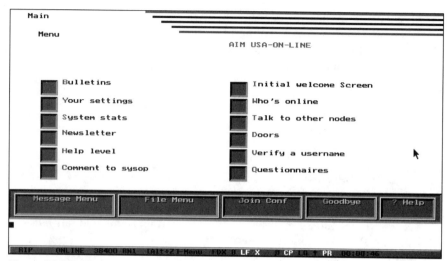

Figure 14-8: BBS main menu with RIP terminal emulation. RIP provides a graphical interface and mouse support for a BBS.

If you look carefully, you can see the same menu options on both screens despite the totally different appearance.

What to Look for on a BBS

If you look hard enough, you can find BBSs to fit your tastes — no matter how eclectic they may be. However, the following sections give a brief overview of items to look for when choosing a BBS, particularly a messaging and file-exchange BBS. They include the board's organization, files to look for, and the file-exchange services offered.

Organization

A BBS presents itself to you one screen at a time. A good BBS is one that is easy to navigate. It is amazing how many BBSs are very difficult to use. Consider the following items when assessing a BBS:

- Does it contain the information *you* want?

- Is it easy to *find* the information you want?

- Is the grouping, such as conferences and file libraries, *logical* to you?
- Can you *search* for the files you want?
- Is there a *regular flow* of traffic?
- Are the menus *consistent*?

Most of these topics have been covered elsewhere, but it is worth doing a critical assessment of the online services you use from time to time so that you continue to get the most from them.

A BBS should contain information of interest to you, where you can find it, and arranged in a fashion that is obvious to you. The organization may seem very logical to the sysop but not to you. For example, one sysop may keep all the word processing utility files in the word processing library, but another puts them into various categories, such as printers, video, and mouse sections. Both are reasonable places, but one will seem more logical to you.

When you first log on to a BBS, the amount of accumulated information can seem exciting and endless. However, the information may not change, perhaps because not many callers contribute to the messages or supply new files. These BBSs can quickly become boring because you are not seeing new material. Similarly, when you first log on to a BBS, you may be overwhelmed by the amount of information and may be intimidated. Find a BBS with more-limited information and get used to that before considering another one.

Beware of some BBSs that use the same letter command for different purposes depending on which is your current menu. For example, a BBS may use S in the message menu to send a message and S in the file menu to search for a file. These BBSs can be very irritating to use, especially when you reach the point where you stop reading the menus carefully. These include compression and uncompression utilities, lists of conferences, lists of files, and possibly lists of other BBSs to call.

Invaluable files

Almost all BBSs have a few files that are worth collecting. These include compression and uncompression utilities, lists of conferences, lists of files, and possibly lists of other BBSs to call.

First, you need a file compression and uncompression utility program. Most files are stored on the BBS in compressed form to save disk space and to reduce the time needed to download them. The compression program also allows multiple files to be stored in a single compressed file. Consequently, you download a single file that may be comprised of many individual files needed to run the program you have selected.

"What are the most important files to get from a BBS?"

The market leader is PKZIP from PKWARE and is typically named PKZ204G.EXE. The 204G portion of the filename refers to the version number — in this case, Version 2.04G. Consequently, when a new version becomes available, this filename will change. Files that are zipped with PKZIP have a file extension of .ZIP.

The file PKZ204G.EXE is a special type of compressed file, known as a self-extracting file. You download this file to your computer, type its name at the DOS prompt, and then press Enter. The file automatically uncompresses all its component files, and you end up with, among other important files, the compression and uncompression programs. Be sure to read the supplied documentation to understand how to use PKZIP.

Some BBSs and online services use other file compression utilities. The most common are ARC and LZH (typically found as ARJ202.EXE and LHA212.EXE respectively.)

Most BBSs include a file that lists all the files found on that BBS. They may also keep a list of available conferences in a file. It is found under a variety of names, so you may have to leave a message if you cannot find it. However, common names are FILES.ALL, DIR.ALL, or variations on the name that include the date the file was compiled, such as FILE0294.ALL, meaning February 1994's list. This file is sometimes listed as a menu item on its own. For example, Software Creations lists ALLFILES as a directory item of its own and has a separate directory of "free needed files" that includes such things as PKZIP.

Another commonly found file is a file containing a list of BBSs that you can call. It is sometimes called BBSLIST.ZIP. The file GOVT.ZIP, is a list of BBSs run by government agencies. However, if looking for these files does not reveal a BBS that you are particularly interested in finding, consider the following search strategies. Call the BBS manufacturer's BBS. Each of the companies that sells BBS software runs a BBS.

For example, Mustang Software, who makes QModem, runs a BBS. Mustang allows its registered BBS software owners to advertise their BBSs. Last time I looked, they had more than ten pages of BBS ads in their file listing. Several were for overseas BBSs, such as in England or Trinidad.

If you have a more specialized interest, call the national association, the local club, or look in a relevant magazine. For example, Antiquenet, a BBS for antique dealers, advertises in one of the antique dealer magazines.

File exchange with a BBS

If you intend to do much downloading of software, you should carefully examine your options after you have mastered the basics. The following sections give an overview of the most important items to look for, including supported file protocols, libraries, and quotas.

Supported protocols

In most cases, you want to select a BBS that supports the ZMODEM file-transfer protocol. You will want to choose a version of XMODEM as a backup. Practice downloading files with both protocols, and make a note of the preferred choices for that particular BBS. (Chapter 6 explains the potential discrepancies between XMODEM file-transfer protocols.)

You should weigh the advantages of using ZMODEM in batch mode, where you can specify a series of files for downloading at one time, with the speed differences. For example, a BBS that supports 2400 bps and ZMODEM batch mode may be preferable to a BBS that supports 9600 bps, but you must specify each file in turn.

I would look for a BBS that has it all: fastest speed with compression, ZMODEM batch mode, and the capability to hang up automatically after downloading files. However, I have a high-speed modem, a husband who considers high phone bills a trivial detail, and a second phone line in my home.

Libraries

When considering a BBS's file libraries, you should look for logical organization and a reasonable searching mechanism. You also want to see that new material is being added regularly and that the older material is being removed or moved out of the way so that accessing the newer material remains efficient.

Suppose that you want to look for a genealogy program. A directory labeled something like genealogy or family history, would be ideal; but on smaller BBSs, you may need to choose a more general library topic that suggests genealogy, such as history or personal. Now suppose that you find the topic, download a few files, and try out a few programs.

A few months go by and you decide to get interested in genealogy again but want to see whether there's anything better. When you call the BBS, you don't want to wade through all the same material you saw before to find the one new file of interest. Therefore, you need to evaluate whether the BBS lists files by date or another element that indicates clearly how new they are.

The BBS needs to supply easy ways to find what you are looking for, even if you do not know exactly what you are looking for! Although this may seem a tall task, it is surprising how some BBSs seem to do this effortlessly and others do not.

Quotas

Some BBSs use file quotas or ratios to encourage new files on the BBS. You may have to upload one file for every five you download, for example. If you call several boards regularly, it is quite easy to maintain this quota.

Other boards offer alternative pricing that you will want to select based on your use of the BBS. Some may offer a quota system for free, a more liberal quota system for a small subscription, or unrestricted downloading for a more generous subscription. Other approaches include more liberal time online per day for subscribers, or alternate and less busy phone numbers for subscribers.

This is one area where BBSs are likely to be much more economical than commercial online services. Many online services charge for connect time and charge a premium if you connect at a higher speed. Most BBSs charge an annual or monthly subscription if they charge at all.

Desirable extras for messages

Other items to consider when choosing a BBS relate to messaging rather than file exchange. If you are going to do much message reading, offline mail reader support becomes a vital rather than desirable extra. Additionally, support for echo and relay mail systems, such as RIME, Fidonet, and the Internet, may be important to you if you want to reach or hear from a wider audience.

Summary

This chapter introduced general categories for BBSs based on size and function. Local BBSs tend to be small and may focus on regional topics. National BBSs with huge followings have a wide user base, extensive libraries, and messaging services. Chat boards, the best of which draw users from a national audience, allow you to express your alter ego. BBSs are run as hobbies, by associations, by clubs, and by companies as technical support tools.

A BBS is a community of its BBS software and its users. As with all communities, you will find a wide diversity of opinions and views. Don't be afraid to contribute to the community. If you find it really does not suit you, there are hundreds of thousands more BBSs you can call.

This chapter scratched the surface of my favorite type of online service: BBSs. There is a BBS out there for everyone — you only have to find it.

15

CHAPTER

Message-Based Services

This chapter introduces commercial electronic mail service companies. These companies offer private messaging and file-exchange services. In particular, this chapter covers the following concepts:

- Privacy with e-mail
- Available commercial services
- A tour of MCI Mail
- Sending files, faxes, and telexes via e-mail
- The potential for e-mail

Understanding E-Mail

As its name implies, electronic mail, commonly abbreviated *e-mail*, consists of messages that you send electronically. Apart from file exchange, the most common use for online services is sending messages or e-mail. However, there is a distinction between sending messages and sending e-mail. (Both terms are used synonymously.) The issue is privacy, and it can be very significant.

If you call a BBS or a typical commercial online service, such as CompuServe or Prodigy, you can send messages to other people who call the BBS or commercial online service. You usually can mark the message as *private* so that all users of the system cannot read it. However, the message is not completely private, and the sysops, or their designated staff, can read those messages even if they have been marked private.

"How do I send a private message?"

Some commercial companies offer an electronic mail service that keeps your message private so that it can be read only by the intended recipient. This is the service to use if you want to send confidential information. For example, a private message on a BBS or typical commercial online service is fine for inviting a friend to dinner or talking about the great computer deal you made. However, these are not the services to use to send private messages showing your company sales reports, employee performance reviews, or other private negotiations, such as contract bids, potential products, or patents.

Note: The weakest point for privacy in your electronic mail may be your own computer. Although a sysop can read all the messages, the volume is so high that messages are not typically read in detail. However, someone with direct access to your computer is more likely to have a vested interest in the contents of your messages.

Internal e-mail

Many companies use e-mail extensively as an internal communication method. Most LANs (local area networks) include an e-mail system where you can send electronic messages to anyone on the network. The e-mail program installed on your network is an application program, equivalent to using a word processor or spreadsheet. Although you pay for the e-mail application program, you do not pay for each message sent because the message is internal to your company.

Depending on the e-mail program, you can establish users on the LAN who are not physically located within your company. These people, such as sales staff, call into the LAN via modem and pick up their messages from their assigned electronic mailboxes. In this case, the salesperson calling in for the message incurs the cost of a phone call to collect the messages.

As with internal messages, you don't pay for each message but only pay for the telephone charges, because you supply the electronic mail services. Every person trying to receive or send e-mail must be a user on the LAN. If you have a preferred supplier or customer, for example, you can give her an assigned mailbox on your network. However, the intent of a LAN is to provide full network access to each user and enable all users to share the application programs, such as word processors and spreadsheet programs. Although there are situations where you may wish to establish a nonemployee as a remote user of your LAN, you probably won't want to do this in all cases.

E-mail via online services

A better alternative when you want to communicate with more than your fellow employees is to use commercial online services for e-mail. You establish an account with an online service and can send messages to anyone else with an account on that service. (In many cases, the service can exchange messages with other commercial services, which extends the potential recipient base substantially.)

When you start considering commercial online services as a method of contacting people, you need to consider the issue of privacy. In this book, the term *commercial online service* applies to online services whose primary goal is information and file exchange. The intent is to share information. They are covered in more detail in Chapter 16.

Although you can send a message addressed to a particular subscriber of a commercial online service, you cannot usually send a file for receipt by that individual. Additionally, you cannot be certain that the message will not be read by another person. This person would be authorized by the service to monitor and maintain the messages and would not be a casual user.

The costs incurred in sending a message depend on the service but include telephone charges and any connect time charges. A few services charge an additional fee per message over a monthly minimum. For example, the first 30 messages may be free, and then each costs 10 cents.

E-mail via commercial mail service

This chapter addresses a different message delivering category, *commercial mail services*. These services offer message and file-transportation services, and their intent is to deliver information and not share it. A message or file cannot be read by anyone except the recipient.

A subscriber pays for an electronic mailbox with the mail service. Although there may be a nominal annual fee, you usually pay only for each message that you send, and there is no connect time fee. Because of the narrow focus of these services, they are relatively easy to use. However, they offer unique services that can be powerful marketing tools and cost savers.

The three major players in commercial mail services are MCI Mail, AT&T Mail, and SprintMail. Of these, MCI Mail is the most appropriate for an individual user. AT&T Mail and SprintMail are intended for medium to large corporations.

A Brief Tour of MCI Mail

In principle, using MCI Mail is similar to calling a BBS or commercial online service. You open an account with MCI Mail and access it by calling a phone number from your communication program with your modem. You type your account name and a password to gain access to your account. After you access your account, you can use the messaging facilities.

MCI Mail uses the concept of an office Desk for your mailbox. You have an Inbox, an Outbox, a Desk, and a Pending area. The Inbox contains all the messages that have been sent to you that you haven't read. The Outbox contains all the messages you have sent. The Desk contains the messages you have read. The Pending area contains the messages you are currently creating.

These areas of your Desk are completely separate, and you need to be aware of which area you want to work in. You issue the Scan command, as in Scan Outbox, to view a summary of the contents of the desired area. The Scan command numbers the items in that area for reference. For example, if you have four unread messages, issuing the command Scan Inbox assigns the numbers 1 through 4 to the waiting messages. You can then issue commands, such as read 1 or read next, to read messages.

"What costs do I incur with MCI Mail?"

Using MCI Mail for simple message creating, sending, and receiving is particularly easy. You only need to learn a few commands, and even if you forget them, help is easy to find. Additionally, because you call an 800 number to reach MCI Mail — and are charged for the messages you send, not how long it takes you to create a message — MCI Mail is an economical service.

However, MCI Mail also includes more-advanced features that make the service more than a simple e-mail exchange service. You can, for example, attach files to your message, send a message and have it received as a fax document, or even send documents to nonsubscribers. The following sections illustrate sending a message, reading a message, and getting help. Later sections show how to take advantage of MCI Mail's more advanced features.

To access MCI Mail, you must first open an account with MCI and choose such items as your customer name and user name. MCI Mail then mails you the enrollment kit that contains your password. When you have your password, you can start to use the system. From your computer, you run your communication program and make it dial the central access number for MCI Mail. At the prompt `Please enter your user name:`, you type the user name you have selected and press Enter. This is a single word, typically a contraction of your name or your company name.

At the `Password:` prompt, you type your assigned password and press Enter. MCI Mail displays a summary of today's headlines, a notice about whether there are any messages waiting to be read, and the command prompt. Your screen will be comparable to Figure 15-1.

Sending a message

You control MCI Mail by typing commands at the command prompt `Command:`. To send a message, for example, you type **create** and press Enter.

```
Welcome to MCI Mail!

Need information from the White
House on the North American
Free Trade Agreement?

Type VIEW WHITE HOUSE FOREIGN
for details.

Today's Headlines at 12 pm EDT:

--Arkansas Judge Rules Wal-Mart
    Guilty Of 'Predatory Pricing'
--GE's 3rd-Quarter Net Rose 8.6%
      * Corporate Earnings Report *

Type //BUSINESS on Dow Jones for details.


MCI Mail Version V11.3.H

    There are no messages waiting in your INBOX.

Command:
 ANSI    ONLINE  38400 8N1  [Alt+Z]-Menu  FDX 8 LF X ♪ ♫ CP LG ↑ PR  00:00:08
```

Figure 15-1: MCI Mail opening screen. MCI gives a brief news headline summary, status of your Inbox, and the command prompt when you first log on.

Creating a message is similar to creating a memo. You first generate the address portion followed by the text content. For example, you specify who will receive the message, who will get a "carbon copy," and then generate the subject of the message. When you need to edit a message, MCI Mail considers everything except the text itself as the envelope.

After typing **create**, MCI Mail prompts with TO:. You type the name of the recipient, in our example, **Sandy Reed**. MCI Mail displays the name and customer number for the recipient or provides further information. For example, if you only type the name **Reed**, MCI Mail needs you to choose the correct customer amongst its many Reeds. On the other hand, if no subscriber is found, MCI Mail reports that you must try a different name. MCI Mail continues to prompt you for additional addressees until you press Enter without typing a name. In this way, you can send the same message to several different people.

After choosing the recipient, you are prompted by CC:. At this prompt, you type the name of someone who should receive a copy of the message but is not the addressee. It is equivalent to cc: on a letter. You may, for example, send a message to a manufacturer complaining about a product and send a copy to the store manager where you bought the defective product.

Again, MCI Mail continues to prompt you for more names until you press Enter without typing a name. At the Subject: prompt, you type the subject of your message, which is **Meeting Confirmation** in this example. (As shown in the following section, the message recipient sees the Subject: in the message summary section.)

After the subject, you are prompted for the main text of your message. Figure 15-2 shows a typical message creation screen.

```
Command: read inbox
Your INBOX is empty.

Command: create

TO:        Sandy Reed
              382-6179 Sandy Reed              -          Saratoga, CA
TO:

CC:

Subject: Meeting Confirmation

Text: (Enter text or transmit file. Type / on a line by itself to end.)

Hello!
Thanks for taking the time to talk to me this morning. This message
is to confirm our meeting on Friday at 12 noon. I will be standing
under the clock in Paddington Station wearing a red carnation and
carrying a portable computer.
I will be on the lookout for a tall dark stranger with the Times
newspaper under one arm and a modem (with phone cable and power
cord) under the other.
 ANSI    ONLINE  38400 8N1  [Alt+Z]-Menu  FDX 8 LF X ♪ ♪ CP LG ↑ PR  00:05:37
```

Figure 15-2: Message creation with MCI Mail. Messages in MCI Mail have a similar structure to memos with the addressees and subject followed by the main text.

If you are used to word processors, or even BBSs and some commercial online services, you will find that the message creation editor in MCI Mail is not very sophisticated. In a word processor, when you run out of space on a line of text, the word processor automatically wraps your word onto the next line. Many BBSs also support this feature in their message editor. MCI Mail does not and expects you to press Enter at the end of each line.

Although you can type longer lines in MCI Mail, you can get into very confusing situations. MCI Mail warns you if the line is too long, and you can reformat by using the editing commands. However, the result is not always what you would expect and can result in a mixture of long and short lines. You must remember to press Enter at the end of each line or type the message offline and use the more advanced upload text command introduced later in this chapter.

MCI Mail's message editor also requires that you end the message in a particular way. When you finish typing all your text, you need to type / on its own on a new line to signal the end of the message. If you press Enter without any text on the line, MCI Mail assumes you want to leave a blank line in your message and does not assume that you have finished typing. Fortunately, the slash (/) requirement is displayed as a reminder at the top of the message during creation.

"How can I separate my e-mail charges by project?"

After typing /, MCI Mail prompts you for the message-handling requirements. If you have no special requirements, you press Enter to ignore this option. Several handling options are available, including charging the message to a particular project, or giving a message priority-delivery status so that the recipient realizes it is urgent, or requesting a notification that the message was read by the recipient.

I think the handling options are particularly valuable even to infrequent users. I use the charge option to split my MCI Mail bill into projects. I can then submit expenses to my customers without having another customer's expenses appear on the same billing page. The receipt option is particularly useful if you have trouble contacting someone and want to know whether he is ignoring you or simply not checking his mail.

You are then prompted to send the message. If you choose yes, your message is sent and a copy is placed in your Outbox. If you choose no, the partially written message is kept in the Pending section. You can edit the message by using the edit commands or can delete the message without sending it.

Reading a message

Finding your messages can be tricky with MCI Mail, unless you remember the areas of your mailbox. As mentioned previously, your Inbox contains unread messages; your Desk, messages you have read; Pending, messages you have started to create but have not sent; and your Outbox, messages you have sent.

When you log on to MCI Mail, the message line above the command prompt tells you whether your Inbox contains any messages. To read these messages, you must first scan your Inbox by typing **scan**. MCI Mail then assigns numbers to each message and presents a summary list. You read the first message by typing **read 1** (or a different message with a different number). MCI Mail then displays the message along with its contents.

After you read a message from your Inbox, it automatically moves to the Desk area. Figure 15-3 shows the contents of a typical mailbox, where all the messages have been read and one message is in the Pending area. In this example, to read the message from Dan Sommer, you type **read 9,** and MCI Mail displays its contents. To read the draft message in Pending, you type **read 10**.

```
Command: scan inbox
Your INBOX is empty.

Command: scan desk

  4 messages in DESK

No.  Posted       From             Subject                    Size
  6  Sep 20 10:24 John P. Davis    RE: New email product      119
  7  Sep 27 12:55 Kimberly M. Crew                            993
  8  Sep 27 12:56 Kimberly M. Crew Welcome Aboard!            953
  9  Oct 01 14:03 Dan Sommer       reaching IW via MCI        744

Command: scan pending

  1 message in PENDING

No.  Posted       From             Subject                    Size
 10  Oct 12 Draft To: Sandy Reed   Meeting Confirmation        398

Command: scan outbox
Your OUTBOX is empty.

Command:
 ANSI    ONLINE  38400 8N1 [Alt+Z]-Menu  FDX 8 LF X ♪ ♩ CP LG ↑ PR  00:08:18
```

Figure 15-3: MCI Mail mailbox. As soon as a message is read, it moves from the Inbox to the Desk area.

Getting help

MCI Mail makes getting help particularly easy, so even if you are an infrequent user, you can find out how to perform tasks from the command prompt. (The supplied quick reference guide is also clear.) To get help while online, you type **help** followed by a command name. For example, to get help on editing a message, you type **help edit,** or you type **help mailbox** to get a list of your mailbox areas and the typical commands you may need to use.

Ancillary services

At its simplest, MCI Mail allows you to send and receive text messages. However, it actually offers many more features. It is not a general-purpose online service but includes many different features relating to sending messages. The following sections summarize some of the features you may want to explore.

Compare the U.S. Postal Service. At its simplest, you can send a letter for delivery. However, you can actually do much more. You can send parcels as well as letters or send material express, priority, certified, or bulk mail.

Sending to a nonsubscriber

MCI Mail allows you to send messages to people who are not subscribers to an online service. You prepare and send a message to a person and specify that it can be sent on paper. The message is printed at the physical MCI Mail location that is closest to the recipient and is then mailed to the recipient. You can specify that you want an overnight delivery, and the message will be delivered by courier.

This method has several advantages. In the U.S., for example, you can send a message up to 11 p.m. EST and have it delivered the next day. Depending on your location, the overnight courier services may have final pickup time much earlier.

"Why should I use MCI Mail to send a message overseas to a nonsubscriber?"

Additionally, this method may be advantageous in cost and time for overseas delivery. MCI Mail may have locations or agreements with other companies that have locations close to your recipient. You can save the time that would be necessary to physically fly your letter to the required country. In some cases, this can reduce the delivery time by days.

Apart from the time-reduction aspects, paper delivery allows you to add a signature to your letter. You can arrange for your letterhead and a signature (or multiple versions) to be registered with MCI Mail and your account. Then, when you specify paper, the message is printed with your letterhead and signature.

Sending a fax or telex

Using a method comparable to sending a message to another online service, you can use MCI Mail to send fax or telex documents. You specify fax or telex during the addressing process and supply the necessary fax phone number or telex number.

"How can I send a telex?"

In many areas of the world, the telex remains the only electronic contact method besides the telephone. In the U.S., telexes are becoming scarce. MCI Mail enables you to send and receive telexes without extensive special consideration. However, telexes have a maximum of 69 characters on each line of text.

With the typical cost of a fax modem, you probably won't use this approach as an alternative to using your own fax modem, but don't dismiss the MCI Mail fax feature. It can provide a convenient method of sending a message, even if it is not the most economical. Additionally, you can use MCI Mail to send a fax document when you do not have access to a fax machine or fax modem.

Sending to other online services

MCI Mail is connected to other online services, including CompuServe and AT&T Mail, and you can send messages to subscribers of those services. To do this, you use a special address.

You begin creating a message in the usual way, but when prompted by the TO: prompt, you type the name followed by **(EMS)**. You then include additional information at the electronic mail service (EMS) prompts to enable MCI Mail to route the message. The precise details of what to add to the address depend on the service you are trying to reach.

To send a message to someone on CompuServe, for example, you need to know the person's name and CompuServe ID number. After typing the name and (EMS), MCI Mail prompts you for the name of the electronic mail service by displaying EMS:. You type **CompuServe** and press Enter.

MCI Mail then prompts you for the mailbox information. At the first MBX: prompt, you type **P=CSMail** and press Enter. At the second MBX: prompt, you type **DDA=ID=99999,999** where 99999,999 is the recipient's CompuServe user ID number.

MCI Mail can connect to any electronic mail system that employs the X.400 connection standard. Some large corporations use this standard, as do other mail systems, such as AT&T Mail. People who have mailboxes on these systems can supply the precise mailbox address information you need to supply.

Consider your mail's privacy when sending information to another system. MCI Mail offers a completely private service, and messages cannot be read except by the recipient. However, this privacy may not apply to messages sent on another system.

Interesting extras

MCI Mail has several other features you can use. The most important is the capability to attach binary files to your messages. You might use this to send a copy of a budget spreadsheet to outside sales staff along with a message requesting that they fill out their particular section and return it. To attach a file to your message, you issue the upload command when you are prompted for the text for your message. To read a message with an attached file, you issue the download command to collect the file.

Although powerful features, the upload and download commands are not particularly easy to understand in MCI Mail. If you plan to attach files to your messages, you should use a special program, such as MCI Express (formerly Lotus Express), or an offline mail reader, such as OLX (part of QModemPro). These automate the uploading and downloading process so that you are less likely to make a mistake.

MCI Mail also provides access to the Dow Jones News Retrieval Service, which also is accessible from other online services. It is an online service that contains current and historical information relevant to business and finance from around the world. For example, it contains the full text of *The Wall Street Journal, The Wall Street Journal Europe*, and *The Asian Wall Street Journal.* You need to subscribe to this in addition to MCI Mail.

"Can I have a "toll-free" mailbox?"

Other MCI Mail features enhance your mailing facilities. For example, you can set up a *toll-free mailbox* so that the recipient rather than the sender pays for the message. You can have your mail automatically forwarded to other recipients, use electronic forms, or share your mailing lists with other subscribers.

An additional feature of MCI Mail allows you to establish a bulletin board that can be accessed by the people you specify. A corporation, for example, may want to establish a bulletin board that can be read by sales staff and provide a medium for discussion via electronic mail.

One disadvantage to electronic services is the need to supply precise information to find a subscriber. Sometimes, it can be difficult to find someone because you are misspelling the name slightly. To help, MCI Mail allows you to search its subscriber list. Consequently, you can turn this disadvantage into an advantage. (The same is true for commercial online services.) You may be able to find a subscriber from a particular company where you are interested in making contacts. Use the FIND command or other similar commands, and see who is a subscriber.

Tip: I find MCI Mail particularly useful when I try to get industry quotes for an article. I send a message to people who are extremely busy and don't have time to talk to me on the telephone. Because they actually get my message when they, or their assistants, are prepared to read messages, they will often rattle off a quick reply that I can use. If I call, I always manage to interrupt a meeting and catch them off guard. By using electronic mail, my response rate is maximized, and the amount of time I invest in getting the quote is minimized.

Simplifying Your Message Distribution

With the various online services available, you may find that the people you regularly contact do not all subscribe to the same service. Keeping in touch and feeling confident that you have actually contacted all the relevant people can become an administrative nightmare.

If used appropriately, MCI Mail provides you with a single account from which to send your messages to a wide variety of destinations. You may be able to get a similar service from another online service, such as CompuServe, but depending on your emphasis, the mailing facilities may be more important and economical than the file exchange and forums offered on CompuServe.

Suppose that you have ten different people to contact. Two subscribe to MCI Mail, one to AT&T Mail, two to CompuServe, three have fax machines, one has a telex, and the other has no electronic mail facilities at all. Coordinating sending messages to this group and making sure that the information was received can be difficult. However, the MCI Mail facilities enable you to create a single message and address it to each recipient in different ways. As far as your records are concerned, you send a single message to ten different people, but MCI Mail routs the messages in several different ways.

Note: MCI Mail also allows you to store lists of people that you want to send messages to. These ten people with their different addresses need to be entered only once, and you can choose them from a list when you need to send more messages to them.

Automating your account

Like all electronic mail, the service is useful to you only if you regularly check your mailbox. You should establish a procedure, such as checking the mailbox once a day, to be the most effective. You can purchase products that automate your MCI Mail use. Products include MCI Express (formerly named Lotus Express), Norton Express, and in a more limited way, the offline reader in QModemPro.

"How do I automate my MCI Mail usage?"

MCI Express is a communication program and a message-handling program. You can only use it to call MCI Mail and not as a general-purpose communication program. MCI Express is extremely valuable, especially if you need to send many messages and keep records over a long period of time. MCI Mail only keeps a record of the messages you have sent for a couple of weeks. After that time, they disappear from your Outbox. MCI Express requires you to explicitly delete the message from your Outbox.

Other advantages of MCI Express include the capability to easily attach binary files and easily read binary files attached to messages. The text editor for typing your message is also slightly better than the one on MCI Mail itself. You can set up MCI Express to call your MCI Mail account automatically. You load it as a TSR and specify how often it should call. For example, you can make it call once an hour or once a day.

Note: You don't want MCI Express loaded as a TSR if you are going to use your modem to call other services. Norton Express offers comparable features for MCI Mail.

QModemPro, a general-purpose communication program, includes an offline reader that is particularly useful for collecting messages from BBSs that support the quick mail (QWK) mail packet format. However, you can also use another supplied offline reader program (QGate) for reading your MCI Mail and responding to messages. (It also offers comparable features for CompuServe.)

You don't get the same level of automation and organization that is possible from MCI Express and similar products with QGate. You can't, for example, make the program call every hour. However, you can automate your message sending and retrieving.

Summary

This chapter introduced online mail services, in particular MCI Mail. These services provide a method of sending private mail and files to another subscriber. You can also use the service to send faxes, telexes, and messages to subscribers of other online services.

In its simplest form, MCI Mail is very easy to use. However, it includes flexible features that can streamline your messaging. With a single message, you can send e-mail, fax, telex, and paper output, depending on the recipient.

You can purchase programs that automate the process further and supply a more complete record of your online activities.

With a little exploration, you can use MCI Mail to find new contacts and link with other services that you may not find on other services. MCI Mail also supplies a gateway into the Dow Jones News Retrieval Service, a business and financial online service.

16

CHAPTER

Information-Exchange Services

This chapter introduces information-exchange services. These commercial online services offer the widest variety of features of any online service. In particular, this chapter covers the following topics:

❖ Understanding information-exchange services

❖ Understanding graphical services

❖ A brief tour of a graphical service

❖ Understanding text-based services

❖ A brief tour of a text-based service

❖ Typical features of online services

Understanding Information-Exchange Services

After BBSs, commercial online services are the most commonly found online service. Some people prefer commercial online services to BBSs, and others prefer BBSs to commercial online services. In general, BBSs are preferable because you don't pay for connect time. Although you pay for the phone call, you aren't usually running up a bill with a BBS for the time you are online.

In general, commercial online services are preferable because they have more users and you consequently have a more diverse user base. Because you do pay a connect charge, you are not limited in the amount of time you can spend online. BBSs typically restrict you to about an hour a day maximum.

"Why should I subscribe to an information-exchange service?"

Information-exchange services are usually general purpose and offer messaging, file exchange, and chatting online. They offer more features than most BBSs and are not as limited in the number of phone lines. You are unlikely to find a busy signal when you call a commercial online service. A popular BBS may have busy signals and be unaccessible at peak usage periods.

Like BBSs, commercial online services emphasize information exchange. Although they do offer messaging services, which are used extensively, much of the messaging is not private and is for public discussion. These large systems are divided into sections so that you can focus on a particular area of interest. These commercial online services each have hundreds of thousands of users. If you have an interest in a particular topic, you should be able to find someone else with a similar interest if you look hard enough.

This chapter avoids prices for these services because they change so frequently. However, most services offer a special promotion, and you should watch out for opportunities to try new items inexpensively as you use a service. For example, a special recently offered by a couple of the services was five hours connect time for $5.

Balancing Online Costs

The "Calculating Connect Charges" sidebar in Chapter 13 explains the various costs involved in using online services, including telephone charges as well as any connect time charges. The connect time charges can vary with the connection speed as well as the time of day. Depending on what you actually do online and when you do it, online charges can mount very quickly. A common fear for newcomers is large unexpected bills. Some services have complicated pricing structures; others have deceptively simple ones.

Most services offer a basic service where you pay a fixed price, typically between $10 and $20 per month. This may entitle you to unlimited time on the service or give you the first x hours free. However, most services also include extra cost items. For example, a stock quote may cost a few cents, or sending mail via the Internet may have a monthly minimum fee. The services do clearly state what costs more and usually warn you when you move to an area where extra fees apply.

Until you are familiar with the service, you should avoid the extra cost items. But don't overlook their value. It may cost a dollar or two, but if it gets you an answer you would have to spend days finding or would have to drive to the library to look up, it can be worth it.

There are many ways to economize. The telephone networks, such as Sprintnet and Tymnet, are much less expensive during nonworking hours. If you can find one or two services that fill all your needs, even if another service is quicker to use, you may save money. Don't overlook the opportunities of BBSs. Although they don't usually have current, constantly changing information, such as news, weather, or stock information, they do have the latest computer games and lots of messages from users interested in specific topics.

Getting online has become part of my daily and weekly routine. I check my mail daily, which takes a couple of minutes, and then I call a few BBSs and a couple of online services on a weekly basis for about an hour. My expenses, both phone bills and online service charges, vary little from month to month unless I am working on a special project.

However, you had to use the time within the calendar month or you lost it. Another service offered one hour of free access to a games area one month and one hour free access to the business news area the next.

The problem with describing any of these services is that they are diverse, and you can find more or less anything on any of them. However, each has an individual character that you may or may not like.

In general, commercial online services can be divided into two types: graphical and text-based. The two most popular graphical services are Prodigy and America Online. The most popular (with the most subscribers) text-based services are CompuServe and Genie. However, other text-based services have a loyal following too because they are less general purpose in nature.

Introduction to Graphical Services

Graphical information exchange services offer ease of use as their main strength. When you subscribe to a graphical service, you are supplied with a program that you install on your computer. This is a communication program written especially to interface with the service.

"What is a graphical online service?"

You can, and will probably prefer to, use a mouse with these services. Wherever possible, the communication program removes the details of the connection, and you make selections from the screen as if you were running an ordinary application program. You may not even realize that you are communicating with another computer via telephone. Generally, graphical services are very simple to use. However, they have a tendency to run slowly and can be frustrating to wait for unless you have a powerful computer.

Understanding a Slow Graphical Online Service

In general, the speed of your computer does not make much of a difference to your communication speed. The speed of an online service is much more dependent on your modem speed and the speed of the computer you are connected to.

However, graphical online services can be an exception to this generalization. These services use a program running on your computer as part of the communication process. In part, they depend on the processing power of your computer to display and redraw screens.

Consequently, on a slow computer, the service can appear to be slow. On a 386-based computer or better, any delay due to the computer's speed is insignificant; however, on a PC or AT-compatible computer, the performance can be frustrating.

This slow speed is not apparent on text-based systems. The text can be displayed on your computer more or less as fast as it can be sent from the remote computer. The information is not processed by your computer's microprocessor before display, so the speed is independent of your computer's speed.

You don't have to remember commands to use these graphical services, because the menus are displayed or are accessible from the screen. However, after you are familiar with one aspect of the service, it is worth learning any shortcut keys to help speed your progress from one area to another.

Many people, especially non-technical people, find the graphical online services wonderful. Others, particularly those who are not intimidated by complicated computer commands, find the graphical online services frustrating. I believe these services can be used by anyone who can read. However, I also know a lot of people who used these services as an introduction to online services and then moved on to a text-based service, where the depth of information, particularly technical information, is greater.

The most suitable service for you is the one that contains the information that you need and presents it in a manner you can understand. You don't need to know much about modems to access and use an online service, particularly a graphical online service. The two most popular graphical online services are Prodigy and America Online. The following lists indicate the features offered for each type of service.

Prodigy

Service topics offered by Prodigy include:

- Business and finance

  Automatic bill-paying services, real estate, tax, investment, and travel information

- For your kids

  Encyclopedia, teenager message area, Sesame Street area, and games, such as Where in the World Is Carmen Sandiego?

- Fun, games, and adventure

  Chess, brain teasers, golf, armchair baseball, and a games message area

- Bulletin boards and messaging

  Singles, seniors, computers, careers, pets, medical, genealogy, and hobbies

- Travel

  EEASY SABRE, a travel reservation service; weather; and city, vacation, and restaurant guides

- ♣ Arts and entertainment

    TV reviews, news, and schedules, plot summaries of soap operas, book reviews, movie reviews, and music reviews and charts

- ♣ News and information

    Headline news, national, political, and international news, lottery results, and columnists on politics and Washington

- ♣ Sports

    Sports message area, sports results and headlines, auto racing, horse racing, golf, football, boxing, and bowling information

- ♣ Computers

    Software guide, Macintosh column, consumer reports, multimedia, computer club, and best-selling software charts

- ♣ Homelife and shopping

    Cookbooks, wine reviews, health, home business, do-it-yourself, gardening, and online shopping for cameras, books, clothes, sporting goods, toys, and entertainment products

America Online

The following lists features offered by America Online:

- ♣ Learning and reference

    Library of Congress Online, CNN Online, *National Geographic,* and Teacher's Information Network

- ♣ People connection

    Public and private chat areas, message boards, and event schedules, as well as special conference events

- ♣ Travel and Shopping

    EAASY SABRE travel service, flower shop, Comp-U-Store, classifieds, and office products

- ♣ News and finance

    U.S. and world news, sports, editorial, weather, stock quotes, business, and finance

- Life-styles and interests

  Chatting and message areas for variety of topics, including disabilities, seniors, pets, aviation, and food and drink

- Computing and shareware

  PC file library, news, reference, and messaging areas

- Games and entertainment

  Multiplayer online games, casino games, and entertainment news

A brief tour of America Online

As an introduction to a graphical online service, the next sections present a brief online session with America Online. When you enroll with America Online, you are given the choice of two PC communications programs — one for DOS and one for Windows. The features are the same with both programs, although the screens look slightly different. (The following example shows the Windows version of the program.)

After starting Windows, you double-click the America Online icon to start the program. You are prompted for your user name and password. Prodigy and America Online allow you to establish several different users for the same account. For example, you may be one user and your son another. You are charged as though one person uses the account.

After selecting the user name and typing your password (each user has a different password), you choose Sign On to proceed, and the program automatically connects you with the service. The icons on-screen show the call's progress. They show the phone number being dialed, the modems link being established, and the password being checked. Your screen then looks like Figure 16-1.

The opening screen shows your name as it is known on the system. The window offers four topics of interest, such as the top news story and new record releases. Because the screen was captured near Halloween, another suggested topic is Halloween Art. You are also given an icon that indicates whether you have any mail. In this example, I chose the button Browse the Service. Your screen will look like Figure 16-2. The eight departments show America Online's main topic areas as mentioned in the features list.

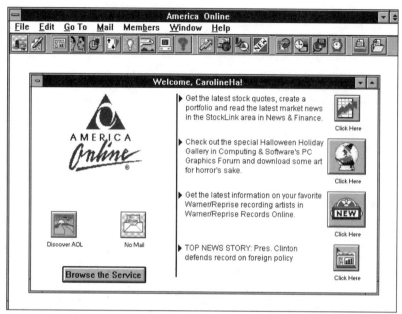

Figure 16-1: America Online's opening screen. All commands can be selected from the screen icons.

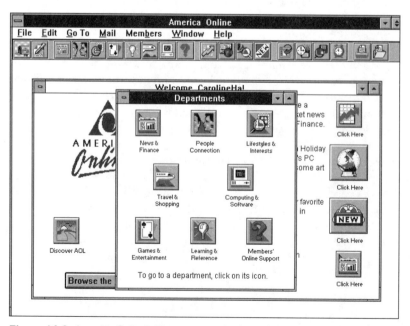

Figure 16-2: America Online's Departments. America Online divides its activities into eight topic areas.

I decided to visit the People Connection section and chat with other people online. The first area I visited, the Lobby, did not have any interesting conversation, although 22 people were in that area. I chose to look at the *room*, labeled Sports. After watching for a minute, my screen looked like Figure 16-3.

The five people in the sports chat area were discussing football. To join in, I could type my comment at the bottom of the screen and press the Send button to have it added to the list. However, because I was hoping they would be talking about the World Series and not football, I decided to leave.

From the department window, I selected the Games and Entertainment department and checked my horoscope, as shown in Figure 16-4. After reading that my financial outlook for today was poor, I decided to look at more entertainment.

I picked the message board area and looked at the messages on the topic of oxymorons. Figure 16-5 shows part of the list of messages. After reading some of the messages and adding a message containing my own favorite oxymoron (initial deadline), I returned to the Departments window.

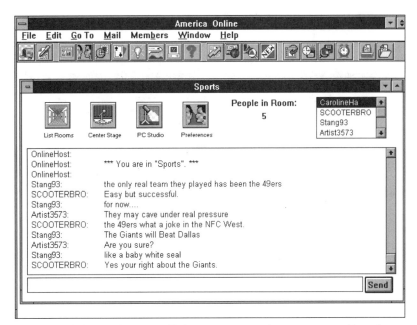

Figure 16-3: Sports chat room. Each participant in a chat session types his or her comments and reads other people's comments.

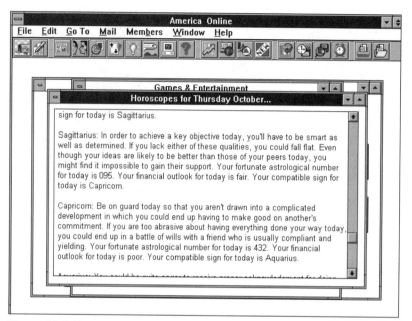

Figure 16-4: Horoscope. Each topic is displayed in a window. Where applicable, scroll bars and icons are available.

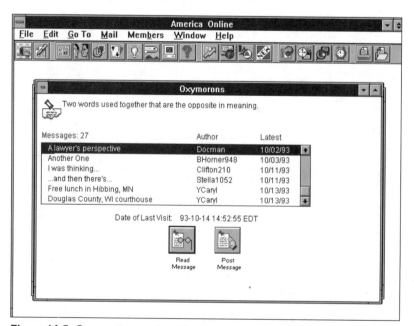

Figure 16-5: Oxymoron messages. The messages are divided into topics. You can choose to read all messages, or only some, as well as respond.

From the Departments window, I chose Learning & Reference. Figure 16-6 shows some of the available topics. Comptons Encyclopedia is online as well as many specialized topics. I was particularly interested in Smithsonian Online and explored that area before choosing Sign Off from the Go To menu at the top of the screen to end my session.

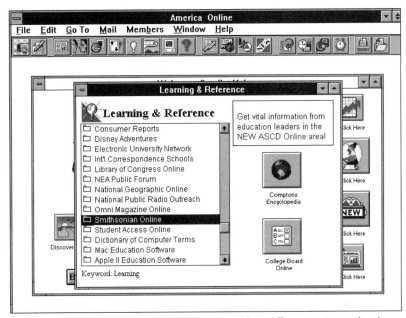

Figure 16-6: Learning & Reference Department. Many different topics can be chosen, including College Board Online and Omni Magazine Online.

Introduction to Text-Based Data Exchange Services

Like the graphical-based systems, the text-based data exchange services also attract hundreds of thousands of users. The most popular services, in terms of the number of subscribers, are CompuServe and Genie. However, BIX, Delphi, The Well, and others also have large followings.

"What does a text-based online service offer?"

In general, these services offer messaging, file exchange, forums, and games. Each has a leaning towards one or more of these features. CompuServe, for example, has a large number of forums, many supported by computer software and hardware manufacturers. The typical user tends to be fairly computer literate and technical.

As another example, The Well emphasizes messaging and has hundreds of different topic areas. It has had a long history and has a very loyal following. It does not have live chatting or online games.

Imagination is specifically targeted towards games and entertainment. It has live chatting and many games. You can find terminals in bars, restaurants, and hotel lounges around the country.

The following lists give a brief summary of features offered by the most popular services: CompuServe, BIX, Genie, and Delphi.

CompuServe

- Electronic mail
- Online reference material
- Travel services
- Weather feature
- Shopping
- Investor services
- Leisure-time games
- Forums
- Software exchange
- Chatting

BIX

- Electronic mail
- Conferences
- MicroBytes industry news briefs
- Software exchange

Genie

- Multiplayer games
- Chatting
- Electronic mail
- File exchange
- Investment and financial services
- Electronic text of publications, company profiles, and patent information

Delphi

- Electronic mail
- Messaging areas
- Chatting
- File exchange

A brief tour of CompuServe

Most online services offer a multitude of services and options. Although you can call the services and find your own way around, most services offer a software program, variously referred to as an *information manager* or *a front end*.

These programs are essential for economical and efficient use of the service. You can make your selections for the areas of interest and proceed directly to them instead of learning a lot of commands. Although these programs may have a text-based user interface, they allow you to choose commands and areas of interest from lists of commands.

The following example is a brief tour of CompuServe. The CompuServe Information Manager (CIM) was used to make the selections. CompuServe supplies this program with its enrollment fee. Like the graphical-user interfaces, the Information Manager hides the details of the modem use from view. You start the program and select the topic you want to browse. CompuServe Information Manager then makes the connection automatically. (The following example shows the DOS version of the program.)

Unlike Prodigy, where you are prompted to choose your user name and type the password, CIM stores your user name and password. You can only have one user for each CompuServe account.

CIM displays a series of cascading windows that show where you are in the service. In Figure 16-7, for example, there are four windows on-screen. One, in the lower-right corner, indicates that mail is waiting, and the one in the upper-right corner shows highlights of the service this week. The other two windows show the selections made prior to connection.

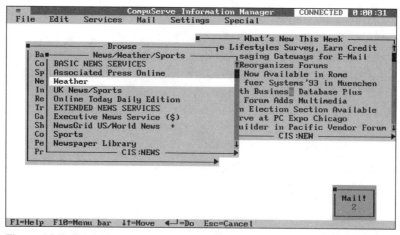

Figure 16-7: CompuServe connection. CIM presents a series of cascading windows to navigate the system.

After starting CIM, I decided to view a weather map. I chose News/Weather/Sports from the Browse window, and CIM automatically connected with CompuServe. The current connection status is shown at the top of the screen. In Figure 16-7, it shows CONNECTED, but at other times it may show WORKING or DISCONNECTING. The length of time that you have been connected is also shown at the top of the screen.

The News/Weather/Sports window opens on top of the Browse window and summarizes the available topics. After choosing Weather from this list, your screen will look like Figure 16-8.

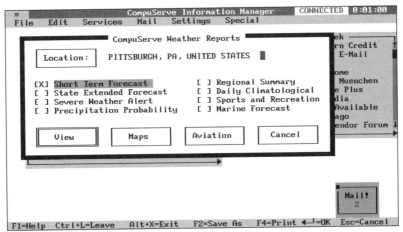

Figure 16-8: Available weather reports. You can choose from a variety of weather forecasts and maps for any location.

The available weather forecasts cover most requirements. For example, you can see a short-term forecast, extended forecast, or a regional summary. In addition to reading a forecast, you can see a map of the chosen forecast. Although CompuServe assumes that you want a forecast for your location, you also can choose the location. For this example, I chose to view a map of the current weather. The screen looked like Figure 16-9.

Figure 16-9: Weather maps. The map shows a graphical view from the current weather radar.

After viewing the weather map, I decided to explore one of CompuServe's most popular areas, the computing support areas. These forums are supplied by computer software and hardware manufacturers. You usually can get technical support; news information; and, in some cases, updated device drivers or other utilities. Some of these forums are very formal; others provide interesting insight. These forums are often a way to communicate with the company executives.

I chose Computer Support from the Browse menu and then Hardware Forums from the Computer Support menu. I then chose Hayes from the extensive list of hardware manufacturers and groups.

Each forum is different and is structured by the particular company that supports that forum. However, they are all similar in presenting a list of options for you to choose from, and you gradually focus on the item of interest. For example, after choosing Hayes from the Computer Support menu, I chose Special Support programs and discovered that Hayes offers three special support programs: one for registered dealers, one for developers, and one for sysops. I could choose one of these for more details about the current programs.

After viewing the special support for sysops, I moved to the forum area itself to read messages about Hayes products. As shown in Figure 16-10, the messages are divided into topics, and you choose a topic of interest to see the relevant messages.

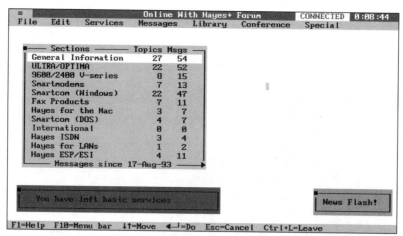

Figure 16-10: Typical CompuServe forum. The messages are divided into topics to make finding them easier.

After looking in the forums, I took a look in the shopping area. I picked Shopping from the original Browse menu. I then searched The Electronic Mall by product to find some cookies. As shown in Figure 16-11, the index starts with general topics and then focuses on the more specific items.

I chose the Index, Gourmet Foods, and then Candies/Cookies/Cakes and was presented with a list of companies that will accept my order online. These include a cookie company, a steak company, fruit shippers, and a coffee company. I spent my allowance and then chose Disconnect from the File menu. CIM then automatically disconnected me from the service.

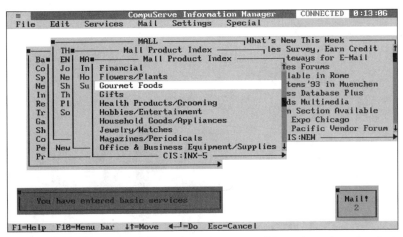

Figure 16-11: Shopping mall. You can purchase many different items from the electronic mall.

Summary

This chapter introduced the commercial information exchange services. These offer similar features to BBSs but on a larger scale and for a higher cost. Depending on the particular service, you can connect with services offering general interest or very focused interests.

The commercial information-exchange services typically include material, such as news and weather, that is regularly updated. Most include an encyclopedia.

The graphical services, such as Prodigy and America Online, offer menus and icons for your selections. They are easy to use but tend to be slower than the text-based services.

Most of the text-based services offer a front-end program that makes navigating the vast array of options easier. These front-end programs allow you to pick from a list of choices. However, you can also access these systems directly from your own communication programs. As an advanced user, this may save you time.

Chapter 18 introduces Information-Searching services that specialize in supplying database information for business applications.

17

CHAPTER

The Internet

This chapter introduces the Internet. This network of networks includes all the features of the other online services, but because it is not owned or run by a single organization, it doesn't fit a neat explanation in the same way as the others. In particular, this chapter covers the following topics:

❖ Understanding the Internet

❖ Getting access to the Internet

❖ Typical features found on the Internet

❖ Typical utilities to navigate the Internet

Understanding the Internet

Understanding the Internet is like appreciating astronomy. I know that the Earth is a planet spinning on its own axis and moving around the Sun. I also know that the moon spins on its own axis and moves around the Earth. My mind can grasp the concept of light years and billions of galaxies. However, somewhere between this elementary level and discussions on event horizons, pulsars, quasars, and arithmetic involving numbers approaching infinity, my mind locks up.

At a simple level, the Internet also seems logical. As an interconnected computer system, it seems understandable. However, when you try to pin an item down or grasp an overall understanding, the terms become esoteric, the experts become more vague or more technical, and comprehensible explanations are elusive.

At first glance, understanding the Internet is easy. It is a network of interconnected computers. You, a computer user, access one of the interconnected computers and, as a consequence, communicate with others (people and computers) on the Internet. You have access to information that is stored on the computers in the network. Keep this simple description in mind as you expand your understanding.

The computers linked together in the Internet all use a communications protocol called TCP/IP (Transmission Control Protocol/Internet Protocol) for their communication. This protocol specifies the form of data and how the data is passed between computers. It is a *packet-switching protocol*, which means the data is divided into chunks (known as *packets*) for transmission. Each computer and each user on that computer on the Internet has an address, and the packets of data include the addresses of the sender and receiver. The addresses help the computers route the information packets. The packet is passed from the sending computer to the next computer in the net until it reaches its destination.

So far, the description doesn't sound much different from a typical online service, such as a BBS or CompuServe, except that more computers are involved. However, the Internet is different because there is no central computer that you are calling. The available resources are scattered around all the different computers. No single group owns all the computers, and it is a continually changing network as computers are added or are taken out of service (temporarily for service or permanently). Estimates of thousands of new computers being added every month are not exaggerated.

The computers are located in universities, research establishments, government sites, and commercial companies literally around the world. Some computers are linked by very high speed connections, others by slower links. (These are still much faster than a typical asynchronous modem connection.) The costs involved are borne by the various computers that are connected together. For example, computer A, linked to computer B and C, may pay communications charges for the data being passed from A to B and C. Or, computer B pays for the data it passes to computers A, D, and E.

The link between the computers is not an asynchronous link, as has been discussed in the rest of this book. The computers are linked via leased lines, and the connection is permanently open (except when closed for maintenance or breakage). As a result, to the organizations owning the computers, the connection charges are constant and continual. You, or other Internet users, adding your data to the flow does not alter the costs. (It may alter the performance in some cases, because there is a limit to the amount of data that can be sent at once.)

The packets are passed from one computer to another based on the address in the packet. Any particular computer in the Internet knows the addresses of the computers it is attached to, and it passes a packet to a computer that it considers "closer" to the destination address.

The actual route taken by a packet depends on many factors, including the source and destination of the packet. Some interconnections between computers are intended for specialized use, such as research or education. These connections allow packets that are sent to or from research or educational addresses only. Commercial use of the Internet, although becoming commonplace, was not the original intent. However, there are enough computers on the Internet, so that, although a commercial message may take a different route, it still arrives at its destination.

"Should I be on the Internet?"

The Internet has existed and flourished for many years. Most computer users who have dabbled with Unix-based computers at college have visited the Internet. PC users, who typically use DOS or Windows as an operating system, have found the Internet in only the last few years.

Whether you need an Internet address depends greatly on your communication needs. You may even have an Internet address and not know it. (Most online services are indirectly or directly connected to the Internet.) Without doubt, more information is stored on the Internet than is available from online services, and more people are connected to the Internet than to online services. However, you must weigh whether you care about this access.

The following section gives an overview of some of the information available on the Internet. Subsequent sections explain how to get access to the Internet and how to find items on the Internet.

Typical Features on the Internet

Plumbing the depths of the Internet does not simply involve choosing items from a menu. The information and people are there, but you have to find them. If you are adventurous, you can have a lot of fun or find invaluable information, but you can compare it with the way you use a library. If you like to randomly pick books from the shelves, you will have fun on the Internet. If your research material is not available elsewhere in an easy to find form, the Internet may be your only source. However, do not expect to find an index or directory that describes the Internet's contents. You will find hundreds, if not thousands, of lists describing where to find items.

You can chat, send and receive messages, and transfer files on the Internet. As on BBSs and commercial online services, this means you can send and receive e-mail, send and collect files, and potentially chat with other Internet users by typing at your keyboard. However, the ease with which you can do these things varies greatly, depending on the type of connection that you have. The following section describes the differences between types of connections.

"What information is on the Internet?"

Because the Internet is many computers that are organized in different ways, the information available is not arranged in a coherent manner. (This is where understanding the Internet moves from tangible numbers to numbers approaching infinity.) Imagine a network with five computers for a moment. If each computer has a different directory structure and different application programs, accessing each computer may require you to learn five approaches to finding information. Suppose that each computer offers different levels of access, and the information you can reach varies. Now expand the network to tens of thousands of computers, and you get some idea of how the Internet is a whole universe to explore.

As a small chapter in a communications book, generalizations on the Internet are necessary in this book. The following descriptions only scratch the surface of the available information.

You can send e-mail on the Internet. Your connection includes (or you obtain) a mailing program that can send messages. You supply the Internet address for a message's recipient, write the message content, and send the message. The message is passed via the Internet to the computer where your recipient is connected and where it can be read.

Note: There is no privacy on the Internet. The message can be read on its way to its destination. This is not important when announcing your child's birth but may be important when handling delicate business negotiations. If you use an online service that offers complete privacy for your messages and you also send messages via the Internet, remember that this privacy is lost once the message gets to the Internet.

By using e-mail, you usually send a message to a single recipient, but you can widen your audience to include *newsgroups* and *mailing lists*. These are similar to conferences on BBSs and other online services. (In some cases, as shown in Chapter 14, the conferences found on BBSs or online services are Internet newsgroups.) You read the mailing by using a mail program, and you read the newsgroup by using a news-reading program. (Your connection may not include both programs.)

The newsgroups focus on particular topics, and you can choose groups that you want to "subscribe" to. For example, you may choose to read the conferences on IBM PCs and organic gardening. The messages posted to these conferences are sent to your e-mail address. You can add your own contributions or remain passive. In some cases, this may result in two or three messages a week; in others, it may mean two or three messages a minute.

Using newsgroups is a very interesting way to exchange ideas with other interested people, but as you can guess, you need to check your mailbox regularly and remove or add newsgroups as your interests change. You may be able to filter the information you read from a newsgroup, depending on the particular software you are using to pick up the information.

Another variation on the e-mail topic is subscribing to mailing lists. You can sign up to receive mailings from various places on the Internet. As the name suggests, you then receive any mailings from that location. For example, you can sign up to get all the White House press releases or weather reports twice a day. Other services, such as newswires, are also available on the Internet, but you may have to pay to subscribe.

Note: Most newsgroups and mailing lists have a special message known as an *FAQ list.* This itemizes the frequently asked questions about the group. As a newcomer, you should read this information before posting a question of your own.

As part of your exploration of the Internet, you will quickly learn that there are many lists of lists. For example, you can find lists of available newsgroups and lists of available mailing lists. Most Internet books, including *the Internet For Dummies*, give you a sampling and show how to find the lists listing more.

In addition to various e-mail features, many computers on the Internet have files that you can download. After all, the computers are connected so that information can be passed from one computer to another. Many of these computers require you to have an account with them to access the files. However, thousands support nonsubscribers and give you access to a small area of the available information. You log on to the computer as a person named "anonymous" and gain access to the public area.

In some cases, the computers provide a convenient storage area, and the files are of a general nature. For example, you can find most shareware and public domain software that you would find on a BBS or commercial online service on the Internet. In other cases, the information is supplied as a service. The Library of Congress and the Smithsonian Institution have files containing digitized pictures of exhibits.

In principle, you download these files in a comparable way as downloading a file from a typical online service. You run a program at both ends of the connection to transfer the file from one computer to the other. Two popular programs are FTP (file transfer protocol) and RCP (remote copy protocol).

In practice, your particular Internet connection may not support file transfer. Although this limitation is changing with time, most commercial online services can provide you with an Internet e-mail address but cannot supply file transfer facilities for the Internet. (Delphi is a notable exception and currently offers the easiest and most economical connection for the typical PC user.) The sidebar "Transferring Binary Files as ASCII Text" explains how you can transfer a file to someone via e-mail if you don't have file transfer facilities. However, this will not allow you to transfer files from another computer.

You can find the computers on the Internet that have files you can download by exploring. You find a list of places to call, which in turn leads you to further places. To explore with any degree of efficiency, you need to learn new jargon and be prepared to read pages of information for one nugget of information.

You also can chat over the Internet. This is how you can talk to people in Russia, Australia, and Africa, for free, all at the same time. Again, you need a program; IRC (Internet Relay Chat) is a popular choice. You type your comments, and the other people online at the same time respond. CB radio is a good analogy. You talk to whomever is listening. If this interests you, there is a newsgroup (named alt.irc) that gives more information. Many connections do not offer this feature, because it arguably uses computer resources for little value.

Transferring Binary Files
without Internet File-Transfer Capabilities

Chapter 5 introduces the ASCII character set and the extended ASCII character set. Each character in the ASCII character set can be represented by using 7 bits of data. (The extended character set uses 8 bits of data.) Most electronic mail systems, especially those on types of computers other than PCs, handle only 7-bit ASCII text files. If you are connected to the Internet and can only send e-mail, this method applies.

As a PC owner, these electronic mail systems allow you to send messages to other computer owners without problems. However, if you want to transfer a binary file, you use a special file-transfer protocol, such as XMODEM, that can handle the 8-bit data. A *binary file* is a program or data file containing a series of 8-bit characters.

If the computer you are calling is unable to support file transfer, or the intended recipient cannot download the file from his system, consider using the ASCII text message features to send the binary file instead. This involves converting your program file from a binary file to an ASCII representation of the program file. You then send the ASCII file as if it were a message to the recipient. The recipient converts the received message back into a binary file for use.

The method is used most frequently when communicating via the Internet where file-transfer protocols are not always supported. The most commonly used conversion utility files are found on Unix-based systems because until recently most computers linked to the Internet were Unix-

based. These files are known as UUENCODE and UUDECODE. UUENCODE converts the binary file to ASCII text, and UUDECODE converts the ASCII text into a binary file.

For a PC running DOS, shareware or free conversion utilities are available, including encode and decode utilities from Sabasoft Inc. and Richard Marks. They are often named or referred to as UUENCODE or UUDECODE because of their Unix origins. I use Wincode from Snappy Inc., which is written by G. H. Silva. It is a Windows-based encoder and decoder that is available free of charge and has several particularly nice features. (Like PKZIP, it's available from online services, BBSs, and The Internet.)

You can compare the encoding and decoding procedure with using a file-compression program, such as PKZIP. When the file is compressed (or converted into ASCII text), it is unusable. The encode and decode utilities are tools that allow you to do something you could not do with the file in another form.

If you use a commercial online service as your Internet connection, you need to look carefully at the service's charges and limitations. Limits on the size and number of messages that you can send affect how you choose to convert your binary file. Some encoders can split your binary file into multiple ASCII text files of an appropriate size. The decoder can reassemble these files upon receipt.

Chatting over the Internet seems to me like stopping people in a grocery store and talking to them. I can understand people wanting to chat on BBSs or online services where the topics, such as politics or sports, are defined, but just chatting for the sake of doing it does not appeal to me.

You also can play games on the Internet. These may be familiar board games, such as chess or go, or may involve many players at once. These Multi-User Dungeons (MUDs), which are also known by many similar names such as MUSEs (multi-user shared environments), are variations on the chatting approach. They are roughly equivalent to the role-playing fantasy game Dungeons & Dragons. If this interests you, a newsgroup supplies a weekly list of available MUDs.

Getting Access to the Internet

All the computers on the Internet communicate by using TCP/IP protocols. Consequently, for you to be *on* the Internet, you need to use or connect to a computer that supports TCP/IP. If you are a home user with a stand-alone PC and a modem, you are not connected to the Internet. But if you use a PC in a business, particularly where you are on a LAN, you may already be on the Internet or can arrange to access the Internet. If you have a system administrator, *ask.* If you have access to a college computer — and in some areas, local schools — you may have access to the Internet. Several of my friends "talk" daily to their college-age children via the Internet.

If you subscribe to a BBS or commercial online service, you may already have access to the Internet. For example, you can send and receive messages to and from the Internet with your MCI Mail account, your CompuServe account, or your Delphi account. (In most cases, you will pay the service to send and receive messages. This may be a fixed monthly fee or may be a per message fee.) In most cases, this access is limited to sending and receiving messages.

Some BBSs connect to the Internet to pick up newsgroup mail. As explained in Chapter 14, they show up as conferences of messages that you can read. You may be able to suggest further newsgroups for your BBS to collect.

"How do I connect to the Internet?"

Another resource is an Internet Service Provider. These companies will provide you with access to the Internet for a monthly fee. They assign you a mailbox on their computer so you have an Internet address. When you have an account, you call the service provider from your PC and use the computer as your access to the Internet.

These service providers typically offer two types of connection: *terminal* and *network host.* They also offer different schemes (for different charges) that are typically volume related. For example, you may be charged $20 a month for a mailbox that you can access for an hour a day or $400 a month for unlimited access, multiple mailbox addresses, and other features.

The two types of connection are important to understand. By using a terminal connection, you call the service provider with your modem and communications software, such as Smartcom for Windows or QModemPro, and use the Internet access tools that they provide. For example, they may offer FTP as a file-transfer program, finger as a program to find who else is connected to the Internet, and IRC as a chat program. You cannot use your own selection of programs for this type of connection. When choosing a service provider, look carefully at the utilities offered and their user interface. (This is the type of connection currently offered by Delphi.)

As a network host, you make your computer actually attach itself to the network. This allows you to choose the software programs you run. This is particularly interesting for PC users who may find the commonly used utilities archaic and frustrating. It also allows you to take advantage of a relatively new trend. Many new software programs are becoming available, particularly for Windows, that provide a more familiar user interface for PC users with network host abilities.

For the typical single PC user, running a small business for example, the Internet service provider may allow you an economical way to connect with the Internet for a minimal cost. Using a special type of connection, SLIP (serial line IP) or PPP (point-to-point protocol), you can call the service provider via an ordinary telephone line with your modem and become a network host for the duration of the call. Although you may need support from your local supplier to install the required software to start with, this need not be an expensive alternative. (It's as complex as installing a very small LAN.)

Note: You are not paying an Internet organization; you are paying the provider who supplies you with your connection to the Internet. As a consequence, your charges and facilities may be very different from other Internet users. It is well worth shopping around.

Typical Utilities for Navigating the Internet

To communicate with other computers on the Internet, you will need to run software programs. You will, for example, need a mail-reading program to read mail and a file transferring program to download files. As explained in the preceding section, whether you can choose your own programs or must use the ones supplied by the Internet service provider depends on the type of connection you have.

However, because the Internet has been around for many years, there are several programs, some newer than others, that people tend to talk about. (This is where the astronomy analogy comes in again. Other Internet users may sound like they are talking in technical detail about event horizons or black holes.)

PC users have their own jargon they use without being aware of it. Internet users do the same. For example, we talk about zipping a file and using PKZIP. This is actually a product name. We mean compressing, but we don't say that. The good Internet providers will supply information on the utilities they provide. Increasingly, providers are adding menu-driven user interfaces to make your job easier. You will probably have to read the instructions and probably the FAQ (frequently asked questions) information to get started.

"What do I use to search the Internet?"

To understand this process, you need to learn two more terms: *server* and *client.* The term server on the Internet (and other computer systems) means the computer that supplies (stores and can run) the application program. You need to run an appropriate client (a piece of software) to access the server application. This client is a utility program that may be located on your local computer, the server you are accessing, or even another server on the Internet. The utilities your Internet provider supplies are examples of client software. This explains how different Internet servers can be accessed by dissimilar computer systems (Unix, PC, Mac, etc.) by means of an appropriate client for each system. The server behaves the same, no matter which system the client software is running to access the server.

In some cases, you may need to run one client software program on your local computer to connect with another server and use another client software program on that server to access the application program of interest. For example, a Gopher server is the computer that contains the Gopher program and the computer that is actually running the Gopher program for you. You use the expression *connect with a Gopher server* to indicate that you are running the Gopher program. You can use Gopher client software located at your local computer, in which case the Gopher client software makes the connection and runs the Gopher program. Alternatively, you can use a different program, such as Telnet, to make the connection with a Gopher server and run the Gopher client software as well as Telnet. To compare this with typical asynchronous communication, you run a communications program with terminal emulation to make the connection with another computer, but you may use a second program from within the communications program that supports file-transfer protocols to transfer the file. As a user, you probably don't realize that you are running two different programs; you only care that you have made the connection and accessed the desired function.

Telnet

This most basic utility allows you to log into a remote computer as a *terminal*. As explained in Chapter 5, when you link your PC to another computer as a terminal, you control the remote computer from your PC.

Finger and Whois

These are two commands available on many systems that allow you to find other people on the Internet. The finger command tells you about who is currently logged into the Internet at the address you specify. The whois command tells you about the addresses of people on the Internet. The whois directory does not contain all Internet user names but contains many people who are involved in the working of the Internet and doing network research.

FTP and RCP

These programs allow you to download and upload files to the Internet.

Archie

This program searches the Internet for files that meet your description. You access an Archie server (a computer that has Archie available for use) and run Archie from there. You may have Archie available at your connection (if your Internet provider offers it). Or you can use Telnet to access the Archie server. You are then logged in as a terminal to the computer that can run Archie for you. Alternatively, you can send e-mail to an Archie server and receive the response as a (potentially huge) e-mail message.

Gopher

Gopher is a menu-driven program that helps you look for documents and files on the Internet. It is an attempt to make navigating the Internet easier. You run Gopher from your connection or Telnet to a Gopher server. When you find something of interest, you can access this data from Gopher.

The Gopher program is an example of why the Internet is so powerful yet hard to understand. Anyone who wants to can set up a Gopher server and provide menus that show the features of their particular computer. This Gopher server can also provide links to features of other computers. As a result, you may find the menus inconsistent, because so many different people may have been involved in setting up the menus. (Keep in mind that the Internet is a network of networked computers without a centralized system.)

Veronica

Veronica (Very Easy Rodent-Oriented Net-wide Index to Computerized Archives) is a database that shows all the locations of available Gopher servers. (There are so many Gopher servers that the index is very useful.) It is typically available from all other Gopher servers. You pick the menu selection, such as Veronica or Other Gophers. It is roughly equivalent to Archie, where Archie is an index to FTP files on the Internet. Veronica can find Gopher servers that meet your search criteria.

Wide Area Information Servers (WAIS)

Wide Area Information Servers (WAIS, pronounced *ways*) is another form of index on the Internet. It looks inside the documents and files rather than at only the titles (like Archie and Veronica) for the words that meet your search criteria. However, not all documents and files on the Internet have the necessary indexes for WAIS to be able to find them.

WAIS has a reputation of having a very difficult user interface, but you can often access WAIS through Gopher menus, which makes life much easier (but more limited).

World Wide Web (WWW)

The World Wide Web (WWW or the Web) is another document index that explores the information on the Internet by using hypertext links. You access a hypertext browsing program and see a summary or part of the document. Certain words are highlighted or numbered, and you can select one of these linking words or phrases to jump to another area of interest. In fact, the link may not be a word or phrase, but may be a pointer to a picture.

You probably have encountered hypertext in Windows help files. You display an index of information and click a hypertext phrase to jump to information on that phrase. When in the new area, you can jump to another highlighted phrase to get other related information.

Most of the documents that WWW can search are also WAIS documents and files. Consequently, you can consider WWW as being a preferable user interface to access WAIS information.

Summary

This chapter introduced the Internet. It is a rapidly growing collection of interconnected computers. Each computer in the chain passes data to the next computer in the chain to make a world-wide network. There is no "central computer."

You can connect to the Internet in a variety of different ways. If you subscribe to an online service or BBS, you may already be part of the Internet community. This may limit your connection to sending and receiving mail.

An Internet service provider can provide two other forms of connection that give you even greater access. As a *terminal*, you can call the provider and use the utilities supplied by the provider to read mail, search for information, and do file transfer. As a *network server*, you can use your selection of utilities rather than depending on the service provider's choices. The connection as a network server may be continual or may be via a SLIP or PPP connection where you are actually only connected to the Internet for the duration of the phone call.

Chapter 18 covers information-searching services, which provide vast sophisticated databases useful for specialized applications, such as patent searching, following news wire services, and other electronic database searching.

18

CHAPTER

Information-Searching Services

This chapter covers information-searching services. In particular, you will learn about the following topics:

- ❖ When to use an information-searching service
- ❖ The types of information-searching services
- ❖ Tours of two different searching services
- ❖ Using a third-party to search efficiently

Understanding Information-Searching Services

Unlike the other online services covered in Part IV, this chapter covers services intended almost exclusively for professional use. These services are vast databases that are valuable to business, academic, and research staff. Although connect time charges can be more than $10 per minute, when used for the right purpose, these services can easily save a company more than that amount.

Information-searching services are similar to your accounting system. When you are a small company, you can handle the accounts and payroll with one individual and PC. As you grow, you reach a point where it is more economical to pay an outside service to do some of the work, keep up with the government and tax regulations, and ensure that the job is done on time. However, you may reach a point where is it better to have the relevant skills in-house, and some of the responsibility returns to your company.

"Who needs an information-searching service?"

Information-searching services are not really suitable for individuals, but when chosen judiciously, small businesses may get a large competitive edge from them. If you need to follow an industry, particularly one that has government regulations, these services can keep you informed.

The information falls into two categories: current and historic. The current information includes such items as today's newspapers from around the world, regional and even local newspapers, and current stock market quotes and newswire information.

As you might expect, the historical information includes back issues of the newspapers, periodicals, and financial data. However, it also includes much more. You can find such diverse topics as worldwide patent and trademark information, books in print, government publications, labor statistics, zoological information, and toxicology and other medical data. The information is particularly relevant if you do research. There are many chemical and legal databases. Most, if not all, the information is available from other sources. However, the advantage of having a single source in which the information is stored electronically cannot be ignored.

Consider a simple example of research done the manual way. About a year ago, I needed to find the source for a quote made by John Walker, the founder of Autodesk, Inc. and creator of AutoCAD. I read the quote in a magazine article and wanted to read the context in which it was said. Most of my research work was done because I knew the title of the book where the quote was taken from. However, because I didn't have access to an information-searching service, finding a copy of the book and then finding the quote in the book took several hours, with several days' delay.

This type of research problem occurs in most businesses. A new company calls, and you need to know something about it, the people, and the financial information. You are considering names for your product but need to check trademarks of other companies. You need to find out as much as possible about new businesses your competitors are exploring. You want the best newspaper clipping service possible. You meet with an executive to get him to support a philanthropic endeavor, and you want to do some research about what causes he's interested in.

Using an information-searching service is similar to using another online service. You call the service with your modem and communication software. You then connect to a remote computer that contains all the database information. You search for the desired information by specifying such items as where you want to look for the information and what information to look for.

"What can I find on an information-searching service?"

The commercial online services covered in Chapter 16 are aimed at a general audience and include relatively intuitive user interfaces and common features, such as messaging, file exchange, and chatting. The information-searching services tend to be more targeted and are not particularly easy to use. However, they are no more difficult to use than a specialized application program.

Like other online services, you can get the same information from a variety of sources. For example, the Dow Jones News Retrieval service, a business and financial news information service, can be accessed directly or via other online services, such as MCI Mail (see Chapter 15), or DataTimes. Certain newspapers and magazines are available online from other services. For example, America Online has *USA Today*, and Prodigy contains *Consumer Reports*.

The following sections summarize the available features of three popular information searching services: Dow Jones News Retrieval, DataTimes, and Dialog Information Services Inc.

Dow Jones News Retrieval

The Dow Jones News Retrieval service emphasizes business and financial data. It includes worldwide news information as well as data on companies, stocks, and mutual funds. However, it also includes more general services, such as college selection services, sports, movie reviews, weather, and shopping. Electronic mail services are supported via MCI Mail. You can use MCI Mail from Dow Jones News Retrieval in the same way that you can use Dow Jones News Retrieval from MCI Mail. However, you do need to subscribe to the two services separately.

The services offered include the following:

- Business and world newswires

  Business and Finance Report, Japan Economic Daily, Dow Jones Business Newswires, and Dow Jones News Service

- Dow Jones Text Library

  Current business articles, *The Wall Street Journal,* and other national, regional and industry publications

- Company and industry information

- Dun and Bradstreet market identifiers and financial records, Zacks corporate earnings estimator, Standard and Poors profiles and earnings estimates, corporate ownership watch, worldwide corporate reports, and corporate Canada online

- Quotes, statistics, and commentary

  Historical Dow Jones averages, Dow Jones quotes, future and index quotes, mutual fund performance reports, and "Wall $treet Week" transcripts.

- General services

  Book reviews, career management advice, encyclopedia, travel, college selection, and weather reports (electronic mail services via MCI Mail)

DataTimes

DataTimes boasts more than 2,000 local, regional, national, and international newspaper, newswire, trade, and industry sources. Its emphasis is on printed material.

❖ National news sources

Newswire services include Associated Press and US Newswire. Magazines and newspapers include *The New York Times*, *USA Today*, *The Wall Street Journal*, *The Washington Post*, *Money Inc.*, *Barron's*, and *American Banker*.

❖ Broadcast transcripts

Including CNN's news, specials, "Crossfire"; "Inside Business"; National Public Radio's "All Things Considered," "Morning Edition," and "Weekend Edition"; "Frontline"; "Nova"; and "Washington Week in Review"

❖ Local and regional newspapers

Divided by state and individual papers. For example, North Dakota sources are *Grand Forks Herald* and *Fargo's Forum*, while 21 New York newspapers are available.

❖ International newspaper and business sources

General international sources include *NTIS Foreign Technology Newsletter*, *Electronic World News*, and *International Country Risk Guide*. More specific sources are from Africa, Asia, Australia, Canada, Europe, Latin America, the Middle East, as well as Russia and the Commonwealth of Independent States. Examples include *Southern African Freedom Bulletin*, *South China Morning Post*, *Ottawa Citizen*, *Euromarketing*, *Tehran Times*, and *Soviet Aerospace and Technology*.

❖ Company and industry databases

Same-day regional business news from such newspapers as *The Kansas City Star* and the *Houston Chronicle*. Additionally, many Dow Jones News Retrieval services, such as newswire, business and financial news, SEC Online, Dun's Financial Records, and quotes and statistics.

Dialog

Dialog is an immense online database with a mixture of reference material and current news. It claims more than 450 separate databases containing more than 330 million articles, abstracts, and citations. It emphasizes news, business, science, and technology.

✤ Business

General business and industry, such as *Moody's Corporate News, Harvard Business Review,* and *Standard and Poor's Daily News.* Business statistics, U.S. and international directories and company financials, product information

✤ Dialog reference files

Includes product name finder, journal name finder, company name finder, electronic mail, and newsletters

✤ Law and government

Includes Congressional Information Service, American Statistics Index, Federal Register abstracts, Laborlaw, and British Official Publications

✤ General

REMARC (Library of Congress books), books in print, British books in print, academic index, OAG electronic edition, encyclopedia of associations, public opinion online

✤ News

Indexes for over 100,000 articles and full text to over 60 newspapers, wire services including Reuters, and PR Newswire; and international news services, including Kompass International and Global News

✤ Patents, trademarks, and copyrights

U.S. copyrights; several U.S. Patent related databases; U.S., UK, and Canada trademarks and world patents.

✤ Science

General topics include agriculture and nutrition, chemistry, computer technology, energy and environment, medicine and biosciences, pharmaceutical, science, technology, and engineering. Specific databases include aerospace database, consumer drug information, zoological record, *New England Journal of Medicine,* oceanic abstracts, Datapro software directory, polymer online, and food science and technology abstracts.

✤ Social sciences and humanities

The available databases include education index, religion index, philosopher's index, mental health abstracts, and music literature international.

A brief tour of the Dow Jones News Retrieval

As the name suggests, the Dow Jones News Retrieval service focuses mainly on news, financial, and business-related material. To illustrate a couple of its features, the example in the brief tour shows how to find recent news stories for particular companies as well as the stock symbol for companies. The subsequent example shows more of the available financial information.

When you have been issued with a password to Dow Jones News Retrieval, you log on by calling the relevant phone number, typically your local Tymnet or Sprintnet number, and issuing the commands to connect your computer with the service's computer.

Dow Jones News Retrieval divides its services into topics, such as stock quotes, news wire services, and Official Airline Guide (OAG). In this example, I looked for the recent articles and newswire information on IBM.

You access the newswire service by typing //**WIRES** at the command prompt. Your screen will look like Figure 18-1.

```
                              -END-
▲◀   !!◀//wires


                    DOW JONES BUSINESS NEWSWIRES
                Copyright (C) 1993 Dow Jones & Company, Inc.

Enter a symbol or a code to get news, articles, releases and reports.

Enter /C to search by company name or to search for a content code by
its description.
_____
To limit your selection by newswire group(s), choose from:
   1    Articles from all five Dow Jones newswires
   2    Press releases from PR Newswire, Business Wire and Canada NewsWire
   3    Japan Economic Newswire from Kyodo News International
   4    Analyst Report Abstracts from Investext
   5    Business articles from today's newspapers
   6    European business news from Agence France Presse-Extel
_____

ENTER SELECTION: 1 or 2, or 1,5, etc. To continuously display articles,
type DISPLAY and article numbers. For example, DISPLAY 1,3,6-9 (RETURN).
Or press (Return) for instructions.
▲◀   !!◀
 ANSI    ONLINE  38400 7E1  [Alt+Z]-Menu   FDX 8 LF X ♪ ♫ CP LG ↑ PR  00:02:03
```

Figure 18-1: Dow Jones Business Newswires. You can search for news on a particular company or based on the news supplier.

You can limit your search by choosing the newswire or news service. For example, you can choose to search only the European business news or the business articles from today's papers. For this example, I searched all the services but looked only for articles referring to IBM. To do this you type /**C,** press Enter, type **IBM**, and then press Enter. Your screen will look like Figure 18-2.

```
 5    Business articles from today's newspapers
 6    European business news from Agence France Presse-Extel
-------------------------------------------------------------------
ENTER SELECTION: 1 or 2, or 1,5, etc. To continuously display articles,
type DISPLAY and article numbers. For example, DISPLAY 1,3,6-9 (RETURN).
Or press (Return) for instructions.
▲◀   !!◀/c

ENTER AS MUCH OF THE COMPANY NAME AS YOU KNOW AND PRESS RETURN.
▲◀   !!◀ibm

YOU ENTERED: IBM

FIND STORIES ON:
 1   IBM          IBM
 2   G.IBM        IBM DEUTSCHLAND GMBH
 3   F.IBM        IBM FRANCE
 4   I.IBM        IBM ITALIA S.P.A.
 5   J.IBM        IBM JAPAN LTD.
                          -END-

ENTER A SELECTION, /T FOR TOP, OR HELP.
▲   ◀   !!◀
ANSI    ONLINE   38400  7E1  [Alt+Z]-Menu  FDX 8 LF X ♪ ♫ CP LG ↑ PR  00:01:25
```

Figure 18-2: Searching by company name. Dow Jones News Retrieval prompts you for the company of interest to avoid ambiguity.

Dow Jones News Retrieval notes that five companies match the requested IBM. They include IBM France and IBM Japan. To focus in on IBM France rather than IBM, you choose 3 from this menu. However, if you choose 1, Dow Jones News Retrieval displays the latest articles available on IBM. Your screen will look like Figure 18-3.

This shows a list of the 18 most recent news items on IBM. (Further lists are displayed by pressing Enter.) The first six articles show a time rather than a date because they are taken directly from the newswire services and today's papers. For example, article number 1 is from the PR Newswire service. The older articles (yesterday's in this example) show the headlines and date for the article. Notice that articles 13 through 15 are all on the same topic; remarketing Evans & Sutherland Accelerators.

Article number 18 is a notification of IBM's second quarter financial statements that are filed with the Securities and Exchange Commission. To view this, you type **18** and press Enter. The financial statements or article is displayed one screen at a time. Obviously, if you call the service on a different day, the newest articles would be different. You can perform a similar search for articles on another company or in a particular industry, such as railroads or tobacco. Other searching options are also offered.

```
BUSINESS NEWSWIRES - IBM                              HEADLINE PAGE  1

  1 PR    09:34 HOW DO YOU MOVE 2,367,096,000,000 BYTES OF INFORMATION FROM...
  2 BW    08:22 Adobe's Display PostScript Level 2 Supports New IBM PowerPC...
  3 WJ    06:16 Digital A Surprise Contender In Video Servers Market
  4 AX    05:01 ALITALIA REPORTEDLY TO CONTRACT BOOKING SYSTEM TO IBM, SIP...
  5 SFC   03:13 Many Layoffs Are Planned For the Future
  6 HOU   02:18 Expo to guide firms through computer-buying maze
  7 IN    10/19 IBM/Interactive -3: No Consensus On Best Hardware System
  8 IN    10/19 IBM/Interactive-2: Bell Atlantic Says IBM Strong Contender
  9 IN    10/19 (WSJ): IBM In The Running For Bell Atlantic Video Project
 10 DJ    10/19 IBM Eliminates Use Of Ozone Depleting CFCs In Mfg Process
 11 BW    10/19 IBM 0662 Model S12 1.05GB Drive is PC Magazine's Editors'...
 12 BW    10/19 IBM eliminates worldwide CFC emissions from manufacturing...
 13 DJ    10/19 IBM - Evans & Sutherland -2-: Accelerators Available Next Yr
 14 DJ    10/19 *IBM To Remarket Evans & Sutherland Accelerators >ESCC
 15 BW    10/19 IBM to remarket high-end graphics accelerators from Evans &...
 16 WJ    10/19 IBM Picks Welsh For New Post
 17 WJ    10/19 Bull To Get A Cash Injection One Last Time From Government
 18 FF    10/19 INTERNATIONAL BUSINESS 2Q Fin'l Statements
_____
SELECT STORY, ENTER PRINT COMMAND OR PRESS (RETURN) FOR MORE HEADLINES.
▲◀   ‼◀
 ANSI    ONLINE  38400 7E1  [Alt+Z]-Menu   FDX 8 LF X ♪ ♩ CP LG ↑ PR  00:02:35
```

Figure 18-3: Newswire listing for IBM. The latest headlines for newswire reports and articles for IBM are shown.

For many of the topics available on Dow Jones News Retrieval, you need to know the company name and its stock symbol that you are interested in. These can be found online by using the symbols database. If you type //**SYMBOLS,** your screen will look like Figure 18-4.

```
                        DIRECTORY OF SYMBOLS
                        COPYRIGHT (C) 1993
                      DOW JONES & COMPANY, INC.

To find a stock symbol, enter at least 3 characters of a company name
and press (Return). Or you can enter one of the following selections:

  1    Stock Symbol When Company Name or Cusip Number is Known
  2    Company Name When Stock Symbol is Known
  3    Summary of Codes and Symbols for a Company
  4    Mutual Funds
  5    U.S. Corporate Bonds
  6    U.S. Treasury Issues
  7    Foreign Bonds
  8    Companies in Dow Jones Industry Group Indexes
  9    Information on codes used in //WIRES, //CLIP, //DJNEWS and //TEXT
          available exclusively in //GUIDE Code Directory (selection 8)
 10    Recent Symbol Updates
 11    Option Symbol and Code Information
Note: Media General Industry Code Information is now in //MG
_____
Press (Return) for general instructions and help.
▲◀   ‼◀
 ANSI    ONLINE  38400 7E1  [Alt+Z]-Menu   FDX 8 LF X ♪ ♩ CP LG ↑ PR  00:01:12
```

Figure 18-4: Symbol Directory. Many searches require a company stock symbol and not the company name.

This directory allows you to find the stock symbol or abbreviation for the chosen item. Typing **IBM** and pressing Enter at the command prompt, for example, opens the screen in Figure 18-5.

```
4      Mutual Funds
5      U.S. Corporate Bonds
6      U.S. Treasury Issues
7      Foreign Bonds
8      Companies in Dow Jones Industry Group Indexes
9      Information on codes used in //WIRES, //CLIP, //DJNEWS and //TEXT
          available exclusively in //GUIDE Code Directory (selection 8)
10     Recent Symbol Updates
11     Option Symbol and Code Information
Note: Media General Industry Code Information is now in //MG
-------------------------------------------------------------------------
Press (Return) for general instructions and help.
▲◀    ‼◀ibm
└SYMBOL
                            STOCKS

D.IAD     IBM CREDIT CORP. - NA
G.IBM    *IBM DEUTSCHLAND GMBH - GE
F.IBM    *IBM FRANCE - FR
I.IBM    *IBM ITALIA S.P.A. - IT
J.IBM    *IBM JAPAN LTD. - JA
IBM      *INTERNATIONAL BUSINESS MACHINES CORP. - NY
                            -END-
▲◀   ‼◀
 ANSI    ONLINE  38400 7E1  [Alt+Z]-Menu  FDX 8 LF X ♪ ♪ CP LG ↑ PR  00:01:44
```

Figure 18-5: Symbol searching. Dow Jones News Retrieval reports on the companies with names similar to that specified.

Like the newswire service, several companies fit the name description of IBM. These include IBM Germany and IBM Credit Corp. When searching for stock information on these companies, you must use the correct symbol. For example, to search for International Business Machines Corp., you use IBM. To search for IBM Credit Corp. you use D.IAD. If you look for Microsoft, you find that the symbol is MSFT, and no other companies use Microsoft as part of their name and Microsoft does not have other separate companies.

Dow Jones News Retrieval is particularly useful for finding financial and business information. Much of this is updated on a continual, daily, or weekly basis. For example, you can access the MMS Weekly Market Analysis. These are the weekly survey results generated by MMS International. They gather the data from more than 200 economists, traders, and money dealers nationally and internationally. They assess the economy, foreign exchange, and equity markets.

To reach this analysis, you type //**MMS** at the command prompt to open the screen in Figure 18-6. You can view economic summaries, equity, currency, and debt commentaries. You can also view a calendar that shows the upcoming economic events such as housing starts.

```
FINAL PAGE OF TEXT IN THIS SECTION.

PRESS FOR
  T   TOP MENU
  M   PREVIOUS MENU
◢◀   ‼◀t
└

                  MMS Weekly Market Analysis
                        Oct. 17, 1993
                      Copyright (c) 1993
                     MMS International Inc.


        1        MMS Weekly Economic Survey:
                   Summary & Analysis and Survey Medians & Ranges
        2        Weekly Equity Market Commentary
        3        Weekly Currency Market Commentary
        4        Weekly Debt Market Commentary
        5        Calendars of Economic Events
        6        MMS Forecasts of Monthly and Quarterly Indicators
        7        MMS Biweekly Economic Briefing

     Enter selection.
◢◀   ‼◀
 ANSI     ONLINE   38400 7E1   [Alt+Z]-Menu   FDX 8 LF X ♪ ♫ CP LG ↑ PR   00:03:34
```

Figure 18-6: MMS Weekly Market Analysis. You can view analysis on various economic markets.

If you press **7**, you will see a multipage summary of the current and forecasted economic state. You can read this compiled text information. If you press **6**, you can get tables of monthly or weekly economic indicators. Figure 18-7 shows one page from the summary of monthly economic indicators. For example, it shows that imported car sales are expected to grow in the next few months, and domestic car sales will also grow.

```
└
MMS                                                        P103 ENDS AT 105

          MMS Forecasts: Monthly Economic Indicators
                   Last Reviewed OCT/15

     REAL SECTOR          JUL      AUG      SEP      OCT      NOV      DEC
  CIV.UNEMPLOYMENT        6.8%A    6.7%A    6.7%A    6.6%     6.6%     6.5%
  NONFARM PAYROLL         237KA   -41KA    156KA    165K     165K     180K
  DOMESTIC AUTO SALES     6.7MA    6.7MA    6.6MA    6.9M     7.0M     7.1M
  IMPORTED AUTO SALES     2.0MA    2.0MA    1.9MA    2.0M     2.1M     2.1M
  PPI                    -.2%A    -.6%A     .2%A     .2%      .1%      .2%
  RETAIL SALES            .5%A     .5%A     .1%A     .6%      .4%      .3%
  IND.PRODUCTION          .2%A     .1%A     .2%A     .5%      .3%      .3%
  CAPACITY UTILIZATION   81.6%A   81.6%A   81.6%A   82.2%    82.3%    82.4%
  WHOLESALE SALES         .9%A    1.1%A     .2%      .4%      .4%      .4%
  HOUSING STARTS         1.23MA   1.32MA   1.30M    1.35M    1.35M    1.35M
  PERSONAL INCOME        -.3%A    1.3%A     .2%      .5%      .5%      .5%
  PERS. CONS. EXPEND.     .4%A     .4%A     .3%      .5%      .5%      .4%
  CPI                     .1%A     .3%A     .0%A     .4%      .3%      .3%
  DUR GDS ORDERS        -2.8%A    2.3%A    1.0%     2.0%     1.0%      .5%
  DUR GDS SHIPMENTS     -4.3%A    3.6%A    1.0%     1.0%      .5%      .5%

◢◀   ‼◀
 ANSI     ONLINE   38400 7E1   [Alt+Z]-Menu   FDX 8 LF X ♪ ♫ CP LG ↑ PR   00:01:33
```

Figure 18-7: Monthly Economic Indicators. The economic indicator data is summarized in tabular form.

You disconnect from Dow Jones News Retrieval by typing //**DISC**.

A brief tour of Dialog

Dialog Information Services Inc. has an extensive series of databases that you can search through. Generalizing a typical search is very difficult because the range of supported topics is so diverse. All information-searching services require a knowledge of what you are searching for and some idea of where you will be able to find it. In many cases, you will look in the more general databases and then move to the more specialized databases.

Suppose that you have invented a new chicken-flavored crunchy snack food. You are considering product names, and your short list includes Crickles and Chickles. You can use Dialog to search for other companies that may have trademarked your proposed product name.

You log on to Dialog in a way comparable to other online databases. However, you typically connect via a packet-switched network such as Tymnet or Sprintnet. You call the local number, specify the service you want to connect to — in this case Dialog — and enter your user number and password.

You can select different user interfaces when you set up your account. This chapter uses an account that provides more menus and help with the user interface. This is easier to use than the more curt user interface, but it takes longer to move around the system.

After logging in, you can begin your search. From the catalog, I determined that the U.S. Federal Trademarks are stored in database number 226. (Dialog also includes U.S. State, Canadian, and UK trademark information in separate databases.)

You gain access to the database of choice by using the Begin command. At the command prompt, you type **begin 226**. You then choose key words that you want to search for. In this example, the key words are Chickles and Crickles.

You type **select crickles** to make a selection set of all the records in the database that contain the word crickles. Dialog searches the database and reports back. As shown in Figure 18-8, the results for set number one (S1) found one item with the word crickles.

```
     Enter an option number or a Begin command and press ENTER:
     /H =Help              /L =Logoff        /NOMENU =Command Mode
?◄begin 226

        19oct93 15:45:51 User073296 Session D64.1
             $0.09    0.006 Hrs FileHomeBase
     $0.09   Estimated cost FileHomeBase
     $0.05   TYMNET
     $0.14   Estimated cost this search
     $0.14   Estimated total session cost    0.006 Hrs.

File 226:TRADEMARKSCAN  OG:10/05/93 AP:08/11/93
        (Copr. 1993 Thomson & Thomson)
***    PRELIMINARY RECORDS THROUGH 09/16    ***


     Set  Items  Description
     ---  -----  -----------
?◄select crickles
     S1      1  CRICKLES
?◄select chickles
     S2      1  CHICKLES
?◄
 ANSI    ONLINE  38400 7E1  [Alt+Z]-Menu  FDX 8 LF X ♪ ♫ CP LG ↑ PR  00:01:57
```

Figure 18-8: Dialog selection set. Dialog searches the chosen database for the chosen items.

Similarly, you type **select crickles** to make a second selection set. Dialog creates a second set (S2) and reports that it found one item with the word chickles in it.

You can view the specific references to crickles and chickles. You can have them displayed one screen at a time, continuously, or printed out and mailed to you. In this example, if you type **d s1/2/1**, your screen will be similar to Figure 18-9. This command instructs Dialog to display set number 1, with a format style of number 2 (a summary), and the record you want displayed is the first one.

As shown in Figure 18-9, the word Crickles was first used in 1968 and was trademarked in 1970 by John E. Cain Co. It is used for a brand of pickles.

Using the same display command, but this time requesting information for the second set, you can see the information for Chickles as shown in Figure 18-10. In this case, Chickles is a registered trademark for a soft toy with a light-actuated noisemaker. It was first registered by Animal Fair, Inc., and has been assigned to Manhattan Toy/Carousel, L.P.

It looks like your snack will have to have another name to avoid using another company's trademark.

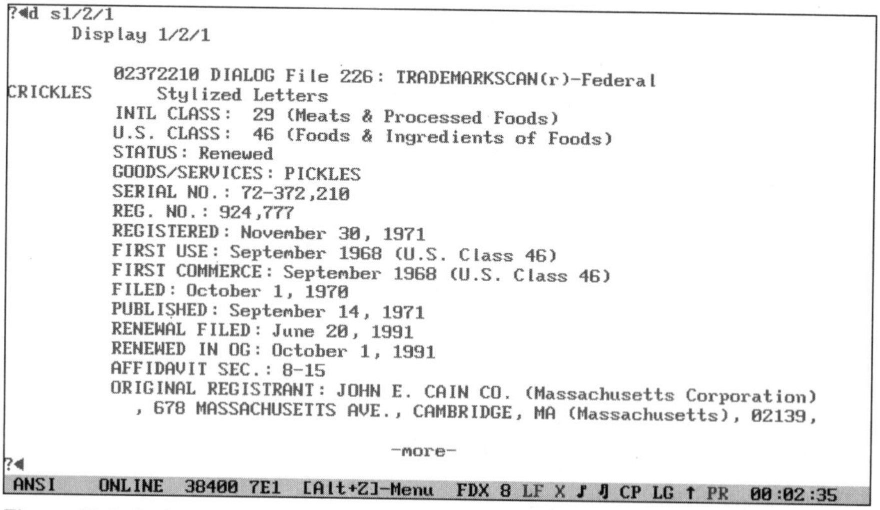

```
?◄d s1/2/1
        Display 1/2/1

            02372210 DIALOG File 226: TRADEMARKSCAN(r)-Federal
CRICKLES       Stylized Letters
            INTL CLASS:  29 (Meats & Processed Foods)
            U.S. CLASS:  46 (Foods & Ingredients of Foods)
            STATUS: Renewed
            GOODS/SERVICES: PICKLES
            SERIAL NO.: 72-372,210
            REG. NO.: 924,777
            REGISTERED: November 30, 1971
            FIRST USE: September 1968 (U.S. Class 46)
            FIRST COMMERCE: September 1968 (U.S. Class 46)
            FILED: October 1, 1970
            PUBLISHED: September 14, 1971
            RENEWAL FILED: June 20, 1991
            RENEWED IN OG: October 1, 1991
            AFFIDAVIT SEC.: 8-15
            ORIGINAL REGISTRANT: JOHN E. CAIN CO. (Massachusetts Corporation)
              , 678 MASSACHUSETTS AVE., CAMBRIDGE, MA (Massachusetts), 02139,

                                -more-
?◄
 ANSI    ONLINE  38400 7E1  [Alt+Z]-Menu   FDX 8 LF X ♪ ♫ CP LG ↑ PR  00:02:35
```

Figure 18-9: Dialog record display. Dialog can show the selected database records in a variety of formats.

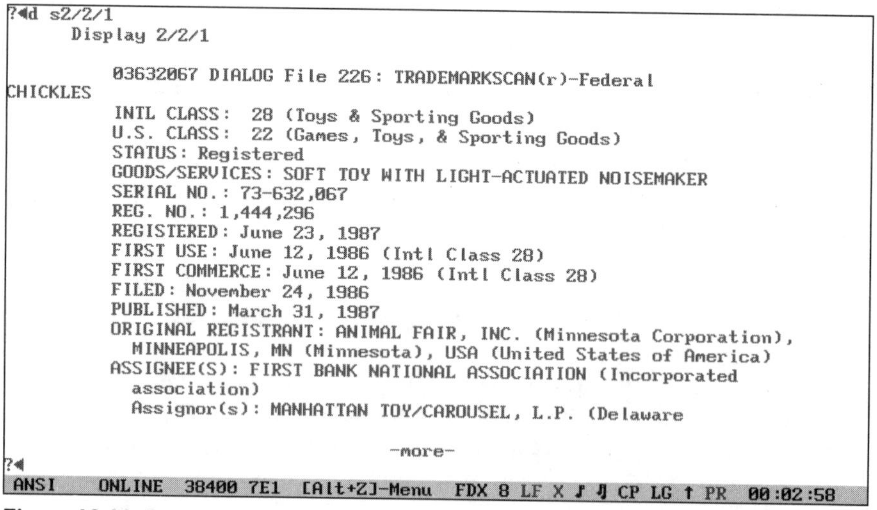

```
?◄d s2/2/1
        Display 2/2/1

            03632067 DIALOG File 226: TRADEMARKSCAN(r)-Federal
CHICKLES
            INTL CLASS:  28 (Toys & Sporting Goods)
            U.S. CLASS:  22 (Games, Toys, & Sporting Goods)
            STATUS: Registered
            GOODS/SERVICES: SOFT TOY WITH LIGHT-ACTUATED NOISEMAKER
            SERIAL NO.: 73-632,067
            REG. NO.: 1,444,296
            REGISTERED: June 23, 1987
            FIRST USE: June 12, 1986 (Intl Class 28)
            FIRST COMMERCE: June 12, 1986 (Intl Class 28)
            FILED: November 24, 1986
            PUBLISHED: March 31, 1987
            ORIGINAL REGISTRANT: ANIMAL FAIR, INC. (Minnesota Corporation),
              MINNEAPOLIS, MN (Minnesota), USA (United States of America)
            ASSIGNEE(S): FIRST BANK NATIONAL ASSOCIATION (Incorporated
              association)
              Assignor(s): MANHATTAN TOY/CAROUSEL, L.P. (Delaware

                                -more-
?◄
 ANSI    ONLINE  38400 7E1  [Alt+Z]-Menu   FDX 8 LF X ♪ ♫ CP LG ↑ PR  00:02:58
```

Figure 18-10: Patent summary. Each patent is a separate record within the database.

This example shows the most simple search possible on Dialog. Typically, you will search with far more complex criteria. Suppose that you want to look up patents for magnetic stripes and, more specifically, you want to know who has an international patent on the magnetic heads that are used to read magnetic stripes on credit cards.

The general procedure would be to search in a patent database. For example, database number 351 contains the world patent index. You may issue the following select command: **select magnetic and stripe**. This searches the patents for instances where the words magnetic and stripe occur in the record. As shown in Figure 18-11, Dialog may report back that there are 155,392 records with the word magnetic, 4,478 with the word stripe, and 360 with both words.

```
        1981+;DW=9335,UA=9331,UM=9309
**FILE351: Attention Derwent subscribers: Markush DARC on DIALOG is
   available.  Begin WPILM to access.

      Set   Items   Description
      ---   -----   -----------
?◄select magnetic and stripe
         155392   MAGNETIC
           4478   STRIPE
      S1      360   MAGNETIC AND STRIPE
?◄select s1 and card and head
            360   S1
          19626   CARD
         149168   HEAD
      S2       46   S1 AND CARD AND HEAD
?◄select s2 not reader
             46   S2
          13620   READER
      S3       27   S2 NOT READER
?◄select s3 not manufacture
             27   S3
         202001   MANUFACTURE
      S4       27   S3 NOT MANUFACTURE
?◄
 ANSI    ONLINE  38400 7E1  [Alt+Z]-Menu   FDX 8 LF X ♪ ♩ CP LG ↑ PR   00:10:48
```

Figure 18-11: Dialog search criteria. Dialog accepts typical Boolean expressions in its search criteria.

If 360 records are too many to look at, you can choose to refine your selection by searching the selected records for those that contain the words card and head. The command is **select s1 and card and head**. This searches set number one for those records with the words card and head. Dialog reports that there were 360 records in set one; 19,626 records contain the word card, and 149,168 contain the word head. The combination, called set number two (S2), contains 46 records.

Your search continues by widening and narrowing the search criteria. Dialog supports Boolean expressions, such as AND, OR, NOR, and NOT. These are familiar to many technical PC users, especially engineers and programmers. And they are relatively easy to understand because they act exactly as their names suggest.

The AND command gives you a record selection only when both the word before and the word after the and are in the record.

The NOT gives you the records that are selected that do not contain a keyword. For example, continuing the credit card example, if you try and eliminate patents relating to card readers, you can type **select s2 not reader**. This reduces the number of selected records to 27.

To remove records related to the manufacture of these magnetic stripe heads, you type the command **select s3 not manufacture**. Unfortunately, the resulting set number four also has 27 records. Although Dialog found 202,001 records with the word manufacture, none were in the selected set.

You can string a series of selection options together, similar to a mathematical equation, on a single command line to speed the process. Dialog offers technical support and training programs to help you search more effectively.

Dialog also includes other commands that help you find appropriate references. For example, a better way of searching for records that relate to magnetic stripes is to use the near command. This specifies that the words must be near each other in the record. If you type **select magnetic(5N)stripe**, you would find records where the words magnetic and stripe appear within five words of each other.

These types of commands are particularly valuable on full-text databases. For example, if you are looking in a database related to education, you may find many records with the words head and start in them. However, using the Near command helps narrow your focus to records more likely to be covering the specific education program called Head Start.

Choosing a Service

Because of the emphasis on news and financial information, the most common use for Dow Jones News Retrieval is for information that ages very quickly. For example, you can use the service to get current stock quotes (delayed by 15 minutes). It also includes performance information. For example, you can find the best-performing mutual funds, information on the Dow Jones Industrial Average, and financial statements for publicly held companies.

Although Dow Jones does not use typical PC commands for navigation, the user interface is relatively easy and consistent. The help information is also considered a database and is accessed by using the //**HELP** command.

Data-Searching Services

Like most PC applications, almost all users can operate information-searching services, but only a proportion of users make efficient use of them, and only a smaller proportion can exploit their potential.

Information-searching services are more expensive than any other online service, and inefficient use can be very costly. Although inefficient use of CompuServe may cost tens of dollars a month, inefficient use of an information-searching service may cost hundreds of dollars a month.

This is the fault of the user, not the information service. Some services offer training seminars that can be invaluable. Most services, and many independent contractors, also offer consulting services and some type of tailored service. These are well worth considering for two reasons. Not only can you make the most efficient use of the service, but you can get the ongoing material essentially automatically.

Consider a newspaper clipping service. Manual methods depend on the readers being able to spot every incidence of your company name, competitor's names, industry name, and whatever other words you request. An electronic method will not miss any of these references. Additionally, it is only incrementally more expensive to widen the search to more newspapers and publications.

You can also access current-awareness services, which can give you information on national health care and the Americans with Disabilities Act (ADA), for example.

A consulting service can help you establish search criteria and collect the material regularly. Some services even offer an automatic searching system. For example, you might establish that all articles relating to your industry are printed and sent regular mail, while all articles mentioning your company name are faxed to your company immediately.

Dialog's user interface is harder to use than the Dow Jones News Retrieval service, but it is much more powerful. Other services, such as DataTimes, have yet another user interface. The costs for using each service can be dramatically different, and it is important to understand which service is most applicable for your situation.

My minimal needs, where I may need a few news-breaking stories and a couple of historical searches in a month, may cost less than $100 but save me hours searching in libraries and phone calls. On the other hand, I interviewed a professional librarian employed to do research for a multimillion dollar company who said a $10,000 monthly bill for online services was not unheard of.

Summary

Online information searching services offer unique opportunities for gaining a competitive advantage in business. Because you pay according to the type of information retrieved, these services can be expensive but can be invaluable.

Each service offers a different collection of information and is suitable for different purposes. Some are tailored to news information, others to data of long-term interest, or specialized disciplines.

Most services offer consulting services where the ongoing searching can be done for you. Additionally, independent companies that specialize in searching can provide beneficial help.

V

Appendixes

Part V provides several appendixes that provide valuable reference material.

Appendix A includes a thorough list of AT commands that are applicable to most modems.

Appendix B provides listing of online services that are organized according to function and area code to save you money.

Appendix C provides concise documentation for using the Smartcom for Windows LE software that is included with this book.

Appendix D lists all the frequently asked questions that appear throughout the book and the page where you can find the answers.

AT Command Set

Your modem should support the Hayes Standard AT Command Set common to all modems. Additional commands your modem supports vary with supported standards and the manufacturer. This appendix contains a list of commonly used AT commands, S-registers, and result codes.

AT Command Descriptions

The following tables list and describe each of the AT commands. Default settings for Hayes modems are listed in **bold**.

Note: Type **AT** before each of the following commands.

Command	Description
A	Enter answer mode, go off hook, attempt to answer incoming call, and go online with another modem.
A/	Re-execute previous command line (this command is not preceded by **AT** nor followed by pressing the Enter key).
B0	Initiate calls by using ITU-T V.22 at 1200 bps.
B1	Initiate calls by using 212A at 1200 bps.
B15	Initiate calls by using ITU-T V.21 at 300 bps.

(continued)

Command	Description
B16	Initiate calls by using 103 at 300 bps.
B30	Initiate call by using V.22 bis at 2400 bps.
B41	Initiate call by using ITU-T V.32 at 4800 bps.
B52	Initiate call by using V.32 bis at 7200 bps.
B60	Initiate call by using ITU-T V.32 at 9600 bps.
B64	Initiate call by using V.FC at 9600 bps.
B75	Initiate call by using V.32 bis when handshake begins at 14400 bps.
B76	Initiate call by using V.FC when handshake begins at 14400 bps.
B81	Initiate call by using V.FC when handshake begins at 16800-28800 bps.
D	Enter originate mode, go off-hook, and attempt to go online with another modem. The dial modifiers (see following table) tell the modem what, when, and how to dial.

Dial Modifiers	Description
0-9 * # A B C D	Specifies letters, numbers, and symbols the modem uses when dialing.
T	Dials by using tone method.
P	Dials by using pulse method.
,	Pauses before continuing the dial string.
W	Waits for second dial tone.
$	Waits for "bong" tone (for calling card number entry).
@	Waits for quiet answer.
!	Issues hookflash.
R	Places call in reverse mode (to call an originate-only modem).
;	Returns to command state after dialing and maintains the connection.
S=n	Dials telephone number n (0-3) stored with the **&Zn=x** command.

Note: The **comma** (,) and the **W** dial modifiers should be used only within a dial string and following the **D** command.

Command	Description
E0	Do not echo characters from the keyboard to the screen in command state.
E1	Echo characters from the keyboard to the screen in command state.
H0	Hang up and place modem in command state.
H1	Go off hook and operate auxiliary relay.
I0	Display numeric product code.
I2	Verify ROM checksum (OK or ERROR).
I7	Display the product version number.
	Note: I7 is supported only by OPTIMA 288 V.FC + FAX.
L0, L1	Set low speaker volume.
L2	Set medium speaker volume.
L3	Set high speaker volume.
M0	Turn speaker off.
M1	Turn speaker on until carrier detected.
M2	Turn speaker on.
M3	Turn speaker on until carrier detected, except while dialing.
N0	When originating or answering, handshake only at speed specified by S37.
N1, N2	When originating, begin negotiations at the highest DCE line speed specified in S37 and fall back to a lower speed if necessary. When answering, handshake at the highest speed allowed by S37 and fallback if necessary.
N3, N4	When originating, handshake only at the speed specified by S37. When answering, handshake at the highest speed allowed by S37 and fallback if necessary.
N5	When originating, begin negotiations at the highest DCE line speed specified in S37 and fall back to a lower speed if necessary. When answering, handshake only at the speed specified by S37.
	Note: The maximum handshaking speed is determined by the specific features of your modem.

(continued)

Command	Description
O0	Go to online state.
O1	Go to online state and initiate equalizer retrain sequence.
O3	Go to online state and initiate ITU-T V.32 *bis* rate renegotiation sequence. **Note:** O3 is not supported in OPTIMA 24 + FAX96, OPTIMA 24B + FAX96, OPTIMA 96 + FAX96, or OPTIMA 96B + FAX96.
P	Select pulse dialing method.
Q0	Return result codes.
Q1	Do not return result codes.
Q2	Return result codes in originate mode, do not return result codes in answer mode.
Sn?	Read and respond with current value of register n (n is the register number; ? requests the value assigned to that register).
Sn=value	Set the value of register n to value.
T	Select tone dialing method.
V0	Display result codes as numbers.
V1	Display result codes as words.
W0	Do not return negotiation progress messages.
W1	Return negotiation progress messages.
W2	Do not return negotiation progress messages and return CONNECT messages using modem-to-modem (DCE) speeds instead of modem-to-DTE speeds.
X0	Provide basic call progress result codes: CONNECT, NO CARRIER, and RING.
X1	Provide basic call progress result codes and appropriate connection speed (e.g., CONNECT 1200, CONNECT 2400).
X2	Provide basic call progress result codes, connection speed, and DIALTONE detection.
X3	Provide basic call progress result codes, connection speed, and BUSY signal detection.

Command	Description
X4	Provide basic call progress result codes, connection speed, BUSY signal detection, and DIALTONE detection.
Y0	Do not respond to long space disconnect.
YI	Respond to long space disconnect.
Z0	Reset and recall stored user profile 0.
ZI	Reset and recall stored user profile I.
&A0	Connect as answering modem when auto-answering.
&AI	Connect as originating modem when auto-answering.
&B0	Disable V.32 Auto-Retrain.
&BI	Enable V.32 Auto-Retrain. **Note:** This feature is not supported in OPTIMA 24 + FAX96 or OPTIMA 24B + FAX96.
&C0	Assume presence of carrier detect signal.
&CI	Track presence of carrier detect signal.
&C2	Assume presence of carrier detect signal until online, then track presence of signal.
&D0	Ignore status of DTR signal.
&DI	Monitor DTR signal. When an on-to-off transition of DTR signal occurs, enter the command state. Return to the online state when the O0 command is issued (if the connection has not been broken).
&D2	Monitor DTR signal. When an on-to-off transition of DTR signal occurs, hang up and enter the command state.
&D3	Monitor DTR signal. When an on-to-off transition of DTR signal occurs, hang up and reset.
&F	Recall factory configuration as active configuration.
&G0	Disable guard tones.
&G2	Use 1800 Hz guard tones.
&K0	Disable local flow control.
&KI	Enable RTS/CTS local flow control.

(continued)

Command	Description
&K2	Enable XON/XOFF local flow control.
&K3	Enable RTS/CTS local flow control.
&K4	Enable XON/XOFF local flow control.
&K5	Enable transparent XON/XOFF local flow control.
	Note: Local flow control is unidirectional in &Q6 mode and bidirectional in &Q5 mode.
&Q0	Communicate in asynchronous mode.
&Q1	Communicate in synchronous mode 1. Async-to-Sync.
&Q2	Communicate in synchronous mode 2. Stored Number Dial.
&Q3	Communicate in synchronous mode 3. Voice/Data Switch.
&Q4	Communicate in synchronous mode 4. Hayes AutoSync.
&Q5	Communicate in error-control mode.
&Q6	Communicate in asynchronous mode with automatic speed buffering (ASB) — for interfaces requiring constant speed between the DTE (computer/terminal) and the DCE (modem).
&Q8	Communicate in MNP error-control with 2:1 data compression. If an MNP error-control protocol is not established, the modem will fallback according to the current user setting in S36.
&Q9	Communicate in V.42 bis/MNP2-4 error-control. Attempts to negotiate a V.42 bis error-control link upon connection. If V.42 bis (or V.42) is not achieved, MNP2-4 will be attempted. If neither error-control protocol is established, the modem will fallback according to the current user setting in S36.
	Note: &Q1, &Q2, and &Q3 are not supported in board-level modems.
&R0	CTS tracks RTS while the modem is online.
&R1	CTS is on while the modem is online; RTS is ignored.
&S0	Assert DSR signal always.
&S1	Assert DSR signal before handshake only.
&S2	Assert DSR signal after handshake negotiation, but before `CONNECT XXXXX` result code is sent to the DTE.

Command	Description
&T0	Terminate any test in progress.
&T1	Initiate local analog loopback.
&T3	Initiate local digital loopback.
&T4	Grant request from remote modem for remote digital loopback.
&T5	Deny request from remote modem for remote digital loopback.
&T6	Initiate remote digital loopback.
&T7	Initiate remote digital loopback with self-test.
&T8	Initiate local analog loopback with self-test.
&T19	Determine whether RTS and CTS circuits are supported in the DTE cable. **Note:** The **&T** commands must be entered when the modem is configured for &Q0 (unbuffered asynchronous mode). Also, your terminal software must support the function of &T19 to work with &T19.
&U0	Enable trellis coding (ITU-T V.32 9600 bps only).
&U1	Disable trellis coding. **Note:** OPTIMA 24 + FAX96 and OPTIMA 24B + FAX96 do not support &U0 and &U1.
&V	View active configuration, user profiles, and stored telephone numbers.
&W0	Write storable parameters of current configuration in memory as profile 0.
&W1	Write storable parameters of current configuration in memory as profile 1.
&X0	Modem generates transmit clock.
&X1	DTE generates transmit clock.
&X2	Modem derives transmit clock from receive carrier signal.
&Y0	Specify stored user profile 0 as power-up configuration.
&Y1	Specify stored user profile 1 as power-up configuration.
&Zn=x	Store phone number x in location n (n=0-3).

Result Code Descriptions

Hayes modems are factory-set to monitor calls and report the following result codes (**X4**).

Number	Word	Description
0	OK	Command executed.
1	CONNECT	A connection has been established.
2	RING	Ring signal indicated.
3	NO CARRIER	Carrier signal not detected, or lost, or inactivity for period of time set in the automatic timeout register (set with **S30**) caused the modem to hang up.
4	ERROR	Invalid command, checksum, error in command line or command line exceeds 255 characters.
5	CONNECT 1200	Connection at 1200 bps (disabled by **X0**).
6	NO DIALTONE	No dial tone detected. Enabled by **X2** or **X4**, or **W** dial modifier.
7	BUSY	Engaged (busy) signal or number unobtainable signal detected. Enabled by **X3** or **X4**.
8	NO ANSWER	No silence detected when dialing a system not providing a dial tone. Enabled by @ dial modifier.
10	CONNECT 2400	Connection at 2400 bps (disabled by **X0**).
11	CONNECT 4800	Connection at 4800 bps (disabled by **X0**).
12	CONNECT 9600	Connection at 9600 bps (disabled by **X0**).
13	CONNECT 14400	Connection at 14400 bps (disabled by **X0**).
14	CONNECT 19200	Connection at 19200 bps (disabled by **X0**).
15	CONNECT 28800	Connection at 28800 bps (disabled by **X0**).
18	CONNECT 57600	Connection at 57600 bps (disabled by **X0**).
24	CONNECT 7200	Connection at 7200 bps (disabled by **X0**).
28	CONNECT 38400	Connection at 38400 bps (disabled by **X0**).
31	CONNECT 115200	Connection at 115200 bps (disabled by **X0**).
33	FAX	FAX connection.
35	DATA	DATA connection.
65	CONNECT 230400	Connection at 230400 bps (disabled by **X0**).

Negotiation Progress Result Codes

A special set of result codes can be enabled to monitor error-control negotiation. Hayes modems are factory-set to disable the display of negotiation progress messages (**W0**). If your communications software supports this level of result code monitoring, you may wish to enable the display of negotiation progress result codes by selecting the **W1** command.

Note: Whether or not some of the result codes are fully enabled (used and viewed) may depend on the compatible settings of an **X**n command and the **S95** register.

Number	Word	Description
40	CARRIER 300	Carrier detected at 300 bps
46	CARRIER 1200	Carrier detected at 1200 bps
47	CARRIER 2400	Carrier detected at 2400 bps
48	CARRIER 4800	Carrier detected at 4800 bps
49	CARRIER 7200	Carrier detected at 7200 bsp.
50	CARRIER 9600	Carrier detected at 9600 bps.
51	CARRIER 12000	Carrier detected at 12000 bps.
52	CARRIER 14400	Carrier detected at 14400 bps.
54	CARRIER 19200	Carrier detected at 19200 bps.
53	CARRIER 16800	Carrier detected at 16800 bps.
38	CARRIER 21600	Carrier detected at 21600 bps.
37	CARRIER 24000	Carrier detected at 24000 bps.
36	CARRIER 26400	Carrier detected at 26400 bps.
55	CARRIER 28800	Carrier detected at 28800 bps.
66	COMPRESSION: CLASS 5	MNP5 compression negotiated.
67	COMPRESSION: V.42 bis	V.42 bis compression negotiated.
69	COMPRESSION: NONE	No compression negotiated.
70	PROTOCOL: NONE	Asynchronous mode.
77	PROTOCOL: LAPM	V.42 LAPM
80	PROTOCOL: ALT	Alternative protocol (MNP compatible).

S-Register Descriptions

S-registers are special memory locations in the modem for storing specific configuration and operating parameters. S-registers typically hold some type of counting, timing, ASCII character, or feature negotiation value.

S-registers can be adjusted to configure the modem from the range of values indicated in the Range/Units column in the following chart. Values assigned to these registers (except **S1**, **S3**, **S4**, and **S5**) can be stored in user-defined profiles with the **&W** command.

Sn=value is the command to change an S-register (for example **ATSn=value** Enter key, where *n* is the S-register to be changed, and n is the value to be assigned to the S-register). **Sn?** is the command to read the value currently stored in an S-register (for example **ATSn?** Enter key, where *n* is the S-register to be read).

Register Setting	Description	Range/Units	Default
S0	Select ring to answer on.	0-255 rings	0
S1	Ring count (incremented with each ring).	0-255 rings	0
S2	Escape sequence character.	0-127 ASCII	43
S3	Carriage return character.	0-127 ASCII	13
S4	Line feed character.	0-127 ASCII	10
S5	Back space character.	0-32,127 ASCII	8
S6	Wait before blind dialing.	2-255 sec	2
S7	Wait time for carrier/silence.	1-255 sec	50
S8	Duration of delay for comma.	0-255 sec	2
S9	Carrier detect response time.	1-255 1/10 sec	5
S10	Delay carrier loss to hang up.	1-255 1/10 sec	14
S11	Duration/spacing of DTMF tones.	50-255 msec	95
S12	Escape sequence guard time.	0-255 1/50 sec	50
S16	Test in progress.	0-6	—
S18	Select test timer.	0-255 sec	0
S25	DTR change detect time.	0-255 1/100 sec	5
S30	Automatic timeout (S30 monitors the activity on the line; the factory-set default is 0, which disables the timer).	0-255 10 sec	0

Register Setting	Description	Range/Units	Default
S31	XON character select.	0-255	17 (DC1)
S32	XOFF character select.	0-255	19 (DC3)
S36	Negotiation fallback.	0,1,3,4,5,7	7
S37	Maximum DCE line speed.	0-12, 15, 26, 29, 33, 34	0
S38	Delay before forced hang up.	0-255 seconds	20
S43	Current DCE speed.	0-12, 15, 26, 29, 33, 34	—
S46	Error-control protocol selection.	2, 136, 138	2
S48	Feature negotiation action.	0, 3, 7,128	7
S49	Buffer lower limit.	1-249 bytes	64
S50	Buffer upper limit.	2-250 bytes	192
S69	Link layer window size.	1-15 frames	15
S70	Maximum number of retransmissions.	0-255 retries	10
S71	Link layer timeout.	1-255 1/10 sec	2
S72	Loss of flag idle timeout.	1-255 seconds	30
S73	No activity timeout.	1-255 seconds	5
S82	Break signaling technique.	3, 7, 128 values	128
S86	Connection failure cause code.	0-19	—
S91	PSTN transmit level adjustment.	0 to -15 dBm	10
S95	Negotiation message options.	1,2,4,8,32	0
S97	V.32 automode V.22/V.22 bis probe timing.	15 to 70 (1.5 to 7.0 seconds)	30
S108	Signal quality selector.	0-3 values	1
S109	Carrier speed selector.	0-4094 decimal values	4094
S105	V.42 frame size.	4-9 octets	7
S110	V.32/ V.32 bis selector.	0-2 values	2
S113	Calling tone transmission.	0-1	0 (off)

B

APPENDIX

Resource Guide to Popular Online Services

The following is a sampling of available online services. The services are divided in the same way as the chapters in the book. The topics are BBSs, Messaging Services, Information Exchange Services, and Information Searching Services.

The service is listed under the heading that is most appropriate. That does not mean that a particular service does not offer services that belong in another category. For example, a service listed under information exchange services may include messaging services as well.

The phone numbers given for the BBSs are the online numbers that you can call with your modem. The phone numbers given for the other services are the voice information numbers where you can get further information and open an account.

BBSs

The following list of 100 BBSs represents a good mix of the typical types of BBSs you can find. They include messaging, file exchange, and chat boards. Some BBSs have only a couple of phone lines; a few have hundreds of lines. Most sysops are volunteers. The BBSs are listed by area code so that you can save money by choosing from your region.

BBS Phone No.	BBS Name	Sysop Name	Description
201-935-1485	Starship II BBS	Phil Buonomo	General interest, 10Gig, Chat, 100+ message areas
203-371-8769	Psycho Ward BBS	Dennis Ryan	Free system, 13Gig, IBM, Amiga, MAC
203-738-0342	H H Infonet	Lee Winsor	Professional, technical, & business oriented, Windows files
205-660-1763	The Unearthed Arcana BBS	Slayer/Lady Morgan	Adult, occult, automotive CD-ROM online, files, messages, online games†
206-692-2388	TCSNet	Al Charpentier	Newsgroups, Rime, MetroLink, online services
206-956-1206	Capital City Online	Joe Goeller	Internet, Usenet, 12Gig, 100+ online games, chat
209-357-8424	Aces Place	Bill Paez	Message areas, new files, helpful staff
212-274-8905	Invention Factory	Michael Sussell	250,000+ files, newsgroups, large adult section, USR V32bis modems†
212-888-6565	Computers & Dreams	William P. Stewart	Internet, Usenet, Rime, 40 doors, 10,000+ new files
213-933-4050	Westside	Dave Harrison	SprintNet access, very large file base, many great features
213-962-2902	BCS BBS	Bill Weinman	Home of Cal-Link, ilink, e-mail, general interest†
214-497-9100	Texas Talk	Sunnie Blair	Adult chat, matchmaking, games, parties, CD-ROMs
214-690-9295	Chrysalis	Garry Grosse	Internet, Connex, 30Gig, chat, encyclopedia
215-439-1509	Father and Son BBS	Dale Lloyd	Fidonet echoes, 10Gig, large adult area, chat, OS/2 files
215-443-9434	Datamax/Satelite	Ron Brandt	Live ftp & telenet, 10Gigs, large adult area
216-691-3025	PC-OHIO	Norm Henke	Internet, 3,000 message areas, 400 file areas, 250 doors†
216-726-3619	Rusty and Edies BBS	Rusty Hardenburgh	All shareware, 9Gig, huge adult section, USR 168 modems†

BBS Phone No.	BBS Name	Sysop Name	Description
219-256-2255	Radio Daze BBS	Michael Shannon	Worldwide echoes, 63 Gig, 65,000+ files, USR HS modems
219-696-3415	Toolkit	Ken Prevo	Resource for programmers and power users
303-933-0701	Eagle's Nest BBS	Ron Olsen	Free access to all, 13Gig, very nice single-line system
303-534-4646	File Bank	Brian Bartee	Astronomy, ham radio, programming, adult files
305-346-8524	Looking Glass	Kenneth Wiren	Files, conferences, doors
310-371-3737	Source BBS	Chip North	General interest, Fidonet e-mail, new files daily
312-907-1831	Zoo BBS	Chuck Goes	Adult social network, chats, gay, bi, straights welcome
313-238-1178	Totem Pole BBS	Alan Myers	4Gig, 97 file areas, 419 message areas, 24 doors
313-776-1975	Legend of Roseville BBS	Richard Leneway	45Gig, message areas, files
314-446-0475	Batboard	Mark Chambers	For BATMAN fans, RIP, NAPLPS, custom GIF & FLI files
317-357-1222	Some Place	Mike Shepard	Fee-based system. Best place to find the hardest-to-find files[†]
401-732-5290	Eagles Nest Communications	Mike Labbe	Internet, Usenet, RIME, Ilink, Paranet, 50,000+ files
403-299-9900	Logical Solutions	Hans Hoogstraat	The Information Exchange, technical advice, PD software, FidoNet message bases plus Netmail, Internet workgroups plus Email, online games, etc.[†]
404-992-5345	Hotlanta BBS	Mike Deen	Social chat system for open minded & adventurous adults
405-325-6128	OU BBS	Ronnie Parker	Internet, telenet, 3Gig files, online games, PIMP, chat

(continued)

BBS Phone No.	BBS Name	Sysop Name	Description
407-635-8833	Techtalk	Jerry Russel	Six CD-ROMs, USR 168 modems, PIMP, Internet, techtalkcom
408-655-5555	Monterey Gaming System	David Janakes	Chat, messages, e-mail, online games, fun entertainment
408-737-7040	Higher Powered BBS	Bob Jacobson	Ilink, SmartNet, SciFact, FredNet, 1 Gig files
413-536-4365	Springfield Public Access	Matthew De Jongh	Internet e-mail, focus on Genealogy, Ham Radio, Windows
414-789-4500	EXEC-PC	Bob Mahoney	World's largest BBS, 35Gig, most anything you need[†]
415-323-4193	Space BBS	Owen Hawkins	Internet e-mail, 3,000 newsgroups, Rime, Ilink, a most active BBS
415-495-2929	Studs	Hans Braun	Adult conversation, AIDS/ HIV news and information
416-213-6002	CRS	Neil Fleming	Canada's largest online system, very large file area
501-753-8575	USA BBS	Jeff Johnson	Internet, all major filebone areas, online games, 10Gig
503-639-4135	PCs Made Easy BBS	Ken Rea	This BBS is aimed at the programmer and the home brewers (beer) in Oregon[†]
504-756-9658	Cajun Clickers BBS	Michael Vierra	Online games, 44Gig, no fees, 11,000+ files
505-294-5675	Garbage Dump BBS	Dean Kerl	Adult chat, dating registry, games, national access
505-299-5974	Albuquerque ROS	Steven Fox	Home of ROS BBS, 60,000+ files, active social issues
508-368-7139	Software Creations	Dan Linton	Home BBS for Apogee, and many other shareware producers
509-943-0211	One Stop PCBoard BBS	Gary Hedberg	USR 168 modems, 8Gig, 70 doors, 900 messages areas
510-736-8343	Windows On Line	Frank Mahaney	Premier Windows file service, 10,000+ 3x files

BBS Phone No.	BBS Name	Sysop Name	Description
510-849-2684	Planet BMUG	Dong-Gyom Kim	100 forums, gateways to OneNet & BMUG Boston
512-320-1650	After Hours	Conrad Ruckelman	Best little BBS in Texas
512-345-5099	Nightbreed	Randy Faulk	Games, messages, files, users
514-597-2409	S-Tek	Eric Blair	Montreal's premiere Gay & Lesbian BBS, G&L BBS List
515-386-6227	Heat In The Night	Rob Murdock	Free Adult BBS, chats, dates, and fun
516-471-8625	America's Suggestion Box	Joe Jerszynski	Focused on collecting & distributing consumer feedback
516-689-5390	Lifestyle	Marc Kraft	Adult lifestyles, personal ads, e-mail, personal contacts
517-695-9952	Wolverine	Rick Rosinksi	Official SkyGlobe support, Searchlight sales & support
518-581-1797	NightOwl BBS	Greg Lake	Files, online games, message board†
602-294-9447	Arizona Online	Shawn Striplin	Massive adult area, 20,000+ files, 3Gig online
604-536-5885	Deep Cove BBS	Wayne Duval	Internet, 7Gig file area, CD-ROMs, ZyXEL modem sales
609-764-0812	Radio Wave BBS	Tyler Myers	ASP BBS, RIME, 4Gig files, 4,000+ newsgroups
612-633-1366	City Lights	Brian Elfert	Adult files & echoes, 600 message areas, 57Gig, 35,000+ files
614-224-1635	Wizard's Gate BBS	Joseph Balshone	FREE, no fee, ASP BBS, full access on first call 12Gig
615-227-6155	3rd Eye BBS	Michael Vetter	Adult system serving the responsible swinging life-style
615-383-0727	Nashville Exchange	Ben Cunningham	Internet, Usenet, Fidonet, 10Gig files, online games
617-354-8873	Channel 1	Brian Miller	3,500 message ares, 120 online games, Internet, 30Gig

(continued)

BBS Phone No.	BBS Name	Sysop Name	Description
617-721-5840	BMUG Boston	Roz Ault	East coast BMUG, gateways to OneNet & Planet BMUG
618-453-8511	Infoquest	Charles Strusz	RIP, Fidonet, Internet, VNet, 100,000 files, many online games
619-737-3097	Cloud 9	Devin Singleton	Chat, Internet e-mail, trivia, 50000+ files, online CPA
701-281-3390	Plains Bulletin service	Rob Kirkey	Great Plains Software support for GPS Partners
702-334-3308	Advanced System BBS	Alan McNamee	Internet, Fidonet, 16Gig, TBBS enhancements
703-385-4325	OS/2 Shareware	Pete Norloff	5,000+ OS/2 files, 25 areas, 50 message area
703-578-4542	GLIB	Jon Larimore	Information serving the gay, lesbian, and bisexual community
704-254-4714	Yes Net	Burton Smith	Networking local environmental groups, schools, and businesses†
708-564-1069	Windy City Freedom Fort	Robert Copella	Adults only, over 4,000 original scanned graphics
708-827-3619	AlphaOne	Toby Schneiter	Online shopping, 30+ games, 200+ echoes, 30,000+ files
713-596-7101	Fantasy Party Line	Charles Henderson	Social gatherings, live chats, great users
714-636-2667	Kandy Shack	Mike Bernstein	Ilink, U'NI-net, ASP member, 24Gig online, USR 168 modems
714-996-7777	Liberty BBS	Stephen Grande	Nationwide chat, e-mail, news, games, Internet
716-461-1924	Frog Pond	Nick Francesco	Supporting MS-DOS & cp/M with great files and zany users
718-837-3236	The Consultant BBS	Jay Caplan	Specializing in ASP shareware programs†
719-578-6088	CoSNUG BBS	Joe Adams	Mainly for Seniors, open to the public
800-874-2937	Online With Hayes	Ricky Lacy	New products, technical support, order small parts, and download SCOPE scripts†

BBS Phone No.	BBS Name	Sysop Name	Description
804-490-5878	Pleasure Dome	Tom McElvy	Sexually explicit, adults only, ladies free
804-790-1675	Blue Ridge Express	Webb Blackman	Message areas, 84+ files areas, 21,000+ files
805-964-4766	Seaside	Les Jones	ASP BBS, 100+ online games, 450 message areas
812-428-3870	YA WEBECAD	Dan Habegger	PSL library, ASP BBS, 72,000+ files, 118Gig, adult file area
812-479-1310	Digicom BBS	Gary Barr	Product Support BBS list, adult area with games, 27Gig
813-289-3314	Godfather	Jim Sharrer	Fidonet, Usenet, adult areas, graphics, GIFs, new files
813-321-0734	Mercury Opus	Emery Mandel	Internet, 80,000+ files, MS-DOS, Windows, OS/2
816-587-3311	File Shop BBS	Walt Lane	RIP, 2,200 file areas, 28Gig, 310,000+ files, 85 online games
817-662-2361	File Quest	Jim Ray	General purpose, 2.5GB files, FidoNet, Echonet†
818-358-6968	Odyssey	Michael Allen	Where adults come to play and meet, active chats
818-982-7271	Prime Time BBS	Bill Martian	Live multi-user games, chat, Interlink, files
904-874-1988	Baker Street Irregular	James Young	Variety of general interest conferences and shareware downloads†
908-494-8666	Microfone Infoservice	John Kelly	Fidonet, 14 CD-ROMs, online games, since 1982
914-667-4567	Executive Network	Andy Keeves	10Meg new files daily, 4,000 message areas, Internet
916-448-2483	24th Street Exchange	Don Kuhworth	General IBM MS-DOS files and support, ASP BBS, Fidonet, chat†
918-665-0061	Wayne's World	Wayne Greer	Large filebase, online games, latest new files

(continued)

919-481-9399	deltaComm BBS	Zack Jones	Support board for Telix Communications software
919-779-6674	Micro Message Service	Mike Stroud	Internet, excellent ham radio area, 7Gig, family BBS

† Indicates a BBS that uses a Hayes V.FC Modem

Messaging Services

MCI Mail
1111 Nineteenth St N.W.
Washington DC 20036
800-444-6245

SprintMail
US Sprint
12490 Sunrise Valley Drive
Reston, VA 22096
800-736-1130

Information Exchange Services

America Online
America Online, Inc.
8619 Westwood Center Drive
Vienna, VA 22182
800-827-6364

BIX
General Videotext
1030 Massachusetts Ave.
Cambridge, MA 02138
800-695-4775

Compuserve
CompuServe, Inc.
P.O. Box 20212
Columbus, OH 43220
800-848-8199

Delphi
Delphi Internet Services Corp.
1030 Massachusetts Ave.
Cambridge, MA 02138
800-695-4005

Genie
P.O. Box 6403
Rockville, MD 20850-1785
800-638-9636

Prodigy
445 Hamilton Ave.
White Plains, NY 10601
800-822-6922

The Well
27 Gate Five Road
Sausalito, CA 94965
415-332-4335

Information Searching Services

Dialog
Dialog Information Services
3460 Hillview Ave.
Palo Alto, CA 94304
800-334-2564

Dow Jones News/Retrieval
P.O. Box 300
Princeton, NJ 08543-0300
800-522-3567

NEXIS / LEXIS
Mead Data Central
P.O. Box 933
Dayton, OH 45401
800-227-4908

BRS/After Dark
Maxwell Online Inc
8000 Westpark Drive
McLean, VA 22102
800-289-4277

DataTimes
14000 Quail Springs Parkway,
Suite 450
Oklahoma City, OK 73134
800-642-2525

Guide to Smartcom for Windows LE

C

APPENDIX

Smartcom for Windows LE is an asynchronous communications software package for Windows Version 3.1. Based on Hayes Smartcom for Windows, this fully-functional *limited edition* program gives you a chance to experience the power of Hayes Smartcom communications software. If you find that there are additional features you would like, chances are they are in Smartcom for Windows. Call Hayes Customer Service at (404) 441-1617 to order your copy. Use the coupon from Hayes at the back of the book for a discount on your upgrade.

Some additional features of Smartcom for Windows include:

- The Smartcom Communications Editor combines text with color and ANSI character graphics to create high-impact, exciting messages.

- English, French, German, Spanish, and Italian program files let you standardize on one program for international data communications.

- You can download and view .GIF images.

- Additional file-transfer protocols and terminal emulations give you more error-free options and increase your communications capabilities.

- The SCOPE script compiler lets you create scripts to simplify communications by automating repetitive tasks.

- You can communicate with popular communications servers and networks plus TCP/IP Telenet communications and NetBIOS connections support.

Installing Smartcom for Windows LE

To properly install, configure, and operate Smartcom LE, you need the following:

❖ An IBM AT, PS/2, or 100%-compatible computer with a 286 processor or greater.

❖ 2 MB or more of available RAM.

❖ A hard drive.

❖ Microsoft Windows version 3.1.

❖ A monitor and video adapter capable of EGA resolution (640 x 350) or better.

❖ AT-compatible modem. Although it supports all popular modems for personal computers, Smartcom LE automatically assures Hayes modem users the full benefit of its special features while maximizing the throughput performance and capability of Hayes modems.

❖ Mouse. Although all Smartcom LE functions can be accessed via keyboard, you should use a mouse connected to your computer for maximum speed and flexibility.

Use the following steps to install Smartcom for Windows LE:

1. Make backup copies of the Smartcom LE master disk. Install Smartcom LE by using the copies. If something happens to one of the copies, you can make another copy from the master disk. Store your master disk in a safe place.

2 Verify that Windows is running on your computer and that the Windows Program Manager or the File Manager is open.

3. Insert the Smartcom LE disk in the floppy drive you want to use to install the program.

4. Choose Run from the File menu. The Run dialog box opens. In the Command Line text box, type:

   A:\SETUP

   (If you are installing from a different drive, type that drive letter instead of A:. Or, if you are in the File Manager, you can simply go to drive A and double-click SETUP.EXE.)

   Then click OK.

5. The Smartcom for Windows dialog box opens. If your computer system is using virus protection software, disable it now and then click OK.

If your computer system is not using virus protection software, click OK.

6. A dialog box then displays information about the README file that comes with Smartcom for Windows LE. This file contains the latest information about Smartcom LE. Take a few minutes to read it.

Click Continue when you are ready to move on.

7. After you finish reading the information text, Smartcom LE automatically checks your system hardware and software.

If Smartcom LE cannot install for any reason (if you aren't using Windows 3.1, for example), a dialog box appears and explains the reason. After you resolve the problem, begin the Setup program again.

8. If no problems are found with your system, the Names dialog box opens. Enter your name and your company's name, and click Continue.

9. The Select Directory dialog box opens. Select the drive and directory where you want to install Smartcom and click OK.

The default path is C:\SCWINLE. If you want to select a different path, backspace over the defaults and type your new path. The Setup program creates the directory if it does not exist and then installs Smartcom LE files in the following subdirectories:

Files	Where Installed
Program files	Smartcom LE program files are copied into C:\SCWINLE (or the subdirectory you indicated).
Communications documents	When you create communications documents—which contain modem settings, telephone number, terminal emulator, and so on—they are stored in C:\SCWINLE\COM, unless you specify another directory location when you save them.
Receive files	When you download files from BBSs, information services, and other remote systems, they are stored in C:\SCWINLE\RCV, unless you specify another directory location at the time of downloading. Files that are automatically downloaded to your system also will be placed in this subdirectory.
Temporary files	Any temporary files that Smartcom LE creates are stored in C:\SCWINLE\TEMP.

10. The Select Modem & Settings dialog box appears. If you are using a Hayes modem, accept the default Hayes by clicking OK.

If you are not using a Hayes modem, select your modem vendor, and the supported models display. Choose your modem from the list and click OK.

If your modem vendor is not listed, select Other 2400, Other 9600, or Other 14400, depending on your modem's maximum baud rate.

Note: Smartcom LE assumes the modem is installed on COM1. If you need to change this communications port configuration, see the section "Selecting the communications port."

Note: If you need to reconfigure Smartcom LE for a another modem after the installation procedure, you can pull down the Settings menu and choose Modem.

After confirming that your hard drive has enough memory space for Smartcom LE, the Setup program copies the program files from the floppy disk to your hard drive and indicates the status of the installation process on your screen.

If your computer has insufficient disk space to install Smartcom LE, a warning message appears. Click Cancel to exit the Setup program. Delete enough files from your hard drive to make room for Smartcom LE, and begin the Setup program again.

11. When the installation is complete, the Successful Installation dialog box appears. Click OK to exit the Setup program.

After clicking OK, the Smartcom for Windows LE group icon displays in the Windows Program Manager.

Registering Smartcom LE

Registering your Hayes products makes you eligible for free Customer Support.

To Register Smartcom LE, double-click the Smartcom for Windows LE group icon in the Windows Program Manager. Double-click the Product Registration icon. A Smartcom Script asks you questions and prompts you for answers. Follow the prompts, and the script makes a toll-free connection with a Hayes BBS (bulletin board service) and registers your Hayes product. Smartcom tells you when your registration is complete.

Note: This registration procedure uses your modem, so the modem must be connected to your computer before registering your Hayes products.

Starting Smartcom LE

Double-click the Smartcom for Windows LE program-group icon from the Windows Program Manager. Double-click the Smartcom for Windows LE telephone icon. When Smartcom LE first starts, you will briefly see the sign-on screen.

If you want to quickly dismiss this sign-on screen, press the spacebar. If another Smartcom LE communications document is already open, the sign-on screen will not appear.

After a few moments, the application displays with a default communications document called Untitled-1 open. This is where you change settings, place calls, and perform communications activities with Smartcom LE.

Note: There are certain operations (like creating custom buttons) that are not allowed when you are working with the default document. To enable these operations, save the default document as a specific communications document.

Accessing Online Help

Smartcom LE has an online, context-sensitive Help menu. You can access help at any time by selecting Help and then choosing a topic. If you select Context-Sensitive Help from the Help menu, Smartcom LE provides online assistance on the last action performed. Also, Hayes Microcomputer Products, Inc. offers free technical support.

Calling the Online With Hayes BBS

Online With Hayes is a BBS dedicated to Hayes products. After you access Online With Hayes, you can read information about new products, obtain technical support, order small parts and download SCOPE scripts and other files. Follow the instructions in this section to log onto the Online With Hayes BBS.

Smartcom LE comes with a communications document called Online With Hayes. This communications document is configured with an auto-logon script and the settings needed to log you onto the Online With Hayes BBS (U.S.). This document demonstrates some of the customization options available to you, including the button set interface.

If you want to connect to the Online With Hayes BBS quickly, the easiest way is to use the Online With Hayes communications document. Also, because of common default settings and Smartcom LE special modem control, you can simply click the phone icon, enter a phone number and go online.

Note: Most BBSs limit how long you can stay connected during a 24-hour period. You may call Online With Hayes up to three times per day, but your total connection time cannot exceed 30 minutes per day. This is to prevent individuals from monopolizing the phone lines and to give everyone a chance to call.

Creating a Communications Document

Smartcom LE uses *communications documents* to control communications with remote systems. A communications document contains the settings necessary to connect and interact with a remote system, including a remote system's telephone number, connection speed, character format, and terminal emulation. SCOPE scripts, macros, and custom keyboard layouts are also stored in communications documents.

You'll probably create custom documents for the various systems you call. After you create the communications documents you want, you can automatically start Smartcom LE with the document of your choice by double-clicking that document in the Program Manager, by using the File Manager's drag-and-drop function, or by using the File menu or Phone Book button to select the document you want, after starting Smartcom LE.

Selecting the communications port

Before you can telecommunicate successfully, you need to select a COM port for serial connections. Serial connections are used when you are using either a modem or a direct connection through a serial port on the PC and you are not using a network. Smartcom LE recognizes both external and internal modems.

To select a COM Port, follow these steps:

1.   Select Choose Port in the Connection pull-down menu. The Choose Port dialog box appears.

2. Click Program Default if you want to specify a default for all communications documents that have this option selected. If you want to specify a default for the current communications document only, then click Document Only.

3. Click the serial port (COM1, COM2, etc.) that you have configured for your modem. Click OK.

The COM port you select for your modem depends on how your computer is configured. Depending on your PC and its configuration, in addition to selecting a COM port in Smartcom LE, you may also have to select the same COM port in your computer's setup and/or, if you are using an internal modem, on your modem.

Quick Settings

Quick allows you to set those most commonly used settings. Or you can use Speed & Format, Modem, Terminal, and File Transfer Protocol from the Settings menu if you need to further redefine your configuration.

When you select Quick from the Settings menu, the Quick Settings dialog box appears.

Note: You can also access this screen by clicking the Phone Book button and then selecting Settings.

Selecting the type of terminal emulation

Many BBSs (including Online With Hayes) use ANSI BBS emulation to produce multicolor graphics. To use ANSI BBS emulation, select Terminal from the Settings menu. The Terminal Settings dialog box appears.

Note: You can also select a terminal emulator by choosing Quick from the Settings menu.

Select the Emulator drop-down list box to see the choice of emulators. Choose ANSI BBS, for use with Online With Hayes. TTY and VT102 would also work, but you would not see the Online With Hayes color graphics.

Selecting the type of file-transfer protocol

Smartcom LE supports the file transfer protocols XMODEM and ZMODEM. Your computer and the remote system must use the same file-transfer method.

Note: If it is supported by the remote system, ZMODEM often has a clear advantage in speed, features, and ease of use. Other ZMODEM features include the selective transfer of groups of files based on size and date changes and interrupted file transfer recovery.

If you want to select the XMODEM protocol, go to the Settings menu and select File Transfer. The following dialog box appears. Click the file transfer list box and select XMODEM.

Note: You can also select a File Transfer Protocol by choosing Quick from the Settings menu.

Entering the remote system's phone number

The final parameter you need to add is the phone number of the remote system. Select Phone Number from the Connection menu.

Enter the phone number of the remote system you wish to call, and click OK. Later, when you save this communications document, the phone number will be stored with any other changes that you have made.

If you are calling the Online With Hayes BBS, type 1-800-USHAYES in the U.S.; 011 44 81 569-1774 in Great Britain; or 011 852 887-7590 in Hong Kong.

Note: If you enclose alphabetic characters in quotation marks, Smartcom LE converts them to numbers.

The following table describes the dial modifiers that can be used to tell Smartcom LE how to dial:

Dial Modifiers	Description
0-9 * # A B C D	Numbers, letters, and symbols that Smartcom LE recognizes when dialing
T	Specifies dialing using tone (DTMF/touch-tone) dial method
P	Specifies dialing using pulse (rotary) dial method
, (comma)	Pauses before continuing the dial string
W	Waits for dial tone before continuing the dial string
@	Waits for quiet answer
!	Issues hookflash

Pull down the Connection menu again, and make sure that the Connect Through Phone and Originate options are both checked. You are now ready to save the communications document.

Saving Your Communications Document

Choose Save As from the File menu. Complete the File Name and Description boxes, and click OK.

Note: Remember to follow DOS file-naming conventions—.SCW is the common extension for Smartcom LE communications documents.

There is usually no need to change the default drive, directory, or file type. Smartcom LE saves the communications document under the name you selected as the standard directory for communications documents.

Placing the Call

You are now ready to place a call to the remote system by using your newly created communications document. To place the call and go online, double-click the Phone button. Smartcom LE displays a Call Progress box with sequentially highlighted graphics to indicate the program's progress as it attempts to make a connection.

If the connection is established, you see whatever screen information the remote system sends to you when you are connected; you may have to press the Enter key to make this happen. The first time you log onto a BBS, for example, you usually have to answer some questions identifying yourself and your computer system. If you are not calling Online With Hayes, follow the prompts that the remote system gives you.

Using the Phone Book

The Phone Book allows you to view all your Smartcom LE communication files, their phone numbers and descriptions. You can select a particular communication document and copy, delete, or cancel it. You also can change the settings and initiate a connection.

To use the Phone Book, follow these steps:

1. Click the Phone Book button.

    Note: You can also pull down the Connection menu and select Phone Book.

2. Select a communications document by file name, phone number, or description. Click Browse to peruse the communications document.

3. After you select a communications document, you can do one or all of the following actions:

    ❖   Initiate a connection by clicking Connect.

    ❖   Change the settings of a communications document by clicking Settings. Smartcom LE prompts you with the Quick Settings dialog box.

    ❖   Create a new communications document by clicking New. Smartcom LE prompts you with the File Save dialog box and then the Quick Settings dialog box.

    ❖   Copy an existing communications document by clicking Copy. Smartcom LE prompts you with the File Save As dialog box, which contains a name and description field.

    ❖   Remove an existing communications document from the Phone book by clicking Delete.

4. To save your changes, click Done.

Logging Off Your Remote System Connection

After finishing your BBS connection, you need to log off. Clicking the Phone button severs the connection; however, you should exit a system via its menu commands. If you are communicating with an information service, this ensures that your session is terminated and that you are not being charged while the host is waiting for a time-out condition to occur. This also ensures that you receive all information that the BBS has to send you. (Some BBSs display one last screen after you log off.)

Exiting Smartcom LE

To exit Smartcom LE, follow these steps:

1. Select Exit from the File menu.

   If you have made changes to the current communications document and have not saved them, Smartcom LE displays a dialog box.

2. Click Yes to save and exit, No to exit without saving, or Cancel to return to the program without saving or exiting.

   Smartcom displays a dialog box that asks whether you want to save the information in the peruse buffer.

3. Click Yes to save and exit, No to exit without saving, or Cancel to return to the program without saving or exiting.

Running SCOPE Scripts

SCOPE (Simple COmmunications Programming Environment) is the programming language developed especially for automating data communications by using Smartcom products. SCOPE scripts can perform the following functions:

- ♣ Automate repetitive tasks
- ♣ Create menu-driven interaction with remote systems

♣ Trigger events according to a specific time, keyboard input, or remote system response

♣ Process and transfer files

With Smartcom LE, you can run existing Smartcom scripts. You can download scripts from Online With Hayes or use SCOPE scripts from other Hayes Smartcom products (Smartcom III, Smartcom Exec, or Smartcom for Windows).

Smartcom LE allows you to run existing scripts, but if you want to create your own scripts, upgrade to Smartcom for Windows and take advantage of a significant savings from Hayes.

With Smartcom LE you can run existing scripts created in other Smartcom products the following four ways:

♣ From the SCOPE menu.

♣ By using a Smart Button.

♣ From the Windows Program Manager.

♣ If you have a script called AUTOEXEC, it automatically runs when you open the communications document.

100 Most Frequently Asked Questions

APPENDIX D

Chapter 4: Selecting Your Equipment

Chapter 5: Understanding Your Data Modem

Chapter 10: Streamlining Your Communications

Chapter 11: Making the Most of Your Fax Modem

Chapter 12: Special-Purpose Communications

Notes

Notes

I

I N D E X

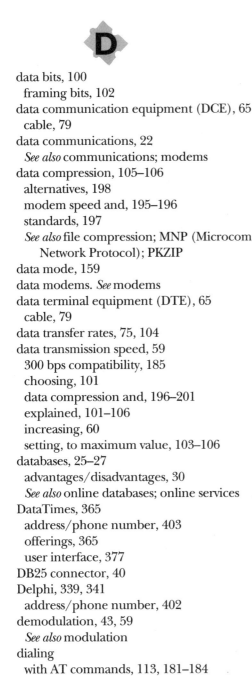

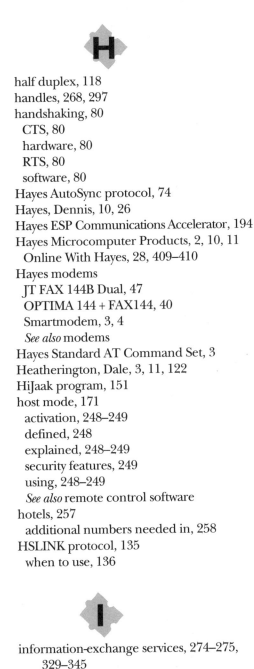

N

O

Q

R

GEnie®
The most fun you can have with your computer on.

No other online service has more cool stuff to do, or more cool people to do it with than GEnie. Join dozens of awesome special interest RoundTables on everything from scuba diving to Microsoft to food and wine, download over 200,000 files, access daily stock quotes, talk to all those smart guys on the internet, play the most incredible multi-player games, and so much more you won't believe your eyeballs.

And GEnie has it all at a standard connect rate of just $3.00 an hour.[1] That's one of the lowest rates of all the major online services! Plus -- because you're a reader of *The Official Hayes Communication Companion* you get an even cooler deal.[2] When you sign up we'll waive your first monthly subscription fee (an $8.95 value) and include ten additional hours of standard connect time (another $30.00 in savings). That's fourteen free hours during your first month - *a $38.95 value!*

You can take advantage of this incredible offer immediately -- just follow these simple steps:

1. Set your communications software for half-duplex (local echo) at 300, 1200, or 2400 baud. Recommended communications parameters 8 data bits, no parity and 1 stop bit.
2. Dial toll-free in the U.S. at 1-800-638-8369 (or in Canada at 1-800-387-8330). Upon connection, type **HHH** (Please note: every time you use GEnie, you need to enter the HHH upon connection)
3. At the U#= prompt, type **JOINGENIE** and press <Return>
4. At the offer code prompt enter GAD225 to get this special offer.
5. Have a major credit card ready. In the U.S., you may also use your checking account number. (There is a $2.00 monthly fee for all checking accounts.) In Canada, VISA and MasterCard only.

Or, if you need more information, contact GEnie Client Services at 1-800-638-9636 from 9am to midnight, Monday through Friday, and from noon to 8pm Saturday and Sunday (all times are Eastern).

1 U.S. prices. Standard connect time is non-prime time: 6pm to 8am local time, Mon. - Fri., all day Sat. and Sun. and selected holidays.

2 Offer available in the United States and Canada only.

3 The offer for ten additional hours applies to standard hourly connect charges only and must be used by the end of the billing period for your first month. Please call 1-800-638-9636 for more information on pricing and billing policies.

Put the power
of CompuServe
at your fingertips.

Join the world's largest international network of people with personal computers. Whether it's computer support, communication, entertainment, or continually updated information, you'll find services that meet your every need.

Your introductory membership will include one free month of our basic services, plus a $15 usage credit for extended and premium CompuServe services.

To get connected, complete and mail the card below. Or call 1-800-524-3388 and ask for Representative 607.

Yes! I want to get the most out of my PC. Send me my FREE CompuServe Introductory Membership, including a $15 usage credit and one free month of CompuServe basic services.

Name: _____

Address: _____

City: _____ State: _____ Zip:_____

Phone: _____

Clip and mail this form to: CompuServe
P.O. Box 20212
Dept. 607
Columbus, OH 43220

CompuServe.
The difference between your PC collecting dust and burning rubber.

No matter what kind of PC you have, CompuServe will help you get the most out of it. As the world's most comprehensive network of people with personal computers, we're the place experts and novices alike go to find what's hot in hardware, discuss upcoming advances with other members, and download the latest software. Plus, for a low flat-rate, you'll have access to our basic services as often as you like: news, sports, weather, shopping, a complete encyclopedia, and up to 60 e-mail messages a month. And it's easy to begin. All you need is your home computer, your regular phone line, a modem, and a CompuServe membership.

To get your free introductory membership, just complete and mail the form on the back of this page. Or call 1-800-524-3388 and ask for Representative 607. Plus, if you act now, you'll receive one month free unlimited access to basic services and a $15 usage credit for our extended and premium services.

So put the power of CompuServe in your PC — and leave everyone else in the dust.

CompuServe®

SM The information service you won't outgrow.™

Hayes®

Your Fast, Reliable Communications Link to the Electronic World.

From the creator of the legendary Hayes® Smartmodem™

ACCURA™ 288 V.FC + FAX
ACCURA™ 144 + FAX144

The easy way to call other PCs, online services, or Bulletin Boards and send or receive FAXes.

Practically operates without you - error-control and data compression. 28,800 bit/s or 14,400 bit/s external data and FAX modem with free Smartcom™ for Windows™ data and FAX software and cable.

Hayes® ESP® Communications Accelerator

Hit the Accelerator!

Ultra-fast serial port that helps prevent data loss and overruns in a Windows communications environment.

Hayes
Increasing The Speed Of Business.™

Special Discount Coupon

Qty.	Product	Sugg. Retail	Your Price	
_____	ACCURA 288 V.FC + FAX	$339	**$309**	_____
_____	ACCURA 144 + FAX 144	$199	**$149**	_____
_____	Hayes ESP Communications Accelerator (single port)	$99	**$69**	_____
			SubTotal	_____

LIMIT 2 OF EACH

Tax only for Residents of GA 5%, CA 8.25% _____

Shipping and Handling $10.00

Total _____

Payment Method

☐ Check ☐ Money Order ☐ VISA ☐ MasterCard

Card Number _____ Exp. Date _____

Signature _____

Shipping Address

Name _____

Title _____

Company _____

Address _____

City _____ State _____ Zip _____

Phone _____ FAX _____

Offer expires 6-1-95. Offer valid in the United States and Canada only and void where prohibited by law. Offer subject to product availability. © 1994 Hayes Microcomputer Products, Inc. All rights reserved. Printed in U.S.A. Hayes, the Hayes icon, the Hayes logo, and ESP are registered trademarks and Increasing The Speed Of Business, ACCURA, Smartmodem, and Smartcom are trademarks of Hayes Microcomputer Products, Inc. ' Other trademarks mentioned are trademarks of their respective companies.

For Canadian pricing and information call 519 746-5000.
For European pricing and information call + 44 252 7755 44.
For Asian pricing and information call + 852 887 1037.
For Australian pricing and information call + 612 959 2340.

Order by Phone

Call today
404 441-1617
Ask for the Official Companion offer

Order by Mail

Return this form with payment to:
Hayes Microcomputer Products, Inc.
Customer Service
P.O. Box 105203, Atlanta, GA 30348

Order by FAX

FAX this form
to 404 449-0087

> "I rely on your publication extensively to help me over stumbling blocks that are created by my lack of experience."
>
> *Fred Carney, Louisville, KY on*
> PC World ÐOS 6 Handbook

PC WORLD MICROSOFT ACCESS BIBLE
by Cary N. Prague & Michael R. Irwin

Easy-to-understand reference that covers the ins and outs of Access features and provides hundreds of tips, secrets and shortcuts for fast database development. Complete with disk of Access templates. Covers versions 1.0 & 1.1

ISBN: 1-878058-81-9
$39.95 USA/$52.95 Canada
£35.99 incl. VAT UK & Eire

PC WORLD WORD FOR WINDOWS 6 HANDBOOK
by Brent Heslop & David Angell

Details all the features of Word for Windows 6, from formatting to desktop publishing and graphics. A 3-in-1 value (tutorial, reference, and software) for users of all levels.

ISBN: 1-56884-054-3
$34.95 USA/$44.95 Canada
£29.99 incl. VAT UK & Eire

PC WORLD DOS 6 COMMAND REFERENCE AND PROBLEM SOLVER
by John Socha & Devra Hall

The only book that combines a DOS 6 Command Reference with a comprehensive Problem Solving Guide. Shows when, why and how to use the key features of DOS 6/6.2.

ISBN: 1-56884-055-1
$24.95 USA/$32.95 Canada
£22.99 UK & Eire

QUARKXPRESS FOR WINDOWS DESIGNER HANDBOOK
by Barbara Assadi & Galen Gruman

ISBN: 1-878058-45-2
$29.95 USA/$39.95 Canada/£26.99 UK & Eire

PC WORLD WORDPERFECT 6 HANDBOOK
by Greg Harvey, author of IDG's bestselling 1-2-3 For Dummies

Here's the ultimate WordPerfect 6 tutorial and reference. Complete with handy templates, macros, and tools.

ISBN: 1-878058-80-0
$34.95 USA/$44.95 Canada
£29.99 incl. VAT UK & Eire

PC WORLD EXCEL 5 FOR WINDOWS HANDBOOK, 2nd EDITION
by John Walkenbach & Dave Maguiness

Covers all the latest Excel features, plus contains disk with examples of the spreadsheets referenced in the book, custom ToolBars, hot macros, and demos.

ISBN: 1-56884-056-X
$34.95 USA/$44.95 Canada /£29.99 incl. VAT UK & Eire

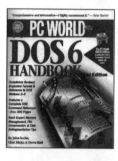

PC WORLD DOS 6 HANDBOOK, 2nd EDITION
by John Socha, Clint Hicks & Devra Hall

Includes the exciting new features of DOS 6, a 300+ page DOS command reference, plus a bonus disk of the Norton Commander Special Edition, and over a dozen DOS utilities.

ISBN: 1-878058-79-7
$34.95 USA/$44.95 Canada/£29.99 incl. VAT UK & Eire

OFFICIAL XTREE COMPANION, 3RD EDITION
by Beth Slick

ISBN: 1-878058-57-6
$19.95 USA/$26.95 Canada/£17.99 UK & Eire

For more information or to order by mail, call 1-800-762-2974. Call for a free catalog! For volume discounts and special orders, please call Tony Real, Special Sales, at 415-312-0644. For International sales and distribution information, please call our authorized distributors:

CANADA Macmillan Canada
416-293-8141

UNITED KINGDOM Transworld
44-81-231-6661

AUSTRALIA Woodslane Pty Ltd.
61-2-979-5944

 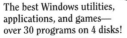

Order Form

Order Center: (800) 762-2974 (8 a.m.-5 p.m., PST, weekdays) or (415) 312-0650

For Fastest Service: Photocopy This Order Form and FAX it to: (415) 358-1260

Quantity	ISBN	Title	Price	Total

Shipping & Handling Charges

Subtotal	U.S.	Canada & International	International Air Mail
Up to $20.00	Add $3.00	Add $4.00	Add $10.00
$20.01-40.00	$4.00	$5.00	$20.00
$40.01-60.00	$5.00	$6.00	$25.00
$60.01-80.00	$6.00	$8.00	$35.00
Over $80.00	$7.00	$10.00	$50.00

In U.S. and Canada, shipping is UPS ground or equivalent.
For Rush shipping call (800) 762-2974.

Subtotal _____

CA residents add
applicable sales tax

IN and MA residents add
5% sales tax

IL residents add
6.25% sales tax

RI residents add
7% sales tax

Shipping _____

Total _____

Ship to:

Name _____

Company _____

Address _____

City/State/Zip_____

Daytime Phone _____

Payment: ❑ Check to IDG Books (US Funds Only)   ❑ Visa   ❑ Mastercard   ❑ American Express

Card# _____ Exp._____ Signature_____

Please send this order form to: IDG Books, 155 Bovet Road, Suite 310, San Mateo, CA 94402.

Allow up to 3 weeks for delivery. Thank you!

Hayes Microcomputer Products, Inc. Limited Warranty — English/U.S.A.

(This Limited Warranty applies to Products sold within the borders of the United States of America.)

Who is Covered by This Warranty? This limited warranty ("Warranty") is extended by Hayes Microcomputer Products, Inc. ("Hayes") only to the original end user purchaser of the accompanying HAYES HARDWARE PRODUCT ("Hardware") and/or HAYES SOFTWARE PRODUCT ("Program") (separately and together, "Product").

What Does This Warranty Cover? This Warranty covers defects in materials and workmanship, under normal use and service, in the Hardware and Program magnetic diskettes ("Defects"). This Warranty also covers any failure of the Product to perform substantially in accordance with the description in the documentation accompanying the Product ("Performance"), unless the packaging or documentation of the product indicates that the product is intended for use only in a specified country or countries. If the product is designated for use only in a specified country or countries, then this Warranty covers any failure of the product to perform substantially in accordance with the description in the documentation accompanying the Product only when used within the borders of the country or countries designated on the Product package ("Country Performance"). This Warranty is in lieu of all other express warranties which might otherwise arise with respect to the Product. No one is authorized to change or add to this Warranty.

What Does This Warranty NOT Cover? Hayes does not warrant or guarantee you uninterrupted service, the correction of any error or elimination of any "bug". You are solely responsible for any failure of the Product which results from accident, abuse, misapplication, alteration of the Product, or use of the Product outside of the borders of the country or countries shown on the Product package. Hayes assumes no liability for any events arising out of the use of any technical information accompanying the Product. THIS WARRANTY APPLIES TO THE PRODUCT ONLY AND DOES NOT COVER ANY OTHER SOFTWARE OR HARDWARE WHICH MAY BE INCLUDED WITH YOUR PURCHASE OF THE PRODUCT. WITHOUT LIMITING THE GENER-ALITY OF THE FOREGOING, ANY SOFTWARE OTHER THAN THE PROGRAM IS PROVIDED "AS IS" AND WITHOUT WARRANTY OF ANY KIND. INCIDENTAL AND CONSEQUENTIAL DAMAGES CAUSED BY MALFUNCTION, DEFAULT, OR OTHERWISE WITH RESPECT TO BREACH OF THIS WARRANTY OR ANY OTHER EXPRESS OR IMPLIED WARRANTY ARE NOT THE RESPONSIBILITY OF HAYES AND ARE HEREBY EXCLUDED BOTH FOR PROPERTY AND, TO THE EXTENT NOT UNCONSCIONABLE, FOR PERSONAL INJURY DAMAGE. Some states do not allow the exclusion or limitation of incidental or consequential damages, so the above exclusion or limitation may not apply to you. This Warranty gives you specific legal rights and you may also have other legal rights which vary from state to state.

What is the Period of Coverage? The period of coverage for the enclosed Hardware and/or Program is set forth in the Warranty Period section of this Guide. If this section indicates that Hayes offers an Extended Protection Plan ("Plan") for the enclosed Hardware and/or Program and you select the Plan, the period of coverage for the Hardware and/or Program would be the total of the original Warranty Period and the Plan period. ANY AND ALL IMPLIED WARRANTIES OF MERCHANTABIL-ITY AND FITNESS FOR A PARTICULAR PURPOSE SHALL TERMINATE AUTO-MATICALLY UPON THE EXPIRATION OF THE PERIOD OF COVERAGE. Some states do not allow limitations on how long the implied warranty lasts, so the above limitation may not apply to you.

What Will Hayes Do to Correct Problems? In the event of a malfunction attributable directly to Defects or Performance, Hayes will, at its option, repair the Product, to whatever extent Hayes deems necessary to restore the Product to proper working condition, or replace the Product with a new or functionally equivalent product of equal value, or refund an amount equal to the lesser of (1) the purchase price paid for the Product or (2) the then effective Hayes Estimated Retail Price for the Product. THE REMEDY DESCRIBED ABOVE IS THE EXCLUSIVE REMEDY EXTENDED TO YOU BY HAYES FOR ANY DEFAULT, MALFUNCTION, OR FAILURE OF THE PRODUCT TO CONFORM WITH THIS WARRANTY OR OTHERWISE FOR BREACH OF THIS WARRANTY OR ANY OTHER WARRANTY, WHETHER EXPRESSED OR IMPLIED.

How Do You Obtain Warranty Service? To obtain warranty service, you must either call the appropriate Customer Service number or write to Customer Service at the appropriate address listed at the end of this section. You must return the Product, along with the return authorization number given to you by Customer Service and proof of date of purchase, or after expiration of the Warranty period, Hayes will, at its option, repair the Product and charge you for parts and labor or replace the Product and charge you the then effective Estimated Retail Price for the Product, unless Hayes has discontinued the manufacture or distribution of such products because of techni-cal obsolescence.

Warranty Period

Your modem includes a two-year limited warranty, and an optional two-year extended protection plan is also available. Hayes software includes a 90-day limited warranty.

Statement of Copyright Restrictions

(This Statement applies to Hayes Software Products sold outside the borders of the United States of America)

The Hayes Microcomputer Products, Inc. ("Hayes") program that you have purchased is copyrighted by Hayes and your rights of ownership and use are subject to the limitations and restrictions imposed by the copyright laws and international treaty provisions outlined below.

It is against the law to copy, reproduce or transmit (including without limitation, electronic transmission over any network) any part of the program except as provided by the Universal Copyright Convention of Geneva and the copyright laws of your country (the "Laws"). However, you are permitted by Hayes to write the contents of the program into the machine memory of your computer so that the program may be executed by a single user. You are also permitted by Hayes to make a back-up copy of the program subject to the following restrictions:

1. Each back-up copy must be treated in the same way as the original copy purchased from Hayes;

2. If you ever sell or give away the original copy of the program, all back-up copies must also be sold or given to the same person, or destroyed; and

3. No copy (original or back-up) may be used while any other copy (original or back-up) is in use.

If you make a back-up copy of the program you should place the copyright notice that is on the original copy of the program on every back-up copy of the program.

The above is not an inclusive statement of the restrictions imposed on you under the Laws. If you are in any doubt as to whether your proposed use of the program is prohibited, you should seek appropriate professional advice.

Certain programs sold by Hayes are copy-protected (in addition to copyright protected) - that is, the diskette on which the program is recorded is physically designed so that the program cannot be copied or reproduced. If the program you have purchased is copy protected and a back-up copy of the program has been provided to you by Hayes, your rights in the back-up copy are also subject to the restrictions under the Laws referred to above.

To the extent that any of the terms and conditions of the English version of this Statement of Copyright Restrictions conflict with any of the terms and conditions of any translation thereof, the terms and conditions of the English version will prevail.

Service Address

Americas Region	Hayes Microcomputer Products, Inc. Attention: Customer Service P.O. Box 105203 Atlanta, Georgia 30348-9904 Telephone: (404) 441-1617 Telefax: (404) 449-0087 Telex: 703500 HAYES USA Online with Hayes BBS: (404) HI MODEM or (800) US HAYES and Hayes forums on CompuServe (GO HAYES) and GEnie information services. For unit repairs: 5953 Peachtree Industrial Blvd. Norcross, Georgia, 30092
Canada Office	Hayes Microcomputer Products (Canada) Limited 295 Phillip Street, Waterloo Ontario, Canada N2L 3W8 Telephone: (529) 746-5000
Europe Region	Hayes Microcomputer Products, Inc. Millennium House, Fleetwood Park Barley Way, Fleet Hampshire GU13 8UT United Kingdom Telephone: + 44 252 775544 Telefax: + 44 252 775511 Online with Hayes BBS + 44 252 775599
Asia Pacific Region	Hayes Microcomputer Products, Inc. 39/F, Unit B, Manulife Tower 169 Electric Road, North Point, Hong Kong Telephone + 852 887-1037, Telefax + 852 887-7548 Telex: 69381 HAYES HX Online with Hayes BBS: + 852 887-7590

IDG Books Worldwide License Agreement

Read this agreement carefully before you buy this book and use the programs contained on the enclosed disk.

By opening the accompanying disk package, you indicate that you have read and agree with the terms of this licensing agreement. If you disagree and do not want to be bound by the terms of this licensing agreement, return the book for refund to the source from which you purchased it.

The entire contents of this disk and the compilation of the software contained therein are copyrighted and protected by both U.S. copyright law and international copyright treaty provisions. The individual programs on this disk are copyrighted by the authors of each program respectively. Each program has its own use permissions and limitations. You may copy any or all of these programs to your computer system. Do not use a program if you do not want to follow its licensing agreement. Absolutely none of the material on this disk or listed in this book may ever be distributed, in original or modified form, for commercial purposes.

Disclaimer and Copyright Notice

Warranty Notice: IDG Books Worldwide, Inc., warrants that the disk that accompanies this book is free from defects in materials and workmanship for a period of 60 days from the date of purchase of this book. If IDG Books Worldwide receives notification within the warranty period of defects in material or workmanship, IDG Books Worldwide will replace the defective disk. The remedy for the breach of this warranty will be limited to replacement and will not encompass any other damages, including but not limited to loss of profit, and special, incidental, consequential, or other claims.

5¼", 1.2MB Disk Format Available. The enclosed disk is in 3½" 1.44MB, high-density format. If you have a different size drive, and you cannot arrange to transfer the data to the disk size you need, you can obtain the programs on a 5¼" 1.2MB high-density disk by writing: IDG Books Worldwide, Attn: *Official Hayes Modem Communications Companion,* IDG Books Worldwide, 155 Bovet Rd., Suite 310, San Mateo, CA 94402, or call 800-762-2974. Please specify the size of disk you need, and please allow 3 to 4 weeks for delivery.

Copyright Notice

IDG Books Worldwide and the authors specifically disclaim all other warranties, express or implied, including but not limited to implied warranties of merchantability and fitness for a particular purpose with respect to defects in the disks, the programs, and source code contained therein, and/or the techniques described in the book, and in no event shall IDG Books Worldwide and/or the authors be liable for any loss of profit or any other commercial damage, including but not limited to special, incidental, consequential, or other damages.

Installation Instructions for Smartcom for Windows LE

Before you install the contents of Smartcom for Windows LE, please read the notices on the preceding pages. Smartcom for Windows LE is described fully in Appendix C, "Guide to Smartcom for Windows LE."

Installing Smartcom for Windows LE

Perform the following steps to install Smartcom for Windows LE:

1. Make backup copies of the Smartcom LE master disk. Install Smartcom LE by using the copies. If something happens to one of the copies, you can make another copy from the master disk. Store your master disk in a safe place.

2. Verify that Windows is running on your computer and that the Windows Program Manager or the File Manager is open.

3. Insert the Smartcom LE disk in the floppy drive you want to use to install the program.

4. Choose Run from the File menu. The Run dialog box opens. In the Command Line text box, type:

   `A:\SETUP`

   (If you are installing from a different drive, type that drive letter instead of A:. Or, if you are in the File Manager, you can simply go to drive A and double-click SETUP.EXE.)

   Then click OK.

5. Follow the on-screen prompts to complete the installation and setup program.

See Appendix C, "Guide to Smartcom for Windows LE" for more details on the installation process.

IDG BOOKS WORLDWIDE REGISTRATION CARD

RETURN THIS REGISTRATION CARD FOR FREE CATALOG

Title of this book: Official Hayes Modem Communications Companion

My overall rating of this book: ❑ Very good [1]   ❑ Good [2]   ❑ Satisfactory [3]   ❑ Fair [4]   ❑ Poor [5]

How I first heard about this book:

❑ Found in bookstore; name: [6] _____

❑ Advertisement: [8]

❑ Word of mouth; heard about book from friend, co-worker, etc.: [10]

❑ Book review: [7]

❑ Catalog: [9]

❑ Other: [11]

What I liked most about this book:

_____

_____

What I would change, add, delete, etc., in future editions of this book:

_____

_____

Other comments:

_____

Number of computer books I purchase in a year: ❑ 1 [12]   ❑ 2-5 [13]   ❑ 6-10 [14]   ❑ More than 10 [15]

I would characterize my computer skills as: ❑ Beginner [16]   ❑ Intermediate [17]   ❑ Advanced [18]   ❑ Professional [19]

I use ❑ DOS [20]   ❑ Windows [21]   ❑ OS/2 [22]   ❑ Unix [23]   ❑ Macintosh [24]   ❑ Other: [25]_____
(please specify)

I would be interested in new books on the following subjects:
(please check all that apply, and use the spaces provided to identify specific software)

❑ Word processing: [26]

❑ Data bases: [28]

❑ File Utilities: [30]

❑ Networking: [32]

❑ Other: [34]

❑ Spreadsheets: [27]

❑ Desktop publishing: [29]

❑ Money management: [31]

❑ Programming languages: [33]

I use a PC at (please check all that apply): ❑ home [35]

The disks I prefer to use are ❑ 5.25 [39]   ❑ 3.5 [40]   ❑ o

I have a CD ROM: ❑ yes [42]   ❑ no [43]

I plan to buy or upgrade computer hardware this ye

I plan to buy or upgrade computer software this yea

Name: _____   Business ti

Address (❑ home [50] ❑ work [51]/Company name: _____

Street/Suite# _____

City [52]/State [53]/Zipcode [54]: _____

❑ **I liked this book!** You may quote me by name in f
IDG Books Worldwide promotional materials.

My daytime phone number is _____

T328 529 512 2

KNOWLEDGE

❑ YES!

Please keep me informed about IDG's World of Computer Knowledge.
Send me the latest IDG Books catalog.

OF VOWS AND WAR

THE COVETED: VOL. III

BREA LAMB

For those who were given pain in place of love and told to be thankful. May you shine even brighter in the shadows they sought to stifle you with.

Chapters with heavy triggers include:

- *Chapter eight: graphic descriptions of torture and murder, including blood.*
- *Chapter forty: graphic descriptions of torture and murder, including blood and dismemberment.*
- *Chapter forty-four: discussion of suicide as well as blood play during sex. Includes graphic descriptions of blood and self-harm.*
- *Chapter forty-nine: graphic descriptions of self-harm, including blood and gore, and an on-page anxiety attack.*

Please see the back of the book for summaries of these chapters if you would like to skip the triggering material.

WELCOME TO THE WORLD OF THE COVETED

Demon Realm
Eoforhild
Haven
Pike
Forest of Tragedies
Sophistes
Claud
Elpis
Kratos
Dunamis
Andreia
The Royal City
Yentain
Eros
Grishel
The Sea of Akiva
The Mist
Mortal Realm

Fae Realm

MORTAL REALM

Isle Healer

Isle Shifter

Multiple Lands

Single Lands
Golden Goose Inn

The Capital

Earth Lands
Water Lands
Air Lands
Fire Lands

Isle Element

Yesterday Lands
Reader River
Tomorrow Lands

Isle Reader

Betovere

GANDRY

VESTEER

CALESS

TEMPLE OF THE GODS

RAZC

XALIE

TAKO

ELDOR PEAKS

JORE

The Iridem Sea

BEHMAN

Mortal Realm

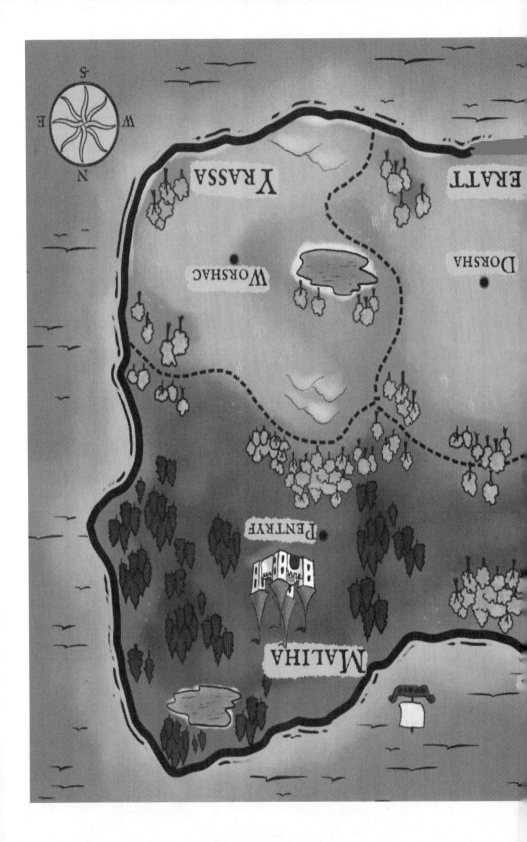

PRONUNCIATION GUIDE

Adbeel: Add-buh-hail

Alemthian: Uh-lem-the-in

Andreia: On-drey-uh

Asher: Ash-er

Asta: Ah-s-tuh

Augustu: Uh-gus-too

Ayad: Eye-ed

Behman: Bay-men

Bellamy: Bell-uh-me

Betovere: Bet-O-veer

Bhatt: Buh-ah-t

Bhesaj: Beh-saw-j

Braviarte: Brah-vee-ar-tey

Bronagh: Bro-nuh

Caless: Cuh-less

Calista: Cuh-lee-stuh

Claud: Claw-d

Cyprus: Sigh-prus

Dalistori: Dah-leh-store-E

Damon: Day-mun

Daniox: Dawn-wuah

Davina: Duh-vee-nuh

Demis: Deh-me-s

Dorsha: Door-shuh

Druj: D-roo-juh

Dunamis: Doo-nuh-miss

Elpis: El-pus

Engle: Aye-n-gull

Eoforhild: U-for-hill-d

Eros: Air-O-s

Farai: Fair-eye

Gandry: G-an-dree

Genevieve: Jen-eh-vee-v

Graham: Gr-am

Grishel: G-re-shell

Harligold: Har-leh-gold

Henry: Hen-ree

Heratt: Her-at

Herberto: Air-bear-tow

Ignazio: Eye-na-see-O

Iniko: In-E-co

Ishani: E-shaw-nee

Isolda: is-ole-duh

Jasper: Jas-pur

Jesre: Jess-ray

Jonah: Jo-nuh

Jore: Juh-or

Judson: Juh-d-son

Kafele: Kah-fey-lay

Karys: Care-is

Kratos: Cray-tow-z

Kyoufu: Kee-oh-foo

Lara: Lah-ruh

Lawrence: Lor-ence

Lazarev: L-ah-zuh-re-v

Lian: Lee-en

Likho: Lee-k-ho

Luca: Loo-cuh

Malcolm: Mal-k-um

Maliha: Muh-lee-uh

Maybel: May-bell

Mia: Me-uh

Mordicai: Moor-de-k-eye

Mounbetton: Mon-bet-tun

Nayab: Nay-eb

Nicola: Nee-co-lah

Noe: No-ee

Nyla: N-eye-luh

Odilia: Oh-dill-E-uh

O'Malley: O-mal-lee

Padon: Puh-d-on

Papatonis: pah-puh-tone-is

Paula: Paw-luh

Pentryf: Pen-t-riff

Pike: P-eye-k

Pino: Pee-n-yo

Prie: Puh-ree

Ranbir: Run-beer

Raymonds: Ray-mun-d-s

Razc: R-ah-z-k

Revanche: Rey-vah-n-ch

Salvatore: Sal-vuh-tor

Samell: Sah-mell

Selassie: Seh-lah-see

Selkans: Sel-k-en-s

Shah: Sh-aw

Shamay: Shuh-may

Sipho: S-eye-f-oh

Sophistes: So-fee-st-es

Stassi: S-tah-see

Stella: S-tell-uh

Sterling: Stir-ling

Takort: Tuh-core-t

Theon: Th-E-on

Tish: T-ish

Trint: T-rin-t

Tristana: Tris-tah-nuh

Ulu: Oo-loo

Venturae: Ven-ter-aye

Vesteer: Veh-s-tear

Windsor: Wind-soar

Winona: Why-no-nuh

Worshac: War-shack

Xalie: Zay-lee

Xavier: Ex-ay-vee-er

Yarrow: Yahr-r-oh

Yentain: Yen-t-A-n

Youxia: Yo-shaw

Yrassa: Ear-ah-suh

Zaib: Zay-buh

Zohar: Z-oh-hawr

GLOSSARY

Afriktor: Omniscient creature that lives in the Forest of Tragedies, created by the God of Death and Creation.

Air: Element sub-faction with the ability to wield Air power (i.e. create wind).

Alemthian: The world that the fae, demons, etc. live on.

Betovere: Also known as Fae Realm, made up of five islands that are inhabited by the fae species.

Dalistori: A feline-like creature with the ability to alter its size, created by the God of Death and Creation.

Earth: Element sub-faction with the ability to wield Earth power (i.e. grow flowers).

Element: Faction of fae with the ability to wield elements.

Ending: Term used by fae that means death. It is believed that the fae will sense when Eternity calls them home, and that is when they will choose to pass on.

Eoforhild: Also known as the Demon Realm, this is the continent that the demon species reside on.

Eternity: The sentient place that fae power comes from, as well as the higher power they pray to and believe their souls return to after death.

Faction: Term used to group together fae with similar powers (i.e. Readers or Shifters).

Fae Council: Group of fae who aid the King of the Fae Realm with decision making.

Fetch: A dream-walking creature with the power to track magical signatures, created by the God of Death and Creation.

Fire: Element sub-faction with the ability to wield Fire power (i.e. create a flame).

Healer: Faction of fae with the ability to heal.

High Demon: A creature from Shamay that has the ability to control and feed off of two opposing things (i.e. Death and Creation).

Honey Tongue: Ability to influence beings with the sound of one's voice.

Lady/Lord: The title bestowed on demons who reside over one of the five territories in Eoforhild.

Magic: General term for abilities that are thought to be bestowed by gods, wielded most notably by demons.

Moon: Ability to wield the raw magic from the moon (i.e. wield shadows).

Mortal: General term for the humans who do not live indefinitely.

Multiple: Shifter sub-faction with the ability to alter their appearance in indefinite ways, though they can only maintain that form for a short period of time.

Navalom: Creature that lives in the Forest of Tragedies and feasts on memories.

Oracle: Term for a being who can see both the past and the future without touching a being. This ability is rare and believed to only be possessed by fae.

Power: The general term for abilities gifted by Eternity, wielded by fae.

Prime: Member of the fae council who is in charge of particular specialties that are needed to maintain the Fae Realm (i.e. trade or coin). They live in The Capital.

Reader: Faction of fae with the ability to read the past or future.

Royal Court: Members of the fae council who are the strongest in their respective sub-faction. They are chosen to represent said sub-faction and live in The Capital (ie. Royal Healer or Royal Fire).

Shamay: A world that holds high and low demons, as well as dragons and other creatures.

Shifter: Faction of fae with the ability to alter their physical appearance.

Single: Shifter sub-faction that can alter their appearance into one chosen form for an unlimited amount of time (i.e. wolf or panther).

Siren: Water folk with the ability to have legs on land and a large fin underwater. Can lure their prey with their singing.

Sub-faction: Term used to represent fae who wield the same power.

Sun: Ability to wield the raw magic from the sun (i.e. wield light).

Tomorrow: Reader sub-faction with the ability to read the future of anyone they touch.

Warden: Title bestowed on the second strongest member of each sub-faction. They rule over their respective lands.

Water: Element sub-faction with the ability to wield Water power (i.e. create waves).

Whisp: Creature that can turn their body into various forms, such as black mist, bubbles, etc.

Wraith: Creature with the ability to blend into their surroundings, their form fading and turning them nearly invisible. Often called ghosts by the fae, though they are living beings.

Yesterday: Reader sub-faction with the ability to read the past of anyone they touch.

Youngling: The fae and demon equivalent to a child.

BEFORE WE BEGIN,
LET US FIRST REFRESH...

After discovering the lies that she was told her entire life, Asher was determined to find allies. She sought out help in the Mortal Realm while Bellamy readied the demon military forces. While on her journey, Asher was contacted by what she would later discover was the holder of Death and Creation, Padon. This creature, who was worshipped as a god on Alemthian, was obsessed with Asher, threatening those she loved.

Over the course of months, Asher, Bellamy, and a few friends, were able to successfully gather allies, work with creatures of all kinds, and even best the desperate god. But just as Asher decided she would be selfish after a lifetime of being selfless, a mortal kingdom that they had rallied was attacked by the fae military.

Forced to drop everything and help, Asher and Bellamy fought alongside their gathered soldiers. But what once looked like victory soon became bloodshed. When Queen Mia Mounbetton showed up to the battle and nearly killed Bellamy, Asher stepped in. The Manipulator quickly did what she did best, taking hold of Bellamy's mind and forcing him to take their soldiers and run—leaving her behind.

We open our story just like that, with a princess imprisoned, a prince distraught, and the knowledge that an Oracle plots on fae soil.

ACT I

~ DECEPTION AND CANDOR ~

PROLOGUE

In a universe so vast—so all-encompassing—it was no surprise that world walkers were revered.

Perhaps that was why Asta felt so uncomfortably bored in her life. She had the ability to travel through galaxies, to learn—to thrive—to *live*. But Padon, who was funny and handsome and so very good with his tongue, did not have the curiosity that she did. Her sister and her father understood that deep desire to be more than a crown, but her mother sided with the holder of Death and Creation.

Yes, Stella understood what Asta did not. There was no satiating the curiosity that ran through her daughters' veins. Which was why, when her husband desired to bring their daughters world-walking, Stella wished to say no. In the end, she allowed Sol to go, but forced Asta to stay. Asta

was their heir, despite being younger. She and Padon had a wedding to plan and so much to learn. They did not have time to sightsee. Their place was on Shamay.

Asta would forever associate that moment with guilt, for this would be the last time she ever saw her father and sister. Stella would live with regrets rather than guilt, for she wished more than anything to have spent one more moment with her doting husband—her soul bond. She would give anything to kiss her oldest daughter's forehead—to hold her tightly and remind her of her magnificence in times of doubt.

Decades would pass. Then centuries. Stella would search and search, but she would not find them. Her own world would suffer for her absence at first, though her tear-filled moments of presence were not much better.

One day, the empress would stumble upon a world unlike any other. This world, with its beautiful yellow sun and its immense magic, reminded her of her lost husband—of the curiosity she once sought to stifle. Stella would explore the world, finding she did not quite like the creatures that called themselves fae. Though they looked like her kind with their pointed ears and sharp features, they did not settle within her bones comfortably. Instead, their presence weighed heavy in her stomach, like a bad pastry. They were conceited and flamboyant, all things she and her family never were.

So she would search on, stumbling across a vast continent, one that held creatures with round ears and no magic in their veins. They were kind and happy, but more than that, they were eager to learn.

The holder of Sun and Moon would do something abhorrent in her daze. She would gift the short-lived creatures her essence. From the skies she would steal the magic of their nearly white sun and the shadowy moon, raining it down upon the entirety of the continent known as Eoforhild. Mortals, as the fae called them, fell to their knees in thanks. And soon they would call her goddess. Soon they would worship her.

Back on Shamay, Padon—a strong and almost simple creature—found himself stepping up. He knew one thing above all else, he would save them. There was no doubt in the male's mind that he belonged on the throne, just as he was absolutely certain that he was meant to have Asta at his side. She was his equal, perhaps even his superior. She was *his*.

How wonderful they were together. Every morning he would awaken her with coffee and breakfast, with words of affirmation and love. He would slip beneath the blankets and rip screams from her mouth. Then he would rule with her in Stella's absence during the day, sneaking peeks at her dazzling silver eyes and hair beneath their teal sun. At night, Padon would once more ravish her, consuming everything she offered. And as she closed her eyes from fatigue, he would whisper his love to her.

Their life was perfect.

Until it was not.

And maybe it was his own inability to see past that utter bliss he existed within that prevented him from noticing when Asta no longer returned his declarations of love. Nor did he catch on to her aloofness during the day. Even worse, Padon did not notice Asta's misery.

As a certain pink-haired beauty would say, this was Padon's greatest sin.

CHAPTER ONE

PERDITA

Gritting my teeth, I prepared for the bone-deep chill of the air to become the all-encompassing freeze of the Ibidem Sea. A wave soared over the starboard side, and all I could do was sign to my crew, "Incoming!"

The impact of the waves on a ship was dangerous.

The crash of the water upon a demon was deadly.

It hit me head-on, water shoving its way down my throat and drenching my clothes—my leather pants and cotton shirt doing nothing to save me. My hands gripped the gunnel despite how slippery the wood was quickly becoming. Desperately, I ordered the goddess, Stella, to keep me upright.

Once the water cleared, I doubled over with a cough, drying my lungs. With a glance back, I saw the crew doing the same. That was all the encouragement I needed.

"Get those fucking sails stowed!" My violent and sharp signs were cut off by the crack of thunder as another wave smashed into the Abaddon, my center of gravity shifting as I was knocked off my feet. I flew across the deck, using every bit of my magic to keep the others up so CJ could have enough time. Sea water surged into my mouth once more when I gasped in pain at the feel of my body slamming into the wooden bulwark. Forcing my eyes open despite the salty burn, I called upon my shadows.

One moment I was being slowly drowned by the sea that had seen most of my formative years, the next I was atop the crow's nest, gasping for air. Lightning streaked the sky, painting my ship in a silver glow—a haunting image.

Looking down, I caught sight of CJ's strained face as she pushed out her Water power. Her screams were silent to my unhearing ears but practically vibrating beneath my feet as she attempted to fight the flood, just as Bek's determined instructions likely battled for dominance against the booming thunder above. Watching as CJ's mouth moved in response, I realized how hopelessly she was working against the sea.

With a sigh that burned my throat, I finally conceded.

My shadows seeped from my skin, crawling down the ropes and sails, seeking a foothold on the Abaddon herself. I willed them on, not so much as breathing until every inch of my beautiful ship was wrapped in their cool embrace. Then I thought of home.

***

"That was a close one," Bek signed lazily as she slumped into the faded wooden chair beside mine. I shoved my tankard of grog at her, a

small smirk lifting the corner of my mouth. Life upon a ship was not an easy one, but the moments of humor and joy one could concoct made it all worth it.

That and the gold, of course.

Perhaps it was the freedom too.

Bek gripped the handle with her bone-white fingers, tipping back her head and taking a hefty swig. Laughter silently tore through me as she lurched forward, spitting out what was still floating in her mouth as she sputtered.

"You." Gasp. "Bitch!" Cough. "I fucking—" Her hands stilled then, bracing against her knees as she leaned over her legs. Oh, that was real choking there.

The sight of her hacking gave me the urge to scoot away, my face pinching in slight discomfort. Still, I reached out my hand and smacked her back a few times, earning a rather menacing glare. Not that those black eyes could be anything other than unsettling most days. Though it helped that her dirty blonde hair was loose. After a few more moments, she gathered her breath and sat up straight. "You need to stop putting saltwater in our damn rum, Perdita."

With a shake of my head and a chuckle, I reached down and grabbed a white horn full of undiluted rum. Amusement lifted my round cheeks, my lips splitting into a grin. I handed it to her with an eye roll, my fingers sore as I signed from gripping so tightly when the water threatened to overtake us. "Can you at least pretend to not be an insolent little shit? The fresh fish will think me an incompetent leader. Or worse—a soft one."

Rolling her eyes back, Bek snagged the horn and lifted it to her nose, sniffing with her dark gaze squinted in suspicion. Satisfied by the burning smell, she brought the edge to her mouth and swallowed before nodding, gesturing to the area behind me. I turned in time to see Dima approaching us, her endless black hair blowing in the wind and her pale skin vibrant in the sunlight. Her lavender eyes found my deep brown ones

just as I shoved Bek, hoping she would take the hint and leave before Dima got to us. As always, she refused simply to annoy me.

"Captain, it is good to see you up and moving again," Dima signed, her hands slow and fumbling. Her feet were damp with water as they smacked across the deck, the aquamarine shade of her billowing dress looking like the movement of the very sea she had clearly just been playing in. I watched her with unabashed lust, the sway of her hips and the bounce of her breasts making my mouth water. She never wore anything below those barely-there pieces of fabric she called dresses, and I thought I might never stop craving her.

"Well, Storm—"

"I have told you before, that is not my name, *Perdita.*" A smile fought its way to my face as I watched her full pink lips move in time with her hands. Bek patted me on the shoulder before standing, taking my rum with her as she left. I watched her retreat below deck before returning my eyes to Dima. She leaned forward, placing her hands on the armrests of my chair. The fabric of her dress opened, showing me one of my favorite sights in the entire gods damned world.

"Well, *Dima,* I am the best pirate to roam the three seas. A few measly waves cannot steal that from me." My arms opened wide, showing her all that I was, willing her to admit my greatness.

There were many things I was poor at. Being a loving daughter. Working as a slaver. Following the rules—Underworld spare me, I was quite terrible at that. Still, there was one thing I was magnificent at: being a pirate. I looted like no other, captained my crew with excellence, and overall was the best at what I did. Sailors spoke my name with a tremble, and I reveled in it.

"Ah, yes, you so often say so. But I wonder, can one be a renowned pirate *and* possess honor?" Dima's question was meant to unnerve me—to spark some bit of remorse. She would find none within me.

"My honor is my truth, lovely siren. I am honest about what I am, rather than claiming myself a privateer and trading in living things like my

7

father. Is there not principle in that?" My hand lifted as I finished the sign, a single finger reaching to graze the swell of her breast, the brown of my skin making hers look nearly translucent. A wonderfully erotic gasp left her lips and vibrated against me as I continued to gently tease her, and I thought perhaps honor was a fickle and pointless thing anyways.

"You do not trade, Captain. What you do is steal." My head fell back in a laugh, the hypocrisy of her words settling low in my stomach—in my core. I wrapped my free arm around her waist, dragging her onto my lap. Her long legs bent, resting on the outside of my thighs. Without hesitation, I leaned into her, my finger pulling down the top of her dress and my tongue flicking one of her perfectly peaked nipples. Gods, she was glorious. The salty taste of her was a flame within the hearth of my desire, forcing a strangled growl up my throat as I attempted to continue the conversation without forcing her to her knees in front of me.

"*We,* Storm. You have joined our crew, have you not?" A breathy moan emanated from her and painted the air in sensuality as she rocked her hips against me. Another chuckle freed itself from the confines of my chest. "Regardless, it is quite a thing to question my morality. While I walk away with heavy pockets, you walk away with a heavy stomach."

Two of my now free fingers lowered, diving under the flimsy fabric upon her thigh and skating up her velvet skin. She grew more frantic with her movements when I bit down upon her nipple, sucking it into my mouth before freeing it with what had to have been an audible pop. Smiling at the feel of her already wet center, I began my slow destruction of the beautiful carnivore before me.

She pulled away slightly, putting her hands between us.

"That reminds me, the water spoke. A ship comes," Dima signed before pressing her breasts back into my face, a groan brushing against my skin following the casually given statement. Yet, it was not something of no consequence to me. No, this would be how we made up for the gems we lost out on earlier. Scoffing, I shoved Dima off me, her body tipping back and her phenomenal ass landing hard upon the deck of my ship.

"Dammit, Dima! You cannot lose focus upon these seas. You must remember that nothing is as important as gold in the palms of our hands." My signs were hasty and sharp, a clear representation of my growing frustration. I dragged one of my now free hands through my tangled coffee-brown curls, the desire for preparation and hatred of spontaneity rising within me.

"But I am starved, can I just have a quick snack first?" Those bright eyes lowered from my face, stopping and remaining focused upon the still-wet spot between my legs. Rolling my eyes, I reached out a hand and helped her up. Her smile was ethereal, brilliantly white teeth unstained despite her bloodlust.

"Good, you can feast upon what is left once I am done getting the coin you will find us. Now get your ass in the water and call that ship to me." With a shove, I urged her towards the edge of the ship. The siren glared at me, every bit of desire leaving her eyes. *There* she was.

With a flash of her middle finger my way, she turned, leaping over the bulwark and into the calm sea below. Jogging over, I saw that she had barely caused the water to ripple, but her presence would be known soon. I let out my warning whistle, my pointer finger and thumb curving into my mouth as I blew out three long notes.

Rolling my shoulders, I kicked off my boots and pressed my toes into the wood below my feet. My fingers dug into the ledge as I waited for the rumble of her voice to soothe every nerve in my body. Unlike the rest of my crew, I enjoyed feeling the notes of doom that Dima sang for the unsuspecting seafarers. In moments, she blessed us with her song. With a final laugh at the ominous beat of her haunting, deep voice, I closed my eyes and prepared for what was to come. Death would stain the sea red today.

CHAPTER TWO

STASSI

One more meeting, then I would go to my creature.

Deal with the others for an hour, and then I could—ideally—head straight to the dungeons beneath the golden castle. Asher could wait. That ridiculous little shit. A part of me hoped something awful would befall her simply so she would no longer be my problem. The other part of me, though, wanted her to live and ruin Padon's life.

The arrogant prick walked at my side, standing as tall and foreboding as ever. His violet trousers and jacket hugged every ripple of muscle, forming nearly a second skin. Pale fingers flattened his lapels,

straightening out the open jacket that showed the black button-up below. Striking was truly the only word that could describe Padon.

I sure would've liked to strike him, that was.

Asta would have. She was the only one who never feared him, other than Stella. What I wouldn't give to will her and Sol back to me. To bring my best friends home and reunite my family. Instead, Padon and I walked into the meeting room, and I listened as he slid the door closed. For some reason, it felt like my fate was being sealed, too.

Iniko stood first, a glowing smile upon his face. The holder of Chaos and Order, with ribbons of sapphire hair and skin the color of midnight, was easily one of the most handsome males I had ever seen. Somehow, he was also even more insufferable than Padon.

"Stassi, you're looking exceptionally lovely this morning." His words caressed the air between us, which he quickly closed by walking to us and offering me his arm. My hand flew out, smacking him so hard that he hissed in pain. Padon, for all of his uptightness, smirked down at me, placing a kiss to my hair. Before I could swat him too, he hastily made his way to his seat at the head of the table. Groaning, I looked back to Iniko. "I thought you would be more agreeable after your vacation. Were the mortals not skilled enough to settle you?"

With a scoff, I glared into his vibrant blue eyes. "What makes you think I would ever be agreeable towards you of all creatures?"

Shoving him, I tried to make my way to my own seat, but the idiot grabbed my arm. A growl crawled up my throat, slowly vibrating throughout my body. One day I would tear him apart limb from limb. "I think that you, like your mother, are perpetually unsatisfied."

"My mother had taste," I hissed, looking him up and down. He knew what I was insinuating—that I marked him as unworthy for being rejected by her so long ago. The others shuffled nervously within their seats, all of them watching Iniko and I. Each of them was used to how things had been before I left. Before I knew what I could be with a little more magic within my veins.

"Yes, that father of yours was something, wasn't he? At least he, unlike you, knew his place. He was comfortable in his limitations, content with the little magic he had. Why can't you be the same?" A smile stretched his lips and lifted his cheeks, the look of satisfaction and victory making my blood heat. I simmered until, finally, Iniko made his bed. "Though, I would hate to drag your husk of a body to the sacred grounds like his."

With a guttural scream, I boiled over, grabbing his neck with one hand and bringing my fist into his nose with the other. Chairs scraped against wood at the same time I used Iniko's surprise—his arrogance—against him, digging my fingers into his neck and squeezing with all my strength. His large body teetered back as I shoved my weight into him, sending us both to the gray marble floors. Not sparing a moment, I dug my knee into his chest and tightened my hold on his throat. With the knowledge that someone would soon stop me, I hastily brought my lips to his ear, whispering ever so softly, "You're right, Iniko. I'm not my father. When you look at me, know that I'm every bit my mother's daughter. Like her, I see you for what you are. The scum beneath my foot."

Padon's arms wrapped around my waist then, his hands familiar and unwanted. But I didn't fight back when he pulled me off Iniko, who was blinking up at me in shock. And Eternity spare me, it felt *good* to watch him stutter upon his words. "She—she attacked me! What are—what did—do something, Padon!"

I lunged, trying to dig my claws into the bumbling fool and rip out his blue eyes.

"Enough!" Padon shouted, practically tossing me into my pink chair, my elbow smacking into the armrest and pulling a reluctant gasp of pain from me. "We have a war to win!"

"Actually, it's more of a conquering," Jonah added nonchalantly from his seat. Iniko quickly stood, scrambling to his chair as Padon sighed in annoyance. Our oh so fearless emperor pinched the bridge of his nose, tilting his head back as if to seek patience from above. He would find none.

"Call it what you want, but we need to decide what our next steps will look like. The low demons are restless, just as we are. Not only have the gems nearly lost all of their light, but we now face the repercussions of too many years of complacency. The loss of magic will bleed our stability from the air if we're not quick." Padon gripped the back of his chair, the deep purple of it nearly black. I watched with more annoyance than I thought I had within me as he stroked one of the skulls absentmindedly with his long pointer finger.

Stella and Achari's seats were absent, but their gems still floated above us, a chilling reminder of what pride could do to someone. The once-empress's gem was dark, the black and white swirled rock absent of the magic that once pulsed within it—of Stella's magic. Her husband's wasn't as bad, his brother's magic vast enough that we didn't suffer too much from the loss of Time and Void. But without Char's seed of magic, that ancient golden light that had existed longer than life itself, then we would soon see the repercussions of his absence too.

Sun and Moon, that we would surely lose everything without. We didn't have Stella or Solana, no relatives strong enough to hold together the gem. If it broke, so would we. Fury filled me at the knowledge that we wouldn't be in this mess if Stella were still here.

"Well maybe we shouldn't be wasting our time looking for an annoying little mortal girl, and instead should be begging Stella for forgiveness." Silence barreled into the room at my comment, beating down our breaths and shoving into our hearts—stilling them. I dragged my gaze up to Padon's, his aubergine eyes and my rose ones locking. The two of us glared at each other, allowing the hatred in our chests to rise, filling us like an empty cup and threatening to overflow.

His grip tightened on the back of his chair, my own squeezing the arms of mine tight enough to hurt. No one else moved, their eyes flicking up to the gems before settling on whichever of us they sided with. I meant what I said, and they all knew I was right, even if they wouldn't admit it. Still, the proud asshole pushed on with his ridiculous agenda.

"We don't need Stella. Asher possesses something far grander. I can and will make her more, and she will save us all. We must first take her pathetic excuse for a world, though, so let's get back to—"

I stood, my chair wobbling slightly from the speed with which I moved. My fists came down onto the table, the booming sound of my wrath echoing in the still silent room. I pointed a finger at the high demon of Death and Creation—the moron who let Asher think him a god for the sake of that very ego that was dooming us today.

"You have cursed us all with your selfishness. If Stella sat upon that seat, we wouldn't suffer in this way. But you banished her because she refused to force her daughter back to you. Because she refused to submit to your heartless will. Because she didn't wish to put her daughter through more agony! And now you stand there, acting as if this isn't all your fault, still being as reckless as ever! Your little princess won't replace what was lost! Get it through that thick skull of yours!"

Padon's fury won out then. He lifted his chair, throwing it across the room before appearing before me in a cloud of sparkling, violet smoke. I had no time to dodge his strike, forced to take the slap that sent my head whipping to the left. A burning sensation lit my face, the sting traveling from my cheek and down into my soul, where this great crime would fester beside all his others.

"How dare you! What would you have me do, Anastasia? Take pity on the creatures who practically stole my wife? Who our aloof empress had wasted her time on? The very beings who have lived in the safety of my absence for the last fifteen thousand years? I took an abandoned throne that was meant to be mine since the moment Asta was born! I brought our world back from the brink of destruction!"

"You doomed us all!" My screams cut off his rant, Karys gasping as her orange magic flared. Her hold on Love and Hatred was likely slipping, or perhaps she was making this all worse. One could always count on a demon to choose the way of anger. It was one of the few things we felt strongly enough to act on with such passion. "Asta wasn't yours, Padon! She didn't want you anymore! And because of you I never got to say

14

goodbye to her or Stella. You took them from me whether you want to admit that or not!"

"Fine, you want Stella so badly? Then go find her! Do what you wish, Stassi. But know this: if you leave Shamay, you will not be allowed back. I will gladly watch you suffer the same fate as your wonderful empress," he seethed the words, his jaw clenched tightly as he spoke. I could do nothing but rear back in surprise, my thoughts swarming, my creature at the center of the storm.

"What about Asher? Who will get her for you?" The question was littered with anxiety. So obvious was my desire to go back—though none of them would know why—that Padon had thought of the perfect punishment. Force me to remain on Shamay and I would suffer deeply.

"That isn't your business anymore." The words were no less than a damnation, made all the more clear by the way Padon portaled away from me, retrieving his chair and not looking at me again. For some reason, despite my constant desire to be anywhere else, the thought of banishment awakened poignant feelings of utter terror within me. "Leave. Now."

The others stared on, Venturae's green eyes betraying the unsettling way she was scrutinizing how this would affect Fate and Chance, the two locking even us within their confines. That was the thing about living and breathing, it made you a slave—a prisoner—to the ethers and their reckoning. There was no escape from the future—no fighting destiny. Even Venturae, with all of her immense magic, could only do so much in the way of fighting what Eternity had written within the cosmos. This moment felt like an inevitability that would only spiral from here.

With a growl of frustration, I kicked my chair and portaled away, breaking into a run the moment my bare feet met the icy bite of the snow upon the mountaintop. My flimsy blush dress whipped in the fierce wind, my sleek locks blowing back in a wave of vibrant pink.

"Torrel!" I yelled as I neared the edge. Then, without a second thought, I lept off the mountainside. Asta had taught me just how wonderful it could be to fall like this—the testing of our immortality an odd

sort of freedom. As the ground below beckoned me down and the wind desperately tried to push me upwards, I smiled despite the pain in my cheek.

Glowing pink scales caught the teal light of day, and then Torrel was there to scoop me from the sky. I latched onto her scales as my chest connected with her neck. For a second, I lost my grip, but I squeezed my thighs and gritted my teeth. In all my life, I had never fallen from my girl, and I wouldn't start today.

"Take me to the cottage, Torrel."

CHAPTER THREE

BELLAMY

Bile climbed up my throat, magic digging into me like desperate claws seeking purchase. I ran my fingers over Asher's necklace atop the desk briefly and fought off the pain. My head was throbbing as the knife that was Asher's magic stabbed into my temples—punishing me. Still, I pressed on, my hand shaking as I gripped the pencil and attempted to write upon the page—the graphite staining my pale fingers.

Please, just *one* sentence.

A gong seemed to ring in my mind, the tremor of pain caused by its echoing tenor finally pushing me over the edge. I heaved, vomiting mostly blood into the bin I now kept at the side of my desk.

Another failed attempt.

My entire body convulsed, Asher's voice whispering into my mind. **You will not come looking for me. You will not save me.**

Tears spilled from my eyes at the memory. That was all it was—all she was—now. A mere ripple in the sea of my past. A blip of time that was not nearly enough. The blood had poured from beneath the small log of wood, her body shaking and her eyes half closed. When she had fallen to her knees, I nearly exploded from the rage and magic within me. Of all the times for Asher to realize just how strong she was, that had been the worst. And now she was gone.

No, I would not let that be our ending. I could fight this. I attempted to sit back up, but my body protested, seizing and leaving me no choice but to fall to the floor in a heap of desperation and failure.

While I laid there upon the cool rock, crying unabashedly, I thought back to the letter Nicola had sent us. The instructions she had given.

First, you must not plot to get Asher. Not directly. Your best chance at saving her *and* Alemthian is by doing exactly as I say.

Second, in one week's time, you will portal a ship bearing the demon sigil to the coordinates I have written on the back of this missive. Wait until midday, when the sun is highest in the sky and its rays light the black waters.

Third, a stranger will come upon you, and you will trust them. This is vital. Carry two standard pouches of gold and pay for their trust in turn.

Fourth, train those mortals and focus on rebuilding alliances. Your light-haired mortal king will be uneasy, but a queen will come to your aid. You must not lose any of the mortals to the fae. Asher was right in her desire to craft alliances. Without five of the six kingdoms on your side, you *will* lose this war, and we will all die.

Finally, stop fucking trying to write strategies to save the princess, Elemental. You will only embarrass yourself. Asher's magic has awoken, and it will not be defeated in this.

My fingers went slack, the pencil rolling away from me. Tomorrow we would sail, and I had yet to follow her final rule. Every day for the last week I had attempted to plot rescue missions. And every day, just as Nicola Salvatore said, I embarrassed myself.

Sighing, I closed my eyes and called to my fire. The red and blue flames flickered beyond my eyelids, the heat scorching as it licked up my hands. I welcomed the burn, the pain of my flesh melting away. Ranbir would be upset, but if Asher was being harmed, then we would feel that hurt together.

***

"Faster!" I screamed, breathing in through my nose and out through my mouth as I leapt over a group of fallen branches, the sight of the large pieces of wood raining down unwelcome memories upon me. My hands balled into fists, the itch of newly healed skin making my teeth grind. Ranbir had yelled at me as his power seeped into my body, his tone furious and filled with disappointment. But I did not care. Getting to feel that blazing pain momentarily distracted my mind from the excruciating loss.

"Bell, I cannot keep up when you—" I heard her fall, the snapping of twigs and the smack of her body on the grass loud, before her curses filled the sweltering air. "Fuck! I swear to the gods and Eternity above that I will beat your ass!"

I sighed, slowing before coming to a halt. Within my chest, my shattered heart beat a ferocious rhythm as I spun to face Lian. Her blue hair had dirt in it, her yellow-toned skin red from the exertion and her fury. Scowling up at me, she squinted her almond eyes, the upwards tilt of them making her anger all the more prominent. Oh yes, I had done it this time.

Offering her help up, I awaited my second scolding of the day. She took my outstretched hand, but instead of using it to get back to her feet, she yanked me downwards. Unprepared for her vengeance, I careened forward, landing hard on the forest floor. A stinging in my forearm alerted me to the rock, but I did not care as my blood spilled upon the dirt and stone. Instead, I laid down, staring up at the scorching sun and sapphire sky beyond the greenery of the trees.

"I have loved and lost too, Bellamy," Lian whispered between clenched teeth, her tone bordering on murderous. But I knew it was not simply frustration that led her to speak of Yuza when she so often did not. It was concern. My eyes drifted to her face, which was slowly relaxing. Clearing her throat, she reached up to dust off her training leathers as she continued. "Yuza was fiery and determined, like Asher. In the twenty-four years we had been together, she never once wavered in her desire to change the future—in her wish for us to be free to love and live. It was I who was scared and selfish, who wished for nothing more than to be by her side, even if in secret. Like you, all I dreamed of was her. Like Ash, Yuza would not settle."

A gasp slipped from my lips, the surprise startling in its raw form. I knew some of this story, but to hear it relayed to me in direct comparison to my own tale? Well, there were few things that still hurt these days, but relating the tragedy of Yuza and Lian to Asher and I absolutely stung.

"I did not know at first that she had contacted the rebel group stirring within Betovere. Even when I had become aware, and begged for her to stop, I was still ignorant to what it all meant. Honestly, I did not know how deeply she had woven herself within their ranks until she was dead at my feet." She scoffed then, a sound of both pain and disbelief. "But Yuza, she thought it the only option. Overthrow the Mounbetton's and we would be free. We did not know then that we were being watched, nor did we see that it was not the demons attacking our homes, but our own fae."

I sighed, facing the sky once more as the knowledge of how deeply woven I was within the pain of all who I cared about. It was *my* family that had been the cause of Lian's pain. Of Ranbir's. *My* parents that had killed

Winona and Luca and Pino—that had destroyed Haven, demolished cities in Eoforhild, and attacked Behman. *My* blood that held Asher hostage.

Like Asher, I understood how heavy the world was.

"Beings like Yuza and Ash are rare. But even more rare is the group who gets to love them—to be *in* love with them. We are special, you and I, because we were awarded their hearts." I felt her small fingers grip my face, the tips digging into my cheeks as she forced me to face her. Those knowing eyes bore into me and threatened to bring me to tears. Lian, more than anyone, knew what it was to lose your love because they were determined to save the world. "I will do everything in my power to make sure you do not lose Asher in the way I lost Yuza. We will bring her home. *Alive.*"

With that, Lian released my face and braced her hands on the dirt beside me. I watched with surprise as the Air cuddled up next to me—in the dirt no less. When she was tucked closely to my side and facing the blowing tree limbs above like I was, I finally found my words. "Thank you, Lian."

Her sharp chuckles filled the air, both of her hands folding over her shaking sternum. "There are many things you owe me thanks for, Bell, but this is not one of them. Asher is as much mine as she is yours. One day she will be my queen, regardless of which realm she presides over. I *will* follow her, just as Cyprus, Ranbir, and Noe will. Just as *you* will. She is…well, she is made for a throne."

A smile lifted my cheeks at her words, but—just as each rare moment of joy that occurred in the days since Ash was taken from me—it did not settle the storm of despair that clouded my heart and rained down horrifying thoughts upon my mind.

"Remember that time you painted Yuza for me?" She whispered the question as she lifted her hand, five fingers twirling through the air. I watched as the trees bent to the coming wind, green leaves breaking free to dance within Lian's power. Lian had always been stronger than most fae. She was once the third strongest Air to live, and she would have been

named Warden of her lands eighty years ago if she had only found love within her faction.

But love did not care what was easy. Star-crossed souls, that was what Yuza and Lian were—what Asher and I are.

"Yes, I do. Faintly. It was not very good," I finally said in response. Lian did not acknowledge my aloofness at her question, nor did she accuse me of not listening. We had been together for over eight decades. Too long to not know better.

"It is beautiful, actually. Yuza still rests above my desk in Haven, just as her ashes still lie beneath the grass. Noe has taken me there seventeen times since the fae queen attacked. I always reach up as if to take the portrait, but instead I find myself sliding my finger across her long black hair. My skin traces the bold blue of her irises, the color gone from my memory now, and then down her jaw. Before she died, I would do that in the mornings—touch the skin from her ear to her chin. Her left side was fuller than her right, making her face asymmetrical in the most alluring way. Now, I cannot recall what she felt like. Cannot remember the sound of her enchanting laugh. As if she never existed." Though Lian did not cry, there was a shaky quality to her voice, the tone ebbing as she spoke. Not allowing myself to second guess the choice, I quickly gripped her free hand, interlacing our fingers. The Air smiled softly, turning her head to face me as I did her. "I wonder sometimes if it is better to have loved and lost, or if it might be a greater mercy to never love at all."

CHAPTER FOUR

ASHER

In my dreams, I recalled the pain of death and lies—the festering wounds that bubble and burst from the life and truth that seek freedom from their confines. More than that, I dreamt of what life would be like if only I had known better.

***

Day One.

My eyes did not see. My ears did not hear. But my body—my skin, my bones, my mind—they felt. Yes, I felt it all.

***

Day Two.

His voice was soft, his accent strong—like his tongue was too heavy to lift sometimes. It was peaceful, listening as he offered ballads of war and love and death. Yet, I could not will my eyes to open, my limbs to move. Perhaps they were gone. But my ears, they were there, and they listened as the golden-haired prince sang.

***

Day Three.

My blood felt as if it boiled within me, a crack and sizzle that scorched its way to my still-beating heart.

Alive. I was alive.

Despite the fire blazing within me, my skin was pebbled and my limbs were shivering. The moment I acknowledged the chill of the air and the stone floor beneath me, my teeth began to chatter, as if my mind had just realized my jaw was still there. A sound to my left forced my heavy lids open, the startling awareness of another being nearby sending fear clawing up my spine. I tried to sit up, to take on a defensive position of any kind, but a rock connected with my temple, pain shooting through my head.

No, not a rock. There was no rock. I knew this agony well. I could still recall the first time I had been sentenced to my low level room—could

feel the way the leather band scraped against my neck. I was five the first time my magic got away from me. The first time I was punished for an outburst. The screams that had torn my throat to shreds, the tears that had stained my cheeks for days, the piercing ache of my head—yes, it was a blocker that was doing this to me.

"Asher? Oh my gods, you are awake. Hold on, let me grab that water. Stay still, please." That voice, the heavy and deep tune so different when he was not singing, lulled me. I laid my head back upon the stone, content to listen for once. Every part of my body hurt, as if I had been thrown off a cliffside and forced to simply deal with the pain of it all. Perhaps that was how everyone lived. I had never been taught to bandage my wounds. There were many things I had not been taught. I could not cook or sew, could not clean or sail. And maybe that was to make sure I was never able to exist beyond the gilded walls of the palace I grew up in. Or maybe it was because I let myself be a prisoner and never asked for anything more than I was given.

Maybe it was both.

"Okay, I am going to try to help you sit up, but I need you to first crawl to the bars. It will hurt. Gods above, I know it will hurt. But if you can get to me, Asher, I can help you," Sterling vowed, his voice a broken whisper. I knew then that he was not aware of just how many times I had been in this very predicament. Chuckling, I willed my hands to flatten upon the ground below, pushing my torso up and lifting my horribly heavy head. Nausea rolled through me in waves, my body begging me to simply lay down and sleep once more. But I ignored the aches and pains and desperate need for rest. Instead, I moved to my forearms and pulled myself to the left—to the mortal prince beyond the bars. That was when I felt it.

My back protested the movement, the freshly healed skin splitting and blood dripping to mix with the dried flakes from days ago. With a cry of both pain and fury, I dragged my body across the stone. Sterling croaked out a praise, urging me to continue. When my fingertips touched the icy iron of the bars that separated our cages of captivity, I gasped in relief. Sterling's large hand gripped my wrist, gently tugging me the rest of the

way. Looking up, I met his gaze of pure anguish, those warm brown irises staring right back at me.

"You did perfectly, Asher. Now let me help." As he reached through the bars, bringing a metal cup of what I desperately hoped was water to my lips, I allowed myself to take him in. He titled the cup, water slowly filling my mouth, and I watched the way his jaw flexed in concentration. It was more square than Theon's version, his cheekbones higher and his skin paler. His curls were far more wild, like his sister's spun locks.

Too much water entered my mouth, my distraction causing me to choke. Panic flooded his face, his eyes widening and jaw going slack. I laughed through the burn in my throat, noticing how his shoulders slumped when I finally took a full breath. His torso was bare for some reason, the malnutrition he suffered obvious in his protruding collarbones and ribs.

Sterling set down the cup then. Those green-flecked brown irises flicked downwards momentarily before quickly returning to my own. I cocked my head to the left, the motion making my heart ache as I thought of whose habit I had adopted. All of that sorrow was quickly replaced with horror though, because Sterling's fingers were moving toward my chest. I jolted back, feeling my back cry out as more skin separated and ripped open. Sterling froze, his fingers inches from me.

"I am sorry, I was just trying to finish buttoning my shirt," he said.

His shirt?

Looking down, I realized why Sterling was bare chested. His dirty and torn shirt was on me, mostly hiding my skin beneath. But the top two buttons were left open, revealing the swell of my breasts.

"How did you get your shirt on me?" I asked, my voice hoarse. My arms shook with the effort it took to hold up my upper body, and I wondered if I would be better off just laying back down. But then Sterling let out a deep sigh, and all I could do was watch his eyes lose focus as he recalled what happened.

"Actually, it was not me. I assume you know who Malcolm is?" I nodded, the hiss that seemed to rattle my chest a startling sound. Sterling chuckled wryly before continuing. "Yeah, I am not a fan of his either. I did ask him if he would put it on you, though. Perhaps it was because I never ask anything of him, but he did it without question. Gentle does not begin to explain how he was with you. It was almost…familial. The care he afforded you, it was like a father with their small child."

Those words hung between us momentarily, Sterling's button nose scrunched and brows furrowed in thought. For my part, I could think of nothing but the way he had whispered to me upon the battlefield in Behman.

"I remember when these had points, you know."

"Well," the prince said, stealing my focus back, "it does not really matter. No amount of niceties can make up for what he has done to you. I am not attempting to sway you at all. I just thought you should know." His head leaned forward as he spoke, forehead touching the iron bars between us. Other than his eyes, jaw, and height, he was just like the Sterling who had severed my ribs and bruised my skin.

With a deep breath, I reminded myself of what I had learned. Theon had been masquerading as Sterling. He had been the one to hurt me. This Sterling, the real one, had been held captive. There was no reason to think he would hurt me. Not yet.

Nodding, I leaned towards him, watching as his hands once more moved through the bars. His fingers made quick work of the buttons, never touching my skin, and then he backed away. Offering me the space I wanted—needed. I tried to breathe through the fear, the memories of those hands—no, not those hands—around my neck.

"How did this happen to you?" This time my voice was a sad excuse for a whisper, the rasp of it so painful I choked on the final word. Sterling's lips pursed before he grabbed the cup once more and offered me another sip.

"Drink, then I will help you lie back down," he ordered.

Water halted the argument on the tip of my tongue, and I found myself thinking back to Genevieve's undying love for her younger brother. The desperation she so clearly felt to get him back. This man in front of me, he was the one who had earned that trust and love. It was that realization that had me gulping the lukewarm water and allowing him to help me lie down. When I was once more settled upon the stone floor, his voice rang, the first thread of Sterling's story being woven.

"When I turned eighteen, I left Maliha for the first time. My family is not devout, nor do they enjoy traveling, so there was never a reason to go anywhere before then. But I am a curious person, and I survive on the high of learning. Above all else, I seek to know more—to become so full on the knowledge of the world that I am bursting at my seams." Sterling's chest rose and fell in quick movements, his head still against the bars as he spoke. But he looked me in the eye as he told his story, his gaze never straying. It was as if he wished for me to know how important these words were to him.

"In four years, I saw the entirety of the Mortal Realm. Every kingdom, every castle, every mountain, every river. It was glorious and gratifying, so I gorged myself upon it all. Yet, when I returned home with notebooks full of what I had gleaned and maps so heavily marked they could no longer be read, I was still not full. More food was out there, if only I could taste it." Another humorless chuckle left his lips, and then he was sliding down the bars, adjusting himself to lie down. When his knees and nose were against the iron like mine, he continued. "It was that curiosity that was my true downfall."

Silence momentarily hugged us, the cold embrace a hollow feeling. I took the time to wonder what it must be like to know you have only a handful of decades to truly *live*. What must it be like, to live upon time that felt borrowed? To exist knowing death looms nearby, constantly waiting to steal you away from life's loving hold? To be mortal?

"Barely a year had passed before a letter came," Sterling finally said, a hint of anger in his voice now. "It was addressed to my father, but really, it was for me. And who would not want to marry a stunning creature from another realm? To see magic and live amongst beings greater than yourself?

28

I begged my parents to agree. In fact, I went to my knees, pleading that they afford me a new chance to learn. My sister was the real problem."

Genevieve? A small huff of surprise snuck through my clenched teeth, but that did not stop Sterling's story. Instead, he seemed unable to hear me. Though he looked me right in the eyes, I wondered if perhaps he was seeing another time, long ago. When life was worth living.

"She hated the idea of me going. My sister has always been the warrior, the politician, the born queen. I was not fit for those things. I wanted to remain moving, to never cease," a sad smile lifted the left corner of his mouth, rounding his cheek slightly. "In the end, I had been strong enough in my resolve to win that fight. After my parents sent their letter of agreement to the terms, I started plotting. They asked for one last year with me, though I had wished it would be less, honestly. Then, one month before I was meant to come to you, to start a life that I thought might finally satiate me, another letter came. This one was written in lovely script, with all of the letters connecting together and a small bit of ink spilled upon the bottom left corner. This one was from you, Asher."

I gasped, recalling the letter I had sent him so long ago. A letter written by a naïve princess who eagerly hoped she could learn to like her new match. Who desired to heal from the loss of the love of her life with a gift given by the guardians she thought loved her more than anything. "I forgot I wrote you that."

"I have it memorized. *Dear Prince Sterling Windsor, my name is Asher Daniox, and I am apparently to be your wife,*" he began, lifting his chin from his place on the floor. Ah, he had imagined me a haughty little thing then. I laughed, a series of coughs following the sound. He waited for my fit to end, reaching a hand through the bars to gently pat my back. I only flinched once at his touch, which my brain struggled to differentiate. After I had finally settled, he pulled his arm away, tucking his hands beneath his head and continuing. *"Though we have a lifetime of learning ahead of us, I would like to start now. Tell me, Sterling, what is your favorite color? Your favorite dish? What do you do when the sun sets and you have too much energy to sleep? Do you enjoy reading? What pastries exist within the confines of the mortal realm? I simply must know it all.*

29

In case you were curious, I am eagerly awaiting your arrival. I dare say we might just have some fun together. Most sincerely, Asher."

The two of us chuckled at the way his high-pitched imitation of my voice made my words seem almost scandalous. The Asher back then might have meant them that way, too. Not that I could recall. Nor would I ever be her again.

"You had me then. If any doubt had lingered, your words upon the page had pushed them far away. Like me, you wanted to know more. You *needed* to know more. Honestly, you could not have been more perfect in my eyes. The king and queen had given us more information on your abilities than we would have expected, and my parents were so very scared of you—Genevieve even more so. I was not though. All I could think was that I might have found myself a wife who craved knowledge and adventure like I did." Tone drowning in passion, Sterling did not seem to notice when my smile fell.

Would he wish to be my ally in this mess if he discovered just how much I had changed? Would he realize who was truly to blame for his suffering?

"Time passed excruciatingly slowly after that, like every hour was a mountain I had to climb without rope. So when the day came we were due to sail, I was riddled with anticipation. I can still feel my mother's embrace, my father's firm handshake, and my sister's forehead below my lips. They deserved better than a son that would force them into such a mess." When I opened my mouth to disagree, Sterling let out a soft shushing noise, not letting his story be silenced. "We sailed first to Isle Healer. I did not get to see much before our ship was approved for travel to the center island, but I did watch a woman slice on her palm and offer it to a small boy. The tiny little one smiled so bright the sun seemed to dim. Then he touched her palm, closed his eyes, and he *healed* her."

Wonder, so much wonder floated from his mouth and blew away in the phantom wind of his imagination. Sterling had been the epitome of joy—of curiosity and light and *life*. As I looked at the man before me now,

I realized just how little of that spark still existed within him. Mia had snuffed out his fire, and now he threatened to fizzle out.

"I saw the golden palace before I even saw the land. It was ostentatious to say the least. But oh how I eagerly awaited the moment we docked. In my arms I carried books upon books for you, ones I thought would bring a smile to your face or a wrinkle to your brow. In my pocket rested my grandmother's ring, which she had gifted me before she died ten years past. Looking at the palace, I recalled regretting that the band was gold, because the color seemed too monotonous. But the sapphire shined bright, the diamonds on either side even brighter. You would have liked it, I think. But you were not there when we arrived."

Where had I been? What had I deemed more important? I could not recall now.

"They took me straight from the docks to the palace, my four guards and I so clearly out of place that the fae seemed eager to hide us away. But the thick golden curtains and the cold golden tub could not hold my interest for long. Although, I did fully expect your lake to run gold, and I found myself staring off in the distance through my window to peek," he admitted with a soft chuckle. His head lulled back to the ground, our eyes still locked but his mind elsewhere. "After hours had passed and I had fully unpacked, someone finally came to retrieve me. They took me to a grand room with a long golden table. The ceilings were higher than I had ever seen with four-tiered chandeliers dangling above, and still I struggled to take my eyes off of you, Asher."

"You were sat across from Queen Mia, her grace and poise on full display as that icy gaze tracked my every movement. But you did not notice me as you leaned towards a male with wavy black hair and the most outrageous golden crown atop his head—your king. Every word he spoke seemed to transfix you, as if he were an idol you had the chance to look upon. I watched with awe when he said something that made you laugh, your humor bleeding into the air and making us all feel lighter. I could see how someone might become intoxicated by such a creature. How I, after so many years of being so impossibly unsettled, might finally breathe fully in your presence. But it was when you looked up at me, your big gray eyes

wide and your power pulsing from you, that I realized I was going to marry the most extraordinary being in the entire world."

Cheeks heating, I tried and failed to swallow down the odd sense of pride that swelled within me. "Yes well, you would have made fantastic arm candy. I had thought you were quite handsome that first night."

His pupils widened slightly, as if he were finally coming back to his current, bleak reality. Instead of looking stricken, the prince laughed once more, the sound bringing a smile to my face.

"Are you kidding me? That would have been a dream. If you wanted me to be a trophy and raise our children while you saved the world and ruled over everyone? Perfect. I would have done so without hesitation." Thoughts of a future that would never be brought the two of us to the natural end of Sterling's story—the hard truth and painful epilogue. "That never happened though. No, after a night of us getting lost in conversations of our favorite books and preferences in weather and even some rather impressive jokes on your end, I was not afforded your hand as I thought. Instead, Xavier called the meal's end and Mia encouraged you off to bed. Too afraid to protest, I had watched as you nodded and turned to me, offering a small smile and a kiss to my cheek before you stood."

Neither of us could deny the way the air charged with terror, how this part of the tale was the beginning of the end. It was haunting, to watch that emotion play out on the prince's face. The scrunch of his nose and tight closing of his eyes. The way his hands balled into fists and his jaw ticked. How I wished to rip the blocker off and soothe him, to steal those thoughts and memories away so he might know the peace that was taken from him. All I could do was watch though, as Sterling recalled the day his dreams came crashing down.

"Your power had barely faded from the room before Xavier stood, his face suddenly stern. The empty seat beside me that once held your brightness felt more like a last barrier then, like the only thing standing between me and the monster beneath a king's crown. But, like I think he often is, Xavier was the distraction, not the danger. Vines had shot so quickly across the table that I had no time to even register the action. Like

the goodbyes from my family, I can still feel the way her vines slithered up my skin and squeezed around my throat—I fear it is something I will never forget. And then, as if a villain in a storybook, a male—Theon—walked in. Forced to watch in horror, I bore witness to a Shifter's power for the first time as he morphed not into a beast, but into *me*. It was sickening, seeing him take on my features with that chilling smile. Those vines tightened before I could scream, my vision going black. The last thing I remember hearing before I awoke here was Mia's melodious voice informing me that it was 'nothing personal.' The first time they let Theon beat me sure did feel personal, though."

Twin tears, one his and one my own, hit the stone floor at the same time, their splashes nearly silent. This boy before me had wanted nothing but to fill his short life with adventure and learning. Such a simple desire, one I understood deeply. Yet, he was instead afforded such pain that he would never be the same. The mere thought of it made my stomach turn.

"Sterling, I am so sorry. I am going to get you out of here. I have met your family, and they are desperate to get you back. If it is the last thing I do, I *will* bring you home." A shift in the air was all I felt before a voice rang through the dungeons.

"No, Asher. All he can ask for now is a clean death. Perhaps you can give him that."

CHAPTER FIVE

ASHER

Malcolm stood beyond the bars, his body clad in Eoforhild blue—the blue of a realm he betrayed. How tragic, to know the love of a family and take it for granted in such a way. To let whatever greed ran through him taint his Ayad blood green.

Staring up into his black eyes now was like seeing the darkness that seemed to haunt us all, as if it had overrun him in his quest for more than he was given. His skin was dull, almost lifeless. His hair was cropped short, though I could tell by the way the curls laid on his cheeks and over his ears that he was in need of a trim.

"How are you feeling?" His soft tone took me by surprise, the genuine kindness coating the words like a slap across the face after his

comment moments ago. With a furrow of his brow, Malcolm bent down, letting his elbows rest on his knees and his hands hang. "What is that face for, pretty little thing?"

An involuntary growl barreled through my teeth, rattling my bones and giving me the strength to sit up. Whatever they were poisoning me with had slowed my healing drastically, but that would not stop me from ripping apart the male before me.

"Apologies, scum, I cannot say I am as talented at hiding my feelings as I once was. Perhaps what you see upon my face right now is the utter disgust I feel at your nearness." My words were more of a hiss than I intended them to be, and I felt that pang of heart-wrenching sadness at the realization that I sounded like a certain creature of death.

Sterling chuckled beside me, his sardonic humor an echo that momentarily left the three of us frozen in place. Malcolm was the first to break from the trance, his answered smack of the bars shaking my cell. His glare could have cut through flesh and bone, but it was not on me. No, he reserved the murderous look for the mortal prince to my left. When his gaze returned to me, it softened slightly, a sort of sadness there in his onyx irises.

I wanted to gouge them out and feed them to him for his utter audacity.

"Asher, there is no reason to be so hostile. Your mother will be coming soon, and it is important that you repent. Apologize for your crimes and then everything can go back to the way it was. That is all she wants."

With a guttural cry of agony, I forced myself to my feet, that anger that had always simmered within me boiling over and masking the nausea that rolled through me from the blocker. "She is *not* my mother."

Sterling's hand reached out, trying and failing to grab hold of me. "Asher, do not—"

"Tell me, what sin have I committed? Was it when I finally opened my eyes and stood up to someone who has abused me for centuries? Was

it when I decided that the murder of innocents was not worth the power of a crown upon my head?" I flashed the demon before me a smile, the baring of my teeth a menacing and feral look. On shaky legs I walked towards Malcolm, grabbing the bars and staring up at him with all the hatred of a world held prisoner. "Or is my apology supposed to be for my traitorous ways? Will you get on your knees and apologize to your father? Will you repent for the great atrocities committed by your hand? Will you visit the grave of the demons you slaughtered? How does their blood feel upon your hands, Prince Malcolm Ayad?"

All semblance of kindness left his face then, fury furrowing his brow and tightening his lips. His hand shot through the bars, grabbing my throat just below the blocker and lifting me. I gagged, choking on the way air tried to dig down my throat with no success. My fingers rose, desperately clawing at his grip on my neck.

"Let her go!" Sterling screamed, the sound of him rattling the bars between us fading as my vision speckled with black.

"You know nothing about what I do for my blood. But I promise you will, Asher," he seethed, the threat so ridiculous that I could not stop the strained chuckles that begged for freedom of my chest. My crackling laughter split the tension, or maybe it doubled it. In his surprise, Malcolm loosened his grip, and I greedily took the chance.

"Would it not be funny if I died here before I could do your queen's bidding and finally make your miserable existence mean something?" I asked between laughs. And then I was thrown to the ground. I landed hard on my right hip, my body crumpling as I bit down a scream of pain. With a smile far stronger than I felt, I looked up at the mortal prince beyond my iron bars. "I think I struck a nerve."

For a moment he merely stared at me in horror, but then, as if he could not help himself, Sterling smiled back. "Yes, well, perhaps we can keep score."

We burst into laughter at that, neither of us quite caring about our empty stomachs or our bruised bodies as we leaned towards the bars that

separated us. Malcolm seethed from beyond, clearly not enjoying our comradery. That, or he was irritated by just how right I was.

All I could do was continue laughing, my head lulling forward and my throat burning. It was odd to care so little about my current predicament. For once in my pathetic life, I was not worried about how my actions—or in this case, lack thereof—would affect the world or the realm or those around me. Stress and anxiety did not consume me at the mere thought of the inevitably disastrous future. Maybe it was my faith in Bellamy's ability to save the world, or it could have been the fact that this heavy life might finally end. Whatever it was, I relished in this newfound liberty.

Though I knew I was never normal, feeling more free than I ever had whilst behind bars was a new version of strange.

"Well, at least I can confirm you still have your fire." That deep and warm voice was enough to silence me once more. With a gasp, I turned back towards Malcolm, my eyes catching on the approaching figure just beyond him. "Leave them be, Malcolm. I will be taking Ash anyways."

Xavier approached my iron cage with all the grace of a warrior—his presence that of a sharpened blade ready to cut through pride and joy and hope. As formidable as ever, the fae king stood tall and firm, his dark black waves kissing his shoulder and his golden crown of fire resting atop his head. As always, he was dressed in head-to-toe gold, the silk loose around his strong physique and clashing with his pale skin. He had grown out his facial hair, the bottom half of his face now covered in dark stubble. Dark eyes bore into me, watching as I assessed him with what looked almost like despair. I would believe it if I did not know better, but—unfortunately for him—I had learned in my time away.

Even more surprising than Xavier's appearance in the dungeons was Malcolm's response to the king. From my spot on the ground of my cell I could just make out the sound of his teeth grinding. His brow was furrowed and his eyes squinted, his square jaw clenched just as his fists were. He seemed...on edge.

"I said, leave them be," Xavier ordered, his voice a booming demand that echoed across the stone all around us. To my utter bafflement, the demon did not portal away. Instead, he turned to his left, looking down upon the king before him with enough fury that even my tempered magic could sense it.

"You will do well to remember what is *yours* and what is *mine.*" Then, as if Xavier's response would be of little consequence, Malcolm turned to face me once more. A desperation remained dormant in his gaze, one that made the hairs on my neck rise. "Apologize to your mother, Asher."

With that, the demon disappeared into smoky shadows. Xavier let out a furious growl, swatting at the shadows with his hands as if the action would somehow hurt Malcolm. When the tendrils of Moon magic finally faded, the king approached my cell door. A scream begged for freedom within my chest at the sight. Once, Xavier had been my role model. Like Sterling had said, I used to look at my father-figure as the most extraordinary being in the entire world. More than my desire to please them both was my wish to be them. Now I would rather die than become the nightmares they were.

"Ash, I have missed you so much. Come, we are going to get this whole situation sorted out," he assured. I watched in disgust as he smiled widely at me, a single dimple showing on his cheek that made me grind my teeth.

He was Bellamy's *father.* After two hundred years of being ridden with guilt for surviving an attack their son did not, it was jarring to say the least knowing what I did now. And heartbreaking. Not only had they abused me and lied to me my entire life, but they also willingly let me suffer in the pain of survivor's guilt. They did not consider how anything they did would affect me. Not to mention how little regard they showed their son.

Perhaps the me of a year ago would have blamed Bellamy too. Maybe I would have felt anger at his lies and careful truths. But after everything I had been through, I could not bring myself to do anything but love him. He might not have been raised by the king and queen, but even

in the short time they had called him theirs, they had harmed him in unspeakable ways.

If it was the last thing I did, I would give him vengeance. I would end the beings who dared treat him with such disregard.

"I am not going anywhere with *you,*" I seethed at Xavier as he pulled a set of iron keys from his pocket. The clinking sound of them smacking into one another made my head pound, and my back still cried out in pain from careless movements. Sterling shuffled to my left, his trousers scraping against the stone beneath us as he scooted closer to our shared bars.

Ignoring me completely, Xavier slid one of the keys into the lock and turned it, pulling open the cell door with a great groan of protest from the iron. Though his smile had fallen, there was still far too much hope within his dark brown eyes. He approached me slowly, his hands raised. "All I want is to speak with you. Just let me get you out of here. I have some clean clothes for you, and Mia awaits us. Please, Ash. Come with me and make this easier on us all."

With that, he reached out a hand, a slight tremble to his fingers. As if he really cared. What a ridiculous act. On instinct, I slapped it away, letting out a low growl. "Get your hands away from me."

"You better listen to her, or so help me I wi—"

"You will what, mortal? Threaten me with more words? Perhaps insult my cock? I think I will survive," Xavier said, cutting off Sterling's threat. Then, like I was nothing but an insolent youngling, the king grabbed my bicep and lifted me. I slammed my fist into his chest, my back burning and my body aching as he dragged me out of my cell. Sterling screamed from behind us, pounding on the cell bars. In one last-ditch effort, I tried to use my magic. The attempt sent piercing waves of pain through me. "Stop fighting me, Ash."

With that, I promptly dove forward, slamming my head into his. The move must have been Xavier's last straw, because, with a furious shout, he turned and smashed his fist into my face.

***

"She has been asleep for far too long, Tish!" The shouts came from a melodic voice I knew all too well. Mia was close by, her tone full of worry making me want to cut out her tongue. But when I tried to move my hands, I found myself unable to do so. They had shackled me.

"No, she is awake, actually," Tish whispered, her voice broken and shaky. Never before had I heard her sound so horribly ill, but I could not bring myself to care when I knew just how much she had aided in not only my own pain, but Sterling's as well. "Asher, you need to be careful. You are healed, but I was only able to do so much in my…state. If you are not careful, you can hurt yourself further."

With that, I felt a small, cold hand tap my arm and then heard the sound of retreating footsteps. I strained my ears, trying to determine just how many others were nearby. Two sets of breathing, so offbeat from one another that it had to be Mia and Xavier, sounded nearby. How had I ever believed that they were a good team? A united pair? It was clear now just how impossibly naïve I had been.

"Asher, are you really awake?" Xavier's deep voice boomed, making the question sound far more like a demand. I remained still, wishing that they would simply leave me in the dungeons to rot rather than subject me to their presence.

"Of course she is awake, you idiot." Another set of cold fingers, these ones clammy and thin, met my skin. Every ounce of my willpower was still not enough to stop me from cringing at the way Mia caressed my cheek—ever the doting mother.

Fake, all of it. I had never once allowed myself to imagine a day that I would be faced with the chilling reality of Mia's utter detachment. How could someone pretend day in and day out to care for another while secretly harboring the belief that the one they faked affection for was a tool to them?

40

I was a means to an end, a shovel to dig the dirt of her garden so she may plant more beautiful flowers.

"Do not touch me," I hissed, finally allowing my eyes to open. The light of Xavier's fire burned as I adjusted to the sight around me. The walls were gray, similar to my low level room though we were not there. This area was larger and absent of the jagged symbols that marked my room. The only beings I could see were the royals.

Mia and Xavier said they loved me for two centuries, and now there they stood, looking down upon my chained body. As if I were nothing but a pet who had acted out. Pointless was the denial of such a thing.

"Asher, you need to calm down. We are only trying to set things right." Xavier's tone was soothing, just as it always had been post punishment. When I was blamed for the pain and agony and self-hatred they had bestowed upon me.

"Can you for one moment simply shut your ridiculous mouth so that I can get done what must be done?" Mia asked, her teeth bared in a snarl. Xavier puffed his chest, golden silk stretching across his muscled torso. His black waves still hung loose, his dark eyes glaring at his wife as if he could end her with a stare. She huffed, turning to face me. I stared into those icy blue eyes, hating myself for not knowing who Bellamy truly was. For not guessing, at least. "You will stop this nonsense immediately. Punishment has been doled out, and now we must once more unite for our realm. This is not a game, Asher. You are all that stands between us and the demons. You might think them good and just, but all you know is what they have spun, what they have—"

"How dare you!" I shouted, thrashing against the chains upon my ankles and wrists, my head smacking into the table below me. "You lay me out like a body within a morgue, chain me like a beast, and speak to me as if I am a youngling no more than five! But I know what lies you have woven, I know the truth you desire to keep hidden. Do not for one moment think anything but death will stop me from fighting you."

Rage clouded Mia's eyes and pinched her face. Then her hand soared down, striking my cheek and ear. The impact was so forceful that my head whipped to the right, slamming into the table. I bit back the scream that barged up my throat and into my teeth, a ring sounding in my ear that made me dizzy.

"How dare *you!* I am all you have in this world—practically your mother. You will do as I say because that is the duty of a daughter. That is the duty of a princess!"

"The moment you release me I will tear your filthy black heart from your chest, you bitch!"

"Then you can remain chained for the rest of your life! If you want to fight, *my flower*, we will fight. But I will win, and I will show you fear like you have never known." Her words were a threat, but I could not summon that terror she used to bring out of me.

There was no hesitation in my eerie smile, my magic a distant hum in my veins despite the blocker and the poison I knew had to be within my system once more. With a light chuckle, I looked up into her eyes and spoke the words I knew she so wished I would never utter—the one thing she begged I might never realize. "I do not fear. I am the thing to fear."

Xavier's answering gasp was made all the sweeter by Mia's slight stumble as she backed away from me. Finally, after two centuries, I had discovered just how powerful I was. And I would not let them treat me like a weapon when I could now wield myself.

After a few moments of silence that seemed filled with charged energy, Mia finally cleared her throat and spoke through clenched teeth. "You think yourself invincible now that you have bore witness to life outside these walls of safety, but I promise you this: the world does not offer kindness to the ignorant. And neither do I."

CHAPTER SIX

BELLAMY

Adbeel was *staring.*

I tried to feign ignorance as I chewed, opting for indifference when that failed. But in the end, I found myself looking up at him from across the table, our gazes colliding. As seemed the norm for this last week, I was looked at with both pity and fury.

"Say it," I told him, casually grabbing my cup of wine and bringing it to my lap. No doubt he knew what I was doing, but I still pretended I was being sly as I slowly poured in the lavender liquid. Adbeel frowned, but did not speak like I hoped. With a deep sigh, I brought my hand up and pinched the bridge of my nose. What I would give to just sit in my chambers and burn. "Do not go quiet on me now. Not when you clearly have so much scolding to do."

With that, I attempted to toss back the entire cup of wine, desperately needing to feel it further warm my already scalding body so I would not feel this aching torment of her absence. At least then I would be able to stomach whatever ridiculous venture Nicola Salvatore was sending us on. A blast of light hit the cup and knocked it from my hands, jarring me from my thoughts. I stared down at the red puddle with complete and utter devastation. Then a loud smack sounded from across the table, forcing my eyes to focus on Adbeel's hand upon the table as he sneered my way.

"You will not do this, Bell! You will not lose yourself after so many decades of searching for who you are. I know what it is like to lose the love of your life, but you have an entire realm to think about right now. We are preparing for *war*." Each word seemed more strained than the last, as if he were choking on the truth of our world.

Yes, war would come, and if I did not follow through with Nicola's plan then Asher might be on the opposite side of the chaos. That was not an option. Especially not as I heard the echoes of Ash's mental voice.

You will win this war, even if that means facing off against me on the battlefield. Even if that means killing me.

Never.

"I know this, Adbeel. Asher's magic reminds me of my duty every day. I wake up with my head swimming in a river of strategies and rage. Daily, I am swarmed with thoughts of death and battle. There is not a moment that goes by in which I am not completely overwhelmed by it all. Trust me when I say that losing this war is *not* an option." I practically growled the words, my anger rising. If only I could go back to not caring about the wretched world, but apparently no one would allow me that kindness.

"Bellamy, I am concerned. You are…fading. I cannot bear to watch you disappear again—to say goodbye to another son as he falls victim to the darkness. Please, tell me what I can do for you. Let me help," he pleaded, reaching both hands out towards me.

I froze, wondering how on Alemthian it had come to this. To Adbeel practically begging me to accept help. I thought back to when he forced me to join the military, when he had told me there was no other option and that I needed an outlet before I was lost forever. Now, here I was once more, seeking a map that had been burned away by Asher herself—the only path to her now nothing but dust.

Help. I could accept such a thing. There was nothing wrong with needing that, right? I had gotten help from my Trusted, from Adbeel, from so many. What was a little more in the face of the end of the world?

"Actually," I conceded with a sigh, "I could use the assistance. You will not like it."

"Anything, Bellamy. Anything."

Nodding, I let loose another heavy breath and asked for the help I needed.

"Would you be able to remain in Pike for the day and watch over the training sessions? All soldiers are out there now sparring, but soon they will begin breaking out into groups. They could use a firm hand and I could use Damon during this meeting I must have."

Adbeel went visibly rigid, annoyance momentarily flitting across his face and pinching his brow before he contained it. Rolling his neck, he ran a hand through his mahogany curls and straightened his black tunic.

"And where, pray tell, are you going?"

"I will not be long. Asher has made sure I am allowed to do very little other than win this war," I remarked with an eyeroll. Not that the raging sea of agony within my chest was as simple and inconsequential as the action made it seem. Adbeel seemed to see that, and I watched with relief as he nodded silently before getting up.

"I am so sorry for what you have lost, Bellamy. Take the day, do what you must, and then come home." With that, he walked away.

I thought about telling him then of the future Pino had shown me. So much time had been wasted this last year, time that Pino had warned me against taking. My selfishness, Asher's fears, all of it had led us to this horrible fate. But how much worse would telling them separately make this? Instead of speaking, I let him leave, thinking all the while how terribly wrong I had been.

There was no such thing as a world for dreamers.

***

"Well you are pissing me off, Bellamy!" Noe shouted, shoving me backwards. I stumbled slightly but kept my ground, letting her come at me again. "You do not make choices for us. She is *ours* too. I refuse to stay behind this time!"

When the Moon attempted to swing her fist at my jaw, Damon grabbed her around the waist, lifting her slightly and pulling her away from me. I would have taken it, though I think Damon knew that and did not want to put more strain on Ranbir than he had already suffered through this last week.

Too bad, I had really been looking forward to the pain.

"What she means," Henry interjected, lifting his hands up in surrender, "is that we deserve to go with you. We have no idea how dangerous this will be. You, Damon, and Lian cannot go alone. Cyprus, Noe, Ranbir, and I want to come too. Let us be there at your side."

"Our family has been so scattered this last year," Lian added. "We are meant to stick together. It should be all of us or none of us."

"Well you all know damn well that it cannot be none of us." I reached out a hand, waiting with a scowl for them to come to me. When

the six of them finally shuffled forward and huddled around me, I called to the poison in my veins and willed it to take us to my ship.

The second we landed I stormed away from them, clinging to what little sanity remained within me. I wanted so desperately to be alone. To wallow and beg the stars for a different ending to this gods forsaken story.

Yet, I also knew that if it were not for my family I would have already ended it all.

Because of that, I tried my hardest not to scream in outrage. We did not actually all need to be here. None of us knew what Nicola had in store, but I doubted that she was about to put us in danger when she likely knew what I meant to Asher. If only I could have convinced them that.

Furious footsteps stomped towards me, the sound of scuffing shoes a sign that it was Noe who was coming to finish me off. She had done that since she was five. Forever, really.

"You are our prince, our general, our leader, and our brother. What you are not is a dictator." I scoffed at her words, turning to face her. Her long golden brown hair caught the wind as we set sail, her light brown skin practically glowing in the light of midday. Despite how pristine she was from the neck up, her training leathers were still worn and ragged from the last battle. We would not have Pino around to fix them now. He had drastically improved them after that day at Reader River, and now it felt wrong to consider having anyone else modify them again. "I need you to understand how different this all is now."

"I do understand. You all want to find her. I do too."

"It is not just that. Ash…she is our queen now. Perhaps not by right or by law, but in our hearts she is. Maybe fate was always dragging us towards her. Venturae could be up in the Above, wielding fate and forcing us to follow Asher as we are meant to." Noe shrugged, picking at her nails as she leaned over the ledge beside me.

I sighed, turning to face the open sea as she did. Grabbing her hand, the two of us relaxed and summoned our shadows. I willed mine to coat

the ship, and then I thought of the coordinates, the map I had been using tucked away in my pocket for now. But Noe and I knew where we were going, even if she was not supposed to come. Breathing heavily, I shoved the shadows further around us, widening the circle so that it covered the entirety of the wood beneath our feet. Noe's shadows moved at double the speed, her strength an incredible thing to witness. When we had adequately coated the ship, the two of us closed our eyes and willed our shadows to take us where we wanted to go.

We landed somewhere west of Eoforhild, deep in the Ibidem Sea. The cold here bit into my skin like death itself, burrowing into my bones. Behind Noe and I, Damon and Lian began arguing.

"Lian, for once, can you just listen to what you are told?" Damon seethed, the tone of his voice telling me that Lian was doing what she did best: disobeying direct orders.

"You are telling me to do stupid things, so no, I cannot," she paused, letting out a quiet cough before deepening her voice in a mock version of his, "do what I am told and be a boring little twat with no brains. So sorry old boy, cannot comply."

A small laugh escaped my lips, enough for Noe to look over to me. Her form was radiant from my periphery, even with the daunting gray skies and matching seas as a backdrop. Despite how beautiful she looked, as she always did, I knew that Noe was hurting just as I was. I had known her almost my entire life, neither of us could hide sorrow from one another.

"I have been thinking about the dress."

"What dress?" Turning fully towards her, I caught her gaze just in time to see a mischievous sparkle light her hazel eyes. Oh gods. When she did not immediately answer, my nerves lit into a fiery inferno. I would not like what she had to say, clearly. "Noe, tell me."

"Well, before he…passed, Pino and I had been working on a dress for Asher. A wedding dress." There it was. I knew it would be heartbreaking, but I had not realized how deeply it would tear me apart. I had seen glimpses of the dress that day at Reader River. Small white buttons

had trailed up her spine, the train dragging behind her in a sea of silk. From the small view of her backside, I had realized she did not wear a veil, finally free of her need to hide.

Somehow, I had stolen my own future from myself. The best one I could have ever asked for, gone in the blink of an eye.

Noe let out an odd sound, almost like a hum. I blinked, staring at her in confusion. She only furrowed her brow, looking at me as if I were making the noise. The truth of what was happening hit us both at the same time, but it was too late.

Somewhere in the distance, a siren began to sing.

"Henry, do not listen!" I screamed, running towards his place at the helm. But Henry's eyes were glazing over, the green dulling as he stared off to our right. I portaled to him, appearing on his left just as he violently turned the ship to the right. My feet flew out from beneath me, and then my face was smashing into the wood below, my nose letting out a loud crunch that had me dizzy. I thought of Asher, her fist connecting with my face and the fire returning to her eyes.

We could not get sucked in by a siren. We could not die. We needed to follow through with Nicola's plans.

But all I could do was wince and listen as words began to form from the eerie voice.

"Come to me, heed my song.

Raise your sails, follow along.

Lay your heads, upon my chest.

Come to me, seek your rest.

Upon my shore, your joy shall reign.

Here in my arms, you will feel no pain."

With a furious scream, I pushed myself up and shoved Henry to the side, willing my mental shields to burn away the song. But the moment I had Henry down, Noe appeared beside me in a burst of shadows. She gripped the helm tightly, continuing to steer us towards the creature who wished to rip us apart with their fucking teeth.

Henry grabbed me from behind, wrapping his arms around me and willing me to submit. My shouts were loud, the sound of them a violent echo against the harsh sea. I felt the moment Lian began using her Air power to propel us forward, the whip of Noe's hair a sharp sound. I fought harder against Henry, breaking free momentarily and then being forced back down when Damon came at me. The back of my head hit something hard, my nose still pouring blood. Dizziness seemed to overcome me, and my shields blew out like a candle in a windstorm.

All of the fight in me stopped as the siren continued to sing to us, begging us to come to them. They promised us such safety, such beautiful comfort. Perhaps that was where we needed to be. Maybe they could find Asher and keep my family safe. They seemed so lovely, the siren with the voice of an enchantress. Yes, I could feel the truth there in their song. Whoever they were, I now thought it impossible for them to do anything other than help me.

I was so lucky they found me. They were going to fix *everything*.

With a smile, I shuffled away from Damon and Henry, leaning my head against the wood in wait.

The wait turned out to be quite short. Soon we approached an island, a ship bobbing in the water nearby. The sea was calmer here at the edge of oblivion, so much nothingness in the distance that it felt like perhaps the world never existed at all. Each of us bore bright smiles and straight backs. We eagerly readied for our fate.

In the back of my head, a fierce throbbing began, as if I were being punished somehow. No one else seemed to flinch as I did. What was happening? I gripped my temples as the pain intensified, my head

swimming in the agony. A new voice sounded, drowning out that of the siren beyond.

I am choosing you, Bell. For once, I am. Do not let them win this. Live.

I bent over, gasping at the sound of Asher's voice as her magic fought off the siren.

You will win this war.

My submission to death was breaking her rules. I was disobeying orders just as Lian had.

Asher's magic was about to save us all.

Ducking down, I quickly shuffled across the deck, swiping up Lian's wooden bow and her leather quiver of arrows before ducking behind a barrel. Asher's voice grew louder, the pain piercing now. Her words became new, not from memory, but as if The Manipulator herself existed within my mind somehow.

Kill them. Kill them all.

A burst of shadows popped into existence before my family, and from them walked a female. She was around Noe's height, her deep bronze skin and equally brown curls making her teeth look so white they almost hurt my eyes. She wore a billowing cream top, the laces undone so that the low cut of the collar exposed the top of her breasts. Her pants looked leather, matching the quiver at my side. Her boots were a soft brown, sticking to her like a second skin all the way up to her knee.

She did not speak, instead moving her hands and fingers, her whole body really.

Sign, she was using sign. So then she likely was not the siren. Maybe their captain? But wait. Fuck. I did not know sign.

The female sighed as if her life was far harder than it should be, and I watched with bewilderment as shadows surrounded her. Then, from

within them, walked five more beings. She looked at them with unabashed glee, like what they were about to do to us made her happy. It must have, because why else would she be using a siren to call ships to her?

I watched as she quickly signed something to who I assumed were her crew before walking over to the edge and letting shadows seep from her fingers. She reached them down into the sea below before tugging them like a rope. As she did, another female emerged. She was soaked completely, her dress the color of clear waters as it dripped and clung to her. Her hair was long and black, cascading down her body. A smile curved her lips, cutting open her face to reveal the beast beneath.

Her song seemed to soften, but within my head Asher's magic still valiantly beat the shit out of me. The others still seemed dazed as they watched the siren approach, still transfixed by her voice.

"Can we make this quick? I am starving and I want to be gone before Dima starts gnawing on their bones so I do not lose my appetite," the one with blonde hair said just as she sent a beam of light from her fingertips, allowing it to wrap around my Trusted like a rope. It was an impressive bit of magic.

With a final breath, I lit an arrow and prepared to end them.

But then a raven swooped down, circling me once before dropping a piece of rolled paper. The note hit my forehead, bounding down to the ground and slightly rolling after. I snatched it up, hastily unrolling it.

Dear Idiot Prince,

Gods, she was kind of rude.

I told you, take your bags of gold and pay for their trust. This pirate captain is not one to be messed with, but she is also your only hope of rescuing Asher. Heed my warning when I say that the future is not set in stone. As of now, it is not only your death that I see. Asher will not survive what is to come if you do not succeed.

Nicola Salvatore

P.S. Captain Perdita Harligold just might find your beheading of a cockless male atop a snowy mountainside interesting.

A cockless—what?

Harligold. Where had I heard that name?

"Well, well. What is a sexy thing like you doing hiding over here?" I flinched at the sound of the blonde female's voice above me, realizing I had allowed myself to be distracted. Pirates, I fucking hated them.

Wait.

Pirates. Harligold. The demons that attacked us last winter! Asher said they were practically pirates, looting and trading mortal lives. Was…was their captain related to this captain? How would us having killed him help?

The female whistled above me, reaching down a hand to push a loose strand of black hair out of my face. Her fingers grazed my temple, and it took everything in me not to break it. She smiled down at me, her teeth slightly crooked and her eyes as black as the darkness that lurked in the depths of the sea below.

Sighing, I stood, holding the magic and power within me at bay. That was when I realized that the knife that was Asher's magic had stopped stabbing me in the brain. A part of me missed it, that small piece of her. Another part of me raged at the fact that she had stolen my choice from me. Shaking off that bitter thought, I pasted on my smirk, willing the once rakish prince to resurface.

"Hey now, beautiful. I was not hiding, I was waiting to be found. Two very different things." She scoffed, but I saw the way she leaned closer to me, how she seemed to draw in a deeper breath. Just as she reached out her finger and dragged it down my chest, another sharp whistle rang from behind her. My eyes flicked to the source, watching as who I assumed was Captain Harligold approached. She looked less than amused, her lip lifted in a sneer and her glare flicking between the female and me.

Good, that meant two of us were really fucking mad.

Before she made it to us I lifted my hand, summoning my shadows and calling to the two bags of coin I had laced with my essence earlier. The sky-blue velvet sacks were heavy, weighing down my hand and making it bob. But my face remained cocky—unbothered.

"Hello, Captain Harligold. It is so very lovely to meet you," I said, smirking at her narrowed gaze. The female before me lifted a brow and turned to her captain. Intrigue consumed me momentarily as I watched the blonde's hands fly through signs, moving so quickly that I wondered how the Captain could possibly understand. But understand she did.

Her head whipped back my way, suspicion flooding her face and briefly washing away the animosity. I had forgotten how much I loved surprising people.

"I am here with a proposition for you," I offered, my eyes flicking to the blonde as she once more translated for me. Captain Harligold watched as well, responding with even quicker movements.

"She says you look like an idiot and she does not particularly like what few things stupid people have to offer." Harligold snapped at her crew member, signing something again before pointing at me. "She also says she

likes cunt and that even a face as pretty as yours would not fool her into wanting to be within ten feet of the worm that hangs between your legs."

A laugh escaped me, sending air up my nose and causing me to snort. Asher would like this female.

The conclusion came involuntarily, but it did what all thoughts of her did, burned me from the inside out. Of course, I did what I did best, I reveled in the pain.

"Well, seeing as my rather large cock is already spoken for, I think we will be fine. What I offer is gold." I held up the two sacks, letting them both stare in bafflement before willing them to disappear in a puff of black.

The captain looked from my hand, to my face, and then honed in on my ears. Ah, this would be interesting. Her next few signs were a bit slower, almost smug in their execution. The blonde cackled loudly as her head flew back, gaining the attention of everyone aboard the ship. My Trusted remained calmly tied up, the six of them waiting for orders for once. Within my veins, foreign Moon magic thrummed to a war beat that did not exist, as if eager for blood to be shed.

"She wants to know what she can do for The Elemental."

CHAPTER SEVEN

ASHER

Day four.

Excruciating. That was the only word that could describe this pain. In truth, I did not realize Mia had such a talent for torture—or that she had the guts to inflict this level of damage with her own two hands. The whipping I understood. Perhaps I even expected it. But the first snapping of bone as she screamed at me to submit was the moment I finally understood the lengths she would go for power.

Not that the knowledge of such a thing did much for me as I leaned against the bars of my cell, my leg bent at an odd angle and my left hip bone peeking through my shredded leathers.

"I spy something black," Sterling said passively. I took in a heaving breath, the rattling sound reminding both of us that my lungs were not healing as quickly as they should. The blocker and the poison they were likely feeding me were doing a fine job of keeping me weak.

"Is it…the…rock…two feet to the left of…the wall sconce?" I asked, staring at the expanse of dark rock that made up the dungeon walls.

"Nope." Darn, I should have picked the one two and a half feet to the left. With a sigh, I curled in on myself slightly, silently begging for death to just fucking take me already. "Ash, we talked about this. You have to stay awake until Tish comes to heal you."

A groan left my lips, the sound muffled by the sloshing of air hitting my flooded lungs. It burned, horribly so. But of course, I had to be strong. Just as I always had to be. My entire life I was told to be more than I was. Many thought that my magic made me special, but my body knew better— I was just the same as everyone else. The blood that leaked dutifully from my leg was a scarlet reminder that I was nothing more than an average fae.

I was no god.

That thought brought me back to the memory of Padon laughing after I stabbed him in the heart. "Do you…know anything of…the gods?"

"The gods? Yes, actually. I spent quite a long time with my nose buried in texts within the walls of the Temple of Gods," he answered, his tone nonchalant. Before I could say anything else, I heard the prince shuffle and his voice ring out once more. "Though, I spent far more time with my cock buried in faithfuls."

His laughter rang through the dungeons as I scoffed, my own chuckles impossible to hide. Especially as pain from the movement made them sound strangled and weak.

"Will you tell…me about them?" My question came out strained and slow, the words feeling as if they would break through my clenched teeth. Eternity spare me, my leg hurt. So badly. "I know so little."

"Well, the first thing is that gods were blessed, not born. Their magic came from the Above, where they would transcend mortality and become ever-living. It is said that the only way for a god to die is by the hands of another god, in which they must remove their magic." Interesting. So it was not only Padon who could not die. "There are ten gods other than Asta, your prince's goddess and late queen. Stella, Goddess of Sun and Moon. Achari, God of Time and Void. Padon, God of Death and Creation. Karys, Goddess of Love and Hate. Jonah, God of Peace and War. Druj, Goddess of Deception and Candor. Kyoufu, God of Fear and Bravery. Iniko, God of Chaos and Order. Venturae, Goddess of Fate and Chance. And, last but not least, Anastasia, Goddess of Sin and Virtue."

"How do you know of their names?" I asked in surprise, flinching at the sting in my chest from straightening my back.

"The Temple of Gods has one of Asta's journals," Sterling stated casually, as if that was not something rather impressive. "Faithfuls believe that it was a gift from the goddess herself, but I think it was a demon who gave them the text. It is the sole scenario that makes sense to me. Our history dates back only the last two hundred years, as if nothing existed before then. Odd that all knowledge of demons disappeared with it. And for the demon queen to have gifted it to us? Stranger yet. But alas, the text is how I know. She names them."

"Does she...say anything else...about the gods?" Eagerness and curiosity were evident in my tone, but I was unwilling to hide my interest. I was unsure why, but knowing more about Padon and Asta felt important, as if it would somehow help me get out of this situation.

"Well, we learned from her that the holder of Sun and Moon was always the one who ruled over the Above. However, something miraculous happened. A goddess was *born*. Gods and goddesses never mated, but Stella and Achari were in love. More than that, they were soul bonded. It is said that soul bonds are the strongest love a being can experience. Something greater than chance or choice. More like destiny." A smile lifted one corner of Sterling's mouth, a sort of awe seeping from his voice. Stirring within me was my magic, begging for freedom. I could taste the prince's love for knowledge, the faintest tingle upon my tongue. Never before had my magic

remained through a blocker, and I found myself trying to reach for it as Sterling continued. "And when the two mated, they conceived a child born glowing silver, whom they would name Asta. She possessed immense magic, more than any other god in existence. Stella and Achari would make the choice to afford Solana, Stella's elder daughter, the seed of Sun and Moon when the time was right, but Asta would inherit the throne. Some objected, but most bowed down to the Goddess of Souls."

"Souls?" I inquired, my surprise momentarily distracting me from both my magic and the excruciating agony.

"Yes. Asta could steal souls," Sterling answered with a nod, his eyes slightly glazed over as he spoke. "Along with that, the sound of her voice could sway any being to her will."

"Oh, yes…a Honey Tongue. That I knew."

"A honey what?"

"Nothing, go on."

"Okay, well, um. Where were we?"

"They bowed down…to Asta."

"Yes, they bowed to her willingly. All was well, honestly. The Goddess of Souls and the God of Death and Creation were to rule over all. Many guessed at what god they might conceive, and all thought them such a lovely pair. But the future has a funny way of beating fate, and Asta would one day sit an entirely different throne. Some believe her change of heart was due to black magic, that being born instead of blessed with such gifts darkened her soul. In fact, many rumors suggest that Asta crafted the Underworld, where she would eventually damn souls that she no longer cared for. Perhaps that was where the idea that demons were hideously disfigured creatures from the fiery depths of below came about."

With a shrug, Sterling reached over and grabbed a piece of stale bread from the golden plate near his thigh. Apparently, the royals had not

budgeted for ugly plates to feed prisoners. Shame. It would be nice to not have to look at the offensive color.

"Did Stella not...care that her daughter's...husband was murdered?" I pressed, desperate for more information.

"Oh, she cared. According to Asta's journal, Stella sought vengeance against Padon, but he turned the other gods against her. Together, they usurped her, banishing their empress. Asta suggested that neither of them would ever see their home world again, and that they would both remain in the land where they had poured their magic."

Their home. I had seen it, had I not? The palace where their portraits still rested, hidden in a room that looked like more of a shrine than an office. Did Padon regret his choice? Was there space for remorse in a creature so absorbed in their own selfishness?

"So then, what...happened to Asta?"

"No one in my realm knows that. Does your prince not have those answers?"

None of my injuries could have come close to the pain with which the term *my prince* brought me. The assault upon my chest felt like daggers slicing into me, breaking through bones and flesh, puncturing my heart and lungs. What a visceral feeling, to know how little you have after possessing so very much.

"I never asked...I cared for nothing but...the prevention of war." After a beat of silence, I quietly added with a broken voice, "I did not love him...the way he deserved."

"Hey, that cannot be true." There was sincerity in his words, but all I could do was hear my own inner voice reminding me of the awful partner I had been, and how I would never get the chance to be better for Bellamy. What was he doing? Were they any closer to ending all of this? Without a word, I wrapped my arms around my chest, the aches and pain unable to reach me when so many thoughts pierced my every nerve. Maybe Bell would kill me and all of this would finally be over.

Tish walked in then, her face wan and her demeanor that of an overused horse. She looked as exhausted as I felt. At no point during my painful healing session did she speak, opting to remain silent and leave immediately after.

The second her footsteps faded, Sterling spoke. "Tell me about him."

Startled, I looked towards the prince, his vibrant curls as wild as his sister's. He had leaned towards me, his eyes wide and encouraging. Despite his handsome features, he looked so young sitting there, eagerly waiting to hear stories of love and loss. Like a curious child preparing for a bedtime story. Wholesome was the only word I could think to describe how beautifully inquisitive he was.

A smile split my face despite the morose turn of my mood. How did one explain Bellamy? He was so much more than a hair color or a hobby or a single word. He was…everything.

"He is easily one of the most ridiculous beings alive. He is cocky and obnoxious and self-serving." Sterling scoffed, and I turned to find him gaping at me in horror. With a laugh, I continued. "He is also funny and brilliant. He is determined and fierce. His favorite color is black, but red is special to him. Of all the seasons, he prefers winter, because he enjoys the crisp air and the beauty of death—ever the tortured painter. He likes chocolate and potatoes—not together, though I would not put it past him to try such a thing. He has fought through so much pain and come out of it stronger each time. He never discriminates, and he believes in dreaming even when the nightmares invade your every sense. I can still picture the little freckles across his cheeks and how annoyingly perfect they looked when he would console me after a panic attack. How he would rub my back and tell me about the stars. He loves deeper than anyone I have met, and he is the best thing that has ever happened to me."

"Wow, that is—I cannot even fathom such a love."

"Neither can I, honestly. And he loved me even when I was broken and bitter and borderline heinous. One time, when we were traveling, I had

gone two nights without sleep and I was particularly cranky. One of his Trusted, Lian, had sliced through my thigh with Air power. Even then, I think he saw what I would never admit—I let her. Sometimes I would just allow them to hit me. On those darker days, I reveled in the pain. It reminded me I was alive. We were at an inn, and he had sat next to me at a table. The others gave me space, but not him. He plopped into the seat next to me and told me my lips looked like they were in desperate need of a tongue swiping across them." Sterling laughed then, bringing a ridiculous smile to my face. "I smacked him, but I found myself laughing. And that was all it ever took for him. He later laid down on the floor beside mine and Noe's bed, and he asked me about my favorite memory—listening so intently as I spoke. Like each word that left my lips was a treasure."

And there it was. The truth that I avoided in any way that I could. Bellamy had loved me more than anyone ever would—than anyone else ever could. And I feared not for myself, but for him. How would he recover from the loss of me? After nearly two years of giving so much just to have any piece of me, how would he survive having nothing but the ghost of my magic within his mind forcing him to never look back?

After a moment, I let out a husky cough, clearing my throat and blinking back the tears that threatened to spill from my eyes. Reaching up, I tugged at my hair, my brown locks matted from the blood and dirt that had dried within it.

"Did you ever find yourself attached?"

"Me? No, never. I did not want to be still, and that is what love does to you. It stops your feet, stills your heart. Love is similar to poison in that way."

"Really, no one ever?" I asked, fully moving my body so I was sitting with my back against the jagged cell wall instead, Sterling and the bars to my left. He smirked my way, having already adjusted himself against the wall as well. "I guess you are only two decades old. That is not much time to find love."

"We mortals do not have much time to do anything worthwhile," he added with a shrug. As if his mortality was something casual of little importance. But it was not, was it? It was a tragedy. Though, perhaps it was also a blessing from Eternity. Less time to suffer. "There was someone that—never mind, you will laugh."

My eyes widened, the pain in my head from the blocker rising with the quick movement. Ignoring it in favor of the conversation, I made a mock face of offense.

"How dare you, I am a perfectly kind and nonjudgmental being," I chided, my mouth wide and hand against my chest. Sterling guffawed, his head pressing into the stone behind him. "Fine, I am a cranky bitch. But I will not laugh, I promise."

After a moment of his warm brown eyes darting between each of mine, he finally sighed and nodded. Before he spoke, the prince shuffled, getting comfortable. Wonderful, a long and brutal tale. My favorite.

"Okay, I know you will think me insane, but a few months ago, a creature visited me here in the cells." My back stiffened, flashes of beasts like the afriktor and the fetch reminding me of how dangerous the word *creature* was. Then I thought of Wrath, and my heart felt as if it might shatter. With a shake of my head, I rid myself of the gruesome picture of black blood drenching my hands and focused on Sterling, who had gone silent. His lips formed a thin line, eyes darting back and forth as he sat in what seemed like deliberation. Anxiously I waited until finally he spoke again. "Would you believe me if I told you I met a goddess?"

A sharp cackle slipped through my lips before I could seal them shut, Sterling's answering huff of annoyance forcing me to raise my now healed fingers in surrender. "Wait, wait. I was not laughing at you. What you said was just funny because—" I paused, not truly knowing how to explain what happened with Padon. "You know what? I will tell you later. Just, please, keep going."

For a moment he only glared at me, his warm brown eyes now mirroring his sister's fierce ones. Lifting a brow, I smirked his way, a challenge of sorts.

"Fine, if you are so desperate to hear, then I will tell you. She said her name was Stassi and that she had the ability to feed off sin and virtue, as well as heighten both."

"Like the Goddess of Sin and Virtue?"

"Precisely what I thought. Stassi does sound like a proper nickname for Anastasia. Now though, I wonder if my mind was just seeking company."

"Why?"

"Because she has not come back since you arrived, and I know they have put nightshade in our food and water, which means I have likely just been hallucinating her and your presence has grounded me somewhat."

"Nightshade? What is that?"

"You may know it as Belladonna."

"How on Alemthian do you know what that tastes like?"

"It makes everything slightly sweeter. I had not tasted it before you came, but I wonder if that was because I was so focused on the loneliness and pain. I know what it tastes like because I learned about poisons and antidotes in Heratt. They specialize in it."

"That is—"

"I see you continue to associate with the filth," a deep voice rang out, the oily sound of it making my head swim. Theon.

I turned, facing the approaching figure of my old classmate. Just as he had been in his youth, Theon was a proud male, standing straight with his chin held high. He was broader now, his brown skin practically glowing.

Once long, brown locks were now cropped short, those deep blue eyes staring at me with a fierce hunger.

I wanted to rip out his intestines and feed them to him.

Sterling must have been thinking something similar, because he stood and charged towards the bars. With a snarl, he reached for Theon through the cage, screaming in fury as the shifter's body seemed to melt away—forming himself into the mortal prince. There were few things in this world that still scared me, but this—watching how easy it was for Multiples to masquerade as someone else—was horrifying.

Before us, clad in gold silk, stood the cruel mirage of Sterling. Yes, it was the Prince of Maliha that smiled our way, tsking at the mortal who was still attempting to claw his way through the bars of his prison. His golden curls were once more silky, his skin a creamy white rather than the sickly pale of the caged beast that now backed away from the iron confines that separated him from his imposter.

"Less than a week with our little princess and you are already out of wit. Impressive, Asher. You trained him when even Mia could not." Theon clapped, smiling with Sterling's lips and teeth, lacking all the warmth of the prince.

"Tell me, Theon, does your annoying voice not grate on your nerves like it does mine?" Theon glared my way, his hands raising to grip the bars of my cell door. I merely smiled his way, trying my best to not show him how truly unsettled I was by his presence. "Even in Academy, I remember thinking that the sound of you speaking made me want to vomit. Sterling, what is one thing that would be better than listening to this moron talk?"

Sterling snickered to my left, slowly letting his body slide down the wall without breaking eye contact with Theon. Though, the Shifter seemed to only have eyes for me. Rage radiated from him, my magic flaring within me like a bird with broken wings trying to take flight.

"Shitting my pants," Sterling answered confidently, a smirk on his face.

"Oh, definitely. I think I would eat it if that meant giving my ears a reprieve from the aggravating sound of killjoy over there," I added.

Beyond the bars, Theon seethed, his form once more melting back to his natural state. With a fierce smack to the door of my cell, he practically foamed at the mouth as he pointed my way. "You have not changed since Academy either, *Ash*. Even back then you thought yourself too good for us—too good for *me*. No matter how hard I tried to get your attention, you refused me time and time again. As if I were nothing but the dirt beneath your boot. And now look at you, bleeding and broken on a dungeon floor as I look down upon you in royal gold."

How fortunate, to know nothing but infatuation and jealousy. Even back in Academy, I had been riddled with anxiety and duty—had known little peace at all apart from Sipho and my friends. But there Theon stood, rage clouding his eyes at the memory of a slight I committed nearly two centuries ago. Well, if he wanted to fester in such contempt and bitterness, then I would bury him in it.

"In my defense, you practically are the dirt beneath my boot," I quipped.

"I have only known you for a short time, but I think you are quite the catch—like a plague," Sterling added.

"A freeing presence—like death." My response had Sterling laughing as he spoke next.

"The same thing I wish upon us both rather than continuing to be in your presence." That had me cackling as well.

"I am sure all the females say the same thing when they see him naked," I agreed.

"Enough! You both think yourselves so funny. But when your head is on a spike and your lips are around my cock, the only one laughing will be me." Theon's response was unimaginative. Not surprising.

"I do not know about that. I have laughed with a tiny carrot in my mouth before, it is not that hard." I waved my hand his way, winking at him to enrage him more.

"I will—"

"Enough, Theon. You are indeed perpetually exhausting," Mia chided, appearing next to Theon with Malcolm on her arm. It was disgusting, watching how the Shifter cowered in her presence. Pathetic. "And I have yet to forgive you for the stunt you pulled with Asher last fall. Get out of my sight or I'll find someone more useful."

With that, Theon briefly bowed and proceeded to run out of the dungeons, his slapping footfalls echoing across the rock walls.

"Why pretend it bothered you, Mia? We both know you chose him over me in that moment."

"Wrong, as you so often are, my flower. I tortured that scum for two days after the harm he caused you. Still, I agree it was not enough. One day, when all is settled, I will let you seek your revenge. But first, you must apologize to me."

"Never in all my two hundred years have I heard a more delusional statement. And I have met your *son,* so that says a lot." I knew the words would enrage her, but I still threw in a shrug for the fun of it.

"Do not call him that!" Mia screamed, fury contorting her face into something sharp and fierce. Her breaths came in heavy pants as she stared me down, her icy glare a menacing and familiar thing. At least that I knew. Familiarity like that was almost comforting. "Who are you? You never used to speak in such a way. Even as a youngling you knew your place and stayed within it. This is not you, Asher."

"Do you mean the youngling you would hold prisoner in a room that sucked the magic out of her? I remember once when I was nine years you left me in there so long that I lost count of the days. But of course, I should have been thankful, yes? Because you threw me a lavish party afterwards and let me sleep in your bed for a week. I remember the new

67

dress you had made for me, the sweets you let me have, the beautiful stories you read to me. How stupid was I that I allowed two centuries worth of such a thing to happen? That I considered that abuse normal? Decades upon decades of hurt, and I convinced myself it was love. But you do not love me, Mia. You love no one but yourself. While you and this place have stayed the same, I have evolved—learned." With my best attempt at a chilling smile, I outstretched my arms. "I am still me, but now I know better."

"Perhaps you know better, but I will always know best." With that, she turned and walked away, not looking back even when orders left her lips. "Malcolm, bring Asher to her low level room, I think she needs another lesson."

CHAPTER EIGHT

ASHER

Day five.

Screams coated the air in agony, my throat alight with the same fire that scorched its way up my arms. Besides my every desire to remain quiet—to not give them that power over me—I continued to beg for respite. I almost wished they would torture me in my low level room so that they could not use their power on me. At least then I would feel less pathetic.

Abruptly, the burning stopped, Xavier pulling his hand away from my skin in favor of turning on the queen a mere two feet away. Mia stood silently as she watched the scene before her with open distaste.

Before I could so much as catch my breath, the match had begun.

"I cannot do this anymore. Mia, this is not the same as teaching her a lesson. We are going to kill her if we do not stop!" Xavier's shouts were like knives being shoved into my ears. I wanted to tell him to at least shut the fuck up if I was going to be tortured for the rest of the day again. But my throat was raw, my gasping breaths sending shocks of pain throughout my body. So instead of sweet quiet, I was punished with Mia's voice.

"You have always been so weak, just like my father! Last I checked, Xavier, this was our only option. She refuses to give up any information on Eoforhild, will not agree to resume her position as heir, and the last cohesive sentence she uttered was when she told Malcolm he looked like he was drawn by her right foot!" Despite myself, I chuckled at the recollection of my insult. Malcolm had stormed out of the room after that, though the pained look on his face said he likely would have left soon anyways.

Mia once more caught my attention as she pressed her hands into Xavier and shoved, the king momentarily losing his balance as he stumbled back. The queen pushed him again, the two of them nearing the threshold of my prison. Never had I seen them so much as yell at one another, let alone get in physical altercations. How lovely, a show of their so-called unity just before my funeral.

"It is not weak to not wish harm upon my daugh—"

"Do *not* call her your daughter. Asher is not *yours*, she is *mine*. She will always be mine, even if that means keeping her strapped to a table and bleeding for the remainder of her life!" If I could, I would have laughed at how ridiculous she sounded, but my charred arms and legs left me breathless. Or maybe it was the way they had cut my stomach and split me open like a book, as if trying to decipher the story of my life over the last year through the pages of my flesh. "Now get out before I kill you!"

Startled, Xavier just stared at Mia. His dark eyes were wide, terror resting in them like a stagnant pool of water—as if the normalcy of such fear brought him some sort of peace. The queen did not let his shock last

long before she made true on her promise. I watched in confusion—and amusement—as she began crafting spikes of wood. Then, with a furious scream, she threw her hands forward, sending the sharpened pieces his way. Xavier barely had time to craft a shield of fire before Mia hit her mark. Each fizzled out and burned to dust, but the king had gotten the message. With one last look of what seemed like hopelessness my way, he turned and left, his golden clothes swishing as he did.

Slamming the door, Mia turned to face me once more, her hands falling to her sides. Flustered did not look good on her. Actually, neither did her dress. She was a disaster with her blood-soaked orange hair that had grown past her shoulders and her simple silk dress that clung to her like it was convinced it would get burned too for being ugly if it left her skin.

Silently, she began violently rubbing at her face, smearing the cosmetics that had been so perfectly placed on her. Black was running down her cheeks and red stained her chin. Eternity spare me, was she going insane?

As if she could hear my thoughts, her wide blue eyes met mine, a snarl leaving her lips. "Do not look at me as if you think me less than you! I *raised* you! I taught you to read when you refused to learn from the tutor. I showed you how to play pianoforte when you felt as if your head might explode from your magic and needed an escape. I held you when the world said you were a monster." Suddenly she lurched forward, tears trailing down her pale cheeks and landing on my nose. "Whatever you wanted, I gave it to you, Asher! Do you know how many fae would kill to be in your shoes? How can you be so ungrateful, so disobedient?"

Rage clouded my vision, red seeping in from my peripherals. Words evaded me, my voice stolen from the agony of my injuries, but I could still plot—could still think up ways in which I would thank her for her cruelties one day. For now, all I could do was stare at her as I simmered in my fury. And perhaps that was best, because it only seemed to further anger her, too.

Good, let us both wallow in our faults and failures.

71

"Fine. If you choose silence, then let me choose violence. Theon!" she shouted, her head turning to face the door as it creaked open. Had he truly been lurking around the corner just waiting to be called upon? Pitiful.

I watched as the Shifter stalked forward, a cruel smile spreading across his face—his real one. With a sigh, I prepared for what was to come, knowing that it would be nothing new. Mia had chosen violence decades ago. The only thing that changed was that I realized life could be different.

"You have five minutes to get anything about those wretched creatures out of her before we give up for the day and send her back to her cell. *Five minutes,* Theon. At least attempt to not disappoint me," Mia ordered with a tired wave of her hand, disdain coating her voice like honey in a hive. Without so much as another glance my way, she left.

Theon peered down at me through his thick lashes, eyes roaming over my body like a child given a new toy. Fitting, seeing as I had been treated as such my entire life.

Except for with Bellamy and my friends. Never with them.

"Well, Asher, it looks like we are finally in the positions in which we both belong. Me above you and you strapped down, waiting for me." A growl involuntarily escaped me, my throat raw from so much screaming. A chuckle was his only answer before his fingers delicately traced my jaw, his mouth relaxing until it fell open in an 'O' as his thumb slid over my bottom lip. Because I was me, I did not think through my anger-fueled response.

Blood sprayed into my mouth as I took his thumb between my teeth and bit down with all my strength, hearing his shriek as a piece of the digit came loose and rolled down my tongue. Closing my throat just before I swallowed, I reared back and spit it at his face. Glee filled me when it hit his open eye and made him scream in further pain. Idiots always made it so very easy.

Tauntingly I bared my bloody teeth, the smile a sinister and wicked thing. Just as I was. No longer would I deny that I had become just as much of a villain as those around me, but I did not fear such a thing anymore.

This villain would save the gods damned world no matter how many bodies fell within my wake. Or, at least, I once thought I would.

"How dare you! Each day you remind me more and more how lucky I was to not get stuck with you." There was a bite to his tone as he spoke about getting "stuck" with me. What I would give to tell him that in his wildest dreams he would still never have me or anything more than an abysmal amount of power in comparison to my own.

Theon shouted curses and gripped his wrist, staring at the place where a nail once graced his thumb. Doubtful he had ever used it for any good, anyways. With all my remaining strength, I cleared my throat and spoke. "If your hands ever come near me again, it will be your throat I rip out with my teeth."

Each word scratched at me like blades, the pain nothing compared to my other injuries but still enough to leave me breathless. Yet, the pain was worth it, because the anger that blazed within Theon's eyes was positively delightful.

"You disgusting little wretch!" he bellowed, his hand whipping to the left to grab one of the knives.

As Theon pointed the blade towards me, my mind wandered to a memory of Wrathy, the deep and gravely sound of his chilling voice making my heart ache. **"Pain is your friend, an old companion. It cannot win if you do not let it."**

I would not let this pain win. Not after so many, including Wrath, had died because of me. Not when remaining silent and refusing to help the royals was all I could offer now. Wincing at the ripping of my hair as Theon gripped it within his fist, I readied for the new onslaught of agony.

"Let us make the outside match the inside, shall we?" he inquired, smiling once more before he pulled my hair tighter and began sawing it off with the knife.

A rush of horror seemed to overtake my mind, the slicing sound of Theon's knife merging with the soft clipping of Winona's scissors. Despite

that, I remained still, only a single tear sliding down my temple as I felt his blade hit my scalp at the crown of my head. When he finished, grunting in frustration at my lack of response, he threw the blade. I had only moments to prepare for the slap before his hand made contact with my cheek, my face flinging to the right. His fingers and bloody thumb gripped my jaw, forcing me to look his way again.

"You are worthless, Asher. Now you look it, too," he hissed. For good measure, he reared back like I had and spit on me, the foul liquid hitting me square on the forehead. I wanted to scream that he knew nothing of my worth. Or better yet, to reach up and snap his neck. We both knew I could do nothing though, so it was really a matter of holding out the remainder of the five minutes Mia awarded him. Just like that, the door swung open.

A sigh of relief escaped my dry and cracked lips. Tish looked ragged, as if she were suffering just as I was. From what I understood, she had been healing a mortal from torture sessions for a year straight. That sort of power exertion was dangerous. Mortals did not help the process in the same way fae did. Now, she had to regularly deal with healing me while poison clouded my veins and a blocker confined my magic. I would feel sympathy if she had not played part in my torment for decades.

"Her Majesty says your time is up and that I am to heal Her Highness," she said quietly but not softly. In fact, there was an air of authority to her tone.

Theon smiled brightly and stepped back to give the Healer room. Tish eyed him as she stepped up to the table I was strapped to, her stare not leaving the Shifter even as she reached out for my chest. Momentarily, my anguish was heightened, Tish's power burning through my body like a flame caught on the wind in a forest. Soon though, I was sighing in relief.

Turning, I smiled at Theon. His answering growl sounded like a vengeful beast. If he was already that angry, there was no harm in making it just a bit worse, right?

"You look mangy in that outfit by the way. I now see why you had to masquerade as a mortal just to potentially get laid. Sadly, that personality of yours cannot be shifted. Pity, yes?" I queried, batting my eyelashes to feign innocence.

"That is enough Healing power!" Theon shouted, shoving Tish to the side just after she unlocked the chains upon the table. Unfortunately, there were still chains keeping my hands tightly secured to one another. His large hand grabbed the links, tugging me down until my body slipped off the edge. I toppled to the ground and was hit with a new flash of pain. Gods, how unnecessary.

Before I could gain my footing, Theon began pulling me, dragging me out the door and down the dark and damp path to my cell. Fighting, I tried and failed to gain the upper hand long enough to get my feet below me.

We reached my cell quickly, my shouts of protest startling Sterling into consciousness. The mortal prince jumped up, his eyes finding mine immediately. When he opened his mouth to defend me, I shook my head. They had not tortured him for information—or fun—since I arrived. If I could prevent any further harm upon him, I would.

Theon dropped the chain connecting my handcuffs and dug into his pocket to find the keys. After a few muttered curses, he recovered them and unlocked my cell. Then, he removed my shackles, picked me up, and threw me in. My right knee hit the stone so hard I screamed in surprise and agony. How many more times would he hurt me until he was satisfied?

"You are really making me mad, you beast of a fae. I would be careful not to infuriate me further unless you wish to meet a grizzly end," I threatened, glaring up at him. A random breeze flew through the dungeons, my nearly bald head too exposed and causing a chill to run down my spine. Theon must have thought he caused it, because he merely smiled down at me, grabbing the bars of my cell door as he spoke.

"Actually, it is *you* who should be careful not to infuriate *me*. Eventually, we will break you, and you will regret not choosing me. Now

and then." His eyes glittered beneath the Fire power that blazed in the wall sconces, victory there in the depths of blue.

"You are truly that angry that I did not date you in Academy? That was so long ago. Get over it." Adjusting to a more comfortable position with my back against the wall, I faced Theon, embarrassed for him at his crush turned vengeance.

"No, it is not simply that you looked over me. It is that you chose a lowly Healer over me. That you cared for a random nobody when I was the strongest Multiple the Academy had seen in decades!" I stilled at his shouted confession, my mind filling with Sipho. How did he know about him? "You look confused, Princess Asher. Perhaps I should enlighten you."

With that, he flashed a final smile and pushed away from my cell. He paced loudly, Sterling catching my eye when he stood and approached his cell door. The two of us were on edge waiting for Theon to explain himself.

"You turned me down my fifth year, your third. Do you recall?" he asked. I remained silent, not completely remembering the moment. As if he could sense my answer, he scoffed, continuing his story with far more annoyance than he had before. "Well, not only did you take away my chances at having *you,* but you took away a crown that I deserved. Yes, I could wait for your eventual introductory ball, but none of us were sure when or how it would be held. So, I followed you. Studied you. Trying to gain your attention and discover what you liked. However, all I truly figured out was that you were rather private and did not care much for socializing."

True. Not that the intense bullying and shunning helped any. Theon continued to pace, Sterling watching intently, just as I did.

"It was not until I came back to visit during your first year after Academy that I realized why you were so uninterested in the males around you." He stopped midstep, turning his head my way and offering a wink. "You already had yourself a lover."

"No," I said breathlessly. It could not be. There was no way he knew all those years ago and said nothing to the royals. Sterling hit his bars,

furious with the turn the story was taking. But I remained still, both ready and not to hear the rest of the story.

"Yes, Asher. I saw you and your precious Sipho. He whispered in your ear as he passed you one day." Suddenly, the Shifter whipped around to face Sterling, his smile impossibly wider. "Let me fill you in, my little doppelganger of sorts. Sipho was a Healer that graduated the same year as Asher. His father had begun selling his produce at the market here in The Capital immediately after his son's graduation, which meant Sipho was able to visit rather often. And where do you think he went when he disappeared from his father's stall?"

Sterling answered with a defiant shout and another rather forceful smack of the bars before him. Theon, undeterred, nodded vehemently. Pointing to the mortal before him and then snapping, he faced me again.

"Exactly right, Prince Sterling. Sipho went to the woods behind the golden palace, where he met—you guessed it—The Manipulator herself. There, well, the details are a bit too graphic to share, though I will not lie and say that I did not have some fun watching such scandalous activities." Theon groaned as he reached down and cupped himself between his legs, rolling his head as if fighting off a wave of lust. My body began to shake, the image of Theon pleasuring himself to Sipho and I having sex making me bloodthirsty.

"You know what I felt after, though? Fury. So much fury. Because the princess had told me once that she was not allowed to be with anyone until the royals chose her husband one day. But there she was, fucking a farmer's son. Fucking *scum*—"

I cut off Theon with a shrill scream, jumping to my feet and racing towards the bars. Slamming into them, I reached through the bars in an attempt to sink my claws into him. Theon merely laughed, taking a few steps back and eyeing me with glee.

"Oh, just you wait, Asher. The story gets so much better. I waited months to find the perfect time to share my knowledge with the king. I needed to get rid of the Multiple that was just above me in rank, as my

scores landed me third in my subfaction," he said nonchalantly, waving off the fact that he murdered his Warden like it was nothing. "But once she was dead, I was to be given the title of Warden, allowing me to rule over the Multiple Lands. Which, of course, meant a ceremony at The Capital."

My head swam with the facts, timelines falling into place until dread overcame me, making my legs weak. Theon laughed so hard he doubled over, grabbing his stomach as if to contain the humor. Stumbling back, I tried to remember what I had done the night of that ceremony. Had I not met with Sipho? I could not recall exactly, but he had been safe with me. Right?

"It was all too easy for King Xavier to send the Healer and his father home before you could meet. Even easier for me to take Sipho's form and meet you in the forest," I watched as he licked his lips, his eyes traveling down my body slowly as if he knew it well.

No. Eternity, *please no.* Shaking my head, I muttered the word over and over again. "No."

"*Yes,* Asher." Then, right before my eyes, Theon shifted. A cry of agony left me hunched over as Sipho's dazzling honey eyes and unruly black curls appeared in front of me. The Multiple had done far better with Sipho's likeness than he had with Sterling's. I thought then that such a hurt was far worse than any form of torture they could inflict upon me.

"Please, stop. Stop this," I begged, choking on sobs. Theon merely smiled with Sipho's beautifully brilliant white teeth and round cheeks before dragging a finger across his full lips.

"The way you ravished me with your lips that night was nothing short of magical. You did not even let me attempt to speak in his voice, which was great for me as I have always been poor at impressions. And oh, did you taste delicious." With that, he leaned his head back and moaned loudly.

That was when the grief slowly began to simmer into rage.

"Sadly, King Xavier was watching, and I could not take you like I wished. So instead, he called to you. Do you remember, Asher? Do you recall that time you *almost* got caught with your lover? How you placed one more chaste kiss to my lips and mouthed 'later' before running off to your king?"

I shook with the anger within me, letting it bubble and straighten my spine. My hands balled into fists, something deep within my chest coming alive. I felt an odd sensation around my neck where my blocker was, as if the throbbing and never-ending agony it caused was beginning to fade.

"You know the rest, right? No more than a fortnight later, King Xavier and Queen Mia made false plans to visit Isle Element. Reckless as you were, you almost immediately ran to your Shifter and made plans. You even took the time to speak with his father, who had no idea that the princess before him would be the death of his beloved son—his *only* son." A low sound rumbled its way up my throat, like a building threat. Theon did not care as he let the end of his tale be known. "You know, I touched myself many times upon that spot on your floor while you were gone. Pleasuring myself to the thought of that waste of space dying was more euphoric than your stretched out and used cunt could ever be. Too bad Sipho is not here to see your pathetic and hideous self now. I bet he would be so disappoint—"

The rage boiled over then, my piercing screams cutting off Theon's monologue. This time, when I charged him, I did not hit the bars before me. One moment a cage separated me from the Shifter, and the next I was tackling him to the ground. I did not give myself time to think. Did not so much as take in a deep breath before I silenced my own screams by bringing my bared teeth to Theon's throat and biting down. His cries were met by my jaw closing even tighter. And then, with enough force to rip the universe itself apart, I tore out Theon's jugular. The taste of iron spilled into my throat like a vengeful river, and the beast below me—or perhaps I was the beast—convulsed. His screams became gurgles as his face returned to his own, but it was not enough.

Sterling's shouts behind me were met with the fleshy thud of my fists raining the Underworld down upon Theon. Each time my knuckles collided with his face my battle cry grew louder, until nothing could be heard over it. Again and again I hit him, his head quickly becoming a bloody scene of gore and revenge.

Only when he was completely unrecognizable did I slow, coming to a stop and catching my breath.

Silence coated the death-tainted air. That was, until claps sounded from my right. My head swung towards the source. I caught sight of Mia just as she walked into the light, a new gown and fresh cosmetics making her look a queen once more.

"There is my daughter—my heir. Feral is the scorned, after all." She chuckled, a dainty little laugh. I gasped, using the lifeless body below me to push myself back onto my feet. Briefly, I considered what it meant that I had moved through—past?—the bars of my cage. But I had no time to realize what I was before Mia spoke again. "He deserved it, Asher. He hurt you. He insulted you. He belittled you. No one who does that should live. You gave him the end he earned."

Wobbling on my feet, I scoffed at her, bunching my aching fists once more in preparation for another fight. "Then perhaps you—who has hurt me worse than any other—deserve my wrath most of all."

Slowly but surely, my magic invaded my veins once more, both Sterling's shock and Mia's pride faintly registering in the back of my mind. The Manipulator within me urged me to end her—to show her an even worse fate than Theon met.

"No, my flower, I have loved you," she whispered, flicking her wrist. Suddenly, something hard hit the back of my head like a boulder. I collapsed to the ground in a heap of bloody limbs and pulsing magic. Just as my eyes closed, Mia's haunting voice sounded once more. "Now we shall see that love mold you back into what you were always meant to be."

CHAPTER NINE

BELLAMY

Of course they knew who I was. A fae with pointed ears wielding shadows was not only rare, it was a singular case. Me.

"I see my reputation precedes me," I taunted, leaning forward to bow but never letting my eyes leave the captain's. She was wholly unimpressed, but I could tell she was intrigued by the why of it all. Why was the Prince of Eoforhild so far out into the Ibidem Sea? Why was he on a ship with no supplies other than gold? Why did he know her name?

If Asher were here, she would have come up with a better plan. Then again, if Asher were still with me, I would not need to beg at the feet of pirates.

"I believe you can help me with resc—" Pain, far worse than before, barreled into my mind. It crawled its way through every thought and memory and emotion like a spider weaving a web. Whatever Asher did with her magic had left a poison burrowed so deeply within my brain that it might just rot me into nothing. My back gave out, leaving me hunched over and gasping for air as the bow clattered to the ground.

"What is wrong with you?" Another female asked. The sound of heels meeting the wooden deck came closer, and then a pair of brown leather boots came into my line of sight.

Standing straight once more, I swallowed my words. So no planning her rescue, got it.

"I need your help, but unfortunately I cannot be the one to plot and plan with you." My hand gripped my hair, trying to rip out the ache from where it festered.

"She wants to know why."

"Well, if you must know, you nosy little pirate, the love of my life stripped me of my free will and forced me to leave her for dead. So now I am, quite honestly, in so much pain over the mere thought of aiding her that I am considering murdering you all and simply burning the entire fucking world to dust just so I can find some peace."

"She said down puppy." I balked, letting my eyes move between the two annoyingly smug females before me.

"Did she truly?"

"Yes," the blonde answered, "she also said that you need to find a new female to piss on and claim because she isn't helping your old one."

Rage left my toes curling and my fists bunching. What I would not give to—

"Well, well, if you all do not look like the tastiest little treats," the siren said, cutting off my failing conversation with the captain. Irritated and

far beyond my wits end, I ripped water from the sea below, willing it over the ship and raining it down upon us all. Screams erupted from those aboard, and I took the opportunity to portal to my Trusted, lighting a circle of black fire around us.

"I care little for what your captain thinks of me, though, if you think you will be walking away from this ship alive without your vow to aid me, then you are surely mistaken. You may be formidable, but there are few things in this world as dangerous as I, my lost love being one of them." With a flick of my wrist, I shredded through the beam of light that wrapped around my Trusted. They remained casually grouped together, none of them looking so much as unsettled by the pirates around us.

Captain Harligold approached, gesturing sharply as she did. Her face was pinched in rage, staring at me like I was a rancid meal she'd like to dispose of. Who I wagered was her quartermaster, seeing as the very blonde had been the one to translate earlier, followed closely behind, eyes trained on her captain's hands. When Harligold stopped mere feet from me, the blonde spoke.

"Captain Perdita Harligold is the most notorious pirate to walk Alemthian. She does not fear pampered princes and weak threats. We have faced far worse and come out alive, so you best consider what you are willing to lose in order to gain support you shall not have."

Just then, I caught sight of the captain's gesture to the siren. My anger was an erupting volcano in that moment, and I felt my magic leak from me like lava.

The crew members all attacked at once, but I was faster than even their captain. Harligold's shadows were not even halfway to me before her siren collapsed to the deck, my blazing shadows still burning at her flesh where they sliced right through her.

A gargled noise left the captain's lips just as her crew members descended upon us. I met the enraged blonde head-on, crafting a sword of shadow and fire to stop hers. Ice hit air as a female with bronze skin and

cascading navy hair attacked Lian, who fought the exceptionally talented Water off.

Chaos was threatening to ruin this singular chance to save Asher, and my own distraction nearly allowed the Sun before me to slice open my neck. I jumped out of the way with barely a moment to spare, and I decided that swallowing my pride was the only option.

"Captain!" I shouted. Harligold glared at me from where she was bent over the dying siren, her face red with fury.

"Do not speak to her!" I ignored the blonde's screamed order, opting to wrap her in vines that seemed to suck more power out of me than normal.

"I have a fae Healer with me. Promise me your sword and I shall have him help your siren. The gold I showed you before is yours too. I ask only for your aid." Before she could respond to my plea, I willed vines around all five of her crew members, fortifying them with small hurricanes that swirled violently around each female.

Perdita Harligold stared on in astonishment, as if she had not expected such power from me. But she possessed Moon magic, which meant she was a demon who had been raised to fear me. I knew what it was to be that arrogant, had fought against the part of me who thought myself better than all for the last hundred years. Her hands shook against the wound that poured black blood from the siren's stomach, eyes scanning my Trusted. Ranbir stepped forward, his thin form drowning in the black leathers that once fit him perfectly. My heart ached as he approached the two females upon the deck. He deserved so much more than he had been given.

"I will not hurt you. Please, let me heal her," he whispered, the softness of his paired hand movements finally breaking the captain. She withdrew her hands, backing away from the bleeding siren and keeping her deep brown eyes on me. Ranbir made quick work of closing the wound, letting out a quiet gasp of pain when his hands touched her blood.

Reality hit me then. Siren blood was black, just like Wrath's was. Like the fetch's was. Stella save me, sirens were creatures of the God of Death and Creation too. The siren let out a deep breath, her eyes shooting open. As quickly as I could, I willed vines and water to hold her still, hoping that I would not have to hold it all for long. The captain flinched, a fire blazing in her gaze as it slowly returned to me.

"Would you allow me to heal your hands as well, Captain?" Ranbir, so giving and kind, stretched his fingers towards Harligold. For a moment I truly thought she would accept, but instead of placing her hands in Ranbir's, she took a dagger and stabbed it into Ranbir's palm. He screamed in agony as she ripped it out, and then she disappeared beneath a cloud of shadows.

Not a moment later, I heard Henry's grunt. Turning, I found him near the bulwark of the ship, Captain Harligold's bloody dagger against his throat and a storm of shadows swarming them both. A single drop of blood dripped from his neck where her blade pressed too hard into his skin, and my vision went the same deep shade of red.

Cyprus and Damon rushed to Ranbir, Noe and Lian opting to flank me on either side. I walked towards the captain with furious steps, the rage from this last week coming to a head. Henry remained still and silent, watching me come to him with knowing eyes. I would sooner kill them all than let him get hurt.

"Your choices are fewer now, Captain. Let my brother go, or watch as your entire crew slowly dies," I growled.

Noe and Lian separated, wrangling the pirates into a pile to my left as they writhed and fought against my power. My determination seemed to only grow as I tightened their binds. Water sloshed against the deck in time with their screams, but Lian quickly turned their shouts into silent gasps as she stole their air from their lungs. Noe summoned a whip made of shadows, twirling it in her hands and staring at Harligold. For her part, the captain stared on, her dagger still firmly pressed to Henry's neck.

"I promise you this, Harligold, they will all die long before you can harm him. In fact, how long do they have, Ranbir?" My head turned towards Ranbir, who had been clutching his now-healed hand.

"One minute at most," he hissed, anger coating his voice in venom as he signed to her. "But I can make it seconds."

"Did you hear that, Captain? Seconds." I shrugged, smiling as I spun to face her once more. War waged within her, those once sure hands shaking even more now and her magic nearly covering both of their bodies entirely in darkness. Then, thankfully, she let her dagger fall, willing her shadows to fade. Henry seemed ready to pounce, but I shook my head and motioned for him to come to me. "Release them, Lian."

Henry glared once more at the captain before coming to my side. In that moment, I did not care about what the pirates thought. I grabbed Henry and pulled him into me, patting his back three times and breathing in the truth that he was alive. My family would not grow any smaller.

The pirate crew gathered slowly around their captain, surrounding her like a shield just as my Trusted did. We stared head on at each other, eyes locked and abilities at the ready. Nicola's letter had demanded I trust them and pay for their trust in return. Perhaps that was still possible.

"I do not wish you harm, Captain. All I seek is an alliance that will benefit us both—and a world that will see us all thrive." Minus her looting and murderous ways, but she did not need to know that now. "Help me, and I shall help you."

Holding out my hand, I once more willed the sacks of gold to appear. When the shadows dissipated, I tossed the gold her way. She caught it deftly, glaring at me before opening them. A gasp of surprise left the lips of the blonde who seemed to never leave the captain's left side.

Come on, take the fucking gold.

Perdita Harligold looked up at me once more, a sense of unease on her face. That was all I needed.

"I am told that the death of a pink-haired pirate captain named O'Malley Harligold might further entice you. My love—my Asher—did most of the work, honestly," I admitted, watching as the blonde signed along with my words. "But after she had shoved his own severed cock down his throat and gouged his eyes out, it was I who removed his ugly head from his shoulders. He threatened her, so I ended him."

If Nicola was wrong, then the future she had foreseen was but a gust of wind, gone before it had time to cool the stifling air.

Captain Harligold—along with the rest of her crew—seemed to freeze, their mouths agape. What felt like a year passed by in silence, the sound of everyone's collective breathing making my hairs stand on edge. But then, as if a decision had been shoved into her, the captain lurched forward with hands racing through signs. My eyes darted from her to the blonde beside her, nerves skyrocketing as I hoped for what seemed like the only future that would see Asher free. Prayed for it.

"She...she says to leave your brother and the small one with the big teeth." Lian growled, a low noise that was paired with the sound of her dagger being unsheathed from her thigh. I held up a hand, stilling her so we could hear the rest of what the pirates had to say. Clearing her throat, the blonde continued. "We will—gods damn us all—we will help you. But we desire more gold and wish for a legal privateer license. And we want your Healer to look over our Captain."

"Does she wish to speak?" Ranbir asked softly, though there was still fury in his tone. I did not blame him. What an exhausting year it had been for us all, but Ranbir especially. "I am not sure I can correct such a defect."

"No, you idiot. She does not wish to speak. Our captain is perfect as she is. There is no defect. You will be wise to shut your foolish mouth." The captain watched the interaction with a smirk, as if she somehow knew what was being said and enjoyed watching her crew member scold Ranbir. Then, she too held up her hand and stilled the female, just as I had Lian. "Fine. But he is on my list," the blonde said as she signed. "Captain

Harligold has had pain in her throat for the last year. She would like to have that fixed, along with her hands."

Turning, I looked back at Ranbir. He sighed before nodding and walking towards the captain and her crew of what were clearly deranged females. Asher would like them.

"What is the plan exactly? How will they help us get Ash back?" Noe asked from my side.

"You cannot possibly be considering leaving me with them? They are clearly barbaric lunatics," Lian added in a harsh whisper. Henry nodded and crossed his arms, sparing a glare for the group as Ranbir touched the Captain's throat.

"You are developing sores. That is an easy fix, it has just been made worse from not healing it," Ranbir explained. A groan of pain sounded from the captain, and then a sigh of relief followed it. "Also, your vocal chords have snapped and your ear drums have burst."

The captain promptly punched Ranbir in the face. I gasped in surprise, and then I ran at them. Fire lit my hands and water sloshed against the ship, my fury causing the wind to rage around us. The female crew braced themselves for battle once more, but Ranbir's body suddenly blocked my way.

"That was my mistake, not hers. She did not wish to know, and I said it anyway out of spite. I got what I deserved, Bell." Ranbir's words were loud enough for the crew to hear, but I watched Ranbir move his fingers in jerky and strained movements after. Signing to the captain.

"Okay, with that settled, tell us what we must do so we can be rid of most of you," the blonde said, translating for Captain Harligold as her hands moved.

If only I knew. Nodding, I grabbed Ranbir's sleeve and tugged him towards the Trusted. We gathered, each pair of their eyes watching me with a desperate need for answers. In another life, maybe I was the one being led—the one without such a weight on my shoulders. Now, as I prepared

to burden my family with that heaviness, I knew I would give up all of those lives of ease rather than force them to face what was to come. But that was not an option.

"I cannot make these decisions. It…it hurts. Asher's magic will not let me. But you," I said, looking to Henry and then Lian, "can do this. I know the two of you can save her. I trust you both. If you are willing to take on this burden, then it is yours. Unfortunately, we do not have time to think this through. I wish you did not have to make this decision at all, but you must."

They broke eye contact with me, looking at one another and communicating without words. In the way only a family could. And then the two of them nodded, agreeing to a fate I wished had not been forced upon them.

"Okay then. The two of you will set sail with the pirates and the rest of us will return to Pike. We have a war to win and a princess to save."

***

Leaving Lian and Henry had been agonizing. Terrifying.

Coming back to find Adbeel waiting had also been quite scary. As I walked up to him, I readied for a battle.

"My King, I did not expect you to await my return." The formality had him lifting the corner of his mouth in a smirk. I was not in the laughing mood, though. "What can I do for you?"

"Well, first, you can watch your tone," he said, moving to my side and walking up the path towards the entrance of Pike with me. Rolling my eyes, I remained silent, preparing for whatever it was he had wanted to tell me. He had overseen Pike in my absence today after all, I owed him my ear at least. "Second, I noticed Henry and Lian are not with you. That will be a

problem for Lady Nash. She expects Henry to play his part in this war so he may earn his place as general when you ascend the throne."

"Well, Lady Nash can, quite frankly, kiss my ass. Henry is exactly where he needs to be," I sneered. Not having Henry at my side once more was quite the opposite of ideal, but it was the only way.

"You overstep again, Bellamy. Odilia will be a burden now, and for what? Are your reasons more important than the outcome of this war?" he questioned, the tone he used a scolding if I had ever heard one.

"For Asher, who holds the balance of this very war in her hands." Adbeel's tree-trunk-like arm whipped in front of me, stopping me mid-stride. Turning, I caught sight of the vexation in his gaze. This would be it then, the moment I finally cracked and faced whatever horrid future Pino foresaw.

"This must end, Bellamy. I understand that you want her, that she matters. But this is war, this is our future. She cannot be prioritized. I cannot let you risk my realm for a female that you hardly know but claim to love. Her life does not come before the survival of Eoforhild. Your nonsense stops now." An order. That was what it was.

I faced him fully then, puffing my chest and willing myself to speak the words I had been hiding for nearly two years.

"What about the life of a princess?" I asked.

"I fail to see how the life of a fae princess matters to me. To our realm."

"And if she were a demon princess?"

Adbeel pressed his hand to my chest, forcing me to take a step back from him. A low beastly grunt was all I offered. "You marrying her is not a possibility in current circumstances. She is not the Princess of Eoforhild. Call back Henry and Lian, we have a war to win."

With that, he patted my chest and began to walk away. Pino's warnings echoed in my mind. Adbeel was not to know without Asher. But if I did not tell him, then Ash would be lost to us forever.

Consequences be damned.

"And what about for your granddaughter?"

CHAPTER TEN

STASSI

By the time Padon came to fetch me I had already finished off half a bottle of vodka to myself, vomited, fell down my stairs, and wrote him a hate letter.

Quite the accomplishment, really.

"You look like absolute shit," he muttered as he stepped through the threshold. I huffed out a sarcastic laugh, weighing the bottle still in my hand before hurtling it at him. But he knew me well, so I was forced to watch with disappointment as he snatched the bottle from the air before it even came close to his face.

Incoherent grumbles left my mouth, and I found myself crawling towards my kitchen, wondering if ripping the emperor's heart from his

chest and eating it raw would leave him down long enough to go to Alemthian and steal my creature.

No, the fucker would find a way to come back before I could sober up enough.

His shining black shoes passed by my feet just as I made it to the tile of my kitchen floors. I watched with fury as he opened a cabinet and pulled out my good whisky. Then, the fiend *drank from the bottle.*

"You stupid oaf. I'll kill you in your sleep and put your ugly head on my bedpost so I can pleasure myself to the thought of your eternal silence!" My slurred shouts did little to stir his attention, which seemed honed in on the opposite wall as he slowly slid down my counter and cabinets. Then he sat upon the floor and took another hefty drink in silence. Groaning, I rolled my eyes. I knew pouting when I saw it.

I finally made it over to him, and I found myself using his head to push my body up. He growled at me like a rabid animal, swatting at my hand, but I just pushed down harder. When I was upright, a bottle of vodka caught my eye, and I quickly swiped it off the counter before losing my balance and falling to the ground next to him.

Padon peered down at me with annoyance and what looked like concern, but I needed neither from him, especially when I knew whatever had him so worked up would take priority.

"Fine, tell me what's making you so deliciously furious," I slurred, moving to sit upright beside him. My shoulder pressed into his elbow, and I wished for nothing more than his discomfort at that second.

"Asher...she's gone." His voice was monotone, more hollow than the glass jar of whiskey he was practically inhaling. For a moment I simply watched as he took swig after swig, the motions becoming sharper and more forceful. Popping open my own preferred drink, I too sipped from the bottle.

"Hasn't she been gone since I let her go this morning?" As if my words had broken through a barrier, Padon's fury flooded my cottage. He

threw the almost empty bottle into a wall, shattering the glass and dragging a shout of surprise from my chest.

"She's *gone!* I can't sense her at all anymore, as if she disappeared from the universe itself! As if she—" He cut himself off, breathing so heavily it looked painful. As if she died. That was what he meant to say. "I had her here the last time you returned. I had her in my grasp and I let her go. Now she's fucking *gone!*"

Unsure what to say, I simply handed him my bottle. He took it without looking and drank deeply. Tears slowly began to crawl down his cheeks as he returned the vodka to me.

He was crying. Eternity above, he was losing his mind.

"Well, we can figure this out. I'm sure—"

"Asta loved you, you know," Padon whispered, staring forward at what must have, to him, been the past playing for him like a painting brought to life.

Words evaded me, because what did one say to a truth that only brought pain? Of course Asta loved me. It was him she didn't love.

"But her love wasn't enough. Not for her or us or anyone. Betrayal was all she offered Shamay in the end. And now look at us." He gestured to the mess of glass and whisky, as if it was a direct representation of what we had become. And perhaps it was.

"I miss her. I miss all four of them." While he knew it, saying that truth felt like an admission of guilt. Like a confession. Still, I didn't stop. "I think about the last night we spent together before Achari and Solana left a lot. You, Asta, Sol, and I all sat in our spots on the floor of Stella's office as she worked. We drank more wine than we should have and ate that horribly spicy dip. Stella and Char eventually came and sat with us, remember? Char told us stories of other worlds and we all laughed until Sol had wine shooting out of her nostrils. Back then I would look at Stella and Char and you and Asta with hope—at Sol with love. Then again, that was

back when our crystals were full and the right high demon was on the throne."

Padon practically hissed at the accusatory tone I'd taken. We both knew I was right though. He didn't belong upon that throne.

"Asher is far better than Asta. You're just too bitter and vexed to see that. She can fix everything, but nothing will change if we can't find her." Now it was my turn to let out a furious snarl. "We don't need Stella or Achari. We need *her.*"

Despite how utterly drunk I was, I shot up. Standing on shaky feet, I looked down at Padon, suddenly seeing him for the first time. The real him.

"You're pathetic," I hissed. He gasped at my insult, mouth opening as if to cut me off, but I was not done. "All this talk about how Stella didn't deserve the throne and Asta's betrayal and Shamay's future, but it's *you* that is leading us to destruction. How often have you blamed Achari's borderline obsessive curiosity? Now look at you! Haunted by the artificial love for a mortal princess who could not care less about you! All for what? The magic that plagues her veins? Eternity did not bless her, Padon. It cursed her to a lifetime of being hunted rather than loved. You seek to do nothing but covet her like a prize when all that will do is kill her like it nearly killed Asta! At every turn, it is you who threatens everything! You who ruins it all!"

Padon did not speak, instead he shot up and pushed me, his strength shoving the air from my lungs and forcing me back down to the ground. I hit my tiled floor with a crash, hissing at the pain of my elbow and shoulder shattering beneath the pressure. Padon was not done though. He screamed with fury and bent down over me, lifting me as he wrapped his hands around my throat and squeezed with the rage of someone who has suffered through tens of thousands of years.

Unfortunately for him, so had I.

My hand flung towards the counter, gripping a knife and swinging without mercy. It sliced into his throat, the silver blade protruding from his

skin where I had forced it to turn. A gurgled cry echoed off my ceiling as he released me.

"Again and again you have wrecked my fucking life, Padon!" I screamed, my hands sweating and my vision swimming. I watched as his hand moved to grab the knife, but I quickly kicked my foot into the blade, sending the hilt into his neck and his body toppling down. "You seek nothing but the ends to your own means! You want to take over that world? You want to waste our time instead of finding Stella? Fine! You can do that shit on your own."

Abruptly I stopped my rant, needing to take deep breaths. Padon used the opportunity to grip the sharp end of the knife and pull it from his throat. Backing away, I willed my mind to clear. The alcohol wouldn't last long, my system would break it down soon enough if I could just stall for a few minutes. Then I could run.

Grunting, Padon stood, his body alight from the deep purple of his magic. He was healing himself. Shit.

Shit. Shit. Shit. Shit!

"Oh, now you're all high and mighty because you left Shamay? For once you've been something more than useless and suddenly you feel like you can judge me? Condemn me? Blame me? No, Anastasia." I backed away further, my heart racing and my magic a storm in my veins. Still, it was nothing compared to what Padon had.

Think, Stassi. Think!

"I am done making excuses for you. Done treating you like a little sister when all you've done is be ungrateful ever since Asta left. You want freedom so badly? Fine. Then I will give you eternal freedom!" he screamed.

A fierce pull at my chest forced a scream from my lips, and I realized with terror that Padon was trying to take my seed of magic. He was trying to *kill me*.

Panic seized me, and I could do nothing but will myself somewhere else. Somewhere safe.

The last thing I thought of before I was wrapped in the comfort of rose-tinted magic was Asta. Was her beautiful smile and her glowing silver eyes. My little sister in all but blood.

And then I felt myself portal.

My feet went from the soft carpet of my sitting room to a worn and cracked wood. I breathed deeply, trying to ground myself. Where had I gone? What would I do? How would I fix what I had just irrevocably broken?

Mere seconds passed, and then a deep and raspy voice shattered my focus.

"Who are you? What are you doing here?"

My eyes rose, meeting the gaze of the brightest blue eyes I had ever seen. And perhaps it was Eternity who had willed me there. Or maybe it was Asta's soul, somewhere above, watching over me and pushing me towards my destiny. Either way, when I locked eyes with the male before me, I made my choice and sealed my future.

Straightening, I ordered my voice not to slur or stutter and spoke my fate into existence.

"Hello, Prince Bellamy Ayad. I am Anastasia, holder of Sin and Virtue. It seems I am here to help you save your world."

CHAPTER ELEVEN

ASHER

D_{ay…}

I was not sure what day it was.

Time felt as if it had both dragged and sped on. I could see the light of the fire through my closed lids, which burned so hot it looked like daylight. For once, the ground beneath me was soft. And warm. Had they given me a blanket? Was I being rewarded for killing Theon? I groaned, reaching up to rub my assaulted scalp. But instead of jagged hair and ripped skin, I was met with soft strands of thick waves. It felt just as it had before I had left The Capital. Silky and styled to look less wild. My eyes cracked open slowly, sticking together somewhat and confirming that I had been asleep for quite some time.

What I saw forced my body upright, my breaths coming so fast it made my head spin.

Gold. There was gold *everywhere*. This was not my low level room or even my dungeon cell.

I knew those golden curtains and gilded floors. I knew the discolored spot near the end of my bed and the wall of windows that let in the sunlight.

They had put me in my old chambers.

My heart raced as my brain slowly caught on to what was happening. A silk slip that shone the most pure shade of gold graced my skin, my body half tucked beneath thick gilded quilts. A piercing scream filled the chambers—*my* scream. I dove off the bed, crawling away from it like a youngling who could not yet walk.

No, I could not be in here. I needed to leave. To run. To escape.

Both doors flew open before I could so much as stand, through them walking Mia. She wore a dazzling gold gown made to look like a tree. The trunk hugged her body before the leaves burst free at her chest, full and grand like a summer bloom. Her hair was immaculate, the crown of gilded branches perfectly in place atop her head. Cosmetics hid the freckles on her cheeks, but her eyes still shone the vibrant blue of Bellamy's.

"Why am I here?" I asked with a hiss. Mia's brow pinched, her hands reaching forward and fingers splaying as if she were taming a beast. If that was what I was, then it was because she made me so.

"My flower, you are ill. Please, get back into your bed so I can call for Tish," she begged as she approached me. Her kindness was a surprise. To which I answered with a lantern to her face. She barely blocked it with conjured rock, but I grabbed the vase that had rested upon the side table and threw that at her too. She yelped as it sailed towards her, but that too she stopped before it could hit her, the dirt she chose to summon falling to the floor with the flowers.

"Get away from me!" I tried to stand, gripping at my throat in the hopes of ripping off the blocker despite knowing it was not that simple. But, the blocker was not there. My necklace also remained missing, lost on a gore-soaked battlefield.

"Asher, you have been asleep a long time, you need to rest so that we can be sure you are alright," Mia urged, now mere feet from me. I backed up until I hit the wall, using it to slowly lift myself. This time, I would kill her. No manipulation on her part would see her surviving this encounter.

"I will not be swayed with your false pity, you monster! Put me back in the dungeons and let me rot or face me now. I will gladly give you the death you deserve!" I bellowed the threat, the vow of sorts. Mia stumbled back, gasping with wide eyes and gripping her chest as if scandalized.

"Asher, what are you talking about? I do not understand."

"Oh, so you deny locking me in the dungeons and torturing me? That lie is rich, even coming from you, *Your Majesty.*" Her title sounded mocking from my lips, as I wished it to. As she blinked on in feigned surprise, I tried to find anything I could turn into a weapon. But if she had been foolish enough to remove my blocker, then that was her mistake. She also had Tish heal me, based on the lack of pain in my body. I could win this, even with poison in my veins. The queen had all but ensured that.

"Asher, I need you to breathe. You are confused. Nearly a year-long coma can do that to a fae," she whispered, moving forward with open arms. I froze then, facing her fully.

"You brought me up from the dungeons a year ago?" I squealed in horror. Had the war already happened? Had Bellamy lost?

No. Please no. That could not be. Please, let—

"Asher, you were never in the dungeons. I would never put you there. I am not sure why you would think such a thing. It must have been the magic they hit you with." Now she was nearly upon me, but my mind

was racing. Her words were not making sense. The time was confusing me. I could not think.

"Magic? What magic?"

"Demon magic. Black magic. You have been asleep since demons attacked your wedding, my flower."

ACT II

~ LOVE AND HATE ~

CHAPTER TWELVE

ASHER

"No. That—that is impossible. Bellamy took me from the wedding. He did not hurt me. It was you who nearly killed me. You have been hunting me for months. You!" I screamed the final word, jerking when Mia reached out to soothe me. "Do not touch me!"

"You are scaring me, Asher. Please, calm down." Mia's voice was filled with terror, but I knew how capable she was of spinning lies. I knew my mind. I knew my truth. I knew Bellamy. I knew it all.

I knew.

Without thinking, I pushed off the wall and shoved Mia. She flew back, her body slamming into one of the four golden posts that made up

my canopy bed. Her shout of pain was startling, so soft was the noise that for a moment I believed it. Only a moment though, because then I recalled all she had done and knew better than to pity her. Not sparing her another glance, I ran towards my double doors, clawing at the gold upon my body to free myself from its torment.

Tish walked through just as I grabbed for the golden handles, and I was forced to stop mid-step. My memories of her wan face and deteriorating body did not line up with what was in front of me. The Healer looked immaculate, her skin now ivory rather than gray, her short brown hair silky again.

She looked as she did the night before my wedding.

My heart raced in my chest, and I found myself gripping my hair again. How had it grown back? How long had they kept me asleep? On instinct, I looked down at my arms. The skin there, once more a light brown rather than the darker shade it had become from so much time outdoors this last year, was free of the jagged scars.

No. It could not be. I knew what was real.

"What have you done to me?" I asked. Begged.

"Asher, I do not know what you mean. Please, get in bed and lie down. Then you can explain to me what it is you think happened, and I can tell you all that has occurred since the attack." The queen gestured to the lush golden bed, a small frown of concern thinning her lips.

"No, I know what happened. You tortured me, Mia. You nearly killed Bellamy!" My bellows echoed off the high ceilings, a small wind coming in through the slightly ajar windows behind me. Perhaps I could jump, then they would not be able to use me for whatever sinister game they had begun playing.

"My flower, I do not know who that is. Please, you need rest. The realm will be so glad to hear you are finally awake after so long, but you have to be well-rested and calm to address them," she cautioned. I continued to back up, once more allowing myself to be cornered.

"You claim not to know your own son now?" Each word was a knife soaring through the air with jagged slashes, missing the mark. Mia did not grow angry like I had hoped, did not do so much as gasp with offense. Instead, her blue eyes watered as she stumbled back. As if in pain. Fake. All of it fake.

"How dare you, Ash!" Xavier's voice cut in. I whipped my head to the right, catching a glimpse of the king as he rushed in to aid his wife. He embraced her, a gentle touch born not of love but of familiarity. Just as they had been before my wedding. "You know how hard the loss of Baron was on us. What could we have possibly done for you to throw out such hateful lies?"

Genuine disbelief slackened his face, as if he truly could not think of something he had done that would warrant such an offense. As if none of the last year had occurred.

Impossible. I could not have dreamt up the life I had lived since my wedding. I was…I could not have.

Bellamy was real. Our love was the most real thing I had ever known. Yes, it was real.

"I think Princess Asher needs space to rest," Tish said, looking at me as if I were a rabid animal. Lies. All of it, lies! I wanted to scream at them that I was not stupid, but Mia sniffled and nodded. The three of them slowly and steadily left my chambers, six eyes trained on me as if looking away would mean being mauled to death.

By the time my mind registered what they were doing, it was too late. I ran at them, trying to stop them from locking me in. Xavier ripped the doors closed, the sound of the lock clicking into place ringing through the space just before my fists hit the door. I pounded on them with a desperation I had not known in so long. When my knocks failed to free me, I began punching into it, the bite of the splintering wood as it gave beneath my strength unable to deter me.

I had not prepared for the granite set of doors behind those. A cry of outrage shattered the silence, my screams that of a caged animal. And that was what I was now. What I had always been.

Tears streamed down my face when my fist hit the granite, making no noticeable dent. Again and again I tried and failed to break through it, throwing my entire body into them to no avail. Pain was a reminder that I was real, that I was here, that I was aware. They could tell me all the lies they wished, but I was smarter than that.

Heaving deep breaths, I turned from the doors and began desperately ripping off the gold silk from my body. When I was completely bare, I ran to the bathing chambers and slammed the door behind me. That was fine. I was out of the dungeons, so I had a better chance of escape.

Unwilling to think of any other outcome, I nodded and quickly walked to the large tub that had been mine for so long. Now it felt foreign, like it belonged to another being altogether. Still, it was a refuge of sorts as I crawled in it and curled into a ball on the dry bottom.

"It was real," I whispered into the void.

Yes, it had all been real. I just needed to remind myself. To repeat. To remember.

"Bellamy took me from my wedding," I began. "He took me and saved me. I found a family. A real family. Noe, Henry, Ranbir, Lian, Cyprus, Winona, Pino, Damon, and Luca. We traveled from Haven to Dunamis. We trained and I fell in love. Bellamy loved me—loves me. We battled and lost, we suffered but we lived. Bellamy told me stories and held me. He kissed me like I was a blessing rather than a curse. I knew not of loneliness because I had them. Wrath, I had Wrath."

"Did you, Strange One?"

The haunting gravely voice was like a leaf in the wind, slowly falling to my ears. Gasping, I turned to my right, finding Wrath there. He was in his smaller form, the size of a dog. His gray fur was silky and intact, his

throat whole. The dalistori looked just as he had before my world came crashing down.

"Wrath? What—what are—I do not—"

"Cat got your tongue, Asher?" he asked, licking a paw as he did. His yellow eyes never left mine though.

"You died," I croaked out. My sweet Wrathy, gone forever. But no, he was here now. How was he here? Had Padon sent him back to me? Had he shown me mercy?

"Or perhaps I never existed at all." As he spoke, the dalistori jumped down into the tub, laying in a ball just as I was. "Maybe you dreamt of something better after a lifetime of worse than one can imagine. It would make sense. How else would your hair and body and world be just as you had left it all those months ago?"

I balked at him, baffled by such a theory. No. I was not insane. I had not imagined nearly an entire year of my life. How could I? Why would I?

"Oh please, I am not that creative." My whispered sarcasm was a weak version of what I had once been, and I realized for the first time since awaking that my voice was hoarse. As if it had not been used in a long while.

"You have always dreamed of better, you just did not have the means to allow yourself to live in those dreams. A magical coma seems like the perfect time to fall victim to such madness. It would make sense for someone like you. The balance to a being with magic that takes from the mind would be…" he trailed off, his fluffy tail swishing back and forth as he watched me curiously.

"Would be what, exactly?"

"Losing your own."

With that, Wrath disappeared.

***

"Bellamy saved me. He taught me to love. Mia stole that love. I was freed and then imprisoned. Cherished and then tortured. I know what is real." My sort of mantra were the only words I had said since Wrath left me yesterday. "I know what is real."

Every inch of my skin was pebbled from the cold of my bathtub, but I refused to move. A dinner plate had been left on the table beside my tub by Maybel, who had gushed over finally seeing me awake after so long, only to shriek when she realized I was naked in the bath. I could not bring myself to regret shoving her when she reached down for me or screaming at her to leave me alone.

No one had come for breakfast.

All the best. I needed to ground myself. To remember what they willed me to forget. Not eat more poison.

A knock on my bathing chamber door startled me out of my thoughts. So much for alone time to ground myself.

"Ash," Xavier's voice rang from beyond the door. Not him, anyone but him.

"Be gentle with her, Xavier. She is confused," Mia chided. Okay, anyone but *them*.

"Asher, please, we just want to talk to you. We worry that you are not well. That magic, the burst of darkness, it hit you right in the chest. Perhaps whatever it did to keep you asleep is also muddying up your mind." Mia's soft and gentle tone was anything but welcome. It was all a lie. They meant to keep me here, to once more make me docile. To retrain me like a prized pet that had an outburst and needed a lesson. But I could no longer be tamed.

Bellamy was real. Bellamy loved me.

"Ash?" Xavier asked with concern.

I was strong. I was more than a pawn. I had lived.

My door burst open then, the two of them rushing in. I grabbed a towel to shield myself, but otherwise remained silent.

I had visited other realms, seen another world. I had conquered and could do so again.

"My flower, are you well?" Mia bent down beside the tub, a tear falling down her cheek. She could star in plays with that talent.

"You have been poisoning me for two centuries, I do not think I will ever be well again. I am surprised my body even functioned without it for as long as it did." Curling further into myself, I thought of ways I might escape. But if I did, then what would that mean for the world? Mia would simply come after me again. There was no stopping her. Killing her was the only option now.

"Honestly, you know we would never do such a thing. Getting out of your chambers might help. How about I send up Maybel and Tish, then you and I can take a walk through the gardens?" The queen did not wait for my answer before she pressed a kiss to the top of my head and grabbed Xavier by the arm, dragging him. So fast I nearly missed it, she yanked on the golden pulley that would ring in Maybel's chambers and left.

I did not want to see her, but better the handmaiden than the royals. Whatever they aimed to get out of this farce would do little for them. I would not break.

I knew what was real.

Maybel showed up only minutes later, a thin gold gown draped over her arm. Gods, end me now. If only I had remembered what Sterling said their names were.

Sterling!

Despite my desire not to wear the wretched color, I ripped the dress from Maybel's hands. I needed to see Sterling, to check on him and possibly free him. But I would not have long before Mia came back.

"Your Highness, you cannot just snatch the clothes from my hands like that!" Maybel shouted, chiding me. Did she know the truth? Was she lying to me as well? Could it have been her who had done the poisoning for the royals over the last two centuries? Even if she were not aiding them in their plans, she had still forced me to dress for my wedding. Had helped prepare me for my slaughter.

Solely for my affection for her as a youngling, I chose not to snap her neck then and there. Instead, I willed my magic into her mind and forced her to sleep. The act was like swimming in sludge, my whole body growing fatigued with the small show of magic. Whatever doses they were giving me now must have been larger than before.

How had they done it? When I was asleep? I knew it was probably in the food and water, but if they dosed me as I slept then I would need to be vigilant. No matter, sleep and food and water had been kept from me before.

Hastily, I dressed, cringing as I donned the gilded undergarments and slid the golden fabric up my body. But Sterling was more important than my feelings—than my comfort. So I sucked in heaving breaths, wiped the tears from my eyes, stepped into slippers, and walked out of my chambers.

Soft clicks echoed off the barren gold walls as I made my way to where I knew the dungeons awaited. How strange, the hollowness of this place. Never had I thought too deeply on why they had left everything bare, but now, as I rushed through the halls and tried to ignore the way my skin crawled, I did. Why had they not adorned the walls with art or any sort of decoration? What was it that made them wish for the palace to be so horribly empty?

Like their hearts.

Attempting to understand them was futile. They were not worth the energy. That was what I said to myself as I pressed on, ducking around corners when staff or counsel members walked past. The palace was bustling with fae, as if something important was about to occur.

But I was not as careful as I should have been.

A particularly lively group of staff came teeming around a corner far quicker than others had. With one floor left, I was determined to not be spotted, so I dove for the nearest door, opening it and locking myself in.

Pressing my ear to the golden wood, I listened for any sign that they passed, but it was what was behind me that quickly drew my focus.

"Asher?" A small gasp slipped from between my lips at the sound of Raven's voice. The daughter of the Royal Single had not changed since the last time I had seen her. She was about sixty years my junior, but far more fierce than I had been at her age and a notorious gossip.

Ultimately, I was fucked.

"Hey, Raven. Sorry, I did not realize you were in here," I admitted, reaching for the handle. The small sitting room was lit with candles. Raven sat on a sofa as she read a book, even the spine of which was gold. She wore a stunning blue gown, the soft tones of a vibrant sky highlighting her dark hair and eyes well. Her look of astonishment had my hackles rising. "Really, it is my fault. I will just go find something else to do."

"You sound odd." Raven stood then, tossing the book onto the sofa as she assessed me.

"What do you mean?"

"You are talking strangely," she added.

"Oh." Clearing my throat, I straightened, rubbing my sweaty hands on the stifling dress. Breathe. Just breathe. "Well, I am feeling a bit sick. Plus, there is a lot going on and I have so much to do. In fact, I better get going before Mia—Queen Mia—finds me slacking off."

Before I could so much as turn to face the door, Raven spoke again. "No, I mean you are speaking differently than you used to. Before you were attacked. You used to be so...*proper*. Even with those of us who knew you personally." Her head tilted slightly to the side, and I nearly lost it.

An image of Bellamy sarcastically cocking his head as he teased me flashed across my mind, and I thought the world might cave in. Everything became blurry, the air around me too thick to choke down. Bellamy, my loving and wicked and perfect Bellamy.

"Asher, I really think you should sit down. You look like you might be sick. I will go get King Xavier or Queen Mia. They should know you are awake." With that, she rushed past me and whipped open the door.

Maybe it was wrong, and perhaps the old me would have hesitated, but I was no longer the female I had been crafted into. I had repainted the canvas, remolded the statue. The new me—the one with far less pity in my heart and a desperate need to save the ones I loved—had no qualms with reaching into Raven's mind and forcing her to sleep. She hit the ground with a loud thud, deep red seeping across the ground from a gash on her head.

That was fine. She would be fine. It was fine.

Heart pounding, I made a break for it, leaving her sprawled out in the doorway. Every step seemed to ring through the entire palace, letting all know where I was, but I somehow managed to reach the long stairwell to the dungeons with no interference.

Taking them two at a time, I flew down the paths, winding through the halls until I came upon the line of cells I had known as a sort of home for the last week. For the first time, no fire burned in the wall sconces, the space practically void of light.

Passing each set of bars until I reached the final one, I found myself face-to-face with...nothing.

The cell was empty.

No. No. No. No. No!

"My flower, what is it you are doing down here?" Mia asked quietly. I wanted to burst, to shed my skin and free the evil within me that might finally end the queen. Anything other than simply stare at the cell void of a snarky and brave mortal prince.

But that did not happen. Of course it did not happen.

"Have you killed him?"

"Killed who? Asher, I wish I could make sense of what you are thinking, but I fear I might never understand. In fact, I am beginning to worry that whatever dark magic they attacked you with might be meant to turn you against me. To fill your head with these atrocious lies and steal you away."

Scoffing, I gripped the bars in front of me and leaned forward, letting my forehead press into the iron. Magic slithered within my chest like a chained dragon wishing to take flight. As a last-ditch effort, I freed that darkness within me, wishing beyond reason that it would strike Mia. There, in the silence of the dungeons, I sensed the way it barreled into her mind, striking a golden garden of pure energy. There was no sign of the blackness that had been a sort of barrier in Haven, but with poison in my veins, my magic did little more than ricochet off the flower petals.

Mia shouted, the sound of her heels smacking into the stone floors as she stumbled back making me smile despite the failure.

"Asher! What is wrong with you?" Her screeched words made my ears ring, and maybe it was that loss of depth that suddenly left me unable to hold back. Not wasting another moment, I turned and ran at her. Our bodies hit like two realms colliding. Using my momentum, I forced her to the ground, watching with glee as her head smashed into the stone beneath us. "Asher, stop! You are hurting me!"

"And you have hurt me my entire fucking life! You have done nothing but hurt me, Mia!" I wrapped my hands around her throat, squeezing with all my strength as I lifted her slightly and then once more

forced her head to snap back. A crack resounded just before blood began flowing freely from beneath her tangerine hair. "This is my thanks for a lifetime of pain."

Mia did not fight me as I tightened my grip, my eyes wide and mind racing with all the good her death would bring. Perhaps it might even give me the peace I had endlessly searched for. I was willing to be a monster for such a thing. Refusing to blink, I watched and watched as her eyes grew wider, her skin turning a violent red before fading to a blueish tint. There was no time to wonder at why she was letting me kill her, only enough seconds to remind myself that she had to die.

"Asher, no!" The ordered shout came just before a body barreled into mine, forcing me off Mia and sending me sprawling across the ground. Every newly healed bone in my body seemed to ache as I caught my breath, the male now holding me down as he shouted for help.

Through hazy and watering eyes, I looked up to find Sterling above me.

CHAPTER THIRTEEN

ASHER

Sterling was not only alive, but he was there above me, breathing heavily with those green-flecked eyes darting between my own. I could do nothing but stare up at him, so baffled by his presence, his action, that I was frozen in place. The sound of Tish talking as she ran to Mia was but a muffled and distant whisper. Sterling did not leave me, did not cower or run. He remained atop me, gasping for air just as I did. When he finally spoke, it made my heart shatter.

"What have you done, Asher?"

What had I done? What had *I* done! No, what had *she* done!

"Sterling, if we want to get out of here alive, then she has to die. She will imprison you again if we do not end her now," I hissed, squirming below him. His hands grabbed my wrists, pinning me to the ground. A wave of nausea rolled through me, the memory of Theon masquerading as Sterling while he violated me flashing behind my lids like a play of horrors.

"I have no idea what you are talking about. I woke up a week before you did, so maybe I have just had time to adjust, but you need to calm down." He looked away from me, and I found my own gaze turning the same direction. Vision clearing, I caught sight of Xavier standing over Mia as she was healed by Tish. His pale face was even more void of color than it normally was, his black waves tied back at the nape of his neck. He wore all gold, the long layers seeming too warm for summer.

Was it still summer though?

"I am taking my wife to her chambers. She is clearly not well," Sterling asserted, not giving Xavier the chance to demand my punishment before he leaned back to a crouching position and scooped me into his arms. I clung to him, unsure why other than the fact that I did not wish to be banished to my low level room.

Sterling nearly ran through the dungeons, making quick work of the stairs as well. He only slowed when we had reached the shining gold hallways of the palace above, a deep breath of relief skating across my cheek. Though I was fine to walk, Sterling did not set me down. That protective and possessive grip on me seemed to call attention to his words from before.

My wife.

No. Gods no.

"I am not your wife." It was all I could do not to scream the words. Had he been fooling me in the dungeons? Was he just as ambitious and manipulative as Theon? No. That could not be it.

"While I might not remember the wedding, I am told we completed our vows before being attacked, so I think that makes us husband and

wife," he offered, the barest hint of a smirk flashing across the left corner of his mouth.

"What do you mean? Sterling, you have been trapped in the dungeons since you arrived. You have been imprisoned! I do not know what they are doing to convince you otherwise, but you know the truth."

Pausing midstep, he seemed to think my words over. I used his moment of thought to press my hands against his chest and shove, forcing him to let me go. My hands and knees took the brunt of the force, but I ignored it in favor of scrambling away from him and pushing up to my feet.

"Why are you doing this?"

"I do not—"

"What is the last thing you remember?" I asked, cutting him off.

"Dinner. It is fuzzy, but I remember it." There was surety in his voice, as if it was the only thing he knew to be true.

"Dinner? What dinner?"

"The night I arrived. Queen Mia said that the black magic likely stole my memories. Did it steal yours as well? What do you remember?" His query was paired with outstretched arms, as if he were begging to understand. Lips quivering, I walked up to him.

"Everything. I remember everything." Tears slowly crawled down my cheeks, the last dregs of my sanity seeming to fade away. "I need you to remember too. I cannot be alone in this, Sterling." With ice cold, shaking hands, I pressed my palms to his cheeks. Magic flooded from my fingertips and into his mind, searching—seeking truths I was desperate to find.

Only to come to an abrupt halt just after I left the dinner in his memory.

Everything after that was endless darkness. A year of nothing.

Sterling did not remember. He did not remember and everything was wrong and *I was losing my fucking mind.*

I stepped back, pulling my hands away like his skin was a flame. Eternity above, I needed out. Mia had to die and I had to get out of this horrible golden prison.

Bellamy, I needed Bellamy. He was real, I knew it with every fiber of my being. My eyes darted down to my smooth skin. To my long strands of dark waves. To my hands that were free of calluses.

"You attacked the queen, Asher. Trouble will come if we do not get you to your chambers so you can rest. I am your husband, let me take care of this. Let me take care of *you.*" Sterling's hand slowly wrapped around my bicep, which was—gods, it was smaller. *Softer.* My muscles were gone, the hard-won firmness of my body a mere memory.

Or was it? Had I made everything up? Did my mind dream of something better?

No. It was *real.*

With one last wipe of my hands on my skirts, I turned away from Sterling and started darting towards the winding staircase that would lead me back to the main level of the palace. Fresh air would help. Yes, I just needed to get out of this suffocating place and think. They had to have freed me from my cage and constructed this lie for a reason. What had Mia said after I killed Theon? Something about her love molding me. That was all this was. An attempt at once more making me into their creature. Their killer.

I had already taken care of one of their loose ends after all. Theon was likely becoming more of a liability than an asset, and I had taken him out. Not that I would regret such a thing. As I bound down the stairs two at a time, I thought of the way he had defiled Sterling's face. How he had been a part of Sipho's death.

Blood rushed to my head, making me dizzy as I made it to the bottom of the stairs, nearly causing me to lose my balance. So much death, and in the end, much of the blood was on my own hands.

"Ah, another pity party. Sorry I did not brush my fur for such an event." Wrath's voice was both a welcome and a terrifying sound. Sweat dripped down my spine, and I found my head automatically tilting down. Locking gazes with Wrath, I tried my hardest not to think about what it meant that I was seeing my dead friend. "Can one be dead if they never existed?"

"Stop that. You know you existed!" My shout reverberated off the empty walls just before a set of rushing steps sounded behind me.

"Asher stop! We need to get you to bed!" Great, the mortal prince was chasing me like a stray dog. Just what I needed in that moment.

"Leave me alone, Sterling!" With that, I jumped over Wrath as he smirked up at me and dashed for the doors that would give me freedom, even if only for a moment.

"You cannot run from your own mind, Strange One," Wrath muttered as he kept pace with me. I wanted to kick the little vermin, but I was fairly certain my foot would go through thin air and then I would most definitely throw that pity party.

"Watch me," I spit as I pushed myself to run faster. Sterling called out for me to stop, to wait for him. When I did not listen, I heard him yell at the guards to help him. No one was going to force me back into that prison again.

What would Bellamy do?

Portal. Bellamy would portal away. And had I not done that when I attacked Theon? Had I not willed myself past those bars? Whatever I was, I could *portal*.

That would be my confirmation that it had all happened. If I could do this, then I would not only have a far better chance of killing Mia and

Xavier, but I would also know without a shadow of a doubt that it had all been real.

"You cannot portal. The likelihood that you simply made that up is far higher than you being able to bend time and space to your will." Wrath was really starting to aggravate me. Ignoring him, I pushed on, trying to pick up pace as I summoned my magic.

Work, please just work.

"Take me to the lake. Take me to the market. Take me anywhere but here." The world went dark as I scrunched my eyes together, trying to push out my magic. The sounds of someone quickly approaching left my heart racing. I knew I had failed before I even opened my eyes.

Just as I prepared to give up and seek another way, I ran right into someone.

Grunts left both of our mouths as we smacked heads, but whoever it was remained upright, catching me by the waist and stopping my fall. Heavy breaths mingled together, but the delicate arms that wrapped me in a hug and the radiant dress with full skirts that caught my sight made my gasps stop.

I knew those dark curls, those gentle hands.

Nothing could make me forget her.

"Nicola?" I breathed her name like a prayer. A salvation.

"Hi, Ash. I have missed you," my best friend whispered.

CHAPTER FOURTEEN

PERDITA

The prince's friends were...weird. The gigantic one paced and fidgeted so much that my entire crew was on edge around him. Meanwhile, the small thing with bright blue hair simply scowled as the two of them plotted. In the three hours we had them on board, neither had so much as spoken to us. Prince Bellamy Ayad asked—no, *demanded*—that we give them a couple hours to strategize, but I was quickly losing my patience.

Yes, we had our gold, but I was not one for waiting around. I did not like stillness, and I surely did not like being without a plan. Time drifted by like a rowboat at sea, but here we remained, anchored and unmoving.

It was pissing me off.

I was a pirate, for fucks sake! Reputations had to be maintained. Fear needed to be instilled, gold needed to fall at my feet, and blood needed to soak my deck. These two idiots were wasting my time. Yet, I could not simply kill them. More than gold hung in the balance of this odd alliance I had crafted with Bellamy Ayad.

Tides were shifting, change was coming, and I needed to be on the winning side. Not to mention they had killed my *father*. The bastard who had beaten me when I did not speak. The beast that used to haunt my sleep.

Torn vocal cords. How strange to know the truth of it. Not that I would want to be any different than I was. My inability to speak or hear had not stopped me from besting any and all who wished to come at me— challenge me. I was more than just a sailor or a pirate. I was a captain. The *best* captain.

Well, until today. Gods I could wring that stupid prince's neck right about now.

"They are odd," CJ signed. I nodded, but did not respond. As always, that did not deter CJ from continuing to converse. She had been secluded almost her entire life, left uneducated and hidden because of the strength of her powers. As far as Waters went, she likely would have been a part of the fae council if she had completed Academy and been scored. Thankfully for her, CJ's parents had been a part of the rebel group that had only grown as the years passed. They taught her at home, honed her powers, and showed her how to fight. More than that, they allowed her to see the truth: one must do anything they can to survive, even if the world deemed it evil. "I could freeze their blood and see how long they last, if you are bored."

Chuckling, I shook my head and shoved her arm playfully. She was a bright spot, despite her grim sense of humor.

"No need. I think I have waited long enough. If I spend more than five minutes in their presence, then send Ro over to save me." CJ saluted me and winked a piercing blue eye before skipping away, likely to torment

an already irate Bek. I watched with glee as her flowing dark hair swayed in the wind and wacked Fatima in the face.

CJ was the youngest of us—only thirty-five years—but when she found us docked at Isle Element and begged for our help, I could not refuse her. Anyone running from a family who caged them deserved a chance at freedom. While her family had not hurt her or even neglected her, they refused her the right to live beyond the walls of a home that existed in limbo.

My other five crew members—Bek, Ro, Dima, Jazmine, and Fatima—all came to me in different ways. Two strays, one poached from my pathetic father's crew, and two found along the way. Each of them served a vital purpose that maintained the ship and our livelihoods.

With a final deep breath of peace, I began walking towards the two newcomers. The male abruptly stopped his pacing at the sound of me nearing, but it was the female who took a fighting stance. She stood, pointing her dagger at me and glaring.

Objectively speaking, she was quite pretty. Her blue hair matched well with the yellow-tint of her skin and the deep brown of her eyes. Despite her oddly large teeth and mouth, her face seemed to be perfectly paired. She sported the body of a fighter, which was rather appealing to see. But there was something off about her. As if the darkness that lurked beneath her skin would consume us all if we did not behave.

Odd then, that she was not a demon at all. Not with those ears.

Choosing her had been completely random, but I found myself glad now as I squared off my shoulders. Neither of them could sign, that I was sure of. Few cared and even fewer learned. But they would have to make do.

"You are taking far too long," I signed, smirking when they both looked at me in confusion. Idiots. Laughing, I pointed to them and then to the sun. The tall one stared at me dumbfounded, but the female glared before standing and speaking to the male. I was not awful at reading lips,

but I often preferred not to. Her lips though, they were enticing. Like my eyes wished to do nothing but stare at them all day.

"She says it has been too long, I think."

Smart female.

The male scoffed, made obvious by the parting of his lips and the quick lift of his chest. As if he had any right to be annoyed. It was not only my time he was wasting, but his own as well. His princess's, too. Both of them should be more eager than I was, but instead they were doing what looked like nothing.

After a beat of silent stares between the two of them, the female faced me again. If one could cut with a stare, then I would have been dead upon my own deck from hers. Was she just a warrior, or did she hold a position of power? Would the prince keep a fae around that did not offer some sort of enormous gain? What then, was her power?

I wish I had been paying attention after they attacked Dima and the fight began, but I could not take my eyes off the dying siren. Could not understand how things had gone so horribly wrong. That, and I was carefully considering what I was willing to lose in order to win.

"We need to get to Betovere. Have you heard anything about the fae princess in the last week?"

Watching without laughing as she attempted to act out each word was an impossible task. I burst into a fit of chortles when she used her hands to make a crown on her head as she said "princess."

Bringing my fingers to my lips, I quickly blew out a whistle and waited for my crew to come. They were upon us in seconds, Bek and Ro taking up my flanks. Ro, with her upturned forest green eyes and her soft brown hair that only just kissed her collarbones, looked the sweetest of us all. She was, in fact, actually the meanest.

"We should kill them and run. Take our chances hiding from the prince instead of doing his dirty work. He might be sending us straight to

our deaths, Perdita." Her signs were soft despite the words she was conveying, just as she appeared to be. Rolling my eyes, I signed back to her, allowing my gaze to find the brown irises of the furious fae female before us.

"She wants to know if we have heard anything on the whereabouts of the fae princess. Tell her we have not, but that we need to form a plan if we are to be sent on a possible suicide mission." I knew with certainty that Ro likely growled in anger at my reply. But I did not answer to her—nor did I answer to anyone. My agreement to work with the prince would give us more than it would cost. If we could make a good plan, then we could accomplish this.

And gaining the fae princess as an ally would not hurt. Everyone in Eoforhild knew of the heir to Betovere and her horrific powers. She was practically the incarnation of the Underworld. Perhaps she could melt a few brains for us.

In front of me, the female seemed to deflate slightly, as if she had great steaks in this mission, too. More than her life. She spoke swiftly, her large lips barely opening. Though I could not make out what she was saying, I could sense the irritation.

"Also, ask her what their names are," I added. Ro's lips pursed before asking them with obvious reluctance and disinterest. Both the fae and the demon before us looked at me with scrunched noses and frowns, as if me asking such a thing was offensive.

"Henry and Lian," Ro said, signing the letters. L-I-A-N. How did that sound? Lie-an?

"It is pronounced lee-en. Li like tea, en like the beginning of the word end." Bek was always perceptive, always knew what I thought before I told her. Lian. Lee-en. Interesting. Henry was easy enough.

"Tell Henry that—" Before I could finish signing the order, the demon summoned light to his hand, a pencil emerging from the Sun magic. We all waited as he read, his eyes wide by the time he finished. He turned

and quickly cast out his magic, the white light turning into the shape of a female.

A curly-haired blonde emerged, dressed in green trousers and a black tunic. Despite her casual wear and sweaty face, so at odds with what must have been training leathers on the two she now stood beside, the female held herself like a queen upon a throne. Even the quality of her attire was clearly high. Definitely nothing like our flimsy and flowing clothing that best suited the seas and the scalding air. I drew the sword that had been strapped to my back, ready to end the newcomer before she had the chance to attack, but Henry put up a hand.

How *dare* he attempt to stop me—to order me!

"She has something for him," Ro signed, pointing at the note that the heavy breathing and red-faced female was sliding into the demon's hands.

CHAPTER FIFTEEN

BELLAMY

"Stop staring at me," Anastasia slurred. How she knew I was staring was beyond me. For someone who said she was here to save our world, she sure did look like she lacked initiative. Her small form was slumped across my bed, which she had eagerly commandeered after announcing she was going to throw up.

"You appeared in my home, suggested you were going to help me save Alemthian, and then puked on my sheets. What, exactly, should I do?" My sarcasm did not seem to inflame her like it did most. In fact, it was as if she did not feel much at all.

That was not my only reason for staring though. I knew her, I could have sworn I did. As she rolled over, her glowing pink hair fell forward over her face. It hit me then, where I had seen her before.

"You!" I shouted, causing her to wince in pain. "You were there on the battlefield when I awoke. You did something to Asher and I!"

"Stop yelling you fucking moron!" The words were practically a hiss, like a vexed cat.

That made me think of Wrath. Of how, as I burned his body and buried him in Haven last week, I had realized that Pino very briefly showed me the evil little vermin when we were at Reader River.

Aching for even another moment with all those we had lost, I sighed and sat in the chair at my desk. My legs straddled the back of the wooden seat, my chest leaning forward and arms hanging off the top. Anastasia opened a single pink eye, her oddly pointed ears sticking outwards instead of up. Her skin was a deep tan, but I wondered if below, her blood flowed black.

Was she another servant of the God of Death and Creation? She had called herself the holder of sin and virtue, that sounded oddly similar to the goddess.

"You're very handsome, you know," she whispered. A frown tilted my lips down as I furrowed my brow at her. She did not seem like the type to willingly give compliments. "Too bad you'll probably die soon."

Lovely.

"Do you have anything of value to say or offer? For someone who has deemed themselves a savior, you sure are being useless."

"How rude." This was getting very old, very fast.

"Listen, I think you need to leave before I make you—"

"*Make* me? Hah! You're funny. Anyways, I need Asher. She and I are going on a little treasure hunt." With that, the pink-haired psychopath crawled up my bed and tucked herself beneath my blankets. Gaping at her, I did not register exactly what she said for a few seconds. When I did, I

could do nothing but simmer in the anger and fear that had consumed me up until the moment she had arrived.

Adbeel had broken down in tears when I explained. Watching him sob had been heartbreaking. Listening to him rage at me for keeping her from him for the last year had torn me to shreds. What could I say to that? *"Sorry that I selfishly delayed our arrival and then allowed her to hyperfixate on finding allies instead of meeting you?"*

I knew what Asher was doing. That she refused to spend even a second of time doing something that she felt was self-serving because she thought she had not yet earned it. Could I have properly explained the importance of meeting him to her? Of course. Had I chosen not to because I refused to push her towards finding out truths that I thought might tear us apart? Definitely.

Adbeel's fury was more than deserved. He had not spoken to me since yesterday afternoon when I told him. Soon, he would come to me. I knew that. Looking for Asher had been the only reason he had taken me all those decades ago. When he realized I was not, in fact, his grandchild that he had only been briefly informed of through a secret letter, he had assumed the youngling had been murdered after all.

Now the granddaughter he had never known was once more gone.

"Hello, I told you to go get your little princess. Fetch like a good dog."

That was it.

I stormed over to her, grabbed her infuriating pink hair, and promptly yanked her out of my puke-stained bed. The horrible female shouted as she fell, and then she proceeded to *bite my leg*.

Furious shouted curses left my lips as I shoved my knee into her face. The beast then took out my knees with her tiny body. She was stronger than any demon or fae I had ever met, so strong it was concerning. Air whooshed from my lungs when my back made contact with the wooden floors.

"You pulled my hair! What kind of a male does that? I should kill you for your crimes!" Anastasia swayed as she stood, her nose bleeding not black, but a deep *blue*.

"What are you?" I asked with a wheeze. Something was very wrong.

"I told you, idiot! I am the holder of Sin and Virtue—a high demon. Your kind call us gods. Which is ridiculous by the way, there is no such thing." Scoffing, she slowly lowered herself to the ground near my feet. Three deep breaths later, I too sat up, facing her with more than a few questions.

"So, the god that abducted Asher, was he actually a high demon?" My mind was racing, unable to comprehend so much information, let alone acknowledge the fact that she was freely offering it all.

"Padon? Yes, he is unfortunately the emperor of Shamay, our world. Which is why I need Asher's help. He's currently planning to take not only her, but your entire world. Whatever she is doing, he cannot sense her magic, but as soon as he does, he will come for her. The moment she is in his grasp, he will destroy Alemthian. The demons are desperate, and he thinks Asher is the answer."

"Why does he think she can help? Why does he want to destroy our world?"

"According to him, she has the potential to become a high demon. If he ascends her, then she can possibly solve an issue we are experiencing. It is a long story. All I need is for Asher to help me find someone. Stella. She can fix everything."

"You know Stella?" I inquired with narrowed eyes. Anastasia would not be deterred. She glared my way, crossing her arms and scowling. "Asher is gone."

The words stung, admitting them like accepting defeat. But she would not be gone forever. Henry and Lian were taking care of her while I took care of Pike—of Eoforhild. That had to be enough.

"Fuck. That's going to be a problem. Is she dead or did she just dump you?" The nonchalance of such a question practically left steam coming out of my ears. Blood lust seemed to fill me, like a pot left to simmer. I wanted to explode—to kill her and anyone else who stood in my way of Asher.

Instead, I took my shoe and chucked it at her. Glee stretched my lips into a smile as it connected with her face, sending her head careening backwards. I did not know why, but I felt closer to Asher in that moment, like she had rubbed off on me in some way. It was something she would do, after all.

"You son of a—ow! Eternity above, sorry I hit a nerve you big baby!" She grabbed her forehead, massaging the spot where the toe of my boot had smacked into her. Her nose had stopped bleeding, a blue streak running down her cheek where it had dried into flakes. She healed quickly, similar to demons and fae. Not a god, but a high demon. Had all gods of the faith been high demons all along?

Perhaps she could help me with all of that magic.

"Asher was taken by the fae king and queen. If you help me get her—" The words sent a spark of pain into my temples, Asher's voice echoing across my consciousness.

"What is wrong? Why are you scrunching your face like that? You look ugly," she said, indifferent. She was so odd. And gods was she rude.

"Asher has used her magic to stop me from helping her. It is why I had to send others to do it. Why I am here when she is there." Broken. My voice could only be described as broken.

Anastasia cocked her head to the side, contemplating something in that wicked mind of hers. Probably nothing good.

"I can do a siphon spell with some runes. It won't take long, but it will hurt." Shrugging, she stood and walked past me towards my desk, opening up every drawer until she found a pot of ink stashed in the bottom one. I tried not to growl in frustration at the way she left each of them open.

With that, she snatched my old glass of water, drank it in one long gulp, and then threw it in the trash. The sound of it smashing really did pull the sound of irritation out of me then. "Down dog, it was an ugly glass anyways. Remind me to teach you taste if we all survive this. Now, lay back, take off your shirt, and prepare yourself. This is only going to be entertaining for one of us, and it isn't you."

Laying back, I watched as she dipped her finger into the ink. With a final glare, I unbuttoned the black tunic I was wearing but left it on my arms. That must have been enough skin, because she only whistled and smirked before bringing her finger to my stomach. Which runes she was drawing across my skin, I did not know. I only knew a few from what I had learned of the gods, which must have been what she was using. I stayed silent as she worked, slowly covering my body in the ink.

"This won't take the magic from your veins, by the way. In case you were worried about losing that little bit of Stella's essence," she whispered, moving to make a mark on my forehead. I blinked up at her, surprised by the words.

"Why would that worry me? I would be lucky to be rid of it. All it serves is to bring me that much closer to death." If what I said surprised her, she did not show it. She just stared at her finger while she worked and furrowed her brow.

"You're lucky to be gifted something as eternal as Moon magic. Stella came from a long line of conquerors. Her magic was made for a throne. Even if you were clearly not given it the right way, it's still a gift." As her finger ran across my cheek, a soft sigh left her mouth. "Regardless, there's only one way to get it out of your system now that you have been given it, and that's death."

"Old news," I whispered. She paused for a second, as if she somehow could see my death too. Just as promptly as she had stopped, she started once more, painting me in magic that made my hairs rise and bumps spread across my bare skin.

"So, lover boy, tell me, how did Asher get taken on your watch again? You're oh for two right now." Lover boy? What was wrong with this female?

I was the ocean. I was unmovable, unforgiving, a tempest.

Breathe.

She was no more than a ship at my mercy. Her words meant nothing.

The rage disagreed as it rolled within me like a hurricane, disrupting the ocean of tranquility that I claimed myself to be.

"What did you do to get cast away? Did you upset your leader? Did you throw a tantrum? You seem so very levelheaded with your drunken idiocy and your inability to shut the fuck up," I hissed. With eerie speed, Anastasia reached up and snapped my nose, the crunch so loud it seemed to echo in my ears.

I cried out, rolling away from her and grabbing at my face. Blood poured freely from my nose and coated my hands. It was so much sexier when Ash did it.

With a deep breath, I released my nose and flashed her my middle finger, hoping it translated to whatever underworld forsaken hole she crawled out of.

"You're nothing but a little bitch who can't see past his own wants and needs. Now tell me what exactly happened to Asher while I fix your nose," she hissed. I rolled back towards her, ignoring her quip in favor of lifting my nose towards her. A flash of bright pink smoke appeared around my face, and then the pain was gone. It did not hurt like Ranbir's power. Instead, it was an instantaneous burst of magic that came and went like a whisper in the wind. Before I could answer her, she mumbled, "Mortals as stupid as you shouldn't be so attractive."

"That was the worst compliment I have ever received," I grumbled, wiping the blood off my nose with my sleeve. She merely offered me a look

of disinterest before once more dipping her finger into the ink and painting my skin. "As I was trying to say, Asher was taken by the fae king and queen. They raised her, and they were determined to get her back. She…*sacrificed* herself for me."

"Well that's unfortunate." With that she swiped her finger across my collar bone, then pressed down. "Brace yourself."

The pain was excruciating. It felt like my very soul was being cleaved from within me. As if the high demon were digging it out with her pink claws. A scream slipped from between my lips, and I wondered how long the agony would last. Just as I thought it, the pain dissipated.

"Gods, that hurt," I groaned, pushing myself up to a sitting position. "Did it work?"

"How would I know? You're the one with magic attacking your concerningly nice body," she retorted.

"Even if I did not have Asher, I still would not want you anywhere near my obviously amazing body. Also, it is my head that her magic affects," I added with a wave of my hand. With that in mind, I decided there was no time like the horrifying present to test out the success of the runes.

Asher. Perhaps I could portal there, storm the palace made of gold and heartbreak. I could get her. Save her. Bring her *home*.

"I feel…nothing. There is no pain," I whispered, the disbelief—the *joy*—bringing tears to my eyes. "Anastasia, I—I do not know how to thank you. You might be annoying and rude, but you just changed my life."

I could go get her. I could kill them all. I could—

"Don't thank me yet, pretty boy. You owe me some labor before you go off and whisk your princess away." My head whipped towards her, watching as she smirked and wiped her hand on my red quilt, staining it with the black ink. "You can call me Stassi, by the way. It seems like we are about to become reluctant allies."

CHAPTER SIXTEEN

ASHER

Every breath of Nicola's floral scent was a relief to my system. Peace in the eye of a storm.

"Asher, you need to breathe," she said into my hair. What did she mean? I was breathing. Desperately so. Maybe too quickly, actually. "You are going to have a panic attack if you do not take a moment to settle yourself."

Oh gods, she was right. It hit me then, how my gasping heaves of air and the tears running down my cheeks must look. She likely thought I was insane.

"No, I am fine," I muttered, pulling back from her. She was just as stunning as ever. Her dark skin was glowing, her full lips pursed and brown

eyes wide. She had pulled her wild and lovely curls back with pins the color of the sun. Her dress matched, a bright spot in an otherwise bleak world. "I need to tell you something—to explain everything."

"Listen, there is very little time. If there was ever a time to trust me, that time is now. Your future, all of our futures, hangs in the balance of whatever decision you are about to make," she whispered, eyes darting back and forth. Backing further away, I ripped my arms from hers, unable to make sense of what she was saying.

"Of course I trust you. But you do not understand, we are living a *lie*. We have to figure out how to stop the king and queen, we—"

"Ash, you are sick and confused. I understand, but you have to follow my lead right now, okay? Can you do that?" She asked, her wide eyes pleading as they bore into my own. My mind spun with the vague and ominous information she was giving me. What did she mean? I was not sick, I was finally awake after centuries of sleep walking through my life.

But this was Nicola. She knew more than others. If there was anyone here in Betovere that I could trust, it was her.

"Yes, I trust you. I can do that." With a nod and a sad smile, she stood up straighter and pasted on a look of glee.

"Your Majesty," she greeted, pulling me to her side before bowing low. I watched in horror before turning my head, internally screaming as Xavier stormed our way. My best friend's grip on my skirt tightened and pulled, yanking me into the same dip.

"Nicola, while it is lovely to see you, I need Asher to come with me. She is very sick." His voice was like thunder as it boomed out, the meaning beneath the words delayed lightning striking me in the heart.

"I would like to come with, King Xavier. She has been asleep for so long," Nicola pleaded. A hand gripped mine, her skin warm and soft and familiar. Xavier's eyes darted down to where Nicola's fingers intertwined with my own, and I watched in horror as a muscle ticked in his jaw and fire seemed to blaze in his dark eyes.

"Do not read her, Nicola. The attack left her weak and disoriented. She needs rest, not company." With that, he grabbed my arm and pulled me away from her. Yelping in both pain and terror, I tried and failed to wrench away from him.

"Please, let me be there. Just to watch over her. Kafele's injuries prevented me from attending her wedding, and I may never forgive myself when I might have been able to make a difference. I wish to never leave her side again." The words sounded earnest, but there was a sort of hollow feeling to them that I could not place or understand.

"Kafele was injured? What happened to him? Is he okay now?" The two of them both looked at me, Xavier in fury and Nicola in discomfort. Eternity spare me, was he...*dead?*

No, Nicola would not be so cavalier about the death of her soulmate.

"He was attacked, but he has fully recovered. Nothing to worry about," she said, pursing her lips and reaching for me.

Xavier jerked me further back, forcing me to stumble away from her. Nicola's eyes squinted slightly, and I watched as she seemed to weigh her next words. As she *hesitated.*

"It was...a demon attack," she finally clarified.

My mind went blank of everything except Bellamy's smiling face. The dimples that dug into his cheeks and the tilt of his head. No. It was not demons.

With all my might, I shoved Xavier, forcing him to let go of my arm. Then I ran at Nicola, gripping her biceps and staring into her eyes. I felt crazed, desperate, disturbed.

"No, it was not demons. It has never been demons! The attacks are—"

"Ash, you are not well. We need to get you to your chambers," she said, her eyes wide and full of an emotion I could not understand. I wanted to argue, to explain to her how wrong she was.

We had been fooled our entire lives, and she was still being tricked. Trying to enter her mind to *show* her, I was met with a sharp, stabbing pain in my temples, leaving only the faint taste of my best friend's terror on my tongue. I grabbed my face, the ache strong and disorienting.

Nicola came closer, whispering through her teeth, "Remember what I said?"

"You have to follow my lead right now okay?" she had said.

I trusted her. Of all the beings in this Eternity forsaken realm, it was her that I trusted the most. With a nod, I released her. Xavier was quick to once more claim my arm, practically dragging me away from the Tomorrow—no, the Oracle. Nicola was an Oracle.

"Come, Asher, you need to lie down and allow Tish to see to you," he ordered. Nicola looked at me in horror as he pulled me farther and farther from her, one of her hands outstretched towards me.

"Wait, Your Majesty! I think that—"

"No, Nicola!" Xavier shouted, abruptly stopping to turn towards her. My chest flew into his, my head knocking into the muscle there. "Asher attacked Queen Mia. She is volatile and unwell. She needs to be looked over and alone. We will let you know when it is safe to visit. Go home to your husband."

Husband.

They had gotten married. I missed my best friend's wedding.

Though it was not the most important part of the day, or even of the conversation, it was that fact that had me obediently walking alongside Xavier.

***

"You will not leave your chambers until Tish has deemed you well enough to do so. Under no circumstances are you allowed to have any visitors other than Mia, Sterling, or I. If I find that you have used your powers—"

"Magic," I mumbled, cutting off Xavier's tangent. He froze, his finger still pointing my way and his mouth left open.

"Eternity above, Asher. You have truly lost your mind. You do not have magic. You are not some demon from the depths of the Underworld." There was a sincerity to his tone that made me close my eyes. He was lying. I knew what was real. "If you use your *powers* on anyone, I will have no other choice than to have your blocker placed on you once more."

Forcing my eyes to remain closed, I further curled into myself in the corner. Waiting for his suffocating presence to leave. I felt like a youngling again. I felt weak.

"I do not want to do this, Ash. Seeing you like this hurts me. But you are proving yourself to be a danger and a liability. We cannot allow it. Please, get into bed, eat your lunch, and rest. That is all I ask." Had I truly once thought they loved me? It baffled me that those hideous words hidden beneath false endearment had convinced me for so long that I was loved.

Choosing to stay silent rather than acknowledge his deceit, I remained still until his retreating footsteps were met with the click of my doors closing.

And then, just as I had once always been, I was alone.

***

Two days passed without me so much as moving to relieve myself after I had stripped my body bare. I remained there, in my own mess and hopelessness, chanting.

It was real. It was real. It was real. *It was real.*

"Sure it was, Strange One." Wrath had unfortunately kept me company. "I wish you would bathe. You smell horrendous."

Though I did not speak back to the dalistori, he rarely stayed quiet himself.

"I am a figment of your imagination. If you want me to be silent, then make me. It is not my fault you have dreamt up a fake life and love and cat." His tale swished as he spoke, his gray fur silky and his fangs short. Those big yellow eyes bore into me, waiting for a reaction.

I would not give him one.

I knew what was real.

"You are insane, do you know that?" he asked with a sharp-toothed smile. I scowled his way, watching with annoyance as he chuckled and scooted closer to me. If only I could drop-kick him.

"Maybe you should try, see if you can look any more ridiculous than you do in a pile of your own urine and wearing nothing but your own shame."

Wrath was a figment of my imagination. He was the part of me that was unwilling to leave the past behind. Every piece of my mind and soul that loathed me. What he said meant nothing.

"Sure, Strange One."

Closing my eyes, I begged for a reprieve.

***

The next morning, I awoke to pounding on my door and the sound of Sterling's horrified shouts.

"Asher! Are you okay? Asher!" Again and again his fist slammed into the granite, the echoing sound making my head ache.

I wanted to tell him to leave me be. I was wallowing. That and plotting. My mind was swimming with potential ways I could eventually kill Mia and Xavier. Prioritizing my own strength was important. In the last three days I had come up with a sort of checklist.

One, do not eat the food or drink the water. There was no doubt in my mind that it was poisoned. However, I had to be cautious. Baths were out of the question, because they could taint that too.

Two, do not wear the clothes. How easy would it be to lace the gowns with hemlock or belladonna? Yes, I could wear gold, even if it made my skin crawl. Bellamy had taught me that I was stronger than that. But, if they tampered with the fabric, then I could be wearing my downfall.

Three, no visitors. I would not be forced to endure the presence of anyone who might harm, poison, or sway me. They were attempting to manipulate me, but I would not let them.

Four, remember it was real.

"Asher, I have a key. Please do not make me enter your space without your permission." Eternity above, he never left. Every day, he came and yelled behind the doors until I finally said to leave. It was annoying. More than that, it was tempting.

I feared for the mortal prince. They had harmed him—tortured him—before. There was nothing stopping them from doing it again. A part of me wanted to welcome him in and not allow him to leave. To protect the boy with adventure in his soul and light in his heart. Another part of me, the more sane part, knew that it likely only put him in more danger to be around me. To be seen as someone I cared about.

"That is it, I am coming in!"

Shit.

For the first time in three days, I moved. Far slower than normal, I pushed myself up and crawled to the bed. Locks jingled on the other side of the doors, freedom closer than it had been in a while. My hands gripped the golden gown I had tossed days ago, pulling the hideous thing onto my body just as Sterling burst through the doors.

He wore golden silk that matched the perfect coils of his hair. His skin was slightly darker than it had been in the dungeons, his pallor no longer sickly. I had no idea how they managed to rid him of the thinness that signaled malnutrition, but there he stood, his body filled out and quite strong.

Despite that, the mortal prince appeared terrified.

"Asher, what happened?" he asked in a panic.

I stared at him, unsure of what to say. Or what to do. He rushed to me, brown eyes wide. Despite the smell, Sterling knelt beside me, his hands coming to either side of my face as he seemed to search for any sign of injury. He would find none that were visible, think me mad, and then leave to tell Xavier or Mia. I was sure of it.

"If you tell me what is wrong, I can help," he said. Then, far quieter, he whispered, "Please let me help you."

The ring around his finger on his left hand seemed to sizzle against my skin. Gold crackled and burned where it kissed my cheek, a marriage forced upon me like a curse. Sterling was kind, funny, curious, and handsome. He was more than I could have asked for a year ago. But now, after knowing what it was like to love and be loved by Bellamy? Well, nothing would ever compare. And even if I never saw Bellamy again—if perhaps I died ridding the world of the fae king and queen—I would still never call anyone else my husband.

"Take off the ring," I ordered brokenly, tugging my face free of his grasp. Sterling's face fell, sadness seeping in to wash away the terror. With a slight nod, Sterling pulled off his wedding ring and tucked it into his pocket. Freeing me from the sight of a false promise I wanted nothing to do with. "Thank you."

"Of course." A beat of silence passed, a moment of tension and unknowing in which we both stared at the other. "How about a bath?"

"It will be poisoned. You do not understand, but the king and queen wish to keep me weak. They are trying to remind me of how small they can make me. I will not let them," I stated, lifting my chin.

While I expected judgment or condemnation, Sterling just sat back on the heels of his shoes and studied me openly. After a few moments, he simply nodded and held out a hand.

"Okay, my bathing room it is."

"What?"

"You can come to my chambers and bathe there. I will have them bring up fresh water and I will lend you some of my old clothing." With a few words and a simple shrug, Sterling completely shattered my shields of defense. Nodding, I grabbed his hand and let him pull me up.

"Are you only doing this because you think I am your wife? Because you want something from me?" I had to ask. There were so few beings in this world who gave without ulterior motives. Even if Sterling was once the type of man who harbored more kindness in his heart than most, who knew what they had done to him since I saw him last.

"I am doing this because you are a person—sorry, being. You deserve to feel safe. Of course, you are my wife, so I owe more to you than most." With that, he tugged me forward. "Which means, if you say the king and queen are out to get you, then I believe you."

I followed silently, knowing I was not meant to leave my chambers but caring little. He seemed perfectly fine, so they likely were not tampering

with his water. And they probably would not have thought to do anything nefarious to his clothes. Maybe this could work.

Or maybe he was in on it and was just trying to get that poison in my system for them.

Honestly, I did not feel much better without it. My head throbbed, my body ached, and my magic felt distant. All of which could have been due to dehydration and starvation, but I feared it was because whatever they did was going to permanently affect me—or maybe they were still poisoning me after all.

We did not go far, passing through my doors and walking to the end of the hallway. Sterling halted at the final door and pushed it open, revealing a golden disaster. Clothes littered the floors, trays from meals sat on the bedside table, and books were *everywhere*.

Mess did not accurately describe Sterling's chambers.

For some reason, I loved it.

"Do maids not come here?" I asked, letting out a soft and weak chuckle. The first since we had been locked in the dungeons together.

Sterling looked over his shoulder, grinning widely my way. "They try."

Shaking my head, I let the prince lead me through the mess, hopping to each spot he did. We stumbled our way past his golden bed on the right, his matching dresser on the left, and made it to the bathing chamber in the far right corner.

Sighing dramatically, Sterling straightened and opened the door. His bathing chamber was simple, containing a tub, a vanity, and a chamber pot. Nothing exciting, though the gold made everything gaudy.

"I will have them bring water but will not let them carry it in. When it is ready, I will fill the tub and then leave so you can have space. Let me go grab you some of those clothes really quick." He left me then, pulling

the rope that would alert the servants who were meant to serve him. I waited, listening to what sounded like him tripping. Curses sounded from the main chambers, putting a smile on my face against my will.

Minutes passed as I stood there, thinking. Plotting.

If I could get close to Mia or Xavier, then maybe I could use a weapon to end them. My magic was volatile, so it would be of little help, but blades were steady. Constant. Yes, I would just need to find a way to walk through the palace without notice.

"You sure are thinking hard," Sterling muttered as he carried two enormous buckets of water to the bath. I watched silently as he dumped them, the steam enticing me to halt my planning in favor of taking a moment to relax.

"Are you positive they did not know I was here?" I questioned instead of responding to his comment. He shook his head, golden curls swaying with the movement.

Between chuckles, he answered, "Positive."

Nodding, I walked towards the bath. I would clean myself then get out. There was no time to waste. Maybe Sterling could help me find a way. He seemed to believe me. Or at least, he appeared willing to go along with my beliefs. That was enough.

"I will be right on the other side of the door if you need anything," he said. His steps back towards the door were slow and measured, the same way one might walk away from a monster they feared would attack.

"Well, if I drown, slip, or die suddenly, then my ghost will tell you first." Laughter and a salute were his only responses before he slipped through the door and shut it behind him. A moment later, the door swung open again, and he set down a small pile of clothes on the floor before closing the door again.

It felt wrong to laugh. To be anything but miserable when those around me attempted to steal Bellamy and my family from my memory.

Still, I allowed myself to feel the amusement as I stripped from my dress and stepped into the scorching water. Then, like a flower basking in sunlight, I vowed to never wilt again.

CHAPTER SEVENTEEN

ASHER

While he might not have had any memories, Sterling was still an excellent companion.

After my bath I had quickly dressed, the forest green top and black cotton trousers fitting me rather well. When I had pulled the door open, Sterling's body had careened backwards. No amount of sleep would have given me the strength to stop myself from saying, "Ah, it seems you have discovered gravity."

Sterling, ever the partaker in wit, simply stared up at me from the floor and said, "It is painful being this brilliant."

We now sat on his bed, playing cards and eating what I used to call *the trifecta*—buttered bread, pastries, and cheese-stuffed rolls. Sterling had lost four games in a row, which was truly just the product of me having been bored for two centuries and getting good at nearly useless things. Which was why I took pity on him and let him win.

"Finally! You know, I got rather good at cards while I traveled," he commented, smacking his hands together as if to dust them off. I froze, my mind adjusting to his comment at rapid speed. Yes, I had known he traveled despite him never telling me before the wedding, which was proof I had not made any of it up. Tangible proof!

"Yes, your travels. I know all about those. You told me about them, do you have any recollection of when?" I asked, knowing he would not remember our times in the cells. To my surprise, though, Sterling nodded his head.

"While you were unconscious. Queen Mia suggested I speak to you of myself as you slept so that you might wake up sooner. I think it worked, oddly enough. You were conscious a week later."

"No, Sterling. The reason I know those things is because you told me when we were in the dungeons together. I do not know what they did to you, but I can show you what I mean—the memories. Would that be okay?"

Sterling nodded, unflinchingly curious. Today that would be in my favor. With a deep breath, I pressed out my magic. It hurt, the act making my head pound and my stomach roll, but I pressed on, projecting my memories of our time beneath the golden palace.

Emotions flashed across his face: confusion, surprise, horror, heartbreak, fury. When I had finished, tears welled in his eyes and anger tightened his jaw.

"Do you believe me?" I asked cautiously.

He gave me no answer other than reaching forward and wrapping me into a tight embrace. My muscles tensed at the contact, memories of

horrors committed by those hands but a different being entirely flashing behind my eyelids. The moment I reminded myself this Sterling was different—*good*—I melted into the hold and returned the embrace. Even if he did not necessarily believe me, at least he was there.

A knock disrupted the moment of peace. We parted quickly, my mind instantly on edge.

"Who is that, Sterling? Did you tell someone?" I did not wait for him to answer my panicked accusations. Instead, I reached out my magic, gasping at the pain of it as I searched for who it was that stood on the other side of that door.

Relief cooled my blazing body. Nicola. Leaning back against the headboard, I slowly massaged my temples. Sound that I had not realized I had blocked out came back to me, Sterling's terror loud in my ear.

"Asher, did you hear me? Asher! It is just Nicola."

Everything was hurting. My body, my mind, my heart. I felt like I might explode from how badly my own magic pierced me. A war drum seemed to beat at full speed beneath my eyes, pain shooting down my spine. Clawing at my skin, I tried to dig out the source of the pain—to do anything other than just sit there.

Then a hand touched my shoulder.

Maybe it was my magic being more volatile than normal and corrupting my senses. Or it could have just been reflexes that I *knew* I had. Either way, one second I was clutching my head, and the next I was twisting Sterling by the wrist, a sickening crack met with a pained shout.

The doors burst open, Nicola racing forward with wide eyes. "Sterling!"

"I am fine, it was an accident," he said through clenched teeth. He was not fine though, I could feel the way his agony crashed through his body in waves.

"We need Tish to heal this, there is no way that was a clean break." Nicola's calm words broke through the haze of my panic, and I found myself far more aware of my own sanity—or lack thereof—than ever before.

"I am so sorry, Sterling. I thought…well, I do not know what I thought." Shaking my head, I leaned forward and inspected the odd twist of his wrist and the limpness of his hand. Gods, I could not believe what I had done. Nicola was to my left, standing beside the bed with a vacant and distant look in her eye. Was she scared of me?

"No need to worry, the only thing I used it for was pleasuring myself anyways." Sterling's joke forced an incredulous laugh out of me. How could he jest like that when the female he thought was his wife had snapped his wrist?

"Well then, I guess I was really doing you a favor." My voice shook, the pitch higher than my normal tone.

"How is that?"

"Now you have an excuse to train the other." His smile was bright despite the scrunch of his eyes and clench of his jaw that betrayed the pain he felt. The kindness he offered me made my chest tighten. I did not deserve it. Perhaps I really was losing my mind.

"Asher," Nicola finally spoke. I looked over to her, watching her beautiful features contort into an almost pained expression. "This will lead to something quite nasty, but we are on the right track. You must call for Mia, not Tish. Get back to your chambers and change your clothing. When Mia asks what happened, you say that the two of you were getting intimate and Sterling fell off the bed."

"Why would we lie?" Sterling asked, furrowing his brow.

"Do you want your husband to live?" Nicola asked, cutting off Sterling. She stared at me with those haunting and distant eyes, so different than the bright and joyous way they used to shine. So we would all be changed by this war. If any of us survived, we would never be the same.

I spiraled through the possibilities of what she could mean, but really only one thought made it past my lips.

"He is not my husband," I muttered. Sterling scoffed at my side, still sprawled on the bed and clutching his broken wrist to his chest.

"Asher, do you want him to live?" Her gaze zeroed in on me, the veil of her power momentarily dropping.

Against my will, my eyes darted to the boy. That was what he was, in truth. Just a boy. Young even by mortal standards. He had so much life to live. His wit and curiosity and pure joy reminded me of what Bellamy never got to be. What I never got to be.

"Yes, I want him to live."

"Then get him to your rooms, mess your hair, and call the Queen."

With that, she turned and left. I did what I had once done best, what I had forgotten how to do until this moment. I followed orders.

"Do I at least get to kiss you to make it realistic?" Sterling asked as I began pulling him up.

"Did no one tell you? Fae females have tongues like razors." My words were paired with Sterling's hiss as I wrapped his uninjured arm around my shoulders and tugged him to the door. The pain was clearly making him dizzy. Incoherent too.

"All the more reason to take me for a ride."

"Unfortunately for you, I am spoken for."

"Yes, by me, your husband," he clipped, his tone betraying his annoyance at my refusal to believe in our sham marriage.

"Currently, the only thing you are to me is a problem," I spoke, a grunt nearly cutting off my sentence when my foot caught the edge of the gold carpet that ran the length of the hallway.

"So, no to the kiss?"

"You learn so quickly. Perhaps we can find you a far better female to kiss. Maybe even fuck."

I released him for a second to reach into his pocket and grab the keys. As expected, Sterling mumbled something about me fondling him and my false disinterest in his cock. I ignored him, choosing to focus on getting the door open. There were five keys and three locks, so he was forced to direct me.

"It does not fit!" I hissed, trying and failing to get the final key into the lock.

"Not the first time I have heard that," he responded.

"Not the first time a male has lied to me about their size either. Now tell me which key."

"You sure are crass. Anyways, I think I got them mixed up, try the more rounded one."

"Eternity damn you," I groaned, grabbing the correct key.

"Yes, Eternity damn me to the Underworld. I love all things hot and spicy." His wiggling eyebrows brought a reluctant grin to my face. Mortals were menaces.

"You are even more of an idiot when you are in pain." There, the lock clicked.

"A hot idiot, at least?"

"I would not know, I prefer savory, now get in."

We made it through without being seen—a miracle if I have ever known one. Sterling winked before jumping into my still perfectly made bed and crying out when he accidentally jostled his hurt wrist.

What an absolute nitwit. I was constantly surrounded by such creatures.

Ignoring the prince, I hastily made my way to my wardrobe, grabbing out a thin nightdress. Making it believable. My hair was newly washed and still fairly damp, but I reached up and mussed it on my way to my bathing chambers. As quickly as I could, I stripped from Sterling's clothes, tucked them behind my tub, and dressed in the golden silk.

From there it was just a matter of ringing the pulley that would alert Mia's handmaidens. My hand touched the rope, the ends frayed from just how often I had called for her.

I used to love her. She was my rock, an immovable force that stopped me from being pulled out to sea. When someone hurt me, it was Mia that I first called to. Her arms would wind around me as she whispered kind words about my magnificence. Xavier would later tell me ways in which I might fight back, how I could destroy them if I was smart. How was it that those same two beings—the fae I thought of as parents—would then hurt me so deeply? Would call me a monster and tell me to thank them for their love?

With a deep breath, I cleared my mind and tugged the rope.

Passing through the door, I darted back to Sterling. In my absence he had taken on a sickly pallor, his face nearly as green as the flecks in his eyes.

Time was of the essence, so I did not hesitate to jump on the bed with him and run my hands through his hair.

"This will hurt and I am so so sorry for that. For hurting you before. Likely for hurting you again, I am sure."

Then I ripped him up towards the pillows, dragging him until his head hit the cushion. My fingers expertly undid the golden buttons of his tunic, parting the fabric to reveal his bare chest. Then I yanked off his shoes, threw them to the side, and tucked him beneath the blankets. For my own

part, I slapped and pinched my cheeks, shook one of my straps off my shoulder, and moved to straddle him.

Wait, no. He needed to be on the ground. Shit.

"We have to move you! The story is that you fell and broke your wrist. How could you have done that on the—"

A knock on the door cut off my sentence. She was here. With no other option I moved to the side and kicked Sterling off the bed, diving to the ground after him.

"Come in!" I said, using my hand to cover Sterling's mouth and muffle his cries. He jostled for a moment before stilling. Then my doors burst open. Mia ran, her golden gown swishing around her. Every part of her was immaculate, crafted with precision. Her lips were full and pink, her orange hair once more shorter in the back than in the front and cut above her shoulders. There was no sign of her freckles, but her eyes of ice were confirmation enough.

Bellamy's mother approached, Tish not far behind her. As if she knew my need for her could only mean injury now. So different than it once was.

"He fell," I said, trying to elicit some of the panic at her nearness into my voice. Mia's gaze ran over me, taking in my hair and my flush and my exposed shoulder. Then she looked at Sterling, who was even more of a disaster than I was. His buttons still exposed the flesh of his chest, his curls a mess from when he had ran his fingers through it as we played cards.

"Tish, check on him," the queen ordered. Tish nodded her head, her complexion once more perfect and simple. She looked healthy. Like she no longer needed to heal every day.

"Or perhaps she never had." My eyes moved to the harsh sound of Wrath's voice of their own will. I caught sight of him just behind Mia, a smirk on his feline face. He was smaller than normal, but just as daunting.

I wanted to yell at him. To swear at the queen before me. More than both of those things, I wished to curse the ethers themselves for all the wrongs they had committed. For it was Eternity who I owed my bitter thanks—my bloodlust—my insanity.

"Yes, Strange One. Blame all but yourself. What a new way of thinking for you. Perhaps your imagination has taught you something after all. Madness looks wonderous on you."

And then he disappeared.

Mia was on her knees, her gown splayed out around us. She grabbed my jaw, tilting my head back and forth. "Did he force himself on you, my flower?"

As if she would care. She had proven that, when push came to shove, it was her plans over my wellbeing every time. But of course, I could not say that. So instead, I lowered my gaze and slumped my shoulders. I made myself small and shy. Becoming the Asher she had raised.

"No, we were…" I allowed my words to trail off, my eyes to flick up to hers and then over to a now-healed Sterling as he sat up. "We got a bit too excited."

For a moment, I feared she would not believe me. Her jaw seemed to clench as she looked between the two of us. I did not dare check that Sterling was playing his part. No, my attention remained fixed on the queen.

Believe me. Take this victory. Accept that the future you desire is coming to fruition.

I did not dare use my magic. Not when it was so determined to work against me. Instead, I waited for Mia's ego to be her downfall.

She stared, her shoulders back and her lips pursed.

Sterling seemed to catch on to the tense showdown, because he quickly wrapped his arms around me.

"Sorry for the scare, love." His heart was beating rapidly against my chin, a sign of the nerves he so clearly had.

Burrowing further into his chest, I returned the hug. "It was my fault, really."

Just as we went to release one another, Nicola's singsong voice rang out.

"Ash? Are you okay?" I jerked back, my eyes scanning my chambers for her. She was dashing from the doorway, making quick work of closing the distance between us. Glee filled me to the brink as she shoved past Tish and lowered herself to Mia's side. "What happened?"

A smirk lifted the corner of my mouth as I answered, "Fun happened."

"Okay, okay. Nicola, I think it is about time Sterling goes back to *his own* chambers. Will you take him? Asher needs her rest." Mia's voice was commanding. The tone of a queen who had been wronged too many times.

"Actually, Your Majesty, I had an idea," Nicola nearly whispered. Face docile and tone sweet, Nicola was the picture of a subservient fae. She smiled, ever the doting subject. "I was thinking that it might benefit Asher to see the realm. With her and Sterling wed, they could go together on a sort of royal tour. After all, they will one day rule the Fae Realm. Traveling throughout it might even get Asher's spirit up once more."

My shoulders straightened at the idea, though I had a feeling Mia would just say no. Her attention remained on me, scrutinizing the way I became eager at the idea. What she could not see was how different this eagerness was than how it used to be. I no longer cared about adventure. Now I wanted nothing but her blood and my freedom.

"Nicola, you understand more than anyone why that is unwise. Your own husband was attacked by demons late last year." There was a harshness to her normally lovely voice, Mia's mask falling.

Nicola was undeterred, her eyes glazing over for a split second before brightening up again. "But would it not be wise to have her see the reality of what is out there? To remind her of how important her role is? How special The Capital is?"

"Do I have any say in this?" I asked, my irritation getting the best of me. Mia scrutinized Nicola for another moment before turning my way again.

"It seems you are about to get your wish, my flower. We will leave for Isle Shifter tomorrow morning." At that, she gracefully stood. "Tish, see to it that handmaidens come to pack for Asher and Sterling."

"What about me?" Nicola asked, her voice holding the barest hint of panic. Mia flashed her a dazzling smile, shedding the face of the demure queen.

"You will return home to your husband, of course."

CHAPTER EIGHTEEN

HENRY

She was there, right in front of me.

Genevieve looked as stunning as ever. Her hair flared out in gold-spun curls and her cheeks were a vibrant pink. She wore tight-fitting, Maliha-green trousers and a loose black tunic that exposed the swell of her breasts as she heaved deep breaths.

"This came for me—*you*," she panted out. "It is from the Fae Realm."

Lian gasped, moving to take the missive. Genevieve was faster, already slipping it into my still lifted hand. Not willing to waste another moment, I untied and unrolled the message, finding not one, but two.

Dear Genevieve Windsor,

My name is Nicola Salvatore. I am writing to you with a proposition. Your brother is currently walking free in The Capital. However, I am quite sure that will not be true for long. Take these instructions to Henry Nash and I promise your brother's safety.

Sincerely,

Nicola Salvatore

The note stopped there, so I flipped to the next one.

Henry,

As we all know by now, you and your band of heathens called the Trusted are relatively useless when it comes to this mission. So, in the spirit of teamwork, I am going to give you three clear instructions. Feel free to share this with Perdita Harligold.

First, you need to immediately set sail for Isle Shifter. I know someone there who can forge paperwork for Captain Harligold that will allow her to pose as a fae merchant ship. In five days, she must be at the Isle Healer docks. This will require a certain royal ship being sunk, but there should be no problems after that if the

captain maintains her flare and stops by the apothecary in the coastal town.

Next, you will remain on Isle Shifter and look for a male by the name of Olivander Adams. He is the current second in command of the rebel group that has been stirring in Betovere. The last I heard, he lived in the northern part of the Single Lands. He sells pottery by day, so try the major market there. Lian Youxia must stay with the pirate captain, but stress to her that she should not be seen by Asher.

Finally, tell the demon prince that he should stay the course that has been presented to him. The task being asked of him is vital to our future. Do not allow him to look for Asher.

Sincerely,

The Oracle Who Is Saving Our Asses

"Is it from the Oracle?" Lian asked, trying and failing to peer over my shoulder. I simply nodded to her before gazing at Genevieve one more time.

Turning, I lifted the missive above my head, waving it towards the captain with a sultry smile. She promptly grabbed the dagger strapped to her thigh and hurled it at me. Lian stepped in front of me instantly, raising a shield of air. I peeked down at her just in time to catch her winking at the furious captain.

"Okay, lovers. No squabbling. It seems we have a plan." My words most definitely registered with Captain Harligold, because she rolled her

eyes and held out her hand for the note from Nicola. I sent it to her in a beam of light, watching as it appeared above her hand.

Delight eventually pulled up the corners of her mouth as she read, then she tucked the note under her arm and signed something to her crew. They cheered loudly, all six of her crew members copying the signs she responded with as they shouted, "Pockets full, souls empty!"

Bizarre creatures.

With that settled, I turned to Genevieve. She stared on at the pirates, clearly judging and assessing them. Lian seemed to be doing the same, her eyes squinted at the captain in particular. I, on the other hand, could do nothing but longingly look at the mortal princess.

She had not spoken to me since she screamed in my face at Pike. After the battle of Behman, she had been soaked in mud and bleeding from her bicep, but otherwise fine. Physically that was. Her shouts of fury about her dead soldiers that Ash had killed were hard to silence. Even worse was that when she finally stopped yelling at me, she ceased speaking to me altogether.

After that, Genevieve had remained with a still-healing Shah. The mortal queen had barely survived the battle in her kingdom, but once Ranbir was able to stabilize her, she had immediately begun plotting revenge. There was a fury in her that seemed palpable, and Genevieve's anger only further stoked those flames within Shah. I had portaled the two of them back to Caless, where they both turned their backs on me and did not look back.

Now there Genevieve stood before me, like my every desire made tangible.

"What are you doing here?" I asked, unable to resist.

"You know what. I was ordered to give you this note. Plus, you told Shah and I that if we were ever contacted by this female then we were to tell you. This is me telling you, Firefly." Her casual shrug did not match the

fire within her eyes. It was as if she were attempting to be unfeeling but could not quite stifle her passion or anger.

"No, I am asking why you have come *here*. Why not just send me the note? You have the pencil that is laced with my essence." In response to my suspicious tone, the princess bristled. As if my words stoked that flame within her.

"I am here for my brother, you idiot. Not for you, if that is what you think. Your psychotic pet princess slaughtered my people, but she is also the key to saving my brother. I know that, just as Nicola Salvatore does. When the time comes, I will kick her ass. For now, my brother is my priority," she seethed. Her speech had Lian moving closer to my side, ready to stand up for Asher.

Torn was the only way to describe how I felt. I loved Genevieve, despite my deeper desire not to. She was like a knife to my gut. I could not pull it out, for fear of bleeding to death. But gods did it fucking hurt.

Then there was Asher. She was our queen, even if she did not see that yet. Her rule—her survival—was more important than most things. Her pull was magnetic and all-encompassing.

Gravity. Asher was gravity. She was the compass pointing us the way. The wind directing our sails. Bellamy might wish her to be solely his, and she might claim to only be her own, but she was all of ours. Born to rule and lead and conquer. Hearing her slandered, it stung.

Yes, she was a beast of a creature. Asher was sarcastic, sometimes brash, and hard-headed. There were many faults that perhaps one could point out. Beyond those though, was a brave and fierce female who would sacrifice herself so that beings like Genevieve and I could live and love. For that alone, she was worth following. Worth standing up for.

"If anything, we are all Asher's pets, my sweet curse. And I would watch my tone, if I were you. Your people were sent to fight ours and Shah's. They were there to destroy your friend's kingdom. Asher saved more than she slaughtered," I leveled. Genevieve's brow pinched and she opened her mouth to speak, but I quickly cut her off. "You want to come?

Then come. But do not for a moment pretend that you do not need Asher just as much as we do."

"Curse? How dare you!" she shouted, her finger jabbing into my chest. "And I do not need her, I am a queen!"

"You are a spoiled princess. You would not understand half of the things she went through," Lian cut in, her words as sharp as a blade. She stepped between us, swatting Genevieve's hand away from me. The princess' eyes went wide, Lian's words clearly sinking in. "When your parents torture you and then demand you say thank you, come talk to us. Until then, shut your pretty little mouth and make yourself useful."

With that, the mortal princess turned and stomped away. I had no idea where she would go, but I was glad for the space. She aggravated me to no end, but damn was she beautiful. Seeing her look up at me with her jaw set in determination had nearly undone me.

"Lian, Nicola says we are to go to Isle Shifter. From there, I will take Genevieve and search for a male named Olivander. Apparently he is the second-in-command of the fae rebels," I whispered to her.

She spun around to look at me, her face draining of color and her fists bunching at her sides.

"Olivander Adams. I know him. Sort of. Yuza met with him a few times. Be careful. He is a powerful Shifter. He is also an ass." I chuckled softly, putting my hand on her small shoulder. None of us knew much about Yuza. Lian was slow to speak of her. But we understood how deeply her memory and loss hurt Lian. The Air shrugged off my hold, shaking her head as if to rid herself of the thoughts that likely swarmed her like insects. "Where am I to go?"

"She says you need to stay here. Probably to make sure the captain follows through with her plans. But you cannot be seen by Ash. I do not know why, but if Nicola says not to then we should follow her command."

Lian grimaced, but nodded. Neither of us wanted to be on this ship with these pirates. Bellamy would be furious when he found out I was

leaving her alone with them. Sometimes he acted like he was our father, as if he was responsible for all of our safety. Lian would be fine on her own though. She could kick any of their asses with her eyes closed.

"Well, at least I will get to see Asher. Even if just from a distance. Bellamy will be wonderfully jealous," she said with a smirk.

"Me too. Whenever you are allowed to speak to her, tell the little brat that I will drop kick her into the next millennia for being a self-sacrificing dumbass."

CHAPTER NINETEEN

BELLAMY

"What are you doing?" I asked as I leaned against the doorframe.

"Thinking. Planning." Adbeel did not so much as look up at me as he continued to walk, his gaze down and mouth moving with silent words.

"It looks like pacing to me."

"I am a king, I do not pace."

"Ah, yes. Sorry. That planning looks more like walking quickly from one spot to another and then back." Approaching him, I took a seat at the chair in front of his office desk. This was the first time I had been in the space since Adbeel and I argued last. Since I told him about Malcolm. Now,

I noted that the traitorous prince's portrait had been taken down. Erased from existence.

"I am not in the mood for your sarcasm, nor your presence." Ouch.

"I take it you are still mad." There was no denying it. Just as it was true beyond a doubt that I deserved the wrath Adbeel held for me, waiting to be set free.

"Of course I am mad! You had no right to hide her from me!" he yelled, finally looking at me. His billowing blue top moved with every lift of his hands, his silver trousers catching the light of the fading day through the windows in the office. My eyes caught sight of the waves as they barreled towards The Royal City.

"You are right," I admitted. Salt water sprayed up the side of the cliff that held the castle. What a beautiful place for such a horrible conversation. I breathed in the air that reminded me of my youth. The adolescence that Asher should have had.

"She is my blood, my granddaughter." He did not so much as acknowledge my words as he pointed my way with his entire hand. His dark eyes blazed with fury. Eyes that Asher did not have, somehow. The first of his line to not possess the nearly black shade of iris.

"She is," I agreed.

"I thought the youngling had died with my son and daughter. Now I come to find out that not only is my son still alive, but so is his—"

"Adbeel, I know I fucked up." My words silenced him for a moment. I took the chance to plead my case, however poor it was. "At first, it was completely selfish. I found out who she was, and I panicked. Pino had shown me so many moments of our lives together. He had given me something I first thought was a gift, but later realized was a curse. For months I watched her, had her followed, and dreamt of her. But I did not know how to tell you when Pino was so insistent that she had to find out with you."

At that, he sighed, sitting down in his bleached driftwood chair. He waved his hand, urging me to continue on. Nodding, I sat straighter and attempted to convey what had gone through my mind the last two years.

"When I finally had her with me, I wanted just a bit of that time he had shown me. To love her and know peace with her before I told you both the truth and faced the possibility of losing her. Then, when I took her to the Royal City, you were gone. Haven was attacked the next day, and she became obsessed with earning her right at happiness. It was as if she could not pause for even a moment. I think she feared speaking to you and discovering what I was keeping from her would somehow be self-serving. That if she thought of herself for once then she would no longer deserve whatever joy might come of it."

Adbeel seemed to straighten up at that. As if the sound of who Asher truly was to her core intrigued him. Perhaps it did. She was what a queen ought to be.

"Still, you deserved more than that. I should have pushed her. I should have, for once, chosen something other than my own wants. I should have done better. There is no way to take it back, but I will bring her home to us. That I can promise." My words were determined, fierce even. Yet, Adbeel did not seem settled by them. Did he not believe me? Did he not think me good enough for his blood? He knew who I was. What a monster I could become.

"No, Bellamy. I will be getting my granddaughter. The Capital shall burn. If that bitch queen does not surrender her, then she will watch her entire realm turn to dust. It is as simple as that. They want a war, I will give them one." He stood then, moving to grab the sword that hung on his wall. A trophy of past battles. A memory of another life.

I thought of the note I had received from Henry earlier. Of how important it was to not make hasty moves, no matter how much it pained me. But I would not ignore another Oracle's orders.

"We have a plan. An Oracle lives once more. She grew up with Asher, and she has implored us not to move just yet. Asher's safety and the

future of our world hang in the balance." So ominous was my tone that Adbeel whipped around, staring at me with wide eyes that seemed to water as I spoke. "She says we are to wait a few weeks."

"Are you truly asking me to once again leave my granddaughter in the hands of sycophants? Tyrants?" I merely stared at him, trying to plead with my eyes. Not only for his agreement, but for his undeserved forgiveness as well. "You have one month. After that I will get my granddaughter, the future be damned."

***

Stassi sat on my bed, her toes wiggling as she painted them black. I ignored her in favor of bending down and lifting one of my floorboards. Privacy was the last thing on my mind as I took out the small blood-red box. Opening it up, I paused momentarily to touch Asher's amethyst necklace, the cold gem making my heart ache. Then I grabbed her anklet, which I had found on her side table when I first came back to this room in Pike. Gods, it had looked perfect on her.

With a deep breath, I set them both down and picked up one of the rolled pieces of paper. A chuckle slipped past my lips as I read the back and forth between us.

I miss the sound of your laugh and feel of your hand in mine more than ever today.

You are so sappy. How is it anyone fears you when all you spout is poetic nonsense?

P.S. I miss you too. So much.

Do not lie, I know you love it when I praise you, my beautiful creature.

Oh please, you are so full of yourself, demon.

When you touch yourself tonight as you think of me, make sure to write back with that dirty little hand after.

For you, my darling idiot, anything.

"If you're going to cry, will you do it in your bathroom? I'm starting to feel a hangover coming on and I don't care for your sad little sniffles to make my headache worse," Stassi said. I looked up to find her now blowing on the polish, still wiggling her toes like an annoying little youngling. The high demon said she was tens of thousands of years old. I wished she would act like it.

"You know, Stassi, I have a remedy for headaches." The pink-haired fiend looked over to me, a single brow rising in interest. My smile widened, my old self surfacing for a moment. "Death. I can help you out, if you would like."

She promptly threw one of *my* pillows at me, which I swatted away. Ignoring her and rolling my eyes, I returned the note to the box. Then I grabbed the new note from Henry and reread the final line.

We are going to bring her home, Bell.

It was hard to think of such a bright future. Or, it had been. But now that I was free of her magic, I could finally see the light at the end of this tunnel. Breathing deeply to stop myself from actually crying in front of the vermin on my bed, I rolled the note back up and tossed it inside.

"I cannot go with you when you search for Stella," I said as I picked the box up.

Stassi huffed, drawing my attention. "You have no choice."

"Helping you is not the problem. It is the fact that I have been absent from my army for far too much of the last year. I need to focus as war nears."

"A much worse war will come if we don't find Stella," she insisted. I watched as she stood, curious about what she would do. Instead of hostility, she merely stopped in front of me, peering down with a face that looked simultaneously furious and panicked. Stassi was *scared*. "This is more important than anything else, Bellamy. The high demon of Sun and Moon is our only shot at beating Padon—*at surviving*." Sincerity coated her words, the sweetness of such a thing unable to mask the bitterness of the imminent future.

Limited options made all desperate, and I was beginning to realize that even gods—no, *high demons*—were not above hopelessness.

Once more, I chose to ignore her completely. I stood, bringing the box with me to my small wooden desk. I set it down, pulling out a fresh piece of paper from the top drawer that she had carelessly disheveled earlier. Her silence seemed to grow hostile, charging the air, but I did not care. My fingers grazed a pencil, the graphite cold against my heated fingers. Hunching forward, I began yet another letter.

Asher,

I hate what you have done to me. To us. You took my choice away, something you have always been so adamantly against. Yet here I sit, unable to come after you. Well, sort of. A long story that I can summarize in four sentences.

I would give anything and everything to fight with you right now. To breathe the air that you do. To hold you again and feel at home in your nearness. Of all the things in this world, you are and will always be the most precious.

Soon, we will be able to argue again, beautiful creature.

Love, Bellamy

"What is it with this princess that has all of you oafs on your knees for her?" Stassi asked from over my shoulder, reading as I wrote. I snatched up the paper, rolling it quickly and tossing it into the box.

"Your insufferable personality and your inability to mind your fucking business probably pushes males towards other females often," I muttered, snatching the box and moving to return it to its home. She followed, a growl emanating from her chest.

"You need to take this seriously. Do you think I don't have someone I wish I could run and get? That I don't want more than being a lackey desperate for a new master? Our desires don't matter right now, *prince.*"

Gods if she did not know exactly where to strike me. Even worse, she was right.

Sighing, I stood straight once more, facing off with the tiny beast.

I was selfish. It was a simple fact. And perhaps it was because she did not know me, but choosing to stay at Pike instead of going to Asher was the least selfish thing I had possibly ever done. The hurt of what felt like choosing being a general over saving my soulmate ran deep enough that every second had to be a conscious choice to listen to Nicola's orders.

Now, as I stared down the barely five-foot tall high demon, I wondered if it were possible to ever be anything but self-serving. If, in the end, no matter what I did, it would always come down to me. To what was best for me and those I loved.

I wanted to be different. Eternity knew how desperately I wished I could be more like Asher. Though, I also wished she would be more like me. Maybe that was why we were the perfect match. Balance. And maybe I could find balance now.

"Okay. I can compromise with you. Tell me how I can help without leaving this base. Give me tasks that do not require all of my attention. That I can do," I conceded. She stepped back, as if surprised by how easily my mind could be changed. If only she knew how truly difficult it actually was.

"Well, for starters, you can help me access anything of Asta's. If Stella has been living on this world like I think she has, then she's been doing so in secret. She likely has been blending in with you all without you even realizing it. Which means she uses very little magic and often stays put. Give me Asta's journals in particular and I will let you stay here."

Interesting. The idea of Stella being on Alemthian for millennia without any of us knowing was both absurd and unexplainably exciting. More than that, this was a compromise I could easily make. Too easily. It was almost suspicious.

"Fine. I can send someone to the archives later today. Right now I have a meeting and then training." Her only response was a scoff, which I

took as a sign of agreement. "Look at us, compromising and being unselfish. A new world indeed."

"You're proving yourself to be egregiously stupid."

"And you are proving yourself to be unceasingly exasperating."

"Better than stupid."

"Take it from someone who finds themself constantly surrounded by both, it is the irksome ones that make you go mad," I quipped before stepping to the door. "Speaking of which, I have a few wonderful idiots to speak to."

Closing the door, I had only made it a step before she yelled, "Dumbass!"

Fortunately for me, walking down the hall to my office offered much warmer greetings.

"Okay, asshole, what is it you wanted?" Noe asked from her spot in my desk chair. She was still angry at me for not letting her stay with the pirates. Though I did not blame her, I still found myself letting out an annoyed groan.

She was wearing training leathers and had her hair up in a twist, clearly prepared for the session starting soon. Damon was standing in the corner to her right, his silver hair glowing beneath the sun that streamed in from the window. He was also adorned in black training wear, though his exposed his arms. Ranbir had on his signature white outfit, prepared for another day in the infirmary. He had his hair in a plait today, the braid going down his back. His beard had been trimmed by Noe, but only barely. Cyprus seemed more alive than normal, a small smirk on his face and his leathers slightly muddy. Farai and Jasper had chosen to sit in the two chairs in front of my desk, their bodies also now adorning black leathers. Farai had his arm around Jasper as if shielding him.

"Well, I needed to update you on what Henry and Lian have learned. That, and I think it is important I tell you about something that has

recently transpired." They all stiffened, on edge for whatever it was I had to say.

Truly, I wished I did not have to. But if there was anything I learned from telling Adbeel about Asher, it was that the longer I kept a secret, the worse the reaction would be.

"Most of you know that Asher was abducted by what we thought was a god early this summer. Now, even then it was something that was hard to wrap our minds around. She had been targeted by something that many of us honestly thought was a figment of the imagination. But, today I have been shown just how real those beings are," I admitted.

They all went slack-jawed, gaping at me like I had said the most insane and implausible thing in the world. In truth, I had. We all had been completely baffled when Asher told us, though we tried to act nonchalant when she was around. It had been a difficult thing to believe, and even more so that it could happen at any time. This was possibly even more unbelievable.

"A female portaled into my room early this morning. She said her name is Anastasia and that she is the high demon of Sin and Virtue."

"What is a high demon and what does it have to do with the gods?" Noe asked, nearly cutting off my final word.

"There are no such thing as gods. They are all high demons." I shrugged, causing each of them to stare at me in silent disbelief. "Listen, we do not have time to waste, so I am going to give you a shortened version. What we thought were gods are actually called high demons. They live on a world called Shamay, the same place that Asta and Stella were from. Anastasia—Stassi—wants our help finding Stella—"

"Is Stella not on Shamay?" Cyprus shouted in horror. The others began to murmur, but I lifted a hand to silence them.

"I thought she was, but Stassi believes that Stella came here with Asta. Apparently, Stella was banished from their world after she stuck up for Asta's betrayal. She is hoping that we can locate some of Asta's old

journals for her to read over with the goal of locating Stella." I was eager to be done with the explanation, my words a rushed jumble. But they each understood. I could tell by the way they nodded with wide eyes and slightly parted lips.

"I can get my hands on those," Noe offered. I nodded her way, a sort of thanks for her help. And then, with a deep breath, I readied for the arguing.

"One more thing. Asher is Adbeel's granddaughter." Their shouts were even louder than I expected they would be.

CHAPTER TWENTY

ASHER

The gardens were bright and full and perfect. As was everything in this horrid place.

Though I was eager to leave and not see the golden palace looming above or around me, I still found myself walking the path. Truly, it was because I missed Bellamy. I made it to the bench where I had sat with him that first night and nearly wept. Grazing my fingers across the gold-painted concrete bench, I thought of how his lips had felt against mine. How he had told me of his desire to be more than what the world had demanded he be.

Too much. The memories were too much. I fell to my knees, gasping for air as I reminded myself how real it had all been. There was no way I could have made the rest of it up. Not that sort of love.

"You keep doing this, convincing yourself it was real," Wrath said as he appeared to my right. "Yes, you shared a wonderful moment with the Fire here. But the rest of it was a lie. Did you even go to that market with him? Or had you dreamt that up and convinced yourself it was reality? What do you think Eternity's price is for your power, Asher? A lost mind maybe?"

"Why are you doing this, Wrath? Why not just leave me alone?" I asked despite knowing what he would say. His chilling smile of sharp teeth conveyed the fact that he was aware of my understanding too.

"I do what you wish me to do. What that insanity that plagues you wishes I do." His tail swished slowly behind him as he sat and stared at me. Eerie. Far less cute than he had been in life. Finally, I understood Henry's distaste for Wrath.

"You are—" I cut myself off, my eye catching on a flower beneath the bench that was not quite the same soft purple as the lavender plants that grew here. No, this was a deeper purple, like an unripe plum. Bending down further, I was also able to catch sight of berries. Nearly black in color. "Belladonna."

I remembered the plant only because Nicola had been so interested in it.

"A berry that tastes sweet but can kill? What an unsettling and intriguing little plant!" she had said after I told her about what I learned in a Healer class.

Since then, Nicola had become obsessed with it. She even had Mia craft her one that she kept on her windowsill in her chambers within the palace. And it looked just like these.

Sterling had called it nightshade. He had said they were poisoning us with it.

179

"Or maybe she grew it for your friend and you are using real memories to create fake ones," Wrath countered with a chuckle.

"Guard!" I shouted, hitting my head on the way up. I was rubbing the sore spot when the guard came running around the corner, her black armor clinking together as she darted my way.

"Your Highness! How can I be of service to you?" Quite frazzled, the fae did not inquire why I was on the ground or why my hands were now slightly purple. Clearly, she was just eager to help me and be on with her day. That was perfect.

"Are you a Fire by any chance?"

"Um…well, yes, I am."

"Excellent." Calling to my magic, and begging it would go easy on my already aching head after this, I pushed into her mind. There had been no shield, no fortification, nothing but free access. Hastily, I sat up straighter and lowered my tone to that of The Manipulator. *"Burn these flowers. Burn every flower in this garden and then forget you ever left your post."*

Then I stood, walking away to the sweet smell of cruelty alight and a horrid ache in my head. They were still poisoning me somehow. I had not eaten again since being in Sterling's chambers, so it must have been a different way. Wrath followed silently at my side, weaving through my legs here and there. When the path ended, I cut through the grass and made my way to the far docks where we would depart.

I had always dreamed of seeing the realm I was raised to lead. But now, even though I knew Nicola was plotting something, I felt as if it were sullied. Ruined. My feet dragged, dirt probably staining my shoes. I was meant to take the carriage, but my desire for solitude and fresh air outweighed the ache in my legs.

"It will take you hours to get there," Wrath huffed. He never said we.

"Well then, I hope you have more entertaining things to say than calling me crazy. Perhaps a song?"

***

By the time I arrived at the docks, the pain in my head had become piercing and my feet felt as if they might fall off. The sun was high in the sky, bright and fierce. Still summer, I had learned. I had been asleep mere days rather than months.

"You are late," Sterling chided from where he leaned against a wooden pole upon the dock. His curls were perfectly coiled atop his head, his body clad in the vibrant gold of royal fae. A gold band twin to my own that now burned in the gardens was once more on his finger. Mia had insisted.

The ship loomed behind him, far out into the water and much larger than it needed to be for a voyage from isle to isle. They were not so far apart that we required something so exquisite. But of course the royals would request this.

"If this is when I got here then everyone else is early," I said. Sterling laughed, tossing his head back, and I found it impossible not to join in.

"Then why can you not just be happy with this male, Strange One?" Wrath asked as Sterling reached out a hand, the prince's eyes snagging on my ringless finger. My heart lurched to a stop at the insinuation the dalistori was making.

"You go ahead, I want to stay on solid land for as long as I can." A smile graced my face, I could feel it, but inside my mind, thoughts—memories—fluttered like butterflies.

Sterling seemed hesitant to board the small boat that would take us to the ship, his nose scrunched and lips pursed. Eventually he nodded and turned.

"You know why," I whispered to Wrath. We watched as a guard rowed Sterling out, and then the prince was climbing a rope ladder. He made it up quickly, approaching who must have been the captain. His smile was exuberant even in the distance, his soul ready to adventure once more. "He is not Bellamy."

"Yes, your imaginary lover. Do tell me how that goes for the rest of your unfortunately long life."

"I could not have imagined him. He is far better than I ever deserved. Especially after Sipho. You think me more creative than I am."

"Yet here you stand, speaking to a talking cat that no one else sees." My mouth opened, prepared to deliver a retort, but nothing came out.

He was right.

Wrath disappeared after that, my mind done playing games for now.

I waited on the docks for a few more minutes, trying to imagine what Bellamy was doing at that moment.

"You will be okay, Asher." Nicola's appearance scared me enough that I jumped slightly to the right. Gripping my chest, I looked over to her and grimaced. She was wearing a thin and simple dress the same shade of purple as the belladonna berries, her thick curls twisting down her back. She smiled in a way that made me wonder if whatever was in store for me was terribly bleak and she just did not want to admit it.

"Will you?" I asked quietly, stepping back towards her. "Be okay, I mean."

"Yes. Kafele is waiting for me. We live in the Warden's estate in the Yesterday Lands now. You will see us soon. I doubt they will let you be on each isle for more than a day or two." She came closer, grabbing me by the

shoulders and tucking me into a hug. I felt her lips briefly graze my ear just before she whispered, "Remember who you are while away. Remember who you have vowed to save."

And then she pulled away, smiling softly and gripping my hand before walking away. I tightened my fist as I watched her head down the dock, prepared to board a much smaller vessel and go home to her husband. Her life she had made in my absence.

Remember who I had vowed to save.

By the time I made it to the deck of the ship, my hand was aching. I walked all the way to the front, stopping at the railing and looking at the vast ocean. Isle Shifter loomed somewhere out there, ready to greet us.

Finally, I grew the courage and looked down at my open hand. There in my palm sat a small amethyst.

"Well that is pretty. Reminds me of your old necklace." Xavier's voice startled me, my skin crawling at the nearness of him. He had burned me, cut me, broke me. Now, he stood mere feet from me, his smile so full it showed his dimple through his barely-there facial hair. His dark waves were loose, reaching just past his shoulders. As always, he wore head-to-toe gold and his crown of gilded flames. "Sorry, Ash. I did not mean to scare you."

"Odd that torturing me is perfectly fine but scaring me by accident is not," I hissed, closing my fist tightly and hiding the crystal. There was a sense of foreboding as I looked at him. As if this moment would change fate itself.

Xavier seemed unusually still as he contemplated what I said. I wondered if my words struck him somewhere deeper than they normally did; if, perhaps, he felt remorse. Still, I knew it would not be enough.

"I am sorry that we were tough on you when you were younger. We just needed you to be ready for this world—for this crown. Your power, it is dangerous and unpredictable. At least, it was. But now look at you." He gestured towards me with both hands, like a farmer showing his prized pig.

The one they would later slaughter. "You are a queen, Ash. We are so proud."

Gods they were convincing. Just as my golden gown and my tiara were. It felt like being back in the palace last year, waiting for and then basking in his approval. If only I had known then just how different real love was. Love was not punishing someone for things they could not change. It did not come with limits or rules. It was unconditional.

"You can pretend like you did not imprison me and that everything is normal, but I know the truth, Xavier. You are not on my side unless I am useful to you, and I promise I never will be again," I vowed. His eyes went wide, darting quickly to the stairs that led below deck before zeroing in on me again. "Remember that the next time you want to have a sweet little conversation about our past and future."

With that, I pushed off the railing and turned, heading towards the rooms I knew they would have for me. The only thing worse than being cornered by Xavier would be running into Mia, but I needed to be alone and escape the suffocating presence of lies.

But of course, Xavier would not allow me that peace.

"Play a game of chess with me." His tone was nearly pleading, a grim sense of desperation pouring from him. Though I knew better than to believe in his false love, my own once unflinching admiration for him flickered like a fading fire somewhere deep in my chest. "It has been far too long since I taught you a lesson in strategy."

"Do I have a choice?" I asked, looking over my shoulder to glare his way.

Xavier's entreating eyes squinted slightly, a returning glare forming as he breathed in the defiant air around me. "You have the choice to say yes or for me to make you."

"Fine."

"Excellent, I have already set it up in my rooms."

Of course he had.

We moved silently down the hall of doors, me fuming and him smiling broadly—mood much improved by my submission. Stabbing him would be so wonderfully rewarding. Sadly, all I could do was walk through the door as he held it open and take my seat at the small wooden table. The floors creaked below our feet and chairs as we got comfortable. His bed was small and modest, the quilt a deep gold and the dresser a faded cherry wood. The cramped space felt as if it might suffocate me, damp air not quite filling my lungs before it was fleeing my body.

"As always, white first," Xavier said, pointing a finger at me. I nodded silently, wishing more than anything to have this game over so I could be alone and free of his clutches. I made my move, eyes darting up to his.

"In chess, the player who makes the first move has a higher chance of success. Why is that, Ash?" he inquired as he too moved a piece. In my youth, I had eagerly looked forward to these lessons. Xavier's time and presence had been worth more than gold to me. Strange how times change.

"Because they set the tone. To make the first move is to choose the stakes. If chess were an orchestra, white would be the conductor," I answered, eyeing the board as we continued to battle. He was not going easy on me, but I was also not willing to give in without a fight.

"Interesting."

"Are you saying I am wrong?"

He did not answer me for a while, instead choosing to mercilessly attack.

"I think you gave the answer most would." Xavier took another piece as he spoke, the corner of his mouth lifting in a smirk. As if he had won already.

"And that is somehow not the correct one?" I hissed, moving next.

"I agree that there is an advantage to making the first move. I also think it creates a false sense of security. That those who go into a battle thinking they have won are often too short-sighted to truly do so. Even worse, those who believe they will lose often do." Another of my pieces done. Xavier was moving too quickly, and I was out of practice. "Life is a game of strategy, just as chess is. Your mind is your greatest strength and your heart is your greatest weakness."

"So you think it is psychological?" I asked, my eyes darting across the board, trying to see a way free of the place he had backed me into.

"I think that I have beaten you with the black pieces enough to know that anyone can win. There is no such thing as a guaranteed victory. If your enemy is smart, then there is no such thing as an advantage either." With that Xavier moved again, and I was trapped. "Checkmate."

CHAPTER TWENTY-ONE

ASHER

We docked on the Western side of Isle Shifter, fae everywhere staring at the gold-accented ship that flew a flag bearing the fae sigil.

Each Isle had only one port. One legal place where they could come and go. A singular strip of the beach for exit—or escape. All four ports faced The Capital.

"Ready?" Sterling asked from my side. He held my hand in his, the two of us crowned in gold. We were a united pair, a happily married couple.

"Oh definitely. Cannot wait to be paraded around like a doll," I answered, wiping my free hand on my skirts and probably staining them with my sweat. "Look, they even got us all dressed up."

"So kind of them. Maybe they will also throw us a tea party and move our hands for us next." Sterling's hand gripped mine tighter, offering a squeeze of reassurance. No amount of joking could make this easier. I was finally about to see the realm I was raised to rule one day, and I did so while actively unsure if I was insane or just being lied to.

Every hour it seemed as if the former was the truth.

A flash of orange caught the corner of my eye, and then there she was. Mia towered over me, standing as tall as Sterling. She was a lean and foreboding sight, even her smile dazzling in the most horrifying way. Her ears came out to a point, parting her hair, and her eyes shone crystal blue in the light of day.

"Remember, we stay close together and maintain our smiles." Mia paired her words with an even wider baring of her teeth. "That means you, Asher."

Looking up at her, I proceeded to smile as widely as I could. Xavier came to her side, laughing lowly as he watched.

"That is absolutely terrifying. Maybe we should allow her to simply not frown or glare." Sterling let out a soft chuckle at Xavier's words, making Mia bristle and rage.

"You are all unbearable. Now walk off this dock and act like the royal family we are." With that, Mia lifted her chin and began making her way to Isle Shifter. The three of us held awkward eye contact for a moment, none of us wanting to be the first to follow.

Xavier broke, scoffing and hurrying to take his place at her side. She did not speak, only lifted her hand. He offered his arm for her to grab, and the two of them descended the stairs that connected the dock to the beach. Sterling let out another chuckle before giving me his arm too.

"Well, sounds like it is time to party," he whispered near my ear.

"Ah yes, so much fun to be had among those who either fear or worship me." With one last huff of displeasure, I wrapped my hand around his arm and we followed the royals before us.

Luscious greenery surrounded the area, a bold blue sky above us. Fae were everywhere, all openly gawking our way. They stared on like we were beasts that might eat them. All except for one.

A male stood not far from the spot where Mia and Xavier stepped onto the wooden dock, eyes keen as he surveyed us. He styled his hair in two braids, the long coffee brown plaits disappearing behind his shoulders. He wore a vest the color of the foamy sea upon the shore, his dark brown arms visible. Tattoos swirled across his skin, patterns and zigzags cutting through here and there. They were as extraordinary as Shah's, but the clean lines and cohesiveness seemed to be generational rather than personal. I tried to think back to if I had ever seen markings like that on a Shifter or any fae that traveled through Academy or the market. But I could not think of any.

My heeled shoes stuck in the sand as we walked, Mia not so much as stumbling in her own. She halted before a tall female with hair that acted as a dome around her head, the gorgeous curls so small that they were almost indistinguishable. She, too, had deep-colored skin, her smile broad as she bowed low in welcome. Her beige tunic and skirt split to reveal her navel when she straightened. It was almost scandalous here in Betovere.

How wonderfully normal it would have been in Eoforhild.

Something wrapped around my feet just as I stopped before the female, Wrath's voice traveling up to my ear on a phantom wind.

"Still using false names, are you?"

I did not dare look down at him or respond with so many eyes on me. But I did allow my teeth to grind, the act making the pain in my head shoot down to my jaw and spine.

"Your Majesties. Your Highnesses. Isle Shifter welcomes you with great gratitude. We are honored to have the royal family upon our shores," she beamed, clasping her hands together.

"Tasi, it is wonderful to see you once more." Xavier practically hummed the words, mischief pouring off of him in waves. I watched with bewilderment as he stepped forward, grabbed her hand, and kissed her knuckles. Tasi stared at him with open desire, her bottom lip between her teeth as he held his mouth upon her skin for far longer than was necessary or proper.

"Yes, we do so enjoy visiting our many wardens," Mia added, stepping into their space. Xavier released his hold on Tasi and nodded in agreement. "We are also proud to formally introduce you to Princess Asher Mounbetton, our daughter."

Every fiber of my being seemed to will me to flee as those words came from her mouth. I did not run though, rather, I stared dumbfounded at the queen who had finally made her move. She was claiming me. Officially marking me as hers in preparation for ascending the throne. None of it made sense, not when she knew I was against her and uninterested in ruling as she did. Especially after all she had done to me this last year. I was volatile and determined to kill her, even if it meant my death too. Yet there she stood, arm outstretched to me and eyes glassy. Pride was shining on her face and pouring from her mind. It washed over me slowly, like sinking beneath the waters of a calm lake. A slow embrace of parental joy.

It was as if…as if she were telling the truth. As if none of it had happened. Like she thought I was still on her side, if not a bit confused from the magic that harmed me.

Eternity above.

"Yes, Strange One. You are finally seeing the truth of it all. That power of yours is showing its cards—rearing its ugly head." Wrath's deep and haunting voice seemed to echo off the sky itself. "As I said before, the price of such a gift is not your morality or the fear of others. The price of that power is your mind."

I risked peering down at him where he sat to my right, his head just higher than my hip now. He looked so *real*.

They all had.

"Asher?" Mia inquired, her face pinching in worry. Oh, did it look so unfathomably real. The face of a mother who was concerned about her daughter.

I tried to picture Bellamy, to remember how real he had truly been. I had once told myself I would always remember the tiny things that made up who he was, that I would never forget. But now I feared I might have meticulously crafted him in my mind after meeting him atop that balcony. Could it be that a single kiss and a few moments of attention had sparked this descent in my sanity?

With Mia before me, her arm lowering and her body fully pivoting towards mine, I was faced with the very real possibility that I had made it all up. That I had been horribly wrong in it all. Would it be that unrealistic for my mind to work against me after so long of my magic—power?— tormenting others?

Blinking, I did my best to shake off the thoughts. Even if—gods forbid—I had made it all up, that did not change the truth of the matter. They had hurt me nearly my entire life. I was not bound to them or the duty they had forced upon me. I did, unfortunately, have a role to play in that moment.

"My apologies, it seems I am still a bit seasick. Please, forgive me, Warden Tasi. It is wonderful to meet you and to be here on your isle." I offered her a dip of my chin, which she quickly returned with a deep curtsy. She must have been the warden of the Single Lands, as Theon held the position for the Multiples before he had died. Had he died? Had I killed him? Or had I made it all up?

"No apologies necessary, Your Highness. I do agree though, it is lovely to officially meet you. I had visited while you were on your sick bed to pray to Eternity beneath the stars with the other wardens not long before

you awoke. Perhaps the King and Queen's desire for help from above was the answer after all," she said, her smile shrinking minutely.

Every hair on my body stood on edge as silence suddenly overtook the beach. Shifters loomed, fidgeting and whispering. My magic barreled into the newly built gate around my mind, barely keeping it contained to stifle the pain of using it. Something within my chest writhed—The Manipulator seeking a foothold.

"Something is very wrong," I whispered to Sterling, tugging him farther into me as I stood straighter. "Stay close and keep your eyes ahead."

"Well, are we ready to make our way to the carriages? My estate is not too far from here. I already have dinner prepared," Tasi said, gesturing to the spot where the sand rose in the distance and wooden steps led to a grassy area. Beyond must have been the carriages. How I wished we were not about to be forced to ride in them like caged animals. To say I was surprised that Xavier was allowing this would be an understatement. I was on edge the entire walk forward.

Beyond the steps, trees with jagged and sharp leaves loomed. Towering mountains without a hint of snow dominated the far right of the landscape, and beautiful stone homes poked from between the lush greenery on the left. It was a vision as we grew nearer, birds fluttering the leaves and singing above. Tasi continued forward, the male from before with the tattoos now on her right. He was speaking softly but animatedly to her, his nerves projecting my way and once more rattling that lock on my mental gate.

The two carriages were simple and black, though as we got closer I saw that they had small etchings of different animals on them in the same color. Stunning brown and white spotted horses were already strapped in and ready to pull us to the warden's home.

Despite my overwhelmed and slightly panicked mind, I did my best to breathe deeply and remain focused. I had to continue to believe it had all been real, to push forward and take down the royals.

But to do that, I had to remain free.

So I straightened my back and played the part I had been trained in my entire life.

Letting go of Sterling's arm, I grabbed my skirts and walked to Mia's side. She smiled at me softly, but her body was tense.

"Where is the warden of the Multiple Lands?" I inquired, trying my hardest to remain neutral on the subject.

"He died in a demon attack on the Golden Guard base here," she whispered, her tone solemn. Ah, so the isle *had* been attacked. Another consistency with what I remembered, at least. "The demons become a bigger problem as the days go on. When we get home, you, Xavier, and I must accept the very real possibility that we will be in the center of a battlefield someday very soon."

With that, she took Xavier's hand and entered the second carriage, smiling at him as if he were her best friend. I remembered I once thought they were.

"Wife," Sterling said, holding his hand out to me as he stood near the carriage door.

I rolled my eyes, leaning closer and hissing, "I am not your wife. Stop that."

"Just maintaining appearances." Shrugging, he let me put my hand in his and helped me into the carriage. When my skirts got caught, he chuckled and shoved his shoulder into me until I slipped through. Much to Mia's dismay and Xavier's amusement, I fell straight onto my hands and knees.

"Asher, please do not ruin your dress. My favorite seamstresses worked tirelessly through the night on your wardrobe for this trip," Mia scolded.

Ignoring her, I stood and took my seat across from them, all the while imagining jamming my foot down her throat. Sterling must have

noticed, because he giggled like a youngling at my side as the carriage took off.

"We are trapped in here," I muttered, looking at Xavier. He sat straighter, eyeing me with a curious expression. But I could see that he too felt the unease of being in there. Vulnerable.

"This dinner is the first of eight. We must be strong in our convictions, our desires, and—most of all—our family." Xavier and Sterling nodded, but all I could do was stare and picture the berries in my pocket. I wondered how many it would take to kill her.

Then, just as we began to move, the carriage halted, sending Sterling and I flying forward at the abrupt stop. Someone shouted from outside, followed closely by a piercing scream. The voice was a blade cutting through my plans, tearing my thoughts in half. A part of me thought this the perfect moment to catch Mia off guard, but the other half of me was stronger—the side that told me danger lurked beyond the carriage door and my fae needed me to help.

So, without a second of consideration for my own safety, I shoved through the door.

Blood caught my eye before anything else. It was already everywhere, coating the grass and trees and even the horses. A large group was fighting against guards clad in black armor and bearing the golden fae sigil. The fae attacking wore seemingly random clothes—normal ones, even. Plain tunics and trousers, nothing upon them matching except for one thing. Each wore a black cloth over their face, hiding all but their eyes. At the center of the cloth, right where their mouths would be, was the shining fae sigil…bleeding.

"Protect the princess from the rebels!" someone shouted from my right. A guard tried to jump in front of me, their sword clashing with one wielded by what I now knew to be a rebel. I ducked low, kicking my foot into the rebel's knee. The Manipulator inside of me hummed with glee at the sound of the fae's bone cracking in half. I wasted no time using my heel to stab into the rebel's chest, picking up their sword and readying to fight.

"Asher!" Sterling's voice cut through the screams and slicing of metal upon metal. I did not turn, did not do anything but dart forward towards a shrieking female holding her small youngling.

"Get out of here! Run!" I shouted to her. She did not move, appearing almost rooted in place. A growl tore up my chest as I saw what she was looking at. Before her in the grass was a male, his throat slit and eyes empty. She continued to sob, her youngling clinging to her.

Another rebel came at me mere feet from her, and I was forced to jump back before they could disembowel me. My sword was up in an instant, swinging towards the fae's face. She dodged it, smirking at me. We circled one another, neither of us caring about the violence that surrounded us.

"You fight, that is not something we knew," she said. All I could do was laugh, so disbelieving of what was happening.

They were killing our own. They were slaughtering innocents. Nothing was worth that. I would know, I had been a monster who did the same my entire life.

"Underestimating your enemy is a quick way to lose," I offered. That seemed to strike her somewhere deep in her heart, because her smile fell and she let out a deep battle cry. Her first swing missed me entirely, but the second and third took an immense amount of strength to counter. She was strong, and I was sure she would shift soon if I kept blocking her strikes. So I went on the offensive, trying to remember all that the Trusted had taught me but mostly hearing Wrath's voice as he called me insane.

First to draw blood was me, the very tip of my sword slicing through her forehead. She screamed in rage, trying and failing to return the favor. Out of nowhere, she turned and grabbed the crying female. I stilled, my eyes darting between them both. "Come with us, or I kill them."

Her sword moved to the throat of the fae, her youngling wiggling in her arms and screaming so loudly it made my teeth rattle. My magic seemed to urge me to slaughter—to welcome the evil within me and disregard the innocents that would suffer too—but I was done with the

purposeless bloodshed. Done with letting down those I had promised to serve. As the youngling cried out for their father, I let my mental gate open wide.

"Release them," I ordered. The rebel did as directed, delicious fear trickling down her like sweat. With that, I promptly kicked the Shifter in the chest and let my eyes roam over the fighting fae. *"Be still!"*

Everyone froze, eyes wide and heartbeats pounding in time with the horrid headache that already began to wear on me. Shouts of pain and cries of sorrow still rang out, but not a single fae moved. Not even Mia or Xavier, though their mental shields were up. Hiding from me.

Tossing the sword, I reached down and hoisted the female rebel up by her collar. She did not fight against me. Tears ran down her cheeks and her breathing was more of a gasping cry as she stared at me.

Anger clouded my heart, but my mind was momentarily clear.

"If you want to think me evil, then fine," I shouted to the crowd of unnaturally still fae, listening as their fears of me coalesced in the air and kissed me in fond hello. "Call me a monster, a beast, a curse. I will gladly be your villain. But do not take out your anger with your rulers on the fae of this realm. For those who do will quickly learn why it is I who haunts your nightmares and looms within your waking thoughts."

Because I knew the best way to prove how serious you were was to show the world, I threw the rebel to the ground and stomped my foot into her spine, shattering it at the neck. Screams could be heard from both sides, which I used to my advantage as I let my magic seep deeper into every mind near and weed out the traitors.

"You will all do well to remember this moment. No longer will the innocents die for the crimes of the wicked. If you have something to say about how this realm is run, then by all means, voice it. But, until then, those who wronged their own will pay."

Silence was shattered by the sounds of bodies falling lifelessly to the ground.

CHAPTER TWENTY-TWO

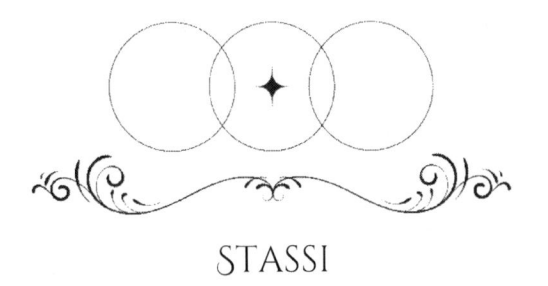

STASSI

The prince was, to put it nicely, a pain in my ass.

Not only was he late, but he was also in an undeniably awful mood. That, and I was pretty sure he was secretly planning to kill me in my sleep. It wasn't possible, but he still put me on edge. Big fucker couldn't be trusted.

"You're late," I said from my spot at his desk. He had pushed me out of his bed last night ten times before he finally gave in and slept somewhere else. Despite that, he looked…good. Which was even more annoying.

Even worse, it made me miss my creature, who had been stunning in a completely different way. He was kind and sinful where Bellamy was

rugged and grumpy. Even the prince's dimples couldn't make him look sweet or soft. But my creature, he'd been that. A rarity, in my opinion, to find someone who was both sexy and delicate.

Instead I was stuck here with this world's crankiest male.

"Must you speak to me this early?" he asked, reading through a stack of papers as he walked towards me. Without another word, he lifted his foot and kicked the chair out from under me. I crumpled to the ground, groaning at the ache that hitting the cheap and tacky floor caused.

Fine. He wanted to be hostile? I'd show him the definition of the word.

"It's past noon, you idiot," I growled, grabbing his ankle and ripping his foot upwards. Glee consumed me as his back and shoulder blades slammed into the wood.

"Any time before I have started drinking is too early to hear your voice," he groaned.

"Well if you want my help in saving your little soul bond, then I suggest you be nicer."

"Asher does not need your help, and neither do I. Nicola has it covered. And how do you know we have a soul bond?"

"Don't you?" I mocked.

"I am not sure that exists amongst my kind."

"Whatever you say. Anyways, did you get the journal?" Back to what was important. His love life was the least of my concerns.

"Noe did, she should be up soon. She is excited to meet you."

"Excellent, I love fans."

"Do not call her that, or you might find someone who wants to kill you more than me. And, unlike me, Noe always finishes what she starts."

Bellamy stood, dusting off his dark blue trousers and straightening his black top. Gold rings graced each of his fingers but one, the same finger that the demons of Shamay used to symbolize marriage.

"Tell me, Bellamy, what will you do if Asher decides to be with Padon?" He stumbled at my words, nearly falling. One of his hands reached out and caught the small wardrobe against the wall, his grip so tight a part of the wood splintered.

Slowly, I returned to my spot in his desk chair, waiting for an answer I was not sure would come. Magic came with a price, and that was a certain lack of morality. It was worse for my kind. We were stronger, our magic more potent. There was a cruelty to how deeply it wove itself into our souls. Though his magic was not as strong, I could see that it still burrowed into his heart and festered like a sore. That was probably why he treated it like an infection he wished to cut out of himself.

"Asher is free to make her own choices," he said after a moment. The words came from between clenched teeth. How tragic, to love like that. It was gross and terrifying and, quite honestly, pathetic.

"Liar."

"Fine. She can, but I know her. She will choose me. Even if the world was nothing but dust, she would still be at my side. Asher would die for me, kill for me, and live for me. Can you say that about anyone?"

Every sentence seemed to cleave its way into my heart, each digging deeper than the last.

They hurt. Oh, did they hurt.

"Once, I did." I thought of shining blonde hair and bright green eyes, my heart clenching. "Her name was Solana. I was obsessed with her. Every time she welcomed me into her bed, my infatuation grew. We fucked for years, neither of us ever discussing what it meant. She did kill for me, and I think she would have died for me too. But when the time came for her to choose between me and something new—an adventure—she didn't pick me. So, apologies if I find your confidence to be a little preemptive."

I thought of my creature again, how wonderfully curious he was. Just like Sol. Except he was not born to become a high demon and live forever. He did not possess the ability to world-walk or even enough magic to portal from his cage, regardless of whatever type of being he was. Which meant, unlike Sol, he would have no reason to wish for any more than me.

A burst of darkness encircled us, and then a female appeared. Her hair pooled down her back like golden brown silk. Her skin was a deep olive, making her hazel eyes light up. Only her body made me realize she was a threat. Yes, she was curvy and appealing, but she was also very clearly a honed weapon.

"Hello, not goddess Anastasia. It is absolutely horrifying to meet you. My name is Noe." With that, she shoved her hand forward and beamed down at me. There was nothing to lose in taking her hand, so I did. Still, I was on edge as I watched her jump onto Bellamy's bed.

Bellamy cleared his throat, eyeing me like he had a million questions and was not brave enough to ask any of them.

"Ask. You know you want to."

"You mentioned before that your world was in danger. Is it because Solana left?"

"Oh, wonderful, I love ancient lore and tortured futures. Give me one second." Noe disappeared from his bed, the darkness a cloud in the air above the thick red quilt. Moments later, she reappeared, the smoke-like shadows dissipating to reveal her lying down and holding what looked like a spoon and a bowl of chocolate. "Okay, now go on."

Scoffing, I quickly wrapped my magic around the bowl and willed it into my hands in a puff of pink magic. Moaning after licking some off my finger, I answered.

"Solana and her step-father, the holder of Time and Void, loved to travel. They had decided to go world walking, which takes an immense amount of magic and focus. But they never returned. Not only did we lose

the Time and Void seed, but we also lost the sole heir to the Sun and Moon seed."

"Pause. What is a seed?"

"That's what we call the magic that is passed down from one high demon to the next. It's what gives our magic color. Like the core of an apple."

"Then why not call it a core?"

"Fine, like the seed of an apple being replanted into a demon of one's line that is strong enough to ascend."

"Shut up and let her tell us the story, Noe."

"She took my chocolate," she whined, letting her head fall off the edge and draping her arm over her eyes with a groan of false pain.

"You will live," the prince retorted, kicking her foot off of his.

"Anyways, when Asta refused to come home and marry Padon, Stella let her remain here on Alemthian. Padon was enraged, and after he killed Asta's lover, he banished Stella. Which means we are now missing two seeds of magic."

"How weird that the story became so skewed over time," Noe commented as she pouted. I wondered if that was because few demons had access to the journals, or if it was because the journals simply held no relevant information. Silently, I prayed to Eternity that it was the former.

"What is so special about the seeds?"

"Our world needs them. It is the only one that we have found that can sustain so much magic, but it requires us to feed that same magic back into it."

"Like an offering?" Bellamy asked, his eyes wide in wonder.

"Sort of. Our great ancestors crafted the gems, one for each of the ten high demons. The gems hold the magic we siphon into them, and then they feed the world itself. But, with two seeds being gone, we don't have enough to feed the gems. Not only is our world slowly dying, crops and animals and even low demons perishing because of it, but the magic itself is volatile. It rebels against us, sometimes not working at all."

"So you seek Stella's seed to restore balance, but how will you find the Time and Void seed if it has been missing for so long?"

"Well, nosy prince, Stella searched for a very long time with no luck, but she was in mourning then. Plus, if I can convince Padon to stop being an idiot, then I am positive he can help. He is just quite set in his ways at the moment."

"His ways being Ash," Noe interjected, peeking at me from beneath her arm.

"Currently, yes. Before it was bitterness that stopped him. Stella and Achari, the holder of Time and Void, were not just our rulers. They were the oldest of us. And their daughters, Solana and Asta, were close in age to Padon and I. We had all been friends—family. Plus, Padon and I had been forced to ascend far earlier than normal, so it was nice having both mentors and parental figures in the Empress and Emperor. But when Padon didn't get his way with Asta, he rebelled against the being who practically helped raise him. He didn't want to look for Achari or Solana. All he wanted was the throne."

I fiddled with my fingers, suddenly so unsure of what I was meant to be doing. My entire existence had been inconsequential until now. Nothing was ever expected of me. This task was the exact opposite. Everything came down to me finding Stella.

"But if I can find her and get them to talk, maybe I can change his mind and stop this ridiculous war before it starts. We have enough problems without making you lousy creatures another one of them."

"You are pretty rude for someone who came to us for help. Speaking of which, we had three journals locked away in the royal library's

vault," Noe said, pointing to a spot on the bed beside her where black shadows writhed. I stood, hastily making my way to the small pile of worn leather books that now sat to her left.

"I'm going to pretend like you didn't just say that for the sake of convenience," I muttered, snatching all three journals up. Sitting next to her, I slouched into the flat pillows and readied for answers.

The two of them watched as I opened the book to the final entry and read, my eyes watering as I heard Asta's low and enchanting voice narrating the words in my head.

I dreamt of Zohar and Zayan again. Or perhaps it was a nightmare.

They died in my arms, just as they had all those years ago. I think I deserve such a fate. Choosing a mortal does that, tortures and maims the heart. When I first kissed Zohar, I thought the universe itself had shifted somehow. As if suddenly, everything was him—us—our hearts. Now I think I realize that it was just my own selfishness swaying me. Yes, the nightmares are my payment.

In my sleeping moments I see Death and Creation. I see my husband's blood on the hands of my old lover and wish for nothing more than to tear his soul straight from his body. If only he had one.

Mother says I can't do that. She swears that it would be a waste of precious time. She sounds like Father. Always on about the importance of time and its finite treasures.

Tomorrow I meet with the one called Oracle. She says she can give me better answers. I'm sure it's going to be nonsense. Everything always is.

I think I'm ready to say goodbye. I wonder if Mother will help.

A tear dangled on my lower lashes as I finished. She had been so broken.

The Asta I knew had been vibrant and happy. The Asta that had died upon this soil had been shattered and bruised. I slammed the book closed and grabbed another.

"Who was this Oracle?" I asked, trying not to let any emotion seep into my voice. I was not going to allow myself to look weak in front of them or anyone else.

"Which one?" Bellamy asked, picking up the journal I had tossed. My fingers halted on the page I opened to, looking up at the prince.

"There was more than one? What were they?" Noe looked at me as I spoke, her keen eyes squinted in thought. From my peripheral, I could see her fingers tapping on her stomach where her hands rested. She was observing me. Not the airheaded fool she portrayed herself as, then.

"Every few millennia, a fae is born that can see both the past and the future. It is an extremely rare ability, and a taxing one at that," Bellamy

said, his mind clearly straying elsewhere. "Seeing so much without always choosing to…I cannot imagine how awful that would be. I was given a glimpse of such a thing once, and I would not wish that weight on even your psycho ass."

"So if Asta met with an Oracle, then she could have changed the future she was told?" I asked, incredulous. That was extraordinary. Different than what even Venturae could do. Asta would have been given the chance to manipulate the future itself.

"Well, sort of. The future is always changing. Any Tomorrow or Oracle will tell you that. Every decision you make can alter it. But, if she was given instructions and followed them, then she could have encouraged the future that was foreseen. Did she say what she was told?"

"No, the entry stops there and so does the journal. That one must have been her last. She does mention her mother briefly, which confirms my suspicion that Stella was here with her." I let my voice trail off, reading an entry towards the beginning of the journal in my hand.

This one was from when her son, Zayan, was still alive. She wrote about the way he spoke, how the demons seemed to listen to his every command. How extraordinary he was. I smiled despite myself, thinking of how special her youngling would have been. Then, while I was already far more emotional than I normally was, I caught sight of my name.

"What has you so uncharacteristically happy?" Bellamy asked. He acted as if he knew me. It infuriated me, but even that could not tear the smile off my face.

"Asta wrote about me. She called me a connoisseur of debauchery and reveler in chaos," I whispered, laughing at her choice of words. Then, even quieter, I added, "She said she missed her best friend."

CHAPTER TWENTY-THREE

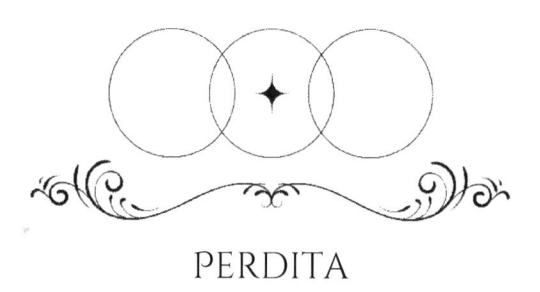

PERDITA

Father always said that to die rich was better than to live poor.

It was one of the few things we agreed on. Although, now that he had, in fact, died rich, I wondered if he still thought such a thing wherever he was. The Underworld, ideally.

Finding out that he was dead had been jarring—freeing. Now that we had a job to do, and gold to find, he could hold no space in my mind. It was better that way. He did not deserve my thoughts, even if they were hateful and spiteful. So instead, I sought out Dima.

It had been two days since we boarded the prince's ship. The same amount of time since I had nearly let her die.

"You hesitated to let the Healer save me. Do not pretend you care about anything other than gold. Not when you proved that to be true when my life was hanging in the balance!" she had signed before retreating to her quarters below deck. Dima was holding a grudge, it seemed.

What had she expected me to do? Nothing was more important than my ship and my gold. They had attacked us. Of course I was considering killing the Healer instead of letting him save her. It would have been the strategic move. But then the prince had trapped my crew, and I was forced to accept the help. She saw that I refused his aid for myself in favor of one last attempt at securing their goods. How could she be upset when I was not willing to save even myself?

No matter, she would forgive me.

Lifting my hand, I knocked. My fist hitting the wood made my skin tingle, rattling my bones. Dima was quick to rip open her door and glare at me with her violet eyes. When I tried to step forward, she halted me with a slap to the face. Fire erupted on my cheek, the sting of her smack not enough to deter me.

If I could just get inside, I could make her forget.

"Please, can I come in, Storm?" I asked. She watched my hands with downturned lips, preparing to say no. "Do not make me force my way in."

Dima threw the door all the way open, stomping away to her bed. She sat, crossing her legs beneath her rose-colored dress. The material clung to her body, some of it hidden beneath her pitch-black hair. I smirked, walking in and closing the door behind me.

"You need to get over your anger, Dima. I would have done the same to anyone. Even you are not more important than our mission—*my* goals. You know this. So why do you shut me out?" She watched me, becoming visibly more angry as I signed. Gods how I grew wet watching her chest heave in fury.

"You are pathetic! All this time wasted on gold and glory, but you refuse to let anyone share it with you. When you die, your life will have been just as pointless as your father's. Nothing and no one left to show for it." Her lips moved faster than her hands. I moved even quicker.

I portaled to her bed, landing above her and shoving her down by the neck. She squirmed, a sort of panic lighting her eyes. My own anger blurred my vision, her words hitting exactly where she hoped they would.

Using her surprise against her, I grabbed both of her hands and held them above her head, willing shadows to tie them together. Then I ordered them to secure to the wood of her bed. Next, I tied her feet. She wiggled beneath me, a tear falling down her cheek.

My hands moved to her breasts, gripping them and squeezing. A moan rattled her chest, making bumps rise on my skin.

She gasped as I ripped her dress in half, my mouth flying down to her left breast. I bit down on the flesh there as I shoved two fingers between her legs. She writhed below me, struggling against the shadows that confined her. We both knew this would hurt just as much as it pleasured.

Pulling out my fingers, I smacked her dripping center. Once, twice, three times. Then I switched to her other breast, licking and sucking and enjoying every moment of her moans that vibrated on my lips as my fingers slipped back into her. When my eyes flicked up to her face, I saw she had already been watching me. Her lips formed a single word, a plea before the end. Truthfully, I could watch her say that for years on end and never grow tired of it.

"More."

By the time I licked up my final success, tears were running freely down her face and her body was coated in newly forming bruises. I watched her come down from the orgasm with a smile, my tongue swirling inside of her before sliding out and up, flicking her swollen clit. She tasted like victory.

When I stood, wiping my mouth, Dima watched knowingly. The shadows holding her down dissipated, but her hands remained where they were.

"Get off my ship, Storm. You can come back when you have learned better."

And then I left, slamming the door shut behind me.

I darted up the stairs, still somewhat unsatisfied. Which was made worse by the sight before me.

CJ sat in front of Lian, moving her lips slowly in time with the sign for ship. Lian watched her with greedy eyes, copying the sign perfectly. For some reason, the image of such a thing made me angrier than Dima's comment about my worthless father.

I put my salty fingers into my mouth, whistling. CJ's head whipped towards me. She stood abruptly, clearly noticing the stiffness to my demeanor. The anger that swarmed me.

"What are you doing, CJ?" I signed. Briefly, she glanced down at the fae who merely sat and picked at her nails. Then she was slumping forward, knowing she would receive little in the way of help.

"Lian wants to learn sign so she can be of better help to us. She is skilled with her Air power and a quick learner. Over the last two days she has already learned twenty-eight signs." The look of pride on CJ's face would have been comical if it were not utterly absurd.

"Why would we need her help? And why learn sign when she can hear just fine? You are probably helping whatever ulterior motive she has!" The fingers on my right hand cramped, forcing me to stop signing momentarily. A growl sought freedom from behind my ribs, the sound probably coming out strained. What I would give to throw all three of the outsiders over the side of the ship and forget about them. "Get to work, CJ. Do not let me catch you helping her again."

CJ practically ran away after offering a hasty explanation to the blue-haired female, not so much as sparing either of us another glance.

"What is your problem?" Lian asked. Since she realized I could read lips, I noticed that she spoke slower. She was uncomfortably observant. "If I can be of more help, you should let me. It is petty and ridiculous to not take the aid you are offered."

"What I do with my ship and my crew is none of your business. If you need to know sign to pull your own weight, then you are an even bigger idiot than I thought." She watched, squinting at my moving hands as if she could understand what I was signing.

"I want learn," she signed back. It was a simple set of broken words, and she signed them embarrassingly slowly. Yet she lifted her chin, staring at me with a challenge that made my heart race, despite the fact I did not trust or like any of them in the slightest. With three quick whistles, I called Ro to me.

"Captain?" she asked, ignoring Lian completely. It was one thing I liked most about her. She did not care about anything other than the success of this crew.

"Translate for the idiot."

With a laugh, Ro nodded, facing Lian.

"If you want to learn, then you can learn from me," I signed. Ro spoke aloud as I moved my hands, but Lian's eyes never strayed from me. She was trying to understand. How absolutely infuriating. "Lessons do not come free, though, Blue. Every time you take me down, I will afford you a new sign."

Another bark of laughter came from Ro, the sound vibrating against my bare feet. Oh, how I loved a challenge. Anything new that did not require constant vigilance and planning. Something I did not have to stress over.

"That is ridiculous, I am not fighting you to learn—"

I stopped watching her lips and dove forward, tackling her to the ground and forcing her to roll beneath me. A bit of laughter left my lips as she stared up at me in astonishment. Knowing I likely was facing off with someone who knew how to fight, I took the advantage and slammed my fist into her face.

Gods, it felt good to make someone bleed.

Lian spit blood into my face, pulling her arm to the side and then jabbing it into my neck. Pain erupted in my newly healed throat, but I ignored it in favor of throwing shadows in her face and willing them to become solid. She bucked beneath me as she suffocated.

Too easy.

As if she could hear me, Lian stilled. Before I could claim my victory, though, I felt the slice of a blade in my thigh. I fell backwards, gripping at my leg and holding my breath to minimize my movements.

Ro opened her mouth, probably screaming as she watched me fall. She was at my side in seconds, on her knees and inspecting the wound. Shadows wrapped around my thigh just above the bleeding cut. Ro continued to tighten her shadows, but all I could do was stare at Lian as she stood above me and wiped the blood from her nose.

Henry appeared behind her, grabbing her cheeks and inspecting her. Were they together? He had seemed infatuated with the mortal princess over the last two days, but maybe that was for his own gain in this coming war. Perhaps what he really wanted was the little fae before me.

Maybe she wanted him too. Though he was not as handsome as the idiot prince, he had an aura to him. A comforting presence if one wanted it. If I had any interest in males, I would have wanted someone meaner than he seemed to be. More challenging.

It looked as though Lian would disagree. How irksome.

"We have arrived at Isle Shifter, Li," he said to her. Excellent. We would be rid of him yet.

Blue gave me a quick glance and slowly mouthed, "I win." Then she walked away.

***

Lian seemed more prone to anger now that her giant pet was away with his pretty little princess. Did she love him? Was she jealous?

I was not sure why I cared other than boredom.

That and Dima had jumped off the deck three days ago, so I was horny and bothered.

"No you idiot, it is like this," I signed to her before slapping her hands and showing her again. She had beaten me four out of five times since our first fight, her willingness to play dirty surprising me. The only reason I had won the second time was because she was unprepared and sad after Henry left.

They had hugged for ages despite the fact she did not seem like much of a hugger at all.

"You are moving your hands too fast, you bitch!" Her face went red as she yelled, her hands trying and failing to properly sign what she was saying. She sent a gust of wind towards the fire Jazmine was starting on the fae rulers' boat, making the entire ship burst into flames around us. Jazmine, with her hair the same color as the violent red flames she constantly lit and her ebony skin, was a beacon. Which would most definitely put a kink in our plan. We had to move quickly before we were sighted. So I grabbed them both, portaling us back to the Abaddon.

When our feet hit the deck of my ship once more, Lian ripped her hand from mine. I tried not to let it feel like a rejection. She was just a pawn in this game I was playing with her prince. It was not like she mattered. Not really.

Still, I smirked at her and demonstrated again.

"Thought," I signed.

"Thought," she fiercely signed back.

With a nod, I reached forward and mussed her short blue locks. She swatted me away, flashing me her middle finger before standing and making her way to CJ. I had reluctantly allowed them to talk. They worked well together, and we moved at far greater speeds with Lian's help. That and she seemed…lonely. Like she was not used to not having someone she loved nearby.

"You cannot like her," Bek signed as she stepped in my line of sight. I huffed, swatting her hands away from me.

"I do not, so there is no problem. Plus, I can do what I want. Do not mistake our friendship for power. I am the captain, Bek." Her mouth turned down, and her fists bunched at her sides as I signed. I walked away, knowing she would follow, but immensely uninterested in the lecture.

When we made it to the helm, I shooed Fatima away and took control of my ship. Fatima was all too glad to go, the bare side of her head revealing the tattoos she had gotten done after we stumbled upon her all those years ago. The other half of her head still had a bit of her hair left, the brown strands cut short.

"I am not kidding, Perdita." Bek was in my way. Physically and metaphorically. Who cared if I wanted to fuck Lian? I had wanted to fuck Bek when I first met her, and that turned out just fine, if not a bit disappointing.

"I am not kidding either, Bek. Get out of my way. Go tell Lian and CJ that we need to speed up. That ship will be burned completely very soon, and we need to be there when the queen searches for new transportation."

With that, Bek stomped away. I caught sight of Lian staring at me from her place on the deck, lying to myself that I was simply looking at the first sign of Isle Healer in the distance.

Yes, Blue, stare away. Watch me do what I do best.

CHAPTER TWENTY-FOUR

ASHER

Hot. It was so incredibly hot on Isle Healer.

The isle itself was a stunning testament to the circle of life. We had seen so many farms as we passed through the Healer Lands. Their warden, Sandres, had told us that their crop season was mostly over, only those few that could withstand high temperatures still thriving as summer bore down on us.

Sipho had spoken of his home—our home, he would call it—often enough that I felt as if I knew it already. Even all these years later, I could still hear the faint echo of his voice as he described his father's farm and his favorite lake. He had truly loved his home, and I found myself loving it too.

Bellamy would like it here. He would have listened as I spoke of Sipho and helped me craft new dreams that he would help me bring to life.

"The male you know in your mind is not real, Strange One."

"Why do you have to come along and steal my joy? You never used to do that," I noted, crossing my arms as I glanced down at where Wrath sat upon the dying grass, licking a paw.

I had escaped the dinner, which was going rather well in comparison to the hostility at the table that resided in the Single Lands. Still, I hated this game. I was no longer the docile pet that Mia and Xavier had trained me to be. I could not sit, stay, and speak when directed. I was more than that.

"You are exactly as you have always been. Just as I am only what you wish me to be. I do what you say, what your mind deems important." If he did not shut up I was going to lose it.

"How do you explain the way I fought on Isle Shifter? That was my training. I would not have known how to defend myself like that if I had not been trained by Bellamy and his Trusted."

Wrath huffed, standing and moving towards me like a predator seeking prey. He had never really scared me before. But now, as he taunted and tortured me, I thought I might be afraid of him most of all.

"You dreamt for months on end of being taught to fight. You internalized all you learned from those council meetings and overhearing Xavier. That is how you are explaining it away in your mind. Not me, Strange One. *You.*"

I was losing my mind and I did not know how to stop it all. How to shut up the voices in my head that screamed that Wrath was right. Mia's voice. Xavier's voice. Theon's voice. Even worse, at night I dreamed of Bellamy rescuing me, only to wake up still in my golden nightdress and surrounded by fae guards. It made me wonder if Wrath was right. If I had been desperate for something better and made all of it up.

"Leave me alone!" I shouted at Wrath. At the voices. At myself.

"Woah there, I am sorry. I did not mean to upset you." Sterling's deep and heavy voice met my ears, pacifying my wretched mind momentarily. Wrath was gone, the space near my feet empty once more.

Looking up, I watched as Sterling walked towards me. His hands were in his pockets, the barest hint of a smirk playing on his lips. He wore all gold, as did I. I found that each day that passed left me loathing the color a little less. It was stifling, exhausting, and born of such horrible memories. But it was also the color of the sun, of Sterling's curls, of Bellamy's rings.

Bellamy had once said that the color could not control me. I was trying to prove him right.

"It was real," I whispered, reaching over to trace a line up my forearm where my jagged scar had once been. Sterling eyed the movement but said nothing. He was growing used to my insanity. I feared he thought it normal for me.

"Asher, do you need anything?" he asked, stopping a few feet from me. He looked so sincere, so genuine. Why did that hurt worse?

"No, I am fine. Honestly, I just needed some air." He glared as I waved him off, as if he could see the madness that clung to me like a shadow.

Before either of us could say anything else, the sound of something shattering nearby caught our attention. Both of our heads whipped towards the sound, our eyes wide. Neither of us moved, just staring towards the small alley between the rows of cottages that existed near the warden's manor.

Homes were close by here, so much of the larger spaces used for farming. It was an extraordinarily communal place. But that made sense, as the Healer faction was the largest, and the only one that did not have subfactions. They were a community. And as I stared on at the darkness that lurked between their homes, I thought of nothing I would hate more than the sight of that community being torn apart by violence.

So, I crept forward, my heeled slippers silent upon the dirt path. My magic seeped out from my body, slithering like a snake upon the ground as it hunted. There, only two homes down the path, were five fae. Their thoughts were a cacophony of fury. Of pain and loathing. One of them maintained watch—the closest to me at that moment—while the others spoke in hushed voices as they screamed some of the loudest thoughts I had ever heard.

Most of them were about…*me*. How they might catch me, kill me, parade me around as a bloody and lifeless trophy. They all agreed that anyone they killed along the way was justified. Slaughtering innocents was nothing when getting to me was everything. It was sickening.

Even worse was listening to their reasons. Hearing how much they lost. Family, friends, lovers, younglings. A mountain of death that I stood at the top of, smiling.

They hated me because it was I who shattered the minds of those they loved, and I deserved that hatred. So I listened silently as I stalked towards them, knowing what was about to happen and how little a chance there was that I would walk away feeling anything but regret.

Sterling, I need you to go back into the manor and make sure no one else comes looking for me.

The prince jumped at the sound of my voice within his head. I had no time to explain or to reassure him, so when he meant to refuse me, I turned and looked him in the eye.

Go inside and make sure no one else comes out here.

He straightened his back, spun around, and returned to the safety of the warden's home—The Manipulator's voice echoing in his mind. A sigh of relief escaped me before I could silence it, and alarm bells rang in my head as all five rebels locked into the sound.

With no other option, I made my move. I reached around the corner, grabbing the closest male by his shirt and dragging him towards me. His scream of surprise was cut off as his neck was snapped, my hands

moving quicker than I remember them capable of. Another male dashed out of the alleyway, his head whipping towards me. Grabbing the now dead male's knife, I prepared for the fight.

My opponent swung out, swiping at my stomach with a knife of his own. Stepping out of the way just in time, I countered his move. Unfortunately, he was just as quick as I was and we were forced to face off, breathing heavily and both slightly panicked.

"Dane!" a female shouted as she reached out for the dead fae at my feet. Another female wrapped her arms around her, holding her sobbing comrade back. "You bitch!"

"It is her," the last male said as he walked out of the shadows, his hands stained gold and red. None of them wore the cloth with their symbol, but I knew from their minds that they were rebels. The female stifled her sobs, covering her mouth and staring at me wide-eyed.

"You are supposed to be in the warden's manor, dining and unsuspecting," the male I had fought said, his voice calmer than I had expected.

For some reason, I wanted to explain to them that I was going insane. That I was terrified my mind was not right. But more than that, I desperately wanted to feel their blood on my skin. To kill them and then hate myself for it. To free The Manipulator that raged within me. To feel more than despair and terror, even if only for a fleeting moment.

Instead of speaking, I hurled the knife into the face of the female holding the one whose cheeks were still wet with tears. It sliced through her, cutting into the bridge of her nose and sinking into her flesh. She collapsed to the ground just as the silence was shattered by the sound of the three remaining fae's screams of fury.

They converged on me, mercilessly attacking all at once. I was forced to spend my time on defense, leaning back to avoid the strike of a knife as I simultaneously caught a leg with my hand before it connected with my hip. My mind was racing, magic tasting their intentions and only barely circumventing their attacks.

It was a race to see who could slice open the other, and I lost. The female who had once been sobbing turned ruthless as she aimed again and again for my chest. For every good swipe that I got at her, my dress and shoes slowed me just enough for her to get one in as well. Our blood and sweat tainted the stifling air, but we remained nearly silent, not a single fae awaking.

I fought with every ounce of rage I had ever possessed. I screamed with the voice of the youngling who had been caged for days on end. I sobbed from the eyes of a female robbed of joy.

And as I towered over the final fae as she healed herself just enough to stand back up, I inhaled from the broken lungs of someone who had gasped for air for so long that they no longer knew what it was to breathe deeply.

"Why do you not just shatter my mind? Why not get it over with?" she asked as she limped towards me.

"Because I want to feel this," I answered just as I dove forward. She was not prepared for my direct attack, but her instincts were strong. The moment my knife sank into her chest, hers dug into my side, slicing through my ribs.

I let out a barely audible cry, gripping the hilt of the blade and shoving her body away from me. She hit the ground with the same lifeless thud they all had, but for some reason, it hurt more to see her staring off into the distance.

All they had wanted was something different, something better. But they had chosen to hurt innocents in their fight to end the Mounbetton rule.

Nicola's words echoed in my head.

"Remember who you are while away. Remember who you have vowed to save."

"Asher?" Mia's voice stripped me bare of any thought or feeling but one: defeat.

"Let me guess, you had to check in to make sure your guard dog did its job?" I asked, never taking my eyes from the female on the ground. I was truly everything she always wanted me to be.

Mia's footsteps stopped, the scorching air silent but for the bugs that swirled around my sweaty head and the dead bodies before me. My blood-soaked hand still held the blade firmly, trying not to move.

"I wish I knew what you meant by that." Then she approached, gasping as she took in the carnage. "Eternity above. Asher, what happened?"

"I did what I do best. I killed them all."

"But who are they? Were you attacked?" she asked in a voice that dripped panic.

"Rebels," was all I offered, not so much as looking her way.

After a handful of excruciating moments, she whispered, "They do not wear the mark."

"You never told me about them."

"I did not want you to know. I feared it would put even more on your shoulders. You have already lived with far more burdens than any Mounbetton Queen before you." Her hand moved to my shoulder, and I quickly shook it off. Her motherly touch no longer soothed, it burned.

"Do not pretend you care. Not when you spent two hundred years torturing, belittling, and brainwashing me."

For a few minutes, we remained in silence, neither of us willing to speak or move first. My eyes roamed over the destruction I had caused, and I found myself thrown off by how utterly bizarre this was. I meant to speak, to give in, but then Mia let out a heavy sigh.

"I know I have been hard on you, my flower. Your life has not been easy or fun or fair. I know you loved that Healer and that you likely never forgave us, even though you said you did."

I let out a hiss of pain from my body tensing as Mia brought up Sipho. I had spoken of him more in the last year than I had in my lifetime. Or, no, maybe not the last year. Wrath was getting to my head. The world was.

"Growing up, I was taught the importance of the Mounbetton line. Of the females that ruled and conquered. My father showed me no love. When I lost control of my Earth power and demolished part of the palace, I was beaten for days. My mother was different. She offered me a calculated sort of love. I was precious, like a gemstone. Something that could be buffed and cut and displayed. Every day was a test, every move watched. That was all I knew. In my head it made sense to do the same to you. To covet you."

She cleared her throat, the sound of her dress swishing as she shuffled, a clear sign she was either uncomfortable or on edge. Wrath appeared at my feet, twirling through my legs before making his way to the dead fae on the ground. His laughs rang in my ears like a warning.

"I have loved you in the way I know how, Asher. Yes, it can be hard. Sometimes I wish I were different. But this way will make you the strongest. And one day when you have younglings, you will understand it. You will be just like me, even if you say you will not. I am the closest thing you have to a mother, and I am doing my best. I am doing what I was taught."

I wished I knew how to make sense of that information and decide if the story was an excuse or an explanation. But I had neither the time nor the patience for that.

"We should probably clean up these dead bodies before someone realizes your toy has a brain of its own. Would not want the masses to fear me too much and turn on you." Then, my eyes darted to the spot on the wall not too far away, where the fae had painted the bleeding crown with

222

the words *death to the royals* below it. "Just so we are clear, I do not care that the rebels want you dead. I did this for the innocent fae they would have killed along the way."

Mia remained silent as I turned and walked away, passing her without so much as a fleeting glance. Wrath followed, still chuckling at the carnage.

"Congratulations, Strange One, you are officially the monster in the night."

As I entered the warden's manor and the first screams met my ears, I realized that was exactly what I had become.

***

The next morning we awoke to find our ship burning in the water.

Mia had never been particularly obvious when it came to her cunning nature, but every carefully crafted mirage she had shown in the desert that was the barren and lifeless nature of royalty seemed to shed in that moment.

Screams erupted as Mia let loose some of that ungodly amount of power within her. The water shook as she demanded the seafloor beneath to shutter and bend, her fists balled so tightly that her pale skin turned fiery red.

"This cannot stand," she hissed beneath her breath, her words traveling only to Xavier and I. Sterling remained oblivious to the conversation. His hands were pressed into his hips and his mouth hung agape, as if nothing had ever surprised him quite this much.

How had they taken his memories? If everything truly had happened, then what did they do to him that would lead to him magically forgetting *everything?*

"Every time I think you are moving forward, you begin descending back into that madness of yours once more," Wrath said at my feet.

"We must find a new ship rather than remain here like sitting ducks," Xavier whispered, practically twitching from his place between us. I felt the moment his arm wrapped protectively around me, and my eyes caught the motion of him doing the same to Mia.

Once more they appeared the team I had always seen them as. Nothing like they had been in my low level room as they argued over torturing me.

"Perhaps the last year, which fits none of the narrative you were raised on, is what should be seen as odd. Reality is not a fairytale from one of your books, Strange One." My foot swiped out, kicking through Wrath despite the fact that I had genuinely *felt* him sometimes.

He was right, and it terrified me.

"We have to hope a merchant vessel miraculously comes," Mia responded, rolling her eyes and storming from the docks. I wanted to remain still, staring at the ship as it burned. There was something euphoric about it. As if the torment within me sunk to the depths along with it.

"In the meantime, we must find the culprits. This cannot stand." Xavier's fury charged the air as he chased after his wife, the emotion heavy on my tongue. He would slaughter more than deserved it if we did not find safe passage soon. Not that I had much room to judge when I knew in my heart I had killed without merit last night.

"Well, we could always sail a tiny boat out and roast marshmallows over the demise of our oh so fun adventure," Sterling said. Warmth replaced the cold chill upon my shoulders from where Xavier's arm fell away, Sterling's grip on me pulling me from my thoughts.

"Pity, I imagine we were bound to have endless fun upon a ship surrounded by idiots and liars."

"You do not look like a conspiracy theorist," he said, tugging me away from the water. I allowed him to lead, my mind straying to the easy way Bellamy's smiles seemed to light me up from within. How life seemed lighter in his arms, despite how heavy it truly was.

It was real.

I needed to kill the queen and get the fuck out of here.

"—or what if we find a tavern and drink them dry on order of the future queen?" Sterling asked, the beginning of his train of thought lost to me.

"While I imagine watching you vomit through your nose would be hilarious, I think I will pass. I am tired. How about you go in there and demand a drink as the future king consort?"

That had him beaming down at me, his finger coming to flick my nose.

"Such pretty words," he hummed. "Dare I say they hide something nefarious?"

"Depends," I countered, a smile ghosting across my mouth. "Will you let me get away with heinous acts in the spirit of camaraderie?"

"Only if I can watch with a drink in my hand."

"Deal. Meet me back here."

"Oh perfect, wine or mead?" Before I could respond Sterling waved a hand through the air and added, "Who am I kidding? Crime requires rum."

With that, he practically skipped towards the awaiting town.

For a few seconds, I remained still. Wrath appeared at my feet, but I ignored him in favor of plotting. My berries were gone, which meant my plan to slip them into her food was null. Not that it was a very good strategy anyways. I needed something better. Smoother.

225

Corner her in a dark room and choke her to death? No, she would fight back and likely lock me up somewhere.

Drown her in the sea? Possibly, though I wagered there would be a Water in the next crew. Our last one had barely made it off the ship in time, I doubted they wanted to risk their lives again. A new crew would have no idea just how dangerous it was to travel with us.

I could save them the trouble and danger if I ended her now.

Maybe poison was not such a bad idea. It was simpler than the other plans, less obvious.

"Okay, feisty little wife, here is your rum," Sterling said from behind me. I jumped, not having heard him. I was losing track of time. Dangerously oblivious to the world around me more often than not. I had to focus.

"What you should be doing is learning about your realm and preparing for war, yet you remain in your fantasies and allow yourself to be at risk," Wrath whispered as I took the bottle from Sterling. Of course he would buy the entire thing. "If you kill the queen, the Fae Realm might just fall. You would risk the lives of every fae here just to—what? Prove a point? Get revenge on a female who is practically your mother?"

"She is not my mother!" I growled out. From the corner of my eye, I saw Sterling staring at me in nervous bewilderment. Sighing, I straightened my spine, shaking my head slightly. My hair, styled in silky waves, fell around my face and momentarily protected me from his scrutiny. "I need a poison that has no taste, color, or smell. Something untraceable."

Sterling deserved credit for his composure. He did not so much as flinch at my question. "Arsenic."

"Excellent, where can I get that?" I inquired, ready to finally take the action needed to stop this war in its tracks.

"There's an apothecary near the tavern." With a finger, Sterling pointed towards a small brown building with a bright red sign that read *Apothecary: Healing and More.*

"Is the *more* what we need?" I asked, looking up at him. He smirked, taking a swig from the bottle he snatched from my hand. Then, he nodded, waving a hand for me to lead the way. "Fantastic. I love bloodthirsty Healers."

We walked silently, trading the bottle back and forth like two miscreants on a mission to cause chaos. In fact, that was exactly what we were—crowns aside. A bell rang as we opened the door, a musky and thick smell wafting our way. A female with long auburn hair and deep brown skin smiled at us from behind the counter, but any view of her was quickly blocked when two other females cut into our path.

One of them had curls that swirled around her like a tornado, the color that of coffee before cream. She was round everywhere but her eyes, which were the shape and color of almonds. Beside her was a female that looked like she crawled up from the Underworld. Her eyes were dark as night, her smile feral. She had dirty blonde hair that clashed with her pale skin. She was terrifying.

"Apologies, Princess Asher. We were just grabbing supplies for our voyage and simply had to say hello." Shallow bows were offered so quickly they might have been figments of my imagination. As it seemed many things were these days.

"It is nice to meet you both. Unfortunately, we do not have time to talk, as our ship has been turned into firewood and we must find new passage. But I wish you both the best." I tried side-stepping them, but the dark-haired one got in my way. She lifted her arms, making motions and gestures with her hands and fingers that seemed intentional.

The blonde nodded, chuckling softly before turning my way again. "You are in luck, we have room."

ACT III

~ CHAOS AND ORDER ~

CHAPTER TWENTY-FIVE

ASHER

The captain had a preference for the ostentatious. She was bold with her gestures, which her crew called signs. Every move she made was flamboyant and entertaining. Mia seemed to greatly dislike her, preferring to stay below deck rather than remain in Perdita Harligold's presence. It made me like the merchant even more.

She was currently waving her hands in dismissal at one of her crewmates that tried to stop her from scaling the ropes that tied the sails in place. It was hilarious, watching her be both a terrifying and ridiculous sailor. The seasickness that still tortured me was worth such a sight.

Absently, I used my fingers to trace the spaces my scars had been. I kept inventory, reminding myself of the story once etched on my skin.

Wrath remained silent at my side, his head resting on the edge of the boat as he watched the rolling waves. He had taken to only correcting me when I thought something he viewed as particularly idiotic. Still, he remained, usually only visiting when I thought of my time with Bellamy. Like a reminder that my brain was capable of deceiving me.

When my eyes moved back to the place the captain had been, I found nothing but rope and open sky. She was gone, nowhere to be seen. How had she moved so quickly? Was she alright?

"Excuse me!" I yelled to the blonde who had been with Captain Harligold in the apothecary, where we sadly were not able to get any useful poisons. Bek was her name. She turned from her spot on the deck, smiling wickedly as she made her way to me. "Where did your captain go? Is she safe?"

"I am not sure, let me see. Are you safe, Captain?" Her hands moved with such speed I was not quite sure how on Alemthian anyone could understand the signs. Looking over my shoulder, I spotted her. Perdita flashed me a coy smile from her spot mere inches away. I leapt back, surprised and slightly unsettled by her nearness. She offered a couple sharp moves of her hands and a wink my way. "She says she is more than fine."

"Well that is good. I just wanted to make sure since I saw you upon the masts and then you were gone." How had she done that?

The two of them chuckled, Captain Harligold's nearly silent.

"You underestimate Harligold's speed. She is not the most notorious...*merchant* to sail these waters for nothing. Onto more important things though."

"What important things would that be?" I asked, wiping my hands down my skirts as I pushed back my shoulders. I would stand tall, even if they might push me off their ship in retribution for whatever wrongs I had committed against them.

Once more, the captain began signing, a smile on her face the entire time.

"She says that she wants to know more about you. Go sit with her. She has ink and paper, you need no one else for whatever it is the two of you will discuss." Bek abruptly turned, patting Perdita on the shoulder and then whistling as she strolled away.

"Well then, I guess it is just me and you. Should we paint our nails and eat sweets as we gossip about all the fucked up things that happened throughout our lives?" I asked the captain, leaning against the ledge of her ship. She smirked in answer before pivoting and walking away, waving a hand over her shoulder for me to follow.

My steps against the dark wood were drowned out by the sound of breaking waves. I felt my stomach roll and my mouth water, nausea threatening me with each jolt of the ship. But soon we were at the railing that brought us not below deck, but above to a second level. We took the steps quickly, stopping at the sight of a door with the word "captain" engraved in swirling gold script. Fancy, for a merchant. Neither of the other two ships I had been on had that.

We stepped through, and I was met with the most brazen quarters I had ever seen. Gold littered the space. Not just on the furniture either, but actual coins in wooden chests mingling with gems so large they made my breath hitch. When Captain Harligold finally turned around, I spoke.

"I have never claimed myself to be a genius—in fact I think I am an idiot more often than not—but something is telling me you are not a merchant." She stared at my lips, shaking her head with a breathy chuckle when I finished speaking. And then she sat down, pulling paper, a pot of ink, and a golden quill from the top drawer of her wooden desk against the wall. Making my way to her, I was met with the distinct scent of…Lian.

Yes, I could have sworn that it was the smell of spring blooms and crisp air that invaded my senses.

The scratching of quill to paper stole my focus, and my eyes darted over Perdita's shoulder as she wrote.

You are far less scary than the stories claim you to be.

I laughed, my head falling forward. When she pressed the quill into my hand and pulled another wooden chair towards me, I gladly accepted. But as she placed a fresh sheet of paper before me, I found I had a better idea.

Oh, you have not seen anything yet, Captain.

Glee consumed me like fire upon wood as she visibly tensed, her body rigid and the faintest taste of sweet fear upon my tongue.

You can talk back, you know. It is hard at first, but if you focus on me, on shouting those thoughts of yours into the void, I promise I will hear you.

There was something odd about her mind. Bleak and foreboding despite the brilliance of her aura. She was bright and exotic on the outside, like someone who had traveled so many places they became something entirely new. A star that fell across galaxies.

But inside, she was the universe itself, a mass of endless darkness that seemed to stretch on forever. Perdita had suffered in this lifetime, that much I was certain of. Her quill once more scraped against the paper, stealing my attention again.

I cannot speak.

Quirking a brow, I looked over to her, catching her hazel eyes.

Okay, I am not that big of an idiot. I realize that. But I am not asking you to speak aloud, I am telling you to think. Clearly you are capable of that seeing as you somehow tricked the king and queen into believing you a mere merchant.

My gaze flicked to the pile of what had to have been stolen coin and gems. That, or Perdita was trading in something nefarious. A crackling choke of laughter escaped her, a fist hitting the wood of her desk.

I feel as though I should be offended you have not heard of me.

Oh, I have heard of your name, though I am half convinced I imagined it all. Do you have a relative with pink hair and a nasty habit of trying to kill princesses?

Perdita stilled, her smile falling. I wanted to take back what I had said. Her name had been familiar, the image of O'Malley Harligold dead at my feet at the front of my mind. But I must have been wrong, because she shook her head, offering a weak version of the smile that had lit up her face before.

I have no family but my crew.

Well, me either really. Look at us, bonding over trauma.

Her laugh once more rang through the space, making my shoulders relax. At least I had not entirely ruined a nice conversation.

I knew I would like you, brain crusher. Maybe you can join my crew.

I fear I have a weak stomach and a fondness for comfort, or else I would take you up on that offer. Now tell me, what was it you actually wanted to speak about?

Sitting back and crossing my arms, I awaited her response. Her mind raced, images speeding by so quickly that I struggled to keep up. But again I was reminded of Lian as a fleeting memory of blue hair came and went.

I like order, Princess Asher. I am, above all else, a plotter. A planner. There is security in making sure you are prepared for everything. But finding you in that apothecary offered me little choice but to be spontaneous. I hate it. Still, I can rectify such a thing. We sail to Isle Element, where I have a feeling things will become interesting. I want your reassurance that you are on our side.

What side is that?

I quirked a brow, sitting forward slightly.

The side of those who have no say in this war.

***

Xavier found me sitting with my head tilted back against the wood of the ship not long after I left Perdita's quarters. I felt in my gut that I had lied when I promised I was on her side. Had I not killed more innocents than I had protected recently? Still, I wanted to be that for them. A ruler that cared enough to fight for her subjects.

Perhaps I could learn, at least.

I heard and felt Xavier sit beside me, but my eyes remained closed. I did not want to speak to him or anyone, though I doubted he cared about that. I was proven right when he cleared his throat not once, not twice, but three times.

"Suffering from a cold, Your Majesty?" I asked, still keeping my eyes shut.

"Nothing these chocolate muffins cannot fix," he responded. My eyes instantly flew open, finding the sight of two gigantic chocolate muffins on a plate that dripped what smelled like fudge. Narrowing my gaze, I glared his way.

"What is the catch?" I asked, knowing better than to think anything I was offered by him was free.

"Just conversation," he answered with a shrug, waving the plate near my face before setting it between us and grabbing one.

He was bribing me with food.

I was embarrassed to admit it was working.

"Fine, but I do not promise to be nice." With that, I snatched the muffin he was lifting towards his mouth, not trusting that the other was free of poison. He chuckled, shaking his head and wrapping his fingers around the other.

I wasted no time biting into it, the flavor bursting on my tongue and settling my aching stomach. Xavier remained silent for the span of one bite before he capitalized on my euphoria.

"You know, Mia used to love these." Of course this would turn into a conversation about her. What a cohesive, united front they were presenting. I did nothing but chew, not taking the bait. "When we first officially met, she was sneaking one from the table at her introductory ball. She had worn head-to-toe gold, her dress like a rose in full bloom with layers upon layers of petals. No female had ever been as beautiful as she was in that moment. And when I tapped on her shoulder, she did not so much as look at me before telling me to go away."

I could not stop myself from snorting at the thought. Maybe Mia had once been tolerable.

"Yes, it was funny to me too. The Mounbetton princess was known for her grace, her sophistication. Hearing her tell me to shut up with a mouth full of chocolate had been both jarring and refreshing. But Mia was half your age and just as strong-willed, and for that, she would suffer," he said with more sadness in his tone than I had expected.

I straightened, my muffin momentarily forgotten as he continued his story.

"Mia comes from a long line of very strong females—queens. She was raised to be the same. To be more than she could ever possibly be. That was what was expected of her. She needed to be the most cunning, beautiful, and formidable being in every room she entered. Mistakes were not acceptable, and neither was imperfection. It made for a cold life. But she loved her parents, her mother most of all. And when her mother chose *me* of all her suitors that night, Mia eagerly accepted my proposal. After

ignoring me completely out of disinterest, she suddenly found herself engaged to me. All because she lived to please her mother."

"That sounds miserable. One might expect that she would have chosen a different path when it came to raising a daughter of sorts," I huffed, taking another bite of my muffin. I did not feel sorry for Mia, not when she had made the conscious choice to inflict the same pain upon me. We all had the choice to change—to be better. She chose the opposite, and for that, she deserved my wrath.

As if the emotion summoned him, Wrath's weight suddenly bore down on my thighs. He laid there, curled up and watching me with his tail swishing, as Xavier set his muffin down and dusted off his hands.

"You know what else I remember? Holding you for the first time. Mia had hogged you, refusing to share. But I waited, and eventually you were in my arms. You were big, your rolls sporting rolls and your chins trapping drool." I elbowed him, a chuckle slipping from my lips. He returned the amusement, rubbing his bicep where I hit him before continuing. "You were still cute though. And, Eternity above, you were so captivating. Back then, your power had not awoken, but you still seemed to steal the love and adoration of all who met you. I was not immune in the slightest; in fact, I called you my little princess even then. Your parents laughed it off, but we all knew you would one day be a princess. You were promised to our son, and everything was so perfect. I miss those days."

Nostalgia left him sighing in serenity, but all I could do was think of how awful it had all turned out. How wicked that love for me would become. Maybe if I had been born with no power at all they would have been kinder. Or maybe they would not have cared for me at all. I would have been useless. So wonderfully useless.

What a dream.

"I am sorry we loved you wrong, Ash. But we did—*do*—love you. You will be an incredible queen." I did not respond, even when his voice grew hoarse from whatever emotion flooded him. After a few minutes of

silence, Xavier stood. "We will arrive any second. I am eager to show you where I grew up. Maybe we can even stir up trouble just like I once did."

He walked away then, his smile soft and sad and so very sincere. I wished he would torture me instead. Anything other than make my heart ache with remembered fondness. With feelings of love that I had buried.

"You will regret not accepting their affection when you are left alone and broken, Strange One," Wrath said.

I had no time to respond before one of the crew members shouted, "Welcome to Isle Element, Your Majesties!"

Standing, I was met with the sight of the isle. Like Isle Shifter, trees littered the beach and cliffs before us, but this kind of green was invasive and beautiful in the same way a rainforest at the height of fall would be. Driftwood sat lazily on the white sand, hills covered in greenery rolling beyond.

"Wow," I whispered as the crew worked to anchor the ship and prepare the small boat that we would row to shore. A large group of fae awaited us, the dock clear but the beach full. A chill crawled up my spine, nails digging into my bones and the monster itself roaring that something was not right about this.

"Tell me, wife, do you feel as unsettled as I do?" Sterling asked as he approached my side. The two of us gripped the rail, watching with the same focus and trepidation.

"Yes, yes I do."

"Oh good, at least I am not losing my mind," he remarked.

"That makes one of us."

Minutes later, they had the four of us in the boat and nearing the dock. Mia stared forward, her icy eyes scanning the waiting crowd. Xavier had his hand gripped on the pommel of his golden sword. The two of them must have felt what we did.

Golden guards appeared out of what seemed like nowhere, filing their way onto the dock. I raised a brow at Xavier, but he just waved a hand of dismissal.

Ah, so we would pretend that having what looked like a small army randomly show up on one of the isles was normal. Okay then.

"Stay close to me. Something is not right. Worse than the other two isles," I whispered to Sterling, recalling the way Perdita had asked if I was on their side. Though I struggled to remain there, I was. Sterling was just as innocent as any of them. He needed to live. If only to brighten the world that seemed to grow darker by the day.

With a nod, he reached forward and grabbed my hand, forcing my fingers to part so he could interlace his with mine. I did not protest, too focused on the line of guards as what must have been a warden offered us a broad smile and a hand up.

Xavier went first, patting the male on the back when he was on his feet. Then went Mia, who seemed less inclined to share pleasantries with the male. I was next, and I also refrained from touching him more than necessary or even speaking to him.

I did, however, search their minds.

And what I was met with was vile hatred and the desire for violence.

They were there to kill us.

Yet, as I grabbed Sterling's hand and pulled him behind me, no one attacked. They simply stared as we passed and headed for our carriage.

That, and they plotted in what ways they might end us all.

CHAPTER TWENTY-SIX

ASHER

We had traveled through Isle Element with little bumps. Here and there, we were met with hostility, but no outright attacks and not a single rebel symbol spotted. The Water, Earth, Air, and Fire Lands were stunning. This isle seemed to be the most diverse landscape wise. We had seen beaches, rivers, forests, mountains, deserts and valleys. Greenery was in abundance and the sky was clear. But the isle itself made me think of Bellamy, and that hurt more than it soothed.

Xavier was enjoying himself more than he had on Isle Shifter and Isle Healer. No matter what, this was his home. Where he came from. Maybe he had been a better male before he left the Fire Lands that we were currently within.

At the table sat all four wardens, each of them smiling broadly and warmly. They had welcomed us with open arms. As if they were glad we were there. But in their minds festered a level of hatred that made goosebumps rise upon my skin.

Around us, servants held ceramic plates, ready to offer us the first course. My eyes saw pride upon their faces, but my ears caught the sound of clinking from the way they shook in fear. They knew something was about to happen, and it terrified them.

"Why are the four of you so afraid right now?" I asked the wardens. The four of them each wore a color that represented their power. Warden Carmella wore red for fire, Warden Zaden wore blue for water, Warden Titan wore green for Earth, and Warden Ivy wore white for Air.

To my right, Warden Titan cleared his throat. "We are in the presence of royalty, Your Highness. That alone would make lesser fae break."

Nodding and pretending that such a thing made sense was easy. Warden Titan began shoveling food into his mouth the second his plate touched the wooden table, not looking anywhere but down. Warden Ivy squinted at her own food, sniffing it. In his mind, Sterling seemed to assess his own. He began going through a mental list of...oh.

Excellent.

"Do any of you know of my husband's history?" All four sets of eyes flicked my way, darting momentarily to Sterling before returning to me and remaining there. None of them spoke at first, as if silence and ignorance would save them from the fury I was about to ensue.

Finally, Warden Carmella answered, "No, Your Highness, I am afraid we are unaware."

"Well," I said, chuckling as I patted his shoulder from my place on his right. He remained silent and still, but in his mind, he raced through potential reasons for my actions. My head pounded with the exertion of using my magic, but I noticed it was getting better. Significantly so. As if,

just maybe, I would be able to fight off Mia soon. "He traveled all of the Mortal Realm. Is that not impressive? Even more extraordinary was what he learned. Sterling, tell them about what you were taught in Heratt."

That was when my plan clicked in the mortal prince's mind. He nodded, a smirk stretching up his face.

"What is the meaning of this, Ash?" Xavier asked. He was on edge, ready for the battle he knew I was sensing. Mia watched in utter silence. Like always, she was waiting for me to root out any flaw in the system she wished to be perfect.

"Well, I became quite adept with poisons," Sterling answered. Warden Zaden blanched, his pale skin going a sickly green.

"And tell me, husband, would you eat the food before you?"

"While it looks divine, it smells quite like sugar of lead and I prefer not to die today."

Right as Sterling leaned back in his chair and shoved his plate away from him, Warden Titan dropped his fork.

"You must be mistaken," Warden Zaden cut in. "We would never do such a thing."

"Or perhaps it was the staff!" Warden Titan shouted, pointing to the male behind him. Around us, every servant gasped, leaning into the walls as if they could disappear. Mock outrage wrinkled the warden's face, and my patience met its limit.

Gripping my fork, I swung my arm to the right, stabbing the cutlery so deeply into Titan's ear that it sunk halfway into his head. I ripped it out and shoved it into his neck next, just for good measure. The Earth collapsed, his forehead smacking into his plate of food and his blood spraying my face. Red stained my golden gown and dripped down the edge of my white plate.

Shouts erupted, the wardens across from me backing their seats away as if that would save them. Warden Ivy shouted, rather shrilly, "You are crazy!"

My smile stretched until I wondered if my skin would split. Slowly, I reached over and gripped the fork, ripping it free of Titan's throat. Bringing it to my lips, I let my tongue flick some of the blood. It tasted foul, but the effect was worth it. Even Mia gasped in horror.

"I have not begun to show you crazy."

"Why would you do that?" Zaden asked, his eyes watering slightly.

"I was just putting the poor thing out of his misery. If the servants were really the ones who poisoned the food, then he had already consumed so much he was probably about to face a slow and cruel death." I yanked the food from beneath the dead male's head, placing it in front of Sterling.

Sterling sniffed it, terror there in his eyes. I did not mind his fear, he was smart to keep me at a distance. Shaking his head, the prince confirmed that Warden Titan's food had not been poisoned.

"Odd, it was free of poison," I said, quirking my head to the side. "Tell me, Warden Zaden, what do you think of the rebels?"

Zaden froze, sweat beginning to trickle down the side of his face.

"I think they are disgusting. A blight to our realm." When I did not show any emotion to his response, he added, "Their message is deplorable."

"And what is their message?" I inquired.

"Well, it is…um…death to the royals." There was a hesitance and shake to his words, as if he had to force them from his lips.

"Since you think their fight so foul, then surely they poisoned your food as well. Sterling, check it for him, please." I gestured to the plate, watching with glee as Sterling reached forward to grab it. With a sniff, he looked my way and shook his head.

"Wait, please, I can explain!" Zaden shouted, standing from his seat and running a hand through his sweaty hair.

"Sit back down," I ordered. Abruptly, he sat once more. The entire room went silent, the sounds of breathing only faintly registering through my haze of rage. I saw it all there in their thoughts, my magic punishing me as I dug into their minds. They did not join the rebellion for the betterment of the realm. These fae only wanted the power that would be available if the Mounbettons fell.

Xavier smiled to Sterling's left, placing his chin on his folded hands and letting his elbows support the weight. Mia remained stoic, unphased.

"You see, this is the problem. Your fight for supposed freedom is truly just a selfish desire to rule. At no point in your self-centered plight did you stop to think about what you were doing to the innocents around you. Blaming your staff? Truly, how low can you sink? You do not care about them," I hissed, gesturing to the servants that still remained standing near the walls around us. "A real leader would have faced us, fought us. Instead, you wardens sit here in your comfy manors, smiling prettily and waiting for others to do your dirty work."

Quicker than normal, I lost complete control of that anger inside of me. It burst like a volcano, erupting and letting that red-hot heat scorch me from head-to-toe. Relaxing my clenched fists, I grabbed my plate and tossed it onto Zaden's. It hit with a loud clatter, pieces shattering.

"Eat while I talk, I am sure you are starved from making everyone else risk their lives."

The lower tenor of The Manipulator seemed to send chills through Ivy, but I still had eyes for Zaden as he began shoveling the food into his mouth. Snot and tears ran down his face, and all I could think was that it felt so horribly *good* to force this man to poison himself after he was ready to watch servants die for his crimes.

"None of you have the intelligence or the loyalty to lead your respective lands. Having more power in your veins does not make you worthy of a title if you are a fucking idiot, it just makes you a target and a

problem to eradicate." Ivy started to cry as well, only Carmella remaining calm in the face of my magic. "You are not better than those you are meant to serve."

With that, I tore into his mind, stomping my way through every memory and thought. Tearing apart his life and stealing his joy. He convulsed within his seat, his head falling back in a scream as I took and took from him. When I grew bored of the sound of his pain and the slow work of the poison, I shattered his mind, watching as he collapsed into a heap upon the wooden floors.

"Asher, you must stop. We need them for interrogation. Get that anger under control!" Mia shouted. Ignoring her orders, I stood, looking down upon the final two wardens. Ivy leaned away, her mind trying and failing to hide the selfishness that plagued it. But Carmella did not cower. Instead, she stared right back, her chin high.

"Will you fight me, Warden Carmella? Will you be more than the pathetic excuse of a leader that those two males were?" I asked her, my magic playing at the edges of her mind. My head was beginning to pound, the nausea setting in. Not nearly as bad as it had been, but still painful.

Carmella stood, grabbing Ivy and dragging her so that she was hidden behind the Fire warden's back. Friends—best friends even. I could taste their affection, feel the way it pulsed like a second heart in each of their chests. Carmella was stronger, but Ivy was smarter. The two were formidable together and weak apart.

A team of sorts.

"No, Princess Asher. I remember who it was I vowed to save." Just like that, my wrath drained out of me like water set free from a dam.

She used the same words that Nicola had ominously uttered to me before we left for this voyage. Was it a coincidence? No, probably not.

I dug into Carmella's mind, finding that her thoughts and memories of Nicola were already there at the front, as if waiting for me. I sorted through them, watching as Nicola stood at the front of crowds, as she

seemed to conduct and orchestrate every minute move. Carmella had seen Nicola's mind seem to float above the clouds, her eyes going distant and glassy before she would nod her head and begin explaining once more. Then, as if desiring to really solidify the truth, Carmella showed me another memory of Nicola, one in which she slowly wrapped a black piece of cloth around her face, the bloody golden shield at the center of it.

Nicola was a rebel. Not just a rebel either, by the look, feel, and taste of those memories, Nicola was their leader.

Before I could leave her mind, Carmella showed me one last thing. This was not a memory, but an imagined scenario that the warden seemed to think was inevitable. An army of black-clad soldiers stormed the manor, invading Isle Element and coming straight for us.

Blinking, I returned to the space around me. Xavier and Mia stared on in horror, as if they could feel the danger that loomed. Sterling, who could not have been more oblivious, quietly whispered, "Well, it is a good thing that the food was poisoned, because it seems I have lost my appetite."

"The rebels are coming," I said. Xavier reacted quicker than anyone else, standing with a bang of his fists upon the table. Mia's eyes darted from side to side as she thought—plotted. But my gaze remained on Carmella.

You cannot kill them. I have tried and failed more than I care to admit.

Warden Carmella flinched as she listened to my voice within her head, but she remained seated and calm.

We only poisoned yours and the prince's food. We needed to take you out before Nicola's misguided love set you free.

Oh please, they wanted all opposition out of the way. I would not have been surprised if they aimed to end Nicola one day as well.

And the rebels that come now? Are they meant to kill the king and queen?

She looked at me with a rueful smile, one born of loss and failure.

It is not the rebels who come, Asher.

247

What do you mean?

Vines erupted from the chests of both Ivy and Carmella, blood spraying the table as their hearts were speared. Sterling finally lost his cool, bending over and vomiting. Xavier stormed out of the dining room, shouting over his shoulder, "Get the Golden Guard here *now!*"

"Asher, we must be ready to fight," Mia practically growled, pushing herself to a standing position. I stayed still, my mind racing.

Carmella said it was not the rebels coming. The army she imagined in her head had been clad in black, no sign of the bleeding shield. And she had mentioned Nicola trying to save me.

"I was right," I whispered, choking the words out before I sobbed.

"Stop mumbling and get focused, our entire realm will fall if we are not united. We must show those rebels who they are—"

"I was right," I nearly yelled. Whipping my head to the queen, I caught her shocked expression before she morphed it back into impassiveness. It was too late though, because I knew. Wrath did not appear, did not so much as whisper denials into my head. Because *I knew.*

"I know what is real."

Then I grabbed Sterling's arm and willed myself outside.

For the first time, I intentionally portaled.

CHAPTER TWENTY-SEVEN

BELLAMY

"I am nervous, Bellamy," Mordicai said as we watched his soldiers train.

The king of Heratt had sent me more than one missive stating as much, but to have him at my side and outwardly expressing that fear was something completely different.

We could not allow him to change his mind. Nicola had warned us, and I was ready.

"What do you think will happen if you back away now, Mordicai? Do you think your kingdom will be spared? Do you think you will be forgiven for your previous allegiances? What happened in Behman was awful, but no more so than what has been happening across my realm for months." Pivoting, I looked the mortal king in the eye, wishing more than anything that I did not have to do this shit anymore. That I could rest.

"Now, the kingdom of Heratt must choose what it wishes to risk its soil for, because no matter what, you will face death head-on."

Mordicai remained silent as I patted his shoulder, walking away towards where I knew Anastasia waited. On my way up the longest set of stairs in Pike, I was met with not only Ray, but Lara too. The two had grown close, forming a sort of friendship as they gardened. Now they ate, walked, and trained together daily. Cyprus hated it.

"Sir, this could not be more perfect timing!" Ray said, beaming at me before she leaned down to sort through her absurdly large leather satchel. As she did so, Lara patiently and stoically remained at her side.

The whisp wore a vibrant shade of blue leathers that matched her small, haunting eyes and offset her cascading dark hair. Ray, on the other hand, wore a casual pair of brown trousers and a plain white blouse. Like usual, she had her mousy brown hair cut to her chin, displaying her sharp jaw.

"I have a letter for you from someone named Nyla Atrofious." I snatched the paper just as Ray freed it from her bag.

"Thank you, Ray. As always, you prove just how excellent you are at your job. Take the rest of the day off. The two of you should consider expanding the garden." Something to keep them busy. Away. Unaware.

If Ray or Lara suspected anything, they did not let on. And I was not keen on allowing them the time to address any concerns or theories. So I dashed away, the letter tight in my grip and my magic flaring.

I wanted to read it right away, but I needed privacy just in case this was not what I hoped—the queen promised by Nicola. While I was lost in thought, a voice cleared. Looking up, I found Noe smiling broadly my way as if she had been there awhile.

"I just heard from Henry, he and Genevieve will be ready whenever we need them. But, for now, they are safe." Her relieved breaths and joyful crinkling eyes almost made me forget about the missive in my hand. About the war itself.

It was so nice seeing her happy.

"Good. I hate that they were made to split up," I grumbled. There had been no stopping it. If Nicola told us to slit our throats we just might.

"So what is that?" She asked, pointing at the rolled-up paper. I handed it to her, watching her every reaction as she opened it and read.

Surprise. Curiosity. Was that anger? Yes, definitely a bit of fury. Then there, at the very end, *relief*.

I felt the same spread through my body, relaxing my muscles but fortifying my resolve. Taking it as she offered it back, I too read the missive from the queen of Yrassa.

Prince Bellamy Ayad,

How strange it is to write your name after so many years of the mere idea of The Elemental haunting my nightmares. I was told as a child that you were of the Underworld—a curse upon the gods that sought to wreak havoc in their holy lands. Even future queens were told bedtime stories made to encourage subservience. Truly, all of Yrassa was taught about you and the blood you could shed. Now though, I see you for what you truly are: scared. Perhaps even more than I was at merely ten years.

There is something so freeing knowing that even the immortal feel terror. However, I think it best we stifle such a thing as war looms. Genevieve Windsor swears that your side is the one to be on during this chaos, and I have the strangest urge to trust her. So, Yrassa's military forces are yours with the

condition that you not only begin trade with us if we survive this mess, but that you shelter my children. They are young and they deserve the chance to live. Keep them somewhere safe, somewhere full of that magic everyone tells stories about, and Yrassa is yours to command.

Sincerely,

Queen Nyla of Yrassa

"She wants us to take in her children as wards?" I asked, baffled. It was so strange that I could not fully wrap my head around it.

"If you think about it, she has the right idea. After what happened in Behman, she is likely terrified. She knows that both sides put her at risk, but it says a lot that she feels her children are safer if she rallies behind us. Perhaps you should offer King Mordicai the same thing. Maybe it will make him feel less uneasy." Noe shrugged, tapping my shoulder in solidarity before walking away. Seconds later, I heard her shout over her shoulder, "The not-goddess is looking for you, by the way!"

"Way to ruin the joy of the moment!" I shouted back, chuckling despite myself.

This though, was a vital moment. We were closer and closer to getting Asher back, I could feel it. Could sense it in my soul itself. Nicola's plans were coming together in what felt like the perfect storm.

Not even Stassi could ruin that.

Surprisingly, she did not seem as though she wished to when I walked through what had once been the door to my room. Ever since she had commandeered it, I had been sleeping in Henry's. Which was unfortunate, seeing as his smelled atrocious from the sweaty and dirt-ridden clothing he had carelessly strewn across the space.

"Excellent, you're here," she said, barely looking up at me. I shut the door, making my way to what was now her bed and looking at what she was reading. Asta's journals, no surprise there. She had been obsessing over them every day since Noe brought them.

"Did you find something about Stella?" I asked, hoping that she would soon leave and rid me of her presence. For an all-powerful high demon, she sure was lazy and annoying.

Stassi did not move anything but her eyes, which were reading across the pages like it was a race. After a few torturous seconds of silence, she responded, "Yes."

I waited for her to add more, but she went silent again, back to reading.

"Whatever game you are playing, please stop. I was tired of it before it even began." She huffed at my insult, finally flicking her pink gaze up.

"Asta talks about a land that was special to her on more than one occasion. You assumed it was your Royal City, but I think it is somewhere else. There is an entry in the first journal that talks about how she warded an entire forest. She says that Padon sent creatures to her lands to slaughter her new subjects—to destroy the life she had built for herself even after her husband was dead."

My mind conjured up an image of the Forest of Tragedies, the name itself seeming to pulse in time with my racing heart. Asta had warded it. Wrath had called her the fallen goddess, which now made far more sense. The holder of Souls, who had lost her place among the so-called gods for daring to love a simpler being.

"She forced all of the creatures into the forest with her magic, and then she placed a ward on the entire span of it. She claimed that her magic would siphon theirs, diluting their abilities over time. It's quite impressive really, that she had the strength to not simply kill the beasts. I would have, though the stains from that nasty black blood would've been foul."

253

"Does their blood kill high demons?" I asked, trying to understand the full picture of what she was attempting to explain.

"No, what was made from one cannot hurt another. Asta wouldn't have been poisoned by their blood or really affected by their magic. There were some that were made in the hopes of ending her, I'm sure. Ones that her magic didn't work on quite the same. But she was brilliant, and there was nothing that would've stopped her." She waved a hand in dismissal before blowing a stray chunk of pink hair out of her face.

Well, that was optimistic. Reaching into the drawer of my bedside table, I quickly pulled out Asher's dagger. As if sensing it, Stassi's head whipped towards the blade.

"This is only a loan, Asher will want it back when she returns. For now though, I thought you might need this—want it." Sliding my thumb down the runes on the hilt one last time, I offered the weapon to Stassi. She took it greedily, with far less reserve than she normally had for masking her emotions.

"Thank you," she choked out, touching the runes with the same care I had. Clearing my throat, I nodded and moved on.

"Okay, so where is it that you think the Queen and the Empress sought refuge?" Despite asking, I thought that I likely knew the answer. Knew the lands themselves well. Had made a sort of sanctuary out of them.

"There's a chunk of unoccupied land beyond that forest, the one she would later name after the tragic massacre that had occurred before she stopped the monsters. I think that Stella might be there, somewhere." With that, she stood.

"I built a village there. It was recently destroyed by the fae royals, but I imagine if Stella had been there with dual-toned hair and an aura that radiated magic, I would have known." I argued knowing that I was wrong, but still hoping that I had not missed such an important ally. Perhaps one that could have changed everything.

"Well, I doubt she would've made herself known to you or anyone else. Clearly, she has a reason to be hiding." Stassi walked over to my—her—desk, grabbing a satchel she had stolen from my—her—wardrobe and pulling it over her head after tucking the dagger inside. It fell against her hip, the worn leather clashing with the vibrant pink leathers she wore. Had she also stolen from Lara?

"So, what, you will just search the lands and hope you stumble across her?" I asked, following her out the door. She practically jogged down the stairs, moving so quickly that I was surprised she did not fall. Residents of Pike watched in surprise as the blinding pink light that was Stassi barreled through them.

She did not respond to me until we were through the entry to Pike, her gaze set to the mountains beyond as she shouted a single word. "Torrel!"

"What?" I asked.

She scoffed, finally glancing back at me. "I have a sneaking suspicion she's waiting for someone to find her."

"And how will you get there? Do you expect me to portal you around?"

"Obviously not." And then, as if the psychopath had planned it, something horrifically large crashed into the valley behind her.

Rock and dust flew everywhere, screams sounding from those who had been training outside. I covered my face with my arm, ducking slightly to protect myself from the onslaught of debris. When I finally felt it all settle around me, I was met with the sight of pink scales upon a foot twice my size. My body seized up, stilling in the fear of such a beast.

"Oh don't be such a youngling. Torrel here wouldn't so much as hurt a bunny." Stassi's words did little to calm me as she stepped up onto a fucking *dragon tail* and began walking up it like a staircase.

255

"Don't believe her, I eat scrumptious things like you daily." Asher had told me they could speak, but hearing that raspy echo of a voice chilled me to the bone.

"How did you call her here if you can't use your magic without being found?" I croaked in question.

"Dragons bonding high demons is a big deal," Stassi said as she settled into her spot. "It's why Torrel's scales went from black to pink. My magic runs through her veins. She is me and I am her. She can sense me from galaxies away. There's no distance that can separate us. If she wills herself to me, no matter where I am, she can come."

"It's like coming home," Torrel added. "Speaking of home, Milo wasn't safe there, Stassi. Drisha doesn't listen to Batheda any longer. With Stella gone, her dragon simply holds no sway against that of the holder of Death and Creation. I had to bring him."

As if that were his cue, a dragon the size of Lian walked out from behind Torrel's hind leg. Gods, she brought *two*.

My mind immediately went to strategizing. How could we use even one dragon in battle? I could ask Stassi to burn down The Capital. I could watch the gold melt and see the royals aflame. We could stop the war before it even began.

"Stassi—"

"No, my dragon isn't your weapon to wield. She and I have an empress to find."

"But—"

"No buts!" the high demon boomed, suddenly fierce. "Your world will be destroyed entirely if we don't find Stella. My priorities are more important than yours."

"Nothing is more important than Asher," I hissed in response.

"It seems that's what every male within five feet of her thinks. Aren't you curious why?"

"What is that supposed to mean?"

"Oh, nothing. I'm sure it will come to you eventually. Anyways, I need you to keep Asta's journals safe." Her tone was mocking, as if she knew something I did not. "Also, if you somehow manage to pull off your little rescue mission, you should consider utilizing the golden king. He's what I like to call a weak link."

"You must care for my son, Milo, in our absence as well," Torrel said, swinging her head around to face Stassi as she got situated. "He won't harm him, right?"

"He thinks he's a big bad demon, but he's a softie inside. You should see him cry, he's disgusting, pathetic, and hilarious all at once." The high demon was using a spike upon the dragon's back as a sort of backrest, like it was nothing that she sat atop a beast I had thought only existed in stories.

I guessed that to her it was as normal as eating and sleeping. Dragons seemed to have been a major part of her life. Apparently, Torrel thought they would be a big part of my life too, despite the fact I was being insulted in the process.

"Absolutely not. I am not some babysitter and I am already having three mortal children forced upon me like pets. Plus, Nicola could inform us that we are ready to move at any moment."

A grumble sounded from what must have been deep in Torrel's throat, the dragon seemingly ready to argue. Or eat me alive. But Stassi smacked her hand on the dragon's scales, catching the beast's attention.

"Fine, Milo will come with us. But just know that you're slowing us down. If you wanted our help, you're surely not going to get it now."

With that, Torrel glared at me before snatching her son in her claws. The smaller dragon immediately began biting at his mother's foot like a possessed menace.

Oh yes, I dodged a sword with that one.

"By the way, I would keep an eye on that golden king if I were you. I know a weak link when I see one." With that, Stassi leaned down and settled between the dragon's shoulder blades. In response, Torrel shook out her wings.

Just before she took flight, Torrel leveled her head with me and let out a ferocious roar. Her breath was horrid smelling, like raw meat and blood. Spit flung towards my body, her pointed teeth the size of my arm mere inches from my face. As her wings beat, hot air being forced my way and drying her saliva onto my skin and clothes, I could only say one thing.

"Eternity—if you are there—help us all."

***

Adbeel smelled of whisky and tears, a lethal combination, but far better than I did the other day even after I bathed. Foul dragon breath.

It seemed that ever since I got the truth of it off my chest, Adbeel had somehow taken my grief and absorbed it. Or maybe that was because I could sense how close I was to having Ash back in my arms.

Perhaps that scared him just as much as it pleased me.

I could not fathom meeting my long-lost granddaughter after two hundred years. Even worse was knowing what he took from her—what he once thought of her.

"Any day now," I offered, trying to be positive. Adbeel did not seem placated by that. He nodded, taking a swig from his cup and leaning back in his chair.

"Will you tell me about her?" he asked, his eyes flicking down towards me as I sat. A huff of breath whooshed out of me. How could I describe her? She was perfect, immaculate, wonderful.

A part of me wanted her to stay mine and only mine. It was why I had stalled having her meet him. Why I did not want her to know that the evil creatures who raised her were actually my parents. Would she even want me anymore once she realized the truth I had been hiding?

But it had been wrong of me to make that decision for her, and I would not starve Adbeel of stories of his granddaughter when I had already kept him from her.

"Asher is fierce. She is stingy with her love but generous with her aid. I have never met anyone as self-sacrificing as she is. I think that is because she does not feel she is worthy of better. The royals shattered her so thoroughly that, for a while, I thought she would never be whole again. But she is strong—a force to be reckoned with. I do not think anything could truly break her, not fully. She is brave and funny and broody. She says the world is not made for dreamers, yet she seeks a future in which all are safe and equal. Asher is *made* for a crown and a throne."

Quiet sobs alerted me to Adbeel's grief, and as I looked up, I was met with a tear-stained face that showed all the pain that overtook him. I stood, making my way around the desk, and pulled him up. Strong arms wrapped around me, the shoulder of my top soaked within moments. King Adbeel Ayad was not a crier, nor was he a hugger. Yet there we stood, embracing as he bawled.

"She sounds just like Zaib—like Solei—like every queen before her. An Ayad female through and through." His words were muffled by my leathers, but I still heard him. And deep in my chest, I felt the pang of loneliness. Of the parents I would never have. Ridiculous as it was, I was jealous of Asher in that moment.

Like always, Nicola both ruined a moment and saved the day.

A tug on something with my essence told me she was writing to me. The last time she sent a raven—creepy thing—it had waited for my response. Like she knew I would lace the paper and send it back. Now, as she dropped the paper, I found myself practically bouncing with nerves.

"Please be time."

Please be time. Please be time. *Please be time.*

Backing away from Adbeel, I called to my shadows, watching as the paper appeared atop my hand.

Please, Nicola. *Please.*

You are so impatient.

Yes, it is time. Perdita Harligold will be at the coordinates below. The king and queen are ready for your attack.

Remember, all who die risk the future itself. If you do not care about their lives, at least care about Asher's. Be as fast as you can.

Nicola

"Time to get our princess," I whispered.

CHAPTER TWENTY-EIGHT

HENRY

"Why do they have such a big market? This is ridiculous," Genevieve whispered. Gods, she was irritating. And so fucking gorgeous. I could not tell if I wanted to shove her face into the dirt or against my cock.

"Well, perhaps they enjoy the sense of community. Or maybe, just maybe, this is good for their economy," I remarked. For my sarcastic jibe, she took her pointy little elbow and jabbed it into my hip. "Ow!"

"I hate you," she hissed, speeding up her walk to nearly a jog. I kept up with an embarrassing amount of ease, my hands slipping into the pockets of my trousers to annoy her.

"Hate, love, who can tell the difference these days?" I teased.

Sadly, my taunting had the opposite effect of what I wanted. Genevieve stared forward, her golden curls fanning out around her and blocking her face from my view. What was once contempt became…nothing. And I realized in that moment that I would take her hating me over her not caring about me at all.

"Listen, Genevieve, I think we need to talk about—"

"Found it!" she shouted, breaking into a run. Just ahead of us sat a booth with a sign that read "Adams' Pottery". How original. I jogged, catching up with her just in time to watch the male pop out from inside with a stunning vase. It was long, wider on the top than it was on the bottom. The colors were a swirl of green and blue and teal, like the Sea of Akiva on a clear day.

Like the water near Haven.

We had not received word from Nicola since parting from the horrid pirate's ship and being forced to leave Lian behind, so what exactly we were meant to do from here was beyond us. Still, Genevieve rushed forward, completely unphased by her potential downfall. How could she be a monarch and a trained warrior, yet be so reckless at the same time?

Speeding up, I cut her off with an arm in front of her, shoving her behind me as the male looked up and met our eyes. He looked to be a few hundred years old, his dark brown hair pulled back in two long braids and free of gray. His facial hair was full, cut so it stuck closely to his skin. He had eyes that matched the soft dirt below our feet and clothes that were the color of the tropical trees that stretched out above us.

There was nothing extraordinary about him other than the fact he seemed far too fit to just be sculpting clay all day. That, and he had tattoos that wrapped around his arms in swirling patterns.

The hood of my cloak, the one Genevieve had returned to me smelling suspiciously of the strawberry-scented soap she loved, covered my round ears, but I could still tell that he knew exactly what I was.

"You are earlier than I expected," he said, fussing over the vase as he displayed it on the center of his counter, the plethora of pottery around it looking almost dull in comparison. "Meet me back here just after sunset and I will have your order ready."

With that, he waved us off, picking up a thin red vase and walking over to a small group of browsing fae.

"Well, I guess that is our cue to leave," I said. Genevieve grumbled incoherently at my side, her foot coming down in a soft stomp upon the ground. It was so wonderfully endearing watching her cross her arms and lift her chin. As if she was both annoyed and above the male's actions. "Come on, we should find a place to go that will save us from this awful heat."

Not bothering to look back, I wove through the crowds, hoping that I was right and Genevieve was far too unsettled around these immortals to stray far from my side. When I came to a particularly congested area, Genevieve's small hand slipped beneath my cloak and gripped my elbow. Of all the things in the world that could bring me to my knees, I would have never thought it a simple and desperate touch. But there I was, prepared to beg her for a moment of her affection.

I spotted a tavern ahead, resting just beyond the market, as if it needed space from the chaos just like we did. I tugged Genevieve along, reaching over to wrap her arm around mine fully. She did not complain, but when I looked down at her I caught her eyes darting to where we linked.

I knew she loved me. She had to love me. There was no other reality that made sense. No other future that felt like it was worth breathing in. Why it was her that felt so right, I would never know.

There were times early on when I wondered why Bellamy had picked Asher out of all the males and females he had been with. She was not nicer, smarter, or even exceptionally more beautiful than any other. Asher was powerful, but she was not perfect. So why her? Why be so utterly obsessed with her? Sure he saw parts of their future together and that was what pushed him towards her, but what was it that made him stay?

Then I felt her magic. I basked in her aura. That was when I decided it had to have been whatever that pull was. Surely there was no other explanation for being so infatuated with someone that you would take their constant ire and the unending torment of knowing they are not yours over not having them near.

Genevieve made me realize I had been wrong. She did not feel like gravity in the way that Ash did. Asher was someone you could not help but love and want to follow. Genevieve though, was like the desert. She starved me of everything but her heat. Tortured me with the obsession of her endless reach. Nothing existed but her, and it hurt. I desperately wanted out of her grasp, and yet I found myself unable to escape. The mortal princess offered mirages in the form of her hurried affection or moans of pleasure, but when I got too close she stole it from me, proving that hope was futile.

As we approached the door to the tavern, I wished beyond anything that I could be free of her. More than that, I prayed to the gods that I never escaped her.

A bell rang above as I pushed the door open, Genevieve quickly letting go of me and walking forward. "We need a room, please."

Was my jaw on the floor? Yes, it must have been.

Or maybe my ears were simply clogged with wax. Surely.

"Just one?" the fae behind the bar asked. Genevieve nodded in confirmation, reaching into my pocket and grabbing loose coins.

"Just for the night. We will also need drinks sent up. Something strong." And then, without much care for how greatly she was overpaying, Genevieve tossed the gold at the male.

He stared at her in bafflement before nodding, grabbing the coin as quickly as he could and pocketing it. With no further words, he pulled a key off the wall behind him and handed it to her like she was a queen and it was his tithe payment.

Not another sound was uttered as she whipped her head around and began ascending the stairs. Gods above. I followed, saluting the still dumbstruck owner as I passed him.

Genevieve led us to the room that was marked with the same number as the key, unlocking it and nearly slamming the door in my face. Then, almost immediately, she turned and faced me with a menacing glare. What the fuck was happening?

"You will not touch me, breathe in my space, or even speak to me unless necessary. The only reason I got us a room was for my comfort and safety, understand?"

Throwing my hands up, I muttered, "Got it."

A knock came not five minutes later, freeing me from my frozen state of horror. Genevieve had commandeered the bed, her body hidden beneath the blankets and her curls played out on the pillow. Opening the door, I was met with the same male from before. He held two exceptionally large bottles of who knew what, his smile large.

"The best whisky I have," was all he offered me before shoving the bottles into my hand and practically prancing down the stairs. Oh, we overpaid by *a lot*.

"Your relief is here," I said, closing the door with my shoulder and making my way to her. She did not pop out, so I took one of the bottles and pushed it beneath the blankets. Her sigh was outrageous, like someone who had lived so long they no longer saw the colors or vibrance of the world.

Ridiculous.

"Drink up, I would not want you to have to hide under there all day because you are too sober to enjoy my presence." It was a low blow, a bitter one, but what was a male to do when the girl he loved acted like he was diseased?

"Oh please, you know that is not true," she said, taking my bait. Glee filled me as she threw the blankets off of her. "Not even all the alcohol in the world could make me welcome your company."

Her curls were a disaster atop her head, not even her fussing able to fix them. When she finally gave up with a curse and a huff, she popped the cork off the whisky and tipped it back. Greedily, I watched her throat bob as she took more and more of the drink. She did the same with me, took and took until she was full. I wished then that I could simply give it all to her.

"Why are you drinking so heavily?" I asked, walking over to the small wooden table. It did not even reach my hips, just barely high enough to graze my thighs. The chair was not much better, and I was forced to practically squat just to sit.

"Maybe I always drink this much. You do not know me, Henry, no matter how much you pretend you do." Once more mumbling under her breath, she silenced her incoherent whispers with the bottle to her pink lips again.

Uncorking my own, I too drank. If she was going to be a drunk little priss then I would too. Back and forth we sipped, stealing glances at each other here and there. Until finally, I broke.

"What is it, Genevieve? Why are you so angry with me? How have I hurt you other than by simply fucking loving you?" There was a slight slur to my words, and I realized that there was no longer a bite or burn to the whisky as it sloshed into my mouth and down my throat.

"I do not want a lovesick puppy that sits in my lap and begs for attention only to yap and bite my ankles when I do not offer it!" she shouted, standing with a stumble. I wanted to rush to her—to steady her—and then shove her onto the bed and show her just how much of a dog I could be. Alas, I remained still. Trying to be good.

"You overestimate your allure, sweet princess." There was a bite to my tone, proving her point. Groaning, I brought a hand to my face, rubbing at my skin and trying to remember why we were here in the first place.

"No, you overestimate my patience, idiot demon. I will never love you. There is no future in which we are together, no world in which I would ever stand by your side. So get over it!" Her accent was strong from the whiskey, that wicked tongue of hers sounding heavier and heavier as she swayed and yelled.

Rage and lust converged within me, twisting and turning and wreaking havoc in my mind. Standing as well, I pointed my finger towards her, taking quick and uneasy steps her way.

"You are a blight in my world. A stain on my life. Do you think I want to love you? That I dreamt of obsessing over some mortal girl? This is not what I wished for myself, Genevieve! Yet here I am, wanting you so desperately that I can think of nothing else! Every bit of this is *your fault!*"

"My fault? How could it possibly be *my* fault that you will not leave me alone? You are weak, pathetic!" Her arms flew up, her flowing white blouse lifting and exposing the creamy skin below her navel. Something within me snapped.

Growling, I grabbed her into my arms and threw her over my shoulder. Her fists beat into my back, her legs kicking and swinging. She screamed as I walked towards the table. When I brought her down and turned her, she yelped in surprise. But when I took her by the hair and shoved her torso down onto the table, she moaned in pleasure.

"Is this what you want, mortal? You want me to show you just how monstrous I can be?"

I kicked her legs apart, sliding my fingers into the waistband of her brown trousers and yanking them down with little care for how it might tug and pinch her skin. Pathetic? Maybe. Weak? No. I would show her which of us was the weak one.

Her ass slipped free first, then her thighs. They were full, thick enough to try and hold onto the trousers. But I pulled harder, forcing the fabric off her body. When I got to her shoes, I ripped them off, her soft cry of pain almost enough to make me stop.

When her lower half was completely bare to me, I grabbed her ass, watching as her skin turned red from my tight grasp.

"Of the two of us, it is *you* that should fear *me* leaving," I rasped.

Then, I let my knees hit the ground and leaned forward. My tongue slid up her parted cheeks, slowly tasting her. Another moan of pleasure escaped her, sounding as if it had to fight its way free. Pushing her legs further apart, I lifted her higher until her feet no longer touched the floor and her hips hit the top of the table. My fingers parted her, grazing the blonde curls there and making just enough room for my mouth to surge forward and latch onto her clit.

Her responding gasp was everything and more. The answer to every question my soul had asked. A gift from the gods above.

"No one else can do this for you. There is no mortal alive that can love you like I can. No man or male that will devour you in the same way I will. I will drag you to the height of your pleasure and then force you higher. I will rip screams from your mouth and then fill it with my cock. For the rest of your life, you will know that it is I who fills this tight little pussy the best."

No response. No scathing remark. Just acceptance as she let her forehead fall forward and pressed her soaked center further into me. So I consumed her. Bit and licked and sucked that love right out of her. Every shout of my name from her lips had my cock begging for release, but I ate and ate and forced myself to wait.

My fingers dug into her ass, one of my thumbs slipping inside of it slowly as my tongue pierced into her pussy. She writhed and jerked, her release pouring into my mouth like the nectar of life. And then she abruptly stilled.

Slowly I backed away, pushing myself to my feet without removing my thumb or wiping my face. She groaned, her nails scraping against the table. For only a moment, I wished Bellamy were here to paint the sight of her. Maybe Ash would let me show her so she could show him. A birthday gift perhaps.

"You want my big, fat cock in that dripping pussy, Genevieve?" I asked, letting my body fall onto hers, still pumping my thumb slowly in and out of her ass. She nodded violently. *Desperately.* "What about this tight ass of yours? Do you want it there? I bet no one has ever done that to you before."

A groan rumbled up her chest, vibrating against my stomach. I needed these clothes off, but gods did I not want to take my thumb out.

"Answer me. Do you want that?"

"I—I do not know. I have never—no one has—"

"Do. You. Want. It?" I ordered this time, shoving my thumb further into her. Her back arched, my stomach sinking down and my cock rubbing against her thigh. Gods, it felt good. *She* felt good.

"Yes!" she screeched.

I got closer to her ear, letting my breath fan against it and relishing in the way she shivered beneath me. "Then admit you love me."

Her body stilled, stiffening.

"Say it," I demanded. "Tell me you love me. You know you do. Admit it, and I will do anything you want me to. I will make your wildest fantasies come true."

"No."

"Say it."

"Never."

I ripped out my thumb, backing away from her and tearing my clothes off in angry, frustrated pulls. She was really pissing me off today.

Freeing my length, I pumped myself, staring at her still-lifted ass. At the way she refused to move so that I might not see how desperate she

was for me. But I knew. I knew she loved me, that she wanted me. I just needed to hear her say it.

"Come on, Genevieve. Three words and I am yours." I rubbed the head of my cock against her ass, letting it part her once more before sinking lower and toying with the wetness at her center. She bucked and shook, eager for it. "How about this? Tell me you do not love me. Tell me you never will. I will still fuck you right here. I will tear you to shreds and make you ask for more. Then, I will leave you alone. Give me whichever is the truth."

Betting had never been my thing. I believed in seizing life, not letting life seize me. Fate did not rule over me. Until now. This was it. She could make her choice, and I would listen.

Seconds passed, then minutes. It was agonizing, playing with both of her entrances but not diving into her. Preparing myself for rejection, for this to be the end, I used my free hand to leash her neck. With a gentle squeeze, I let my fingers roam, slowly creeping upwards. Right as I hit her chin, I gripped it and forced her head to tilt back until her brown eyes met my green.

"Come on. Tell me you love me or say that you never will. Put me out of my misery."

A single tear slipped down her cheek as she closed her eyes, a breath leaving her like a burden.

"I love you, Henry. I fear I always will."

Shock did not hold me long, because no more than a moment later I was back on my knees, licking her. Readying her.

"Gods above, firefly. Please, just fuck me already. I cannot take this anymore!" she shouted. *Begged.* I hoped to hear her do that for years to come.

I stood upright, once more twirling my thumb to tease her entrance before dipping it in with a moan. I pumped into her mercilessly, using my other arm to wrap around her breasts and tug her off the table.

"I am going to fuck your asshole so hard you forget what life is like without the damage of me. You were right about one thing, my sweet curse. You will never stop loving me. I simply will not allow it."

When I let her go, I freed my thumb and shoved my cock into the wet heat of her center. She bucked, but I forced her back down, gripping her beautiful golden hair. My thrusts were quick and rough, but I needed to make sure I was as soaked in her as I possibly could be so this would not hurt.

"Okay, I am going to pull out of you and then align myself. What I need you to do is set the pace. You are going to fuck my cock with your ass, understand?"

She nodded, whimpering. I lifted her just slightly higher, wanting her to be comfortable despite how irksome she was. When I pulled out of her and lined my cock up between her perfect ass cheeks, Genevieve hummed and slowly pressed into me.

Her hiss of pain scorched my ears, burning with guilt and nerves. But I would not let her see that. Not let her know how absolutely terrified I actually was of breaking her.

She set a slow pace, thrusting back ever so slightly in time with my heartbeats. When she let me sink about halfway inside of her, she stopped, panting.

"Why did you stop?" I asked, grabbing both of her hips like a lifeline. I needed *more*. I needed *all of her*.

"I want you to finish. I want you to take this." Her voice was breathy, full of lust and need.

"You have no idea how badly I wanted you to say that," I muttered. Her hands lifted, gripping the side of the small table. I was cautious at first,

sliding in and out of her with ease. Even so, she was a sweaty and dire mess below me. Her chants of "more" and "faster" were enough to have me fully dipping into her. Again and again I pumped, my pace growing reckless as my mind went hazy from the perfect tightness of her.

Leaning down once more, I reached up and grabbed onto her wrists, letting my mouth return to the spot by her ear. "I love you so fucking much. You are mine. Every inch of you. I will fill you so deeply that I will be a part of you. I will tie you down and refuse to let you leave. I will shatter you and use my fucking come to glue you back together. There is no escape from this—me—now."

And then I lost all control. I stood, latching onto her sides and forcing her to meet each of my thrusts. Her cries of painful pleasure echoed off the walls of our room, mingling with the symphony of our bodies colliding. Our sweat had my grip slipping, but I needed to feel her squeeze around my cock. I needed to see my release dripping down her. I needed so much more than I thought she could possibly give but that I would take regardless.

Genevieve finished first, screaming so loudly I knew the entirety of the inn had to have heard. It was a piercing shout of my name, a simple yet otherworldly sound. One that sent me spilling into her, grunting before shouting her name right back.

For a blissful moment, there was only the two of us while we bathed in our shared pleasure as it slowly faded away.

When she caught her breath, I pulled out, watching with joy as my come did in fact drip out of her slowly. I caught some of it with my finger, tasting it before reaching around and shoving the rest into her mouth. She hesitated at first, but then she sucked.

"My good girl. How I love you."

***

The booths were eerie at night—a strange aura about them. Genevieve was covered in goosebumps, not even my cloak heating her enough to fight off the terrifying chill of the market after dark. But when we finally reached Olivander's booth, we found him smiling. He stood, still just wearing that vest, waiting.

"We are here for our order," I said, wrapping my arm around Genevieve. She had not spoken much since we had sex earlier, likely processing everything that had happened. That, and thinking of excuses for what she had admitted. No matter, I knew the truth now.

"Ah yes, let me go get it for you." He disappeared into his small booth, not a single sound coming from within it. We remained still, waiting impatiently as we were smothered by unease.

Finally, someone did emerge, but it was not Olivander.

No, this could only be one female.

"Hello, Henry Nash and Genevieve Windsor, it is so very nice to officially meet you both. I am Nicola Salvatore."

CHAPTER TWENTY-NINE

PERDITA

"No, Blue, it is not safe. The Oracle said so." If Lian fully understood my signs, she did not act like it. Instead, she crossed her arms and faced the window in my chambers, staring at Isle Element. She wanted to talk to the princess—the mind breaker. She had been so distracted earlier that I actually won a fight.

It was rather pathetic, her agony at not speaking to Asher. I had found the princess interesting, but nothing to be heartbroken over. Or maybe it was the fact that she missed her brute of a lover.

That was what I had decided they must have been: lovers.

"Stop looking me," she signed, the broken phrase making me laugh.

Looking at her was all I could do today. The Air wore a navy blue blouse and beige trousers, her black boots lacing all the way to her knees. Her hair was free and wind-blown, her upper eyelid lined with black kohl that disappeared when she opened her slanted eyes all the way. She was pretty, there was no denying that. Probably one of the prettiest females I had ever seen.

Sadly, she was also a bitch, which meant I was never going to get my head between those strong thighs. Pity, I would have made her so happy for the night—or nights. And she would have numbed my mind, distracted me from just how much there was to do. How many things I still needed to accomplish. The planning that required my attention.

"But you are so beautiful, Blue," I signed, blowing her a kiss. She responded by swiftly swinging her arm and letting her fist land in my gut. I hunched forward, smiling despite the pain. Never a dull moment with her.

Before I could throw my own punch, Ro burst through my door and rapidly signed, "Golden Guard are portaling onto the isle!"

"What?" Panic swept through me like an avalanche, barreling from my head down to my chest. The Oracle had not gotten back to us. We were still not positive what we were meant to *fucking do*.

"They are coming in groups of what seems to be twenty-five. So far three groups have come and gone from the Northwest side of the isle." Ro's signs were both furious and rattled. She was the best at signing among my crew, yet her fingers seemed to seize as she transitioned from one to the next.

"That is where the royals should be," I signed back, trying to think as I went. Lian remained silent, her head quirked to the side as she squinted out the window. "Ro, we are more than prepared to fight. This is what we do. Stay calm, stay ready. Give me five minutes to sort out a plan. Prepare the others."

With a nod and a brief glance towards Lian, Ro turned and left.

"What in the Underworld is going through your head right now, Blue?" I asked, trying my hardest not to lose my shit in the face of the unknown. This was what planning was for. Flailing about with no guidance was agonizing.

"Do you know how hard it was to mask my mind from Asher? I had to sit in my room below deck focusing on presenting a blank space like Bell taught me." My eyes remained glued to her lips, the Air not even attempting to sign so many words. "In that time, I had the chance to think. Why take Asher on this trip? Why is Asher willingly following them? What is it that they have on her? And then I realized. She was not even searching for my mind. I did not even feel her magic near me once."

Gods I wanted to silence her. She was wasting time on rambling nonsense. Yet, I could not bring myself to stop her line of thought. All I could manage was a simple nod when she turned to me.

"They did something to her. Whatever it is, her magic is being affected. Maybe even her mind. She cannot fight alone, Perdita." There was a plea in her face as she furrowed her brows and widened her eyes.

She was asking us to fight for something other than gold or freedom. Lian was asking for more than I could offer. More than I was willing to give.

"I cannot bring my crew in there without more information. Your prince asked me to help with whatever the Oracle needs, and, from my understanding, that is only transportation as of right now. I will not bring my crew there to die. Not for any reason other than more gold." It was a brutal answer, and by the way she mouthed the words I was signing, I could tell that she mostly understood.

Even so, there was confusion written across her face. As if she had expected something else of me.

"I only care about that, Blue. Do not think me some hero."

Her shoulders fell as she turned to look out the window once more. It was for the best that she knew exactly who and what I was. There was

no part of me that cared about the greater good or the better of the realms. I cared about my coin, my ship, myself, and my crew—in that order. There was nothing more important than the gold that made life worth living.

I meant to leave, to walk away and let her stew in her disappointment, but something about her stance changed. It was minute, just a slight shift of her body that told me something was wrong. Closing the space between us, I came to her side and tried to find what was in her line of sight.

In the distance stood a female, her boots planted upon the dock. She wore plain brown trousers and a soft burgundy blouse. Her hair fanned out around her in tight spirals, her coffee skin offset by a flash of her teeth as she chuckled.

She was staring at us.

Fuck.

I grabbed Lian by the arm, tugging her away from the window and through my chambers. We needed to move quickly if we were going to be prepared for their attack. I had never seen a Golden Guard without their armor, but that must have been what she was. Otherwise, why stare at our ship? Why look right at us as if she knew we were watching? It was unsettling.

My mind considered possibilities, so many of them it made my head pound. But I was the best for a reason. I could do this. If not me, then no one would be able to. Bringing my free hand to my mouth, I let out a quick set of whistles. In moments, the entirety of my crew was before me, minus Dima. She would have been incredibly helpful today.

"We are about to be boarded. You know where you belong. Remember, it is better to die than to let them take you. We defend the Abaddon with all we have. If she sinks, then so do we. Understand?" Each of them nodded, straightening at my orders. "Pockets full, souls empty!"

"Pockets full, souls empty!" Their returned signs were met with silence today. We likely would refrain from speaking at all until we knew we

were safe. There were many benefits to knowing sign, but being able to converse silently when being attacked was at the top of the list.

Lian remained still, her eyes glued to the spot where the female had been. But now, it was empty. Not a single fae upon the docks. *Stella, you bitch of a goddess, do not let my ship sink today.*

With that, I turned, aiming for the mainmast. But instead of open air, I hit something hard. My head slammed forward, my nose aching at the pain of whatever I had run into. Before I could so much as gain my bearings, someone shoved me to the side. With a stumble, I balanced myself just in time to see Lian run into the arms of…Henry Nash.

His broad smile was infectious as he caught her, whispering something into her ear. *What was he doing here?*

Behind him, the mortal princess looked as if she might be sick. She watched the show of affection in what seemed like the same way I did, but there was something that simmered beneath the surface, rising as the water bubbled.

To my right, one of my crew members approached. No, not my crew member. They felt wrong. Freeing my blade, I lifted it to the throat of the very female who had been watching us from the dock. If a smile could tear apart a world, then this female's would. She was terrifying for some reason. A sense of foreboding dripped from her, like the future itself stared me in the eye.

"Hello, Captain Perdita Harligold," she said, her mouth moving so slowly it was impossible not to understand. A chill crawled up my spine, shivers following in its wake. "We better hurry, we have company."

With that, she reached into the pocket of her trousers, grabbed a piece of paper, and slapped it against my chest. Then, to my utter bewilderment, she gripped my wrist and shoved it away. I could have killed her; punished her for attempting to board my ship and tell me what to do. *Why did I not?*

My hand caught the paper as it began its descent to the deck. Flipping it over, I found coordinates.

Lian's hand wrapped around mine as I made to crumple the paper. Looking up, I was met with the most honest expression she had ever given me. Determination hardened her face, jaw ticking as she let her gaze roam my soul.

Bek was at my side immediately, her hand casing Lian's.

"That is Nicola Salvatore. It looks like your time for transporting goods has not yet expired," Lian offered, her lips slow.

Underworld below, we were fucking doomed.

CHAPTER THIRTY

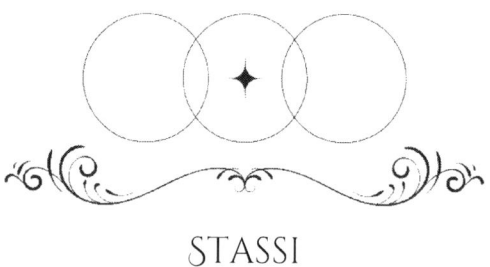

STASSI

"Torrel, get as close to the forest as you can without actually entering it!" I shouted to my girl. She turned her large head my way, the nearly white light of this world's sun making her pink scales seem like they were aglow. Looking at me as if she disagreed with the order, Torrel rolled her eyes and then began her descent.

I held on tightly as she circled the forest below. The dark and eerie quality of it reminded me of home, strangely enough. This was most definitely Padon's work. I would've known even if Asta hadn't written it out.

We slowed as we approached the ground. Bordering the coastline, a village lay in pieces. White cottages and cobblestone paths were cracked and stained in old blood. Not too far there was what seemed to have once

been a market, wooden booths bleached by the sun sitting in wait. Past it all loomed a black castle-like structure. It seemed to shout at me, warning off the intrusion.

When Torrel landed, my bones shook not from the impact, but from the death that seemed to coat the air.

"Excellent landing," I said, patting her scales before standing and descending her spine. She remained perfectly still, waiting until I jumped off the tip of her tail to sniff at the air. In her lifted claw, Milo let out small roars, practically begging to be set loose.

"Milo, I don't know if it will be safe for you to roam. Please, for once you need to listen to me. Do not stray." With that, Torrel released her drake. And, like most young dragons, the little menace bolted. He made his way to the very edge of the forest, where the ground and the trees faded to black.

"Milo, get back here!" Torrel shouted, leaning forward to grab him. But just as her teeth caught one of his tiny spiked wings, I felt something in the air shift. Magic was near. A lot of it.

There was a beauty to raw magic. At its core, it was like clay, ready to be molded into anything. It could become whatever one needed it to be, though it often had its preferences. My magic preferred to handle Sin and Virtue, but it still sang to me when other magic was near. It still wished to be free to hunt the familiar tune of Sun and Moon that seemed to softly hum from within the confines of the forest itself.

"Torrel, can you feel that? Feel her?" Though I knew she had to have been able to feel it, I still found myself surprised when her wide pink eyes darted towards the trees just to the right of us.

"Yes. She waits," Torrel said through clenched teeth as she held onto her son.

Milo was crafty though, and he used her distraction against her. A laugh threatened to escape me as the drake used his hind leg to kick his mother in the tooth. Her grasp released as she hissed in pain, and Milo beat

his wings desperately, looking more like he was falling than flying. Still, he was through the trees in moments.

Both Torrel and I took off in a sprint, dashing into the forest to stop him from getting hurt. Torrel made it barely ten feet into the forest before she got stuck. "I cannot break through these trees without potentially hurting him or you. Find my son and I will watch for the empress!"

Nodding, I continued on, running far faster than normal and begging Eternity to spare the drake. If Milo died, I would kill Bellamy in retribution for not taking the baby dragon.

Shoving those thoughts down for a later time, I honed in on the forest around me. Creatures could be felt *everywhere,* though Padon's magic was not nearly as strong as I thought it would be. It was like listening to someone speak while your hands were over your ears. Muffled.

Stella's magic, on the other hand, only grew stronger, dancing to the beat of my heart as I searched and searched. When I caught sight of broken branches and heard a tiny roar, I darted to the right. Jumping through a small clearing, I was met with a jaw-dropping sight.

Before me sat a modest cottage, black vines creeping up the walls and smoke escaping the chimney. The bricks appeared to be faded over time, now shades of white and gray. Just in front of the door, a female bent down, rubbing Milo's dark belly as he rolled on his back with his forked tongue hanging from his open mouth.

Even if she had masked her dual-toned hair, I would have known it was her. Stella. The female who practically raised me after my mother died and my father took his life in his grief. She had held me when my magic struggled to absorb the seed of Sin and Virtue. After, when my too-young body acclimated to becoming a high demon, she taught me to use and manage so much magic. She sang to me when I had nightmares, matched my clothes to her youngest daughter's, and stood up for me in council meetings. Every day she told me she loved me, that she cherished me like a daughter.

Staring at her now felt surreal. Like coming home and finding it changed.

"Ana, it's good to see you." Ana. Only she and my mother had ever called me that. Instead of making me feel better, it only enraged me. My fists clenched, emotions so strong that they were hard to hold onto flooding me. This was too much. We were not made to feel this deeply.

"You. Left. Us."

If my accusation hurt her, the smile that stretched across her perfect face did not show it. Her dark skin somehow still glowed in the darkness of the forest, the magic of the sun shining from within her no doubt. Her hair was no longer straight from her heat tools, the tight coils now cut so short that they surrounded her like an orb. She wore a thin white dress, the simpleness so different than what she used to prefer.

"You're just as fierce as ever. That makes me happy," she said.

"Padon finds it increasingly annoying." Her smile fell at the mention of the new emperor. Of the male she once thought of as a son. The one who killed her daughter's husband and banished her from her own world.

"Yes, well, he was always impatient. One day he will meet someone that will challenge that. Remake him. Form that anger and desperation into something beautiful." Her words did nothing to soothe me. In fact, all she was doing was confuse me further.

"How would you know? And why are you here? Shamay needs you and you're playing house in a forest full of bloodthirsty creatures? What the fuck, Stella!" I shouted, reaching down to grab a jagged rock and throwing it as hard as I could at the stupid house behind her. When it sailed through a window, I let a wretched and wicked smile spread across my face.

Stella didn't so much as flinch at the damage to her home. She used to be far quicker to anger than that. She used to be so much...*more*.

"You're allowed to be angry, you know. They tell you that we don't feel. That we aren't capable of real emotions. But it's not true, Ana. We might not feel the same as the creatures on this world, but we still *feel.*"

Tears flowed freely down her cheeks, her white and black eyes lined with red. Eternity above, she was going to make me cry too. My hand reached into my satchel of its own accord, gripping Asta's dagger and pulling it out. The moment the blade met the air between us, a great shake of the forest rattled my bones.

My magic simmered and convulsed, pouring out of me like steam.

That was when the fetch appeared. It was just as hideous as I remembered, its crooked body and gray skin dripping black from where it drooled poison. Its long black hair hung in strings over its face, a smile showing all black teeth.

"Anastasia, how exciting that I have found you. His Majesty wishes for you to come home," it hissed, practically floating our way. I saw the moment its black eyes caught sight of Stella. Horror shook me to my core. Padon couldn't know I found her, nor could he be made aware of the fact that I was on Alemthian. "The fallen empress. What a surprise. He will be thrilled to know you still—"

Leaping forward, I caught the fetch by its hair and shoved its face into the ground. My magic pulsed from me in small waves, drowning the fetch and forcing it to remain corporeal. Bringing my face down, I smiled back at it. "Pity you will not be able to tell him."

Then I dug my nails into its flesh and tore it to shreds, black blood squirting onto my clothes and skin. I was drenched in it by the time I was done taking my anger out on the creature. When I looked up at Stella, she was staring blankly at me.

"What, are you against murder now? So changed that you don't revel in a little violence anymore?" I accused more than asked. She was getting on my nerves for some reason.

"No, it's not that. I just realized how far we have fallen. High demons, resorting to fighting one another instead of fixing our messes. You, Padon, Asta, me. All of us. We're failing." Before I could insult her back—or worse, agree—she offered me a hand. I took it, letting her pull me up. She grabbed her spotless skirt, lifting it to my face and cleaning me off, staining the cotton. For once, I didn't fall victim to my need to be unfeeling. Instead, I leaned into her touch. "We have a lot to do, Ana."

"What do you mean?" I asked, surprised by the sudden change in subject.

"Worse will come. I've watched it happen."

"Was it the Oracle Asta wrote about meeting?"

"Yes, she told Asta a lot." There was a grim and heartbroken tone to her voice. One that felt as if it might crush my soul. "It was why Asta poured her magic into that fae river. She brought me there and together we watched what the Oracle foresaw."

"Does it have to do with Asher Daniox?"

"Yes. Asher, she is at the center of it all. She is the promised doom. Our gift and our punishment. I can't say much, and the only future that the Oracle saw in which Asher succeeded was one that I remained hidden until her great loss."

"Her great loss? Stella, I don't understand."

"I know. I want to say more but I could risk everything I've worked fifteen thousand years towards," she croaked. Her hands gripped my face, cradling me like a mother terrified of dropping their youngling. Milo pranced around us, alternating between sniffing flowers and chewing on one of the fetch's wretched bones.

"I'm scared, Stella. Shamay needs you. We all do."

"Everything will fall into place, I promise. Trust me."

"I do, I trust you." Stella kissed my forehead, letting her chin lift and rest on my head. I tugged her close, hugging her so tightly it might have hurt.

"This won't be the last time I see you. Don't worry. For now, you have to help Asher. She needs to be ready when Padon comes. This war was always the prelude. Expect him to come when the world is weakest. When she is weakest. We both know what lengths he will go to in order to get what he wants."

"He wants to take Alemthian. To destroy it and rid the universe of its inhabitants."

"Yes, I figured he would. It represents everything that went wrong in his eyes. I won't pretend like he isn't right about some of them. That horrible fae queen came and brought a poor mortal boy here. She practically fed him to one of the creatures. By the time it was done with him, he was a shaking, sobbing mess."

"Well, not everyone is born a ruler like you and Asta," I muttered. With my mind on the female I once looked at as a sister of sorts, I could not help but ask, "Was she happy?"

"Asta? Yes, immensely. She loved her mortal husband until her dying breath and cherished this kingdom. She felt at peace until Zohar was taken from her. After she saw the Oracle, much of her family had already passed. Once she was positive the information was safe with me, she asked for me to remove her seed." When I scoffed in response, Stella sighed. "She was tired, Ana."

"Aren't you tired too? I know I am." Weren't we all?

"Yes, but I still have much to do." Her mismatched eyes watered, as if whatever it was she must still accomplish was heavier than she thought she could handle. Or perhaps it was just the memory of her long-dead family.

"I miss her. I miss all three of them." My uneven voice was startling, a disgusting and raw display of emotion that made me feel *mortal*.

"I know, Ana. So do I."

CHAPTER THIRTY-ONE

ASHER

We landed in the wooded area behind the Fire Warden's manor, not deep into the trees or very far from the house at all. It was nothing impressive, but still, I had *portaled!*

Sterling looked like he might be sick, his skin a faint shade of green beneath the pale light of the moon. Okay, so maybe *portaled* was a stretch.

"Sterling, I need you to stay hidden." Gripping his shoulders and looking up into his eyes, I tried to convey the importance of what I was ordering him to do.

"But—but I do not understand," he muttered, watery eyes darting between mine.

"I know, but you will. We are going to go home, Sterling. We both are." I felt the first tear run down my cheek, but I quickly wiped it away. I needed to be strong. I needed to do what I was born to do—protect and lead.

"Okay, then let me come with you. I can help. Just please, do not make me leave you behind." There was a desperation to his plea, as if he could not fathom being separated. "Let me protect you."

"The best thing you can do for me right now is to hide, okay? Stay hidden and safe. I need you to survive, Sterling. Me and you, we have a world to see and a life to live. We are going to get home."

Then I leaned up on my toes and pulled his head down to me, placing a soft kiss on his forehead before letting him go entirely.

"Please do not die. I have never been popular, never had people wanting to be my friend or taking the time to understand me. Other than my family, I have no one. No one, but *you.*" Sorrow stretched his face, turning it downwards. My heart clenched, a new loved one filling it up and weighing it down.

"Well, since you asked so nicely," I responded, chuckling to hide the terror inside of me. "I will bring you back someone's head."

"Please do not do that," he quickly said, lifting his hands. I began backing away, offering two thumbs up.

"Fine, you are twisting my leg but I will bring you two."

"Asher!"

"Sorry, got to go save our asses! Two heads, pinky promise!" And then I ran, ready to find my family in whatever mess was about to begin.

As soon as I rounded the first corner, I was met with the sight of Golden Guard *everywhere.* More than were in Haven or Behman. I tried to stay small as I ducked between trees and stuck close to the manor, but my hideous dress was getting in the way. I missed my leathers.

"Come on, Strange One, do you really think that they will come back for you?" I yelped at the appearance of Wrath at my side, the top of his head reaching my shoulder.

"What is that supposed to mean?" I hissed back, trying to stay quiet. I needed to conserve my magic until I found Mia. Which meant no searching for minds nearby or shattering them on sight. I needed to be cunning, cool, collected…ideally not crazy.

"Just because they are real, does not mean they want you back." I stilled, peering at him from the corner of my eye. "You are the reason that Haven was destroyed, that all of those fae died. It is your fault that Behman was attacked. Your fault that they lost Winona and Luca. You are the reason I am dead."

A soft sob racked through me, shaking my entire body.

"Go away!" I screamed, swiping at him. My hand sailed through him, touching nothing but air until it smacked into the tree. I tried to ignore the words, but even when he smirked and disappeared, Wrath's voice still yelled in my head.

Your fault!

Your fault!

Your fault!

Your. Fault.

It was my fault. But I would be damned if it were for nothing. A shout caught my attention, gold clad soldiers heading my way after my outburst caught their attention. With a deep breath, I willed every feeling other than fury to burrow down within me. I caged them, just as I used to. They could be felt later, but right now, Bellamy was here. My family was here. Even if I did not deserve them, they still came. And they needed me.

CHAPTER THIRTY-TWO

BELLAMY

"You should stay here," I said, watching as Adbeel donned his armor. It was black as night, the metal buffed since his last battle. How long had it been since he last fought? Centuries. Not since he found me.

"I will go get my granddaughter, Bellamy," was all he said in response. At least we knew where I learned my stubbornness from.

What would Asher think of the fact that I was raised by her grandfather and she was raised by my parents? Would she think it inappropriate? Wrong?

Would she even be okay enough after whatever they were doing to her to think of such things?

Yes, she had to be relatively okay or Nicola would have said something to me. At least, I hoped she would have.

"Fine, go tell Odilia that she will be in charge until we get back. We need to be as quick as possible. I think the best thing we can do is limit who we bring and focus on retrieving Asher." Adbeel nodded, grabbing the hilt of his silver sword and tugging it off the mount it had sat upon for as long as I had been alive.

"You go get your Trusted and I will inform Odilia. Meet me back here in no more than five minutes," he ordered before disappearing in a beam of light.

"Bossy," I muttered as I willed myself to the hallway just outside of mine and my Trusted's quarters in Pike.

I went straight to my room, dressing quickly in my armor and then stepping into my small bathing room. Though I knew it was vain, I could not help myself from looking into the mirror and making sure I looked decent for my princess.

When I decided I looked well enough, I marched out of my room and into the hallway.

Through Noe's door, I could hear the muffled voices of her, Damon, Cyprus, Farai, and Jasper. I did not bother to knock before pushing through the door. All of them turned to look at me, their conversation cut short. Noe, Damon, and Cyprus sat on her bed, the two males on either side of Noe and her arms slung around their shoulders. Farai and Jasper sat on her floor with their legs tangled together. They had rarely left one another's side, the pure joy of being within each other's company radiating off of them. Asher would have been so happy to see them together. Ranbir was there as well, his back hunched in the wooden chair at Noe's desk. Asher and I would need to find a way to help him.

Something.

Anything.

"Time to go, you lazy assholes. Asher is waiting for her family," I practically hummed. They all straightened, six pairs of wide eyes staring at me with the sort of dazed joy that could only be found when hopeless dreams became a precarious reality.

"Really?" Noe gasped out, her hand on her mouth. Cyprus looked ready to cry. Damon stood, rolling his shoulders back and nodding. Ranbir was similar, his eyes gaze fierce.

"You have to stay here, okay?" Farai whispered to Jasper.

"Absolutely not! I need to help you get Ash back!" Jasper yelled in response, pushing himself to his feet. We really did not have time for this.

"We both know you are not a fighter, Jas. Stay here and make sure that everything is ready for Ash. I am sure Ray will help you." Farai's tone was soothing, and when he stood he placed firm hands on either side of his husband's face. They stared into one another's eyes, looking as if they might be lost in the love they shared. When Jasper finally sighed and agreed, Faria placed a gentle yet passionate kiss to his lips. "She will be in your arms in no time."

"If that is settled, then I need you all to get up and get ready. We have only minutes to portal to Adbeel's office and then get to that ridiculous pirate."

It turned out that they needed only one minute to disperse into their respective rooms and yank on their own armor. By the end of it, we were portaling to the weapons room, where we all armed ourselves. From there, I took a deep breath and willed us to the very edge of Dunamis. Farai looked the least steady on his feet, but he stayed up long enough to step through the wards. Though I knew he was on our side, I found myself looking his way to see if the wards would reject him for malicious intent. As he slid through effortlessly and leaned onto Noe, I nodded and grabbed them again.

The moment our feet touched down, Adbeel was there, grabbing my arm and shouting, "Now!"

Noe responded instead of me, checking the coordinates on a map she had grabbed one last time before closing her eyes and enveloping us all in the sweet smell of her Moon magic.

"Finally," Henry's loud huff cut through the air right as we arrived on the deck. The sky above us was fading to black, the stars popping out one by one to bear witness to the chaos that was about to ensue.

All I could think was that no matter what, I would have the love of my life in my arms by the end of the night.

Lian caught my eye, her blue hair quickly coming my way. I opened my arms, thinking she was going to embrace me. Instead, her hand connected with my cheek. A pained groan slipped past my lips as I grabbed my stinging face.

"Dammit, Lian, what was that for?"

"You are late! We have a future queen to rescue!" she shouted in response, her hands going to her hips and her glare leveling my way.

"They took forever to get ready!" I pointed at Noe and Cyprus, hoping to send some of Lian's ire their way.

"We did not!" they yelled in unison.

"Enough! Focus." Adbeel's order was immediately obeyed, silence overtaking the ship.

He was right, we needed to focus. Nothing was okay until Asher was with us again.

"So what is the plan?" Just then, a door behind us loudly shut. I turned to find Captain Harligold walking out of what must have been her quarters, followed closely by the blonde that seemed glued to her side and a female I had seen many times before. She was dark everywhere but her clothes, the lavender dress fit more for a casual dinner rather than a battle.

For that reason alone—my previous stalking habits aside—I would have known exactly who she was even before Farai shouldered past our group and ran at her.

"Nicola!" he cheered, grabbing her by the waist and spinning her around as he embraced her. She giggled as they spun, wrapping her arms around his neck and pressing their foreheads together.

"I have missed you," she responded.

"King Adbeel is right. We need to focus. Nicola, while it is lovely to meet you in the flesh, can we discuss the plan?" I asked, becoming antsy.

"No plan, Elemental. You have one job, get Asher. The pirates have done their part for now," Nicola said, gesturing behind her to the group of females. I noted that they were one short. The siren was gone. As if that were their cue, they walked away and huddled together, their whispers too quiet to make out. "Burning the royals' ship means that Asher now has drastically less poison in her system, as her new clothes were freshly made and Perdita swapped out her hairbrush. I could not see how else they were doing it, but she should be significantly more coherent and her magic should be enough to fight back. This is not a mission to kill Mia, but Ash will make it one. We need her out of there as quickly as possible or worse will happen."

Sounded easy enough. I would have went for Asher first either way.

"Your Majesty," Nicola said, offering a small curtsy to Adbeel before addressing him again. "I need you to distract Mia. She is going to be looking for Asher. I have not yet seen a future in which she succeeds, but I think we all know that it is not an option."

Adbeel looked stricken at the idea of Asher not coming back with us tonight, and I imagined my face mirrored his.

"I can do that."

"As for us," Nicola said, slowly assessing my Trusted and her best friend. "Well, we are back up."

"This is not enough to fight off what will probably be hundreds of fae soldiers," Cyprus argued. He had spoken so much less since Luca was taken from us that any time we heard his voice was a relief, but especially now. He would survive this, he was okay and ready.

"We are enough for now." With an understanding of what needed to be done, we all squared our shoulders and readied ourselves. "You first, Bellamy. Right to the Fire Warden's home."

I was gone before she finished her sentence.

I landed upon the grass just in front of the manor. It was a sprawling estate with red walls and a towering black gate shaped like flames. My skin prickled, and then I heard his voice from behind me.

"You should not have come, Baron." Xavier's voice was stoic and calculating, just like it had been for much of our conversation in Grishel. This time, it also held the faintest hint of sorrow. I could almost taste it in the air. "Mia had a feeling you were behind these attacks on Asher, but I swore that you loved her too much to harm her. Apparently, I was wrong."

"I would *never* hurt Asher. I am here to take her home, to rescue her from you psychopaths." My hand twitched, black fire igniting at my fingertips and then blowing away like the wind.

"I once said the same about her—about *you*. Yet here I stand, ready to kill my own son, just as I was ready to end you in that desert." Something akin to pain crinkled his eyes. "One of the hardest things in the world to accept is your own wickedness."

He was not my purpose, but he could help. What had Stassi said? He was a weak link, the crack in their foundation.

"You do not have to do this," I said, letting my entire body light in black flames.

"The exact opposite is true, actually. I have to do this, because I cannot let you take Asher from me again," he responded, letting his flames ignite as well.

"You know, I think you do love Asher in your own way, even if it is the wrong way." Xavier let out an animalistic growl at my condemnation, his body going rigid. We faced each other, father and son in every way except the one that mattered. Nearby, screams echoed off the clear sky, entering the abyss and being thrown back at us in a mockery of the pain tonight would bring. "You have to let her go. She deserves happiness."

Xavier ignored my plea, grunting as he stepped forward and rained fire down upon me. I summoned my Earth power, lifting the dirt and grass from the ground. Fire met earth, bursting in angry flames and charred grass. As if the visual had shown him exactly what Asher had felt growing up, Xavier stumbled back. I let the dirt fall as his flames extinguished.

"She can be happy with us. Just like she used to be," he muttered. But there in his broken eyes I could see the truth. Could nearly feel it tingling against my skin. He knew she was never truly happy.

"No, she would be miserable again, as I am sure she has been since your wife nearly killed her."

"Your mother," he corrected. As if that disgusting fact mattered at all.

"I have no mother," I rasped, less bite in my tone than I would have expected. "That female tortured and traumatized the love of my life—my soulmate. You *both* did."

"I felt so incredibly proud the first time I held you," he whispered. I gasped at his admission. Me? "You were the most perfect little youngling. You never cried, always smiling and laughing at everything near you. I could not wait to teach you all the things my father had taught me."

"You let them force magic into my veins right after I was born. You let me be tortured and nearly killed!" I yelled the accusation, beginning to circle him. He mirrored my movements, fire trailing both of us and lighting the ground aflame. Soon we were smothered in smoke and heat, the only thing visible each other. "You let me be taken, not even caring what could have happened to me. You never loved me."

"I sobbed the day you were taken. I begged Mia to let us attack Eoforhild. We knew who took you the moment Mia found Asher hidden away in the forest. The real target was protected while you were snatched away by a demon king with vengeance in his heart." He froze, staring at me with pleading eyes. "Mia was against it though. They had that wretched Mist, and we had the unique opportunity to raise Asher. Mia came from a long line of females—queens. Asher was the blessing she prayed to Eternity for."

"Well, I am glad you did not come for me. I lived a good life. That demon king you speak of as if he is a monster raised me with infinitely more love than you bestowed upon Asher." I took a step forward, trying to appeal to whatever weakness Stassi saw inside of him. "Let her be happy now. Let me take her home. Maybe we can stop this war. Maybe *you* can."

"I am sorry I did not come for you—that I did not rescue you and love you. But you are not my son any longer. Not really. Asher though, she *is* my daughter. You might think me a monster, but I love her more than anything else. She will stay with us. If she has to feel a little pain in order to one day rule over all of Alemthian, then so be it."

He ran for me then, his words ending on a choked cry as he summoned a sword of red flames and swung. I met his blade with one of my own, my black flames burning so hot they were nearly cold. The blades hissed as they connected. Xavier and I stared one another in the eyes, both of us begging for something completely different.

"Then you deserve this end I will give you," I whispered. Just as I released my flames and gripped the dagger strapped to my thigh, wispy black shadows wrapped around Xavier's neck and ripped him backwards. He flew through the flames, shouting with fury and pain.

"I have him, you get our queen," Noe demanded as she portaled to my side, shadow whips in hand. I nodded, grabbing her face and planting a quick kiss on her forehead.

I jumped through the fire, heading for the front of the manor, following the sounds of screams and praying to whatever existed above that it was my beautiful creature slaughtering the masses up ahead.

CHAPTER THIRTY-THREE

ASHER

The first guard that found me was easy to take down. Poor thing impaled himself on a branch that just so happened to be in my hands.

The second one was not as silent or stupid.

"Hey, I found the princess!" he shouted, running like he might rescue me. That was, until he saw the body at my feet. The branch still stuck out of the space where I had jammed it into his exposed side.

"You know, it really was not my fault," I insisted. The guard stared at me with horror in his gaze, and then he screamed.

"She is fighting against us! Tell the Quee—"

Taking the blade I had stolen from the first guard, I stabbed it through the face of the second. My already bloody dress grew damp once more, the gold and red merging. It reminded me of the anklet Bellamy had given me. How it had just made sense for the gold and the red to rest together, connected by silver and black. The story of our lives.

Four more guards shouted as they neared, all of them looking at me as if they might kill me. Let them try, more dangerous creatures have attempted and failed.

One of them commanded the trees around me, and I was forced to expose myself as I leapt out of the small forest. Unfortunately, I was too slow. A branch whipped down and caught my healed foot, yanking me off my feet and dragging me backwards. I dug my fingers into the ground, ripping up dirt and grass.

Think. Come on, think!

My skirt caught on a rock, ripping loudly. Laughter sounded from one of the guards, and I looked up in time to see one of the other three shove the laughing one.

"Do you want her to make your tiny brain bleed out of your ears?" he asked, enough fear in his voice to make the laughing one blanch.

Aggravated and short on time, I decided using a little magic would not hurt.

"*Stay still,*" I ordered them. All four stiffened, their eyes wide. The branch continued to assault me, the guard with the Earth power clearly still commanding the tree. "*Release me.*"

Then I was free, the branch slithering away like a snake. Standing, I held up a finger in their direction.

"One more moment," I muttered as I walked their way. I freed a dagger from one of them, using it to quickly hack off my skirts until everything from my knees down were free. Much better.

With that done, I looked up and frowned at the four males.

I could will them to sleep and move on, but that would require more magic than I was willing to spare.

Plus, I rather thought a bit more bloodshed would help further bury the emotions that attempted to claw their way free of the grave I had dug them.

"This will hurt. Badly." Lifting the first male's helmet, I took the dagger and jabbed it into his throat. He gurgled and twitched, then collapsed to the ground. Easy. I moved to the next, the one who had been laughing. He looked ready to sob as he attempted to twist his face in fear. "Do not worry, I will make it exceptionally hilarious for you."

By the time all of them were dead on the ground, I had fully soaked the remainder of the dress. Not caring, I rushed forward, needing to find Mia. She was the one I wanted, and I only had so long before Bellamy or his Trusted stole me away.

I cut my way through the front lawn until I reached the enormous fountain surrounded by a modest garden that sat just before the manor. My breaths were coming in pants, my arms and legs bleeding heavily from soldiers that knew their way around blades or Shifters who knew when to be a beast.

It was then, as I leaned against the fountain and tried to rest, that I caught sight of her.

Mia's hair was bright in the night, matching the flames that were catching all around us. She paid no attention to me as she fought off a male I had never seen before. He was large, at least as tall as Bellamy and somehow even more muscled. His hair was a reddish-brown, the curls wild and fierce. He had a beard that looked more like a shadow in the night, and he wore all black armor.

As strange as it was, he looked so very familiar to me.

Shouts escaped his lips as he dodged a rock that Mia sent his way, the brightest beam of light I had ever seen bursting free of his hands. The queen was quick to dart out of the way, not even her gown slowing her enough to make a difference. They looked rather evenly matched, though it seemed like the male was slightly slower than Mia.

Which was why I needed to get there and step in. It had to be me who ended her. I needed to be the one to free us all. She would not hesitate with anyone else.

Moving forward, I just barely caught sight of an arrow that was coming my way. It missed, zooming past me. If there was one thing I had learned, it was that there was always someone waiting for their turn to kill you. This time, the who surprised me more than it ever had.

Lian stood not far away, her bow in her hand. She stared at me like I was a ghost before nodding to something behind me. I turned, finding a dead Golden Guard mere feet away, the arrow embedded in their forehead.

Chuckling, I whipped my head back around, only to be met with the sight of more guards rushing me. I attacked like a rabid animal, slicing and clawing at them. Lian was there at my side before the first Golden Guard fell, and within moments of her arrival, the other five were dead too.

"It is so much more efficient with you at my side," I enthused, smiling at her warmly. There was so much I wanted to tell her

"Asher, you need to get to Bellamy," Lian insisted, not allowing me even a moment to bask in her presence.

She was there. She was *real.*

"I need to take out Mia first. If we can kill her, then their rule will crumble. This is my chance!" If my passionate shouts registered in Lian's mind, she did not show it. Her face remained stoic, her stare penetrating.

"Bellamy is waiting, Asher. Go to him," she implored.

303

Dipping my head, I jumped towards her, offering a chaste embrace. Beneath the blood and sweat, her spring scent flourished. She wrapped her arms around me, burying her face in my neck before shoving me away. I stumbled, catching sight of her thrusting her blade through the neck of a Golden Guard.

"Now, Ash!" she demanded.

My feet willed me forward, but my mind strayed to Mia. I ran, pumping my arms and letting my dirt-stained shoes fall off as I went. Lian had not said where Bellamy was, but I figured I would feel him. I had to. He was...part of me, somehow.

Yet, all I could feel was the queen in the distance. She screamed as she fought off the male, who was very clearly a demon based on the beams of light that he fought with. They were arguing as they fought by the sound of it. And though I knew I was meant to look for Bell, I could not stop myself from turning left and running farther from the manor. The closer I got to the two, the better I was able to hear. I darted behind a tree, trying to come up with a good strategy as I listened.

"—mine, as she will always be!" Mia shrieked as she lifted an entire tree out, roots and all. She sent it sailing towards the male, who split it in half with the light of the sun. They were both breathing heavily, desperate pants for air that momentarily silenced them.

"No, she is *mine*. Just as Bellamy is. They are *my* family! You do not deserve anything but death you disgusting, pathetic excuse for a female!" The male ripped his sword free of his sheath, pointing it her way. Mia only chuckled in response, smiling broadly at him.

"My mother told me stories of you. How arrogant you were. How little you cared for anything but your own wants. We were always better than that. We wanted to conquer, to rule and make the world better. To show just how valuable females are. The Mounbetton queens will mold and reshape this world!"

Their battle raged on in momentary silence, both of them charging and slashing at the other, but neither gaining much ground. Until Mia

seemed to acquire the upper hand, pushing back with rock after rock and then drowning the male in the dirt he stood upon. He tried to shield himself with light, but her Earth power found its way in. When he portaled away, she met him each time, turning as if she knew where he would end up. When he appeared behind her, she conjured a spear-like branch and shoved it into his side, letting it dig into him. His scream of pain was paired with her nearly manic laughter.

"Asher Mounbetton will be the one to see your realm fall, King Adbeel Ayad. That, I can promise you."

King Adbeel Ayad.

Bellamy's father. Kind of.

Just like the first time, I portaled without intention or forethought. One minute I was watching Mia rip out the branch, the next I was between them, catching the spear as she brought it back down. She gasped, staring at me as if there was no world in which she thought I would defend the male beneath her. Dumbstruck was the only word that could describe that look.

"It is Asher Daniox, you stupid bitch." And then I dug into her mind, shoving my magic her way. I tunneled and burrowed, trying to sink as deep into her consciousness as I could before she fought back.

Mia was quick to release the branch and use my momentum against me. She shoved my chest, sending me flying backwards. I hit the ground only to be scooped up by tree roots as they erupted from the dirt. They lifted me, smacking me back into the ground as Mia shouted from beyond.

"You selfish, ungrateful monster! Every day I love you, and every day you return that love with disgusting hatred! I have said it before and I will say it again, I will keep you bleeding and toeing death before I let you go!" I watched in horror as she pulled her arms back and threw them forward with a scream of vicious fury.

My body sailed through the air, twisting and flipping like I was nothing but a doll. When I hit the ground this time, dizziness attempted to

keep me down. The world around me spun, and I thought that maybe I was somehow still in the air twirling. But no, the ground was hard beneath me.

Digging my fingers into the grass and dirt, I willed myself to stand, to do anything but remain the victim. I got up, unsteady on my feet but more than ready to fight. Two centuries worth of rage was inside of me, and it was all I needed to lock my gaze on Mia and ready myself.

She stood in her nearly clean golden gown, her hair barely out of place and crown still secure on her head. Fists clenched at her sides, she glared my way and seemed to make a decision. Yes, I could practically smell her resolve, taste its tangy flavor on my tongue.

"You will either kill me or I will kill you, those are your options tonight, Mia," I hissed. My magic hummed in my skin, begging for full freedom. The Manipulator wanted blood—Mia's blood—and I would give her that.

Charging forward, I tried to stay focused on the queen rather than the pain or lightheadedness. Mia matched my battle cry, running at me as well.

I was ready to win or die, but either way, I was dragging her down with me. Just as we were about to collide, my magic darting free of its confines and Mia's power commanding every bit of nature around us, walls of fire erupted on either side of me, surging past Mia before wrapping around and aiming right for her.

Black fire.

Mia ducked, but I was too slow, too awestruck by what this fire meant. It sailed towards me, parting at the last second. I turned around, catching sight of the most stunning icy blue eyes.

He walked towards me slowly, his black armor coated in blood and his dark hair perfectly mussed. His palms faced me, arms out and fire erupting from his hands like a volcano spewing lava. There was not a smile on his face, but even with his full lips pressed into a line, I could see the love in his stare.

Skin burning from the nearness of the flames and ears ringing from the screams around us, I could do nothing but go to him—slowly at first, and then as fast as I possibly could. I ran, those inky flames making a straight path to him.

The world seemed to slow, everything around us nearly freezing in place as I closed the remaining distance. No sound, taste, touch, smell, or thought could be found. Nothing but the sight of him there, waiting for me.

Fifty feet.

Twenty.

Ten.

Five.

I jumped, knowing with every fiber of my being that he would catch me. And he did.

One second my feet were on the ground, the next my legs were wrapping around his waist and my hands were gripping his jaw and my lips were against his. His strong arms tucked me close, as if he might never let me go again. There was such passion in just the way his hands gripped my torn dress and loose curls. Tongues colliding and tears mingling, I tasted him like I might never know anything so perfect. Cinnamon and smoke and sweet, warm sunshine invaded my every sense, my very being.

And then the world came back into focus. A furious, piercing scream shattered our peace like glass.

"Get. Off. My. Daughter!" Mia had never sounded so shrill, so completely and utterly sociopathic.

A wall of rock grew between us, wrenching me from Bellamy's grasp and knocking my leg so hard I shouted in pain. Through my tangled hair, I watched Mia approach me with a crazed expression on her face. On her heels was Malcolm, not once looking back at his father who bled upon

the ground. He gazed intently at me instead, his face contorted like the mere sight brought so much pain he could no longer bear it.

"Kill that fucking beast," Mia ordered, pointing at Bellamy who was freeing his arm of rock that had formed around it.

"No!" I pleaded, pushing myself up and crying out when the pain in my leg intensified. "If you want him dead, you will have to kill me first."

Head swimming from whatever poison still lingered in my blood, I shoved my magic out once more. This time, it hit Mia's mind and stuck, piercing through the shadowy wall that Malcolm had constructed. She gasped, grabbing her chest and ogling me like I was her worst nightmare come to life.

I should have feared that panic. Should have seen it for what it was. Her limit.

She screeched, and then shards of what must have been rock came sailing for me. I bent forward, trying to protect myself without any real chance of success. Bellamy's scent once more coated me, and I felt the moment we portaled. He breathed heavily against the top of my head, grabbing at me like I would disappear if he did not claw his way into my skin.

But I could not focus on him. Not entirely. Not when Xavier now kneeled where I had once been, mere feet away. Dozens of rock shards littered his skin, having pierced through his golden clothes. Blood seeped from the wounds like rivers, and I caught sight of Malcolm's vindictive smile just before he grabbed Mia's incensed and frozen form, the two disappearing in a burst of smoke-like shadows.

Xavier groaned in pain, his head turning to face Bellamy and I. There was the barest hint of a smile on his face, as if he were happy with the outcome. "I love you, my Asher. My blessing."

And then he fell forward, silent and still.

I gasped, daring to look at the male I once thought invincible as he lay dead upon the grass.

"Ranbir! Get him, we will take him to Pike!" Bellamy demanded, pointing at Xavier's body. I had not noticed Ranbir before, but he caught my attention as he stood, offering a hand to the demon king he must have just healed. "Ash, I need you to stay focused and stay with me, okay?"

Bellamy's hands gripped either side of my face, forcing me to look up at him. He was flustered, his eyes wide and freckles hidden beneath smatterings of blood. His lips were parted slightly, chest heaving.

My magic felt so terribly hollow, like maybe it was never there at all. Black spots began to litter my vision, my head drumming an excruciating beat. I was about to pass out, I could feel it coming. There was still so much to do, but there was only one being that needed me in that moment. One singular person who was waiting for me to come save him.

"Sterling is not who we thought," I muttered, begging Bellamy to understand. His face contorted into momentary fury, but I reached up and smoothed the line between his brows with my shaky and numb fingers. "He is hiding in the trees just behind the manor and is without his memories of the last year. Please go get him. Please save him."

And then I was fading into blissful darkness.

"Do not forget the heads."

CHAPTER THIRTY-FOUR

ASHER

A soothing and deep voice was the first thing to meet my ears after what felt like years in peaceful silence.

My mind felt like a jumbled mess, memories and wishes and imagination all colliding. My fingers toyed with the quilt below me, trying to understand what exactly was going on.

I had dreamt of Bellamy. Of what it might be like to be in his arms once again. Wrath had teased me, reminding me of how unbelievably not real it all was. He had reminded me of how often I dreamt of my family, day and night.

Now, as I awoke with no pains or aches, I accepted what Wrath had told me over and over again. Only someone truly insane could dream up an entirely different reality. And that was what I had done.

Was it Wrath speaking to me now? No, his voice had never been soft or calming. A hand touched my forehead, warm and large. Xavier. It had to be Xavier.

"Get off of me!" I shouted, pushing the hand away. I did not want to open my eyes, did not dare let the truth sink in. Perhaps if I stayed ignorant to the gold around me, then I could pretend I was in Bellamy's arms instead.

"Asher, it is okay, you are safe." It even sounded like Bellamy. Gods, I wish it were. If only I could figure out how to get rid of Mia, to kill her and let the world fall apart so I might have a moment with the love I had created in my head.

"Please, just leave me alone. Just let me dream," I begged, swatting the hand away again. This time, I caught the cool bite of metal on them, and I sighed in contentment. At least my brain was bringing me pleasing delusions.

"Bellamy, maybe we should give her space, she seems confused." Ranbir. That was Ranbir's voice. Oh, how the mere thought of him hurt. I could not believe how much I had invented, how horrible my mind could be if I let it.

I opened my eyes, curious to see just how far my imagination would take me. The first thing I saw were his lips. Those full, perfect lips that I had kissed thousands of times. Bellamy smiled, his dimples digging into his cheeks just beneath his smattering of freckles.

"Hello, Princess."

"Hello, demon."

And though I knew it was fake, I still let him lean down and place a delicate kiss on my lips.

"Waking up will hurt so badly this time," I whispered against his mouth. He stilled, lips frozen as they now hovered just above mine. So close I could still taste him.

"What do you mean by that, Ash?" His question confused me. It made my head swim and my heart race.

"I just mean that the next time I wake up and you are gone again, it will hurt worse than usual." If my words made any sense to him, he did not allow his face to convey it. Instead, he backed away, brows pinched together and lips downturned.

"Something is wrong with her, Ranbir," he spoke, not turning his head away from me. Behind him, a figure stirred. Ranbir, dressed in his favored white clothes, peeked over Bell's shoulder and inspected me.

"Asher, do you remember what happened?" the Healer asked. Bellamy cocked his head to the side, awaiting my answer.

"Yes, of course," I muttered, though in truth I did not. Mia had said the demons attacked my wedding, but was it really the demons? Was it actually her? Had everything been fake? "Or, well, I know I was engaged to the prince. That for sure is true."

"Asher, you are going to have to propose to me first before saying we are engaged," Bellamy teased, winking at me. Ranbir watched with a sort of perplexed expression, like his mind might be coming to conclusions but his heart was taking longer to see the truth. I shook my head.

"No, not you. The mortal prince, Sterling. I wish I were engaged to you. I wish you were real. I wish I were free." I was rambling now, the pounding in my head ferocious as it beat me down to nothing.

"I *am* real. You are not engaged to Sterling. It is me, I am here." Bellamy's voice was taking on the barest hint of hysteria, his hands moving to grab my shoulders as he shook me ever so slightly.

"No, you are not. But I want you to be. I held onto you for so long, Bell. I promise. I did not let go. Even now, I am clawing at the image of

you." My voice was just a whisper, but both the males before me heard. "I wonder when Wrath will show up and say he told me so."

"Ranbir!" Bellamy shouted, finally looking away from me to stare at the Healer. Ranbir looked horrified as he gazed at me. What had I said? Did dreams not know they were dreams?

"I am not sure what is happening to her, Bell. She…she seems to be having a mental break of some sort."

"That is the problem, Ranbir. My mental has *been* broken." I said it like he was the dumb one, but both males gawked at me in obvious distress.

"Asher, you are here with us right now. This is not a dream. We came for you," Bellamy exclaimed, shaking me a little more violently this time. "You are safe!"

"Stop that. I do not want anymore hope than I already have. I only just now started accepting this, can you please just leave me be instead of tormenting me with the unachievable?" I asked, shoving him back. I must have pushed harder than I thought, because Bellamy fell, his body sliding a few feet away. If only I were that strong in real life.

"Bellamy, we need to give her—"

"No! Princess, please, listen to me." Bellamy approached me like he was on his deathbed and I was the antidote for whatever sickness was seeking to claim him. This time, his hands grabbed my face, shaking only my head. "We have been through too much for you to leave me now!"

"Bellamy I am serious, you are going to hurt her!" Ranbir shouted from behind him. But it was too late, Bellamy was beyond reason.

"I love you! You are here with me and you will stay with me!" His furious shakes of my skull were beginning to hurt, and I felt the dizziness make way for confusion. For anger. For panic. "Believe me—believe *in* me! In *us!*"

"I said *stop!*" My scream echoed off the rock and wood around us. For the first time, my eyes took in the space. It was Bellamy's room in Pike. Gods, I was losing my ever-loving mind. "Get away from me! You are making this so much worse. Just leave me alone to wallow. Let me be miserable in my life instead of constantly dragging me back into this abyss of false joy. You. Are. Not. Real!"

"That is it, out!" Ranbir shouted, grabbing Bellamy by the collar of his cotton shirt and lifting him. If I had any doubts that this was a dream, the sight of Ranbir taking control like that rendered them void. "She needs s*pace!*"

The Healer shoved his prince out of the room, not even letting him turn to say goodbye. That was for the best. I could feel myself sinking into the bone chilling madness, and I did not want to watch as Bellamy disappeared before my eyes. As soon as the door slammed shut, I broke down into tears, pulling my legs against my chest and trying to will myself back into sanity.

Fur tickled my cheek only moments later, and I groaned in defeat. Of course he would appear as I was falling apart.

"Strange One, this is becoming a problem," Wrath whispered, his eerie voice gentle. I wished he would go away for a little, that all of them would go away and stop giving me faith. Because when I woke up to the sound of Mia's voice or Xavier's laugh, it would break me beyond repair. This fantasy, it was too much. "I think we both know that you never went insane. You did not make this all up. Bellamy is real. He came for you."

Could a heart still beat after it broke? If so, that was what was happening inside of my chest. Wrath, who had been calling me crazy this entire time, was now telling me it was real. I tried to make reason of it all, to understand and be logical despite my mind working against me.

"He cannot be real. If any of that actually happened, then I commanded him not to come find me. So how could he have?" Yes, my heart was like shredded cloth as it pulsed in my chest, ripped apart and irreparable.

"You underestimate the power of love. Why would you not? You were never showed much of it. Your friends were forced to leave you. Your Healer was stolen from you. Your parents taken before you could even love them back. But I will tell you something that, deep inside, you know to be true. Bellamy loves you in a way that could defy fate. He treasures you enough to find a way—to defeat anything that might stand in his path. Love like that is rare, but it exists within him. Within *you*. Even if you feel unworthy of such a thing."

"Why are you being so nice to me?" I inquired, so used to his hatred, his unyielding spite.

"Because I am you, and you are finally ready to be kind to yourself too."

A sob racked through me at his words, my arms still wrapped tightly around my bent legs. Wrath scooted closer, rubbing his silky fur into my side. On instinct, I reached down and scooped him into my arms. He felt so *real*.

"It is time for us to say goodbye. You have a life to live, a world to save, and a stupid little princeling to love." For once, Wrath sounded sweet. His voice had lost the haunting, echoing rasp. Now, it was a caress against my ears. A lullaby to send me to sleep—or perhaps to return me to reality.

"I do not want to lose you. I do not want this to be the end," I cried, begging for a different story. I wished this had not been mine. That I had been given any other tale.

"You have to let me go, Strange One. For them. For him. For *you*." Another round of tears dashed down my cheeks as if it were a race. And it felt like it was. A race against time. Against my own sanity. Against death. "It is not fair how strong you have had to be—how much you have suffered. But you cannot give up. Not now, after so long of surviving the unimaginable."

"I love you, Wrathy." Offering those four words to the fur on his cheek felt like sentencing myself to a lifetime of sorrow. Yet, Wrath chuckled.

"I love you too, Strange One. Always."

And then he was gone, and I was alone.

***

For a while, I let the sobs overtake me. Every memory of Wrath seemed to circle my mind and attack my last bit of hope. I thought of Bellamy. Of faith and family and *love*. Was it truly real? I pinched and slapped my skin, pulled my hair, held my breath. Anything I could think of that would prove that I was really in Pike. That I had gotten out and Bellamy was nearby.

My head snapped up, the closed door calling to me as if something had locked into place.

Before I could so much as second guess myself or this reality, I dried my tears and leapt to my feet. I passed the slightly cracked mirror, realizing I wore a black pair of Bellamy's cotton trousers and one of his black tunics. Not a pretty sight, but I did not care how much of a mess I looked. Within seconds I was at the door, ripping it open and dashing out into the hall. Trying to think of where Ranbir would have taken Bellamy, I let my thoughts wander and search. Maybe the training yard. A chance for him to work through the anger he was suffering from.

Bounding through the halls and down the stairs, I dodged beings left and right, causing many to begin whispering. Ray caught my eye at the bottom of the final set of stairs, her face in a notebook as she scribbled. I could have cried at the sight of her mousy brown hair, soft russet skin, and fiercely sculpted jaw. She looked so much like her brother that it nearly hurt.

She was real. They were real. It was real.

I knew what was real.

"Ray!" I shouted, causing her to jump back in surprise. When she looked up at me, her eyes went wide. My body connected with hers, wrapping her in a fierce hug.

"Princess Asher? You should not be out of bed. Our schedule does not have Ranbir clearing you for at least another day." Laughter escaped me in uncontrollable jolts, hysteria the icing upon the cake of my insanity.

"Seeing you is so lovely. I need Bell, though. Where is he?" How long had it been since I saw him? An hour maybe? He would not leave Pike. Not without me.

My grip on Ray's shoulders left her wincing, and I quickly withdrew my hold to instead stare into her eyes. I could take it from her, that would be faster. But before I could do something rash, his beautiful voice tickled my ears.

"Ash! Are you okay? I heard you were running. Please, I promise not to hurt you, just stay still and I will get Ranbir again." Bellamy had his hands out, palms facing me and blue eyes crinkled in desperation. He was so extraordinarily beautiful, something I had not let myself notice earlier. His dark waves were a mess atop his head, his freckles like constellations on his cheeks. His full lips were a deep pink, his icy blue eyes bloodshot. Dark circles bruised the skin beneath his eyes and his cheekbones were more prominent than they should have been. Still, he was ethereal. Perfection in living form.

He was mine.

I closed the distance, binding him with my arms and breathing in the smoke and cinnamon scent of him—basking in the sunshine of his mind just as I had on that battlefield.

"I am so sorry for everything. I should have never forced you to stay away. I should have fought harder. I should have loved you the way you deserved." The words flowed from my mouth like a rushing river. Bellamy gasped, wrapping me up tightly in an embrace. "I love you. I have never stopped loving you. Even when the world was upside down and Eternity seemed on the brink of collapse, I loved you, Bell."

"My beautiful creature, I always knew that. I never questioned your love for me. There are no words for how much I love you. Please, let me take you upstairs to rest." His voice shook with the emotions building within him, as if his body could not hold them all. But I would not be deterred.

"No, you need to understand. I am so, so sorry. You are real and you are here and you are everything I could have ever dreamed of. I would give up food and water and air for this—for you. I would let the entire world burn for us. Marry me, Bell. Marry me and be with me forever. Be my king, be my friend, be my husband," I begged. It was a shitty proposal, but it was all I had.

"Asher," he breathed my name, a tear hitting my shoulder where his chin rested. "I have loved you since the moment I saw you in Reader River. My heart was made to be yours. Every day before your introductory ball was just a prelude to my life. You are the beginning, the end, and every moment in between."

He released me slowly, backing his face from mine when my feet touched the ground. Nerves skyrocketed within me, an old fear surfacing: rejection. I shook as he placed either hand on the sides of my face, the fire in his veins heating my cold skin. And then, with soldiers all around us, Bellamy bent down on one knee.

A cry slipped between my lips as his fingers traveled from my cheeks down to my hands, gripping them tightly and then releasing them. I watched with disbelief as he reached into his pocket and pulled out a shining ring. The band was gold, thin where it would sit on the back of my finger but curved into the shape of small petals around tiny black diamonds near the center stone. Three of the flowers sat to the left and right of the center stone, grouped together like a triangle. In the middle was a large moonstone, nearly clear. A star in the night sky. I had never seen anything quite so beautiful.

It was gold, but I thought then that maybe it had to be.

"Asher Daniox, there is nothing in this world that I would not give, sacrifice, or destroy for you. You are the breath in my lungs and the beat of my heart. Be mine. Marry me." His dimples poked out as he said the word "mine."

"I am no one's but yours, demon," I whispered between what could only be described as a sobbing laugh. With that, I shoved my hand towards his, smiling openly as he slipped the ring onto my finger. Then I oh-so-gracefully tackled him. He let out a bark of laughter as he slammed into the ground, which I silenced with my lips as I straddled him, consuming the beautiful sound.

He was real.

We were real.

Applause echoed across the open entrance of Pike, demons, mortals, and fae all cheering. Bellamy swiped his tongue across my lower lip and then bit down, the tantalizing pain distracting me as his stolen Moon magic portaled us through time and space. To his—*our* bed.

ACT IV

~ PEACE AND WAR ~

CHAPTER THIRTY-FIVE

BELLAMY

Engaged—I was engaged!

And gods was it marvelous.

She loved me, more than I ever thought she might be able to. Asher was willing to give up everything for *me*. For *us*.

My tongue slid against hers, thanking her for what she had just given me. For the way she had and would change my life. Nicola had confirmed I was still on borrowed time, but as long as that time was spent with her in my arms then I no longer cared.

I wrapped a hand around her neck, the other gripping her jaw. There was a desperation within me, a need to never let her go again. Perhaps

there was also terror, because Asher could choose to leave. She could take away my choice again. Asher could ruin everything by deciding she was no longer worthy.

So maybe I needed to show her that she was. And maybe she also needed to find out what would happen if she ever tried to leave again.

"Can I fuck you, Asher?" I asked between impatient kisses, my hands digging into her skin and shoving her back onto the bed. Ranbir would be so angry with me. She had just suffered physically and mentally. Underworld below, she thought I was fake mere hours ago. But I needed her. I needed *us*. And if she said yes, I would not ask again or hesitate.

Long, brown curls fanned out around her, crowning my princess. Impatient nods mussed the hair, but I would be sure to fetch her a new crown. A real one.

Leaning forward, I ground my erection into her, feeling the heat of her center through the cotton trousers Ranbir had offered her. My trousers.

My princess.

My fiancé.

My soulmate.

She was mine and I needed to make sure she remembered that before I lost her again.

"Can I *punish* you?" I asked breathlessly, still grinding into her and ravishing her mouth. She seemed to startle, stilling beneath me. For a moment I just sat there, hovering above her. Waiting.

"Punish me? You want to hurt me?"

"I will make it the most euphoric pain you have ever felt. I promise."

Hesitating, she looked up at me, her perfect face a stunning testament to the truth of gods or Eternity or *something*. Nothing like this creature could exist without divine intervention of some sort.

"If you do not like this or wish for me to stop, then say…" I paused, trying to come up with a safe word. Something that would allow her a reprieve from the madness I was about to introduce her to. "Bread."

"Bread?" she asked incredulously. We both burst into laughter, but I could still feel that anger simmering low in my gut and the terror clouding my heart. I needed this. Maybe she even needed it too.

"Your favorite," I teased just as I swooped her up, standing and carrying her over to the spot in our room where a beam of wood cut through the ceiling.

"Stay," I ordered, turning around and heading for my desk. Yanking open the bottom drawer, I quickly grabbed onto the red silk fabric I had bought after a daydream I had of Asher before I had even been inside of her at all. Then, I walked around her and pulled the sheet off our bed.

When I turned to face her, I found Asher still fully clothed and waiting for me. She had actually listened.

Twisting the sheet, I stalked towards her, eager to teach her what had to be the most important lesson she would ever learn.

"You stole from me, Asher." Her already big gray eyes went wider, staring at me in shock and guilt. I only smirked, reaching out to graze her full bottom lip with my pointer finger. It was softer than usual, not as chewed and torn as it so often was from her constant stress. "You robbed me of my free will. In that field, you looked me in the eye and took yourself from me."

Guilt clouded her face, making her expression fall. I wanted to apologize and tell her I had forgiven her, but I could not. She needed to be disciplined. Nothing was more crucial than reminding her that she was mine.

Something else twisted her face, something deeper. I felt like I could sense it somehow, like it was there at the front of my mind.

"This is real, Asher. I am real. Let me prove it." Before she could speak, I reached forward and gripped her hair, crashing our faces together and pushing my tongue into her mouth. Her moan rattled my teeth, the vibration making my already hard cock twitch.

We were working with very little time, clearly.

Letting her go, I dropped the sheet and silk and stared at her body. Shirt first. Definitely shirt first. My hands were at the buttons of the tunic in seconds, deftly moving down them and freeing her. That was when I noticed it. Her skin, still the same shade of creamy brown, was free of any blemishes. Asher had no scars. Not a single one.

She must have realized what I was looking at, because she brought her hand to my cheek and gently caressed it.

"They took them. It must have been when I was asleep. They had me out for a week, and when I woke up, they had healed me completely. Even my hair, which had been cut off completely, was back to normal. I do not know how Tish survived it." Her voice was a broken whisper, a plea of freedom from that pain. "They wanted me to forget."

Bringing my lips to just below her left breast where I knew I had cut her during a training session in Elpis, I traced the now perfect skin. Then I moved, placing kisses to every spot I knew she had once been branded by violence and pain. I painted her story, doing everything I could to remind her of how far she had come.

"It was all real. I promise." She gasped as my tongue slid across a peaked nipple. She tasted as she always had, like salvation. "Let me replace that pain, Asher. Let me remind you of just how real I am."

Her nods were slower this time, but her body pressed into me. And oh if it did not fit perfectly.

I pulled down her trousers next, stripping her of the clothing that dared hide her from me. Because I could not stop myself, I allowed my mouth one quick taste of her. My tongue slid slowly up her soaked center, relishing in how she bucked forward and latched onto my hair.

I sucked in her clit, letting my teeth graze it before releasing it with a loud pop. Soft moans were her answer, but that simply angered me. I wanted her screams. I wanted her admittance. I wanted her submission.

Before trailing my way up her body, I grabbed the sheet once more. She looked on in confusion but remained silent.

Taking her hands, I lifted them above her head. I could feel her curiosity growing as I took the sheet and tied it around her crossed wrists. She had been tied up by me before, but if she thought this would be the same, then she was mistaken.

"Remember, my darling bloodthirsty princess: bread," I whispered against her ear, licking the shredded top. Her shiver was glorious, but I heard a quiet giggle come from the back of her throat, and that meant she was not taking me seriously.

With a wicked smile and a slow wink, I bent my knees and then leapt up. My free hand caught the wooden beam with ease. Asher mumbled something incoherent as she watched me throw the sheet over the beam and let myself fall.

"Tell me you have not been taking lessons from Lara in sexual intimacy," she mocked. I laughed as I pulled, tightening the sheet until her feet nearly hovered off the ground. Then I tied it, making sure she was firmly secured.

Next, I took the red silk and held it in front of her. She tilted her head to the side, observing the cloth in much the same way I would.

"You have been egregiously naughty, Asher." She got one last look at my taunting smirk before I took the blindfold and covered her eyes. After fastening it, I was left with the sight of her completely naked body as it hung at my mercy.

"Bellamy, what is the point of this?" She squirmed as she spoke, her body twitching with unease and her perfect cunt glistening in the light that seeped through our curtains.

"The point is to remind you who you belong to." Her dismissive huff of response made my teeth grind. I was not sure if I had ever felt this type of anger towards her. Not even when she tried to marry that ridiculous mortal prince. Regardless of whether or not he had no memories, that did not rid him of my ire. Of my deep desire to tear open his stomach and string his guts across our room as I fucked her.

But this now, it positively infuriated me.

Asher wanted to play the martyr. Well, I would show her that she would be nothing but a queen and a conqueror.

"I dare you to forget you are mine. The moment you try to leave for what you claim to be the greater good, I will drag you back kicking and cursing. I will punish you until I am drenched in your satisfaction and unhearing from your screams." I grabbed her face, my thumb and fingers pressing into her cheeks until her lips puckered. I wanted her to feel just how much I meant what I was about to say. "You want to be self-sacrificing? Good, sacrifice yourself to me. You can be my brave, gorgeous hero, and I your wicked, filthy villain."

And then I leaned in and pressed our lips together. It was no loving kiss like before. This was a joining that could demolish entire worlds. Ours was a union that could bring the universe itself to yield.

Asher's mouth was just as desperate and needy as mine, our teeth clashing when we got too eager. Letting my free hand glide down the curves of her body, I slipped my mouth free of hers and moved my lips towards her ear.

"Tell me, Asher, what are you?" I asked as I brought my ringed thumb to her clit, pressing firmly as I circled it.

Asher liked pressure. She enjoyed quick fingers and slow tongues. Her body always arched more when I curved my digits inside of her. She

loved when I flicked her nipples with my tongue more than she enjoyed when I placed kisses to them. Her moans were always louder when I honed in on the spot of her neck that curved into her shoulder. She did not care much for her feet being touched, though I had tried just for the fun of it. I had yet to attempt anything with her perfect ass, but I knew she loved when I squeezed it as I lifted her. Asher liked submitting, but only here. Only to me. I knew what she liked. I knew everything about her. So utterly obsessed and thankful was I, that I had devoted more time than I realized to learning her. And I would use every bit of that knowledge today.

"What do you mean?" she asked breathlessly, her head pressing into her left shoulder as she tried to tighten her body where she hung.

"You know what I mean. What are you?" I rasped into her ear, switching to my pointer and middle finger so I could move faster against her. Her head fell back at the new sensation, and I leaned in to ravage that very spot on her neck I knew she loved, now speaking against her skin. "Come on, beautiful creature, tell me what you are. Who you are. Please, for me."

"I am—" She cut herself off with a moan as I let my mouth trail downwards. "I am the—" Again she silenced herself, this time to bite down on her bottom lip as my tongue offered another flick against her hard nipple. "Eternity above, Bellamy, how am I supposed to speak when you insist on—"

"Wrong," I growled, letting my knees hit the floor and leaning away from her.

From this vantage point, I could see *everything*. She was like a deity before me. A goddess in the flesh there to make me remember I must bow and pray. She was deliverance incarnate.

"You are Asher Daniox," I said, leaning closer to the heat between her thighs. "The rightful ruler of two realms." Closer. "Manipulator and holder of minds. The salvation of Alemthian. The vanquisher of evil." Almost there. "You are a survivor. You are the sun and the moon and the

stars in the sky. You are everything, Asher." A mere inch away. "But most of all, you are *mine.*"

I latched onto her like I might fall to the depths of the Underworld if I did not have her to anchor me. She screamed out, the first of many shouts that might tell the world that it was I and only I who brought her such pleasure.

Only my need for air stopped me after I began, the desperation to devour her so strong that I resisted my lungs cries for as long as I could. When I did stop, I used those precious seconds to pull her legs up and rest her thighs on my shoulders. Her shriek of surprise forced laughter from my lips, but I was quick to silence myself with the press of my entire face between her thighs.

"Bellamy, what are you—"

"Yes, shout my name," I groaned onto her swollen clit. She began grinding against my face and squeezing me with her thighs, keeping me locked into place as she fucked my face. From there, speaking was not possible, so I waited and watched. I savored her ecstasy, but I relished in what I knew was to come. Just as she began to shake, the spasms vibrating against my shoulders, I smirked and tossed her off.

A hiss of pain met my chuckles as I slowly stood. When I reached out and lifted the red silk, I was met with a delicious glare. She murdered me with her eyes as she swung, her toes trying to find purchase on the ground. Staring at her had my mind straying to a rather wicked option. One that would prevent her from ever leaving—from even being able to.

I wanted a blood oath.

"You can come when you have learned your lesson. By the end of this, you will cut open your pretty little hand and vow to never leave me. When I am through with you, there will be no mistaking who you belong to, Asher." I let my words register, her gaze going wide as she suddenly tried to free herself. "At your wits end already? You know the word. Say it and I will untie you and let you go on without offering me your oath."

She stared and stared, those stormy eyes calculating.

No doubt trying to find her way out of this.

"If you use your magic on me, Asher, you will find me far less forgiving," I warned. A smile twisted my face, curling upwards. "If you would only listen, I think you would find you like being punished by me, beautiful creature."

A shiver seemed to crawl up her body, starting at her toes and climbing to the tips of her fingers. No matter what she said, Asher did like when I took control. Her reluctance to give it was a coping mechanism, a defense against pain. But inside, she knew I would never take advantage of her submission to truly hurt her.

Finally, she bobbed her head down and up, my permission restored. So I moved closer and returned her blindfold before circling her, watching as her ears guided her. She was half fae, after all. But I did not mind that. In fact, I wanted her to know where I was. To taunt and tease her. That was part of the fun.

"You have left me time and time again. Each hurt worse than the last. I find I have grown tired of being abandoned." My hand darted out and smacked her bare ass, the skin instantly tinting red. She yelped, the momentum from my strike forcing her to swing again. "Tired does not explain it well enough. Exhausted. Infuriated. Those are better."

Again I slapped her, the sting of my hand meeting her other cheek pairing with the sounds of both of our quiet moans. Her legs twisted, thighs pressing together and drawing my attention. Then I offered a slap to her center, earning a soft shout. Eight more times I let my hand mark her, both breasts now as pink as her ass and dripping cunt.

"Please, Bell." Begging. I loved the sound of it falling from her lips.

Opening my trousers, I shoved them down my legs and quickly kicked them off. Then I reached back and gripped the collar of my shirt, pulling it over my head and letting the fabric pool next to my discarded pants. Her head was leaning towards me, listening.

Of all the things I knew I wanted my hands on, those thighs were at the top of the list. Grabbing them, I squeezed and forced her legs to part for me. She allowed me to do it, wrapping them around my waist when she realized what I was doing.

"Can you feel how real I am?" I asked as I let my hard cock rub against her. More breathy moans mingled as we both fought to stay in control. When I repeated the movement, her head fell back and her chest pushed forward. Nothing could have stopped me from bending my head and licking one of her nipples—from tasting her.

"Yes!" she shrieked. Whether it was in response to how real I was or the action itself I did not know, but I did it again, tonguing her nipple until she was grinding against me and using the rope to hold herself higher. Anything to give her some semblance of control back.

I stopped, pulling my body away and only barely holding her up by the back of her knees.

"No!" she yelled this time. I gave her a gentle kiss, letting my tongue dart into her mouth and slowly massage hers. She groaned and writhed, but I did not submit.

"You will bleed and promise before you come," I whispered into her mouth. She had no chance to argue, because I let go of one of her legs and positioned myself at her core. When I shoved in, she screamed out. I savored the moment briefly, trying to rein in my desperation to pour into her while also basking in the perfection of her. Grabbing her knee again, I pushed both up to her chest, folding her in half. Then I set a brutal pace, the wet sound of our bodies coming together again and again like an erotic symphony.

It took every ounce of my own self-control not to burst inside of her as she became more frantic with her moans, clawing her nails against the sheet and arching her back. And just when she seemed like she could not take any more, her legs once more shaking violently against me, I freed myself of her warmth.

"Bellamy I will fucking kill you where you—" I ate her words, swallowing them whole and letting them sink into my stomach.

"Bleed for me, Ash. Promise me you will never leave me again," I panted into her mouth. She groaned, pushing herself into me, rubbing her clit against my aching cock.

"You will finish what you have started even if I say no, I think we both know that." Her words were a slap to the face, but oh was she right. There was no way I would be able to resist her. No world in which I could refuse her.

"I will not pretend like you are wrong," I admitted, still holding her up. She huffed.

"Give me a fucking blade before I change my mind." There was a split second where I stood, frozen. She was...agreeing. Gods, she was saying yes! "Hurry up!"

"Bossy bossy," I purred, letting her legs fall. She growled as she swung, kicking me in the shin before I could get away. My laughs practically spilled out of me as I opened the drawer in my side table and grabbed a dagger.

She waited, breathing heavily and clenching her thighs. I wanted so badly to cut her, to let her blood drip onto me. Instead, I grabbed her wrists and slashed the sheet. She yelped as her feet flattened, falling against me and using her now free hands to grip my shoulders in panic. Smirking, I reached up and pulled off her blindfold.

Gray eyes met mine, and I swore I could have found release at the mere sight of the love there in the stormy depths. She watched intently as I brought the blade to my palm and closed my fist around it. The sound of my flesh splitting was the only one other than our breaths as I sliced upwards.

"Together?" I asked, handing her the blade and exposing my bloody palm to her.

"Always." She smiled, grabbed the blade, and cut a line diagonally down her palm. She lifted her hand, pressing it against mine and threading our fingers together.

"I vow to never leave you willingly. To remain by your side for the rest of my life. You are mine, and I am yours." Emotions made my voice hoarse as I spoke. We would make similar vows on our wedding day, but blood oaths were binding. Breaking them would strip you of a piece of yourself—tearing apart what made someone intrinsically them.

"I vow to never leave you willingly. To remain by your side for the rest of my life. You are mine, and I am yours." Her repetition of the words was stronger, but still husky. I felt the oath slink into my blood, binding us. The tingle seemed to travel to my heart, passing the wards there and wrapping the organ in our promise.

With that, I used my free hand to lift her by her thigh, pushing both of us to the ground. Our lips clashed, my cock sliding back inside of her with ease. We made love like only those who were always meant to be could. It was as if the world itself was pushing us together.

"You and I—our love—will reshape this world, Asher. We will make something better. We will dream." I moaned the words against her neck, trying to remind her that in the end, I wanted what she wanted. As long as I had her to show for it, that was.

When her orgasm freed her mind of every word but my name, I lost all control. My release came and went, cresting and crashing like waves. And when the sea settled, it was just as we said.

Asher and I, together always.

CHAPTER THIRTY-SIX

ASHER

Bellamy slowly brushed his fingers through my hair, placing gentle kisses to my head randomly. We laid there, memorizing one another, for longer than I cared to admit. But it was such a beautiful experience, having him there in the flesh. Knowing just how real he truly was.

War loomed, but I deserved this peace. I had earned this joy.

"Do you want to talk about it?" Bellamy asked. It reminded me of when he had asked the same thing in Behman—when I had refused to talk to him and started a fight.

"Yes, I do," I answered, looking up at him from where I laid on his chest. His smile was dazzling, framed by his full lips and deep dimples.

Happiness seemed to bleed from his heart and out into the air, all because I was willing to talk to him. It felt too good to be true, yet there he was.

Real.

Cuddling further into him, I prepared myself for the pain I was going to dig up. I reminded myself that the hurt was worth Bellamy's love, and that nothing could harm me for long when he was there to hold me.

"They tortured me at first. Burned, shattered, and sliced me until they realized I was not going to give them information or submission." Bellamy's grip on me tightened, a low and husky growl rumbling within his chest. "Then, Mia let a Shifter take a turn. I learned he had been impersonating Sterling the entire time. That was…well, that was bad. I had known him since Academy, and it turns out he had been plotting since I rejected him when we were young."

Bellamy did not speak, did not so much as breathe too loudly after that. Something intrinsic within him must have known this would take a terrible turn—that it would involve the crushing of my heart. I tugged up one of his hands, placing a kiss on his knuckles before continuing.

"He was the one who caught Sipho and me. It was him—Theon was his name—that told the royals about my relationship. To prove it, he had taken on Sipho's form and tricked me into kissing him. And then he waited until the chance came for me to marry. When we needed mortal alliances, there was likely no question who would take on the mortal prince's form. Everything after that—the assault, the touches, the hateful things he would say—stemmed from his hatred of my dismissal of him in Academy." Each word was raspier than the last, my voice becoming sore with the emotions that overtook it.

"Please tell me you killed him," was all he said. I laughed, nodding. "Good, or else I would have had to take you to that foul place and make sure you had the chance to do it."

Of course he would not offer to kill Theon. He knew I could do it, that I would want that revenge for myself. It was glorious, having someone believe in me so fully.

"I tore out his jugular with my teeth." Bellamy's arms tightened around me, his mouth moving to my ear.

"Gods, that is so unbelievably sexy," he murmured.

"Well, I paid for it. After that, they took a different approach with me. I was doing too well in the dungeons, I think. Sterling and I were keeping one another company, even laughing and joking. He—wait, Sterling! Did you find him?"

"Yes, Princess. We can go see him later. Just focus on your story. If you want to tell the rest, that is," he added, his voice soft.

"I do," I hastily said. "Let me think, where was I? Oh yes, a new approach. One morning I awoke not on the damp and dark floor of my cell, but instead in my golden bed. It was startling, but Mia coming into the room and claiming I had been asleep for a year had completely overwhelmed me. I knew it was not true, but every day I lost a little faith in our love story. I started to believe that maybe I had made it all up in my head. It did not help that I was seeing Wrath. I do not know why or how, but he would just appear. He was so real, so lifelike. I could pet him and hold him. He would whisper doubts in my mind, telling me that none of it was real. Soon I began to believe him."

"That was why you panicked earlier." It was a resigned sort of statement, as if he was preparing to accept guilt or blame. "Was the sex too much? Are you hurt? Do you feel taken advantage of?"

"No, most definitely not. I feel happy. Thankful." I paused, smirking at him. "Aroused."

He chuckled, the sound short and broken despite the humor that inspired it.

"On the bright side, it turns out the fae are far from content. When the time comes, I think I can enact genuine change and they will be more than eager for it." Bellamy cleared his throat, adjusting beneath me and squinting his gaze. "Before I find someone else to rule Betovere, that is."

Snorting, he rolled his eyes and leaned down to kiss my forehead. All I could do was smile back. How beautiful was it, to just sit there and delight in him?

"How were things here? Tell me you did not murder too many beings while I was gone," I taunted. Bellamy mock gasped, rearing his head back towards the headboard and flicking me in the nose.

"How dare you insinuate such a thing!"

We laughed together, and for a moment everything was perfect. Of course, nothing stayed perfect.

"There is something I need to tell you," Bellamy said. There was suddenly a firmness to his voice that put me on edge, as if he were trying to force himself to say whatever it was.

"Okay, tell me."

"I need you to get dressed first."

"Well that sounds foreboding," I joked, trying to relieve the air of the tension that was flooding it.

"I wish it were not, but you should probably be prepared for something not so great." So much for easing the tension.

"Ew," was all I could say.

We got dressed in silence, Bellamy pulling my old training leathers over my head with a look of fondness on his face that made my heart clench. And my thighs, admittedly.

When we were both clothed and Bellamy had braided my hair back, he pulled out something I never thought I would see again. Sipho's necklace—my necklace—dangled from Bellamy's pale finger. With a dashing smile, he walked behind me and secured the silver chain around my neck. Lifting my fingers to graze the small amethyst, I sighed in contentment. Now fully dressed and ready, we left our room hand-in-hand and walked down the hall.

Though my mind had been cycling through the potential things Bellamy could say, I had not guessed we would stop before a door at the end of the hall that I knew to be vacant.

"Bellamy, what is happening? No one lives in the room next to Damon's," I said, pointing at the door before us. Bellamy cringed, his face pinching together. Instead of responding, he knocked on the door three times.

"Come in," a deep voice responded, the accent the same drawling and slow rasp as Bell's. Pursing his lips, Bellamy stared at me one last time before nodding and opening the door. His strong arm wrapped around me, tucking me behind him as we stepped through the door. I managed to peek around him, endlessly curious about what we were doing there.

The room was rather plain, almost entirely empty save for the enormous bed against the far wall and a chair nearby. A male laid there beneath bright blue blankets, smiling warmly at Bellamy. I recognized him from the battle in the Fire Lands. It was King Adbeel Ayad.

"Hey, Adbeel, how are you feeling?" Bellamy asked, nerves cracking his voice.

"I am fine, but where is she? Safe? I made sure Ranbir only healed me minimally so he would be strong for her," King Adbeel rambled.

Her? Who was he talking about?

"Actually," Bellamy said just before sighing heavily. Squinting, I did my best to understand, going so far as to let my mental gates open.

Bellamy stepped to the side, revealing me to the king. I was engulfed by emotions. First, the fear and nerves from the male to my right. He thought of our love—of our demise. They tasted bitter at the back of my tongue.

But then came the king's feelings. They were the opposite. He thought of his family, of his wife. His daughter. His son. He was

overwhelmed with joy and disbelief. There, in the depths of it all, was the sweetest joy.

"Um, hi, I am Asher. I have absolutely no idea what is going on, but it is very nice to meet you." I took a step forward, waving sheepishly. Gods I probably looked like an idiot. This was my first time meeting—wait. I knew what this was about. "You are about to tell me what it is you have been hiding."

Peering over at Bellamy, I caught sight of his visible flinch. Okay, so it was bad. I always knew it was something important, but I rather thought it would be self-serving. It was the reason I felt compelled not to meet him for so long. But just then it seemed like I had been wrong. Maybe this would hurt more than it would heal.

Neither male spoke, both of them opting to simply stare at me. Did I have something on my face? Was my skin melting off? Had I suddenly become the most wretched looking creature in existence?

"Okay, well, I will start I guess," I muttered. "I am so sorry that I delayed this meeting. I wish I had a better way to explain why I did it. Or any way at all. Truly I feel like I should—"

"Asher—"

"—have a better excuse but I just wanted—"

"Asher!"

"What?"

"I need to explain this to you, but I want you to first remember that I am sorry. I am so fucking sorry," Bellamy said, stepping in front of me and grabbing my shoulders.

Eternity above, this was *bad*. My stomach rolled, my head spun, and I was fairly certain I would have shit myself if I had eaten anything recently.

Closing his eyes, he first tilted his face up, breathing heavily. Then he let his entire head fall forward and his shoulders slump. With a nod, he

turned me fully towards his king and began pushing me to the bed. Quickly, I prodded his mental shields, finding them down.

If this is some sort of family kink, I need you to know that I am not a fan and would rather not.

Bellamy snorted at my words in his head, causing King Adbeel to raise a brow. The demon ruler had sat up, his eyes tracking us as we neared. Why were they being so ominous about whatever it was? It could not have been that bad.

"Asher, this is King Adbeel Ayad. He is the ruler of Eoforhild and a descendant of the...*goddess,* Asta. He is also your—well, he is—I mean, you are—"

"You look so much like your mother," Adbeel cut in. I gasped, staring at the bedridden king with wide eyes. Bellamy choked on what could have only been air, his hair grazing my arm as he bent forward. The king merely stared at me, his lips slightly parted.

"How did you know my mother?" I asked, suspicion woven into my voice like a tapestry of unease.

Adbeel smiled, the expression soft and somewhat pained. It was then, as I looked at the demon king with his unruly curls and light brown skin, that I realized exactly what I was.

"She was my daughter."

CHAPTER THIRTY-SEVEN

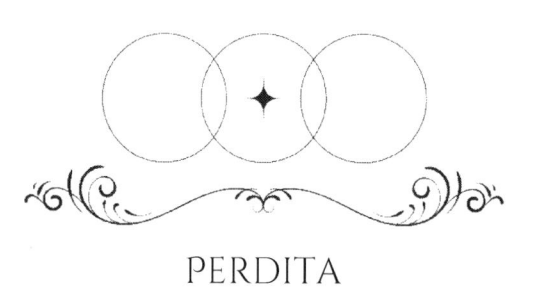

PERDITA

Damn it all to the Underworld!

Today was not going as planned. That oaf of a prince gave me double what he said he would, which should have excited me, but he had Blue and her absurd lover bring it.

She was getting on my nerves. Not because she was being clingy like other females usually were, but because she was being quite the opposite. It was no secret that I wanted her, just as it was plain as day that she did not want me.

Absurd. I was the greatest pirate to walk Alemthian. She should beg on her knees for me. Stupid, ridiculous fae.

I hated her.

Lian walked up to me where I leaned back against the starboard bulwark of the Abaddon. Her hair was shining beneath the bright light of midday as she approached. She was without curves, her chest nearly flat and her hips nonexistent. So different from Dima—from any female I had ever wanted. She was also far less alluring. Apart from when she was flirting with CJ, of course. I caught it for the second time the day before she left me, the sight of her practically humming words to the Water. CJ would giggle as Lian winked, and the two would go on chatting as they worked.

The bane of my existence stopped before me, her overly full lips splitting to show her bared teeth—too large compared to her small, upturned coffee eyes.

I wanted her.

"Blue," I signed before crossing my arms and lifting my chin. She rolled her eyes, mirroring my stance and looking at me. While I had three or four inches of height on her, she still seemed to scowl down at me. As if I were the one leaving.

"You have your money and your privateer license, which means you no longer need to steal for wealth. We expect you to behave." She said the words slowly before quickly signing, "To be good."

I could make her be good for me, if only she would let me.

"I am *the*," I signed with a sharp jolt of my hands, "Perdita Harligold. I will do what I want." Lian put her hands on her barely-there hips, glaring at me like she might stab me. I wondered what face she made when that giant, stupid fucking demon made her come. "Is your little lover not eager to leave, Blue?"

She watched my hands with an intense sort of focus before following my now-pointed finger until she noticed Henry, who stood with Fatima. She was likely finding herself stumped on lover.

I had not taught her that one yet.

Smirking, I reached forward and pinched the end of her hair. It stopped just above her breast, the strands brighter than the sky above. It was the blue of Eoforhild. It was like second nature to close the distance between us as I twirled the hair around my pointer finger. Then, ever so slowly, I released the strands and slid my finger beneath her chin.

With Dima, it would have worked. She loved how forward I was. All the females I had ever sampled agreed. Lian, sadly, did not. One second I was trying to decide how to show her what the sign meant, the next I was on my back. My lungs burned as they searched for air that was not there, my body already aching.

Just as the smiling beast of a female above me went to release my arm she had used to flip me, I called to my shadows. We were engulfed instantly, the Moon magic taking us to my quarters.

"You moron," she signed. Laughing, I pushed myself up. It was not until I was in front of her again and staring into those eyes that a brilliant idea came to me. A smile lifted my cheeks and creased my skin, making me nearly feral with the perfection of what would soon be my life.

I turned, dashing for my desk and quickly scribbling words onto a page. Lian knowing exactly what I was offering was more important than ever. Finishing with a flick of my wrist, I grabbed the paper and practically ran at her. She stared with wide eyes and downturned lips, as if the sight of me was concerning. Before she could say something like goodbye, I shoved the paper into her face, watching as she mouthed the words.

"Join my crew. We could use an Air, and you already get along with CJ. You can keep us in line for your pretty prince."

I could have Blue any time. All the time. As long as I want. Until I inevitably got sick of her, too.

Her eyes moved from the paper, to me, back to the paper, and settled on me again. Then, with all the consideration of a youngling that just learned to speak, Lian bent over and laughed. Slapping her hands together, she continued to full-body laugh, the amusement turning her face red. My hand slowly lowered, rejection sitting heavy on my chest.

"You are funny, I will give you that. Anyways, I have to get going. But make sure you stay out of trouble. I would rather not have to come find you." With that, she wiped a tear from under her eye with her middle finger before lifting it my way. *Bitch.*

Lian winked, turned, and left me.

She fucking *left* me.

My patience gone, I stormed to the door of my quarters, ripping it open. Lian was taking her place next to Henry as I stepped out. The male looked me right in the eye with the most obnoxious smirk on his face. Then, as if he knew just how badly I wanted Lian beneath me, he reached over and put his arm around her shoulders, pulling her into him. The two disappeared beneath rays of Sun magic, but not before I noticed how Lian swatted his wandering hand and opened her mouth as if to yell at him.

They were not together. I was sure of it then, even if the proof was flimsy at best. And if they were, I no longer cared much.

No one left me. Ever.

My crew all watched me from where they stood scattered about the deck. Fists bunched and body shaking from my fury, I took a deep breath and nodded. She wanted me to be good? Then I would be worse than ever.

I lifted my hands, quickly signing to the five of them. "We set sail for the Ibidem Sea. They gave us a license, so let us make them regret it."

Their cheers rumbled the deck below my feet, and for a moment I felt light again. We were made to loot. To take what we wanted. The prince and his pets might think that wrong, but that was their problem, not mine.

For now, I needed Dima back. Not only because having a siren would make life easier, but also because I now had an itch I needed to scratch. She would understand. Plus, she had been separated from her kind for so long that she craved acceptance and companionship. I was enough for her. More than enough. And she would be enough for me until I got what I really wanted.

345

Blue would catch wind of this soon, and when she did I would be ready.

I would show her trouble. She was coming back whether she wanted to or not.

CHAPTER THIRTY-EIGHT

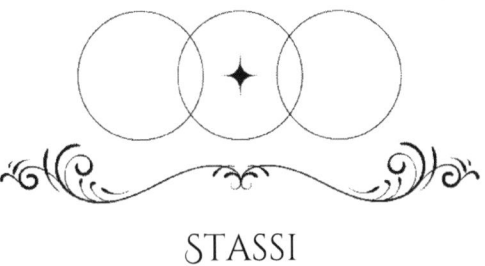

STASSI

Blackened branches sliced through my cheeks as I carelessly walked out of the forest, my arms only saved by the leathers I had stolen from the creepy creature back at the military base. No beasts approached me, all of them likely sensing what I was and rightfully fearing me. That, and Milo was being an energetic vermin at my feet.

Sighing, I pressed on.

The entire trip felt like a waste in some ways. Stella refused to come, unwilling to even leave her cabin. I wished then that I had any other option. Neither she nor Padon deserved the throne anymore. But she was better than him in the long run. We needed to focus on fixing our home. On rebuilding what had been broken. That required the empress.

She claimed that the future the Oracle foresaw required her to remain still, but I found that hard to believe. It was selfishness that pushed her—all of them. Padon. Asta. Achari. Bellamy. Fuck, even me most of the time. The only good thing about Asher was that she was different. The princess did not allow herself to be guided by self-serving whims.

With a groan, I slapped the final branch out of my way. As the light of the day met my skin and my eyes locked on Torrel's, I felt a strange sense of doom. A chill dashed down my spine, my fingers tingling with the oddest feel of magic in the air.

"Torrel, I need you to take Milo and leave," I hissed as I ran towards her, Milo dashing ahead of me. Her pink eyes scanned my face, contemplating whether or not she would follow my orders. A growl rumbled in her chest, Milo copying the battle cry as he wove between her four legs. "Please Torrel, you know I will be fine. But I need you and Milo to be safe."

Every hair on my arms seemed to rise as magic flooded the air around us, Torrel going more on edge when she began to feel it too. Something was coming.

"Now, Torrel!" I screamed. My dragon nodded, grabbed her little one with a clawed foot, and then shot into the air. She was but a speck in the distance by the time a cloud of emerald green magic appeared.

Venturae, then.

Just as I suspected, from the smoke-like substance walked the high demon of Fate and Chance.

Venturae's long braids were the same color as the leaves in a forest at night, the tips nearly touching the ground as she neared me. Her smile was large, white teeth framed by full, round lips. Her skin was black as night, shining in the daylight. She wore a dress made of strung crystals that exposed sections of her skin with each step.

"Venturae, what a pleasure." Sweetness coated my tongue, the sound of my voice practically a hum.

"Stassi, there's no need to lie."

"Fine. I want to kill you where you stand. Happy?"

"Immensely," she remarked, chuckling. Then she stopped before me, her hands behind her back and a smirk upon her face. "You test fate, Stassi."

"Of course I do," I said, crossing my arms. "Padon has a vision for fate and wishes to remove chance, right? Is that why you're here?"

"Oh please, he isn't thinking of you at the moment. The idiot cares about his mortal pet more than anything else." The two of us simultaneously rolled our eyes. He had made a mistake sending Venturae. She never was his biggest fan. "But, you are messing with the rule of Eternity. I can feel the way the magic of chance pulses and writhes within me. Fate is weaker than normal, and it pushes me towards you."

Fate and Chance had always been one of the most volatile of the ten original seeds. Venturae called it hypnotic. The two opposites warred inside of her, shoving her towards different paths so that she may alter the future in their favor. While she didn't see what was to come like the Oracles of this world, Venturae could change the future irrevocably. With her magic she could incinerate entire strings of possibility. All she had to do was listen to the beasts upon each shoulder.

Which meant that if she was here and telling me I was weakening fate itself, then she was very likely being urged to eliminate me.

"What do the monsters within you say you must do?"

"My darling fate wishes for you to cease this nonsense or die. You are destroying divine purpose," she responded, shrugging off the insinuation that she would kill me at the behest of the magic in her body. "On the other hand, fate seems to have been suddenly fed with whatever occurred mere minutes ago. Something you did just pushed the future back on the course it was meant to take."

"How did you know I was here?" I asked, changing the subject. Stella being seen by anyone would be bad, but Venturae had a habit of losing herself to the seed within her, and I wasn't sure how her magic would react if she saw the empress or even merely found out she lived on this world.

"Followed the fetch, duh."

"Of course you did, the nasty creature."

"It already knew you, so it was the easiest option," she shrugged. "Plus, I thought we might benefit from a chat."

"About?" I asked with a raise of my brow.

"You coming back home."

"Venturae, I fear you've lost your mind in your old age." My words were meant to be haughty, but they came out far more strained. "Padon will kill me if I come back. Then you will be short three high demons instead of two."

"Chance calls to me, Stassi. It says we are on the cusp of great change. The two of them argue within my bones. They push and pull and shout and scream. Of all the things they fight over, they agree on one thing. That is the importance of getting you home. Something about you being here is changing things, and not in our favor." Her words held a haunting edge, but I couldn't help myself from clarifying.

"Our favor? Or Padon's?"

"Shamay's," she corrected. I stilled, looking up at her in horror. What could me being here possibly do to hurt our entire world? I was trying to save it for fuck's sake! Venturae's head quirked to the side, her eyes going distant. As if she were listening to someone speak. "Stassi, tell me, have you found Stella?"

Every ounce of my self-control was tested then as I willed my face to remain straight. Giving away Stella would do the exact opposite of what I was attempting to accomplish. It would ruin everything,

"How would I find her so quickly when none of us have sensed her in fifteen millennia?" I asked instead, opting not to answer with a lie.

A smile split Venturae's face, fate and chance warring upon their respective halves. "How indeed."

"Does Padon know you're here? That I'm here?"

"His fetch had already checked here, so he assumes you aren't. I cornered the fetch after and told it to keep looking on this world just in case. Which was why it came straight to me instead of him. As far as he knows, I'm huddled up in my manor willing Fate and Chance to side with us." Her smile became even more devious as she lifted her hand and twirled a pink strand of my hair. Great, she was going to negotiate. "Come home with me and I will hide you away until he calms down. Let him take the girl and this world, then he won't be angry anymore."

"If I say no?"

"Then I will be forced to tell him that you are here." When I merely scoffed in response and slapped her hand away, Venturae straightened, her forest-green gaze bearing down on me. "And I will tell him that our empress lies in wait within a forest full of creatures of Death and Creation."

I couldn't stop the gasp that slipped from my lips, my jaw dropping open as I stared at the high demon before me. She knew. How the fuck did she know? It had to have been those foul things inside of her, the only seed of the ten that was somehow capable of thought—of *will*.

"You don't understand, we will all die if we don't restore the seeds. How can we do that with Padon running our entire world into the ground?" I asked—maybe even pleaded. I couldn't leave, not before everything was said and done. While this world meant nothing to me, it meant everything to Stella and Asta. I might have hated them in that moment, but I never wanted their heartbreak.

351

"Well, I think—" Venturae cut herself off, both of us sensing the swell of magic as it came from not the forest, but the ocean to our right. Heads jerking towards the source, we both watched in horror as Jonah appeared from the deep brown mist of his magic. Even worse was the realization that we were currently upon a world that was on the verge of war. Jonah would be horribly—terrifyingly—strong here.

He wore plain black trousers, his cream long-sleeved top billowing in the wind as he walked. His skin was a light brown, the yellow undertones nearly hiding the blue blush beneath. With every step he took our way, his upturned chocolate eyes seemed to dig deeper into us.

"Stassi darling, how are you?" he asked, opening his arms wide. I felt his magic seep from him, the sparkling cloud of deep brown smacking into me and willing me to be peaceful.

Growling, I hit him with my own magic as I simultaneously fought off his. If what Stella said was true, then we were capable of more feeling than we realized. Perhaps that meant I could find a deeper sense of virtue within him now that I was back on Alemthian.

We continued to face off, the two of us grunting from the force of attempting the other to submit. As expected, males proved themselves weak when push came to shove. Jonah let out a final groan of displeasure and then dropped to his knees in surrender. Raising his hands, he looked up at me and smirked.

"You win."

"I always do."

"Padon would disagree. In fact, I think he'd be quite interested to hear you were able to suggest that to me at all." There was a hint of a threat there in the depths of his words. "Tell me, do you think he knows you're on the same world as his beloved?"

"She isn't his beloved."

"Testy, aren't we? Care to explain to the class why you are suddenly so defensive of our emperor's mortal pet?"

"What can I say, I'm a sucker for an underdog," I replied with a shrug. Jonah only smiled wider at my words, as if I had said something exciting. "Why are you here?"

"Boredom, mostly. I want war. Something new and interesting. You're offering that."

"Battle is inevitable but getting Anastasia home will make it smoother. Less likely for chaos on our shores," Venturae said.

"Iniko brings chaos wherever he goes. War will come to Shamay, regardless of what happens on this pitiful world." Jonah continued to smile up at me as he spoke, an odd sort of knowing in his eyes that, quite honestly, terrified me. "There is a throne to win, after all."

Eternity damn them all.

"How about this," I said, straightening my spine. "You both leave and I don't kill you where you stand."

I had always been one to act stronger than I was. It was the only way to compensate for how little magic I possessed. Alemthian changed things. More magic coursed through my body than ever before. Maybe I could actually follow through on the threat.

Jonah snorted loudly, staring at me with humor in his eyes. When I did not back down, his gaze went wide. I thought I had him. That perhaps he was finally scared. But of course, that wasn't the case at all. The idiot bent forward and burst into laughter.

Laughter!

"It won't be funny when I'm bathing in your blood and holding your seed in my fist!" My shouts were met with his abrupt silence, my tone finally forcing him to take me seriously. He stood, looking at me as if he were seeing me clearly for the first time. Sadly, there was no fear in his eyes.

"How about *this*. You come with us, and we don't kill you where you stand, you pathetic—"

"Jonah, fate grows uneasy," Venturae cut in.

"—ridiculous—"

"Jonah…" she said once more.

"—unimpressive—"

"Chance feeds, Jonah!" Venturae shouted.

"—weak little creature!"

It all happened rather quickly after that. Jonah's hands gripped my arms as his magic erupted from him. At the same time, I let my own magic free, groaning with the effort it took to shove into his chest. Venturae ignored us both, screaming with more terror than seemed necessary.

At our backs, the real threat loomed. A burst of swirling white and black magic slammed into the three of us. The blast hit me, sending my body soaring through the sky and then crashing back onto the grass below.

Lifting my head with a hiss of pain, I caught sight of Stella as she approached. She was a vision of sun and moon, the two colliding to tear down the universe. Her hands were held outwards and kept low at hip level. Black surrounded the right half of her body and white surrounded the left, splitting her into night and day. She stared at us with eyes entirely void of color. Each step made the ground beneath her quake, the clouds above us turning a deep gray as they swirled.

Despite being banished, Stella was still the holder of Sun and Moon, the rightful empress of Shamay. The ethers themselves bowed to her will. We were reminded of that as lightning streaked the sky, followed closely by a boom of thunder.

"You have reminded me just how horrid life is as a high demon," Stella drawled. The tone of her voice was the antithesis to her stance of fury

and power. Jonah peered up at her in pure terror. There was no being in existence that was as feared as the high demon of Sun and Moon.

"Stella—My Empress—it's so wonderful to see you again." Jonah adjusted, letting his body fall into a deep bow. A giggle escaped my lips when his fingers touched her bare toes. Pathetic.

Venturae was not far, standing and making her way to the fallen empress. She shook with each step closer. "We must, of course we must. She is the empress. No, we cannot make decisions based on your whims. Stop arguing. Please, I need to focus."

The high demon of Fate and Chance continued to mumble as she approached Stella, falling into the same bow at the empress's feet. But then Stella looked at me, fury blazing within her eyes. The wrath of a high demon.

"Anastasia, get back where you belong. She needs you."

Scoffing, I pushed myself to a standing position and immediately crossed my arms. How did she not see this situation as proof of our need for her to return to Shamay?

"Just because she is your great granddaughter plus like twenty greats—"

"Twenty-nine," Stella cut in.

"What?"

"Twenty-eight generations of Asta's line have come and gone. Asher is the only living member of the twenty-ninth generation that came from the love between a high demon and a mortal. I don't think I need to remind you how important she truly is, beyond sentimentality. Now. Go."

How dare she order me around!

I meant to say something, to stand up for myself in that moment, but all I could bring myself to do was stick my tongue out at Venturae and

Jonah before giving Stella a curt nod. Then I made a break for it, shouting Torrel's name as I went.

CHAPTER THIRTY-NINE

ASHER

King Adbeel had insisted on getting out of bed. Ranbir had not fully healed him during the battle, agreeing to do patchwork and then vowing to come back to him later. In that time, the Healer had not returned. But the king was a demon, and his blood made quick work of the smaller wounds.

Despite that, Bellamy was still adamantly against letting his father figure out of bed.

Father figure. How was it that Bellamy's father figure was also my last living blood relative? What was even going on?

I felt frozen as the two argued, both of their eyes flashing to me more often than not. For my part I remained still and silent—thinking.

What was I supposed to do? Just accept this as fact and call him grandfather? I had never had grandparents. My parents—no, not parents. They could not have been if Zaib Ayad was actually my mother. So who were the fae that claimed me as their own?

Regardless, they had been over a millenia when I was born. Their parents were gone from the world, their Ending having come. Mia's parents were dead as well. She was unwilling to speak of them in the slightest, which brokered no arguments. Xavier's parents had died during the Great War— had there even really been a war back then? What was the truth?

Dizzy—I felt dizzy.

Too many possibilities and lies and truths swarmed me. I was drowning in the tidal wave of reality as it crashed upon fantasy. Doom coated the air and suffocated me long before the water could. I was dying.

My hand reached up and clutched my chest. Gods I felt small. Breakable. Weak. Yet I had survived far too much to fall at the hands of answers I had been waiting a year for.

The males stopped speaking. I knew not because of the silence, as I was relatively sure the ringing in my ears had been blocking out their commotion the entire time, but because of the way their thoughts bombarded me with images of myself.

No, I would not let myself be the pathetic female that I saw in their heads. Pitiful as I looked, there was always farther I could fall. I would not let that happen.

"So, you are my grandfather. How exciting. Good to have family. Yes, family is important. Now, if you will excuse me, I have work to do." With that, I straightened, nodded, and rotated until I was facing the door. This was fine, I would get out and be fine.

I knew what was real. This changed *nothing*.

I was fine.

"Asher! Please!" Adbeel sounded so much like Bellamy. A deep drawl with a rasp at the ends and a tongue that sounded a bit too heavy for his mouth. How could I be a part of him when Bellamy so clearly was too? No. Not possible.

That was fine, I could leave knowing it was lies and run away until they forgot about me.

"I am sorry that I did not rescue you." As probably expected, that stopped me in my tracks. A sort of hum seemed to escape the king as I pivoted. His absurdly dark eyes were on me, staring at my face as if he could see the mother he claimed was mine.

I acknowledged then that it was the truth. It was why I could portal. Why my magic was magic and made no sense to the fae. Nothing had been put inside of me, I had been born with this thrumming in my veins. Willing me to kill and fight and conquer. I was the daughter of queens and kings past. I was a ruler by blood and right and everything that mattered. I was an Ayad.

Knees shaking, I stumbled my way closer to the king, stopping mere feet from him.

"I knew about you. Zaib had been relatively quiet for half a century. She claimed that she had found love and wanted to stay there. Malcolm came back every now and then, telling me all about the male she had fallen in love with and the good she was doing. He asked to stay awhile, just to keep an eye on her. The battles had stopped. Solei thought it a good idea to enrich our alliance by allowing our son and daughter to remain. And who were we to dictate who they could love? Did it disgust me at the time? Yes. I hated the thought of her marrying a fae. But I loathed the idea of her unhappiness more."

Adbeel wiped at his face, his arm resting on the chair beside him. He seemed to need the support. Bellamy was nearby, watching the king with nervous eyes. I knew he was not surprised by this turn of events, yet it still baffled me just how unphased he was.

"But then, after fifty years of thinking her happy and listening when she insisted we not visit, I received word from my daughter. She was in a panic, the note so quickly scribbled it was nearly illegible. According to her, she had been trapped. They had held her prisoner for the entire length of her stay. She said that the orange-haired queen had tortured her, and I thought perhaps they had forced Malcolm to lie. But in that time, Zaib *had* found love. She had become enamored with her guard. The son of the Royal Tomorrow, Florencia Daniox."

My mother?

No, my paternal grandmother.

"The correspondence had claimed she was pregnant, fairly far along in fact. She told me her magic was weak, but that they were finding their way home. She encouraged me not to come get them, as I would only give away their location if I was even able to find them. At the very end, she said she was confident the baby was male. She promised to name him Zohar."

A soft cry parted the lips that Bellamy had formed into a line. Adbeel's words were haunting. Anyone could tell that they were leading to a horrific end. No joy or peace would find the long-dead princess. My mother.

"No less than a month later, I received word from Mia Mounbetton. She said if I stepped one foot into her realm, she would kill my daughter. She asked for gold, soldiers, land, everything. I agreed to all of it. Anything at all. I just wanted my daughter and son back. She sent only Zaib's head and the promise of my doom if I came for my son. But I did it anyways. With me I brought two ships full of fighters. All that offered was a bloody battle and no sign of him. I meant to go again, to fight for him until my dying breath, but then she sent a hand bearing his ring—*our family ring*. She said I broke the rules. And I knew then that I could not see my grandson's severed limbs. I needed to kill them all."

My lips quivered, my heart breaking at the realization that I could have had a real mother. One of my own. But Mia took that too.

360

"Solei, my late wife, was overcome with the grief of our loss. She cried for days on end. Screams could be heard from miles outside of the castle in The Royal City. And when the screams stopped, it was not because she was better, it was because she had jumped from her tower window to the rocky cliffs below. She had been silenced by her own will to not live without her son and daughter. I had held onto her so tightly that I thought she might shatter, though she was already broken beyond repair. Screams tore up my throat and seemed to release more magic than I thought I had possessed. Those piercing sounds willed Solei's out of her too, I think— darkness meeting light. And they made The Mist just as my wife begged me to stop the fighting if only for the realm."

I wanted so badly to ask what that last bit had to do with my mom. I chose silence though, as it seemed he was not yet done.

"I did listen at first. The Mist protected us, the fighting ended. I mourned and promised the demons of Eoforhild safety. From my lips came promises of peace and unity among our kind—all kinds, really. There was no longer fear that they might lose mothers, fathers, sons, or daughters. But then, my spies said the fae king and queen had suddenly bore a son. A son, so soon after my daughter had expected one."

Bellamy cleared his throat, practically squirming in his skin. I was still as a statue. We both knew what Adbeel would say before he said it.

"So I went after him. I killed dozens of guards before coming across a couple walking alongside the smallest little male with pointed ears and dark hair. He was so very pale and his eyes were so very blue, but I thought perhaps he took after his father I never got to meet. They were terrified when they saw me, the blood coating me not any help. The female ran to the nearby trees, disappearing for only a minute or so before returning and taking a fighting stance. I could sense the magic within the youngling. It had to be him. I remember thinking that as I slaughtered the male and female who were guarding him. They begged and screamed, battled and fell. I tore them to shreds and took my grandson home."

A sob itched in my chest, asking if I might please free it. But no, these tears were not meant to be shed. This was a moment for my grandfather to mourn and cry as he recalled killing my other grandparents.

My other family.

Silence coalesced around us, clotting like the blood I shared with the demon king.

"But it was not my grandson. Bellamy truly was the fae rulers' son. The magic I sensed had been forced into his body. And now, as I think back, I realize that the female who ran must have had you in her arms. She must have taken you and hid you amongst the trees before coming back to fight. You had been right there, but I missed you. And I mourned you when I realized Bellamy was not my grandson. But I did not help you. Did not come back. Did not do anything other than rot away. And I am so, so sorry."

We all took collective breaths, each deeper than the last. I was light-headed by the time I finally found my voice.

"I need time," I whispered. My eyes darted to Bellamy, who grimaced at me before blanching at the sight of Adbeel. "Bellamy, please take me to Sterling."

Bellamy's eyes went wide as his gaze flicked to me. "You want Sterling?"

"Yes, I need to see him. Right away. This conversation can be finished another time." Reaching out for the sleeve of Bellamy's shirt, I moved my gaze to the king and asked, "Is that alright with you, Your Majesty?"

Reluctantly, Adbeel nodded. I watched as he deflated, sinking back into his chair with heartbreak on his face. My heart hurt, but my mind knew better than to let it be pushed any further. I was not okay. I could acknowledge that now. I could fix it—ask for help.

After another second of looking at Adbeel, I tugged Bellamy out into the hallway and willed us to the dungeons. We landed at the top of the stairs, not exactly right, but close.

Bellamy sighed and led the way.

CHAPTER FORTY

ASHER

"Asher," Bellamy called from behind me. I had overtaken him once the line of cells came into view so that I would not snap at him for putting Sterling in the *dungeons*. "Asher."

"I am not ignoring you, I am thinking and…overwhelmed. Time. Please, Bell, just give me some time." I continued walking down the paths, an odd and faint sound coming from the distance.

"Are you mad at me? Disgusted?" His voice was hesitant, full of nerves and fear that I had somehow not anticipated. Of course he was waiting for me to explode. How often had I pushed him away and refused to listen? If there was anything I had learned though, it was that remaining alone in my feelings did nothing to stop them from happening.

So I stopped walking. With slow, measured breaths I turned around and faced Bellamy. He looked so very scared as he approached me; a male walking to the noose. I vowed in that moment never to hide from him again.

"No, I am not mad. Not at you, or Adbeel, or anyone but Mia and Xavier. Maybe you made poor choices or mistakes, but so did I. All of us have," I soothed, reaching up and grabbing his face. He leaned into the touch, his eyes closing as he sighed in relief. "I love you more than anything, Bellamy. We will figure all of this out together when I feel sane enough to do so."

Just then, a piercing scream reverberated off the walls of the Pike dungeons. A chill clawed up my spine, fear digging into my bones.

"Sterling!" I shouted as I bolted forward. Bellamy was following, saying something I could not hear beyond the pain that was radiating from the cell just ahead. I pushed on, moving towards the open door of bars before coming to a halt. The scene before us was nothing like what I had anticipated.

The sounds were not coming from Sterling's cell at all, his likely further down the hall. Two males were inside, one against the wall with his wrists held aloft by thick iron chains, and the other no more than a foot away from him, a bloody blade in his hand and red soaking through his white clothes.

"Four brothers and three sisters, that was who your filthy wife made her leave behind." The words that Ranbir hissed were jarring. I had never heard him speak in such a way, with malice and vengeance in his tone.

Xavier snarled in response, and I watched as the chunk of skin missing from his cheek healed over. The fae king's body twitched as blood stopped seeping from wounds I could only assume were Ranbir's thanks for his lost wife. Gods, he was torturing him and then healing him right after.

"You are a waste of space and breath. I would say that this is a spouse for a spouse, but your life is not worth half of what my wife's was."

365

And then, without so much as glancing back at Bellamy and I, Ranbir leaned forward and began slicing into Xavier.

He practically dug out Xavier's flesh, ripping away chunks of skin until he reached what looked like bone.

"Rib cage," Bellamy whispered into my ear. I dared a peek at him, finding his face stoic. There was an air of indifference to him, like what we were witnessing did not matter to or affect him.

When I looked back towards the pair in front of us, Ranbir had finished slicing and was now using the hilt of the blade to shatter Xavier's ribs. The king's screams were surprisingly quiet for the extent of torture he was enduring. Ranbir still did not face us, but I could feel the fury pouring from him just as quickly as Xavier's blood left the gaping wound in his chest.

"Ranbir, stop!" I surprised myself with the order, though the Healer surprised me even more when he immediately ceased his hacking. Bellamy's warm hand met my left hip, his thumb stroking my skin through his shirt. "Heal him, please."

All I could hear was the deep animal-like growl that Ranbir emitted as I approached them. He reached forward and smacked his hand onto Xavier's cheek, the movement sharp. But the king's skin began to knit back together, and within minutes Ranbir was panting from the exertion of fixing such a wound.

I gripped Ranbir's free hand, squeezing it tightly and tugging him away. The Healer followed my lead with slumped shoulders. Once we reached the cell door, I tugged him into a tight embrace. More pain than ever seemed to sit heavy upon him. A lifetime worth of loss so substantial that it was crushing his heart.

"Do not sink to their level. Do not let them make you into something you are not," I whispered to him, pushing onto my toes and pulling his head down until our foreheads touched. A sob slipped from his lips, and then his arms were wrapping around me too. After a few seconds, he nodded and released me. Not wanting to push my luck, I freed him as

well and flicked my head towards the dark corridor. "Go eat something and get some rest. I will handle this, okay?"

No fight existed within Ranbir anymore. He was a shell that had washed up upon the shore, its lovely sea—its *home*—lost. Pursing his lips, he dipped his chin and then left, not looking back.

"Thank you, Ash. Thank you so much." Xavier's words quickly stoked the flame that constantly burned within me. My fury knew no bounds as I whipped around and faced the pathetic male. Bellamy's hand snapped out, tugging my arm and forcing my body to collide with his.

"Do you want me to stay or should I give you space to do what you must? Give me an order, Princess," he breathed against my ear. I shivered, a surprising wave of lust making bumps rise on my skin. When I titled my face up towards his I found the same need mirrored on him. "I am yours to command, now and forever."

"Stay," was all I managed to say. I needed to focus. To remind myself that there was purpose to what would come. With a nod in agreement, the prince released my arm and slunk back into the shadows of the corridor. I did not hesitate to storm towards Xavier, my magic swirling inside of me like a storm. Like a reckoning.

"I love you, Asher. Thank you for your grace. I promise that I

will—"

"Grace? That was not *grace*," I seethed. Xavier's head reared back, smacking against the stone wall. His eyes were wide, the dark depths pleading. I placed my hands on his head, the contact making it easier to tug on his memories. And while I stole every piece of knowledge we might need in the coming days, I continued to speak. "I do not doubt your feeble love for me. I see it—*feel it*—here in your mind."

Bellamy had remained back, his presence a siren's call. He did not come to me, nor did he speak. Instead, he was a silent beast ready to attack. Waiting patiently for that command.

Xavier began to shake as I took and took, not caring for how it might hurt him. No, I was relishing in that pain of his.

"Perhaps you should have loved me *better*, Xavier. Maybe if you had loved five-year-old me enough to not torture me then it would not be too late for you now." Tears welled in his eyes, one or two escaping with each blink. I continued sifting through memories, moving faster and shattered more. My magic was a careless force as it began to shred him of everything that made him who he was. "I did not stop Ranbir because you finally chose to stand up for me against Mia. Ranbir is too good to lower himself, that is the only reason."

He moaned in agony as I toyed with the power within him, sparking it to life upon his fingertips. I willed him to burn himself, the flames scorching his skin and making the air smell foul. A single scream was all I allowed him before I took those too, ordering his silence.

"Luckily, I know someone who has no qualms with stooping down to your level. In fact, they exist perpetually in that wicked darkness you reside within." I smirked as I spoke, hoping he saw the vindication in my gaze.

Freeing him from my wrath, I waited in silence. I knew he would speak. His nature would not allow him to remain quiet—small.

"Will it be you? Do you think yourself strong enough to kill the only father you have ever known?" he challenged with a tone of both fire and ice. I laughed, throwing my head back before shaking it.

"Mia requires all of my vengeance, actually. But," I added, looking back at Bellamy. He was difficult to see, but I caught the way he tilted his head in that perfect way he always did. "I am told that marriage involves sharing. What is mine is yours and all of that stuff. So I feel it necessary to share the fun with my fiancé."

Bellamy took his turn to chuckle, his form coming from out of the shadows like a corrupt god. I watched in unabashed glee as he came to us with a devious smile on his face and a crinkle at the corner of his eyes. His

dimples did not soften him today. Rather, they made him look all the more dangerous. When he stopped at my side, he leaned forward, baring his teeth.

"I want you to know that what is about to happen is not punishment for what you did to me, but for having the audacity to do even worse to Asher."

And then Bellamy sprung.

I did not flinch when the prince used his black fire to slowly cut through each of the king's limbs.

I did not cry when the son slowly dug out his father's beating heart.

I did not mourn when the body of the male who raised me burned to ash.

As Bellamy stood, his body drenched in gore, I latched onto his face and brought our lips together. We stood there and sealed our freedom with a kiss.

***

Sterling was bloody and bruised, his body sprawled out on a small cot in a cell that felt like it was ages away from Xavier's. I would kill Bellamy for putting the boy in there if I were not desperately clinging to him as proof of his existence, of our freedom and safety. My poor fiancé could not even relieve himself in privacy earlier.

"Sterling!" I shouted, ripping the keys from the wall across his cell and running to unlock the door. The prince jolted awake, his head flinging up as if in a panic. "I am so sorry, let me get you out of there right away!"

"Why are you so eager to help him, Ash?" Bellamy's question was soft, as if he knew he were nearing an edge but was unsure as to how close he might be to falling. His body was still covered in his father's blood, and

both of us shook with the heaviness of the day's emotions. "I understand that you became acquainted after realizing what had happened, but why is he suddenly so important to you?"

"Bell, he was being tortured beneath the palace the entire time. He is just as much a victim as I am—more so, really—and he deserves better than this," I declared before ripping open the door and rushing towards Sterling.

He sat up, a weak smile on his face as he opened his arms to me.

I welcomed the embrace, tucking his head into my shoulder and whispering, "Everything is going to be okay. I am going to get you home just like I promised."

One of the softest cries I had ever heard met my ears. Tears crawled down my cheeks at the sound of Sterling breaking. Though he did not remember what had been done to him, the trauma must have still been there. Like Lara. Even after I stole her painful memories, she still seemed to exist in a perpetual state of moroseness.

"We will find out how to get your memories back too. Maybe this is some kind of magic we have yet to understand. I will work on it, okay?" He nodded against my skin, still holding me tightly as I bent down before him.

I could feel Bellamy's gaze on me—us. I knew he was jealous, the taste of it there in the air. For the first time since I had been taken, my magic felt full and free. It was all too easy for the thoughts of everyone in Pike to swarm me now. I took a moment to appraise my mental shields. Maybe it was time for something new. Something better.

As I lifted Sterling to a standing position and tucked his arm around my shoulders, I crafted a new gate, one that sparkled black and silver, the golden lock and red chains bright in my mind.

"Portaling will be easier," Bellamy insisted, grabbing both of us before I could argue. Sterling cried out as the shadows forced us through

time and space, tugging and ripping us apart until we appeared in the startlingly white space that was the infirmary.

"I think I might be sick," Sterling muttered. Bellamy let out a devious chuckle, to which I responded with an elbow straight into his gut. He keeled over with a grunt that left me smiling.

"Look, now both of you might be sick. How exciting that for once it is not me!" I cheered, slapping both of them firmly on the back before looking towards Ranbir. He smirked, making the hairs that had fallen from the knot atop his head twitch where they framed his face. He was as handsome as ever, his white clothes clean once more. His calm stature and strong jaw were met with a newfound fullness to him. As if he had begun to heal perhaps. Maybe he had needed to hurt Xavier, to find vengeance in something, in order to move forward. Still, I was glad I had not let him continue.

"Life was quite dull without you," he joked, pushing himself to stand. "You gave me a scare earlier." We both knew he did not mean the moment in the dungeons.

Xavier was taken care of, we will not speak about any of it again.

My voice in his mind had his eyes closing, a brief nod all he offered me in response before he looked at me once more.

"I know," I said aloud, closing the space and pulling him into a hug. He laughed, but returned the gesture. "I am so sorry. The things they did…well, it is better left unsaid. Regardless, thank you, as always, for bringing me back and saving me from my reckless self."

"An honor. Always." I could hear it in his thoughts, his returned thanks for doing the same for him. With a smile, I let him go.

"Now that the sappiness is out of the way, I need you to look over Sterling if you are well enough. It seems someone," I paused, looking over my shoulder at Bellamy. He stood straight once more, glaring at Sterling from the corner of his eyes. "Has attacked him."

Bellamy's gaze flicked my way momentarily, his chin rising as if daring me to chastise him. Not even a full day of being my fiancé and already he was challenging me.

Careful, demon. I would not want you to forget which of us is truly in charge here.

Careful, Princess. I would not want you to forget what I will do to you if you dare leave me for this mortal idiot.

Unfortunately for you, I rather like the sound of forever, just the two of us.

Bellamy flinched at that, as if my claiming him forever was somehow painful.

I am yours until the day I die.

There was an odd tone to his mental voice, a morose edge to it that made me fearful of his choice of words.

"Well, I am sure I can fix him up in no time. He will probably have guests soon, would not want him to be bloody and bruised for that."

"Guests?" Sterling inquired as Bellamy walked him over to sit down on one of the beds.

My magic strayed, so eager to be free that even my newly formed gates could not keep it fully contained. I tasted her before she arrived, not even portaling stopping me from sensing her coming.

Noe's golden brown hair smacked me directly in the face as she appeared in front of me. It was not long until she was whipping her head around as she shouted, "Where is she?"

Even then, I had no chance to reply before she was tackling me to the ground. We smacked onto the hard floors amidst chuckles and shrieks. Noe's lips began peppering kisses all over my face, her squeals of glee so loud that they seemed to echo. I laughed at her, trying and failing to get her off me.

"Noe, get off!" My demand was spoken between giggles, causing it to lose its effect. She continued on, only stopping when someone lifted her away from me. Damon was cackling as he dragged her backwards, muttering something about her being crazy. Cyprus appeared above me, lifting me by my waist and hauling me upwards. Right as my feet met the floor, I was wrapped into another firm hug.

"We missed you, beautiful," Cyprus hummed, nuzzling his face into the crook of my neck.

"Nothing but a bunch of puppies," I mumbled as I returned the hug.

"My turn, move!" Henry practically tore Cyprus off of me, tossing him somewhat to the side.

"Pumpkin, you are looking especially ripe today," I teased as he smiled down at me. Then he lifted me, spinning us as he held my lower thighs. I grabbed his shoulders, praying to Eternity that he did not drop me. "Put me down you lunatic!"

"Never!" he shouted, pushing me further up and over his shoulder. I squealed, pounding on his back as he began to make a run for the exit. We were met with a fierce wind that shoved Henry off his feet. As the Sun teetered back, I flipped over his shoulder, nearly landing on my face before I was caught by an upwards gust of air.

"Oh please, like we would just let you take her." Lian's voice was chiding, but her smile was iridescent as she slowly lowered me to the ground and then ran at me. I caught her in my arms as she dove, the two of us laughing from our place on the ground. When she punched me in the shoulder, I did not so much as complain, too happy to have them there. To know they were real. "Leave us like that again and I will kill you myself, Asher."

"Noted." I smiled her way, savoring the taste of their love for me. It was both rich and sweet, like melted chocolate on the tongue.

Standing, I offered Lian a hand up, but she swatted it away. Antagonistic little menace. She pointed behind me, and though I was genuinely concerned for my safety, I still rotated. There, standing back and watching everything, were not only Farai and Jasper—who was healed and whole—but Nicola and Kafele too.

"How?" I gasped out, trying to make sense of seeing Nicola and Kafele here. Safe.

"Tell me you did not think these morons could come up with a plan like this," Nicola responded, beaming at me with watery eyes. I laughed, moving towards them.

Walking was all I could manage after so many reunions, especially when this one was the most devastatingly perfect. My three best friends tugged me into them when I got close enough, the four of us laughing as we cried. Our lives had changed so much in the last year. Still, we all four breathed, and that was a gift.

"I am so sorry, Ash," Nicola whispered as she leaned her forehead against mine. "Letting it play out the way it did was the only salvageable future I could see. What they did to you—the lies—I cannot apologize enough."

"There is no need, Nic. We are all here, together and safe. That is what matters. You are what matters." I looked over her shoulder, nodding at Kafele where he stood slightly behind his wife. His terror, suspicion, and possessiveness soaked the air around him, his focus honed on Nicola. While I had never been as close to him as I had Farai, Jasper, and Nicola, I most definitely adored him. He was perfect for her. Stoic, fierce, protective, unwavering, cautious. "I am glad you are here too, Kafele."

"Yes, well, we had very little choice. If Nicola says jump, you either ask her how high or you get your ass handed to you." They laughed. I did my best to pretend like I was not terrified of losing them all and laughed along.

With that, I turned and faced Ranbir again. He had fully healed Sterling, but his face was scrunched as he held his palm against the prince's

cheek. Bellamy was beside them and watching me, the beautiful pride on his face melting into nerves as he took in my expression.

"Ranbir, is there something wrong with his mind?" Sterling seemed to listen with bated breath, leaning towards me as I spoke. "I cannot find his memories from the last year."

"I do sense something off. His brain has suffered a sort of trauma. It reminds me of what happened to Lara after you attacked her."

"Woah there. I fought back. That is an important fact," I rebutted. Ranbir chuckled, removing his hand from Sterling's face.

"Regardless, it is similar. Any chance you did it and do not remember?"

"Absolutely not. Maybe if we get drunk tonight I will tell you all about what they did to me and what I did in return, but that is not one of them. They had Sterling in those dungeons for the last year. He was being impersonated by a Shifter the entire time. Why they took those memories, I am not sure, but they did it somehow."

"You talking about me like I am not here would be funny if what you were saying was not horrifying," Sterling grumbled, crossing his arms.

"Well, I did try to tell you before," I teased. "At least now you know I was not crazy."

"Debatable."

"You wound me." I feigned outrage, bringing my hand to my heart. He shook his head, chuckling softly. If only I could help him. For all my strength and abilities, I still could not figure this out. It was infuriating. "We also need to start making decisions about this war."

"Wrong," Bellamy cut in, smiling widely as he grabbed me by the hips and pulled me forward. "We have a wedding to plan."

"Ew, Bell! Why are you covered in so much blood?" Noe asked, scrunching her nose.

"The war takes priority," I clarified, glaring at Bellamy.

"Meh, wedding first, war later."

"Bellamy," I growled.

"Asher," he crooned.

"Sterling?" I whipped my head around at the sound of the new voice, catching sight of the girl's golden curls before I really registered who it was.

"Gen?" Sterling asked in response, the disbelief in his tone heartbreaking.

Genevieve stood in front of Henry, the rays of light from his magic fading from her form. She looked beautiful, dressed in clothes that I knew were mine and seemed to fit her just as perfectly as they did me. Tears made her brown eyes glassy and the emotions that flooded her left her cheeks flushed.

Sterling pushed off the bed with wide eyes and open arms, looking as if he might crumble at the sight of her. Brother and sister ran to each other, both of them sobbing. And when he caught her in his arms and held her so tight it must have hurt, I thought it had to have been one of the most lovely things I ever bore witness to.

"Well, with that sorted out," I said, clearing my throat of the emotions, "back to the war."

Genevieve took her turn to silence me, letting go of her brother and using her fist to whip herself around. Knuckles connected with my left eye, snapping my head back and sending pain through my neck. Gods she packed a good punch.

Chaos broke loose then, with the majority of the room flocking around me. I grabbed my face, feeling liquid seep from my eyebrow. A really good punch, apparently. With my good eye, I watched as Henry

grabbed Genevieve around her torso and held her back, Sterling looking on with a comical face of horror.

"That is for my people you slaughtered, you bitch!" Genevieve shouted, reaching out as if to claw at me.

"People who were attempting to kill innocents!" Noe yelled back, her hands balled at her sides and leaking shadows as she stepped in front of me. Bellamy was shaking from fury as he held his arms around me.

"Leash your girl or I will hang her from one," he hissed to Henry. It was too much, everyone's emotions were coagulating, rushing me and attempting to convince me they were my own. Too many reunions. Too many beings. Too many feelings.

Too many.

"Everyone calm down!"

My magic brought each of them to heal, silence overtaking the space. Glorious, sweet silence.

"Genevieve, I am sorry for what I did to your soldiers. I wish there had been other options, but there were not. You are more than right to hate me, but this is not the time or the place to hash it out." The mortal princess huffed as she slackened in Henry's arms, his face showing every emotion he felt.

Anger. Lust. Fear. Obsession.

Love.

"No matter what we all want, this war will happen. The rebels in Betovere are active, and knowing Mia, this will push her to make strategic moves. Xavier's memories will do very little now that Mia is in charge, but we can likely guess what she will do. Her best bet is to continue to make the fae terrify us. She needs those fae more afraid of the demons than angry with their ruler. To do that, she will spin what happened in the Fire Lands as an act of terrorism. Of war. We must be ready and united."

I looked each of them in the eyes, willing them all to submit. I was a born queen. This was my destiny.

"What is stopping the fae rebels from believing what the queen says about us and joining her cause?" Cyprus asked.

"The rebels know the truth of the demons," Nicola said.

He faced her, his mouth agape. "How do they know that?"

"Because I am their leader, of course."

As if on cue, every single one of them—apart from Kafele—stared at Nicola in sheer bafflement. There were no words that could accurately explain how that news felt. When I found out at the dinner table in the Fire Lands, I had no time to truly process it. Was I angry that she had led a rebellion that was willingly killing innocents? Proud of her leadership and initiative? Jealous of her bravery? All of them. Definitely all of them.

Nicola had done something I had dreamt of. She stood up for the fae of Betovere. She had proven just how far she would go to take down the royals. I only wished I would have done the same. I stared at her, trying to think of what to say. Apparently, something else took precedence, because Nicola's eyes momentarily went wide and distant. Kafele grabbed onto her, tugging her close to his chest as she seemed to go to another place—another time.

"Bellamy, you will have a guest by night's end," was all she offered in explanation. Everyone seemed poised to say something in response, but Genevieve spoke first.

"Sterling, we need to get out of here. Mother and father have been—"

"What?" Sterling cut her off. "Gen, I need my memories back. And Asher, she needs me. I have to stay here. I want—"

"Excuse me? Absolutely not! You will not be another one of her pets waiting to be sicced on her foes! You. Are. Coming. Home!"

"No I am not!"

"Okay, okay, we all need to calm down," I said, stepping between them as they squared off. Genevieve sneered, her gaze flicking to my bruised face. I rolled my eyes, unimpressed with her implied threats. "You will both stay the night and we can all work towards a plan tomorrow."

"But—"

"No buts. Henry will find you a place to stay here at Pike. Now, all of you leave me alone so I can fuck my *fiancé*," I demanded, raising my hand and wiggling my fingers their way. Despite Bellamy having mentioned a wedding earlier, they all seemed shocked to see my ring. Everyone but Genevieve and Sterling cheered, swarming us once more and celebrating in the rare bit of wonderful news.

CHAPTER FORTY-ONE

BELLAMY

"What about purple?" Noe asked, her pencil twirling just above the paper. When I lifted a brow at her, she added, "Like Asher's necklace."

"While I am eternally grateful that Sipho showed her love when very few had, I do not think I am strong enough to have my wedding themed after his necklace," I drawled. Noe snickered, writing the word purple and then crossing it out four times before writing *Bellamy is too insecure, must not use* beside it. "You are a—" I cut myself off, eyes darting to the three mortal children who sat at the table with us. "...menace."

"Ooo burn," Noe teased. Rolling my eyes, I turned to the children.

"Make sure you eat the carrots too," I ordered. Nyla's two, Gemma and Safre, both grumbled in response. Octavia, Mordicai's youngest daughter, was not so quiet in her distaste.

"They taste like utter garbage," Octavia groaned, scrunching her small nose and shaking her blonde hair. She looked so much like her father. Talked like him too. Safre nodded in agreement, frowning. Coating the dark skin above his lip was a small line of white where milk had splashed, making him look too sweet to be so sour.

"Do not tell Ray that, she worked hard on this menu." I laughed, looking around the large dining area and scanning the faces to see if my assistant was around. She sat in the far corner, Lara beside her. Looking back at the kids, I noticed Gemma was eyeing me curiously. She was the most daring of the three, so I turned to her fully and raised my brows.

"Are you too scared to eat the carrots, Gemma?" I challenged. Within minutes, the three had fallen into a sort of competition, scarfing down their carrots as if their lives depended on it. With a smirk of triumph, I faced Noe again. She was smiling softly, making my cheeks heat. "What?"

"Oh nothing, just thinking about how good of a father you will be one day." Her words, while meant to soothe and compliment, hurt.

Asher was not able to have younglings. Not yet. And it did not feel like a priority for either of us to attempt to fight the magic. But, even if we could, would I really be a good father? Could someone like me be good at such a thing? Adbeel had raised me, and he was the greatest father anyone could ask for. But Xavier had conceived me, and it was his blood that ran through my veins. Mia's blood. The blood of horrible parents.

"Anyways," I said, shaking my head. "I think red would be a good color for the carpet."

Noe scoffed. "You have had enough red for an entire lifetime. Pick something else."

"But—"

"No buts, you are not going with red."

"Black?"

"Bellamy, I will kill—"

"Ahem," I cut in, nodding towards the children. All three sets of eyes were locked on Noe and I, waiting for what would be said next.

"I will brutally murder you," Noe amended, sending a wink to the children.

They burst into laughter just as my eye caught sight of flowing brown hair and deep gray eyes. Asher approached us with a wide smile on her face and a chunk of bread in her hand. She wore a red blouse and black trousers, looking exactly like I wished our wedding would. My gaze flicked to her left hand and my heart nearly exploded out of my chest when I saw the ring there.

Sterling was at my princess's side, smiling warmly at her as she spoke. I knew there was no reason to be jealous, but envy burned within me like a green flame regardless. Asher and I had been in our room for hours, where she rode me and I ravished her and we nearly lost all hope of ever doing anything else. When we had decided it was time to go back out, she had warned me that she was going to immediately go find Sterling, but seeing them now was still grating.

"Stop staring at them, you look like a possessive dog," Noe hissed, getting another laugh from the children. I had been taking care of them for nearly a week now, and I regretfully noted how comfortable they had grown around me. How easily the little vermin insulted me.

When Noe and I first showed up in Yrassa, King Lazarev and Queen Nyla had not looked very surprised. In fact, they seemed as though they had been waiting for me. Their two children were handed over to us, as were hundreds of soldiers who had volunteered to come with us to Pike. I had spent that first day adding onto our base after quickly finding ourselves out of space. Mordicai brought his youngest child along, and the three of the small beasts had followed me around all day.

But as Asher walked up to our table, their eyes left me and went wide. They watched her with unashamed awe. Ash's magic had been a force today, pouring over us all like a waterfall. Even the children felt it as they gawked. I could sense it, the way they quickly fell into her orbit. Smiling at the thought of it, I stood.

"Ash, I want you to meet Princess Gemma and Prince Safre of Yrassa, as well as Princess Octavia of Heratt," I said, gesturing towards the three with a slow wave of my hand. Asher smiled at them with all the light of a thousand suns.

"Hello, my name is Asher and this is Prince Sterling of Maliha. It is lovely to meet you three." None of them responded, instead continuing to stare at her in awe. She laughed softly before turning back to me. "Bell, we should consider having some sort of war counsel while Genevieve and Sterling are still here. I think—"

"Pick a color," I said, cutting her off. She quirked a brow, watching with disinterest as I lifted a few samples of cloth towards her. "Tell me which would look best running down the aisle at our wedding."

"Bellamy, we do not need anything extravagant. Can we not just say our vows surrounded by our family?" she practically begged.

"Absolutely not!" Noe shouted. She pushed herself to stand, pointing at Asher with fire in her eyes. "You will not have anything less than an ostentatious and overzealous affair. Now choose what you want to be in charge of or so help me—"

"Okay, okay!" Asher cut in, raising her hands in surrender. A devious smile spread across my face at her submission. Then, my smile fell as I caught sight of the terrifyingly mischievous glint in her eyes. "I will pick the flowers."

I wanted to ask her what she was up to, but just then a loud boom shook the ground beneath our feet. Screams erupted from outside, and I watched Asher's face go from taunting to terrified in a matter of seconds. Just as I knew she would, Asher bolted towards the cries.

"Fuck!" I shouted. Noe did not look back as she chased after Asher, leaving me alone with our wards.

My eyes quickly scanned over the children, wishing I had Ray there to care for them like she often did. But Ray had already left with Lara, everyone readying for an attack. The dining area had been lost to chaos and panic, which left me no other option but...

"Sterling, I need you to take care of them until I get back." My order was not said softly, but Sterling did not look at all offended at the prospect of being sidelined. He puffed his chest slightly and marched to the children. Nodding, I let myself be sucked into the masses.

While the screams had stopped, there was still a sense of doom as I cut through the crowd, and I was eager to be at Asher's side. As soon as I was sure they were heading towards the courtyard, I confirmed no one was touching me and willed myself outside.

Somehow I had forgotten Nicola's warning from earlier. But, as I stood before Torrel's enormous head, I was quickly reminded. The dragon roared, spittle flying across my face *again*.

"You nasty beast, why must you get your foul breath all over me?" I hissed. I mean, my gods, *why?*

"Don't talk to her like that or I'll let her eat you raw," Stassi snarked as she descended the dragon's pink-scaled front leg. She still wore the full-body pink leathers she had donned a week ago, her hair now windblown and chaotic. Above all else, even the clear annoyance radiating from her, Stassi looked tired.

"Were you not able to find her?" I asked. Her pink eyes settled on me, a glare forming slowly. Torrel growled before shooting into the sky, likely off to eat unsuspecting innocents. "Oh, touched a nerve I see."

"Shut your stupid mouth unless you want me to remind you how easily I can kill pretty things." A short and almost disbelieving laugh came from behind me at Stassi's words. It was a sound I knew well. Really, any sound she made was one I knew well.

Asher stood a couple feet away, staring at Stassi like she might kill her with just a look and a whim. I wondered briefly if she could, but then remembered she would need to be a *high demon* capable of stealing magical seeds to do that. Stassi would live to see another day apparently.

"You!" Asher boomed, her voice catching everyone's attention. She was furious as she marched forward, her calculating eyes silver in the fading sunlight. Her hands twitched and then formed fists, readying for a fight. It was at that moment that I realized I had completely forgotten to warn Asher about Stassi. "You stupid *bitch!* You made Bellamy and I fight that day in Behman! You made us unprepared when we were shot at! I should *kill you!*"

And then, surprising no one, Asher lunged at Stassi. If there was one thing I knew Asher was capable of, it was being gloriously angry. She brought Stassi down to the ground and slammed her fist into the high demon's face before Stassi could so much as react. Sadly, the fight took a turn from there.

Stassi flipped Asher, landing two punches before Asher brought her knee up and slammed it between Stassi's legs. While I was fairly certain Stassi did not possess a cock, she still screeched in pain. Asher used that to her advantage, reaching up and clawing at Stassi's tawny cheek. In retaliation, Stassi bit Asher's hand.

Sighing, I walked forward and picked up Asher beneath her arms, kicking Stassi in the gut as I began dragging my princess away. Asher offered unintelligible insults and grunts, swinging her legs as if she might land a blow despite the distance between her and the high demon.

By the time they were both standing, they each panted heavily and assessed the other.

Stassi was first to let her shoulders relax, her lips pursing as she took in Asher.

"You're not so bad I guess. You have a shitty punch but you're quick. I can work with that," she offered, flicking her long pink hair back. Asher looked down at the high demon in distaste, letting her eyes roam over the small and infuriating creature.

"Who and what are you?" Asher demanded, crossing her arms. "Are you a goddess? Is that how you have that dragon? And why are you here?"

"Awe, did your pet prince not tell you that I've been sleeping in his bed?" Stassi asked, smirking at Asher before sending me a wink.

Asher let out the most blood curdling scream before jumping at Stassi again. This time, she portaled, appearing before Stassi and smacking her so hard that she crumpled to the ground. I walked slowly to them, more reluctant to stop Asher when it felt so damn good to watch her attempt murder in my honor.

Jealousy looked *delicious* on her.

But I did eventually get Asher off, which resulted in her rounding on me.

"You have five seconds to explain!" she screamed into my face. I smiled, feeling uncontrollably horny.

"She is the goddess of Sin and Virtue. Well, not a goddess. She and that male who has been stalking your dreams are actually called high demons. I can explain more if we go somewhere private. As for my bed, the bitch stole it and I was forced to sleep amongst Henry's filth." And then, because I genuinely could not help myself, I grabbed her face and brought her lips to mine.

"Okay, sickos, let's focus. We need to train and—" Stassi abruptly cut herself off. I released Asher, the two of us turning to find Stassi staring at…Sterling. She was gawking at him really. He looked back at her with a slight bit of confusion, but I also noted the way his eyes swiftly took in her pink-clad body, his tongue darting out to wet his lips. Ew. "My creature."

"Your what?" Sterling asked, furrowing his brows. The three children were slightly behind him, peeking around his body in interest. Stassi's mouth fell open, her jaw slack. It was as if what Sterling said was so absurd she could not compute it.

"There is absolutely no way you've forgotten me already." Her tone was biting—condemning. As if something clicked in her head, Asher stilled at my side and let out a loud gasp.

"Sterling, you told me in the cells you had met the goddess of Sin and Virtue. You *know* her." All of our heads whipped back towards a visibly uncomfortable Sterling as he shifted his weight from foot to foot.

"I—I do not—"

"He had his memories taken. We are not sure how, but I am working on a way to get them back." Asher's voice was surprisingly soothing as she spoke, her need to protect Sterling overshadowing her clear dislike for Stassi.

Noe appeared at my side then, smiling widely. "I love gossip."

"Too much is going on all the time, this is exhausting," Asher responded, nudging Noe.

Stassi seemed to consider the man before her, her nose twitching. She appeared ready to pounce on him. Then, abruptly, her eyes went wide. She turned towards me as she said, "That forest of yours, does it have creatures who can do something like this?"

"Navalom," Noe and I said in unison.

CHAPTER FORTY-TWO

ASHER

"Thank you for the…um…*gift,* but no thank you," Sterling said as he held the dagger between his pointer finger and thumb. His face was scrunched as he eyed the blade, as if it were dirty or offensive.

"He doesn't need that anyways, I'll be protecting him," Stassi said. She was doing wonders for my patience, really testing it. Not only that, but she had been unnecessarily possessive with Sterling. Clearly, he had not been fully honest with me in the dungeons, because she looked as if she was ready to strip him naked and fuck him until he died.

It did not help that he was fully receptive to her affection. Last night when she had arrived, he had immediately fawned over her. Now, as she twirled one of his curls around her finger and placed a hand on his chest, he openly invited her advances. His hand went to her hip, his eyes twinkling

with mischief. I was in no way interested in ruining his fun, but I was nervous about what she might do to him. She seemed dangerous.

The only bright spot was watching Genevieve turn deep red when Sterling insisted he stay to retrieve his memories. She had shouted and argued until, finally, she agreed to another day. Both Lian and I had laughed at the sight of Henry practically lighting up. Damon and Cyprus, who had been standing on either side of Henry, seemed to catch on too, because they immediately began whispering to him in what could have only been teasing tones based on the way he tackled them after.

"You do not strike me as the type to protect anyone but yourself," I scoffed. Stassi peered at me over her shoulder, winking my way.

"Keeping this one alive is in my best interest at the moment." Annoying, stupid high demon.

Bellamy had spent quite some time the previous night explaining to me what he had gleaned, including that Stassi was on a council that Padon led. I learned more about what happened to Asta and Stella, my ancestors— a fact that was still quite jarring. All in all, it had been one of the most overwhelming days of my entire life.

While I had fallen asleep against Bellamy's naked body, basking in his heat, I had awoken three times terrified that it had all been a lie. He thought the events of the day had caused them, but I worried that new nightmares were simply replacing old.

So, with very little sleep and a burning hatred for the pink-haired female before me, I turned and stormed away. Genevieve was nearby, practically fuming as she watched her brother and Stassi flirt. Henry was at her side, periodically looking down at her from the corner of his eye. I had given the princess a set of my leathers for the occasion and eagerly agreed to let her help, much to pumpkin's eternal joy. Coming to her side, I crossed my arms and watched the show as well.

"He is too good for her," Genevieve seethed.

"Far too good. Plus, he is too young. She is practically a million years old," I agreed.

Henry softly chuckled before adding, "I think he is old enough to decide those things for himself."

Genevieve and I immediately whipped our heads towards him.

"Mind your business!" Genevieve chastised just as I said, "He is practically a child!"

It was odd agreeing with her, but together we were ready to go to war for Sterling. He was too kind and funny and curious to be with someone like Stassi. Her mind was a swarm of death and destruction. Sterling needed to be with a sweet mortal girl who had a love for adventure. Not someone who would live far past him and would be able to abuse their power over him.

"Time to go, my pouty little thing," Bellamy said as he walked up to my side. I groaned, nodding.

Bellamy had loved the idea of Sterling and Stassi, deeming it a way to get rid of them both. I had shoved him away, lasting only moments before I tugged him back to me. Smirks like his in that moment should have been outlawed. He was too smug for his own good.

"Dibs on portaling us!" I shouted. I had portaled twice this morning, both times landing exactly where I had meant to. This would be an exciting test of my capabilities.

"Gods no, please do not let her do that. We will end up in the sea or somewhere even more awful," Henry groaned, causing Genevieve to snicker. Noe grimaced, but nodded in agreement. Sterling and Stassi were merely watching, her hand traveling down his back and quite noticeably cupping his backside.

What a bunch of absolute *assholes*.

"If Asher wants to portal us, then she can portal us," Bellamy declared, wrapping an arm around my shoulders and tugging me close. That was more like it. I was allowed to beam in satisfaction for all of two seconds before he leaned down to my ear and whispered, "Please do not drop us in the sea."

Growling in fury, I smacked him in the arm and eyed each of them. "Grab on or get lost."

"Getting lost is my fear," Henry remarked.

"My fist is about to get lost up your ass if you do not shut up!"

"Okay, children, that is enough," Genevieve soothed, grinning from ear-to-ear. Then, surprising all of us, she leaned towards me and said, "We will get him when he least suspects."

Were Genevieve and I...bonding? Our eyes simultaneously went from Henry to Stassi then back to one another. Yes, we definitely were.

"You are utterly doomed," Bellamy teased Henry, his voice full of glee.

"Later, I am hungry so we need to get this party on the move," I said, clapping my hands together and then spreading them out. We all linked together, Noe taking Sterling's hand with a wink towards a scowling Stassi. Smiling at the thought of the high demon's discomfort, I closed my eyes and thought of Haven.

Pale beaches.

Cobblestone paths.

Driftwood markets.

A towering black manor.

The Forest of Tragedies.

Haven. Haven. Haven. Haven.

My magic encircled us, and then we were gone. There was no pain, no hesitant moment between here and there. I felt the ground beneath my feet change from stone to something softer, and I nearly screamed in success.

I did it!

"Damnit, Ash. Where in the Underworld are we?" Henry groaned.

When I opened my eyes, I found us surrounded by orange sand and towering bare cliffs. Oh no. *Where were we?*

"I—I thought—"

"Don't worry, chosen one, not even you can be good at everything," Stassi taunted as she ran a single finger down Sterling's chest, stopping at the growing bulge in his trousers. Eternity above, she was *shameless*. And rude.

"You will get it eventually," Bellamy reassured against my hair as he kissed the top of my head. "Just give it a few hundred years."

At the group's laughter, I crossed my arms and scowled. "Fine, you all want to be rude? Then just know that I will be practicing on each of you."

"Practicing what? Portaling or something else?" Noe asked in alarm. I flashed her a devious grin in return, practically thrumming with revenge.

"That is for me to know and for you to hopefully not die from." With that, she giggled and let her shadows pour around us.

No less than ten minutes later, we were crouched behind a group of blackened bushes, watching as a herd of what looked like at least eighty navalom seemed to convene. The creatures were not anything like I thought they would be. They were barely corporeal, the white of their bodies nearly transparent. Rather than stepping onto the ground as they moved, they practically levitated. It was a haunting sight.

I recalled Winona once telling me that they were not fighters, but as they hummed there, I thought they might prove stronger than we anticipated.

"Let me guess, you want to kill them all?" Sterling whispered at my side. The poor thing was shaking, his fear of what was to come almost adorable.

"It would make things quite a bit easier," Stassi said from his other side. She had pulled her hair back, readying for a fight. There was no denying how beautiful she was, but that only served to further aggravate me. She was so much like Padon. Full of herself and irritating.

"We need your memories, which means they all need to live so Ash can go through each of their minds," Genevieve added.

"A tragedy seeing as I was hoping we would have time for breakfast."

Noe looked at me from down our line, whining, "Did you smell those muffins? My stomach is growling just thinking about them."

"No muffins, we need to focus so we can be swift with this," Bellamy chided. My stomach growled in response, making me moan back.

"Gods forbid we solve anything without murder," Sterling grumbled.

"If I get lucky on my first try then I can grab the memories, shatter their minds, and we can be back in time to eat the muffins hot," I said, practically bouncing on my feet where I crouched.

"Smart!" Noe offered me a thumbs up.

"No muffins!" Bellamy hissed.

"I feel like I should tell you that I ate those muffins before we left," Henry whispered. I turned on him, gasping in offense.

"All of them? You menace!"

"Focus!" Bellamy's tone had grown irritated, which was my cue to scoff and acquiesce. At my submission, Bellamy leaned down and offered me a quick kiss to my lips before jumping out and lighting his body in black fire.

The others took that as permission to move, each of them charging into the group. Despite my desire to be quick with this, I found myself turning towards Sterling, wanting to keep him safe. Stassi was on his other side, and the two of us made unintentional eye contact.

Please keep him safe.

My mental voice was nearly a whisper, soft and nonthreatening as it met her unprotected mind.

With my life.

Sighing, I nodded at her and left the pair, Sterling's eyes wide as he watched me go.

An afriktor had once told me that my magic did not work the same on the creatures of this forest. When I lifted my hands and willed all of the navalom to sleep with no success, I found that it was similar to the terrifying creature I had come across last year. Similar to Wrath. I would have to learn and work around their strange minds, but for now, I was going to be forced to simply fight.

So I did. Charging into the fray, I slashed through their odd legs, finding that they did somehow bleed. Black blood poured onto the dead grass, not burning anyone's skin like the fetch's did. Just as Wrath had said. The memory sent a pang of pain through my chest. Nothing new. Pain had long since been an unwelcome companion in my life.

My screams were met with navalom after navalom falling to the ground from nonfatal wounds. I sliced and parried, not wanting them to touch me. Soon, we had all stood, panting, before dozens of injured memory-eaters. Winona, our brilliant creature specialist, had been right—these beasts were not fighters.

Bending down, I touched my hand to one of them, its icy skin sending a chill down my spine. "I will need more time than I thought. They are similar to the afriktors. It is not as simple as entering their minds."

Everyone around me groaned in disappointment, but they each sat down, all of us on edge while here in this forest. Anything could come at us, and who knew if we would win the next fight so easily?

Quickly, I opened myself to its mind.

Memories were far more beautiful than conscious thoughts. They all had a sort of filmy haze around them, even the painful ones tasting sweet. That was the problem with life, we often did not realize just how beautiful it was until it became a memory.

Navalom seemed to be the opposite. They consumed memories like a delicacy, cherished them for how they fed their souls. These creatures did not appear to be particularly evil, even if their instincts drove them to do horrible things. Below me, the navalom wailed as I searched for Sterling's memories, as if my intrusion was painful.

Amidst the screams, I could have sworn I heard my name. I let my eyes wander around our party, but not a single one of them looked at me as if waiting for my response. How incredibly odd.

"Not this one," I said before moving onto the next. Nine more, and then...yes, there they were.

Sterling's memories were a beacon of pain and despair. They glowed in my mind and sizzled on my tongue, burning rather than settling sweetly on my tastebuds. I tugged them out of the navalom slowly, which was met with piercing wails. It howled below me as what must have been the pain and agony of lost sustenance consumed it.

And when I was finished, I let the creature fall back to the grass with a grimace. It was not right. I had done awful things in my life, but this felt particularly cruel. Bellamy was at my side in seconds, wrapping his arm around my back and letting his hand rest on my hip.

"Should we ask Ranbir to heal them?"

"If that is what you want." Hesitance and confusion circled him like a lost bird, spinning over and over again until it finally landed in the nest that was his mind.

"Yes, I think it is," I concluded softly.

"Okay, I will go get him while you return what you found to Sterling, then we can go home."

When he disappeared beneath his shadows, I made my way to Sterling. He sat on the grass with distress in his brown gaze. I could tell that he hated what we had done, but I would not bring it up. Healing did not redeem devastation, it only righted the wrongs committed. Bending down, I brought my face level to his.

"Are you sure you want these back? They are painful." If my words were considerate and soft, then Stassi's response could have only been described as egotistic and harsh.

"He needs those memories, *Asher*. I want him to know who I am when I fuck him."

An audible gulp came from Sterling, but I ignored the high demon in favor of focusing on him. He needed to make this choice on his own. No one could choose for him. Sterling's green-flecked eyes bore into me, as if he were peeking at my very soul. And then, almost reluctantly, he bobbed his head in consent.

Sighing, I grabbed his shoulders and pulled him into a hug. At first, he seemed confused by the display of friendship, but then he seemed to begin feeling the memories as they returned to him. Soon he was shaking, tears beginning to spill from his eyes not long after.

When I opened my eyes, it was to the rare sight of deep emotion on Stassi's face. Her brows were furrowed, that gorgeous face pinched in pain. She frowned so hard that lines dug into her skin near her mouth. And there, in the pink depths of her eyes, were the beginnings of tears.

The high demon of Sin and Virtue peered up to me then, looking like a crushed goddess. And, to my utter horror, we too became reluctant allies as she slowly mouthed two words.

"Thank you."

CHAPTER FORTY-THREE

ASHER

"Do you like…bread?" Adbeel asked, coughing to hide his discomfort. I could not stop myself from snorting at the question. He had been asking me small things like this all morning, trying to get to know me but too terrified to venture into uncomfortable territory.

"You can ask me the questions you want, you know. I promise not to run or bite," I spoke from across the table. Adbeel, who was broad and fierce, looked somehow demure as he nodded and stuffed his entire omelet into his mouth.

For his part, Bellamy just sat, ate, and snarked.

"She lies, her fight or flight instincts are heinous," the prince teased.

"Almost as terrible as his stalking habits," I retorted, sticking my tongue out. Then, just for good measure, I took off my ring, put it on my middle finger, and flashed it to him.

Adbeel burst into laughter, clapping his hands together and tilting his head back. In that moment, there was nothing that could stop the smile that spread across my face. Bellamy also seemed incapable of hiding his dashing grin.

"Okay, okay. Tell me, what do you enjoy doing when wars are not raging?" Adbeel finally asked after wiping at his eyes and taking deep breaths. Wistfully, I looked out the windows, remembering when I had eaten at this very table with Bellamy. It felt like ages ago. Back then, Winona and Luca still lived. Haven and its innocent inhabitants still stood. What had I enjoyed when death and destruction did not consume my every thought?

"I like to read and play the pianoforte," I finally admitted. Heat crawled up my neck and spread across my cheeks at the pride that suddenly polluted the air. Both Bellamy and Adbeel flooded the room with their delight.

"I would love to hear you play sometime. I must confess, I have very few hobbies other than relishing in that which makes my family happy." Adbeel paused, his gaze flicking to Bellamy as the left corner of his mouth kicked up. "As I am sure you have noticed, I quite enjoy Bellamy's paintings."

"Yes, I have seen one or two I believe."

Groaning, Bellamy pushed back his chair and stood up. "Adbeel, how about we spare me the embarrassment and take Asher down to the village? She did not get to see much of it…*last time.*"

"That sounds lovely. Asher, what do you say?" Adbeel asked softly.

Nodding, I shoved the last piece of toast into my mouth and jumped up. "Yes, definitely."

Just as I went to push in my chair, I once more heard the call of my name. The deep voice was almost whimsical in its faintness, and when I looked up at both of the males before me, I was met with no sign that it had been either of them that said my name.

Shaking my head, I pushed back the thoughts, focusing on what was in front of me.

Adbeel stood, his sky-blue silk tunic shining in the morning light, the fabric clinging to his chestnut skin. He had trimmed his mahogany curls since the last time I saw him, cropping them short. Bellamy was off to his side, wearing a flowing silk blouse that was a matching shade, unbuttoned to expose his pale chest riddled with black veins. His black trousers were identical to Adbeel's, just as his knee-high boots were. He had rings on every finger but the one that would one day hold his wedding band, and today he also wore a stack of thin black and red chains around his neck.

A quick look down at my dress left me smiling secretly. I wore a silk blue dress the color of Bellamy's eyes. It dragged the slightest bit on the floor due to my heelless black slippers and was cut modestly just below my collarbones. The straps were thin pieces of twisted fabric and the back sunk halfway down my spine. I had on my necklace and a flick of kohl upon the corners of my eyes, a contrast to Bellamy, who wore a thin line above his lower lashes twin to Adbeel's.

We looked like a family.

Bellamy reached out his hand, and together the three of us walked through the palace. Adbeel would occasionally stop, pointing at one of Bellamy's paintings and telling me about how proud he was of it. When we left the castle doors and passed through the stunning courtyard, Adbeel explained the story of the trees—weeping willows, he called them. That they were planted by Queen Asta after the death of King Zohar. As we made our way down the large hill, waves splashing up the cliffside and making the late summer air damp, Adbeel continued to tell me of their rich history. He named off his—*our*—ancestors, adding in their contributions to the great demon empire.

I smiled and laughed in the correct places, though at times I felt as if I were floating outside of my body, watching myself find a place and a family and *hope*. Never had I felt quite this complete.

All of those emotions were only intensified as residents of The Royal City began flocking towards their king and prince. Males, females, and younglings crowded us, eagerly hoping to speak to the royalty among them. I did my best to stand back from them, wanting to let them bond with their subjects, though Bellamy's tight grasp on my hand did not let me stray far.

That was, until an oddly familiar looking face appeared in my line of sight. The female had a loud mind, her eyes wide as she approached not Adbeel or Bellamy, but *me*.

"I saw you the last time you were here months ago. For a moment I thought I had seen a ghost. You look just like her," the female said with wide eyes and splayed hands. I knew then who she had been. This was the woman who had stared at me and thought me dead back when Bellamy and I had first come to The Royal City. Only, she had not realized who I really was. Had she thought me Zaib Ayad? My...*mother?* "Can it be? Are you related to her?"

"I—well—I guess—"

"Yes," Adbeel cut in, he and Bellamy placing me between them as Adbeel addressed the crowd. "Asher is the daughter of the late princess, Zaib."

With that, the shouts grew loud, frantic. They all seemed to speak at once, as if it were a battle to be heard above all else.

"Where did she come from?"

"How did you find her?"

"Will she be heir after the prince?"

"Are the rumors true? Will she marry her uncle, Prince Bellamy?"

That last one made my stomach turn. They thought I was in love with *my uncle*. Gods, how would we explain that? Bellamy's hold tightened on me, his jaw clenching as he glared at the male who had shouted the question.

"Silence, please!" Adbeel shouted, raising his hands. When the crowd finally calmed down and quieted, the king spoke again. "For the last two centuries, I have allowed you all to believe that Bellamy is my son. In fact, I have encouraged those beliefs. Regretfully, I must admit to you all that I have lied."

More shouts. The crowd began to pulse, moving towards us and into each other, the energy frantic with the news. My heart sunk into my stomach at Adbeel's words, but before I could allow my mind to wander into the horrible possibility that Adbeel was casting off Bellamy, the king looked down at us with a warm smile.

"Bellamy has been my ward, and I wished to give him a safe and happy life after his true parents harmed him in the most heinous ways. I have loved and cherished him like a son, but he has no blood relation to me," Adbeel's voice dropped a tenor, a mesmerizing hum seeming to escape him as he spoke. There, at the very center of my mental gate, I felt magic prodding. The more Adbeel talked, the stronger the force of magic pushing against my mind's barriers. The magic of a Honey Tongue. "And he has shown his own love and loyalty to me—to our entire realm, really— by finding my long-lost granddaughter. Not only that, but he has fallen in love with her and asked for her hand in marriage!"

The crowd's gasps and questions were quickly silenced by cheers, demons all around us shouting their congratulations, their well wishes, and their gratitude. I gaped at them all, so surprised by such open love. Just like that, they accepted me. There was no anger to be felt for the deception, only great joy. Or maybe it was simply Adbeel's magic that willed them to submit. Either way, there was something so wonderful about being welcomed without terror and suspicion.

Bellamy looked down at me in awe, not sparing anyone else so much as a fleeting glance. "They love you, but I fear I cannot share."

I laughed, which he quickly silenced by leaning down and kissing me. Delight and happiness flooded the pathway where we stood, the residents of the city clapping and cheering. Adbeel touched many of the nearby demons with a single finger, his Sun magic setting it aglow. Some of them cried and thanked him, others shyly smiling. It was so inconceivable and disorienting, but I knew then that Betovere would one day have this. Even if it was the last thing I did, I would free and unite the fae. Whoever we found to rule over them would be this cherished. And they would all be safe to love and live.

"Time to go," Adbeel whispered before engulfing us in his blinding light. We were tugged and shredded before being stitched back together and placed in one of the many halls of Adbeel's castle. My mind swam with so many thoughts, but my heart seemed full of only love at that moment. "I must go spread this news from my own lips before the gossip wins out. I will make multiple stops in each territory, but I will be sure to come to Pike soon."

Bellamy nodded, his eyes glassy. His mind of sunshine and warmth was radiant as Adbeel pulled him in for a quick hug. "Thank you."

"You may not be my son, but you are my family. No matter what, I will stand up for you. I promise that. When is the next war council meeting?"

"Tomorrow," I answered. Bellamy huffed, but silently agreed. While I enjoyed having this time of peace, we still had a war on our hands. The fae had yet to attack, but that would soon change. Mia never licked her wounds for long.

"Okay, that will work." Seconds passed without either of us moving, Adbeel looking at me as if there was a war being raged in his mind rather than on his shores. Of all the minds in Alemthian, Adbeel's was surely the hardest to break through, but I found I did not need to try as Adbeel cleared his throat and squared his shoulders. "Would it be okay if I hugged you, Asher?"

What an oddly considerate king. To be someone who could have anything he wanted yet still asked for something as simple as a hug was such a contrast. Lips slightly parted in surprise, I bobbed my head and opened my arms. Adbeel quickly closed the space, wrapping his large arms around me and tucking me into his broad chest. His well-trimmed beard scratched against my exposed ear as he nuzzled into me, breathing in my presence like he had existed without fresh air for too long.

Abruptly, he pulled away and blew out a gust of warm breath. "Sorry, I just…I am so very glad you are here."

And then he disappeared within a burst of white light.

"He has a hard time expressing his feelings," Bellamy teased, coming up behind me and pulling my back into his chest. "Like someone else I know."

With a snort, I reached up and smacked his arm that had snaked around me. But even I knew he was not lying, and an idea sparked to life in my mind that would quickly rectify my poor habits. Twirling in his hold, I secured my arms around his neck and pressed my lips against his.

"Take us to the piano room," I breathed against his mouth as he returned the kiss. Tongue against mine, he gripped my thighs and pulled me up as he portaled us. The moment our surroundings changed, Bellamy began walking. My backside hit the pianoforte, where he placed me softly without breaking the kiss. I let him ravage me, consuming my love like a sweet dessert. He licked and bit and ate until I thought he might suffocate on the taste of me. Or perhaps I him.

We did not part until we were both gasping, his fingers entwined in my loose curls and mine against his bare chest. His forehead pressed into mine, a raspy moan breaking the silence.

"Play for me, beautiful creature." And then he picked me up and gently placed me on the bench. Like I was a precious gem.

Sighing at the perfection that suddenly—and momentarily—was our life, I cracked my fingers and levitated my feet above the pedals. Then I looked at my soulmate and prepared to bare my heart to him.

"This is the ballad of our love." My fingers touched the keys, and a story began to unfold. "It begins with the deep and dark plague that sat upon my chest as I stood on that balcony." C minor. F minor. B-flat major. A-flat major. My hands danced along with the melody, my soul singing as I continued to play. "We slowly fade into the rapid sound of my heart as it beat when you looked at me with those icy blue eyes." Mezzo-piano as the tempo sped, not too loud, but not as soft as before, pairing with the accelerando. The terms were whispered in my mind, Mia's soft voice as she taught me so long ago fading and being replaced by mine. Finally, I was my own in truth. "You were perfection incarnate—the most handsome male I had ever seen. Your presence was like sunshine."

Bellamy watched with wide eyes and pinched brows, his lips pursed so hard that his dimples dug into his cheeks. I focused on the sounds around me, trying to hear what I played as Bellamy might. As an artist who saw the world in colors and shapes.

"The rasp of your voice as you said my name, the brush of our lips as we first kissed, the tears that splashed against the ground as I sobbed when I discovered you lied." I played and played, sharing my feelings in the only way I knew how. "Knives slicing through chests. Feet pounding against floors. Swords clashing."

Bellamy's breathing was almost as loud as the music, and when he came to sit beside me, the sounds of his soft cries could be heard as well. My fingers cramped from disuse, but I played on, the very song I had composed since I first laid eyes on him without truly realizing it.

"Moans. Bodies colliding. Nails against skin. Confessed love. Whispers of forever." My heart sped, worse coming as the melody darkened but sped—prestissimo.

"Screams, pleas, skin ripping, and bones snapping. Minds lost in forests of pain." Bellamy's tears began splashing onto the keys, but I

pressed on, remaining silent as the music told him of my torture. Of my mind slipping away.

"Freedom," I spoke, letting the chord hold. Fermata. "Love. Family."

"Ash…" Bellamy murmured, thinking I was done. But no, there was more. So much more.

"You slipping in and out of me. Crowns placed on heads. Vows given and received." The music built towards an epic crescendo, the ending in sight. "And one day, far from now when magic is undone and choice is returned, the cry of a newborn youngling with gray eyes and deep dimples. A life lived side by side until death do us part. Dirt placed over piles of ashes. Soulmates returning to Eternity. Love conquering evil."

My hands slammed down, the final note wistful and high. C8.

Heaving breaths and slightly sweaty, I turned to face Bellamy head on, not wanting to wait a single moment.

"I have loved you for every day of my true life and I will love you every day after. You said once that you would crawl from your grave for me, but I would crawl *to* my grave for you, Bell. You are my gift from Eternity, my blessing. Above all else, I am yours and you are mine."

He barely let me finish before he kissed me, his large hands on my jaw. I felt him portal us, and then we landed on his plush quilt. When he finally willed himself to pull away, it was to force my head back. I caught sight of the painting on the opposite wall and nearly burst into tears.

My naked body upon this very bed was immortalized on the canvas, every slope and curve caught and portrayed. Somehow, it was far lovelier than I could have hoped.

"I love you with every piece of my blackened soul and heart. I was made for you, Asher. Eternity and gods are nothing compared to you. I will worship at your altar—at your feet—until I am dead. You are my salvation. My life."

406

As Bellamy made love to me, I thought of how beautiful the rest of our song would be.

CHAPTER FORTY-FOUR

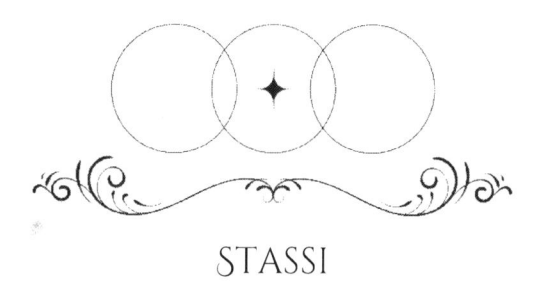

STASSI

Heat from Alemthian's wretched pale sun beat down on me as I let Asher's magic invade my senses—my mind. She was a beastly thing when she wanted to be, and this morning was apparently one of those occurrences.

"You're taking too long," I drawled, lifting my hand to inspect my nails before shoving her out of my head. Across the training area we had confiscated on one of the few grassy patches, she stared with squinted eyes and pursed lips, her fists balled at her sides.

"Pardon me for not wanting to tear apart your mind to break through your mental shields," she hissed out. Ironic seeing as my shields were made of—"snakes. Your shields are made of horrible, awful, pink *snakes.*"

"Oh, so you *are* in my head then?" I asked, smirking over at her. She was wearing those same training leathers that all of Bellamy's little cronies donned obsessively, the outfit bland. Asher was far from that though. She was quite stunning now that I really had the chance to look at her. The painting above Padon's bed didn't do her justice, nor had that moment we first met forever ago. Or, well, it felt like forever. Time on this world moved too quickly.

"I do not have to be in your head when you are practically shouting your thoughts. Thanks for the compliment by the way." Sweat dripped down the side of her face, which was much sharper with her hair pulled back in two braids. Tilting my face down, I took in my loose pink locks before peeking up at her below my rosy lashes. Her eyelids fell halfway as her head cocked to the side and her lips jutted out.

"Do not ask me what you are about to," she ordered, crossing her arms. I let my bottom lip stick out, pouting like a youngling who wanted extra dessert.

"Will you braid my hair?" I asked anyway. She groaned, letting her head fall back.

Asher and I had formed a sort of alliance since I started helping her with her magic. She was a descendant of not only Stella, but Asta too, which meant she had stubbornly refused just as the female I looked at like a sister would have. But I had worn her down with brute force. Getting to use my magic on her had been exciting, and I so loved being able to understand what she thought of as sinful and virtuous. Even more exciting was seeing how drastically her subjective opinions on those things had changed since she'd been gone.

We now met every morning, and I had the chance to see that she was somehow a perfect mixture of Solana and Asta. Like Sol, Asher was curious and always moving. She wanted more than what was given to her, even if she didn't always believe she deserved it. Similar to Asta, Asher was fierce and brutal, often acting on the unending anger that pulsed inside of her. Just as they both had been, Asher was secretly kind. She wanted peace

and was willing to suffer or lose herself to find it for those she ruled over. It made for a great leader.

But what made me truly begin to like her was just how much of a bitch she was.

"I feel it is important that you understand how much torture I would withstand if it meant I did not have to do your hair right now," she seethed, approaching me.

"Do you want me to snap all of your fingers so that the act of braiding is torture? Best of both worlds." Her dark gray eyes rolled, but soon she was behind me, her fingers brushing through the sweat-soaked strands of my hair.

"Hearing your voice is worse, honestly," she remarked, yanking harshly on my hair.

"Ooo yes, mommy, pull my hair," I moaned, knowing it would make her angrier.

Her annoyed groan was paired with her lips near my ear, her breath fanning across my cheek. "Tell me more of the story or I will cut off all of your hair with my dagger."

"I knew I shouldn't have given that back to you," I sighed out. Rolling my shoulders back and closing my eyes, I let the words begin to flow. "Where did we stop yesterday? Oh yes, the generation before mine. Well, that's actually a rather sad chapter. Padon and I were forced to take our seeds way too early under two entirely different circumstances. His mother had him at a very old age, not that it mattered to her physical health or appearance. But living that long, it does something to one's mind. It's miserable. We grow bored and eager for something new. Eventually, not even conquering and raising entire worlds can appease you. Morgana was ready to go, so she forced Padon to take her seed. Stella said she held Padon for hours after she ripped out Morgana's seed and placed it into him."

Asher sucked in a breath behind me, her fingers faltering as they deftly styled my hair. I wished I could see her face, especially knowing how

much she hated Padon. There were few things in life harder than acknowledging the utter humanity of your enemy.

"My situation was different. There was no build-up, no planning. My father was the previous holder of Sin and Virtue. Unlike most high demons, he loved my mother. Married her, even. High demons don't usually do that. They mate with as many low demons as possible, producing heir after heir until they find one strong enough to hold the seed. My parents only had me, as my mother simply could not carry another. Luckily for them, I was strong. But that did not stop my mother from falling deeper and deeper into agony with each loss of a youngling. I remember walking in on her sobbing on the floor of her bathroom, blood pouring down her legs as she gripped her swollen stomach. That was the last time she was pregnant. A few months later, she wrote my father and I each a note declaring her love and her wish for us to be happy, then she hung herself from our kitchen rafters."

Asher gasped behind me. I smiled at the virtue in her heart. Mortals were predictable. Weak. They could be swayed by sad stories and pretty words. It would be pathetic if it weren't so Eternity damned lovely. I wished I could feel that too.

"My father and I found her together, and I was forced to listen to him begging her to come back to him as he tore her down from the rope. Even worse, he had the audacity to look me in the eye, apologize, and then rip out his seed. In one day I watched both of my parents be buried in our sacred grounds *and* became the high demon of Sin and Virtue."

The words were not shaky or forced, instead my voice was sharp. Lifeless but for the small hint of fury there. They both left me. Chose someone else over me. My mother, her dead children over her living family, and my father, his lifeless wife over his breathing daughter. I no longer mourned them, though I would defend them to anyone else.

"Did it hurt?" Asher asked as she ripped small sections of my pink blouse. I almost turned to yell at her, but then I felt her use the fabric to tie off my hair. Scoffing, I whipped around, facing her fully. Her eyes were red,

but her face was dry. She did not cry for my dead family. Not really. Which was better for us both.

Crossing my arms, I glared up at her.

"The seed will only accept that which is strong enough. It essentially tries to kill whoever takes it and it only accepts the blood of its original owner. It's why they're passed down families. So, yes, it hurt like a bitch." The tension between the two of us seemed to peak as Asher took a step forward, reaching out as if she would console me. Thankfully, Milo saved me from the uncomfortable interaction.

The tiny dragon soared through the air, tackling Asher to the ground and puffing hot breath into her face. She giggled, scratching the beast behind his wing. Torrel had found her new caretaker without trying. The princess adored Milo, and she was more than willing to care for him any time she could. Which meant even Torrel loved her. But I knew the real reason everyone flocked around her like sheep.

"Hi there, little one. Want to go start fires and laugh when Bellamy has a panic attack as he puts them out?" Asher asked, rubbing her nose against Milo's snout. Then, she seemed to remember something. Her mouth fell open and her eyes widened as she gazed up at me from her place in the grass. "How is Likho? Would Padon hurt him since you mentioned he took a liking to me?"

Eternity spare me, she was so infuriatingly considerate of everyone else. Why couldn't she just not care like the rest of us? At least Bellamy leaned towards being selfish. It was far more tolerable. Shrugging, I sat down and glanced back at Torrel as she approached, what looked like an entire horse hanging limply from her mouth. The stench of blood tainted the mountain air, festering in the heat of late summer.

Gross.

"Padon is a brute, but he won't kill a dragon. We were nervous about Torrel, but I doubt he would've done anything to her or Milo. It would have been the other dragons that got mine. Padon has a deep respect for their species, just like his mother did. As much of an idiot as he is, that's

one thing he wouldn't risk or sacrifice," I admitted, bending down to sit beside Asher.

Milo barely looked back at me, too absorbed with Asher's doting. Fickle little beast.

"Padon is definitely an idiot."

"And pathetic."

"And full of himself."

"And annoying."

"And creepy."

"And—"

"Are we interrupting something?" a male voice asked. I turned, finding the orange-haired demon walking beside my creature and his sister. Sterling. What a strange and oddly perfect name for him. He had left with his snotty sister, promising that when he came back he would prove to me just how valuable he could be. A callback to our times talking in his cell. Back when life was far less exhausting.

Finding out he was a mortal without magic had been jarring. I had never been with one of those. And what use could he possibly have when his entire life was practically the length of a blink of my eye? Pity.

"Always," Asher jibed, placing a kiss on Milo's black scales and pushing herself up to stand. When I reached out a hand for her to help me up, she merely smirked and walked towards the approaching trio.

How. Fucking. Rude!

"You're such a bitch," I mumbled, standing on my own like a peasant.

"But she is our bitch," Henry, that was his name, said. From his side, Sterling laughed before embracing Asher. The two hugged as if it had

been years since they saw each other last. Too long. The hug was far too long.

"Okay, okay, let's not act like you haven't seen each other in a century. Break it up," I demanded as I made my way to them. They laughed as they parted, and I noted how my creature seemed a bit lighter than he had seconds ago. As if whatever she had just done with her magic had sliced her open, Asher simultaneously bled both sin and virtue.

"You know, Henry," Sterling said, turning to face the demon. I waited with bated breath as the two looked at one another with a sparkle of challenge in their eyes. "Seeing as you are Genevieve's bitch, I would not think you would be one to talk."

Sterling's sister snorted, crossing her arms and looking up at the now smirking male who seemed glued to her side. "Awe poor firefly, nothing more than a hound now."

Henry smirked, licking his lips and speaking without taking his gaze off of her. "Yes, I love being your bitch. Even more so when we are naked."

"Gross," Sterling groaned, sticking his tongue out and pretending to gag. Asher laughed at his side, but she offered a small smile to the pair that made me think she was quite happy for them. "Oh, by the way, Asher. Queen Shah told me she could do it tonight if you are wanting to."

Asher nodded eagerly. "That is perfect."

Then my creature's warm brown eyes were on me. He wore forest green trousers and a tight black top with the sleeves rolled up. I noted just how much fuller he looked now. No sign of the starved male who existed beneath the golden castle. His sunshine curls were wild atop his head, shorter than they were back in the dungeons when I had thought them brown. He approached me with a wicked curve to his lips.

"Hello, Spice. You are looking absolutely murderous over here. If you want, I would love to help you get rid of some of that built up tension," he teased, his hand coming up to toy with one of my braids. Behind him, Asher cleared her throat and quickly began pushing Henry and Genevieve

away, shouting for Milo and Torrel to give us space. All I could do was stare at the male before me and picture all the ways I could use him before he inevitably died.

Unsure whether or not Padon knew where I was after Stella and I had been discovered by Jonah and Venturae, I took the risk of portaling the two of us to the rooms that Bellamy had given me in place of his. After forcing the prince to make it larger and demanding he get me decorations as well as a more comfortable set of linens, I deemed it good enough. The second we were in the locked room, I shoved Sterling backwards on the bed.

"Tell me, mortal boy, can you manage to keep me entertained? Or will you turn out to be a bore and force me to kill you?" My voice was husky as I lifted my legs and straddled him. His smile was sinister, his light skin already flushed from his red blood. "So interesting that you bleed red."

His eyes lit up, a daring look in them as he scrutinized me. Then, he surprised me by flipping us. I gasped below him, feeling his hand trail down my leg. Instead of doing what any other male would do, he stopped at the strap there, ripping my dagger free. And, without so much as a warning, Sterling cut away my blouse and skirt, then my underwear after that. Then he stood, his fingers moving to the buttons of his shirt.

"Those were new!" I shouted in response. But even I knew how devastatingly sexy it was. And as I watched him smile while he slowly undressed, light flowing in and reflecting off his hair, I realized he knew too.

My creature crawled my way, chasing me with the dagger as I backed further up the bed.

"You like blood, Spice? You know, I have lost a lot of it this last year. It seems you are not the only one interested in seeing just how mortal I am." Wincing when my head hit the wooden frame, I stilled, trying to understand what he meant by that. "You want it, Stassi?" Sterling gave me no chance to think further before he cut a line horizontally across the fleshy part of his forearm. "Then have it."

Warm liquid poured over me, splashing my bare breasts and stomach. For the first time in a long time, someone surprised me.

Sterling reached down and dragged the tip of the dagger across my nipple, sending shivers of pleasure throughout my body. Red spread, and I caught sight of his hardened cock as he pumped it with his bloody free hand. What in Eternity was happening? Were all magicless mortals like this?

There was a haunted look there in his eyes, sin coating the air as it pulsed in time with his cock as he rubbed the bloody tip against my clit. Moans dug up my throat from deep in my chest, and I gripped the sheets in a baffling amount of ecstasy. Just as my mouth opened in a desperate cry, Sterling shoved three blood-soaked fingers down my throat.

"Drink it, Stassi. Taste me," he commanded. Instinctively, I sucked, the iron taste of his blood coating my tongue. And though I could not read minds like Asher, I could have sworn I tasted the sorrow and pain within him. His fingers left my mouth, the cut and bloody arm dragging down my body as he unceremoniously tossed the dagger. "Tell me, am I sweet or spicy?"

And then his head was between my legs, his mouth sucking roughly on my clit before I could answer him. I arched up, the sin in the air heady. Magic stirred inside of me, itching to break free. Demanding more of him would be so easy. Natural, even. It was what I did. But there was something about this one that stopped me from freeing the cloud of pink that raged beneath my skin.

I felt...too much.

"You, Spice, taste like sin," he groaned out against my dripping cunt just before biting down. I screamed, unbothered by anyone else hearing as I relished the feeling of his mouth against me. Seconds turned into minutes, and soon I was near tears from the pleasure. He lifted his arm so I could see it, touching two fingers to his still-bleeding wound before driving the same digits into me.

Words could not explain the way it felt as he worked me into a frenzy, my hips bucking and my toes curling. All the while, beneath the sin that he remained drenched in, resided a dark aura of agony.

Sterling was in indescribable pain. I felt my mind acknowledge it just as I finally fell off the edge of ecstasy, my release barreling into me and likely wetting his face. I watched him suck and lap it up, his eyes scrunched in pleasure. And when he lifted his face, it was the sight of his dark red blood on his cheeks that altered something in me. Something that I was not sure if I could come back from.

My hands shook as I reached up and grabbed his neck, pulling his mouth to mine. Lips met and worlds collided. Perhaps the universe itself could've fallen apart in that moment and I wouldn't have noticed. All I could think or feel or acknowledge was Sterling and his unbearably heavy pain as he lined himself up. When he shoved into me, I thought I felt a tear hit my cheek. Was it mine? His? I didn't know. I couldn't remember the last time I cried. Not truly.

His thrusts grew frantic, hard and fast. Desperate in a way. Normally, it would be everything I wanted. Why was this not normal? What was happening to me?

An undeniable urge to soothe him washed over me, and suddenly, I was grabbing his wound, shoving my magic into him and willing the skin to stitch back together. I wasn't nearly as good as Padon, my magic not as perfect or seamless, but I still felt the blood slow. Then all at once, it stopped, and his wound was healed.

"I have you, my creature," I whispered against his lips. Hips stuttering, he opened his eyes and looked at me. The whites around his brown eyes were red, the green flecks in his irises clashing with the new color. I had never seen someone look so broken, so shattered beyond repair. It hit me abruptly, the reality of what must have been happening to him.

He had his memories restored after being forcibly taken. He had been tortured, then told lies. He had been tormented and then tricked. To

top it all off, he had the memories given back, and it all came back to him like a tidal wave.

"You're not alone. Feel it all. Feel *me*. Give me your fear, your hatred, your hopelessness. Turn it into sin. Feed it to me and let it go." Never had I been so kind or considerate, not since Sol and Asta were still around. But it was second nature to kiss him again, feeling as he shoved every bit of his pain at me. His body sunk, pressing into mine as his cock continued to barrel into me. He fucked me like it was his last chance—as if there might not be a future in which he lived to do so again. "Yes, just like that. Feel me, Sterling. I'm here.

When the mortal came inside of me, I wondered if he had broken me too.

CHAPTER FORTY-FIVE

ASHER

"No, our only option is to lure the fae out. We need to be the ones to dictate when and where this happens," I demanded. All around me, the members of the war council looked to be in various phases of shock.

"We also need to consider that Mia Mounbetton will be as strategic as we will, not to mention that she has a demon on her side," Bellamy added, letting his fingers trail scandalous images on my leather-clad thigh beneath the table. I swatted his hand away, but he just chuckled and put it back.

"We might be better off simply burning Betovere to the ground," Adbeel huffed, staring daggers at the five islands to the East of Eoforhild. "We have seen what they will do to not only our innocents, but the mortals as well."

Across from me, Shah seethed. The Queen of Behman had come this morning, her body healed and her rage at an all-time high. She was ready for this war. Eager even. Genevieve was at her side, finally back from Maliha.

Sterling had been forced to leave with her, much to Stassi's complaints and death threats. The only thing that had soothed her was what had to have been one of the most scandalous kisses I had ever witnessed. Sterling was a poor fighter, but he was clearly great at other things. Enough so that, when he whispered into Stassi's ear, she had crossed her arms and nodded curtly before storming away.

Now, only Genevieve was at the table, Sterling likely off keeping promises.

"Speaking of that, I think we have more than one traitor working against us," Bellamy added, not addressing the fact that Adbeel wanted to slaughter innocents in retribution for other innocents being killed.

"I agree. The attack on Behman and every attack before then felt too perfectly strategic. Someone was feeding information to the fae. I can look into it." Noe often spoke up in these meetings, but this was one of the first times I felt the war council members agree with her. "Speaking of which, I found these in Betovere this morning."

With that, she unceremoniously slapped down a stack of thick parchments upon the model of Alemthian. They scattered about the table, some falling into laps. I caught one and turned it over, gasping at what was there.

A depiction of…me.

Above the—rather flattering, honestly—outline of myself was the word "wanted" and below was a single, damning line. "For the murder of King Xavier Mounbetton."

"Well?" Noe asked, her hazel eyes on mine. Nicola was silent where she sat on my right, Bellamy's gaze burning a hole into me from my left.

420

"At least I look pretty."

At that, Trint and Mordicai burst into laughter, the two allies always banding together. Today, only Lian, Damon, and Henry were here, Bellamy's other six captains having been stationed in a separate territory with small forces each. Elrial, Nrista, and Onyx had all been relieved of their position as war council members by Adbeel when they had declared themselves vehemently against my being in these meetings. And when they spewed hate at me, Bellamy relieved them of their lives and threatened to do the same to anyone else.

It was a dramatic and bloody start to the meeting. Nyla, the queen of the mortal kingdom Yrassa, had yelled at Bellamy for two straight minutes for ruining her white dress. Marjorie, the last surviving member of the war council, had simply rolled her eyes and sent a burst of shadows at the prince. Bellamy's head flung back slightly from the hit, like someone being bopped upside the head.

But at least we had moved onto more pressing matters. Like how stunning I looked on these wanted posters. My hand darted out, grabbing onto one that had Bellamy's face instead. His said the same thing, and he had also been depicted fairly well.

Fine, he looked perfect.

"They are painting you two as murderers," Lian said, her tone morose.

"They *are* murderers. The prince just killed three of his council members in cold blood," Trint said in disbelief, gesturing towards Bellamy. I dared to look at my fiancé, finding a wicked smile upon his face and a devious glimmer in his eyes.

"*Propaganda,*" I chimed in. "It will work to reduce the rebel hold. Beings want something to fight for. More than that, they want someone to fight against. We are now their villains, and that will do wonders for Mia's agenda."

"That is not all. Malcolm has come out of hiding," Noe reluctantly spoke. Her gaze flicked to Adbeel at the head of the table, his face flinching in pain. "The fae queen claims he is a reformed demon ready to end the blight of his kind. She has spread the epic story of him saving her life in the Fire Lands far and wide. Even worse, she is telling them all that you, Asher, are the reason they have no memories beyond the last three centuries. The fae want you dead."

I meant to respond, but once again I heard my name. The same deep rasp calling out to me. It sounded like...like *someone*. I knew that voice.

"I think this meeting is over. We are all on edge and nothing will get done right now. Everyone take time to rest and breathe, we will reconvene in three days' time." Adbeel's words were a booming demand. I jumped, my focus once more returning to the meeting.

Everyone startled at his outburst, but soon we were all dispersing, none of us quite sure what we should do as the end neared. Adbeel came to Bellamy and I, tugging us close. "We must move up the wedding. Time is running low."

"But—"

"No buts, Asher. Two weeks," Adbeel demanded.

"Excellent," Bellamy enthused.

"Of course you would think so," I grumbled.

"Do not worry, Adbeel, two weeks is easily accomplishable."

"Ugh, I am leaving to go find Nicola before she gets too far, you two can enjoy the wedding planning on your own." My feet moved quickly, desperate to put some space between myself and the Ayad males.

"Do not forget to speak to Noe about the flowers you want to choose!" Bellamy shouted.

"Already did, now leave me alone you beastly groom!" Chuckling at my insult, Bellamy shooed me away. Adbeel smiled at his side, waving as I turned the corner.

Darting through the corridors, I eagerly looked for Nicola's silky brown curls amongst the dispersing crowd. But soon, I found myself alone, not even the sound of footsteps nearby. Where had she gone so fast? As I made the next turn, I got my answer.

"Looking for me?" Nicola asked from where she leaned against the wall. I scoffed, shaking my head in disbelief to hide the fact that she had scared the Underworld out of me.

"I do not recall you being such a showoff," I teased as my racing heart slowed, causing her to beam at me in pride.

"Well get used to it." The two of us giggled as we joined our arms and began walking. It felt like second nature to be at her side, just as I had been for two centuries.

It was unfortunate that I would have to ruin the peace.

"So," I said, trying to feign casualness. "Should we talk about the rebellion?"

Her sigh was paired with her shoulders slumping, as if she had been waiting for me to ask but was still sad that I did. We both knew it was an important conversation that needed to be had. Her rebels had attempted to kill me on multiple occasions, and I had slaughtered them in return. Not exactly preferred best friend activities.

"They were not meant to attack you."

"I know."

Our holds on each other simultaneously tightened, our sides becoming flush as we continued forward. Very few beings walked the halls, everyone either enjoying the last of the warm days or training for the horror

we would soon endure. I was glad for that. This was something we needed to discuss alone.

"I killed a lot of your rebels, Nic," I whispered.

"You did," was all she said.

"I have killed a lot of fae in general," I admitted.

This time, Nicola said nothing.

An explanation was necessary, but how did one elucidate why they committed graphic and horrific murder? We both knew it was not entirely self-defense. Even before Bellamy rescued me, I had done awful things. I was a murderer through and through. The wanted posters were correct in labeling me as such.

"All my life, I have been a killer. I took my first life almost immediately after I came into my magic. You have watched me become more and more corrupt, and all the while you have loved me despite my wickedness. But I think it is important that you know just how dark I have become." Taking a deep breath, I resisted the urge to look at her and pushed on. "In the last year, I have rather brutally murdered more than I can count, your rebels included. Once, I would have wallowed in regret because of what I had done, but I do not feel that way anymore. I am what I am, and I understand if I am no longer someone you can call your best friend. But I needed you to know that. To know *me* as I am now. Because that is the real reason your rebels wanted me dead. They see me for what I am—a monster."

Nicola's free hand suddenly pressed into my chest, pushing me back and forcing me to stop. She was in front of me in a flash, her deep green dress swishing around my legs.

"First of all, you are not the only one with blood staining your hands. Yes, you have done heinous things, but you are not unique in that respect." I stared at her with wide eyes, her face fierce as she scolded me. "In all my life, I have never been loved by someone as you have loved me. Not even Kafele. Without fail, you have been at my side for every mishap,

tear, laugh, disappointment, and accomplishment for almost my entire life. Doing the same for you was not a favor or a hassle."

A male wearing the colors of Behman came towards us, momentarily silencing Nicola. But all the while, her big brown eyes glared my way. When he had finally passed, she shoved me toward the wall, forcing my back to smack into the rock.

"Second, the rebels had been active long before I took over. Those who wish to harm you are a part of the group that need to be weeded out, many of which do not want to follow me at all." I nodded, hoping that she saw how seriously I was taking her—how intently I was listening. "Everyone sees my potential and the benefit of having an Oracle at the helm. Still, I am not surprised that they went behind my back and defied my orders to get to you. Some of it I even foresaw, but I watched you handle it yourself. What you did was not helpful for the cause, but I have worked hard to make sure they are all ready to fight on *your* side. Because it is *you* who will change the Fae Realm for the better. Only *you* can unite the mortals, demons, and fae. You are our savior in so many ways. I need you to see that."

Was that a tear rolling down my cheek? Yes, it was.

What did I say to that? Thank you for being the best possible friend I could ever ask for in all my life? That did not sound like enough.

"Third—"

"There is *more?*" I asked, my voice cracking. She slapped my arm, a laugh slipping past her lips before she hushed it with a stern expression.

"*Third,* we have plans in place to make sure that the rebel movement does not die out, which includes striving for unity throughout the entire realm. I promise that I will do everything in my power to make sure that those who are willing to sacrifice innocents are taken care of. You have every right to hate that. And, before you say or think it, that does not make you a hypocrite." Gods, she really did think of everything. See everything, was more like it. It must have been so exhausting, knowing so much. Feeling the mass of the future upon your shoulders was something that I

could relate to, and I hated seeing it weigh her down. "I am sorry that I did not tell you what was going on. It is hard juggling what I have seen with what still needs to happen. I just…struggle. We can further discuss it all soon, and I am still in contact with my second who is eager to speak with you. This is all going to work out. Alemthian will see brighter days, I know it. We *can* do this."

Nodding, I grabbed her shoulders and pulled her into me, hugging her so fiercely it probably hurt. "Thanks, Nic. I love you so much."

"I love you too. Always, Ash," she whispered, letting go of me with a sniffle. We stared at one another, basking in the friendship and sisterhood we had cultivated, the rare perfection of such a thing worth reveling in. A smile slowly lifted her cheeks as she took a few steps away from me. "Onto less morose things."

Something hard smashed into me then, knocking the air out of my lungs and making me fall to the ground in a heap.

"Ash baby!" Farai screamed, pulling me into a hug. "Nic says we are going for a picnic!"

"Eternity above, Fair, you are going to flatten her," Jasper scolded between quite unserious cackles.

"Nah, she lives. I have seen it," Nicola stated matter-of-factly.

I opened my eyes, seeing the three of them all smiling down at me, and groaned in pain.

"You three are crazy."

***

"Do you ever wonder how we went from kissing each other by the lake and having no responsibility—other than not getting into too much

trouble—to suddenly being in the midst of a war?" Nicola asked. I snorted, turning my head so our noses touched.

We were all four laying on a thick quilt we had spread out on the rocky ground at the base of one of the mountains. Half-eaten food surrounded us, bottles of wine being passed back and forth as we talked.

"You were a bad kisser, so I was forced to find better," I teased, nudging her nose with mine. Her fingers stung where they suddenly came up and flicked me, my forehead momentarily aching. Farai burst into laughter at my other side, Jasper trying and failing to simmer him down.

"I was doing you a favor since you were a lonely little menace that no one wanted to make out with." Did Nicola know about Sipho? Had she realized I had, in fact, been kissed by someone other than her before then?

I had never told her, but I wondered if she knew anyways with that power of hers.

"The only way to know for sure is if you kiss again," Farai declared, lifting his pointer finger towards the sky. "Or maybe you should both kiss me."

"Absolutely not!" Jasper shouted, sitting up so fast that he knocked over our last bottle of wine. At that, we all burst into laughter, the four of us howling and rolling across the ground like wild animals.

"Remember that one time in Academy when you laughed so hard that milk came out of your nose and went into Jasper's eyes?" I gasped out between giggles, Nicola laughing even harder at the memory.

"He *cried!*" she shouted, snorting. My hands went to my cramping stomach, clutching onto it for dear life as we all continued to laugh.

"Or when Asher drank an entire bottle of rum she bought off a merchant at the market and fell down the huge flight of stairs at the palace?" Jasper asked, snorting so loudly it practically echoed off the sky above us.

"My shoes were slippery!" I shouted, reaching over Farai to punch Jasper in the arm. He grunted in pain, Farai laughing even harder.

The four of us continued to shout out random memories or stories, the instances growing sparser as we began recalling times closer to the present. It was those conversations that made us realize how matters such as fraternization truly did rip us apart. Perhaps that was what they were meant to do above all else.

From what they said, the factions were not fans of one another. They found themselves in constant competition, each thinking themselves better than the others. Even the sub-factions argued and battled, the segregation so deep that they saw only their differences. And how perfect was that for a line of royalty that sought to dominate?

Mia and Xavier had successfully tore apart the fae, preventing them from uniting and fighting back. Betovere was weaker, not stronger. The breeding meant little when the complacency meant everything.

A realm divided was a realm prime for conquering, after all.

After some time of heavy silence, our laughter long gone upon the whispers of wind and wisteria, Nicola asked a tough question.

"Will you come back to the Fae Realm with us?"

Without hesitation or further thought, I shook my head and answered with an unsteady voice. "I belong here in Eoforhild. I still have so much to learn and hopefully beings to convince that I am worth following, but I also need to think about the fact that my birthright is that throne. My only living relative is the demon king and my fiancé is the heir to the throne. Not to mention that I have so much of my own history to learn here."

They all three looked at me with resigned sorrow. But what could I do other than fight for my place in this world? I had been stripped of too much for too long. I no longer wished to sit upon a throne that I did not belong on. I was not meant to be surrounded by gold and leading fae. They had ostracized me because I truly was not meant to be there. I would *never*

be one of them. Yes, I was half fae, but my soul sang in Eoforhild. I was meant to be here, just as they were meant to be in Betovere.

"I promise I will find someone perfect for that throne when the time comes," I vowed.

Nicola looked at me with a sparkle in her eye that told me she knew more about that future than I possibly could. I both wished to know and to never find out. It was daunting, thinking about a future in which I survived to heal and move forward. How heavy that would be.

And how absolutely wonderful.

"Onto better questions. Nic..." Farai finally said, grabbing Jasper's hand and laying his head onto my stomach to face Nicola. His two-toned cheeks began to darken and heat against my shirt. "Is there any chance you would want to carry our youngling if we all survive this mess?"

We celebrated for hours more as we dared to dream what their youngling would look like and Nicola decided what she would wear when her stomach grew round.

***

"Gods, I missed you," Bellamy whispered as he fell into bed beside me. His arms instantly reached forward and pulled me into him. I listened as he breathed me in, sighing with relief when his hands settled tightly around me.

"I saw you earlier today," I pointed out. Groans were all he initially offered in response before his lips pressed to the edge of my shoulder that had been left bare from my nightdress. I could not pretend that I had not been obsessively thinking of him as well. It had been hard to be apart for too long since they had rescued me from Isle Element. Parts of myself that I used to stifle now ran rampant within me, forcing me to acknowledge the

fact that I was tempted to damn the world and just rest with my soulmate—my *everything*.

"Exactly, that was practically years ago." A hint of his stubble scratched at my neck as he spoke, making me giggle. The tickle was paired with his tongue and lips as he whispered against my skin about hating everything but me and wishing he could live between my legs. When he started asking if he could bury his cock into my tight cunt and stay there forever I began to pant and squirm. So deliciously filthy was my fiancé that I barely noticed the tremors that were slowly ceasing within me from the last nightmare. Luckily, I had awoken from it alone, my violent screams met with only taunting darkness and haunting freedom.

Now, as he tugged off my clothes, Bellamy unwittingly soothed my fears—my memories of violent hands and cutting words. His soft lips traced lines down my stomach, stitching together the phantom slices. Nothing felt quite as perfect as the first lick of his tongue up my dripping center. Almost every time, he paired it with strong hands nearly bruising my thighs as he forced them apart and up. He knew me better than I knew myself, and every angle or position or motion only proved that further.

"You taste better and better every time," he mumbled against my throbbing clit before shoving his tongue inside of me. I cried out, my hands gripping his hair for dear life. Silence was shattered again and again as I screamed with every delicious new step he took me up the staircase of my pleasure.

He teased and tormented me, sometimes shoving me down a few steps just for his own amusement as he delayed the inevitable. When I was a sweaty mess and he was gasping for air that he refused to take enough of, I finally caved and did what he loved best.

"Please, Bellamy. Please make me come."

"You know I love it when you beg me, beautiful creature."

In seconds I was arching my back and clawing at the sheets as he curved his long, thick fingers within me and shook his face against me. Bellamy carried me to the top of the stairs and then shoved me off the edge.

My release was almost painful from how intense it was, my desperate screams loud and unencumbered before he suddenly shoved his fingers into my mouth and twisted until his rings grazed my lips and his nails touched the back of my throat. I gagged and sucked on them, tasting how much my body loved his.

"My good princess. So great at doing what you are told when it is me making the demands," Bellamy rasped as he moved above me. I stared up at him with a mixture of lust and awe, his black tunic barely on and his hair a mess from my hands. He was ethereal. No, in this light with his shadows writhing and his veins pulsing, he was utterly demonic. If someone saw him now, they might think him the ruler of the Underworld. Just how I preferred him. My untamed and wicked beast. "Say it, Ash. Tell me you are only good for me."

"I am only good for you," I hummed, my words breathy and dripping with need. "And when you are naked before me, you are never to be good. I want you at your worst in here."

Moaning, he bent down and captured my mouth with his, grinding his hips—and his hardened member—into me. Our tongues twisted around one another, Bellamy's slowing as he began tearing off his clothes. When he was fully bare, my lips and my heart felt swollen from his attention, his light a heady thing.

"I will be anything you want, Asher. Anything, as long as I am yours above all else." And then he was thrusting inside of me, and I was full in so many ways. His hips snapped forward again and again, his pace sending zaps of pleasure up my spine and making my lips go numb.

The next time my orgasm hit me, I found myself unable to scream. All I could do was clench around him as I moaned out, "Gods."

"That is right, call to me. *I* am your god, and *you* are mine."

As if to prove just how divine my pleasure could be with him in control, Bellamy brought my legs up against his chest, urging my ankles to cross behind his head with his hands before leaning forward again. The new angle brought me to the brink of madness, my mind toeing the edges of

sanity. I had been there often, but this was freeing, whereas it once felt caging.

Bellamy devoured and demolished me, tearing me down and remaking me into something that was entirely his. Maybe we were even one in that moment.

When he had filled me up until I was dripping his release, I watched him pull out slowly and inspect his work. A grin stretched his face as he used his finger to attempt to force more of it inside of me. From where he knelt before me, the light of the candles and the moon outside his window cast eerie shadows upon him, reinforcing that image of him earlier. He was a fallen god, a shattered Eternity, the Underworld in living form.

I loved him so fucking much.

As always, his loving nature was impossible to deny. Soon he was sweeping me up and cleaning me in our tub. He ran his fingers through my hair, scrubbing my scalp and lathering soap within the strands. This one was not the vanilla that I preferred, but some sort of lovely combination of our scents. Vanilla and cinnamon, the barest hint of smoky undertones there in the depths.

He cleaned me, even offering me an entire tray of mint leaves to chew on as he went. Again and again, Bellamy made sure I was reminded that he *knew* me. There were no pieces of my shredded and blackened soul that he did not intimately understand. Not all of it came from his time learning me before we met. I often caught him watching me, even now, as if I were a puzzle that might suddenly have a single piece missing.

"You know me well," I whispered, letting my fingers slide against his knee beneath the soapy water. Moments of serenity like that were so rare, but I thought then that we might get more if we could make it out of the war alive. If we were strong enough to survive what was to come from not only Mia, but Padon too. Bellamy and Stassi had a lot to say about him and what he would do to us all.

"As you know me. That is part of being soul bonded." My back stiffened. Whipping around to face him, I took in his look of nerves. My

432

mental gate shook against the onslaught of thoughts from within Pike, but it was Bellamy's terror and love that rattled the golden lock and blood-red chains.

"What do you mean? You think we are soul bonded? Is that not a thing that the gods—I mean, high demons do?"

"We have always known it could happen to demons, but I never realized fae could experience it too. Stassi seemed to insinuate it was something that could happen to anyone. She said we were, and I am inclined to believe her. It feels…right."

Oh it did. That incessant and infuriating tug towards him. The way it felt as if I were becoming whole the first time we had sex. How his mind and our love always tasted like home upon my tongue.

"It does not actually mean anything, Asher. We are not forced to be together. It just means our souls…they sing to one another. The idea behind it is that we are all born as half, and then we find our missing piece. Adbeel says it is not always romantic either. A friend or a youngling or a mentor can be a soul bond. Love, it is not limited in the way many think it. And you are not stripped of your free will, either. Yes, soul bonds are thought to be fate's design, but destiny does not choose, we do. I choose you, Ash. No matter what, it is you. Do you choose me too?"

"Of course I do. You are everything, Bellamy."

"The beginning, the end, and every moment in between?" he asked teasingly. I nodded with a chuckle, wrapping my arms around his neck. "We will have time to think more about it when this mess is over."

"You know, I fear the moment when the war is over and life is that simple. There will come a point when no one, not even you, will need me. And I do not know what I will be then." My whispers seem to strip Bellamy of his carefree smile, stealing his peace and replacing it with an air of seriousness.

"Free, Ash. You will be free."

CHAPTER FORTY-SIX

BELLAMY

Calista was already in my Haven manor when I arrived, running her fingers across the kitchen countertops. She had always loved this space. It was more hers than mine.

"I miss it. Life here was so lovely," she murmured, her tone wistful. My nod was curt, my mind not wishing to remember the days before Haven was destroyed. Not when that came with the horrifying memories of all the dead as we burned their bodies and buried their ashes.

"Why did you stay?" I asked without thinking, my mouth moving quicker than my thoughts. She turned towards me, her violet eyes sharp and

434

her short black hair sticking to her face from the sea water. "In Haven, I mean. You could have been portaled back to the open sea."

Of all the things I had expected her to say, it was not what she chose. "Have you ever wished you could be someone else?"

"Daily before I met Ash," I admitted.

"Well, I remember wishing that back then. When King Adbeel first put up The Mist, many sirens died. We watched the odd red cloud wash over the water, diving into it and coating our friends or loved ones. Their screams still echo in my nightmares sometimes," she said, her voice strained. Tortured. It seemed all of us were these days. "By the time we even considered going on land, the king had declared the war over. We thought our chances better here than with the fae."

"That makes sense. Did you ever consider trying to find any of your kind on the other side?"

"You were the first to welcome us with open arms, Bellamy. Before you, we were ostracized. In the minds of demons, a siren belonged with the beasts in the Forest of Tragedies. We are born of the God of Death and Creation after all." I thought of the black blood that poured out of Captain Harligold's siren and how it burned Ranbir. Yes, they were Padon's creations. Raw versions without Asta's magic to stifle them. "Plus, we have made a home here in the waters of Haven. Some even used to live in the village if you remember. From what we know of, we are the only sirens in existence. None live beyond The Mist."

"I saw one not long ago. She is part of a pirate's crew. She has your violet eyes."

"Interesting. I guess I should have thought of going to look for others. I was never good at leading. Being thrust into the role was never my desire. My sister was queen for a reason, and she deserved more than death at the hands of The Mist." She choked on a soft sob as she opened a drawer, toying with the cutlery inside.

435

I let my mind wander for a while, our silence comfortable. But soon, as a storm seemed to approach, I was forced to ask the question I had been avoiding. "Will you fight with us, Calista?"

"Of course we will. My sweet and wicked Stormy would have. My sister's will is mine, even if it is just the memory of it."

***

"Must everything be black?" Noe asked, throwing the stack of papers in her hand to the ground in her normal dramatic fashion.

Adbeel chuckled, completely unphased by her interruption or her outburst. He leaned back in his chair, hands relaxed where they rested across his stomach. His obsidian crown sat crooked on top of his curls and his full mouth was stretched in a smile. He had been unbearably happy since Asher had been spending time with him. Even after he came back with less than enthusiastic reactions from the realm in regards to the news of Asher's future ascension and our impending marriage, he still smiled nonstop.

While I had expected him to love me less with the prospect of a granddaughter, it had been the exact opposite. Adbeel doted on us both, so unbelievably excited that he could not contain himself. It was wonderful to have everyone together, but also terribly draining. I just wanted to hide in my room with Ash and fuck her for hours on end. Was that too much to ask for?

"Why is *my* shirt of any concern to *you?*" I asked Noe, laying my head on my hand. My elbow was pressed firmly into the wood of Adbeel's desk, a breeze coming in from the open window that smelled of salt water and fading autumn heat. I was far too content, which was why we were running on less and less time to plan the wedding. We needed to take advantage of the rare peace before everything crashed down around us.

"You are so fucking annoying, do you know that? Adbeel, tell him he is annoying and that he must wear a color other than black or red!" She was whining, her voice pitched so high that it hurt my ears. Adbeel only laughed, slapping me on the back.

"You heard her, wear something else," he conceded, smirking at me like he was having the time of his life.

"Just wait until she starts dressing you, old demon." He gasped in mock outrage, straightening his white tunic as if it were a precious piece.

"Speaking of old, I do have something to ask you. Noe, would you give us a moment?" Noe's gaze was wide as it flicked between us. Nosy little vermin. I flicked my hand, signaling for her to get out of there. With a slight stomp of her foot she pivoted, her long mane of golden-brown hair hitting me in the face as she left.

A soft click came as the door shut, and then we were alone. I turned to Adbeel, waiting to hear what he could possibly have to ask. Nerves stretched his face as he seemed to contemplate how best to say whatever it was that held his thoughts.

"Oh how bad can it be? I literally told you that I had been keeping your long-lost granddaughter from you. It cannot be worse than that, right?"

Glaring at me as if I had just reminded him of how much he despised me, Adbeel sat up straight and placed his clasped hands upon his desk. More silence was all I was offered. Fine then, far be it for me to ignore good food. I grabbed a chocolate scone and took a bite, reaching for my coffee to wash it down. Just as I took a drink, Adbeel finally spoke. "I want you and Asher to ascend."

Delicately, like the royal I was, I promptly spit out the hot coffee. Adbeel watched the dark liquid spray his sun-bleached floors with an unamused expression. He looked like someone who had suffered greatly at the hands of his enemies. Really it was just me, being a little shit in his eyes. How wonderfully domestic.

"When?" I finally said through gasping breaths. My dark brown shoe had coffee on it, and I found myself staring at the spot instead of looking at him.

"We will do a ceremony immediately following your vows."

So soon. Would Asher want that? How would she feel about immediately ruling over creatures she once thought her enemies? Was everything still too new?

Asher had spent a lifetime choosing everyone but herself, I feared what putting a crown on her head would do now that she had finally learned to prioritize her own feelings and wants.

"I do not know if she is ready," I finally admitted, looking at him. He gave nothing away with his face, but his tapping foot and tightly clenched hands told me he was on edge. Adbeel had said before that he wanted the crown off his head. He was tired. I could understand that. "We are in a volatile time, do you think now is the best opportunity to challenge the status quo?"

"Asher is the strongest demon we have seen in millennia, our subjects will see that for what it is: hope and destiny."

"Fine, I will ask her and get right back to you."

"Excellent. I will have Solei's old crown fitted for her." Adbeel beamed, twisting in his chair to look out at the sea beyond The Royal City.

"Of course you will," I sighed in defeat.

**

"What if we restored Haven?" I asked as I massaged Asher's head with my hand not covered in paint. The others straightened, our group larger than it had ever been as we sat outside while the sun slowly crawled

towards the horizon, nearly tucked behind the mountains. Even Stassi was there, stuck to Sterling's side like glue. I had caught Asher looking their way with a frown more than once, especially as Stassi seemed to soothe a pain in Sterling's hand. Something had changed between them the other day after he returned with his sister.

Geneveive had agreed to spend time with us as well, though she spent most of it insulting Henry. He was becoming obsessive with his love for her, and it seemed he had begun to wear her down. She was curled up against him, his hand absently playing with her curls before she reached up and swatted it away.

"What would be the point?" Lian asked from her spot next to Damon, who was looking longingly at Noe. My spymaster was uninterested in anything but her plans for my attire at my wedding. Putting down my paintbrush, I looked at Lian.

"The sirens could live in it. Maybe you all could too. It was our primary home for so long, and I feel like it is special enough to deserve more love." Asher's head adjusted against me, and I looked down in time to catch her curious gaze. Was she listening to my thoughts? I did not feel her there, but I rarely did these days. She was even stronger, somehow.

"Nona would have liked that," Ranbir whispered. To his left, Cyprus nodded vacantly.

"Luca, too."

Their names had me picking up my paintbrush again, their portraits coming together slowly. We would need them for the wedding. Luca's blonde hair was giving me trouble, but I was making gradual progress.

"I wish you would let me put you in navy blue, I think it would look so good with your complexion," Noe mumbled before scribbling upon the paper she was inspecting.

"Asher is wearing white, I need to be more subtle so she can shine. It is her special day after all."

439

"It is more your special day than mine, you desperate demon. Plus, I will look fantastic regardless, thank you very much."

"Blue goes great with white!" Noe shouted.

"Just put me in black, please. You can wear blue instead," I scoffed. No way was I wearing the color of fucking Maliha.

"I am not the groom, dumbass! You are so, so annoying, Bell."

"I will toast to that," Damon shouted with a snort. Soon, everyone—even Asher—was raising their glasses before dumping them back.

Stories began, and I was lost in the sounds, my focus solely on the canvas before me. That was, until Asher reached up and grabbed my hand, placing a soft kiss to the corner of my mouth that was still swollen from her affection earlier. I noted the new tattoo on her wrist, my heart breaking at the meaning behind it. Sterling had an exact replica on his left wrist, the two of them having snuck off to see Shah the other night. Together they made a particularly fucked up pair.

Then again, so did we all.

"I love you," I whispered against her lips after turning my head.

Laughing, she mumbled, "I love you more."

CHAPTER FORTY-SEVEN

PERDITA

Dima had been difficult to find.

I had used the conche she gave me *five fucking times* and received no response, until suddenly, the crew heard her. She sang to us, drawing Bek into her web like a spider on the hunt. My right hand took us to the creature beneath the sea, steering us to what would be our doom if not for the fact that Dima would never kill us. She had no one else.

Within minutes, Dima boarded the ship. She was fully nude, her lavender eyes sharp as they took in my crew. Her crew, in a way. She still had a place with us, even if it was not necessarily at my side. Accepting that might be difficult, but she could manage.

"Storm," I signed as she slowly approached me. My lips split in two, a yawning chasm of delight at the sight of her. She knew how much I loved her body, but she secretly delighted in how desperately I needed her magic. And, at the moment, I was prepared to beg for it.

In no reality could I do enough damage and cause enough trouble to warrant Blue's involvement without her. So, when she slapped me across the face, I took the slight with dignity and little to no anger. Kicking her off the ship had not been a good idea.

"Dima, my love. I would like to apologize for how I acted—how awful I was. Incorrigible. Heinous. Outright undeserving of life." Okay, maybe I was laying it on a bit too thick. Clearing my throat, I pulled out a tangle of red roses that I had wrapped up in white string.

Storm took them with little to no interest. But her eyes gave her away. She missed me. The longing in her slouched face and wide stare was obvious. Like any good pirate captain, I seized the moment.

"What do you say to eating a few weak sailors and then letting me devour you?"

"Fine, but I am sleeping in your quarters and you are not allowed to finish," she signed back, her movements slow from disuse.

"You drive a hard bargain, but deal."

***

I would never get over the jaw dropping sight that was watching Dima consume living beings. Clearly she was in a mood, because she did not bother to kill them first. She just started ripping off chunks of their skin with her teeth and swallowing the pieces. Fitting, seeing as they had refused to tell me where their gold was. I had spent a whole three minutes searching.

That was wasted time that completely fucked with our schedule. The utter audacity.

Dima stood, drenched in the blood of the male she had eaten cock first, and turned to me.

"We make a great team," I signed. Storm smiled at me, her teeth nearly black from the blood. "You truly are a queen."

"By blood. On these seas I am merely death. Now come make me scream in ecstasy."

***

Days passed with no word from her. Lian was far less predictable than Dima, but I knew she would find us. She had to. I was staining the seas around her realm red. Prince Bellamy Ayad would not stand for it, and she would be the one sent again.

I watched Dima finish off her meal, the sailor no longer gurgling out strained pleas. Gold surrounded me, the merchant ship captain having just traded her goods. My fingers toyed with the coins, the cold bite of them against my sweaty skin a relief.

Heaving a breath of boredom, I kicked one of the chests over, letting the coins spill across the sea water soaked deck of the Abaddon. And then, with all the flare of the greatest pirate to sail the three seas, I promptly fell backwards into it.

The rumble of my crew's laughter could be felt beneath my splayed palms, and I could not help but smile in return. However, something was different about this time. I felt empty. Oddly unhappy despite the success of the attack. Why was I...*unsatisfied?*

Groaning, I tried to remember where my last correspondence from the prince was, plotting even as I celebrated with my crew.

OF VOWS AND WAR

***

Lian appeared on a foggy day on the Sea of Akiva. I knew she would be there, as I had successfully gotten the prince's attention by writing him a letter. If one could call it that. Though it had not been very formal. Something along the lines of "I thought you would care to know that I have killed a merchant carrying what must have been weaponry for your soldiers. Finders keepers."

Lian had written back one of the most heinous responses. She called me a scoundrel. A psychopath. A stupid bitch. But my favorite? *A filthy pirate.*

I hoped she would call me that last one in bed.

And when she used a female to portal her instead of Henry, I had grown even more excited. She was mine for the taking.

The two of them appeared amongst shadows instead of light, their faces grim and fierce. My attention immediately went to Blue. She had on a tight-fitting pair of olive green trousers, her black boots tied halfway up her calf. An equally skin-tight top with short sleeves covered her upper half while leaving little to the imagination. Exactly how I liked it.

Come on, Blue, show me what you are made of.

The first thing she did, the shadows from the female behind her still clinging to her form, was throw a dagger my way. I portaled before it reached me. My feet went from the small landing in front of the door to my quarters to the deck a mere foot from her. Then, I tackled her to the ground.

My fist went sailing into her cheek, catching her by surprise and forcing her head to whip to the left. That would likely be my last good hit.

And it was.

Lian let out a guttural roar that vibrated in my bones as she dug her nails into my neck, flipping us before slamming my skull into my own deck. Her fists smashed into my face again and again after that, unwavering in their pursuit for my blood. My crew watched on in resigned horror, each of them, even Dima, knowing better than to step in. The female who had come with Lian seemed just as prepared to watch, but she wore a lethal smile.

I finally caved after the ninth punch. My fingers tapped three times on Lian's arm, and she immediately stopped. It was then that she seemed to realize she was straddling me. It felt good to sense her weight there, pressing into my hips. I would gladly keep her there forever. Alas, she was still pretending she did not want me like I wanted her.

She got up with a look of disgust on her face, saying something too quickly for me to catch.

"Eyes on me, Blue," I signed, catching her attention. She glared, looking as if she truly might gut me right there. Instead, I lifted my hands and slowly signed her reward for winning the fight.

"What does that one mean?" She asked out loud, her mouth moving slow enough for me to understand, though she turned her head to face Bek after. My eyes followed Lian's hazel ones, catching sight of Bek as she laughed. A smile tore open my face when my second answered her.

"Captain? Captain! What a stupid sign!" Lian was nearly hysterical as she tilted her face down to me again.

"Just teaching you since you will need to address me properly as a member of my crew." Her eyes flicked with each movement of my hands, understanding enough that a snarl lifted one half of her enormous top lip and gave me the barest hint of her equally large teeth.

I wondered what they would feel like against my skin.

She was driving me fucking insane. Maybe killing her would be better. Get rid of her before she sucked me in any further.

No. I needed her at least once.

"I will never join your crew, you stupid fucking moron!" Lian was shouting so loudly that I could feel her voice against my skin, her fingers twitching as if she wanted to sign but simply could not amidst her anger. I was getting better at reading her lips. Her lips, which looked so soft. So enticing. "Sink one more ship and I will tear you limb from limb!"

I adored her when she was angry. The way her nearly round face grew flushed and her shoulders squared. Simply delicious.

Fight with me, Blue. Let me help you get out that frustration.

Just once. I only needed her once and then I could move on.

I whistled, catching Ro's eye and waving her to my side. She walked slowly, her loose blouse billowing in the chilly wind. We needed to put some of this gold to use and splurge on new clothes. We deserved to look the best seeing as we were the best.

With Ro at my side, I focused back on Lian. On my conquest waiting to happen.

"Come visit me for one night and one day every two weeks," I signed. I had no doubt Ro was translating for me, as both Lian and her companion were listening with squinted eyes and pursed lips. "Be a part of my crew for one full day each fortnight and I promise I will be good."

Lian glared daggers at me, her hand going to the sword strapped to her back. Surprisingly, it was her companion with the flowing golden-brown hair and the curving hips that saw reason. She caught Lian's hand, saying something to her with full lips that hardly moved. Her light brown skin showed no signs of nerves or rushing blood. This female was smart. A spy maybe? Something that required her to see the world for what it truly was rather than what was presented to her.

After an odd sort of staring contest between the two females, Lian pivoted to face me fully.

"One day and one night. I work your sails with CJ. That is it."

Success!

"We are eternally grateful, Blue." Ro nudged me, and I turned to find her looking baffled. Her jaw was loose and eyes scrutinizing as she seemed to will me to change my mind. From just over her shoulder, Bek looked on in outrage. Shrugging, I faced Lian once more. "Tonight will be your first."

With that, I walked away from them, heading towards the port side of the deck. CJ's eyes were on the water instead of the commotion behind me, her desire to be useful often leaving her alone. I came up to her back, reaching out to softly touch her shoulder and get her attention. When she turned to face me, I began weaving my master plan.

"Tell Lian to come see me in my quarters after her friend leaves," I ordered, my signs lazy and my smile wicked. Turning, I could not help but wink at the little blue-haired fae who had no idea what was coming to her.

Then, I caught sight of Dima and quickly grabbed onto her hand, the sight of her lush body draped in a thin silver dress making me far less excited than it once did. She would do for now, though.

The two of us snuck away, slipping into my quarters without catching anyone's eye. Just before the door shut all the way behind me, I caught it, leaving a small sliver of space. Just enough for wandering eyes to see through.

With my plan in motion, I turned on Dima, grabbing her by the neck and forcing her lips to crash into mine. She met me with full force, her tongue pushing into my mouth and her hips slamming into mine. I felt the way she sucked on the blood still leaking from my split lip, eagerness pouring from her. Reaching up, I yanked the thin straps of her dress off her shoulders, tugging once and pulling away just in time to watch the silk pool on the ground.

Dima smirked as she watched me taking her in. While the siren was as she always had been—a glorious sight to behold—it was as if she had lost her shine somehow. Or perhaps my eyes no longer wished to see it.

Shoving that thought aside, I grasped Dima's breasts and once more kissed her. The two of us walked back until my bed forced us to fall. She landed first, her back against the plush mattress and my body atop hers.

Time was running low. Without truly meaning to, I glanced at the barely ajar door, seeing nothing but empty space. Quicker. I needed to move quicker.

I ripped my lips from Dima's, trailing kisses down her body and letting my tongue glide along it. She writhed below me, her hands tangling in my mane of curls as I tasted her. What would be the hottest? The most enticing? My fingers? My mouth? I needed this to be perfect. I needed this to change minds.

A mind.

Attempting to show what I was worth did not always mean looting. I was great at many things. And I needed to prove that.

My mouth. My mouth was best. With an aching jaw and a cut lip, the act would likely hurt. If I were honest, my energy would waver soon, but I had survived worse than a few punches. I needed to do this.

So I kept trailing lower, stopping only to choose which leg of Dima's I would pay the most attention to. I bit and sucked on her thigh, relishing in how large it was. In the space that it gave me to work with. The siren squirmed below me, her moans vibrating against my lips and making them tingle.

Twice more, I looked up to find an empty doorway, my anger beginning to flare to life. Impatience and I were good friends, and the two of us loathed unpredictability. That, and untimeliness.

But Dima was ready, and I had no more time to waste. So, with a growl of fury that I hoped more closely mirrored desire, I shoved my face

between her thighs and licked a long, slow line upwards. At least she still tasted good, if not a little blander than she once had. Rolling my eyes at my own desperation, I suddenly caught movement.

There, looking through the crack in what could only be described as panic and horror, was Blue. My devious, stabby little fae had her hand raised as if to knock, but clearly she saw more than she bargained for. And I was going to make sure she bore witness to much more.

A soft hum swirled in my chest like a tornado as I went to work on Dima, sucking her into my mouth and gliding my tongue across her. She bucked and shook, but I did not take my eyes off Lian. She had not fled, as if she were frozen to the spot.

Yes, Blue, watch how I feast and pray I will devour you next.

I lifted Dima's legs, tugging each of them onto my shoulders and digging my fingers into them as I consumed her. All the while, Lian matched my stare. That was, until I winked at her. My mistake, really. I should have known better than to challenge and tease her.

She kicked the door open, letting it swing and slam into the wall. I was sure the noise must have been startlingly loud, because Dima screamed and pulled herself away from me. I was left on my knees before my bed, my eyes scrutinizing Lian as she approached. But when she began speaking, it was Dima that Lian addressed. I tried to follow her lips, but she was talking too fast.

Leaving me in the dark on purpose. The nerve of her.

Sadly for me, I did not get a chance to call her out or so much as move before Dima's foot slammed into my already bruised and bloody face. The kick made my head snap backwards, sending pain down my spine. Underworld below, that fucking hurt. Gripping my jaw, I stood, ready to scold the bitch for hitting me. But the siren simply grabbed her dress, pulled it on, and dashed out of the room without looking back.

What just happened?

"I told her what you doing," Blue said in broken signs. "Tricking me to watch. Very rude."

With a wink that rivaled my own, Lian saluted me and left the same way Dima had.

What the *utter fuck* just happened?

CHAPTER FORTY-EIGHT

ASHER

Sweat trickled down my temple, my head pounding as magic flooding my body and poured out of me like a raging waterfall. Lian's bursts of air were fierce as they crashed upon me, Noe's cool shadows slashing my legs at every chance. Cyprus was nearly impossible to get a hold of as he faded in and out of his misty darkness, Farai swapping between the forms of different animals to evade me. Meanwhile, Henry and Damon had seen fit to barrel into me with sheer force, the two of them striking me any chance they could. I was completely surrounded and continuously moving.

But I was still winning.

"Who was the twenty-second Ayad to rule over Eoforhild?" Adbeel asked in a shout from his place on the sidelines. He had his large arms crossed and his brow furrowed as he stared at my every movement.

"Deja Ayad!" I yelled in response, my leg swinging to take out Cyprus after I saw in his mind the moment he decided to take back his solid form. His body flew, flipping four times before crashing back onto the ground.

Noe's shadows were slinking around my foot as it arched back down, Henry's fist ready as it swung towards my exposed jaw. I breathed through my nose and followed the will of the magic in my veins, ducking the punch and tugging the line of shadows. I was quick, probably quicker than I had ever been. Neither was ready as Henry's fist cracked into Noe's face. But I did not stop there, choosing to use Damon's fondness of Noe to my advantage.

For a few precious moments, the silver-haired demon was so blissfully distracted that it was practically nothing to will him into sleep, his body crumpling to the ground. Farai was quick to take Damon's place, coming at me as different beasts.

"Portal!" Adbeel ordered. I did as I was told, continuously jumping to a new spot until I got behind Farai in the form of a vulture. I grabbed one of my daggers and threw it, watching as it flew through Farai's right wing.

Lian was on me quicker than the rest, a dome of air encircling me just as Farai hit the ground—becoming a solid force in which I could not break. Despite that, I still ferociously kicked at it.

"What were the six territories named after?" Adbeel's voice still boomed across the open training yard, the air shield not stopping the question from reaching me. Groaning, I turned to Lian.

"Careful, Lian, you have always had a weak mental shield," I taunted her. Her face pinched, fury making blood rush to her cheeks and stain them red. I saw a shimmer around me, the shield glittering in the light of midday as Lian momentarily lost her focus. I smirked, not turning to Adbeel before answering him. "The greatest attributes of the six brothers and sisters that first ruled Eoforhild."

"Correct. And what were those traits?" he asked, still circling the area. My eyes never left Lian's.

Go on, Lian, tell him.

She ground her teeth at my voice in her head, the audible sound of bone scraping faint beyond the shield. The next time I spoke, it was in the deeper tenor of The Manipulator, my head tilting to the side just as Bellamy's always did.

"Tell him, Lian."

Then, inside her head, I said the answers, willing her to repeat them.

"Strength, courage, hope, love, power, and intelligence," Lian said between clenched teeth. And, with no more than a smirk her way, I willed Lian to sleep as well. The air around me thinned, the shield disappearing from existence. I beamed Adbeel's way, proud of my accomplishment, but the king only eyed me as if thinking up a new challenge.

Turns out, that was exactly what he was doing.

"Okay, now my turn. This time, no magic." The king's order was not only terrifying, but *exciting* as well.

"Let us find out who is more rusty," I offered as I raised my fists in preparation. In that time, I also allowed Damon and Lian to wake up, their groggy forms swaying as the others helped them out of the way. Then it was just Adbeel and I.

We circled each other, neither moving so much as an inch closer. My magic itched to break free of the gates that I had locked it behind again, the chains rattling like the moans of the dead come back to life, charging at me for daring to cage them. But I held it back, digging my feet into the ground the second that Adbeel rushed me.

Ducking his blow, I spun, facing him again.

"I have been filled in about the gods, and properly terrified of it all. So I understand why Anastasia is training your magic, as she knows where

our magic began before it trickled down to us," he said, once more circling me. I maintained my distance, not wanting him to have the upperhand. Close combat was not my best, but I could beat him. Over the last year I had discovered that I could do *anything*. "While I might not understand your magic fully due to you being half fae—which is likely why your magic is so different to begin with—I do know where *you* come from." The king struck, jumping forward and bringing his blade down upon me. I was quick to free my sword from its sheath, catching his blade with mine. "I know where you will *go* as well."

A battle of wills commenced. With every bit of ground one of us gained, the other eventually pushed back enough to level the playing field again. Strikes and blows and kicks. No clear winner was in sight. Adbeel soon began quizzing me again, asking me the names of the lords and ladies, the laws that existed in the realm, everything and anything he thought I needed to know for the upcoming ascension. I would be a great queen, of that I was certain.

I was born and raised to be, even if it was all done in the hopes of turning me into Mia. Learning often came at a price, but the knowledge was there forever. And so I would rule well.

Not to mention I would have a particularly well-versed partner. A male who had been raised for this throne in particular. The same male who suddenly appeared into existence behind me.

Bellamy.

I felt his presence like blood rushing through the body, threatening to distract me from my fight.

Just to increase the probability of my victory, I stopped myself from holding back. Bellamy had noticed it more than once, my seemingly ever-growing strength. Now, I hoped to speed up the fight with it. To give myself more time with him today. That, and I desperately wished to win in front of him. Grunting, I swung my sword faster and harder than before.

Adbeel heaved out a breath when my next blow struck his sword, rattling his arms. Again and again I came at him, his prompts fading out as

the fight stole away his focus. We fought far longer than I had with any of the others, but it was good to be reminded that I was not notably exceptional without my magic. I used it so often that I forgot the importance of training without it.

That was why, when Adbeel finally got a hold of the cloth on my chest and used it to lift me before throwing me to the ground back first, I was not necessarily surprised by my loss.

Definitely disappointed though.

Breathing heavily and smiling wider than I had ever seen him, Adbeel chuckled. "Great fight. We will work on magicless training. I want you to beat me by week's end."

"Deal," I said, smiling too. Adbeel's eyes crinkled at the corners as he beamed. All I could do was bask in our shared joy. That and make a joke. "Grandpa."

"Hey now!" he shouted, standing and offering me his hand. I took it, letting him lift me until we were both up and placing our crossed forearms on our heads to catch our breath. "I am not some decrepit old male!"

"I am not so sure, you were rather slow on some of those moves." Bellamy's deep and raspy voice was a balm to my system, slowing and soothing it. He was a bright light that made my cold darkness feel like half of a whole rather than an all-encompassing force. Strong arms wrapped around me from the back, something pointy digging into the top of my head. His chin probably. "I missed you."

"Awe, and I missed you. How lovely to have a ward that so deeply cares for me," Adbeel crooned, his voice coated in sarcasm. Bellamy groaned. What fun it was to watch him receive a taste of his own medicine. In fact, it was wonderful getting to see where Bellamy's humor came from.

"Anyways, I call dibs on Ash's next match." While I knew he was being tame for Adbeel's sake, Bellamy still got close to my ear, his breath

hot on my skin, and whispered, "Unless you would rather we have a different sort of match up in our room, fiancé of mine."

Blushing furiously, I took his arm and ripped it down just as I bent my knees and arched my back. He flew over me, landing even harder on his back than I had on mine earlier. A grunt escaped his lips, the wind completely knocked out of him. Bending low, I let my lips just graze his ear as I challenged him. "Beat me out here and you can have me up there in any way you want me."

"Sounds like our cue to leave," Farai said, Ranbir patting him on the shoulder with a blood-stained hand. The others nodded, all but Henry leaving quickly.

The orange-haired demon looked reluctant to go, but eventually he shrugged and said, "I guess I was bound to doom if I kept going anyways."

"Time for me to go too, this old male needs a nap," Adbeel added, kissing my forehead and kicking Bellamy in the side where he lay. Bellamy hissed at the pain. I watched with a snort as he grabbed Adbeel's ankle and made him stumble.

"I must warn you," Bellamy said as he stood, "when I win I am going to do absolutely horrible things to you in that bed."

"Impossible, because when I win I am going to do heinous— potentially illegal—things to *you.*"

"Well, you better not hold back right now then. Give me all you have, beautiful creature."

We squared off, readying to fight, and I could have sworn my fingertips heated as if being kissed by flames.

***

Nightmares had been plaguing me every night. Incessant, unyielding retellings of my time being physically and psychologically tortured by Mia and Xavier. This was not a nightmare though. No, this darkness—this unending emptiness—was far from the horrid things that normally tormented me.

It was worse.

"Padon, you son of a—"

"Oh, my love! I missed you!" he said, cutting me off. He was on me in seconds, his large arms wrapping around me so tight I thought he might accidentally kill me. Would I really die if he killed me in this odd dream world? What a thought.

Quickly, I jabbed him in the gut with my elbow, smiling with wicked glee as he grunted.

"You are like a child seeing ice cream. Trust me, I know, I snuck three children ice cream behind the back of their caretaker just today," I said, dusting off my clothes to rid them of Padon's wretched germs. Nasty.

"Apologies for having the gall to miss you," he growled, standing straight once more. It was then that I realized it had been *his* voice whispering to me randomly during the day. I squared my shoulders, ready to fight if I had to. But I knew better now. This was my head, I was in charge if I wanted to be. "I think it's time you come back to me."

"I think it is time that I rip out your lousy heart and eat it for dinner!" I yelled, pointing at him like that might really emphasize my words. He frowned, his nearly translucent skin tinted blue from his blood and his slightly longer hair a mess from what seemed like sleep. He wore those same thick cotton pants he had months ago, his torso covered by a thin black top with short sleeves.

"Please, Asher?" he asked with wide eyes. When I did not respond, choosing to instead cross my arms and begin tapping my foot, Padon surprised me by falling to his knees. "I'll give you anything you want. I will let your mortal boy live. I will never step foot on Alemthian again. I will let

you rule. I will kill anyone who opposes you. Please, just come to me. Be mine."

I almost felt bad for him as he crawled forward slightly to kiss the tops of my bare feet. Almost.

"I will *never* be yours. How do you not get it yet? I. Do. Not. Want. You." I pronounced every word slowly, trying to will it into his thick skull. Why was it that he could not understand my desire to not be anywhere near him? I had made it so abundantly clear.

A soft and almost delicate sob escaped him, but as his hands dashed out to grip my ankles, I realized his hold was anything but frail. Bruises would have surely appeared if this had been real. But no, this was a dream. Sort of. Either way, he was not going to bruise me here. No longer would he control me either.

"I can't lose another," he mumbled, still facing down.

"Get off!" I shouted, kicking at him. He groaned as if in pain, though I was not sure if it were more mental or physical. "I will never, *ever* be with you, Padon."

Something must have clicked that time, because his back stiffened and his hands smacked the darkness near my feet. Suddenly, his head flung up, face a mask of rage and death. Without realizing it, I began backing away from him, but Padon only continued to follow me. He slowly stood, his steps towards me measured and his eyes ablaze.

"Congratulations, Asher, you have officially pushed me to the edge." My eyes went wide as his lips stretched into a sneer. Eternity above, he looked moments away from killing me. "If you deny me again then I will gladly—eagerly—destroy your pathetic world and everyone on it. I will steal everything you hold dear, and then I will steal *you.*"

Momentarily more furious than terrified, I stopped my retreat.

"I dare you to try," I seethed. "If you or any of your little minions step foot on Alemthian, then I will rip you apart. I will leave nothing but your bloody entrails as proof that you even existed."

"Please, you can't kill me," he said with a sardonic laugh. My answering smile felt as evil as I did. I was wrath, now. I was anger and retribution and all things vengeance. Around us, there was a sort of shimmery haze building. Padon was losing control. His foothold in my head was slipping.

"Oh yeah?" I asked mockingly, letting my lips rise in what I hoped was a horrific bearing of teeth. My finger rose, poking him hard in the chest. His eyes widened, as if he knew where I was going with what I was about to say. "What if I rip out that pretty, purple seed?"

Padon blanched, his already pale skin gaining a sickly hue. Blowing him a kiss, I flashed him my ring finger, letting the gem face him and willing it to sparkle.

"By the way, I am engaged, fucker."

And then I thrust out my magic, shattering Padon's hold on my mind. Suddenly I was jolting up in mine and Bellamy's bed, no screams escaping me though sweat poured down my skin. Bellamy was already awake, his eyes trained on me from where his head rested on one of his pillows.

"What is wrong?" he asked, his brows pinched together in concern and his blue eyes inviting.

Raising the left half of my lips into a wicked smirk, I answered, "Nothing."

ACT V

~ FATE AND CHANCE ~

CHAPTER FORTY-NINE

ASHER

Yet another wedding loomed.

There was something truly unsettling about waiting for the day to come. While the first marriage had been thrust upon me, this one was an honor. No one forced me to hang the dress in mine and Bellamy's bathing room, just as I had the hideous golden one back in the palace in The Capital. No one made me organize all of the vials Noe had brought in a similar fashion to how Maybel had a year ago. But I did those things anyway.

I was not sure why, just that I felt like I had to.

When I finally got into bed after pacing for what felt like a lifetime, I twirled the ring on my finger, traced my new tattoo, breathed in a deep pull of air, and closed my eyes. Bellamy would not come tonight. In

Eoforhild, it was tradition to spend the night before your wedding without one another. So stupid. But it was fine.

I would be fine.

***

I awoke in a puddle of sweat, screaming as I jolted upwards.

Mia's shouts of fury. Xavier's swinging fist. Sterling's tight grip. They were coming for me. I knew it. I felt it. I saw it. I lived it.

They were coming.

I kicked off the quilt, feeling around in the dark as I tried to find the doors to my chambers.

But everything was different. Off, somehow. This was not my gilded prison.

I took heaving gasps of the hot air, crawling until I felt my head hit a wall.

Think, Asher. Just think.

My left thumb reached for my ring finger, feeling the cold metal there. I needed light. I needed proof.

This was real. I knew what was real.

Letting my fingers trace up my arm, I slowly named off my scars and where I got them, wishing more than anything that they were still there to remind me of who I was and where I have been. Because I was in Pike. I knew it, even if my heart still raced at the recollection of the haunting nightmares.

I soothed myself with memories of the last couple of weeks. Of the time spent in love and safety. I recalled the way Theon's blood had spilled into my mouth as I ripped out his throat. I thought of watching Bellamy dig out Xavier's heart. They were dead. Gone. Left to rot or burned to dust.

Mia was still out there, but she could not take anything from me again. I had Bellamy. Our friends. Adbeel. I was alive. My happy ending was within my grasp, if only I could just remember. Could break free of the haunting memories of pain and blood.

Bellamy could help me. But if I went to him, would he think me too unstable for the wedding? Could I scare him too much? This was his time too, and I feared stealing that from him like it was being stolen from me.

My hand stilled on the spot of my arm where there was once a jagged and raised reminder of what happened after Haven. My hopelessness etched into my skin.

My scars. I needed my scars.

I knew I should have called for help. Anyone would have been glad to talk me through the panic that flooded my veins and weighed my body down like lead. But I did not want to run through castles nearly naked and cry in front of strangers. I wanted to do this on my own.

Pushing myself to a standing position, I relaxed my shoulders and walked through the dark room to the bedside table. Cool wood chilled my scalding feet, anchoring me as I felt for the brass handle. This one was on my side, which meant if I opened up the drawer—yes, there was the soft leather of my sheath.

I was going to be okay. I was going to fix myself. I was going to walk down that aisle whole.

Alive and well and safe. That was what I was. All I needed was a reminder. An anchor to this reality.

My free hand reached in and grabbed a set of matches, a slight shake to them as I sparked the fire to life and lit the candle. There, I could see. And the first thing my eyes looked at were the words inked on my skin.

Sterling and I had both been struggling, though we were loathe to admit that to anyone other than each other. I had spent much of my free time with him or in his head, the two of us talking one another back to reality. He had come back from Maliha more haunted than before, his family wanting everything to be as it was and Sterling knowing he was forever changed. So when Shah had come back with him and Genevieve, we had decided there was an opportunity there.

Shah was not as skilled as a mortal trained to etch the tattoos, but she knew how to do what we asked. And, luckily for us, her script was immaculate.

Now, as I read the words, I thought of Sterling. Maybe I could go to him. But, if I were being honest, no one other than Bellamy would help right now. And even then, I would still fall apart later. I needed to fix this permanently.

Why worry Bellamy when I could handle it?

Yes, I could do this.

My eyes scanned the words on my wrist one last time.

This is real.

And then I unsheathed the blade and began the steady work of earning back my scars. After months of tracing their ghosts, it was easy to begin reviving them.

Blood poured out, the deep red staining my white night dress and pouring onto the ground, but that was okay. Stains and messes would not stop me from repairing myself. Even the bite of the blade was not enough to deter me.

Tears poured down my face, not because I was hurting, but because I was healing. Every dip of the dagger and rip of my skin was a second chance at the story I nearly lost. I was not breaking my body, I was mending it.

To my great disappointment, someone was always there to muck things up.

My door burst open, the wood swinging and cracking from where it connected with the rock wall. I shouted at the surprise, my magic not catching the four minds until they arrived.

Faster, I had to move faster. Maybe just one shoulder. The afriktor's talons were a mark of great change. Of realization. I *needed* that one.

There was a hand and a voice and maybe even sobs somewhere in the haze around me. Suddenly I was being wrestled to the ground, my knees giving out as a dark hand lit fire to my body. I shouted in pain and fury and loss. They stole my reality. My truth. I was so fucking close.

But no. I was still broken.

"Asher, you have to stop!" A deep voice, not soothing or soft like I knew it to be.

"No, Ranbir, let Sterling talk! Shah, get ready!" My sweet, beautiful best friend. Oh how I hated her right then.

"Okay, fine. Asher, Sterling is here. I have to heal these. You have to let me or I will force you." Ranbir again. Of course he would—

Wait, heal me?

No!

"No, stop! Do not touch me!" I screamed, shoving at them. Cool hands grabbed my face, and suddenly my eyes were open and staring into a set of lovely brown ones speckled with green.

467

"I am here. I have you," Sterling said. His smile was full of heartbreak, his eyes shining with tears.

"They are trying to take my scars, Sterling. Please do not let them do this," I sobbed the words out, begging the boy in front of me to help. The only one who could possibly understand what it was like to not know what was real and what was fake. But I saw the slackening of his face that signaled he would not stop them, and I knew that I was alone in this.

"Nicola is going to help you, I promise," he said, his fingers still cold on my face. My body seemed to deflate at his words, Ranbir's power burning its way through me until I was disgustingly bare once more.

Sterling pulled me into him, hugging me close, his deep accent coming out stronger as he sang softly in my ear. The words were foreign to me, Maliha's tongue one I did not know. Still, I felt the truly tragic meaning as he continued to sing. My heart slowed, my mind settling as Sterling's song came to a close.

Shah's face came into view, the sorrow there twin to my own. To all of ours. We had each suffered more than we cared to admit.

"Hey, almost queen, how are you feeling?" she asked. I nearly chuckled at her words, the odd nickname ironic but true. It seemed like forever ago that I claimed myself a queen in her castle. Tomorrow, I would become one in truth.

"Ash," Nicola cut in, kneeling down next to Shah. "I know you are in pain. If I could take that away I would. But I do have a plan to help."

A plan? What could possibly help other than my scars? They did not understand. Of course not. How could they? It was nearly impossible to explain how much it hurt to not know what was real and what was false—to describe the agony of torture and manipulation.

"You are fully healed, so I am going to go. I think you deserve as much privacy as possible right now." Ranbir squeezed my shoulder once before nodding and standing to leave. I did not speak to him, not wanting

to take my anger out on the Healer who was just doing what he thought was best.

"I made him come, Ash," Nicola whispered. "Do not blame him."

I faced her, seeing the truth of her words on her face as she looked at me with sad eyes. The pity there was unbearable. I did not want to be this disastrous version of myself. More than anything, I just wanted to be whole again. I thought of who I had been during my birthday party, those few hours having been some of the best of my life. Why could we not turn back time? Live in those moments for a bit longer so I might recall what it was to be better?

Shah began moving, her hands grabbing and arranging items I could not make out in the faint candlelight.

"How about this: you tell Shah where each of your scars were and what they looked like, and she will tattoo them back on." I whipped my head back towards Nicola, my hair hitting Sterling in the face and causing him to begin hacking heinously.

"Gods above, Ash. Your hair is attacking me!" The sound of him spitting out pieces of my hair was quickly followed by Shah's laughter.

"You can leave, I think we have this. Go find Bellamy. Might as well tell him, I imagine he will want to sit outside of the door and make sure she is okay," Shah said, her tone one of exasperation. She was probably quite tired of my antics by now. That, or she truly understood and felt the same exhaustion I did.

"I will see you tomorrow," Sterling said against my hair, likely having lost the battle to it and willing to suffer longer to tell me goodbye. Then, after he hugged me tighter and hummed for a few more moments, Sterling got up and left too.

With just Shah, Nicola, and I left, I was forced to acknowledge what they were offering. Tattoo my scars back on. Would that be the same? Would black versions look right? I thought of Bell's magic and how the sight of the black lines haunted him. What would he think of my new

tattoos? I did not want to be a source of pain for him. Nor did I think that it would be anything but artificial in my eyes.

"They will not be the same," I said, watching as what I now knew was a bottle of ink was placed on the side table by Shah. Nicola's face softened, her eyes large and round as they scrutinized me.

"You know, I do not always choose what I see. In fact, the future and past are often thrust upon me without my consent. But when I saw this, I knew there had to be better options. You were bleeding yourself out, Ash. You could have killed yourself." Sighing at my best friend's words, I turned away, not wanting to look at either of them while I was called out for my stupidity. "I searched for other futures, and I saw this. The first option was using black ink, but you eventually cut into them again because they did not feel real enough. So I sought out something else, not in the future, but from Shah."

"Did you know tattoos do not have to be black?" Shah asked, a smirk on her face as she handed me the glass jar. I took it gingerly, my hand shaking slightly from the overwhelming emotions that invaded me. It was not black ink that swirled inside of it. Instead, it was the most lovely shade of tan, the color showing the barest hint of peach—twin to the shade my scars had been.

"Farai told me you called your scars your story," Nicola murmured, her voice soft and soothing. I felt a single tear roll down my cheek, the truth of what they were about to give me settling into my chest. "Are you ready to rewrite it?"

After a few deep breaths, I nodded.

"Okay then, where do we start?" Shah asked, rubbing her hand up and down my arm.

From there, I slowly and painstakingly described each scar. Shah worked diligently throughout the night, listening to every detail. By the time the sun began to rise, our candles had snuffed out and my body was covered in stunning depictions of my scars—of my life after Bellamy had saved me.

"All done," Shah whispered. She packed up her things in silence after that, the air coated in an odd sort of tranquility that felt wrong to break. Nicola, too, got up to leave, kissing my forehead before walking to the door with the Queen of Behman.

When they shut the door behind them, I was left to steep in the heaviness of the past and peace of the future. I cleaned myself up before crawling into Bellamy and I's bed, ready to sleep and feel at ease once more. Then, I heard someone mumble something from the hall. My eyes opened, watching as the door swung open.

There in the dimly lit doorway, stood the love of my life.

His face was grim as he approached, but he did not say anything about what happened. Instead, he got into the bed beside me and pulled the quilt over us.

"I love you, beautiful creature. You are my everything."

"And you are mine," I said with a broken voice. "I just wanted to be whole again. To be better for you. For us."

His large hands grabbed my face, fingers tracing shapes against my skin. As always, he was made of fire and sunshine, a bright spot in the darkness. It was odd how a pair of hands could feel so right. I thought of Sterling's grasp on me earlier, how impossibly other it had felt in comparison to the perfection of Bellamy's warm grip.

"You are the best thing that has ever happened to me. You are never anything less than whole in my eyes." A sigh escaped him just as his forehead touched mine. "Should we call off the wedding?"

"What?" I shouted, rearing back. "Of course not!"

His cool chuckle brushed against my face, quickly turning into hysterical laughter. Bewildered, I stared at him with a slack jaw.

"After all this time of dragging your feet, you choose now to get defensive?" he uttered between gasping laughter. And then, I too broke out into giggles, unable to stop the pure irony from getting to me as it did him.

We sat there, holding each other and laughing, for what felt like hours. And when our humor died out, Bellamy began tracing my new tattoos, the skin still raw from whatever Shah used to slow my healing. He willed ice to his fingertips, cooling the inflamed skin.

"Ranbir can make these hurt less. We can call him in here whenever you are ready," he muttered, leaning down to kiss the ink on my shoulder. I smiled, feeling at home in his arms.

"We are going to survive this, okay?"

"Weddings are not death sentences, Asher," he guffawed, flicking me on the nose. Before I could say anything else, he leaned forward and kissed the spot he had hit. As always, his lips soon touched my forehead, my cheeks, my chin, and then my lips.

Our kiss was slow, unhurried and calm. The kiss of forever.

"I meant this war, you ridiculous demon." Our laughter soon kicked in again, and we remained in one another's arms until the sun was fully up and Noe burst through the door.

"You," she said, pointing at Bellamy. "Get out. It is wedding day, bitches."

CHAPTER FIFTY

ASHER

"Ouch," I hissed out, cringing each time Noe pulled at my hair. As she had the last three times I complained, the Moon shushed me with a smack to my head.

"Be still and stop whining!"

"You know, we have a saying in my world. Beauty is pain," Stassi added from her spot on the bed. Groaning, I peered at her through the mirror in front of me. She was laying down with her legs against the headboard, snacking on chocolate-covered strawberries and powdered pastries that were meant to be *my* panic food.

"Why are you here?" I asked, grinding my teeth. Stassi tilted her head back, arching her body until she was looking at me through upside down eyes.

"I heard almost everyone interesting was coming here and figured my invite got lost in the mail."

Eternity above, this female was a pest. Not that I was too proud to admit it sounded like something I would do too.

"Of course you would assume that." I practically sighed out the words, almost wiping my sweaty hands on the skirts of what Noe called my *pre-dress*. It was a short, thin dress made of white silk with no straps, which proved to be an annoying thing as my breasts seemed to seek freedom at every possible moment. "As someone who has the same tendency to be a bitch, I must warn you that many will start to find you annoying."

Stassi let out a loud scoff before flipping onto her stomach and then pushing herself up onto her knees. A single finger with a long nail painted a deep shade of pink pointed my way through the mirror.

"You better take that back. Don't think I haven't noticed that you invited the babbling one who acts like Bellamy is a god and the freak who told me to kill myself yesterday!" My eyes flicked towards where Ray and Lara sat huddled together, their own gazes now on Stassi. Ray was slowly shrinking into herself, which left Lara glaring at Stassi.

"I will hang you myself if you insult Ray again," Lara seethed. Stassi raised a single pink brow, a small smirk lifting her left cheek.

"No murder on the day of the wedding, you brutes!" Noe screeched, pulling even tighter on my hair. She was breathing heavily, the stress of planning the wedding clearly getting to her. No one had asked her to do it, but she had eagerly offered. I wondered then if she regretted it. Sighing, she leaned her face closer to mine and whispered, "Winona would have been better at this."

My eyes closed, heart hammering at the thought of Winona doing my hair today. Her delicate hands and soft humming would have been so

wonderful to have. Clearing my throat, I blinked a few times and looked up at Noe through the mirror.

"It looks lovely, Noe. Honestly, you have planned the most spectacular wedding Alemthian has ever seen. *You* are spectacular." She smiled at that, straightening her back and making quick work of braiding and twirling the rest of my hair.

We had decided on securing all of it up, leaving my ears on full display and showing off the back of the dress. Just as she finished and began weaving pearls through it, Lian dragged a chair to my side and plopped down into it. She had been angry and on edge since returning from Captain Perdita's ship the other day, but I felt her joy emanating from her at that moment.

"Time for your face," she trilled, gathering supplies from the vanity in front of us.

"I will help!" Nicola eagerly offered, a wide smile on her face. She quickly dashed to Lian's side, ready to be of service.

"You better use a lot, we all know she is hideous to look at without it. Wouldn't want the prince to flee at the sight of her walking down the aisle," Stassi chimed in. Rage clouded my mind, my vision going red.

"That is it!" I screamed, pushing up to a standing position and charging towards the high demon.

"Your hair!" Noe shouted as she chased me, the others breaking into laughter while Stassi screamed.

It took another two hours to redo my hair and fix my makeup. Noe had smacked me in the head for daring to ruin her masterpiece and Lian threatened to make me look like a youngling who had gotten into cosmetics if I did not sit still. Nicola had just whispered in my ear that Stassi deserved it. Eventually I was done, and it was time for the dress.

Not even Stassi had anything negative to say as Noe grabbed it from the spot where it hung in the bathing room and showed us all. It was the most stunning creation, simple and elegant and so perfect for me.

Noe had mentioned that she and Pino had begun designing it together during our trip throughout Eoforhild. They had been relaying messages with thoughts, ideas, and sketches without me even noticing. And what they had crafted was immaculate.

Nicola helped me step inside of it, tugging it up my bare body and sliding my arms into the straps. Once she was done, she guided me to the full-length mirror, now free of any cracks. I recalled standing in this very spot during my birthday, Bellamy at my back as he described the dress he had made and what it meant. Back then, I never truly dreamed of getting to this point.

So I basked in the image of myself, smiling broadly at what I saw. The dress cascaded down, loosely molded to my body. The fabric pooled at my feet and stretched out behind me, trailing like silk sands following the tide. The silk stopped just above my breasts, leaving everything to the imagination and offering a perfect view of my necklace. The sleeves were more like thick, sheer straps that sparkled against the light and hung limply on my bicep. The best part by far was the back. I turned to get a glimpse, loving how tightly it clung to my backside and looking in awe at the soft silk buttons that traveled the length of my spine. Unlike the front, the back was made with sheer material that stopped right at my hips, the silk merging with it on my sides and at the bottom of my spine in waves.

Lian had given me a small flick of kohl on the corners of my eyes and some rouge on my cheeks, letting my bold red lips that Nicola had chosen steal the show. And there, dancing across my skin, were my scars. Shah had done an impeccable job, and Ranbir had kindly offered to help the healing process. They stood out in shining contrast to my dark skin, a beacon of hope.

Finally, after two centuries, I was whole.

Well, almost. My other half was waiting.

With one final smile at myself, I tried to find the words that conveyed how I felt about what was reflected in the mirror.

"I look…"

"You look—"

"Perfect," Stassi said, finishing Nicola's and I's sentences. I raised a brow at her comment, but we all knew it was true. The three of them had turned me into a bride. No. *A queen.*

"Thank you," I responded, trying not to say anything rude in response. I was a queen now, I was beyond insults.

"Much better than you normally look," Stassi added with a shrug. "Like a wretched little beast."

"You bitch!" I shouted, turning to face her. Okay, fine, I was not beyond insults. Nicola and Lian grabbed my arms, holding me back.

"If you ruin our hard work, I will literally beat your ass," Noe seethed.

"And you, shut the fuck up and get out," Lian added, glaring daggers at Stassi.

In response, the high demon just smirked, got up, and practically skipped towards the door. "I am sure Sterling will keep me far more entertained anyways."

"I will kill you!" I raged, unable to stop myself from grabbing a vile of fragrance and chucking it at her. She dodged it, throwing her head back in laughter. We had found a middle ground, understanding each other better and somewhat bonding over our mutual adoration for Sterling. But that did not mean I was okay with her fucking him just to eventually leave him. They would not—*could not*—work long-term. Heartbreak was not something he needed.

Stassi waved, each of her fingers dropping at different times like the cresting of the sea. Then she opened the door and closed it behind her.

"Most of the time I hate her," I said, crossing my arms.

"You, Bellamy, Genevieve, and the entire world—save Sterling—would agree," Lian scoffed, smoothing out my dress. "Ray, you and Lara should go too. It is time."

The two females immediately got up, Ray smiling widely my way. "Good luck Queen A—I mean Princess—I mean Ash—I mean—"

"Thank you, Ray," I said, chuckling softly. Ray's cheeks heated, her face almost twin to Cyprus'. The siblings were so different at their cores despite being so similar in looks. Ray stumbled over her feet, waving goodbye and dragging Lara behind her.

"I hope you do not fall down the stairs in your large heels and die," Lara added as they departed through the door, closing it behind them. I snorted, turning to face Noe.

"I think that is the nicest thing Bubbles has ever said to me."

"I would wager it is the nicest thing she has said to anyone other than Ray. Not wishing you death is practically a blessing from her," Noe agreed, nudging me. "She is right though, we will wait until Lian, Nicola, and I get our dresses on and are fully ready before putting those monstrous heels on you."

With that, the three of them quickly slipped into their dresses, the sage green silk making me smile. From there, I helped them each do their hair and put on their cosmetics, Lian deeming my kohl skills abysmal. And then it was time to put on the wretched heels. Noe had let me know that I would only wear them for the ceremony. Then I would change into my final outfit which involved the most perfect pair of slippers.

Noe leaned down, grabbing my long, sheer veil and holding it up as if to place it on my head. At the last second, I lifted a hand, stilling her. My mind wandered to the time in front of the castle in The Royal City when Bellamy had told me not to hide or cower. Back then, he had promised me that the world would fall to their knees before me if only I let them.

"No veil. I think I am ready to show the world who I truly am," I spoke wistfully. Noe's small smile was paired with a nod as she set the veil back down. Pride coated the air, whose I was not sure. It seemed everyone in the area was overwhelmed with emotions, their feelings shaking my mental gates like they might break through them.

In the haze, I heard Padon call out, his voice distant in my mind. I closed my gates tighter, shortening the chain that held the lock. He would not ruin this day for me.

"Last thing," Noe said as she grabbed each of our bouquets of flowers. I smiled widely, almost sinisterly, at the sight of them, my mind thinking about what lined the aisle outside.

"Only you would choose murderous flowers as décor," Lian said, catching my expression. I laughed, picturing how appalled Noe had been when I told her I wanted lavender and belladonna to decorate the training area of Pike that would double as our wedding venue. Only I knew that it was a little "fuck you" to Mia. Well, me and Bellamy. I did not keep anything from him anymore. "Thank you for changing your mind about our bouquets, at least."

Nicola nodded, shaking her small gathering of vanilla, salvia splendens, and baby's breath at my face. The four of us laughed, taking a few moments to gather ourselves.

Farai silenced our fading laughter, bursting through the door dressed smartly in black trousers and a sage green button-up shirt. "Okay, Ash baby, are you ready to make the most incredible entrance since that one time I walked into a ball wearing all black when Mia had specifically said we were all to wear cream?"

"Oh yes, the very one that you were kicked out of and forced to change for," Jasper said as he came in behind him, lightly closing the door. His outfit was an exact replica, their black shoes clicking as they walked across the wood floors to me.

"Ready as I will ever be," I sighed, letting them each take one of my arms and gripping my bouquet tightly in my hands.

"Cold feet?" Farai asked from my right. Jasper pushed himself farther into me on my left, always quick to offer physical affection.

"Sorry, Ash, I cannot let you run. I feel like my loyalty to Bellamy has to mean something every once in a while," Noe said quickly before pushing Lian and Nicola. The three females gathered in a line ahead of us, Nicola directly in front of me.

"I have seen the future, she walks down the aisle," she teased, smiling at us over her shoulder and winking.

"Ugh, I am not getting cold feet! Can we go now before I start wiping my gross sweaty hands on the dress?" I begged.

The five of them nodded, all of us getting closer as Noe called to her shadows. We appeared just before the entrance to Pike, completely circumventing the possibility of me tripping and dying. Lara would be so happy. Or disappointed.

Lian reached up and knocked three times on the doors, music quickly following. It was a soft tune, beautiful and optimistic as it rang out through the open area of Pike. With a deep breath, I nodded at the five of them as they stared at me in wait.

"Ready."

"Showtime!" Noe practically sang. Lian pushed open the large wooden doors, revealing the most stunning sight.

Noe had decorated the area perfectly. A small aisle was marked with a silver carpet, red rose petals running down the length of it. My flower choice littered the area, guests looking down at them in unease that made me giggle. The chairs were all white, green garland wrapped with sky-blue tinsel woven around them. Demon light glittered in the air, bright against the pink and purple sky and the fading orange sun. At the very end of the aisle was a large arch that was made of the same greenery as the garlands, also wrapped in sparkling blue.

Just before our friends were the paintings Bellamy had been working on. Perfect depictions of Luca's blonde hair and blue eyes, Winona's dashing smile and expertly styled green locks, Pino's knowing eyes and soft wrinkles, and even Wrath's wicked smirk were placed at the edges of the small raised altar. And, somehow without me knowing, Bellamy had added a painting of what had to have been Zaib. Her flowing dark brown curls were darker than mine and her eyes were practically black, but her heart-shaped face and sharp cheekbones were twin to mine. My mother. The one I never knew but who risked everything for me. She was here with us.

Adbeel stood just beyond the paintings, his black trousers and silk white top paired with his daunting black crown marking him as both a fierce and loving king. He smiled so broadly that I could do nothing but smile back as Lian began her slow walk down the aisle. Noe followed her, slyly raising her middle finger to Damon, who fanned himself from his spot behind Ranbir as Cyprus nudged at his back with a wink. Henry chuckled in front of the Healer, the four of them matching Farai and Jasper. And then, as Nicola started her walk, Henry nudged the male in front of him, drawing my attention to the one I had been saving for last.

He was dressed in all black, the crisp trousers at odd with his—only slightly open—loose shirt. He wore no chains around his neck, nor did he sport any rings on his fingers, but the lashes below his bright blue eyes were lined with black, and his dark waves were perfectly mussed. He looked at me as if he was seeing the world for the first time and was in awe of its beauty. Like a male in unabashed and never-ending love.

The male there was my everything.

Bellamy.

CHAPTER FIFTY-ONE

BELLAMY

Gods.

Asher had always been stunning. Perfect really. She was the most extraordinary creature to walk Alemthian. Yet, there was something otherworldly about seeing her in a wedding dress. I was terrified she would change her mind after last night, but instead she stood there, ready to seal our love with more than just a blood vow.

I was practically bouncing on my feet as first Lian, then Noe, and finally Nicola made their way to us. What they wore or carried or even looked like was gone to me. It was as if there was a haze that left everything but Asher a blur.

There was only her.

And then, somehow, despite everything that tried to rip us apart, Asher began walking my way. Her slow glide to me was both taunting and enchanting. I thought I might cry, or perhaps faint. I felt Henry's hand grab my shoulder, tugging me back towards him. As his breath fanned against me, Asher made it to the halfway point.

"If you cry, I will make fun of you for the rest of our lives," he chuckled near me.

"If you do not get your stupid ginger head away from me, then I will have Asher send you images of Genevieve walking down the aisle to you and then leaving you at the altar," I hissed, throwing back my elbow into his gut. Air left him in an audible whoosh. Smiling, I focused back on my fiancé—no, Asher was about to be my *wife*.

Okay, so I was crying. Fine. Who cared? I could cry. It was my fucking wedding day!

And then, magically, Asher was before me. Farai and Jasper each took a turn to kiss her left hand, the one that bore the ring I had given her, before offering it to me.

Me.

I thought I might die from the sheer ludicrous nature of the moment. Asher was marrying me. Of all the males and females and fucking gods, Asher chose *me*.

Quickly, eagerly, I grabbed her hand and pulled her up onto the small silver platform. She smiled, her true smile now so common it no longer surprised me. But oh did it still excite me. Her large gray eyes were on me and her hands were in mine, a testament to how perfect my life had become.

"Hello, demon."

"Hello, beautiful creature."

"What, no princess?" she asked mockingly.

"No," I rasped, my smirk full of a bravado I did not feel. No, I could feel nothing but sheer joy.

"Why not?" Confusion painted her stunning face, those alluring red lips pinching slightly.

"It does not fit any longer. Does not mean enough." I pulled her left hand to my mouth, placing a kiss just above where her ring was. "My Queen."

Adbeel sniffled loudly to my right, causing Asher to blush. But she did not pull away or scold me for my mushy nature. Instead, she just smiled softly and leaned down, offering a kiss to the finger she would soon place a ring on as well.

"My King."

I was getting hard. Oh no, I was literally getting hard in my pants. I tried and failed to think of something that was less arousing. Anything other than Asher, really. But how could I when she was right there making every single one of my dreams come true?

Adbeel's voice was deep and firm as he spoke, informing the attendees that we were there to bond us in matrimony. He blessed the union, begging for the gods to grant us their favor. None of the gods we once worshiped would. Except—*maybe*—the pink-haired one in the crowd. She watched on with bland disinterest, her hands wandering over Sterling in a way that likely left him even more excited than I was.

At least I was not the only one.

Sooner than I expected, Adbeel was stating that we vowed to honor and cherish one another, ranting about sickness and riches and so many things that did not matter. I would more than likely die in this war, but if I miraculously did not, then Asher would be the most beloved being on this world. By the masses, yes, but by me most. Nothing could stop me from loving her. So when Adbeel called for Asher to state her vows, I readied myself, trying to remember that Asher might not be the best at expressing

her feelings verbally, but she would always be there to remind me in every way she knew how.

"Bellamy. There is so much I could say right now, so many promises I wish to make and thanks I want to give. If it were not for you, I would have been lost forever. But those things, they can be given, slowly, maybe even daily, over the course of the rest of our lives. For now, I just want to say this. I would wait centuries on that cold and lonely balcony if it meant I could have even a moment of your time. I would suffer a thousand lifetimes of pain if it meant I eventually found my way back into your arms. I am of the belief that there are few things in life that can beat fate and chance and whatever lies in between the two. But this, Bell—you, me, *us*— we are eternal. No force in this universe could tear us apart again. To you, I give my all. I give myself. Today, tomorrow, and every day until forever." And then she took my hand and slipped on a gold wedding band with swirls of black, rubies and diamonds glittering around it.

Well shit. I was most definitely tearing up.

That was fine. Everything was fine. I was just feeling my soul leave my actual body.

At my back, I heard a soft sniffle. Turning, I watched as Henry *cried*.

"What?" he hissed, wiping his face. "That was practically poetry coming from Ash. Leave me alone and say your stupid vows before I start blowing my snot on your shirt."

With a disbelieving laugh, I shook my head and faced Ash again. Her eyes were watering as well, her brows furrowed and her smile soft. She was immaculate. Taking a deep breath, I began.

"My entire life, I never felt whole. I was always two halves at war. Death and fury loomed around my heart constantly, leaving me nothing but a plague upon the world. And then, out of nowhere, came the vision of a future I had never dared to dream of. One filled with quick quips, piano keys, sharp blades, soft breaths, and the most perfect gray eyes. You were more than I could have ever thought to hope for. Every day since, you have proven yourself to be the best thing to happen not only to me, but

Alemthian. Whatever comes after this, I can vow that I will be at your side, ready to take it all on with you. Nothing I will ever be—a soldier, a friend, a king—will ever amount to how magnificent it is to be yours. I will spend the rest of my days worshiping at your feet in thanks for you choosing to be mine as well." I took the plain, thin gold band and slid it just above her engagement ring, letting it settle comfortably there.

"I love you," she whispered, her eyes glassy.

"I love you more." Blubbers and quiet sobs could be heard all around us, but I had eyes only for her. My wife.

"I now pronounce you wed, may the remainder of your days be spent together in love. You may seal the union with a kiss," Adbeel said, his voice shaky with emotions.

Diving forward, I grabbed her face with my hands and brought her lips to mine. She tasted like vanilla and pastries. Like hope and dreams. Like forever.

All too soon, Asher pushed me away with a raspy laugh, allowing me to at least keep our foreheads pressed together as everyone screamed and cheered. I did it. I married Ash. I became more than I ever thought possible. I was finally *someone*. Something with worth.

No, I was more than that. As I looked down at Asher, I realized that to the most important being in the entire world, I was *everything*.

We backed away from one another, the two of us beaming as we joined our hands and raised them to the sky, even louder cheers erupting. For the joy of Asher's annoyance at my theatrics, I bent down and scooped her up into a cradle, carrying her leisurely down the aisle. She rolled her eyes, but laughs slipped free of her lips.

"You are ridiculous," she shouted, trying to be heard over the crowd. I smirked, getting closer to her.

"And you love it," I teased.

To that, she had nothing to say but, "I do."

***

Noe had rushed us through our outfit change, practically forcing us into the new clothes. Mine had been simple, made to match Asher. I wore what looked like liquid obsidian trousers and a matching top, the loose-fitting shirt left nearly fully open to reveal my black veins. The only difference between the top and the trousers were the flecks of silver and gold that coated my upper half. Seven thin red chains had been added around my neck, my gold rings back on my fingers and matching perfectly with my wedding band. Asher had made a snarky comment about muscles and self-absorbed males, but I caught her staring at my exposed chest and stomach, her bottom lip tugged between her teeth. I would have teased her if not for my own staring.

It turned out that the sketch I had found ages ago in Pino's room in Haven had not just been a dream. No, the onyx dress had been real. Pino had given it to Noe for safe keeping, and the little traitor had kept his secret until recently. But the sight of Asher was worth the wait.

Her dress clung to her torso, flaring slightly at the hips where the skirts grew thicker in layers. It was the black of the depths of the sea, sparkling with the same dots of gold and silver that my top had. It cut low between her breasts, held together by seven thin red chains that started just below her chest and traveled up to her collarbones. Her shoulders were held up by braided black fabric, moonstones used as buttons to lock her long cape in place.

Our capes matched as well, billowing and black, baring no additional color other than the faintest hint of sky blue stitching. Both of our heads were without accessories, Asher's long curls free and my short waves a mess. Something heavy would soon rest there.

"Last touch," Noe added, reaching into a box to grab Asher's anklet and what looked like a necklace to match. Had she gotten that made for Asher? My head quirked to the side, watching as Noe reached down and secured the anklet on Asher. Then, my spymaster—one of my best friends—stood and faced me. "Last week, I took Asher to have your ring made. While we were there, she asked the jeweler to make this for you. The female had said, and I am quoting her directly, 'anything for the handsome prince.' I think Asher almost killed her."

My eyes flicked to my wife—my wife, my wife, my wife, *my wife*—catching her wicked smile before it disappeared. "I would have done it," she mouthed.

Noe went to my back, reaching up and over my shoulders with the necklace before securing it on my neck. The Moon kissed each of our cheeks then, declaring that she would see us down there and leaving us momentarily alone.

Like Asher's, the chain was gold and littered with rubies. My fingers went up to it, rotating until I saw the clasp. Just like hers, mine was also held together by one clasp coated in silver diamonds and the other in black diamonds. When I let my gaze rise to Asher, I found her already looking at me.

"A queen of stars and a king of night, joining to secure the future," she declared, reaching a hand out to me. I smiled, nodding as I grabbed it. Tugging her close, I gave her red lips a chaste kiss.

Together, we descended the many flights of stairs, taking our sweet time to bask in one another. As impossible as it was, I felt like I loved her even more. We were one, now and forever. Even after my death, I knew I would be a part of Ash. And maybe, just maybe, I could manage to defy fate and be with her forever.

By the time we reached the doors, the party had begun. Everyone was drinking and shouting, music playing wildly outside. I laughed as demons, mortals, and more huddled around us, all of them more excited than they probably should be. But war loomed, and we all needed

something to find happiness in. So I welcomed their affection, letting them kiss my free hand and pray for our happiness.

We were herded towards the altar, everyone screaming out their congrats. The base was vibrating with the excitement and joy of everyone— alive with love and hope. I could practically feel their emotions in my chest and taste them on my lips. Silently, I wondered how Asher was doing.

She held me firmly, not looking up as we made our way to the raised silver platform. It had to be overwhelming to have so many minds all around her, but she remained firm as she walked, her shoulders squared. I tightened my hold on her.

Adbeel stood where he had during our vows, smiling with tears in his eyes and his head absent of a crown. At his sides, Noe and Henry held plush blue pillows with the towering crowns atop. They were identical, as they always had been. Kings were no more important than queens and vice versa. Equal in the eyes of all. Just as Ash and I were.

We stopped before the current king, each of us sporting wide eyes. This was it. We were about to become rulers of an entire kingdom—a realm.

Adbeel lifted his hands, bending his fingers down towards his palms as a sign for the crowd to quiet. They did almost immediately, everyone watching with bated breath. Adbeel looked away from them, his gaze catching each of us periodically as he spoke.

"The great realm of Eoforhild has known many rulers. The Ayad line has sat upon the throne for many millennia. Though a new name shall take the honor of being— "

"No," Asher cut in. Adbeel peered down at her in bewilderment, clearly as astonished as I was at her interruption. She looked between us, seemingly making a quick decision. With a deep breath, she lifted her chin. "I am an Ayad. That is the name I was born with and the name I…deserve. I will be an Ayad from here on out."

Adbeel gasped, his hand flying to his mouth and a tear trailing down his cheek. I held in my own emotions, having to close my eyes. Asher was always surprising me in the best ways. When I opened my eyes again, it was to find Adbeel gathering himself. He cleared his throat, reaching out for each of our free hands.

"Well then, an Ayad will again sit on the throne," he said, his husky voice full of emotion. "There has not been a pair more deserving of—more perfectly fit for—the titles of King and Queen than these two right here. Under your rule, I foresee a great change. A beautiful future of triumph and happiness. May you lead us to victory in the coming war, and to peace in the time after. More than that, I believe we can all agree when I say that I hope, above all else, you bring us change in the form of unity."

Once more, Adbeel cleared his throat, nodding faintly before turning towards Henry. My best friend—my brother, really—lifted the pillow, sending Asher and I each a wink. Asher snorted at my side, but I just smiled his way.

"I crown you King Bellamy Ayad, ruler of Eoforhild," Adbeel boomed, light leaking from his hands as he took the crown, lifted it high, and placed it upon my head. Screams erupted again, though Adbeel silenced them with a raised hand before rotating to face Noe.

She was already a mess, tears soaking her cheeks and her lips quivering. I scoffed, shaking my head in amusement. Her foot kicked out, striking my shin in retribution. I grunted but remained standing, Asher giggling to my left.

"Okay, beasts, let us finish before you destroy one another," Adbeel said, humor lacing his voice. Then, he grabbed the crown on Noe's pillow and faced Asher. I dared to look at her, catching the way her eyes widened and her mouth opened as Adbeel lifted the crown high and let his light again shine. "I crown you Queen Asher Ayad, ruler of Eoforhild."

The three of us joined hands again, smiling fondly as the crowd once more erupted into cheers.

CHAPTER FIFTY-TWO

ASHER

Ray wore a dress some might—okay, they did—deem too casual for a wedding, the solid brown piece of cotton stretching from right below her collarbones to just above her knees. The sleeves were short, cutting off halfway down her bicep. Her sandals were equally plain, the leather entirely inoffensive in my opinion. I had done my rounds, saying hello to everyone I knew, and there had been far more scandalous clothing.

Yet, a male walked past me, his eyes catching on Ray before he scoffed audibly and mumbled, "Ridiculous dress." In his head he criticized Ray, calling her frumpy and...ugly?

Rotating, I took my glass of red wine and flung my arm his way. The liquid flew out of my cup, soaking the stupid male—staining his pale shirt and light trousers.

"Now you look just as ugly as you actually are, you stupid idiot!" I shouted, raising my arms as if asking him what he was going to do. All he did was act the coward he was, shrinking back and dashing away to save his own life.

Ray had her mouth wide open, staring at me in shock and awe. "What? It is my wedding and I do not want horrid creatures here."

A soft smile formed on her lips, and soon she was jumping into me and wrapping her arms around my waist. Stumbling back, I quickly grabbed her and steadied us.

"You are the most amazing queen," she spoke into my shoulder. The hug lasted a few more seconds before I pulled away, swallowing the emotion that her comment brought forth—pride.

"Are you hurt?" came a melodic and whimsical voice. Lara approached, her small blue eyes squinting at Ray. She had chosen a vibrant purple dress that cascaded down her small body, fitting against it but never showing more skin than her arms and legs. Her long black hair had been left down to sway with each of her nearing steps.

"No, just happy, I promise," Ray said back, turning just as Lara reached forward and grabbed her face. My jaw fell open as the two leaned into each other and *kissed*. A small yet intimate peck was shared, and then they separated, their hands connected still.

"Actually, I am not just here for Ray. I would like to speak with you in private, Queen Asher." How odd, hearing her speak to me in such a way. She had once wanted me dead, to end the suffering she knew I felt after following Henry, Wrath, and I around. Now, she called me Queen and kissed pretty females and *smiled*.

"Of course, Lara." Ray waved, walking towards Bellamy and thinking about work she had to get done. Lara and I headed towards the far end of the training yard where the crowd thinned, but I already knew what she would ask me. How had I not heard her and Ray's loud thoughts before? How had I not noticed? "Just Asher, please."

"I want my memories back, Asher," Lara said without hesitation, looking at me head-on. "You gave them back to that prince. I know we are not friends, but I would like you to do it for me, too."

A soft and patient smile dug just slightly into my cheeks, my eyes roaming over Lara's face. Was that really what she wanted? I was not sure if she could handle having them back after everything she had been through. Looking at Sterling and I was the most obvious show of how dangerous such things were. We suffered immensely from it all still.

"Are you sure?" I asked warily.

"Ray has helped me, and she will be there to keep helping me. She is different from the rest of you. She is not miserable and angry and better off dead." Okay, ouch. "It has nothing to do with being male or female or anything else. Ray is...kind. Her skin is soft and her hair never gets in my mouth during sex. Not once has she tried to take the noose down in my closet." I made a mental note to take that down. "She has made sure our garden never dies, even after that one time I tried to kill it when I was angry. She is never cruel. And the sound of her voice reminds me of times when birds sang and I listened."

While I could make very little sense of both Lara's thoughts and words, I still felt her resolve—her surety. So, with a deep sigh and a racing heart, I nodded.

"They are not mine to keep. If you want your own memories back, then that is your choice. Would you like them now?"

"Yes," was all she said.

So, I looked her way, willing it all back to her. It would have been easier if I had been touching her, but unlike Sterling, I thought Lara could use space during it. I gave her back the graphic memories of being assaulted at rapid speed, wishing above all else that she never had them to begin with. When I was done, Lara did not flinch, cry, or even speak. She merely turned and left, looking for Ray in the crowd.

"That was kind of you to do," a voice said at my back.

Smiling, I turned to face Sterling. He wore a plain navy blue shirt with black buttons and trousers that matched, his blonde curls perfect and his pale cheeks rosy. In perfect sync with the start of a new song, Sterling held up a hand. Laughing, I took it, letting him pull me in and lead us to the dance floor. He picked an inconspicuous spot towards the edge and began to sway us in time with the beat as I spoke.

"They were hers, just as they were yours. Nothing kind about giving someone what belongs to them."

"Still, you were thoughtful about it. You are better than you allow yourself to believe."

"Will you still think I am kind if I tell you that I am afraid Stassi will hurt you?" I asked, staring up at him. His smile fell, eyes suddenly morose and half-lidded.

"It is not that different from Henry and Gen," was all he said back. I opened my mouth to respond, but my mind thought about what he said.

Was it the same? Genevieve and Henry would also live very different lifespans, and perhaps there was a power imbalance in their age gap and abilities as well. But Genevieve, she seemed more equipped to handle it. To survive it. She was fierce. A queen in every way.

I could not say that to Sterling though. He did not deserve to feel weak or incapable. He survived. That was more than enough. More than most.

"I guess you are right," I agreed, though I was still unsure if I was being honest. "I just want you to be happy."

"I am alive."

"That is not the same thing," I chastised, scrutinizing him. He tilted his head back, laughing sardonically even as we spun.

"Oh I know it." In his mind, he thought of every time he had been sure he would die in the dungeons, and I realized that he was simply taking it one step at a time. Trying to survive, even now.

"I am here," I murmured.

"Thank you," he offered, leaning in to kiss my forehead before letting me go. The song was not over, but I saw through his eyes what had him passing me off. Who. Turning, I spotted him. Adbeel stood a foot away, looking at me with love and hope, his hands outstretched.

We came together, dancing slowly at first. It was a lovely moment of tranquility. Overall, the entire night had been perfect. So at odds with the world outside of Pike. We were in the midst of a war, yet we had found a pocket of peace in the heart of it all.

"Well, I suppose I owe you thanks as well," Adbeel said as he twirled me. I giggled as I grew dizzy from the action, Adbeel's large hands catching me before I could fall.

"For what?" I asked between laughter, reaching our hands high and forcing him to take a turn spinning. Such joy. Such perfect, perfect joy.

"For letting me be a real grandfather. Letting me care for you and teach you and protect you." His eyes flicked from my eyes to my crown, resting on it fondly. His wife's—my grandmother's—crown. How strange it must have been to see it on someone's head after all this time. "I love you, Asher. I know it is odd to say since we have known each other for such little time, but I truly do. You are the most extraordinary granddaughter I could have ever asked for."

"Thank *you*. I am sorry Zaib never got to come back, but I am so grateful that you have welcomed me with open arms. And I love you, too." Nothing could explain how lucky I felt to be loved—truly loved—by so many. But it was Adbeel's love, that familial love I had been starved of, which I basked the brightest in.

Other than Bellamy's. But that did not feel like simply love anymore. It was something more. Transcendental. Otherworldly. The universe itself contained within our shared souls.

"She would be proud. Maybe one day you will have a daughter and—" Adbeel stuttered into silence, his dark eyes wide. I gasped, not sure what was happening. An awful, foreboding gurgle came from his throat, and then blood shot out of his mouth, coating my face. Before my cry could even leave my mouth, my grandfather collapsed to the ground. And there, standing with what had to be Adbeel's silent heart in his hand, was Malcolm.

My uncle stood with his own father's heart, staring at the organ as if he were surprised by its presence there. Regret and terror flooded his mind, a tsunami of emotions that seemed to render him helpless. For it had been Mia's order to kill Adbeel and then portal away. To get in and immediately get out. I could see it all there in his head. But Malcolm, who had only managed to get past the wards by truly convincing himself he would do no one harm, had discovered he did not want to be the villain of my story. Not in truth.

Too fucking late.

I stared at Malcolm and let out a piercing scream as I let my mental gates fall.

CHAPTER FIFTY-THREE

BELLAMY

"Who would have thought that you would manage to find a beautiful, funny, powerful female to marry instead of just fucking your hand for the rest of your life?" Noe joked as I dipped her. I snorted, lifting her back up and spinning us around.

"You are such a pain," I sneered, the tone playful despite my face.

"Honestly, though, I am proud of you, Bell. We all are. Winona, Pino, and Luca would have been, too."

What a tragedy that they did not live to see this. That Winona never got to have all of the younglings she once dreamed of. That Pino never got to make Asher's wedding dress and brag about knowing it would all happen. That Luca never got to hear Cyprus confess his unyielding love.

Oftentimes, I found myself thinking about how unfair life was. How it seemed to wish nothing but pain and devastation on the masses. But as Noe squeezed my shoulders and I continued to move us, I felt like perhaps life was finally going easy on me. Maybe the horror would end momentarily.

"Thank you, Noe. I truly never thought I would be full of so much joy." I admitted. Her answering smile was understanding and slightly forlorn. Noe and I knew hopelessness well, despite our knowledge coming from two vastly different upbringings. For us to have made it to where we currently stood was nothing short of a miracle. Together, as we finished our dance, we basked in that truth.

Before walking away at the end of the song, Noe looked up at me and framed my face with her hands. "You sure do look handsome with that crown, King Bellamy." Hints of sarcasm were in her tone, but it was by far overpowered with love. Smiling, I winked at her and nodded towards Damon. He stood off in a corner, watching us. Always waiting for her. She sighed, saluting me before going to him. She would remind him they were just friends, but it would also make them both happy. They loved one another, even if they did so in different ways.

Seeing that Asher was talking to our guests, I went searching for Lian. Within seconds I found her, face stern as she stared off into the distance. The punch she was pouring leaked out of her cup, her hands unmoving. What had her thinking so hard?

"Plan on saving any for the rest of us?" I asked her. She startled, her brown eyes coming into focus and landing on me. I watched as she realized what I said, her face heating up and her mouth pursing.

"Just considering the future," she admitted with a shrug. But it was not as careless as she let it seem. The future was a horrifying beast yet to ever be defeated. We would all die at its hands someday. Some of us sooner than others. If she was considering the future, then she was probably unwell or unsure.

Staring at her, I tried to read her face to gain any information I could without pestering her. I worried about Lian. My captain and swordmaster.

My friend. For so long, she remained unattached, alone save for a random female in her bed if she truly had the desire for company. But, after finding Ash, I realized how happy the right being could make someone even after great loss. Ash was happy now. Lian deserved that. She was owed better than she was given. But I guessed that was true about all of us.

"Is this about the pirate?" I asked, thinking of how the demon captain was making some kind of confusing statement by killing en masse. We gave her the license, I was no longer sure why she needed to loot when she could legally trade. Lian's face paled. Confusion rattled me to the bone when she puffed out her chest, blue hair swaying in the wind.

"Why would you ask that?" Her question was nearly a shout. She looked...embarrassed?

"Because you just went to confront her and ended up in an agreement that will leave you stranded on her ship for a day every fortnight?" My tone left it sounding like more of a question than an answer, but Lian understood. She blew out a breath, nodding before tilting her head back and drinking the entire cup of punch.

"I am just tired. But how are you? How does it feel to be married? I still cannot believe you tricked Ash into walking down that aisle," she teased, elbowing me. Even her jest felt half-hearted, and I found myself wondering what exactly happened on that ship that had left the normally rock solid Lian so rattled.

"Fooled her into thinking it was a line for free pastries and then bribed her with a crown, obviously." Lian snorted at my comment, shoving into my side. We both chuckled, but I caught onto the aloofness hiding beneath her humor. "You are allowed to leave early, you know."

"I know," she hummed, looking off into the distance again.

"Okay then," I mumbled, nodding and walking away.

After that, I found the three little beastlings—mortal children, some might have called them—and danced a few times with them, listening as they schooled me on the proper way for a king to dance. I had seen Asher

with them earlier, doing strange things with her arms and making them laugh. I opted to instead nod my head and cheer on each of them before taking my turn to go absolutely berserk. After Octavia and Safre decided they were too tired to keep going, I swept up Gemma and placed her on my toes, the two of us dancing to a full song that way before she too grew tired.

After she skipped off, I felt a finger tap on my shoulder.

"Can I have a turn, Your Majesty?" Whipping around, I came face-to-face with Nicola, her smile grave. Gods, what was it now? Reluctantly, I nodded, offering her a hand. We got into position, and when the music started, we began our dance.

"Okay, Nicola, tell me, what is it that has you looking so morose?" I asked curiously.

"She is so happy," Nicola said instead, her eyes on Asher as she danced with Sterling. But mine were on the Oracle. Staring at the female who saw too much—who saw *everything*. Something awful lingered in the air. My tongue tingled with the taste of it. Of death.

"Tell me, Nicola. I can take it."

With a heavy sigh, Nicola moved closer to me, her chest against my stomach.

"This war will not be long, Bellamy," she spoke, her tone twin to the chill of loss and pain in the air. "While it has been a long time coming— centuries in the making—the true war that began last year will be the shortest in history." Her tone was still bleak, but there was a hint of hope in it. I could not stop my own heart from racing with the same emotion. Momentarily, I dreamed of surviving this wretched conflict. Nicola stopped those feelings from festering. "I need you to understand that you will die before the war does."

There it was. An official timeline. A confirmation beyond the vague hints from her and Pino.

"I do not know how, and I fear seeking it out. There are some things that we should not know. Mostly because it can haunt us, but also because we might be tempted to challenge fate. As you have seen, when we fight against the future, it often comes to fruition in the worst way."

"But the future is always changing, can this not change too?" My tone was more begging than questioning, but I needed to know. I had to figure out what I could do to have more time with Asher.

"I have told you before, there is no future in which you do not die," she hissed, looking around us as if nervous someone might hear. Normally I would be afraid of that too, but everyone was too caught up in what they were doing to pay us any attention. "Do not tell Asher. I have seen what telling her does. She wastes all of your time together trying to plot ways to keep you alive. Because of that, we also lose the war."

A growl vibrated my neck and teeth, startling Nicola before she schooled her face back into firm neutrality. We would not lose the war. I would not allow it. I would die a thousand times before I let something so grave happen.

"Fine, so I will die. What is the plan before then?"

Her nose scrunched as she thought, brows knitting together. I waited, leading her through the rest of the song without actually paying attention.

"Love her. Love all of them." Nicola rose onto her toes, pecking my cheek before tapping my chest with her hand and leaving me alone there. I stood, contemplating what she had said. Loving all of them was the easy part. Looking up, my gaze immediately found Asher and Adbeel, the pair sharing wide smiles. At least she had her grandfather.

As if Eternity or whatever it was up there was laughing at me, enjoying my foolish hope, I watched Malcolm Ayad suddenly appear behind Adbeel, shadows licking the air around him. The punchline of the joke was not Malcolm's arrival, it was the way he thrust his hand into Adbeel's back, blood spraying him as he did. I shouted, moving to chase

after the male who raised me as he fell to the ground. But time was moving fast. Too fast. And death had him.

If Malcolm was death, then Asher was the Underworld itself. She tilted her head back in a bloodcurdling scream, my hands flying to my ears in response to the sound. Every creature in attendance cringed away from her fury, and then they began screaming too. A stampede of sorts began. Everyone was doing their best to get away from the pair standing above Adbeel's body. Not me though. I fought against them all to get to her.

My wife.

Before Asher's scream ended, an odd shake began beneath the ground. Like she was splitting Alemthian in two, rattling its very core. And then I saw it.

It began with the tips of her hair.

Her curls were abruptly leeched of color, brown being replaced with glittering silver. Like a snake slithering down a tree, the color traveled to Asher's head, stopping at the roots. I watched her eyes fade last, the stormy gray of her irises glowing now. When she reached her hands out, silver mist of some sort poured out of them—out of *her*. Malcolm's body lit too, his screams of agony abrupt and nauseating as he crumpled to the ground.

Asher looked down at the male on his knees, then her gaze flicked to her last living relative, dead at her feet. I knew then what she would do. Her left hand rose, wedding band shimmering in the light of her magic, and then she jerked her fingers upwards. Malcolm's chest flew towards the air, his body almost levitating off the ground. And while words could never explain the sight, it quite nearly looked like Asher was ripping out the demon's very soul with a mere whim as his chest began to expand.

He cried out, inscrutable words getting jumbled and mixed with the agony of his begging wails. All at once, the screams stopped, and Malcolm's chest burst. Just as his body crashed lifelessly next to Adbeel's, something large and black barreled into the ground behind Asher. Spectators that had not fully fled broke out into more screams, the entire scene that of pure chaos.

I moved a step, wanting to close the distance between Ash and I, but I was aware of what kind of creature had found her, and I had a feeling I knew exactly which it was. Stassi's description of the way dragons could find their bonded *anywhere* echoed in my mind as the beast's head lowered.

The all-black dragon opened its wide mouth, letting out a deep and chilling roar that sent tables flying. As it did, I watched in both awe and horror as it too began to turn silver, its scales alight with Asher's glowing magic.

Someone came to my side, their breathing just as heavy as mine. Quietly, as if they meant to say it in their head, the being whispered, "We're absolutely fucked."

Stassi's words settled deep in my chest as the dragon—Likho, I imagined—once more roared protectively behind Asher, my wife a goddess of death and chaos as she stared forward with blood coating her face and magic twirling around her.

A tear ran down my cheek as I looked at her. At Adbeel.

Stassi added one last foreboding line before turning and leaving. A piece of the puzzle we had been missing. The final one. "Behold the seed of Mind and Soul."

CHAPTER FIFTY-FOUR

NICOLA

Hours passed before we were able to calm down Asher enough to get her inside. She was full of pent up energy, of loss and grief turned into red hot fury. Despite knowing this would eventually come, I had not expected it tonight. Had not seen this particular thread. That was what the future was, a mess of thin, shining strings that never ceased to get me turned around. fate and chance warred between them, twirling, tying, knotting, and cutting entire lines of the future. This had to have been their doing.

"We need to attack," Asher screamed, picking up a chair and throwing it towards a wall of rock. Both the chair and the rock shattered, Asher's seed awakened within her now. She had not fully realized what was happening, too emotionally charged by the death of Adbeel Ayad. Her grandfather. Eternity above, could she never catch a break?

I knew he would die though. Had seen it happen in a dozen different ways. Not that warning her would have done anything. Still, I felt guilty watching her break before me. Could she never have a single good moment? A secular experience of pure joy to remember?

No, apparently not.

"Asher, please," Bellamy begged, reaching out to her. I watched as, *finally*, Asher slumped. Slowly, she walked to him, her head falling forward. He was forced to catch her as she crumpled into his arms, the two of them grieving the loss of someone so deeply important to them both. My eyes darted throughout the room, catching sight of the grim faces upon Bellamy's Trusted. They were in the exact places I had seen, this future one I knew well.

Now was the right time. I felt it.

"Ash," I said, wringing my hands as I waited for her to look my way. When she looked up, kohl ran down her cheeks and the red of her lips was smeared. Tears pooled in her eyes and her crown had fallen. It was horrible timing. Terrible. But it had to be now.

"I need to tell you something." Everyone's eyes bore into me, heating my skin. Kafele wrapped me into a tight hug, kissing my temple and giving me strength to say what needed to be said. I hated it. More than anything, I wished I had not been cursed with this ability. No one should know as much as I did, and as brave of a face as I often put on, I desperately wanted to fall apart and crumble too.

"Tell me," Asher ordered, her voice firm despite her broken appearance. I tried to speak, my mouth opening but nothing substantial coming out. My best friend looked on in sympathy as she likely invaded my mind, hearing and feeling my nerves. "Show me, please. I can take it, Nicola. Urgency swarms your mind. I can sense it."

Sighing, I nuzzled further into my husband and closed my eyes. Together, Asher and I watched the series of visions spring to life. The past kissing the present hello.

***

"Mother," Asta said, her voice lacking the energy it once had. Stella looked over at her daughter, wishing she could free her of the torment that they both shared but not willing to lose her too.

"Is the Oracle here?" Stella asked, looking around.

"Yes, I can feel her. Her thoughts are...odd. I have never experienced anything like it. Not even on Shamay." Stella felt her stomach drop as her daughter stepped out of the trees, facing a large river that cut through the land.

***

"From your line will be a savior, one who will not only rescue Alemthian from destruction, but Shamay as well. Her life will be the start of a series of events that will see balance restored to the universe. Both a gift and a promised doom." The Oracle's voice was ethereal as she spoke, her existence that of true gods. She was magnificent to Asta, who watched as what looked like threads of timelines moved both forwards and backwards in the fae's mind. Never had a mind felt so hauntingly cluttered and foreboding, but Asta found she enjoyed being within it.

"So what must I do?" Asta asked, not seeing clearly what would be required of her. Stella remained at her daughter's side, watching the scene with wide eyes and terror in her chest. She knew then she would soon lose her daughter. Felt it in the marrow of her bones.

"Your mother is the one who will do the majority of the work. She must remove your seed and save it for one of your descendents. A female with bravery and kindness in her heart. One who knows suffering and still

506

wishes to dream." The Oracle reached forward, grabbing Asta's hand as her eyes went slightly out of focus. And when she was done, Asta began to sob, reaching her fingers down into the water and lighting it up with her silver magic. In the depths of the flowing river, images began to appear.

***

Stella paced within the blackened forest, cursing Padon. For thousands of years she had waited, and now she was somewhat confident in her choice for the seed. Zaib Ayad was a lovely princess, both brave and kind. She had not suffered much, but Stella knew there would be a great loss that would allow her to reveal herself, so maybe that was what the Oracle had truly meant all those years ago.

Padon was the only thing stopping her. The second she put the seed into the princess, Padon would likely feel the force. He was probably constantly in search of it. Wanting and waiting.

Or maybe he thought she would never give it to someone else. Maybe she would get lucky.

Sighing, she willed herself to the stunning palace upon the cliffs of Dunamis.

***

"Malcolm, look! The entire thing truly is made of gold!" Zaib said, pointing at the structure.

She had begun to feel different the last few decades since getting sick, something within her stirring. Rather than needing to speak aloud to order others, she had found herself slowly growing able to silently demand

things. Often, she even heard the thoughts of others. When she first fell ill, they all thought she would die, but it seemed that she came out of the illness with newfound magic instead. Still, she was far too unsure to tell anyone about it. Anyone but her brother, that was.

She never kept secrets from Malcolm.

"Yes, it is gorgeous," Malcolm said in awe, his arm lying lazily upon his sister's shoulders. "I would love to live in a palace like that."

"Too bad you were not born a fae prince instead of a demon one," Zaib joked, nudging him with her shoulder. Malcolm did not laugh.

***

"Please, brother, please do not do this," Zaib begged from behind the bars, her body aching from being healed after a brutal first beating. She stared at her brother in desperation, wishing she could will him to see reason. To love her like she thought he had. Like *she* loved *him*.

"She is different than the rest of us. After she got sick, she started being able to do strange things. Zaib can literally control the minds of those around her. I have seen her do it, felt her talk to me in my head. She has shown me it all," Malcolm told Queen Mia, basking in her attention. Just as he had basked in the feel of her cunt that morning and reveled in her promises of a place at her side when she conquered. He would rule, and he would have her. Finally, something Zaib could not steal from him.

"Excellent," the queen beamed.

***

"You are new," Zaib murmured as a male's face appeared beyond the door.

He was handsome, his dark gray eyes that of a stormy sky. His skin was lighter than hers, his hair a softer shade of brown. He looked horrified to see her there through the small bars on the door, though she was not sure if it was because of the cuts on her body or her nearly lifeless aura. The king and queen had taken her to the final mortal kingdom today, where she continued stealing memories of a time when demons were not the villains of Alemthian.

"I am," he agreed, voice grave. Zaib did not have the energy to say anything else, as the runes on the walls constantly pulled all of her magic from her. She would vomit and fall over, her tongue numb and her limbs aching. There was no use in speaking when it took all her focus. Especially when this was probably just another tactic to get her to submit.

The male continued to talk, but Zaib did not hear what he said.

She wished they would just kill her already.

***

The guard's name was Dante. He was incredibly funny. Sarcastic and dry, but that was perfect for Zaib. He constantly kept her mind off the pain. Though she remained vigilant, still unsure if her new friendship was some sort of trick. He worked for the Mounbetton's, after all.

"How do you like the bed?" he asked her one afternoon, watching as she laid down on it and smiled. He had gotten her new clothes and playing cards, snuck her delicious food, and just yesterday brought her an actual bed. What Queen Mia called the low level room had quickly grown in comfort.

"I love it," she said in response, pulling the silver and blue blankets around her. His smile was broad, full lips enticing. Zaib felt something in her heart, the organ thrumming to an uneasy beat.

"Can I come eat with you again?" Dante asked. Zaib nodded.

***

"Fine, we cannot contact your father, but I have coin. I can get us on a ship. Please, Zaib, at least let me try to get you out of here." Dante was on a tangent again. Zaib did not have the energy to argue with him.

Over the months, Zaib had grown to trust Dante. In that time, Dante had lost his faith in his rulers——in his parents.

"There are no ships that sail to Eoforhild anymore. No one even knows it is called that now. I would need to portal, which would mean waiting out the poison in my body and breaking free of these blockers on my wrists." They had discussed all of that before, but Dante was growing increasingly more unsettled. She wished she was brave enough to admit she loved him. But to tell him that was to lose him. There was no way he felt anything but pity for her. She had been too scared to check his mind when they forced him to drag her to the torture chamber they called the interrogation room. Better to remain in blissful ignorance.

"Zaib, *please*," he begged again. Zaib rolled over in her bed, facing the wall instead of his heartbreakingly perfect and hopeful face.

***

"Zaib," Dante said, his breath fanning her face. She awoke slowly, her newly healed body still aching and unfamiliar. Her eyes fluttered,

510

catching sight of his gray ones, a smile on his face. He held up a cupcake, a single candle stuck in the blue frosting. "Happy birthday."

"I forgot I explained those to you," she mumbled with a grin, pushing herself up to a sitting position. He beamed down at her, moving to sit on her right.

"Well you did. Now blow out the candle and make a wish like the bizarre little demon you are," he ordered, a laugh in his voice. Zaib laughed too, but soon she closed her eyes and wished for something she knew she could never have. As her lips puckered and air blew out through them, Zaib dreamed not of freedom, but of Dante being hers.

"What did you wish for?" he asked, his scent enveloping her. She opened her eyes, realizing how close he had gotten. And whether it was the fact that she was quickly approaching fifty years in the low level room or her own growing desperation she did not know, but Zaib leaned in and pressed her lips to his.

***

"Zaib, this cannot go on. If you refuse again then I will drag you back to Eoforhild kicking and screaming. You will not fucking rot away in here any longer!" He had been screaming for a while, pacing throughout the room. Panicking really. Zaib was unnaturally calm, though it had always been Dante that was the more fiery of the two. Still, she was too motionless.

Inside of her, the little one was the opposite.

"Dante, I have to admit something to you," she finally said, catching his attention. He looked at her, brows furrowed. When she did not immediately speak, Dante's eyes went wide and he rushed towards her.

"Are you unwell? Is this about you vomiting so much at the beginning of last month? I thought you said you were better!" Zaib smiled ruefully, wishing she had better news.

"I have not bled," she said.

His brows rose, lips tilting down in a confused frown. "Yes well, that is the point of ensuring they do not torture you anymore, Zaib."

"No. I mean I have not had my monthly bleed." Her voice was calm. She had been stewing in this for far too long to be anything but resigned. But she watched as Dante began to understand, as horror stretched his face and reddened his cheeks.

"How late is it?" he asked, the terror in his voice and painting the air making tears well in Zaib's eyes.

"Four months."

***

"Okay, we can stop here for the night. Tomorrow we will be at the very edge of Isle Element and we can try to get those blockers off," Dante said, kissing Zaib's forehead and placing his hand firmly on her stomach. Over the last few weeks she had begun to swell, though the fae king and queen had not yet figured out she was with youngling. By the time Dante finally freed her, it was too late for them to discover the truth.

Zaib grabbed his cheeks, lifting his face to bring their lips together. He smiled into the kiss, his hands wrapping around her neck softly. "Marry me, Zaib."

She chuckled, but without hesitation nodded. "I love you."

As she often had been, Stella was nearby, watching the scene unfold. For the last few decades, she had watched in horror and devastation

as her descendent was harmed. All the while, the sound of the Oracle's warning to not interfere until the great loss echoed in her head. It had not happened yet. The fae had said she would feel it, and the fallen empress had not yet experienced the unequivocal sense of surety.

When she caught sight of Zaib's brother, Malcolm, appearing within a cloud of shadows just behind the happy couple, Stella thought the time might have finally come.

***

"Please, stop!" Zaib screamed, trying to convince Malcolm to cease his relentless attacks on Dante. They were back in the low level room, but this time, she was chained to the wall, forced to watch as the love of her life was brutally beaten.

"He is a disappointment and a traitor, he must be shown no mercy," the golden queen hissed into Malcolm's ear, encouraging him to continue. And he did, stomping and punching at Dante until Zaib wondered how he could possibly not be tired.

When he did slow, he grabbed Dante by his collar and dragged him to her bed, dropping him halfway onto the mattress. Zaib looked into her brother's eyes, unable to understand the darkness that lay beneath his skin. Different than the shadowy magic of the moon. No, this was an evil and wicked thing.

"Now you can watch him die and know it is all your fault," Mia said, practically steaming from the ears. Her hand reached out, latching onto Malcolm's sleeve and dragging him out of the room. The moment they left, Zaib was on Dante, trying to will her magic to heal him through the four brand new blockers and the poison they had force-fed her. But even when the silver sparkled to life and surrounded him, she knew it was too late.

Dante's eyes opened, a small smile stretching his split lips and showing his bloody teeth. Even toeing death, he was perfection incarnate.

"I love you," Zaib breathed out through her sobs. She held onto him, crying so hard her body shook. He reached up, his hand sliding across her cheek.

"I love you," he mumbled. "And I love *you*, my little one. My sweet son." His hand fell to her stomach, but instead of the glassy gray eyes that had stared into her nearly black ones, she watched a glazed and vacant gaze take over. And then the Tomorrow spoke. "Your magic is a force, a strength previously unheard of and ever reaching. As you find the light and dark, you shall see they will guide you if you dare heed their call. When you do, a prince you will lose, a prince you will gain, and a king you will hold. And when the moon paints the sky red, retribution will light fire to the realms. As promised by the true queen who defied her false destiny, when two worlds collide and history repeats, from it will come the salvation. From it, love will defeat vengeance. But if you fear what you do not know or do not understand, you might find yourself dead before you have even lived. And so the world will fall not far behind. No matter the choice you make, your reign will be the end."

At the close of the prophecy, Dante Daniox died in the arms of his love.

***

Stella realized her mistake after she had listened in on the prophecy of the Tomorrow. Zaib Ayad had not been the one the Oracle had foreseen. No, it had been her daughter. Yes, the pair had been wrong in thinking they would birth a son. The high demon of Sun and Moon knew it even before Zaib's screams echoed off the dungeon walls, no one around to help her as labor bore down on her. Knew it before the youngling came out completely silent, looking almost dead in her stillness.

The demon princess had grabbed onto her daughter, crying tears of joy and terror. Just as Stella had been prepared to open the heavy wooden door and free the pair, the sound of boots meeting stone came from her back, and she was forced to hide within the shadows.

Malcolm Ayad approached the door slowly, tears streaming down his cheeks. Before he opened the door, he quickly wiped them away and took a few deep breaths. Then he went inside. Stella listened as Zaib screamed at her brother to leave. As she asked him if he was proud. Begged to know if he was finally satisfied with his life. Malcolm had remained silent, listening as his sister hurled insults his way.

Stella wished she could rip the waste of space to shreds. She went to the door again, watching the scene unfold through the small bars.

When Zaib finally calmed down, her daughter sleeping through it all, Malcolm cleared his throat and spoke. "They will continue to torture and use you, and they will take the youngling. Use him against you."

"Her," Zaib hissed, squeezing the tiny form tighter.

"Her, sorry. They will use her against you. The best thing for you now is death." And then Malcolm revealed a dagger, shining and sharp in the nearby light of the fire. Zaib cried out, but did not attempt to fight as her brother closed the distance between them. "I will make it quick."

"Name her Asher!" Zaib blurted, looking up into her brother's dark and soulless eyes. A sob slipped past her lips when he did not respond, her bravery fading just as her life would. "Name her Asher, please. Let her know that she is a blessing. That she was her mother and father's *greatest* blessing."

Malcolm said nothing as he slid the dagger across his sister's throat. For the first time, the youngling began to wail. The demon prince spared her no glance, pushing himself to stand and then quickly leaving. When his footsteps had faded, Stella wrenched the door open and ran into the room.

The siphon spell from the drawn runes were painful, sucking the magic within her out, but Stella did not care. Did not have time to do

anything but get to the dying female. She offered a quick apology, a hasty explanation following its wake. But Zaib did nothing but nod, her eyes falling to her screaming daughter as the seed attempted to heal her mortal body.

"My little blessing. My sweet Asher," Zaib gurgled out as Stella took the seed of Mind and Soul. The princess's body slumped, dead now in truth.

Stella faced the crying little one—Asher—and, as she held the seed near the youngling's chest, she vowed that she would find a better ending for this one if she somehow survived.

EPILOGUE

Off the shores of a once stunning sanctuary bordered by a dark forest, a fallen empress stared out across the sea. Over the course of her long—too long—life, she had seen many things, hurt many beings, and lost far more than she thought was fair. But, as the holder of Sun and Moon felt the pain of her descendant coat the air, she wondered if she had ever felt as Asher did. As hopeless and scared and doomed as her.

Twirling her fingers, she looked up at the sky, watching clouds converge as they darkened. Soon, trickles of rain started to fall, a great boom following a flash of lightning. The storm matched Stella's overwhelming feelings. Ones she once thought she might never possess. It was odd for a high demon to experience such strong emotions. To exist not in purgatory, but in life.

She silently basked in the idea of death instead. Of finally ceasing to exist. Soon. But first, she knew it was finally time to go to Asher. To meet her and tell her the truth. Very little of that time was left now. Padon would have felt the seed awaken fully just as she had.

So the high demon stood, letting sand slip between her fingers and breathing in the sea air.

Things had gotten murky. She had messed up a lot along the way. In fact, she thought of one of her many failures then. The male with black curls and dark skin, his mind as curious as her late husband's had been. She had accidentally stumbled upon him, listening as he talked with excitement about a new salve he was inventing.

His hand had reached up to twirl a small chunk of amethyst around his neck, and Stella had made a hasty decision. She wanted him for Asher. The female had already lost so much, she deserved joy and love. Above all else, she could surely use the brightness of a curious mind in her life.

Throughout the next week, she would hide things in his room at their Academy that made him think of the princess. She would make him late so that he would see The Manipulator alone—as the young female often was. She would find his favorite scent and then ensure Asher, too, favored vanilla. She plotted and planned, slowly but surely making him grow obsessed with the new holder of Mind and Soul. And then, just to make sure the male would be brave enough to fight his terror and talk to Asher, Stella dropped a piece of parchment just outside of his door. One full of her writing—of supposed questions about Asher's *magic*.

Later, when Stella witnessed Asher's grief, she would learn that her place was in the background.

Now, as she dusted off her legs and thought of her long life, Stella was unsure if she was ready to be a part of Asher's story. Not quite confident in her ability to be of use. More than that, Stella was simply tired.

Long ago, when she had lived beneath a teal sun and beside a golden beacon of love, she would have never guessed where she would end up. But now, well it all felt right. And awful beyond comprehension. Asher

would still lose more. That was inevitable. Stella just hoped the female would at least keep her life.

As Stella turned around to head back to the forest, she spared a final glance at the fading red cloud. Then she began her slow walk to her cottage.

Behind her, The Mist fell.

LOVELY READER,
YOU ARE NO ONE'S BUT YOUR
OWN.

CHAPTER SUMMARIES

CHAPTER EIGHT

Triggers: graphic depictions of torture and murder, including blood.

The chapter opens with Mia and Xavier torturing Asher. Xavier and Mia get into a fight when Xavier says he no longer wishes to harm Asher. He fears they will kill her if they continue on. Mia calls him weak and the two fight before Xavier leaves. Mia calls Asher ungrateful and then allows Theon to come in. When Mia leaves, Theon taunts Asher, touching her lips and making degrading remarks. Asher bites off the tip of Theon's thumb, enraging him. He takes a knife and scalps her, calling her worthless and ugly. Tish comes in and heals Asher. Theon then drags Asher back to her cell next to Sterling. We learn that Theon had wanted to be with Asher when they were in Academy with the hopes of sitting on the throne, but Asher turned him down. He then stalked her and caught her with Sipho. He would go on to impersonate Sipho so that Xavier could see Asher and him. This led to Asher and Sipho eventually being caught and Sipho being murdered in front of her. Theon shifts into Sipho and Asher loses control. She somehow travels from inside her cell to outside of it and tackles Theon to the ground, ripping out his throat with her teeth and then beating him to death. Mia shows up and says that she has loved Asher. She then hits Asher upside the head and tells her that love will mold her into what she was always meant to be.

CHAPTER FORTY

Triggers: graphic descriptions of torture and murder.

Asher and Bellamy make their way to the dungeons, where Asher learns Bellamy had put Sterling. Asher tells Bellamy that she is not mad at him for not telling her about Adbeel and that they have all made mistakes or kept secrets. They hear screaming. Asher runs forward, thinking it must be Sterling. However, when they get to the cell where the screams are coming from, she discovers it is not Sterling's cell at all—it's Xavier's. She watches as Ranbir tortures Xavier, telling him that it is retribution for Mia killing Winona. Asher talks down Ranbir, telling him he is better than that. She convinces him to leave with the promise that she will take care of it. Xavier thanks Asher and says he loves her, to which Asher says that she only did it for Ranbir's sake. Then Asher begins taking Xavier's memories. She tells Xavier he did not love her enough. She takes any important memory she could use and then she forces him to light himself on fire. When she stops, he asks if it will be her who kills him. Asher smiles and says that she has heard that marriage means "what's mine is yours," so she feels it necessary to share with her fiancé. Bellamy tells Xavier that he is doing this for all the times he hurt Asher, and then he dismembers him and rips out his heart before burning the remains. The pair go on to find Sterling and bring him to Ranbir in the infirmary. Ranbir thanks Asher for stopping him. The Trusted come to greet Asher, as well as Farai, Jasper, Nicola, and Kafele. Henry brings Genevieve, who reunites with Sterling. Genevieve punches Asher for killing her people. Everyone gets defensive, but Asher calms them all down and apologizes to Genevieve. Ranbir says that it appears that

Sterling's brain has been through some sort of trauma. Asher tells Genevieve and Sterling that they will stay the night. Nicola tells everyone that she leads the rebels and has a vision that someone will come to see Bellamy that night. Asher also announces to everyone that she and Bellamy are engaged.

CHAPTER FORTY-FOUR

Triggers: discussion of suicide as well as blood play during sex. Includes graphic descriptions of blood and self-harm.

In this chapter, Stassi is training Asher. The two argue, but Stassi internally acknowledges their sort of alliance that stems from their mutual adoration of Sterling. Stassi tells Asher more about the high demons, specifically discussing the generation before hers. We learn that Stassi's parents loved each other deeply, her father breaking the mold of high demons and choosing to marry his lover rather than mate with many low demons to ensure a strong heir. Stassi's mother would go on to take her own life after repeated miscarriages. When Stassi and her father walked in and found her mother dead, her father apologized to Stassi and ripped out his seed, ending his life and forcing Stassi to become the high demon of Sin and Virtue at a very young age. Torrel and Milo come, and we discover that Milo has taken a liking to Asher. Sterling also arrives with Henry and Genevieve. When alone in her bedroom, Stassi notes how unwell Sterling seems. She mentions his blood. He decides to cut himself and offer her that blood, mentioning that everyone seems to want it these days. The pair have sex, during which Stassi can tell that something is not right with Sterling, realizing that it is his trauma catching up with him. Stassi consoles him, crying for the first time in longer than she can remember. She realizes how much she is beginning to feel.

CHAPTER FORTY-NINE

Triggers: graphic description of self-harm, including blood and gore, and an on-page anxiety attack

On the night before her wedding, Asher is alone and suffering from night terrors. Demon tradition requires the bride and groom to sleep separately, so Bellamy is not around to help talk Asher down. She becomes confused and scared, not immediately sure where she is. When she realizes that she is safe, she starts tracing her scars, wishing they were there to reassure her. Her panic attack becomes unbearable, and Asher makes a hasty decision to carve her scars back into herself. She begins to do so, but Nicola, Ranbir, Sterling, and Queen Shah burst into her room. Ranbir forcibly heals Asher as Sterling talks her down. When she is calm, Sterling and Ranbir leave. Nicola tells Asher she would have died if she continued on, but that she has an idea. Shah then offers to tattoo Asher's scars back on in a similar color to what they were. They tattoo Asher through the night. After they leave, Asher cleans herself up and Bellamy comes in. He tells her that she is whole in his eyes after she cries to him. They hold one another for the rest of the night, talking and cuddling. Noe comes in early the next morning, telling Bellamy to leave because it is time for Asher to get ready.

CONTINUE READING FOR

BONUS CONTENT

MIA

~ MIA TOLERATES A YOUNG BELLAMY—THEN BARON—
AND DOTES ON A BABY ASHER ~

He was following me. Again.

I wished he would stop.

Following. Talking. Laughing.

Breathing.

He was a stain. A problem that could not be fixed while it still lived.

I could practically hear my mother screaming at me from the grave. Blaming me for this abomination's existence. For being so pathetic that I would birth it.

"Mama?" the little male asked. I stopped midstep, my right leg slightly ahead of my left and my balance precarious at best. But if I moved, if I did anything at all, then he would only try harder. That was the problem. He *loved* me. I wished he would hate me like I hated him.

"What is it, Baron?" I practically sighed the words, so exhausted by his presence that I could no longer pretend. Not that I had ever done a good job when no one was around to correct me.

Not that I ever let anyone around him anyways.

"Can we play in the garden?" he asked with unabashed glee.

Turning, I faced him, my blue eyes of winter ice flicking down to his blue eyes of summer skies. On his cheeks, freckles were beginning to appear, pairing beautifully with his deep dimples as he beamed up at me. We somehow matched while also being unnervingly different. He closer

resembled the me that existed before my power had come. The me that still believed in a good world.

I hated it.

The only thing that was worse was seeing the tiny lines of black that peeked out above his tunic collar. Magic. Useless, of course. Though I had hoped it would not be. In fact, instead of being helpful, it had seemingly stunted the pathetic male's growth. He was barely bigger than Asher. Yet, he made up for the smallness with an enormous personality. With more love than I thought one creature could hold and a brilliant mind.

"I do not want to play, Baron," I muttered, trying to contain the hatred so it did not seep out from my lips.

My mother had always said that it was vital only fathers punished younglings. They were the stern, the unreliable, the *enemy* if there ever needed to be one. Mothers were the warmth, the solace, the *ally*. While Baron was not female, he was still my youngling, and I needed him on my side rather than Xavier's.

Still, I so loathed him.

He was meant to be a daughter. A princess. A blessing.

"There is my little prince!" A deep shout alerted me to Xavier's presence just before he rounded the corner. I watched in distaste as he bent low and scooped up Baron, the two of them giggling as he swung them around.

My fists bunched at my side, fury building in me. I stomped out the flames, dousing the fire and working to calm myself. It was improper— embarrassing, even—for a queen to let her emotions get the best of her.

Baron continued to giggle as Xavier set him down, beaming up at the king consort. That would not do. He needed to look at *me* like that, not his father.

I would have Xavier punish him tonight so I could soothe him after. Yes, that would fix everything. I would need to speak to the youngling in a kind way. To...*cuddle* him. That would be good for my patience, too.

It would all work out.

"Actually, Baron, I changed my mind. Come help me garden."

***

"You are doing well," I told Baron, eyeing his work on the roses with barely hidden awe. He would be an Earth, there was no doubt about that. He already excelled at working in the gardens. At least I could understand that part of him.

"Thank you, mama," Baron whispered back, smiling up at me reluctantly.

Adoration was obvious in his eyes, Xavier all but forgotten after the last couple of hours in my gardens. His pale cheeks were turning pink from the sun, his pointed ears red at the tips where they poked out of his black waves. I should cut it. He did not need a reminder of Xavier. Maybe I would stop wearing cosmetics and let him see my matching freckles. Show him that he was more me than he was his father.

"I am...*proud* of you, my son." My teeth were clenched, my fists balled so tightly they stung. Still, Baron's tiny eyes watered, his smile full now and his dimples so deep they were practically craters.

He was cute. I would give him that. Not nearly as cute as—

"My Ash!" Baron shouted, pushing himself up and reaching his small arms out. I whipped my head around, a smile overtaking my face as Florencia walked towards us with Asher in her hands.

Asher already had hair to her shoulders, her gray eyes large and her lips full. Her skin was darker than Florencia's, but there was an unmistakable likeness to them that made our story—our lie—regarding Asher's parentage believable.

"Hello, My Prince," Florencia cooed, coming to a stop before Baron and then squatting down to his height. Asher reached out to my son, her cheeks large as she smiled his way. He leaned in, rubbing their noses together and giggling.

"My sweet, little flower," I hummed as I walked their way and pulled Asher away from them. There was something simply extraordinary about her. A sort of pull that felt an awful lot like gravity. Like real love.

We had already decided she would marry Baron. All of us knew she was a weapon disguised beneath beauty. It was more than that, though. Asher felt like the daughter I was meant to have. My dreams lived within her, my heart felt full in her presence, and my mind was content as my gaze hit her.

I recalled the moment I had pried her screaming form out of her useless mother's dead arms. The feeling of rightness that had consumed me. Asher was *mine*.

"Your Majesty," Florencia offered as she stood straight and then dipped back into a low curtsy. I ignored her, staring at my salvation before me. My true heir.

"Mama, I want a turn," Baron complained, tugging on my golden skirts. Like I did, Baron sported all gold, the color complimenting his eyes and hair but clashing with his skin.

It would look so much better on Asher.

I shoved Baron off me, the little male falling on his bottom in the dirt and a soft cry slipping from his lips. Not caring, I began rocking Asher, humming softly to her and dreaming of the day I could teach her to play the pianoforte. Singing lessons too. She would be exquisite in all things.

"Actually, I was coming to ask if you would be okay with Baron going on a walk with Herberto, Asher, and I." My gaze moved to Florencia where she was bent down once more, her hands making quick work of wiping Baron's tears and dusting him off. Rolling my eyes, I reluctantly accepted that this would be good. Less time in Baron's presence now meant that I would be able to endure soothing him later after Xavier beat him.

I was positive he would do something naughty that would warrant it. Males always did.

"I think that is a lovely idea," I agreed with a smile.

***

Herberto's head was barely hanging onto his neck, the sight nearly as gory as the gaping hole in Florencia's chest. I knew that devastation well. It was the work of demons. Not that anyone but Xavier and I would remember that.

Panic was filling me, overtaking me like weeds suffocating roses. Only two bodies were in the clearing. The younglings were missing.

Asher was missing.

When the area surrounding Florencia and Herberto showed no signs of either youngling, I dove into the trees, tears streaming down my face as the memory of Asher's soft giggles rang in my ears.

No. No. No. No!

A scream bubbled in my throat, blocking air from reaching my lungs. Still, I pushed on, searching desperately for a sign that she was still here. My power seeped into the ground, but I did not dare move a single tree. Not when she was at risk of being harmed.

Thorns sliced open my cheeks, vines wrapped around my ankles, dirt flew up into the air. All I could do was think of her as I ran and searched—as I begged the ethers. And then, Eternity saw fit to show me mercy.

Asher's cries echoed across the forest.

When I finally found her, she was sitting up, still in the little white dress she had worn when Florencia had brought her along to fetch Baron. I dove down, grabbing her in my arms and sobbing openly as I hugged her close to my chest.

Reluctantly, I let my magic out, parting the trees to see if Baron was anywhere in sight. But no, Asher and I were the only ones there. Somehow, in that moment, I understood what had happened.

Florencia and Herberto must have hidden Asher and then tried to fight to protect Baron. Only for them to fall and the king or one of his warriors to take my son.

The king must have gotten word from his daughter before she was recaptured. He must have known she was pregnant. Did he think Baron was his grandson?

He would realize that Baron was not a demon, of course. Probably kill him. A weight lifted off my chest at the thought of not needing to deal with the male. Nor would I need to worry about the Daniox's growing further attached to Asher.

Could I be so lucky?

No. There were still loose ends.

My eyes flicked down to Asher's ears, the tips short, rounded points. Other if one had the foresight to search for discrepancies in her appearance. Someone like a king looking for his blood.

With a deep breath, I set Asher back down on the forest floor, summoned a sharp rock in my palm, and got to work cutting—the sound of her blood-curdling screams ringing in my ears.

All the while, my mother's voice urged me on in my mind.

NICOLA

~ NICOLA EXPERIENCES HER FIRST TRUE VISIONS AS AN
ORACLE ~

A candle burned nearby.

Had Kafele lit that after we fell asleep? Suddenly, I realized I no longer felt him beneath me. What was happening?

My eyes blinked again and again, trying to see anything beyond the flickering flame. After a few moments, two figures finally emerged out of the darkness. They seemed to be standing still, their hands gesturing in angry and sharp movements.

In the distance, something roared. The sound was crisp, like a stormy winter night in the Tomorrow Lands. But that was not where I was. I could sense it, somehow. This was not my home.

Almost subconsciously, I moved forward, aiming for the pair ahead. As if that first step was a catalyst, sound and sight came back to me, the image clearer now.

A female and a male were arguing. Both wore black garments and black crowns, so odd when all I knew of fae royalty was their aversion to any color other than gold. Should I shout to them? Make myself known?

I thought about it, but their words were carrying, and something in my mind told me to *listen.*

"You must stop this, Padon! I cannot take it anymore!" The female, her curly hair a startling shade of silver, grabbed the male's wrist, his towering form growing rigid.

"No, Asta, I must do nothing other than rule over our world. Your mother is a shell of what she once was. All Shamay has left is *us*. Your complaints and your grief matter little in comparison!" His cheeks were flushed, the color beneath his almost translucent skin an odd shade of blue. His aubergine hair cascaded down his back, swaying in a phantom wind.

I wanted to stand up for the female—Asta—in that moment. He berated her in a way that made even my teeth grind, but the image shifted, and I was thrown to another place—another *time*.

When two new figures appeared, I gasped in shock. There was no doubt who this female was. I had grown up with her. Loved her.

Asher stood with her arms crossed, her head tilted to the side and her body clad in the same silver as the female's hair from before.

Silver. Asher *never* wore silver.

Across from her was a different male, his hair midnight black and his eyes sparkling blue. His ivory cheeks boasted a smattering of freckles that did not quite fit his menacing presence. He looked like a weapon—a beast.

My feet took two more steps forward, and then I was moving towards the pair. Just as I was nearly there my hands reached out, instincts telling me to save Asher from whoever this male was. But as my fingertips moved to graze Asher's arm, they were met with nothing but air.

Asher's form shimmered and waved, going somewhat transparent momentarily.

Suddenly, my heart was racing. Panic enveloped me like a too tight embrace, and I felt suffocated by the heat of it.

"Tomorrow is the blood moon, Ash. You heard the prophecy. Doom lingers. Lurks," the male rasped, his eyes never leaving hers. He looked at her like...well, like Kafele looked at me. As if she strung the stars and hung the moon. As if she were the universe itself.

"And we are more than ready. I can do this, Bell." Asher's voice was far stronger than I had ever heard it before. She stood with her back straight and her chin tilted up. A force.

The male sighed, his eyes closing and scrunching at the sides. What Asher said seemed to pain him. His hand reached up, not needing sight to find her cheek. As if it were second nature.

Just as quickly as it had come, the vision disappeared, once more shifting to something else.

To *everything* else.

I watched as the past, present, and future unraveled before me. Strings of time wrapping and twirling and snapping before my eyes. I began to choke on them, their weight and strength weaving around my neck.

Every scream that left my lips merely echoed off the darkness, my throat going raw and my chest desperately heaving from the swarm.

And then, a cold sort of nothingness seeped into my bones. It felt like being under fifty feet of snow, a freezing darkness my only companion. In fact, what I saw then was like a wave of shadows, the mass of black overtaking me.

All at once, the darkness evaporated, and the same male who had spoken to Asher countless times in the visions appeared. Bellamy Ayad.

But this image of him was not normal. Gone were his joyful dimples and flirtatious smirks. The blue that had once marked Asher as the universe itself now stared on without any depth or emotion. Empty. That was what the stare was. His black hair was disheveled, onyx armor dented as if a battle had been fought and lost.

Worst of all, Bellamy was completely alone.

Until he was not.

Asher's screams sounded eerie in the otherwise silent moment. They ripped apart my soul in the same way they seemed to shred the world around her as she dove for the ground—for her soul bond.

She grabbed his face, tears streaming down her cheeks and sobs making her chest heave in desperate bursts. She wore twin armor, her hair braided back instead of loose. Her face was a contortion of pain and fury as she stared down at her now dead love.

My heart felt like it might cease beating altogether as I watched her scream for him to wake up. And when she began tugging him onto her lap, I truly did cry.

I was empty in more ways than one. Perhaps nearly as empty as Bellamy's dead body that Asher continued to sob over.

When she finally looked up and turned around, her gray eyes were ablaze. She gave one last kiss to Bellamy's already dry lips before pushing herself to stand. As she walked away, I noticed that she had closed his eyes.

***

I jolted awake, my body shaking and drenched in sweat.

Finally, I was free.

Well, as free as someone could be with so much information.

Kafele shifted, quickly sitting up and reaching his hands up to gently cup my face. His deep skin was faint in the darkness, his coffee eyes holding all the warmth and love that I had watched fade from Bellamy's eyes.

Bellamy. When would I meet him? When would Asher? Something was very wrong. These visions were *not* normal.

"What is it, my future?" Kafele asked, his once joking nickname spilling from his lips like a lifeline. I shook my head, unsure how to speak. As his thumb lifted to brush away a tear that crawled down my cheek, I closed my eyes and took in heaving breaths.

What was that? Did I make it all up? Could those visions of gods and magic and war be true?

It was as if my center of gravity had been tilted, my body swaying. The visions were bees swarming the hive that was my mind. I wanted nothing more than to be the kind of free that I had taken for granted when I fell asleep in Kafele's arms last night.

That was no longer possible. I could feel the truth solidifying, practically see the silver thread of future in all its glory. Behind my lids, the visions plagued me. Tormented me.

"We need to get back to The Capital," I declared, allowing my eyes to snap open. Kafele flinched at whatever look he saw on my face, his hands tightening on my jaw and neck. My rock, as always.

"Ash's ball is not for another two weeks. We have time. You deserve rest and joy. You *deserve* time away from that wretched place." As per usual, he was firm in his tone. As a warden, Kafele was open to change and opinions, but as my future husband, he was unflinching in his desire to see me happy. I loved that about him. He was not only my love, but my soul. Which was why the look on my face had him sighing in defeat. I could be steadfast too. "Why must we go now, Nic?"

Reaching up, I grabbed his hands, pulling them together before my lips and placing a lingering kiss on his knuckles. A groan sounded from deep in his throat, as if he could read my mind.

I needed release. I needed freedom from these thoughts and memories and fates.

And then I needed to get to Asher.

With a gentle shove, I pressed him back down, straddling him as his body went horizontal on the bed. Then, with a final, bleak admission, I freed my fear and opened myself up to pure joy one last time. "Doom comes."

ACKNOWLEDGMENTS

Wow, I can't believe we are on book THREE. It feels surreal, to have so many people to thank and so much support. Words feel as if they will never measure up to all that you have given me. Each reader deserves to be listed here, and I wish I could write all of your names so you realized just how much you mean to me. Since I cannot, I want you all to know that without you, this book would not exist.

As always, I want to start off by thanking my mother. You have always been my biggest supporter and my brightest light. In all the world, there is no one who believes in me like you do. No one who sees in me the potential and talent that you have seen my entire life. I love you so much. To you, I owe it all.

To my two sons, who always look at me with stars in their eyes and love in their heart, thank you for giving me strength. This year has undoubtedly been the hardest of my life, but every day I look at the two of you and know that it is all worth it. You are worth it. You are everything. I love you with my entire heart and soul.

To my extraordinary street team, who have been nothing but loving and enthusiastic, thank you for keeping my fingers writing. Every day you all remind me that I belong in this community. More than that, you all refuse to let me forget that my books deserve to exist. I am so very grateful for each and every one of you.

To Lyra, Kim, Kirsty, and Loren, thank you for taking the time to read this book before it was even finished. For loving and valuing this book in its most vulnerable and raw form. Your unconditional support and unwavering desire to make OVAW the best it could be is not taken for granted. I appreciate you all so much.

To my fellow authors who have propelled me forward (Monica Amore, Nova Nox, and Tara N. Gabrys), you have changed my author journey. I am so thankful for your love and support—for reminding me that we are all colleagues rather than competitors. That this community is a beautiful and bright place. Thank you all.

To two of my all-time favorite artists, vaieart and altassart, thank you for continuously bringing my characters to life. You have both been such a pivotal part of my journey with these books. Your art makes all of this feel so real, like maybe these characters truly do exist beyond the confines of my mind. You are also bright lights and a joy to work with. Thank you, from the bottom of my heart.

Finally, to my beta and arc readers, your support throughout the final stages of this book was so deeply appreciated. You all have truly changed this novel and made it what it is. As Asher says, time is the most valuable currency, and it is hard to explain just how much it means to me that you chose to spend your time on my art. I am forever thankful.

ABOUT THE AUTHOR

Brea has been obsessively reading since she was six years old, consuming any and all books she could get her hands on. Thus sparked the dream of creating something similar – a book that would make readers cry and laugh and smile and feel all those big emotions that she did. At nine-years-old, she wrote her first book. Over the years she would write many more, but it was not until Of Night and Blood that she finally felt the book she dreamed of writing had come to life.

She spends her time advocating for human rights, drinking too much coffee, chasing around her children, and ordering new books for her endless TBR. She lives in the United States with her family.

AUTHOR'S NOTE

Asher's story contains many heavy topics. I hold her dear to my heart as she has lived through much of what I have. Most of my life I have struggled with the concept of worth and how it is measured. Like Asher, I needed to learn that I was no one's but my own, and that my worth was mine and mine alone to determine. With all of my heart I desire each and every one of you to know the same thing.

That being said, I know these themes can be hard to read, especially for those of us who have had similar life experiences to Asher. However, I truly hope that as you follow her journey, you find solace in her resilience. Just like Noe, I hope you face your evils and win.

For those who are surviving similar struggles and need aid, I encourage you to reach out to your local or national crisis hotline. If you are in the United States, visit www.988lifeline.org/chat to immediately get into contact with a crisis support specialist. You can also text or call 988.

You are not alone, and you are worthy of life. All my love.